WITHDRAWN

MEDIA

AN INTRODUCTORY ANALYSIS OF AMERICAN MASS COMMUNICATIONS

The Third Edition

Peter M. Sandman

Cook College
Rutgers—The State University
of New Jersey

David M. Rubin

New York University
at Washington Square

David B. Sachsman

Livingston College
Rutgers—The State University
of New Jersey

PRENTICE-HALL, INC., ENGLEWOOD CLIFFS, NEW JERSEY 07632

Library of Congress Cataloging in Publication Data

SANDMAN, PETER M.
    Media: an introductory analysis of
American mass communications.

    Includes index.
    1. Mass media—United States. I. Rubin,
David M. II. Sachsman, David B. III. Title.
P92.U5S24   1982   302.2′3   81-13834
ISBN 0-13-572545-3   AACR2

To Tina and Judy, Alison and Jennifer,
Jonathan and Susanne,
And to William L. Rivers, our teacher

Editorial/production supervision and interior design by Fred Bernardi
Manufacturing buyer: Harry P. Baisley

10 9 8 7 6 5 4 3 2 1

ISBN 0-13-572545-3

PRENTICE-HALL INTERNATIONAL, INC., London
PRENTICE-HALL OF AUSTRALIA PTY. LIMITED, Sydney
PRENTICE-HALL OF CANADA, LTD., Toronto
PRENTICE-HALL OF INDIA PRIVATE LIMITED, New Delhi
PRENTICE-HALL OF JAPAN, INC., Tokyo
PRENTICE-HALL OF SOUTHEAST ASIA PTE. LTD., Singapore
WHITEHALL BOOKS LIMITED, Wellington, New Zealand

Contents

PART II   RESPONSIBILITY   76

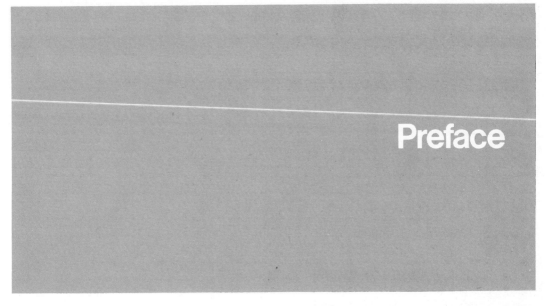

Preface

We began writing the first edition of this book in 1969 because we saw two crucial gaps that needed to be filled.

First, we wanted to produce a text that did not assume its readers were planning a career in journalism. Though we saw the serious need for better-informed journalists, we believed that the need for better-informed readers and viewers was at least as critical. Consumers of mass communication, we felt, need to know what it is doing for them, what it is doing to them, and what they can do about it.

Second, we wanted to produce a text that would itself embody the characteristics of the best of modern journalism—solid evidence, written in a light style, structured by forthright interpretation. Even an introductory book, we insisted, should be thoroughly documented, thoroughly readable, and thoroughly interpretive.

Many things have happened to the media since the first edition was published in 1972.

Perhaps the most important change is a phenomenal growth in consumer interest in the process and effects of mass communication. Today, more people than ever before are aware of the media as a social and political institution that affects their lives. More people than ever before are trying to affect the content of the media. And more people than ever before are considering communications careers.

The goal of this third edition is identical with the goal of the first two editions—to help media consumers and future media professionals understand the media, so that the former can consume more cautiously, so that the latter can perform more effectively, and so that both can join in the struggle to improve the content of the mass media.

PETER M. SANDMAN
DAVID M. RUBIN
DAVID B. SACHSMAN

Introduction: The Power of the Media

Communication involves the sharing of information, attitudes, and experiences. While interpersonal communication is a delicate process controlled jointly by the source and the receiver, mass communication is much more brutal and one-sided. The mass communication audience—you—has little control over content; sources and the media themselves make most of the content decisions. In the United States, those decisions are determined mainly by the profit motive, leavened with some concern for social responsibility.

COMMUNICATION

Communication is the process of transmitting a message from a source to an audience via a channel. Consider, for example, a conversation, the most common kind of communication. The person who speaks is the source. The person who listens is the audience. What is transmitted is the message. And the spoken voice carried through the air is the channel.

Now consider a more complicated example, an article in a newspaper. The message is everything the article says, everything it implies, and everything a reader might infer from it. The audience is everybody who reads the article or even glances at it. The source is everybody who contributes in one way or another to the article; this includes the newsmakers who are quoted, the reporter, the editor, and even the proofreaders and printers. The channel is, of course, the printed word, the newspaper itself.

What is a communication *medium?* Strictly speaking, a medium is a channel—the spoken word, the printed word, or whatever. But the term is often used to mean both the channel and the source, and sometimes even the message. It includes everything that reaches the audience. When we speak of the "mass media," for example, we usually mean not only the channels of mass communication but also the content of those channels and the behavior of the people who work for them.

Wilbur Schramm thinks of communication as a sharing process. He puts it this way:

> *Communication* comes from the Latin *communis,* common. When we communicate we are trying to establish a "commonness" with someone. That is, we are trying to share information, an idea, or an attitude. At this moment I am trying to communicate to you the idea that

the essence of communication is getting the receiver and the sender "tuned" together for a particular message.[1]

Effective communication, then, is communication that succeeds in establishing Schramm's "commonness" between the source and the audience.

In a telepathic society, communication wouldn't be worth studying. Source and audience would be able to read each other's minds, and every attempt to communicate would succeed. Communication is interesting because we cannot read each other's minds. This permits sources to be deceptive, to design messages that reflect not what they themselves think but rather what they want their audience to think. Even more important, it forces sources to "launch" their messages with no guarantee that the audience will receive them correctly. Much writing about communication had been dominated by the bullet metaphor—the source aims the gun and pulls the trigger, then hopes that the bullet will strike the target.

Switching metaphors, anything that interferes with effective communication can be called "noise." This bit of jargon is borrowed from electrical engineering, where "noise" refers literally to the static in an electrical system that lessens the precision of the transmission. A misspelled word, a fuzzy TV picture, and an ink splotch are all examples of noise in a communications channel. Similarly, a speaker who uses words the audience doesn't know is an example of "source noise."

Most of the noise in a communication system is contributed by neither the source nor the channel, but rather by the audience. People are enormously proficient at ignoring, misinterpreting, and misremembering communications that for one reason or another don't appeal to them. At least three psychological strategies are relevant here:

- *Selective attention.* People expose themselves primarily to communications they like. If you

are not interested in buying a car, you will read very few automobile advertisements. If you are interested, you'll probably read all the ads you can. But once you settle on a Plymouth, you are likely to read only the Plymouth ads.
- *Selective perception.* Once exposed to a communication, people tend to interpret it so as to coincide with their own preconceptions. If you show a middle-class audience a drawing of a white man brandishing a razor in the face of a black, many will "see" the razor in the hand of the black instead.
- *Selective retention.* Even if they understand a communication, people tend to remember only what they want to remember. After reading a balanced discussion of Soviet Communism, anti-Communist students recall mostly the drawbacks of the system, while pro-Communist students tend to remember mostly its advantages.

It is worth stressing that selective attention, selective perception, and selective retention are noise only from the source's point of view; they make it harder for the communication bullet to hit its intended target. From the viewpoint of the audience, on the other hand, these are eminently sensible strategies for controlling the communication process. As audiences, we do not think of ourselves as targets. We use the messages around us for our own purposes, focusing on the ones we find interesting, interpreting them in terms of our own values, and remembering only the parts that are useful to us. There is a balance in communication: the source controls what is said, but the audience controls what is heard.

When a teacher lectures to a class, for example, it is the teacher, not the class, who decides the content of the lecture. But if a student is bored or offended by what the teacher is saying, he or she may tune the teacher out and think about something else. Or the student may unconsciously misinterpret the lecture, perhaps "hearing" that there will be one term paper when the teacher has said there will be two. Or the student may simply forget those parts of the message that are least appealing, such as the reading assignment. The teacher is likely to take a dim view of these lapses, but he or she is just as guilty as the students. In grading papers, for example, teachers tend to "see" the right answers in the papers of students whose work they admire.

Selective attention, selective perception, and selective retention are universal and necessary. Without this audience noise, communication would be a dictatorship of the source.

Audience noise is most potent when the message is controversial; simple and unthreatening messages, on the other hand, tend to be received relatively "clear." As a result, it is next to impossible for any communication to convert an audience from one viewpoint to another. It is much easier to create a new viewpoint where none existed before. And it is easier still to communicate information that tends to support the established viewpoint of the audience. All communicators—advertisers, politicians, reporters, even teachers—must work within these constraints.

So far we have talked about communication as if it were a one-way street; the message moves in a straight line from the source to the channel to the audience. In reality, every good communication system must work both ways. The mechanisms for transmitting messages backward from audience to channel, from audience to source, or from channel to source are known as "feedback loops." When a television actor checks the monitor to see how he looks on the screen, he is getting feedback from the channel. When an actress reads her fan mail, she is getting feedback from the audience. And when the network management looks over the show's ratings, it too is getting feedback from the audience.

The technical vocabulary of communication will be used sparingly in this book. Of course we'll be talking a lot about sources and audiences, but very little about channels, and even less about "noise," "selective

attention," "feedback loops," and the like. Nevertheless, these are vitally important concepts to bear in mind. When we speak later about the influence of news bias, we will be describing a kind of noise. When we discuss the ineffectiveness of editorials, we will be referring to a special case of selective attention. And when we complain about the problem of public control of the media, we will be noting the absence of sufficient provision for feedback.

MASS COMMUNICATION

Interpersonal communication is the process of transmitting information, ideas, and attitudes from one person to another. Mass communication is the process of transmitting information, ideas, and attitudes to many people, usually through a machine. There are several important differences between the two.

First, the sources of a mass communication have great difficulty gearing their message to their audience. They may know the demographic statistics of the audience—its average age, its average socioeconomic status, etc.—but they cannot know the individual quirks of each individual reader, listener, and viewer.

Second, mass communication systems typically include much weaker feedback loops than interpersonal communication systems. When you talk to friends, you can usually tell whether they are listening, whether they understand, whether they agree or disagree, and so forth. All this is impossible in mass communication.

Third, the audience of a mass communication is much more likely than the audience of an interpersonal communication to twist the message through selective attention, perception, and retention. People turn off the TV (literally or figuratively) if they don't like what it's saying. It's a lot harder—though still possible—to turn off someone talking to you.

This is a book about the mass media, so we will treat "mass communication" as though it were synonymous with the media. But just for the record, television and radio, newspapers and magazines are not our only mass communicators. Architecture, too, consists of messages aimed simultaneously at many people. A restaurant is a mass communicator. So is a library, or a museum, or a religion. All of these institutions depend for their survival on conveying to audiences the messages they want conveyed.

In a 1979 book entitled *Beyond Media*, communication scholars Richard W. Budd and Brent D. Rubin argue persuasively that we cannot appreciate the impact and dynamics of mass communication in our society until we expand the definition to cover these non-media communicators.[2] Look around the room you are in right now. What is its message? How is that message affecting you? In the years ahead communication researchers may begin asking—and answering—these sorts of questions.

Fourth, and perhaps most important, mass-communication systems are a lot more complicated than interpersonal communication systems. Each message (an article in a newspaper, for example) may have as many as a dozen sources, with different points of view and different goals for the communication. The channel, too, is typically a complex organization (such as a newspaper), composed of many individuals, whose viewpoints and goals may vary widely. Every mass communication is in a sense a committee product.

All four of these factors tend to lessen the effect of a mass communication on its audience. The power of the mass media is based on the size of their audience, on their ability to reach millions of people in one shot. But in dealing with any individual member of that audience, you'd be a lot more effective if you sat down together for a chat.

When people sit down for a chat, however, the things they talk about and the attitudes they express are often derived from the mass media. In 1940, Paul F. Lazarsfeld and his colleagues studied the voting behavior of a group of citizens in Erie County, Ohio. They discovered, to their surprise, that very few people decided how to vote on the basis of information learned directly from the mass media. Most voters made up their minds as a result of interpersonal communications—conversations with a friend, a neighbor, a union leader, a spouse.

Only a minority of Erie County's citizens made significant use of the media for voting information. Members of this minority then sat down with their friends and neighbors and transmitted the message of the media through interpersonal communication. Lazarsfeld called these minority members "opinion leaders." He concluded that "ideas often flow from radio and print to opinion leaders and from these to the less active sections of the population."[3] This is known as the "two-step flow" theory of mass-media influence.

More recent research has shown that the two-step flow theory is greatly oversimplified; "multi-step flow" would be closer to the truth. For one thing, the distinction between "opinion leaders" and their followers varies from issue to issue and from group to group; each of us is a leader occasionally and a follower usually. Think about which of your friends is most likely to talk to you about the quality of recently released movies, the risk of war in the Middle East, and the health effects of various birth control methods. Chances are each is a different person, who follows one topic carefully in the media but pays only casual attention to the other two.

In addition, the communication patterns of opinion leaders and their followers are much more complex than Lazarsfeld suggested, often with far more than two links in the chain. Opinion leaders talk to each other, crystallizing their views into a consistent stance. That stance may or may not be the media's stance; often an opinion leader will rely on the media for up-to-date information but integrate that information into long-held values, using the media more for ammunition than for guidance. And opinion leaders pay attention to their followers as well, intuitively realizing that if their distillation of media content conflicts too strongly with the group's customs and norms, the group is very likely to find itself another leader.

Finally, it turns out that nearly everyone absorbs some media content directly. We may not all pay as careful attention to a topic as opinion leaders on that topic do, but we all spend sizable portions of our lives with the media. Inadvertently, we pick up information and even values about the topic. If you want advice on what brand of bicycle to buy, you will probably consult an opinion leader—but if you're not shopping that carefully you may just choose one yourself, and the bicycle advertising you have encountered will play an important role in your choice.

Despite all these qualifiers, Lazarsfeld was right about the central point. Mass communication and interpersonal communication are interacting networks. Much of the impact of the mass media is indirect, filtered through our conversations with friends.

AMERICAN MASS COMMUNICATION

The American system of mass communication has at least three characteristics that distinguish it from systems in other countries.

1. Pervasive influence.
2. Freedom of the press.
3. Big-business domination.

None of these characteristics is unique. There are other countries with powerful media, other countries with free media, other countries with profit-oriented media. But the United States embodies all three traits to an extent unmatched in the rest of the world.

1. Pervasive Influence. A fish could no more tell you what it is like to live out of water than an American could tell you what it is like to live without mass communication. As soon as American children are old enough to distinguish between two different makes of midget racing cars or fruit-flavored brands of toothpaste, they are bathed in a constant stream of messages from radio and television. They approach the daily newspaper through the comics or sports section; these lead them to comic books and sporting magazines, and then perhaps to more serious books and magazines.

By the time they enter kindergarten, most American children have already been exposed to hundreds, perhaps thousands of hours of radio and television. They have attended dozens of movies and browsed through scores of children's books. They have cut pictures out of magazines and scowled at the newspaper in unconscious imitation of their parents. All these experiences have taught them something—something about literacy, perhaps, something about violence, something about America. They are in a real sense children of the mass media.

For most adults, meanwhile, the mass media constitute the only advanced education they receive after high school or college. It is obvious that the media offer every American a continuous course in modern world history. But it is not so obvious, perhaps, that the very basics of community living come to us through the media: births, weddings,

In 1922, the distinguished political columnist Walter Lippmann wrote a book on *Public Opinion*. He began the book this way:

> There is an island in the ocean where in 1914 a few Englishmen, Frenchmen, and Germans lived. No cable reaches that island, and the British mail steamer comes but once in sixty days. In September it had not yet come, and the islanders were still talking about the latest newspaper which told about the approaching trial of Madame Caillaux for the shooting of Gaston Calmette. It was, therefore, with more than usual eagerness that the whole colony assembled at the quay on a day in mid-September to hear from the captain what the verdict had been. They learned that for over six weeks now those of them who were English and those of them who were French had been fighting in behalf of the sanctity of treaties against those of them who were Germans. For six strange weeks they had acted as if they were friends, when in fact they were enemies.

Lippmann's point is that much of what we know about our world and our relationship to it reaches us indirectly, through media rather than personal experience. This indirect information may come quickly or slowly; it may be true or false; we may interpret it accurately or inaccurately. But "whatever we believe to be a true picture, we treat as if it were the environment itself." Thus Lippmann begins his analysis of public opinion with this axiom: "We shall assume that what each man does is based not on direct and certain knowledge, but on pictures made by himself or given to him."

Lippmann called his first chapter "The World Outside and the Pictures in Our Heads." Decades before television, he insisted that society is molded by the interaction between media content and the media audience.[4]

deaths, weather reports, traffic accidents, crimes, sales, elections.

It is hard to imagine an efficient system of democratic government without an equally efficient system of mass communication. Citizens would learn of new legislation only after it passed, and then only if they visited their representative in Washington. Incumbents would probably serve for life, because no challengers could make themselves known to the electorate. Corruption would go largely unchecked. News of foreign affairs would remain the monopoly of the president and the State Department. And on the local level, mayors would be free to run their cities as personal fiefdoms. Political information is political power. Without the mass media to transmit such information, the American people would be powerless.

Dwarfing even the educational and political roles of the American media is their entertainment function. Television offers a seemingly unending stream of soap operas, thrillers, comedies, and star-studded specials. Radio spins records and conversation. Newspapers lighten the weight of the news with puzzles, advice to the lovelorn, comics, sports, and back-fence gossip. Books, magazines, and films supply entertainment packages for more specialized audiences. The Number One source of recreational activity of almost every American is the mass media.

Of course the media are pervasive in other countries as well. Transistor radios are always among the first manufactured products to be imported into any unindustrialized area of the world. Newspapers and government-sponsored radio and TV stations follow soon afterward. Nevertheless, few observers would dispute that Americans are more a product of their media than any other people in the world.

2. *Freedom of the Press.* The American government was founded on a radical political theory: representative democracy. According to this strange notion, the people of a nation should control the government by electing officials to carry out their will. The mass media necessarily play a central role in representative democracy. It is through the media, presumably, that the people get the information they need to decide what they want their officials to do. And it is through the media, presumably, that the people find out if their officials are doing it.

For this reason the First Amendment to the U.S. Constitution forbids the government to make any laws "abridging the freedom of the press." When it was first written, this provision was unprecedented. Other governments had assumed the right of the king to put a stop to any publication he deemed damaging to the nation. The American Constitution denied Congress and the president this fundamental right. The real threat to a democracy, so the argument went, is a mass-media system in chains. As long as every publisher (though not necessarily every reporter) is free to print whatever he or she wants to print, the truth will make itself clear, the people will be informed, and the democracy will flourish.

Today, many foreign governments have copied our First Amendment into their constitutions, and some even practice the freedom they preach. The American government, meanwhile, restrains its media with the laws of libel, obscenity, and privacy, the licensing of broadcast stations, the postal regulations, and so forth.

Despite these limitations, few mass-media systems in the world today are more free from government interference than the American system. In the 1970s a number of very high officials attacked the media for "irresponsible" opposition to government policy. Some interpreted these attacks as attempts to control the press, and so they may have been. But it is a testimonial to the almost incredible freedom of the American media that the attacks consisted mostly of speeches, denunciations, and largely futile attempts at intimidation. The government could *do* relatively little. You need only consult the latest news of national politics for fresh evidence of America's freedom of the press.

The purpose of a free press, you will remember, is to insure that the people will be well-informed. Well, we have a free press. Do we have an informed population? Pollster George Gallup often quotes a survey of college graduates which found that only four in ten could name the two senators from their own state; only half could cite a single difference between capitalism and socialism; only half had an accurate idea of the population of the United States; and only one in three could list five of the Soviet Union's satellite countries in Eastern Europe.[5]

The notion that freedom of the press is the basic requirement for an informed population is known as the "libertarian theory." The authors of the First Amendment firmly believed that if every newspaper were free to print precisely what it wanted to print, somehow truth would emerge victorious from its open confrontation with falsehood. The only responsibility of the media was to tell it the way they saw it. The only responsibility of the government was to leave the media alone.

In recent decades, many observers have begun to question the libertarian theory. In its place they have proposed a social responsibility theory of the press. That is, they argue that the American mass media must recognize their obligation to serve the public—to be truthful, accurate, and complete; to act as a forum for conflicting viewpoints; to provide meaningful background to the daily news; etc. Social responsibility theorists claim that if the media do not voluntarily live up to their obligations, then they must be forced to do so by the government.

Though the social responsibility theory is gaining in popularity and influence, it is not yet established. The American mass media today are free—free to serve the public or not as they choose.

3. *Big-Business Domination.* Perhaps the strongest weapon in the arsenal of the social responsibility theorists is the Big Business emphasis in the modern American media. The United States is one of the few countries in the world whose major media are all privately owned. Like General Motors and U.S. Steel, American newspapers, magazines, and broadcast stations spend much of their time worrying about stockholders, dividends, and profits. They may have too little time left for worrying about service to the public.

Like every business, the mass media have a product to sell. In the case of the book and film industries, the product is the medium itself; part of the price of a book or movie ticket is the manufacturer's profit. For the rest of the mass media, the product is you. Newspapers, magazines, and broadcast stations earn their considerable profits by selling your presence and your attention to advertisers. Articles and programs are just a device to keep you corralled, a come-on for the all-important ads.

Editors and reporters don't generally feel that way, of course. They do worry about serving the public. But their ability to do so is necessarily constrained by the paramount need to earn a profit by delivering audiences to advertisers. Why, for example, are local television newscasts so often dominated by violent crime? Few news directors believe that a local murder is really the most important news of the day—but most believe (correctly) that the murder will attract more viewers than, say, a budget debate at city hall. These extra viewers make TV news profitable.

In subtler ways the profit motive affects how the media define serving the public in the first place. Executives of the three television networks can argue very convincingly that light entertainment is an important public service, helping America unwind from its daily grind. Executives of our major metropolitan newspapers can argue very convincingly that "reader service"—articles on how to shop for imported wines and the like—is an important contribution as well, more

meaningful in our daily lives than dissections of foreign policy. But the choice of these ways to serve the public, rather than other ways, is an economic choice. If documentaries earned higher ratings and foreign policy attracted more readers you would hear quite different arguments from media executives.

The image of media entrepreneurs struggling to turn a profit suggests a hotly competitive contest, with each paper or station trying its own strategy and rising or falling on the results. There is indeed considerable competition left in the American media system—among local radio stations, for example, or national magazines, or the three TV networks. But the media business owes more to monopoly than to competition. Chains dominate the newspaper industry, buying out the independents until the average community has at most two local papers to choose between. Despite the growth of cable and satellites, the networks still control the bulk of television programming, providing identical shows each evening to audiences from Maine to California. The book business is dominated by a few giant companies on the east coast, the movie business by a few giant companies on the west coast. Competing with the biggies in any of these fields, though it can be done, is incredibly costly and hazardous.

Several conclusions follow from these facts. First, since the American media are businesses first and foremost, they are likely to choose profit over public service when the two come into conflict. Second, since the media are owned by business-oriented people, they are likely to reflect a business-oriented notion of what's good for the public—which may not be everybody's notion. Third, since the media are close to monopolies, they are likely to offer the audience only a single viewpoint on public affairs, instead of the rich conflict of viewpoints envisioned by the Founding Fathers. And fourth, since the media make competition extremely difficult, they are likely to "black out" positions and groups of which they disapprove.

Pervasive influence, freedom of the press, and the profit motive—this is the combination that makes the American mass media unique. Nowhere else is such a powerful social force so little controlled by government, so much controlled by self-interest.

THE FOUR FUNCTIONS

The mass media in general, and the American mass media in particular, have at least four basic functions to perform. They are:

1. To serve the economic system.
2. To entertain.
3. To inform.
4. To influence.

We will consider each in turn.

1. To Serve the Economic System. The fundamental economic purpose of the mass media in the United States is to sell people to advertisers. Economically, the articles in your newspaper and the programs on your radio and TV sets are merely "come-ons" to catch and hold your attention. Advertisers buy that attention from the media, and use it to sell you their products and services. In the process, both the media and the advertisers earn substantial profits.

It is possible to conceive of a mass-media system not dedicated to profit through advertising. Such systems exist, in fact, in many countries. The British Broadcasting Corporation (BBC), to give but one example, is financed in part by a special tax on radio and TV sets. It accepts no ads and earns no profits. Even in this country there are nonprofit broadcast stations and publications—not many, but a few. And of course some of the profit-making media, such as books and movies, earn their money directly from the audience. But the most influential media in the United States are fueled by advertising.

This dependence on advertising has many important implications for media content, which is inevitably designed to attract the sort of audience advertisers need in the sort

of mood advertisers want. But advertising is also important for its own sake. Through advertising, the mass media bring buyer and seller together. Advertising creates the demand for new goods and increases the demand for old ones. It thus helps keep the engine of industry running. No one knows exactly how much of the U.S. gross national product is the result of advertising in the mass media, but most economists agree that advertising's contribution to the GNP is substantial. Regardless of whether we approve or disapprove of advertising, this service to the economic system is certainly a central function of the American mass media.

2. To Entertain. Entertainment is by far the biggest service of the American mass media. This is especially true from the viewpoint of the audience. Political scientists may evaluate a television program in terms of how much information it imparts. Advertisers may ask what kind of climate for persuasion it offers. Station owners may wonder how much profit it brings in. But with rare exceptions, viewers want to know only how entertaining it is. Television is undoubtedly the nation's Number One entertainment medium, but recordings, film, and radio are not far behind.

Even the print media succeed or fail largely in terms of their entertainment value. The best-seller lists for hardback and paperback books usually include a few works of significance and value. But the bulk of every list is always pure entertainment, and even the "important" books must be entertaining to succeed. Magazines, too, must season their informational content with a heavy dose of fun and games. The least entertaining of the mass media is undoubtedly the newspaper. Yet even that offers the reader dozens of comics, humor and gossip columns, and human-interest features in every issue.

Because the public demands entertainment from its media, the media owner who wants to succeed has no choice but to try to be entertaining. Many critics have deplored this fact, complaining that mere entertainment was a waste and a degradation of media potential. Such an attitude ignores the important social role played by entertainment—the transmission of culture, the enlargement of perspectives, the encouragement of imagination, etc. And even the most virulent opponents of media entertainment must admit that the opportunity to relax and unwind is vital. Entertainment is not merely an economic necessity for media owners; it is an integral, essential function of the media.

But that is far from the whole story. The media have other functions besides entertainment. Moreover, the media *choose* the kinds of entertainment they wish to use. They are subject to criticism for their choices.

It is extremely difficult to come up with a clear-cut standard for distinguishing between

"good" entertainment and "bad" entertainment. Nonetheless, most observers will agree that in some sense *Harper's* is better than *True Romances,* "Sesame Street" is better than "Bugs Bunny," and Hemingway is better than Erle Stanley Gardner. The media must cater to public tastes, but they also help to mold public tastes. If the media choose violence, or pornography, or the lowest of lowbrow culture, then they must take responsibility for the choice.

3. To Inform. Entertainment may be what the public wants from its mass media, but information is probably their most important function. No doubt many people read *Time* and *Newsweek,* say, because they find them entertaining; and certainly the newsmagazines try to entertain their read-

WHAT WE WATCH

Judged by the ratings, the following were the most popular TV shows the week of November 24-30, 1980:

1. "Dallas" (CBS)
2. "60 Minutes" (CBS)
3. "Dukes of Hazzard" (CBS)
4. "The Love Boat" (ABC)
5. "M*A*S*H" (CBS)
6. "Trapper John, M.D." (CBS)
7. "The Jeffersons" (CBS)
8. "Charlie's Angels" (ABC)
9. "That's Incredible" (ABC)
10. "Alice" (CBS)[6]

Except for "60 Minutes," a slick amalgam of muckraking exposés and human-interest features, every show on the list is pure entertainment. We learn from these shows, of course—everything from wartime medical techniques to the lifestyle of wealthy Texans. And we pick up attitudes from them too—toward doctors, toward corporate executives, toward middle-class blacks, toward cruise passengers. What we learn may be true or false; the attitudes we absorb may be humane or oppressive. But none of that is what the shows are "about." They are entertainment.

NBC executives were doubtless very unhappy about the results of this particular week's ratings. As they plan their programs for future seasons, they will try to do a better job of providing what the public wants to watch: entertainment.

ers. But the best newsmagazine is not necessarily the most entertaining one. It is the one that successfully conveys the most information.

The power of the mass media to inform is almost incredible. On November 22, 1963, at 12:30 in the afternoon, President John F. Kennedy was assassinated. Within half an hour, two-thirds of all Americans knew of the event. Ninety percent knew within an hour, and 99.8 percent had heard the story by early evening.[7] Some got the news directly from the mass media; others were told by family, friends, or strangers on the street, who had themselves heard it on the media.

There was an immediate rush to radio and television for more detail. During the days that followed, 166 million Americans tuned in to the assassination story on television. The average TV set was on for roughly eight hours a day.[8]

Most of the news supplied by the mass media is more routine than a presidential assassination. Weather reports, stock listings, and movie timetables are among the best-read features in your daily newspaper—and among the most informative. We tend to dismiss these services not because they are unimportant, but because they are easy to prepare. Similarly, news reports of natural disasters, crimes, accidents, and the like are genuinely useful. Since they are standard fare for the media and difficult to handle poorly, scholars pay them very little attention—perhaps less attention than they deserve.

The more difficult a story is to cover, the less likely the media are to cover it well. The informational problems of the media are many and varied. Is a story so complicated that no reporter can understand it, much less repeat it? Is it so technical that few readers are likely to enjoy it or finish it? Does it require days of hard-nosed investigative digging among sources who would much rather keep their mouths shut? Might it insult or embarrass an advertiser, an important newsmaker, a friend of the publisher, or even a reader? Such stories may or may not be more

important than the easier ones. But because they are difficult to cover, the way they are handled is a good measure of the media's responsibility to their informing function.

Perhaps the most important information of all is information about the government. The purpose of the First Amendment, after all, is to insure that the media will be free to report and criticize the actions of government officials, free to inform the public about public affairs. When a television station carries live the speech of a president, it is performing a valuable public service. When it offers intelligent commentary on the content and meaning of that speech, it is performing a much *more* valuable public service.

It is worth mentioning that everything in the mass media is in some sense informative, whether or not it is intended that way. Even a soap opera tells us something (true or false) about how people live, how they dress and talk and solve problems.

For centuries, Italy was a country with two different populations: the wealthy, cosmopolitan North and the poor, rural South. The two were so different they even spoke different dialects, and were almost completely unable to understand one another. Then, in 1954, nationwide Italian television was introduced. In just a few years, television began to unify the country.

A university professor commented: "Some intellectuals call television the 'opium of the people.' That may be so in a city like Milan or Turin. But can you imagine a modern bathroom appearing on TV screens from Naples southward?" And a historian added: "There's been more change in Italy's linguistic situation in the past fifteen years than in the century since Rome became the capital."[9]

The bulk of this book is devoted to an assessment and explanation of the informational performance of the American mass media. This is not because media owners, or advertisers, or audiences consider information the most important role of the media. Many don't. We do.

4. To Influence. The power of the mass media to change people's minds directly is very limited. People don't like to have their minds changed, and so they ignore or misinterpret attempts to do so—usually successfully. If influence were limited to changing people's minds directly, the media would not be particularly influential.

But influence is more subtle than that. When William Randolph Hearst's *New York Journal* championed the war against Spain in 1898, he didn't achieve very many conversions. But through slanted news coverage and sensational writing, the *Journal* did manage to help create a climate of war fever. No doubt most readers viewed Hearst's style of journalism as entertainment and information, not influence. Yet he helped make them go to war.

More than a century before Hearst, Thomas Paine wrote a political pamphlet called *Common Sense,* urging an American Revolution. And some 80-odd years after Hearst, in 1980, Ronald Reagan engineered a television campaign urging his election as president. Paine didn't convert many Tories, and Reagan didn't win over many Carter enthusiasts. But Paine did succeed in crystallizing the gathering resentments of many colonists into a consistent revolutionary ideology. And Reagan succeeded in crystallizing the gathering frustrations of many Americans into a Republican vote. So Paine got his revolution, and Reagan got the White House. The mass media played a vital role in the success of both.

The most obvious and prevalent example of mass media influence is advertising. Media ad campaigns have a lot going for them. Through careful intermixture with entertainment and informational content, they gain a captive audience. Through bold colors and imaginative graphics, they make you pay attention. Through catchy slogans and constant repetition, they make you remember. Through irrelevant appeals to sex, snobbism, and the good life, they make you buy.

The very existence of newspapers, magazines, radio, and television testifies to the persuasive power of advertising. For if the ads were unsuccessful, there would be no ads. And if there were no ads, there would be no newspapers, magazines, radio, and television in the form we know them.

Not every media attempt to influence the public is successful, of course. Politicians and manufacturers may spend millions on the media and still lose out to the competition. Editorialists and polemicists may devote page after page to an urgent plea for action, and get no action. Not every revolutionary book foments a revolution; not every TV appeal to voters captures the White House. But it is nearly impossible to foment a revolution without a book, to win the White House without a TV appeal. The persuasive power of the mass media, though limited, is undeniable.

The remainder of this chapter is devoted to exploring the impact of mass media on society, especially the impact of American mass media on American society. This is an enormously complex and confusing topic.

Before we begin, consider the following facts that have already been mentioned:

1. Mass media pervade the lives of all Americans, adults as well as children; we are all in some sense products of our media.

   but

2. The media audience can easily avoid conversion to new attitudes (and even exposure to unpleasant truths) by ignoring, misunderstanding, or forgetting what it doesn't want to know.

   but

3. We learn from entertainment too, and are influenced by fiction and "straight" news as well as by intentional persuasion.

   but

4. Sources of mass-media content cannot gear their messages to individuals in the audience, and cannot easily judge how the audience is responding in time to change the message accordingly.

but

5. Interpersonal communication is often based on information and attitudes that people have absorbed from the mass media.

but

6. The mass media are so complex, and so diverse in their sources and channels, that a single viewpoint cannot usually dominate the media for long.

but

7. Even though advertising and propaganda are not always successful, they achieve enough that few manufacturers or ideologues would try to do without them.

An adequate picture of the impact of American media on American society must make sense of all these conflicting facts.

The persuasive power of the mass media is neither as great as the alarmists warn us nor as little as the optimists assure us. The media are rarely able to convert their audience to an opposing viewpoint overnight, but they can reinforce old attitudes, create brand new ones, and in time even achieve some change. Readers and viewers are active participants in this process, using the media for their own purposes and needs. This may protect us from specific influence attempts, but it does not keep the media from creating the reality in which we live and to which we respond. The media "environment" plays as big a role in the lives of many Americans as the first-hand environment of their own experience.

PERSUASION AND PROPAGANDA

People have thought about the effects of communication on attitudes and behavior at least since the time of Aristotle. And the special power of mass communication to change the way we think, feel, and behave has been a source of concern (especially to governments) since the invention of the printing press. But the modern science of communication research was born out of psychology, sociology, and political science only in the 1930s. There were two immediate reasons for its quick development at that point in history. First, advertisers wanted to know how to spend their money more effectively. And second, American intellectuals were worried about the propaganda efforts of Nazi Germany.

The research tradition that developed over the next thirty years was devoted to answering one basic question: What factors determine how much impact a particular piece of communication will have on the attitudes of its audience? Hundreds of books and thousands of journal articles were written about various aspects of this question.

By way of example, here is a more or less random list of six findings from this type of research:

1. It is usually better to state your conclusions explicitly than to let your audience draw its own conclusions.[10]

2. Arguments presented at the beginning or end of a communication are remembered better than arguments presented in the middle.[11]

3. Emotional appeals are often more effective than strictly rational ones.[12]

4. When dealing with an audience that disagrees with your position, it helps to acknowledge some validity to the opposing view.[13]

5. Attitude change may be greater some time after a communication than right after it.[14]

6. High-credibility sources (such as doctors) provoke more attitude change than low-credibility sources (such as patients), even if the reason for the credibility has nothing to do with the topic of the communication.[15]

These findings—and hundreds more like them—were very helpful to advertisers, who used them to design more effective ads. They were very helpful to the war effort, which used them to counter Nazi propaganda and later to produce Allied propaganda. And they are still very helpful to marketing experts, political candidates, and anyone else interested in using communication to change people's attitudes.

But as the studies accumulated, attitude change turned out to be a more complicated phenomenon than the early findings had seemed to imply. Later research had to specify the conditions under which the various "principles" of attitude change did or did not hold true. As time went on, and more and more conflicting findings turned up, it became harder and harder to specify which principles were valid under which conditions.

Researchers began to suspect that there was something fundamentally wrong with the way they were studying the effects of communications. In fact, there were at least four things wrong with it.

First, the majority of the early studies were conducted in the laboratories of academic social scientists, using students as subjects. Whole theories of communication emerged from the unpaid efforts of undergraduates in introductory psychology courses. This was convenient for the researchers and made for neat, methodologically controlled studies—but it was unreal. The occasional pieces of real-world research almost invariably found much less attitude change than the lab studies had led everyone to expect. The complexities and counter-pressures of reality just couldn't be duplicated in controlled laboratory experiments.

Second, most of the studies dealt with topics of some intellectual importance but practically no audience involvement—such as dental hygiene, currency devaluation, or the future of movie theaters. The way attitudes are changed around these sorts of topics turned out to be almost irrelevant. Most propagandists were interested in more gut-grabbing topics, such as race prejudice, "welfare statism," or the upcoming presidential election. Audiences already had strong emotional commitments on those issues, and a speech on race relations yielded a lot less attitude change than one on the future of movie theaters. Advertisers, meanwhile, were

interested in topics of zero intellectual interest to the audience, like the choice of a breakfast cereal. By 1965, Herbert E. Krugman was arguing that people are influenced by advertising without paying attention, and without changing their attitudes at all.[16]

Third, most attitude-change research was based on an oversimplified model of how attitudes are related to information and behavior. Many studies assumed that if the audience learned the message, its attitudes would therefore be changed. Even more studies assumed that if attitudes (as expressed on a questionnaire) were changed, behavior would inevitably change too. By the 1960s these assumptions were falling apart. In 1964, Jack B. Haskins surveyed twenty-eight different studies of information, attitudes, and behavior, and concluded that there was "no relationship between what a person learned, knew, or recalled on the one hand, and what he did or how he felt on the other."[17] In the same year, Leon Festinger reviewed the meager research literature on how attitudes affect behavior, and found no evidence of a consistent relationship there either.[18]

Fourth, the early research on attitude change virtually ignored the audience. All the care and creativity went into figuring out the different effects of different kinds of sources, channels, styles of presentation, etc. The audience was viewed as just being there, passive, receiving the message and then changing or not changing depending on the source's skill and know-how. But in fact, people are not just sponges who soak up media content. We *use* the media for our own purposes, and we are therefore active participants in the communication process. How the media affect us depends very largely on who we are and how we are using the media.

In a sense, everything that was wrong with traditional communication research resulted from underestimating the audience. *You* know that you respond differently to an experiment in a psych class than to an editorial on television. *You* know that your views on currency devaluation are more thoughtful than your views on breakfast cereals, and less emotional than your views on race prejudice. *You* know that you can learn things without believing them, believe things without doing them, and do things without learning or believing them. It took communication researchers thirty years to acknowledge these truths fully, because for thirty years they concentrated on the source and the message and almost ignored the audience.

THE MEDIA AUDIENCE

Most Americans, it must be said, are happy with their mass media. They have complaints, of course—too much depressing news, too many commercials, and so forth. But on the whole they are quite satisfied. When survey researchers go into the field and ask people what they would like from the media that they are not already getting, almost invariably the response is "Nothing." It is possible, of course—perhaps even likely—that there are public needs which are not adequately served by the mass media. But if so, the public is largely unaware of them.

What, then, are the public needs that are served by the media? In other words, what do we use our media for, what functions do they fulfill in our lives?

Play is obviously one of the most important ways we use the media. From the very first time your parents read you a story, you have been taught that media use is fun. And for most of us it *is* fun. Not just explicit entertainment, either—many people watch commercials and read newspapers for pleasure, and certainly advertisers and reporters work hard to make their writing pleasurable. At least one scholar, William Stephenson, argues that fun is both the greatest impact and the greatest public service of the media; his book is called *The Play Theory of Mass Communication*.[19] Other observers complain that media "escapism" distracts people from more active sorts of entertainment and from the serious problems of the day. But no one denies that we use our media for play.

Time-filling is related to play, but a lot more passive. When New York's newspapers went on strike in 1945, Bernard Berelson asked people what they missed. Most readers talked about the importance of newspapers as part of the routine at certain points in their daily schedule—over the breakfast table, for example, or while commuting to and from work. They resented the disruption in their lives caused by the strike, and many resorted to scanning cereal boxes or subway ads just to have something to read.[20] Similarly, we listen to the radio while driving and the TV while doing chores mainly to fill up the time.

The mass media also make interpersonal communication flow more smoothly. In a

THE AUDIENCE IS PEOPLE

Not only do people use the media for different purposes at different times. They also have different personalities—and our personalities greatly affect how we respond to a persuasive argument. Authoritarian people are more easily persuaded than independent thinkers, especially by a high-status source. People with high IQs are more influenced by logical arguments than people with low IQs, but they are less influenced by emotional ones. Some psychologists have even suggested that persuasibility is itself a personality trait.

Age, sex, income, social class, occupation, and other demographic variables also influence our response to persuasion. So do the groups we belong to or want to belong to. The mass-media audience is made up of real people who lead real lives, not robots who do whatever the media tell them.

complex and mobile society, many people spend much of their time in interaction with near-strangers. The media provide a steady supply of topics to keep the conversation going. News events and entertainment plots are a safe way to establish and maintain a casual conversation, to begin building a sense of commonality. Communication scholar Lee Thayer argues forcefully that "the primary use to which people put the media and their fare is that of providing something to talk about in ritual, non-vital encounters with other people."[21]

This is by no means the only social role played by the media. Many magazines are purchased for the social status they confer when mentioned in passing or spread out on the coffee table. Television gives families a chance to spend time together peacefully. People go to movies to get away from their kids, or to get away from their parents, or to get close to someone else. In these and many other ways, the media are closely entwined with our relationships with each other.

Innumerable psychological needs are met by the media as well. Studies have shown, for example, that when family fights break out, children turn to television for solace; when their egos are bruised by failure, they read more "Superman"-type comic books. Similarly, many women (and some men) use serials for vicarious enjoyment of open emotion, while many men (and some women) use racy magazines for vicarious enjoyment of open sex. The catharsis of a Shakespeare tragedy, the violence of a police story, and the self-confidence of a news commentator all meet important psychological needs in the audience.

Among the most important psychological needs met by the media is the need for stability, for the reassurance of unchanging routine. The "real world" and real people may be dismayingly unpredictable, but the world and people of the mass media can be relied upon to behave as they have always behaved. The crooks always get caught at the end of the television show, today's newspaper looks exactly like yesterday's newspaper, your favorite DJ will play the same music tomorrow as today. Sudden changes in media content—or media schedules—typically generate a furor of audience resentment; even new characters on a TV series take some getting used to. They disrupt the cherished stability of the media in an unstable world.

Closely related to stability is the mythic role of the media. American society, like every society, is guided by an assortment of "myths" that embody its core values—technological progress, social mobility, rugged individualism, and the like. The media teach these myths to young people. Just as importantly, media content reaffirms the myths for adults, reminding us that this is what we believe and how we live, that our core values survive unchanged and unshaken. Virtually everything in the media, from news to novels, has mythic content—usually the same mythic content.

Information-seeking is another reason why people turn to the media. Not just news, but also quiz programs and advertisements capture our attention in part because they offer us information. And one early study found that people went to movies partly in order to learn how higher-status Americans dress, behave, and make love.[22] Sometimes the information is sought for its own sake; our society considers it a civic virtue to be well-informed whether you take action or not. Sometimes the information is sought for reassurance—people who just bought a Ford, for instance, read Ford ads to collect information showing they made a wise choice. Sometimes the information satisfies a psychological need, or confers social status. And sometimes it's just useful: Why, after all, do you read the weather forecast?

Finally, people use the media for guidance in problem-solving. When a decision needs to be made, we seek out not only relevant information but also relevant influence. We look for someone to tell us what to decide. Self-help books, editorials, advice columns, "how-to" articles, and the like obviously meet this need for help. Other sorts of media content meet it less obviously. A classic study of radio soap operas, for example, found that many listeners used the shows for guidance in their everyday activities. One faithful follower commented: "If you listen to these programs and something turns up in your own life, you would know what to do about it."[23]

We have listed several reasons why audiences use the mass media: play; time-filling; conversation and other social needs; stability, myth, and other psychological needs; information-seeking; and guidance. What happens to your attitudes in response to an attempt at persuasion will depend largely on whether you are paying attention for fun or for status, for information or for reassurance, for guidance or just to kill time.

The media entertain us when we want to play. They pass the time for us when we are bored. They help us relate to each other or avoid each other. They make us feel better about ourselves. They provide us with information when we are looking for it. They tell us what to do when we need guidance. There's nothing covert or manipulative about any of this. It's what we want from our media, and it's what our media do for us. Persuasion is a sideline.

This emphasis on the media audience is known in communication theory as the "uses and gratifications" approach. It flourished in the 1960s. Before then, most research on communication effects was dominated by the bullet metaphor. The source shot the message at the audience, and if the source's aim was true the desired effect was inevitable. By stressing the audience as an active participant in the communication process, uses-and-gratifications research helped scholars understand that the source is not all-powerful after all. Many theorists, in fact, deserted to the opposite extreme, advancing a "limited effects" model of media impact whose central premise was that sources are nearly impotent beside the overwhelming power of the audience to decide how it will use its media.

In the 1970s, communication theory slowly moved back toward the middle. The mass media do affect their audience. The nature of that effect is controlled jointly by individual sources, by individual members of the audience, by the social system surrounding both source and audience, and by the media themselves.

PERSUADING THE AUDIENCE

What, finally, can we say about the impact of the mass media on our attitudes and behavior? Can we do any better than Bernard Berelson's truism: "Some kinds of *communication* on some kinds of *issues,* brought to the attention of some kinds of *people* under some kinds of *conditions,* have some kinds of *effects.*"[24] Yes.

First of all, conversion through the mass media is extremely rare. Hundreds of social philosophers have worried about it, hundreds of researchers have looked for it, but it just doesn't happen very often. In fact, the opposite is far more likely. Regardless of the issue, the mass media usually reinforce the existing attitudes and lifestyles of their audience. They are far more often a force for stability than a force for change.

The active participation of the audience insures that this will be true. People very seldom want to be changed; we usually want to be reassured that what we believe and do is what we should believe and do. Conversion is not one of the ways we use the media. In fact, it is inconsistent with several of them—it isn't fun, it doesn't pass the time innocuously, and it creates psychological and social conflicts instead of resolving them. Selective attention enables us to avoid communications that might threaten our personal status quo. Selective perception helps us misinterpret those we can't avoid, and selective retention helps us forget those we can't misinterpret. Our group memberships and allegiances keep us from straying too far from the group's norms. We talk mostly to people who agree with us, and we use mostly the same media they use. The diversity of the media assures that a threatening communication will soon be supplanted by a supportive one. And the media's profit motive guarantees that most communications will pander to our prejudices, not challenge them. In the face of all this, conversion is highly unlikely.

The fact that the media tend to reinforce our attitudes is itself an important effect. Our views are strengthened by ammunition from the media. They give us new facts to cite, new sources to quote, and above all a sense that we are right and others agree with us. Imagine a hot local debate over a school bond issue, where the bulk of the news happens to favor the supporters. Most opponents probably won't be converted—but that isn't really necessary. If the supporters are getting lots of reinforcement from the media, they'll be much more likely to speak up in conversations with their friends, and to vote on election day. Lacking this reinforcement, opponents of the bond issue are more likely to keep quiet and forget to vote. A crucial piece of every persuasion strategy is to increase the fervor of your allies and dampen the enthusiasm of your enemies. This the media do very, very well.

And what about issues with a lot less audience involvement than voting, such as the choice of a breakfast cereal? Here the audience has no strong attitude, perhaps no attitude at all. We rarely seek out information or guidance on breakfast cereals, but we don't resist it either—we barely pay attention to it when it comes our way. Through repetition alone, an advertiser can thus build in our minds a sense of the product's appropriateness. And so when we go to buy a cereal, or a detergent, or anything else we don't much care about, we usually buy an advertised brand—not because we believe it's better (we don't believe anything about it, really), but just because we've heard of it and it somehow "seems like a good one." An established attitude, a habit, a group norm,

a recommendation from a friend, a bad experience with the product, or just about any other influence can overcome this "learning without involvement." But if nothing else is happening and we don't bother to think about it, mere repetition in the media is enough to determine what we buy.

Advertisers don't have to rely only on low-involvement repetition for their impact. They know that we use the media to satisfy our needs, and they know that the media are good at reinforcing our values. Nothing is easier than tying a product to those needs and values. And so we get the toothpaste ad that promises social and sexual success in return for our purchase. Of course the needs triggered and reinforced by the ad—sex, status, and the like—are not really satisfied by switching toothpastes. We know the connection posited by the ad is irrational; we don't really believe that Ultra Brite gives us sex appeal. But unless there's an opposing influence somewhere in our social environment, the reinforcement of our sexual needs and values is often enough to make us switch to Ultra Brite.

Once we make the switch, we may begin to feel a bit silly. People like to have reasons for what they do, even if what they do isn't reasonable. So we start looking for information that will make sense of our new behavior[25]—and suddenly we're reading Ultra Brite ads with unusual interest. In the case of Ultra Brite, it probably won't work. We can't find any information that one toothpaste is better than another (maybe because it isn't), and so the only thing that keeps us using Ultra Brite is habit and the constant repetition of those sexy ads.

But suppose the new behavior is something a little more defensible, like recycling used newspapers, cans, and bottles. Many people start recycling for the same sorts of irrational reasons that determine their choice of a toothpaste—peer pressure, pressure from their children, etc. But once they start, they begin looking for information to make sense of what they're doing. And they find it in the

WHAT DO YOU KNOW ABOUT WOLVES?

The power of the media to change us through mere repetition is not limited to advertising. There are thousands of noncommercial topics about which we could care less, about which we know almost nothing, and about which everything we know comes from the media. If what the media tell us on these topics is always the same, and if nothing in our non-media environment says anything different, we will predictably wind up believing what we're told. It may or may not be true.

For example, what do you know about wolves? Apart from zoos, most Americans today have absolutely no personal experience with wolves, nor are they something we talk a lot about with our friends and neighbors. Nearly everything we know and think about wolves comes to us from the media. It starts with "Little Red Riding Hood" and "The Three Little Pigs." It continues with the Wolfman and his imitators, and with references to the "wolfish leers" of oversexed men and the slyly disguised threat of a "wolf in sheep's clothing." It ends with our constant battle to "keep the wolf from the door." These and similar metaphors are constantly repeated in the media, from which we pick them up for conversational use. Little wonder, then, that most Americans consider wolves to be vicious, destructive, cunning, dishonest animals. Ecologists know that this image is untrue (wolves hunt only for food, and seldom attack people or pigs), and that it leads to some very unwise extermination programs. But ecologists don't often write for the media.

We are not very committed to our image of wolves, so it is easy to overcome. A 1969 NBC documentary called "The Wolf Men" was seen by more than 24 million people, and resulted in 16,000 letters urging natural resources agencies to protect the wolf.[26] But without such an opposing influence, even a casual, low-involvement image can significantly affect our attitudes and behavior.

media. News about the value of recycling probably doesn't do much to get people started; for that you need the sort of manipulative persuasion found in toothpaste ads. But news is absolutely essential to help us make sense of what we are already doing, and thus to keep us doing it.

Information in the media also helps us apply our existing attitudes to new circumstances. News of the Watergate scandals, for example, didn't make people any more opposed to political corruption than they already were, but it did focus that opposition on the behavior of Richard Nixon. Similarly, the information that a product contributes to pollution can't create an attitude against pollution—but if you're already worried about pollution, that information can turn you against the product. As early as 1948, Paul F. Lazarsfeld and Robert K. Mer-

ton acknowledged this role of the media; they called it canalization.[27] In the midst of the Iranian hostage crisis of 1979, advocates of energy conservation canalized the widespread hatred of Iran's Ayatolla Khomeini and that country's sizable oil industry. Hundreds of billboards went up on American highways, featuring Khomeini's face and the two words "Drive 55."

Paradoxically, the media can even change attitudes while reinforcing those attitudes. Psychologists have found that every attitude has a so-called "latitude of acceptance" around it. A communication that falls within our latitude of acceptance, even though it's slightly different from our own view, will be accepted as essentially what we think. In the process of accepting it, we move our own opinion in the direction of the communication. Our latitude of acceptance moves too, and a more extreme message now becomes acceptable.[28]

It is thus possible—intentionally or unintentionally—to guide an audience toward a whole new value system. A single message advocating the new value would fall outside the audience's latitude of acceptance, and would probably boomerang, moving attitudes in just the opposite direction. But a series of messages can accomplish the change in baby steps. Thus we may gradually adjust to the notion that homosexuals are unfairly persecuted or that manufacturers should be forbidden to dump their toxic wastes or that high unemployment is a tolerable price to pay for reducing inflation.

We have listed six ways that media content can affect our attitudes and behavior:

1. The media can provide ammunition to support our attitudes, thus increasing our commitment.

2. On low-involvement issues where there are no competing influences, mere repetition in the media can change our behavior directly.

3. By catering to our existing needs and values and linking them to a new behavior, the media can get us to act without changing our attitudes.

4. Information in the media can be used to justify or rationalize behavior initially based on needs, building attitudes to support that behavior.

5. The media can relate an existing attitude to a new object by providing information that ties the two together.

6. With a series of messages starting near the initial views of the audience and gradually becoming more extreme, the media can produce major shifts in audience attitudes, one step at a time.

None of these six effects is inconsistent with the general principle that the media are more a force for stability than a force for change. All six involve reinforcement, not conversion. Yet they do change what we believe and what we do.

THE IMPACT OF MEDIA

So far we have talked about the impact of the mass media only in terms of persuasion. We have seen that the alarmists are wrong in attributing to the media the power to convert us from our most deeply held beliefs in a few carefully manipulated minutes. But we have also seen that the media can reinforce our attitudes and values, build new ones on issues we don't care much about, and even change us some over the long haul.

As you might have guessed, persuasion is by no means the only impact of the media on their audience. It's the one that gets most of the research, but there are others. We will talk about four of them:

1. Agenda-setting.
2. Norms and culture.
3. Modeling.
4. Apathy.

1. Agenda-Setting. On any given day, the typical metropolitan newspaper or broadcast station has available more than ten times as much ready-to-go content as it has space or time to use. The media are therefore obliged to play the role of gatekeepers, deciding what information to transmit and how much emphasis to give it. The editorial decision that a particular event is not news is a self-fulfilling judgment; if the news media ignore it, then it cannot be news. Conversely, any event given major play in the mass media becomes by definition a major event. There is plentiful evidence that the media audience absorbs the "agenda" of the newspaper front page and the TV news show far more completely than it absorbs their content. In this sense, even when the mass media do not tell us what to think, they tell us what to think *about.*

Any group that has ever tried unsuccessfully to get news of its activities into the media can testify to the importance of agenda-setting. As Lazarsfeld and Merton put it in

1948, "the mass media confer status on public issues, persons, organizations, and social movements" merely by reporting them.[29] In the 1960s, the media may or may not have changed the racial attitudes of white Americans (the evidence is mixed)—but for sure the media convinced us all that racial discrimination is something important to think about. What is important to think about in the 1980s? Most people are watching the media to find out.

The agenda-setting function is not confined to news. In the 1970s, television and movie entertainment quietly began dealing with themes such as women's liberation, abortion, and homosexuality. Most of these shows probably didn't change many people's attitudes, but their cumulative impact over several years made an important contribution to getting us thinking about those issues.

Of course the media don't usually do their agenda-setting on purpose. In fact, the media get *their* agendas mostly from the public; reporters tell us about what they think we're interested in, not what they think we should be interested in. Still, the media are often ahead of the audience in their interests, and they help bring the audience along.

2. Norms and Culture. The media tell us what our norms are. American society is made up of many subcultures, divided by age, income, religion, geography, etc. Most of our personal contacts are with people who share our subculture, but through the media we interact with those from other cultures as well. How argumentative, how flirtatious, and how drunk can you be at a party and still stay within the bounds of good taste? Which grievances justify a fist fight, and which should be settled less violently? When is an adolescent old enough to stay out all night? What is the proper attitude for a "right-thinking" American to hold toward China, extramarital sex, and cheating on one's income tax? How often should you wax your car? The media suggest answers to

these questions, which may or may not be the same answers our friends and neighbors propose.

The result is a tendency toward the homogenization of culture. The media expand our horizons by telling us what other people do, and in the process they make us more like those other people. In a variety of ways—in language, in dress, in child-rearing practices, in ethical standards—Americans become more and more alike every year, largely because of the influence of the media. Some subcultures, of course, are strong enough to withstand the homogenizing assault of the mainstream American media. But in the battle between cultural diversity and the melting pot, the media are securely on the side of the pot.

3. Modeling. The media not only tell us what other people are doing; they also tell us how we can do it too. Long before most children are ready to go to kindergarten, they have already picked up many behavior patterns their parents never taught them—from television. Kids frequently imitate the posture and vocabulary of their favorite TV hero. More important, they pick up the hero's style of dealing with people and situations as well. And how many adults, for that matter, have modeled pieces of their own behavior in precise imitation of Humphrey Bogart or Raquel Welch, Walter Cronkite or Mary Tyler Moore?

Most of the research on modeling has centered on the effects of media violence, a key issue to many critics of the media. In one typical series of experiments, children watched films of an adult model aggressively kicking or punching a pop-up "bo-bo doll." When the children were later intentionally frustrated (by having their toys taken away) and then put in a room with a bo-bo doll, sure enough they kicked it and punched it more than kids who had seen a different film.[30] They had learned from the model how to abuse the doll. In much the same

"DEVELOPING" A COUNTRY

In the United States, the mass media are privately owned businesses; their job is to earn a profit, and any impact on society is almost accidental. In most of the so-called "developing" countries, by contrast, the media are government-controlled monopolies, and they are used with the overriding purpose of "developing" the country.

Does it work? Sometimes. Media campaigns have successfully changed traditional lifestyles in many countries across the globe, from China to Costa Rica, on topics ranging from literacy to family planning, from sanitation and health care to political indoctrination. But just as often, such campaigns have failed dismally. The most successful ones usually involve dissemination of a new idea of obvious value to the audience and no great threat to the traditional culture—such as a new strain of wheat that yields better crops. Even in these cases, custom and conservatism have often led people to reject or distort the message. When the innovation really threatens traditional ways and values—such as family-planning campaigns—success is rare. In countries where children are the only plentiful form of "wealth," asking people to control their family size is like asking Americans to stop making money.

way, scores of airplane hijackers learned from the media how to vent their feelings most effectively.

The evidence is not conclusive that violence in the media makes us *feel* more violent. But media violence does set a very tolerant norm for us, telling us that physical aggression is All-American. And through modeling, media violence teaches us new and satisfying ways to be violent ourselves. That's enough.

4. Apathy. We have talked a lot about the things the media make us do. What about the things the media keep us from doing?

At the most obvious level, most Americans spend more than four hours a day passively watching television, reading newspapers or magazines, or listening to the radio. One of the most common criticisms of the mass media is that they replace genuine participation with a kind of vicarious, passive pseudo-experience. The result, it is charged, is an apathetic and uninvolved public.

This argument is usually made about media entertainment, especially television, but it may apply to news as well. News in the media is mostly information about the actions of "important" people. In their effort to be objective, reporters seldom tell us what we should do with the information, or even what we could do with it. The speed of modern mass communication and the complexity of the world's problems encourage us to conclude that informed action is impossible, and perhaps even inappropriate. Let the government handle it.

The very format of media news presentations is aimed at rewarding the reader, listener, or viewer for the mere act of reading, listening, or viewing. Reporters are taught to "round out" their stories, to work at creating the impression that all relevant questions have been asked and answered, that the job (reporter's and audience's) is done. The result may be a redefinition of the obligations of a citizen. Instead of feeling obliged to do something about the world's problems, we may come to feel that it's enough just to know what the problems are. G. D. Wiebe calls this the syndrome of "well-informed futility."[31] Most of us call it apathy.

Lazarsfeld and Merton described this vitally important impact of the media back in 1948:

Exposure to [a] flood of information may serve to narcotize rather than to energize the average reader or listener. . . . The individual reads accounts of issues and problems and may even discuss alternative lines of action. But this rather intellectualized, rather remote connection with organized social action is not activated. The interested and informed citizen can congratulate himself on his lofty state of interest and information and neglect to see that he has abstained from decision and action. . . . He comes to mistake *knowing* about the problems of the day for *doing* something about them. His social conscience remains spotlessly clean. He *is* concerned. He *is* informed. And he has all sorts of ideas as to what should be done. But after he has gotten through his dinner and after he has listened to his favored radio programs and after he has read his second newspaper of the day, it is really time for bed.[32]

Agenda-setting, norms and culture, modeling, and apathy have little to do with persuasion. But they have a lot to do with our lives, and with the media's impact on our lives.

MEDIA AS ENVIRONMENT

Every moment of our waking lives, we learn from our environment. Some of this learning is through our rational faculties. Some of it is through our senses, our intuition, and our feelings. We learn from the smell of the air in a meadow or on a city street. We learn from the conversations, glances, and half-glances of the people we meet. We learn from the feeling in our muscles after a hard workout. All of these are educational materials, inputs to the human biocomputer.

Before the invention of the printing press, people spent nearly all of their time experiencing life in these ways. Before the invention of television, most of us spent a good deal of our time doing so. Even today, very few people live their lives entirely in the mass media. But more and more of our time, especially our leisure time, is devoted to the pseudo-reality of the media instead of the genuine reality around us.

This *must* make a difference. Think about watching television for four hours a night—just sitting there, eyes wide, body still, room dark, other people reduced to vague shadows, images pouring into your brain. Regardless of what's *on* the tube, all those hours in front of it must have some kind of impact.

Communication researchers have seldom studied these sorts of questions, because there was (and is) no methodology to study them rigorously. Until the 1960s, what little we knew about the effects of media irrespective of content came to us from anthropologists, who recorded the reactions of primitive cultures to new communication technologies.

Consider this excerpt from a book by Edmund Carpenter, describing his experiences in the village of Sio, in New Guinea:

We gave each person a Polaroid shot of himself. At first there was no understanding. The photographs were black & white, flat, static, odorless—far removed from any reality they knew. They had to be taught to "read" them. I pointed to a nose in a picture, then touched the real nose, etc. . . .

Recognition gradually came into the subject's face. And fear. Suddenly he covered his mouth, ducked his head & turned his body away. After this first startled response, often repeated several times, he either stood transfixed, staring at his image, only his stomach muscles betraying tension, or he retreated from the group, pressing his photograph against his chest, showing it to no one, slipping away to study it in solitude. . . .

When we projected movies . . . there was absolute silence as they watched themselves, a silence broken only by whispered identification of faces on the screen. . . .

When we returned to Sio, months later, I thought at first we had made a wrong turn in the river network. I didn't recognize the place. Several houses had been rebuilt in a new style. Men wore European clothing. They carried themselves differently. They acted differently. . . . In one brutal movement they had been torn out of a tribal existence & transformed into detached individuals, lonely, frustrated, no longer at home—anywhere.[33]

Except for anthropologists and philosophers, no one writes very much about the impact of the mass media simply as *media,* irrespective of content. Systematic research on the question is virtually impossible. So you are as free as Marshall McLuhan (see box) to guess in what ways our society would be different if the printing press or the TV picture tube had never been invented. But even though we can never measure such global

---

THE MEDIUM IS THE MASSAGE

The notion that mass media communicate something quite apart from their content was popularized in the 1960s by a Canadian scholar named Marshall McLuhan. McLuhan, who died in 1980, entitled one of his books *The Medium Is the Massage,* purposely turning the title into a pun in order to emphasize that the real "message" of a medium is the way it pokes, jabs, and kneads its audience—not what it says.[34]

Media, says McLuhan, are either "hot" or "cool." A hot medium is one that provides a lot of information, and therefore permits the audience to remain passive. Print is a hot medium. Cool media, on the other hand, make the audience do more of the work by providing less complete information. Interpersonal communication is a cool medium; it requires participation and involvement. McLuhan thinks television is also a cool medium—a fuzzy collection of thin electronic lines that the viewer must turn into a coherent picture.

Based largely on this distinction, McLuhan divides history into three stages. The first may be called the "tribal" stage, and is characterized by local, oral, "cool" communication. The second stage begins with the invention of the printing press. Because print is a hot medium, it inevitably led to a wide range of social changes—privacy, nationalism, scientific cause-and-effect rigor, linear one-thing-at-a-time thinking. The printing press caused the "detribalization" of human societies. McLuhan's third stage begins, of course, with television, a cool medium that "retribalizes" the societies it touches, creating a "global village" of citizens who interact with their media.

McLuhan's theories struck a responsive chord in the chaotic sixties. The first TV generation was in college, much of it loudly insisting that seminars taught more than lectures, that passion was worth more than logic, that action took precedence over reflection and the sense of community over the sense of privacy. McLuhan seemed to make sense of these phenomena when no one else could. With much help from the media themselves, who popularized his ideas incessantly, he became a "guru" of the 1960s. Older scholars objected that some of McLuhan's pronouncements were internally inconsistent, that many of them conflicted with people's subjective experience with the media, that most of them had no experimental proof whatever. To McLuhanites these objections seemed only to show that McLuhan was right; the older generation was hopelessly linear, mired in the outmoded age of print.

In the 1970s, another TV generation somehow regained its interest in lectures, logic, reflection, and privacy. McLuhan's ideas no longer seemed so compelling, the media stopped quoting him, and communication theory moved in other directions. He left behind one lasting legacy: a sense that television is somehow different from print in ways that have nothing to do with content—even if no one can be sure just what the differences are.

impacts, it would be irrational to suppose that they weren't there. Print and television have shaped our society so thoroughly that we simply cannot determine what its shape would be like without them.

For that matter, much less global effects of the media are similarly unmeasurable. The typical media impact study examines how a particular message (a TV series, a news story, an advertising campaign) affects individual members of the audience. This is done by comparing the attitudes or actions of people who were exposed to the message with the attitudes or actions of those who were not. If the two groups started out the same and ended up different, the difference is presumably an effect of the message.

But how would you measure the effects of an entire content category—say, television soap operas—on an entire audience? Soap opera viewers don't start out the same as non-viewers. Suppose we can show that soap opera viewers are less sophisticated than non-viewers. Would that prove that soap operas diminish the sophistication of the audience, or just that soap operas appeal more to unsophisticated people?

We know that media content systematically endows female characters with different personalities than male characters—and that the values of most Americans reflect similar sex stereotypes. We know that advertising constantly repeats the message that consumption is the road to happiness—and that American society is thoroughly materialistic. We know that violence dominates many movies, TV shows, novels, and news stories—and that fear of violence preoccupies many Americans. It is impossible to prove from all this that the media are responsible for American sexism, materialism, and fear. But it is also impossible, or nearly so, to find an expert who doesn't believe that the media deserve at least part of the blame.

The proved effects of the media are enough to justify our view that studying what they do and how and why they do it is important. The unproved—and unprovable—effects of the media are probably far greater still.

Notes

1 Wilbur Schramm, "How Communication Works," in *The Process and Effects of Mass Communication,* ed. Wilbur Schramm (Urbana, Ill.: University of Illinois Press, 1954), p. 3.

2 Richard W. Budd and Brent D. Ruben, *Beyond Media* (Rochelle Park, N.J.: Hayden Book Co., 1979), *passim.*

3 Paul F. Lazarsfeld, Bernard Berelson, and Hazel Gaudet, *The People's Choice,* 2nd ed. (New York: Columbia University Press, 1948), p. 151.

4 Walter Lippmann, "The World Outside and the Pictures in Our Heads," *Public Opinion* (New York: Macmillan, 1922), ch. 1.

5 George Gallup, "The Importance of Opinion News," *Journalism Educator,* Fall, 1966, p. 113.

6 "TV Ratings," *New York Times,* Dec. 3, 1980, p. C30.

7 Wilbur Schramm, "Communication in Crisis," in *The Kennedy Assassination and the American Public: Social Communication in Crisis,* ed. Bradley S. Greenberg and Edwin B. Parker (Stanford, Calif.: Stanford University Press, 1965), pp. 14-15.

8 A. C. Nielsen Co., "TV Responses to the Death of the President," pamphlet, New York, 1963.

9 "Talking Like a Native," *Newsweek,* March 9, 1970, p. 57.

10 C. Hovland and W. Mandell, "An Experimental Comparison of Conclusion Drawing by the Communicator and by the Audience," *Journal of Abnormal and Social Psychology,* 47, 1952, pp. 581-88.

11 P. Tannenbaum, "Effect of Serial Position on Recall of Radio News Stories," *Journalism Quarterly,* 31, 1954, pp. 319-23.

12 G. Hartmann, "A Field Experiment on the Comparative Effectiveness of 'Emotional' and 'Rational' Political Leaflets in Determining Election Results," *Journal of Abnormal and Social Psychology,* 31, 1936, pp. 94-114.

13 C. Hovland, A. Lumsdaine, and F. Sheffield, *Experiments on Mass Communication* (Princeton: Princeton University Press, 1949).

14 *Ibid.*

15 C. Hovland and W. Weiss, "The Influence of Source Credibility on Communication Effectiveness," *Public Opinion Quarterly,* 15, 1951, pp. 635-50.

16 Herbert E. Krugman, "The Impact of Television Advertising: Learning Without Involvement," *Public Opinion Quarterly,* 29, 1965, pp. 349-56.

17 Jack B. Haskins, "Factual Recall as a Measure of Advertising Effectiveness," *Journal of Advertising Research,* 4, 1964, pp. 2-8.

18 Leon Festinger, "Behavioral Support for Opinion

Change," *Public Opinion Quarterly*, 28, 1964, pp.
404-17.

19 William Stephenson, *The Play Theory of Mass
Communication* (Chicago: University of Chicago
Press, 1967).

20 Bernard Berelson, "What 'Missing the Newspaper'
Means," in *Communication Research 1948-1949*, ed.
P. F. Lazarsfeld and F. N. Stanton (New York:
Harper, 1949), pp. 111-29.

21 Lee Thayer, "On the Mass Media and Mass Communication: Notes Toward a Theory," in Budd and
Ruben, *Beyond Media*, p. 64.

22 H. Blumer, *Movies and Conduct* (New York: Macmillan, 1933).

23 Herta Herzog, "Motivations and Gratifications of
Daily Serial Listeners," in *Process and Effects of
Mass Communication*, ed. Wilbur Schramm, pp.
50-55.

24 Bernard Berelson, "Communications and Public
Opinion," in *Mass Communications*, ed. Wilbur
Schramm (Urbana, Ill.: University of Illinois Press,
1960), pp. 527-43.

25 Leon Festinger, *A Theory of Cognitive Dissonance*
(New York: Harper & Row, 1957).

26 David L. Erickson and G. Norman Van Tubergen,
"The Wolf Men," *Journal of Environmental Education*, Fall, 1972, pp. 26-30.

27 Paul F. Lazarsfeld and Robert K. Merton, "Mass
Communication, Popular Taste and Organized So-
cial Action," in *Mass Communications*, ed. Wilbur
Schramm, pp. 492-512.

28 Muzafer Sherif and Carl I. Hovland, *Social Judgment* (New Haven: Yale University Press, 1961).

29 Lazarsfeld and Merton, "Mass Communication,"
pp. 492-512.

30 A. Bandura and R. H. Walters, *Social Learning and
Personality Development* (New York: Holt, Rinehart and Winston, 1963).

31 G. D. Wiebe, "Mass Media and Man's Relationship
to His Environment," *Journalism Quarterly*, Autumn, 1973, pp. 426-32, 446.

32 Lazarsfeld and Merton, "Mass Communication,"
pp. 492-512.

33 Edmund Carpenter, *Oh, What a Blow That Phan-

tom Gave Me (New York: Holt, Rinehart and Winston, 1973), pp. 132-33.

34 Marshall McLuhan, *The Medium Is the Massage*
(New York: Bantam Books, 1967).

Suggested Readings

BLUMLER, J. G., and E. KATZ, eds., *The Uses of
Mass Communication: Current Perspectives on
Gratifications Research*. Beverly Hills, Calif.:
Sage Publications, 1974.

BUDD, RICHARD W., and BRENT D. RUBEN, *Beyond
Media*. Rochelle Park, N.J.: Hayden Book Co.,
1979.

KARLINS, MARVIN, and HERBERT I. ABELSON, *Persuasion*. New York: Springer Publishing Co.,
1970.

KLAPPER, JOSEPH, *The Effects of Mass Communication*. New York: The Free Press, 1960.

McCOMBS, MAXWELL E., and DONALD L. SHAW,
"The Agenda-Setting Function of Mass Media,"
Public Opinion Quarterly, Summer, 1972.

McLUHAN, MARSHALL, *Understanding Media*.
New York: Signet Paperback, 1964.

POOL, ITHIEL DE SOLA, and WILBUR SCHRAMM,
eds., *Handbook of Communication*. Chicago:
Rand McNally, 1973.

SCHRAMM, WILBUR, *Men, Messages, and Media: A
Look at Human Communication*. New York:
Harper & Row, 1973.

———, and DONALD F. ROBERTS, eds., *The Process
and Effects of Mass Communication*, 2nd ed.
Urbana, Ill.: University of Illinois Press, 1971.

WEISS, WALTER, "Effects of the Mass Media of
Communication," in Gardner Lindzey and
Elliot Aronson, eds., *The Handbook of Social
Psychology*. Reading, Mass.: Addison-Wesley,
1969.

PART I
DEVELOPMENT

The trouble with history is that you have to know a lot about the present before the past seems useful or relevant. And yet you can't really understand the way things are until after you have discovered how they got that way. Ideally, then, everyone would read this chapter twice—once now, to get a feel for the development of the media; and again after finishing the rest of the book, to get the background of the problems that will be discussed later.

If you haven't read the rest of the book yet, the best you can do is to try to keep your own catalogue of important issues and how they grew. There are dozens of them, all discussed some place later on, but let us suggest a few of the most crucial ones here:

1. *Trends in government control.* For many centuries, all governments maintained strict control over the media. Then they began to loosen the reins, allowing greater and greater measures of freedom of the press. How and why did this happen? Was it entirely a good thing? How has it affected the nature of the media today?

2. *Trends in individuality.* Throughout most of their history, the media have been very much the tools of individual writers and editors, who disagreed violently with each other and competed viciously for the allegiance of the public. This is much less true today. What caused the change? How has it affected the tone and function of the media? What can be done about it?

3. *Trends in the audience.* The mass-media audience in the seventeenth century was limited to the literate upper class. Slowly it expanded to include merchants, factory workers, immigrants, farmers. How have the media adapted to these new audiences? Which ones have tried to reach all the public, and which have specialized in certain classes or groups? What implications does this have for democratic processes?

4. *Trends in technology.* Books were the first mass medium, followed by newspapers, then magazines, then film and radio, and finally television, cable, and satellites. Along the way came such revolutionary technological advances as the high-speed press and the telegraph. How has each new medium affected the older ones? Have the media made use of technology, or merely succumbed to it? How can they be expected to respond to future developments?

5. *Trends in influence.* At various points in history, the mass media have influenced the course of social change in many different

ways—and have, in turn, been influenced by social change. What determines the power and influence of the media? Are they aware of their power? Do they use it wisely?

6. *Trends in news definition.* How the media define the word "news" determines the topics they cover and the way they cover them. How has this definition changed over time? What caused the changes? Which is the "right" definition?

7. *Trends in partisanship.* The principal goal of the mass media has varied greatly throughout their history. Sometimes it has been to inform, sometimes to entertain, sometimes to persuade, and sometimes merely to make money. And quite often media owners and media consumers have disagreed about the role of the media. How did these varia-

tions come about? What effects did they have on the content of the media? What should be the main function of the media?

8. *Trends   in   professionalism.* Media owners once viewed themselves as professional advocates; today they are more profit-oriented. Reporters and editors, on the other hand, were once mere employees; today they see themselves as professionals. Why did this turnabout take place? In what ways has it affected the structure and content of the media? How, if at all, is the conflict resolved?

This is only a partial list. Make your own as you go along. Above all, bear in mind the three basic questions of any historical survey: How did things get to where they are? How else might they have turned out? And where are they likely to go in the future?

Chapter 1
Development

Today's mass media, like all complex social institutions, have developed over a period of centuries. The events of each century had a lasting effect on the structure and performance of the media. To understand the modern media in the United States, then, it is necessary to examine their roots in medieval Europe, Elizabethan England, and colonial America.

Medieval Europe was a land-based society. The fundamental economic and social unit was not the city or the country, but the self-sufficient feudal manor. Travel from one manor to another was extremely difficult. Except for churchmen, soldiers, and cutthroats, it was also pretty pointless. Literacy was equally irrelevant. The local serf tilled his land. The local lord managed his serfs. The local priest memorized and recited his prayers. Neither serf nor lord nor priest had any reason to be interested in events beyond the horizon.

Throughout the Middle Ages, the monasteries had a virtual monopoly on literacy. Dutifully the monks hand-copied and hand-illustrated their meager supply of books. Some of the most beautiful were sold to the secular elite, who used them as decorations

and status symbols. But it was an unusual nobleman who could do more than admire the colorful designs of his Bible.

Feudal society began to crack in the thirteenth century. Towns and then cities grew up midway between the great manors. They were inhabited by a new middle class—independent merchants and artisans. The nobles soon learned the advantages of trade. Messengers traveled from the manors to the cities with money and surplus crops; they returned with cattle, weapons, woodwork, cloth, and luxuries of all sorts. They returned also with news: news of war, news of taxes ordered by a faraway king, news of a special bargain in satin or spices.

Oral messages were painfully inaccurate. Written ones were better. So monks were assigned or persuaded to teach the sons of feudal landowners to read. In time the family Bible became no longer merely a piece of decoration; it was a book.

Learning was suddenly a valuable commodity. Dozens of universities were founded throughout Europe to teach the sons of the nobility their Latin. The artisans and traders in the cities, meanwhile, taught themselves to read the vernacular—German, French, Spanish, or English. Both groups,

20,000 B.C.	Cave painting, the earliest form of written communication, reflects pre-historic people's conception of their surroundings.
3500 B.C.	The Sumerians of Mesopotamia develop cuneiform, the first known pictographic writing.
3100 B.C.	The Egyptians develop hieroglyphics.
2500 B.C.	Papyrus, a paperlike substance made from reeds, is invented in Egypt. It quickly replaces clay as the main writing material.
1800-1600 B.C.	The first real alphabet is developed in the Mideast. It will eventually be carried by the Phoenicians to Greece.
1580-1350 B.C.	The first book, *The Book of the Dead,* is written in Egypt.
540 B.C.	The first public library is founded in Athens.
200-150 B.C.	The Greeks perfect parchment, a new writing material made from animal skins.
100 B.C.	A full-fledged publishing system develops in Rome. Parchment scrolls are copied and sold. Public libraries, copyright laws, and some government censorship already exist.
48 A.D.	Roman soldiers invade Alexandria and sack its library, destroying over 500,000 scrolls.
105	An inexpensive method for making paper is perfected in China.
150	For the first time, parchment is folded into pages to make books instead of scrolls.
400	After the fall of Rome, Catholic monasteries become the sole centers of learning in Europe. They will retain their monopoly for 800 years.
676	The Chinese art of papermaking has spread through Persia to the Arabs. Not until the thirteenth century will it be introduced into Europe.
1221	The Chinese develop movable type made of wood.
1200-1400	The Renaissance of learning in Europe. Fifty great European universities are founded during this period.
1445	The Chinese construct copper movable type.
1450	Johann Gutenberg of Mainz, Germany, introduces metal movable type to Europe. Six years later he will print the famous Gutenberg Bible, ushering in the European age of printing.

the upper class and the middle class, demanded more and cheaper books.

Whenever a new need develops in society, an industry is likely to emerge to meet that need, for a profit. Just as television today "gives the public what it wants," so did printing in the fifteenth century. The illuminated manuscripts of the monasteries were incredibly beautiful, but they were also incredibly expensive. What the fifteenth-century reader wanted was lots and lots of books—cheap, portable, and permanent. There was a healthy market for books. The printing industry developed to exploit that market.

The first printing presses were modeled after wine presses. Words and illustrations were carved into large wooden blocks. The blocks were inked, then covered with a sheet of paper. Pressure was applied (by a screw-and-lever arrangement) until the paper picked up an inked version of the carving. The result was, literally, a block print.

This method was infinitely faster and cheaper than the hand-illumination of the monks, but it was still pretty inefficient. After a few hundred impressions the letters began to crack and a new block had to be carved. In the 1440s, Johann Gutenberg found a better way: movable metal type. Gutenberg manufactured individual pieces of metal type for each letter of the alphabet. Hundreds of such pieces were wedged together into a wooden form to make up a single page. After the first page was printed, the type was reorganized into the words of the second page. No new "carving" was required.

By 1500, more than 15 million copies of 35,000 different titles were in circulation throughout Europe. Nearly all of them were printed by Gutenberg's method with movable metal type.

But the greatest literary need of the commercial classes was not for books, but for news. By the middle of the sixteenth century, many large companies found it useful to circulate handwritten newsletters among their employees and favored customers. These newsletters naturally stressed shipping and financial transactions, but they also included news of political events that might affect the business community.

The first printed news reports were "newsbooks," like the 1513 English pamphlet that recounted "the trewe encountre of the battle of Flodden Field." Most were printed by the government. In the 1560s, for example, the government of Venice produced a series of reports on the war in Dalmatia. Sold for one gazetta (a small coin), these publications came to be known as "gazettes."

By the early 1600s, German, Dutch, and Belgian printers began publishing their own regular newspapers, aimed at the commercial audience in various European cities. Most were one-page weeklies, concentrating almost entirely on financial news. The outbreak of the Thirty Years War in 1618 greatly increased the demand for political news as well. Printers cheerfully went along with the trend, and newspapers started looking a little like newspapers.

AUTHORITARIAN ENGLAND

William Caxton, an English merchant, was also a curious man. He traveled to the European continent to study the new craft of printing. In 1476 he returned to England with a printing press.

For nearly fifty years, Caxton and his successors printed whatever they liked without government interference—books, newsletters, even political satires and street ballads. Then, in 1529, King Henry VIII decided to take control of the printing industry. Every printer, he decreed, must have a royal patent (a license) to set up shop. Licensed printers held their patents only so long as what they printed continued to please the king. Certain books were absolutely forbidden; many others were known to be "questionable." In return, English printers were granted local monopolies, while on the national level imported publications were outlawed.

To all intents and purposes, Henry "nationalized" the English printing industry. His reasons seem more religious than political from today's perspective, but at the time there was little reason to distinguish between the two. In 1529, Henry was a devout Catholic, a king by "divine right." He controlled the press mainly in order to halt the distribution of heretical Protestant tracts. Four years later, Henry broke with the Vatican and founded the Church of England. He now controlled the press in hopes of banning Catholic writings. When Queen Mary came to the throne in 1553, Catholicism again became the state religion in England, and Protestant writings were again forbidden. Five years later Queen Elizabeth re-established the Church of England, and outlawed the publications of both Catholics and Puritans. Religion was *the* political issue of sixteenth-century England. It was an issue that made books dangerous and government control inevitable.

Despite the penalties, unauthorized "broadsheets" describing particular political events were openly hawked on the streets of London. So were ideological "newsbooks," pamphlets, and the like. As the literary black-market grew, government reaction intensified. In 1584 William Carter was hanged for printing a pro-Catholic pamphlet—perhaps the first English martyr to freedom of the press.

By 1610, regularly appearing newspapers were common on the European continent, but in England they were unknown. The English broadsheets came out irregularly and reported only a single event. This lack wasn't remedied until 1620, when Nathaniel Butter began importing Dutch newspapers (printed in English). A year later, Butter teamed up with printer Thomas Archer to pirate the news from the Dutch papers. These earliest newspapers contained only foreign news, concentrating on the Thirty Years War. They were immensely successful.

Unfortunately, King James I felt that the Thirty Years War was an affair of state, not to be discussed or debated by mere citizens. In 1621 he ordered Butter and Archer to stop carrying news of the war. The order was ignored, and Archer was imprisoned. Butter then joined up with Nicholas Bourne, and petitioned the king for permission to print a weekly newspaper. They agreed to submit the text of their paper to the government for advance approval. Such precensorship was

---

CHRONOLOGY

1476	William Caxton establishes the first printing press in England.
1529-1530	Henry VIII forbids the publication of certain books, and requires all English printers to obtain royal licenses, the start of authoritarian control over the press.
1550	The major trading companies of Europe circulate handwritten commercial newsletters among their employees and customers.
1609	The first primitive weekly newspaper appears in Germany, followed soon by weeklies in Holland and Belgium.
1620	Nathaniel Butter imports Dutch newspapers and distributes them in England. Called "corantos," the papers specialize in foreign news.
1621	Butter and Thomas Archer print the first English coranto, which soon meets with government repression. Nicholas Bourne joins the team, and government permission is obtained for *The Continuation of Our Weekly Newes,* the first regular newspaper in England.
1644	English poet John Milton publishes *Areopagitica,* advocating a free marketplace of ideas and urging an end to press licensing.
1694	England abandons licensing of the press.
1702	The first English language daily newspaper, the *Daily Courant,* appears in London.
1709	The first modern copyright law is enacted in England.
1712	England adopts the Stamp Tax, a heavy tax on newspapers and other publications.
1709-1720	Richard Steele, Joseph Addison, and Daniel DeFoe produce the *Tatler,* the *Spectator,* and *Mist's Journal,* collections of magazine-type essays in newspaper format.

to become a hallmark of authoritarian control over the press.

Butter and Bourne published their first issue in September of 1621. Entitled *The Continuation of Our Weekly Newes,* the paper carried the legend: "Published With Authority." It ran only one page, on a sheet a little smaller than a piece of typewriter paper. As soon as he was released from jail, Archer joined the team. From 1621 to 1632, *Our Weekly Newes* was the only official weekly newspaper in England.

The decade of the 1630s was marked by intense conflict between King Charles I and the English Parliament. By 1640 Parliament was clearly the winner. It celebrated and consolidated its power by granting increased civil and religious liberties to the nation, including a relaxation of press censorship. Poet John Milton was among those whose voices were raised in favor of freedom of the press. In his monumental *Areopagitica,* Milton argued:

> Truth and understanding are not such wares as to be monopolized and traded in by tickets and statutes and standards. We must not think to make a staple commodity of all knowledge in the land, to mark and license it like our broadcloth. . . . Give me the liberty to know, to utter, and to argue freely according to conscience, above all liberties. . . . And though all the winds of doctrine were let loose to play upon the earth, so Truth be in the field, we do injuriously, by licensing and prohibiting, to misdoubt her strength. Let her and Falsehood grapple; who ever knew Truth put to the worse, in a free and open encounter.[1]

Spurred on by the new permissiveness, a series of daily reports called "diurnals" developed throughout England. They chronicled the tail end of the conflict between Parliament and Crown. That conflict ended in the mid-1640s with the Puritan Revolution. A victory for Parliament, the revolution soon proved a defeat for freedom of the press. Its leader, Oliver Cromwell, quickly estab-

lished himself as a virtual dictator of England. Unlicensed printers were harshly dealt with, while licensed printers were subjected to incessant censorship. Ironically enough, it was John Milton himself who became the nation's chief censor under the Puritan regime.

The restoration of the monarchy under Charles II brought no immediate improvement for the press. But the power of the king was on the wane, and libertarianism was in the air. Instances of censorship were rare throughout the 1670s and the 1680s, and in 1694 licensing of the press was abandoned completely. By the time the *Daily Courant,* England's first daily newspaper, was founded in 1702, the English press was more or less free to write what it pleased, so long as it avoided criticizing the government. The journalism of England in the early eighteenth century was to serve as a model for the young printers who introduced newspapers to the American colonies.

COLONIAL AMERICA

Two of the Pilgrims who landed in Plymouth in 1620 were skilled printers. They had published illegal Protestant tracts in England, and watched the production of primitive newspapers in Holland. But they brought no press with them to the New World. They realized that their tiny outpost in the wilderness would have neither the time nor the need for newspapers.

The Massachusetts Bay Colony, which settled Boston in 1630, was larger, wealthier, and better educated than Plymouth. All Puritan children were taught to read, and the brightest boys were sent to Harvard College to prepare for the ministry. In 1638 the first printing press in the New World was established at Harvard to produce religious texts.

In England the Puritans had been revolutionaries; in Massachusetts Bay they were the Establishment. Like other Establishments of the time, they feared that a free press might threaten the government and promote religious heresies. Printing was therefore strictly controlled. By the mid-1600s, various presses in Massachusetts had published lawbooks, volumes of sermons, poetry, and a history of the colony. But it was not until the last decade of the century that a printer dared to produce anything resembling a newspaper.

Benjamin Harris had come to Boston in 1686, after publishing a number of seditious pamphlets in England. In 1690 he printed the first issue of *Publick Occurrences,* a three-page newspaper roughly 6 × 9 inches in size. Featurey by today's standards, the paper included the following item of special interest:

> The Christianized *Indians* in some parts of *Plimouth* have newly appointed a day of Thanksgiving to God for his Mercy in supplying their extream and pinching Necessities under their late want of Corn, & for His giving them now a prospect of a very *Comfortable Harvest.* Their Example may be worth Mentioning.[2]

The paper also gossiped about the presumed immorality of the king of France, and complained that the Indian allies of the British had mistreated French prisoners. These were bold topics—perhaps too bold. The colonial governor and the Puritan elders immediately ordered the paper suppressed. *Publick Occurrences,* America's first newspaper, died after one issue.

By 1700, the thriving commercial city of Boston was ripe for a second try. John Campbell, the local postmaster, met the need for news with a handwritten newsletter, which he distributed to shippers, farmers, merchants, and government officials throughout the colonies. Campbell was in an ideal position to run a newspaper. As postmaster, he was the first one to get a look at the English and European papers. Moreover, his postage-free "franking privilege" enabled him to send his newsletters through the mail without charge. Throughout the colonial period,

the job of postmaster was closely linked to that of publisher.

In 1704 Campbell began printing his newsletter. Aptly called the *Boston News-Letter,* it was precensored by the governor and "Published by Authority." The single-page paper, printed on both sides, was sold by subscription only. By 1715 Campbell had perhaps 300 regular readers.

The *Boston News-Letter* was strictly a commercial newspaper. It emphasized local financial news and foreign political developments, the latter pirated directly from English papers. A smattering of births, deaths, and social events made Campbell's paper even more appealing to the economic elite of the colonies—but it was not a publication for the average citizen or the intellectual. As a commercial paper, the *News-Letter* was an obvious candidate for advertising. The very first issue carried this notice:

> This News-Letter is to be continued Weekly, and all Persons who have Houses, Lands, Tenements, Farms, Ships, Vessels, Goods, Wares or Merchandise, &c to be Sold or Let; or Servants Run-away, or Goods Stole or Lost; may have the same inserted at a Reasonable Rate, from *Twelve Pence* to *Five Shillings*. . . .[3]

Before long, Campbell was earning a considerable profit from ads.

After losing the postmaster job in 1719, Campbell decided to continue printing his newspaper without the franking privilege. The new postmaster, William Brooker, hired printer James Franklin to publish his own paper, the *Boston Gazetite.* Competition had come to the colonies, and both papers were livelier as a result.

Two years later Franklin left the *Gazette* and established a third newspaper, the *New England Courant.* Franklin was an intellectual of sorts. His interests were secular and political, not religious or commercial. The articles and essays in the *Courant,* often written under pseudonyms, viciously attacked the Puritan clergy and its control over the Boston government. The third regular newspaper in Massachusetts was anti-Establishment.

Among the staff of the *Courant* was Franklin's younger brother Benjamin, an apprentice printer. Apparently without his brother's knowledge, Ben Franklin was also the author of several satirical essays in the paper, run under the byline "Silence Dogood." In 1722 James Franklin was jailed for three weeks for his attacks on the government, and "Silence Dogood" came out with an eloquent plea for freedom of the press. James soon got out of jail, discovered the identity of "Dogood," and jealously ordered his teenage brother to stick to the printing end of the business.

The *Courant* kept up its attacks on church and state, and in 1723 Franklin was ordered to submit his paper for precensorship. He got around the command by making Ben titular publisher, a tactic that enraged the religious leadership of the colony but amused its citizens. Franklin was arrested for contempt of the censorship order, but he was so popular that the government (headed by Increase Mather and his son Cotton) didn't dare to try him. He was soon released and resumed control of the newspaper. Precensorship had failed in Massachusetts; it would never again succeed.

The American colonists were, by and large, an independent lot. Schooled in religious dissent, they took naturally to political dissent as well. At the end of the first quarter of the eighteenth century, most colonial governments still had licensing and precensorship laws on the books. But they were seldom invoked, and almost never invoked with success. The *New England Courant* was the first outspoken anti-Establishment newspaper in America—but it was by no means the last.

The first American printing press outside Massachusetts was brought to Philadelphia by William Bradford in 1685. A book publisher, Bradford found the censorship laws in that Quaker city too stiff for comfort. So in 1693 he moved his press to New York.

Bradford's son Andrew soon returned to Philadelphia, and in 1719 he established the *American Weekly Mercury*. The *Mercury* was the first American newspaper outside Boston, and the third regularly published paper in the colonies.

Never as outspoken as Franklin's *Courant,* the *Mercury* was nevertheless in constant trouble with the government of Philadelphia. Bradford was ordered "not to publish anything relating to or concerning the affairs of this Government, or the Government of any other of His Majesty's Colonies, without the permission of the Governor or Secretary of this Province."[4] Bradford often disobeyed the order. Once, after an especially damning satire, he was arrested. But by this time the spirit of liberty was strong even in Quaker Philadelphia, and Bradford was never prosecuted.

Young Ben Franklin, meanwhile, was bored with working for his brother in Boston. In 1723, shortly after James Franklin was released from prison, Ben ran away to Philadelphia. Six years later he founded the weekly *Pennsylvania Gazette*. A shrewd politician, Franklin managed to publish the brightest and wittiest paper in the colonies without government interference.

In 1741, Franklin inaugurated his *General Magazine;* not to be outdone, Andrew Bradford began the *American Magazine* in the same year. Neither was successful. The American public was not yet ready for such heavy doses of philosophical and literary commentary.

When Andrew Bradford left New York for Philadelphia, William Bradford stayed behind. In 1725 he followed his son's example and founded New York's first newspaper, the *New York Gazette*. The poorly printed two-page paper carefully avoided antagonizing government officials. But stronger papers soon developed in New York: the *Weekly Post Boy*, the *Evening-Post*—and the historic *New York Weekly Journal*.

By the end of the 1720s, a political power struggle was underway in New York between the rising middle class and the Tory Establishment, headed by Governor William Cosby. In 1733 the leaders of the anti-administration group decided that they needed a newspaper to champion their cause. They founded the *New York Weekly Journal,* and asked printer John Peter Zenger to be its editor.

Zenger immediately set about attacking Cosby and the aristocracy, urging a more representative government for New York. Twice Cosby asked the grand jury to indict Zenger for seditious libel (criticizing the government), and twice the grand jury refused. Finally, Cosby's council issued its own warrant for Zenger's arrest, and in November of 1734 the crusading editor was sent to jail. His *Journal* missed only one issue. Later editions were dictated to his wife through a "Hole of the Door of the Prison."[5]

The Zenger case came to trial in August, 1735. Andrew Hamilton, a famous lawyer nearly eighty years old, was brought in from Philadelphia to handle the defense.

Hamilton began by admitting that Zenger had, in fact, published the articles in question. Under existing law, that should have been the end of the case; criticism of the government, whether true or false, was illegal. As the prosecuting attorney explained: "I think the jury must find a verdict for the King; for supposing they [the libels] were true, the law says that they are not the less libelous for that; nay, indeed, the law says their being true is an aggravation of the crime."

It was precisely this point that Hamilton disputed. He argued what was then a novel legal contention: "The words themselves must be libelous, that is, *false, scandalous, and seditious* or else we are not guilty."

The judge sided with precedent and the prosecutor, ruling that truth was irrelevant. He refused even to let Hamilton try to prove Zenger's anti-government accusations. Hamilton then appealed directly to the jury:

> The question before the court and you, gentlemen of the jury, is not of small nor private concern, it is not the cause of a poor printer,

CHRONOLOGY

1638   The Puritans establish the first printing press in America at Harvard College.

1685   William Bradford brings to Philadelphia, and later to New York, the first printing press in America outside Massachusetts.

1690   Benjamin Harris publishes the first American newspaper, *Publick Occurrences.* It is suppressed by Boston authorities after one issue.

1704   John Campbell's *Boston News-Letter* becomes the first regularly published newspaper in America.

1719   William Brooker and James Franklin found the *Boston Gazette;* Andrew Bradford establishes the *American Weekly Mercury* in Philadelphia.

1721   James Franklin emphasizes political and social criticism in his *New England Courant.*

1725   William Bradford founds the *New York Gazette,* the first newspaper in New York.

1729   Benjamin Franklin begins publishing the *Pennsylvania Gazette* in Philadelphia.

1735   John Peter Zenger, publisher of the *New York Weekly Journal,* is acquitted on charges of seditious libel. After Zenger, colonial juries will refuse to convict journalists for printing the truth, however injurious to the government.

1741   The *General Magazine* and *American Magazine* are founded in Philadelphia. Both are unsuccessful.

nor of New York alone. . . . It is the cause of liberty . . . the liberty both of exposing and opposing arbitrary power (in these parts of the world, at least) by speaking and writing truth.[6]

The jury returned a verdict of not guilty, and Zenger was released.

The importance of the Zenger trial is not that it established a new legal principle. In fact, truth was not officially accepted as a defense in seditious libel cases until the Sedition Act of 1798. What the Zenger trial proved is that the average American colonist—in this case the jury—was unalterably opposed to authoritarian government. The trial recognized and solidified the role of the colonial press as critic of government and defender of liberty. It thus paved the way for the important part the press was to play in bringing about the American Revolution.

The American press in the last half of the eighteenth century was less interested in news than in comment—philosophical, social, literary, and political. Most colonial newspapers were quickly radicalized by the hated Stamp Act, and thereafter they led the cry for Independence. After the Revolution, the papers split into two camps: the elite Federalists and the populist Republicans. Each newspaper was written for readers who agreed with it; no newspaper tried to be objective in the modern sense. Political partisanship was to characterize the American press until well into the nineteenth century.

THE REVOLUTIONARY PERIOD

There were twelve newspapers in the American colonies in 1750, serving a population of just over one million. By 1775, the population would rise to 2.5 million, while the number of newspapers would jump to 48. Five successful magazines would be established during this period, and innumer-

able book publishers. The American mass media were thriving.

The typical newspaper of the times was a four-page weekly, 10 × 15 inches in size. The paper was rough foolscap imported from England; it was mottled and ugly, but surprisingly durable. Headlines were rare, and illustrations rarer still. A hand press was used to produce perhaps 400 copies of each issue.

The content of such a newspaper was mostly philosophical-political essays. Even reports on specific local events were generally written in essay form—but most "articles" were not tied to an event at all. Libertarianism was the philosophy of the day. Every colonial newspaper devoted considerable space to reprints of English and French libertarian tracts, not to mention the wisdom of home-grown philosophers.

The English Stamp Act of 1765 provided a new focus for these libertarian essays: the evil of King George. The Stamp Act imposed a heavy tax on paper; it thus hit newspaper publishers harder than anyone else. Not that the tax itself was anything new. It was first levied against *English* newspapers in 1712. Still, never before had the English government imposed such a tax on American newspapers, and the colonial press was unanimous in its opposition to this "taxation without representation." Several papers announced that they were suspending publication in protest. They later reappeared without nameplates, claiming that they were broadsides or handbills and thus exempt from the tax. Before long they resumed their original titles, but no colonial newspaper ever carried the required stamp or paid the required tax.

The Stamp Act was repealed in 1766—but it was too late. The experience of uniting in opposition to the established government is a heady one. From that experience the colonial press never recovered. After 1765, most American publishers were committed to Revolution in one form or another. Their newspapers were devoted to that cause.

The *Boston Gazette*, often edited by Samuel Adams, was typical of the militant papers of the day. With each new imposition of British rule, Adams and other radical writers throughout the colonies strove to stir up resistance. The following is the "lead" of the *Gazette*'s story on the "Boston Massacre" of 1770. It is thoughtful and contemplative, but hardly unbiased:

> The Town of Boston affords a recent and melancholy Demonstration of the destructive Consequences of quartering Troops among Citizens in a Time of Peace, under a Pretence of supporting the Laws and aiding Civil Authority; every considerate and unprejudic'd Person among us was deeply imprest with the Apprehension of these Consequences when it was known that a Number of Regiments were ordered to this Town under such a Pretext, but in Reality to inforce oppressive Measures; to awe and controul the legislative as well as executive Power of the Province, and to quell a Spirit of Liberty, which however it may have been basely oppos'd and even ridicul'd by some, would do Honor to any Age or Country.[7]

To be sure, there were some moderates and even Royalists among American publishers. John Dickinson, for example, published his influential "Letters from a Farmer in Pennsylvania" in the *Pennsylvania Chronicle* of 1767-1768. A businessman, Dickinson resented English control over American foreign trade. But he was unalterably opposed to revolution.

Yet men like Dickinson could do little to halt the effect of revolutionaries like Sam Adams—or Tom Paine, editor of the *Pennsylvania Magazine,* whose pamphlet "Common Sense" sold 120,000 copies in the spring of 1776.

By 1775, war had become inevitable. Publishers were forced to choose sides, becoming either radical Patriots or steadfast Loyalists; there was no middle ground left. Isaiah Thomas, editor of the *Massachusetts Spy,* headlined his article on the Battle of Lexington: "The shot heard round the world." His lead paragraph left no doubt where he stood:

> Americans! forever bear in mind the BATTLE OF LEXINGTON!—where British troops, unmolested and unprovoked, wantonly and in a most inhuman manner, fired upon and killed a number of our countrymen, then robbed, ransacked, and burnt their houses! nor could the tears of defenseless women, some of whom

---

CHRONOLOGY

1765   Colonial newspapers refuse to pay the tax imposed by the English Stamp Act—thus taking a giant step toward radicalization.

1767   John Dickinson publishes the first of his moderate "Letters from a Farmer in Pennsylvania" in the *Pennsylvania Chronicle.*

1770   Boston publisher John Mein is attacked by Patriot leaders and forced to fold his Tory *Boston Chronicle*—a sign of growing polarization.

1772   Sam Adams, a regular contributor to the radical *Boston Gazette,* organizes the Committees of Correspondence, a network of agents "covering" events throughout the colonies on behalf of the Patriot press.

1773   James Rivington founds *Rivington's New York Gazetteer,* the most powerful Tory newspaper of the Revolution.

1776   Tom Paine's pamphlet, "Common Sense," is widely circulated throughout the colonies; the Declaration of Independence is carried on the front page of most colonial newspapers; the Revolution begins in earnest.

were in the pains of childbirth, the cries of helpless babes, nor the prayers of old age, confined to beds of sickness, appease their thirst for blood!—or divert them from their DESIGN of MURDER and ROBBERY![8]

At first, the war was hard on both Patriot and Tory newspapers. Neither were allowed to publish or circulate in territory controlled by the enemy. But as the Thirteen United States of America won victory after victory, the Loyalist press quickly disappeared. Wartime commerce, meanwhile, brought heavy loads of lucrative advertising to the pages of revolutionary newspapers. And public interest in the war itself gave some Patriot papers as many as 8,000 readers. The end of the Revolution left the American mass media—books, magazines, and newspapers—stronger than ever before. They had waged a battle, and they had won.

THE PARTISAN PRESS

The Revolutionary War had united rich and poor in the common cause of independence. But as soon as the war ended, this unity ended as well. Merchants, bankers, manufacturers, and large property owners—the "aristocracy" of America—urged the establishment of a strong central government. Small farmers and wage earners, on the other hand, feared the power of the monied interests; they supported a loose confederacy of local governments.

The agrarian-labor types were in control at the close of the war. The Articles of Confederation they passed in 1781 gave nearly all the power to the states. Without even the right of taxation, the new national government was too weak to cope with the postwar economic depression. Moreover, the propertied classes soon gained control of the various state legislatures. In 1787 they convened the Philadelphia Constitutional Convention to rewrite the Articles of Confederation and strengthen the federal government. The dele-

gates to that Convention were nearly all propertied men, advocates of strong national government. The new Constitution reflected their aims and interests.

Once the Constitution was written, it was sent to the states for ratification. The battle was joined. The conservative, monied group now called itself the Federalists; the agrarian-labor bloc was known as the Anti-Federalists or Republicans. Again, newspapers throughout the thirteen colonies (now the thirteen states) were forced to choose sides. One was either a Federalist or a Republican; once more, there was no middle ground.

Alexander Hamilton, James Madison, and John Jay wrote a total of 85 essays urging ratification of the Constitution. Collectively called *The Federalist,* these essays first appeared in the *New York Independent Journal.* They were carried by Federalist newspapers throughout the nation, and were circulated in pamphlet and book form as well. Anti-Federalist papers responded by publishing Richard Henry Lee's *Letters from the Federal Farmer,* which opposed the Constitution as a document of the propertied classes.

One bone of contention was the conspicuous absence in the new Constitution of specific guarantees of individual rights, including the right of freedom of the press. Nine of the thirteen states already provided for such freedom in their state constitutions, and the Federalists presumably felt that that was enough. The Federalists were not by nature sympathetic to press freedom; the Constitution itself was debated in strict secrecy. As Alexander Hamilton wrote:

What is Liberty of the Press? Who can give it any definition which does not leave the utmost latitude for evasion? I hold it to be impracticable; and from this I infer, that its security, whatever fine declarations may be inserted in any Constitution respecting it, must altogether depend on public opinion, and on the general spirit of the people and of the Government.[9]

The Republicans, by contrast, believed freedom of the press to be crucial to the survival of American democracy. Thomas Jefferson, by birth an aristocrat but by choice a "friend of the common man," was the acknowledged leader of the Republicans. In a letter to a friend, Jefferson wrote:

> The basis of our government being the opinion of the people, the very first object should be to keep that right; and if it were left to me to decide whether we should have a government without newspapers, or newspapers without a government, I should not hesitate a moment to prefer the latter.[10]

In 1788, after a year of bitter strife, the Constitution was finally ratified. The Federalists easily dominated the first Congress of the new nation. In an effort to reunify the country, they proposed a Bill of Rights. It included what is now the First Amendment: "Congress shall make no law . . . abridging the freedom of speech or of the press." In 1791 the Bill of Rights was ratified by the states and became law.

The Bill of Rights did little to bridge the gap between the two factions. General George Washington was the unanimous choice for president. His vice president was John Adams, a Federalist. His secretary of the treasury was Alexander Hamilton, also a Federalist. His secretary of state was Thomas Jefferson, leader of the Republicans. Throughout the Washington administration, Federalists and Republicans were at each other's throats.

Not content with the support of independent publishers, both parties established "house organs" to serve as direct pipelines between political leaders and their followers. Federalist funds were responsible for John Fenno's *Gazette of the United States* and Noah Webster's *American Minerva,* both in New York. Hamilton personally set editorial policy for both papers. Not to be outdone, Jefferson appointed Philip Freneau official translator for the State Department, in return for Freneau's agreement to publish a Republican party organ in Philadelphia. Policy for Freneau's *National Gazette* was personally set by Jefferson. Other publishers throughout the country looked to one or another of these newspapers for guidance on how to handle the news.

In 1796, Federalist John Adams was elected president; Jefferson, the loser, became vice president. The most divisive issue of the moment was the war in Europe between France and England. The Republicans, who had applauded the populist French Revolution several years earlier, supported France. The Federalists, with control of both the presidency and Congress, supported England. The United States prepared to go to war against France.

With war fever at its highest, and rival journalists brawling in the streets, the Federalists made their move to squelch the opposition. In 1798, Congress passed the Sedition Act. Under the Act, it became a federal crime to publish any false criticism of government officials.

The Sedition Act is remembered for two conflicting reasons. On the one hand, it established the "Zenger principle" by explicitly accepting truth as a defense; only *false* criticisms of the government were illegal. On the other hand, it was also the most outstanding piece of repressive legislation in the early history of the United States.

The Federalists used the Sedition Act to purge the nation of anti-Federalist thought. Federalist editors were allowed to continue their defamatory attacks on Jefferson and his supporters—but seven leading Republican editors were prosecuted and convicted for similar invective against the Federalist leadership. The plan backfired. In 1800, public resentment of the Sedition Act helped sweep Jefferson into the presidency. War preparations were immediately halted, and in 1801 the Sedition Act was allowed to lapse.

The last quarter of the eighteenth century was the heyday of the Partisan Press. There were no words so insulting that Federalist and Republican editors were unwilling to use them to describe their enemies. Benjamin

Franklin Bache (grandson of Ben Franklin) was publisher of the strictly Republican *Philadelphia Aurora.* In 1797, he celebrated the retirement of George Washington in the following terms:

> The man who is the source of all the misfortunes of our country is this day reduced to a level with his fellow-citizens, and is no longer possessed of power to multiply evils upon the United States. . . . Every heart in unison with the freedom and happiness of the people, ought to beat high with exultation that the name of Washington from this day ceased to give a currency to political iniquity and to legalized corruption.[11]

This was too much for William Cobbett, the Federalist editor of *Porcupine's Gazette,* also in Philadelphia. Putting aside politicians for the moment, Cobbett attacked Bache directly:

> He spent several years in hunting offices under the Federal Government, and being constantly rejected, he at last became its most bitter foe. Hence his abuse of general Washington, whom, at the time he was soliciting a place, he panegerized up to the third heaven. He was born for a hireling, and therefore when he found he could not obtain employ in one quarter, he sought it in another. . . . He is an ill-looking devil. His eyes never get above your knees.[12]

Neither of these quotations, by the way, comes from an "editorial." Throughout the eighteenth century and well into the nineteenth, it was customary for newspapers to intersperse news and opinion, often within the same article. By 1800, a few papers, including the *Aurora,* had set aside page two as an editorial page of sorts—complete with the editorial "We." But opinions were found on the other pages as well. Objectivity in the modern sense simply wasn't a characteristic of the Partisan Press.

Almost without exception, the dedicated Federalist and Republican newspapers were weeklies. There was no need to hurry a vituperative essay into print; next week would do as well as tomorrow. Urban merchants, on the other hand, were desperate for daily reports on ship arrivals and other commercial news.

The first American daily newspaper was the *Pennsylvania Evening Post and Daily Advertiser,* founded in 1783. A year later the *Pennsylvania Packet and Daily Advertiser* appeared. It was a better newspaper than the *Post,* and despite its expensive price (fourpence), it soon forced the competition to fold. In 1785, two more dailies appeared— the *New York Morning Post and Daily Advertiser,* and the *New York Daily Advertiser.* By 1800, there were twenty daily newspapers in the United States.

As their names imply, the new daily papers depended heavily on advertising. Many were able to fill sixteen out of twenty columns with ads, leaving only four for news. This was all right with their readers, who often found the advertisements as useful as the editorial copy. They cheerfully paid as much as eight dollars a year (roughly the cost of a barrel of flour) for subscriptions. The *New York Daily Advertiser* pioneered the use of half-inch-high headlines in its ads; large type would soon be used for news headlines as well.

The partisan weeklies flourished right along with the commercial dailies. By 1800, there were roughly 200 weeklies in operation, all but a few dozen of them founded after the Revolution. Subscriptions averaged $2.50 a year; the number of subscribers averaged 600 to 700. As much as half the space in a successful weekly might be advertising.

Most of these weeklies served small cities and towns, pirating their news from the larger metropolitan papers. They were able to survive largely because of the Post Office Act of 1792, which set a low one-cent rate for the mailing of newspapers. The Act also provided that publishers could exchange their papers by mail without charge, enabling frontier papers to get all their news free. The government supported the newspaper industry in other ways as well. Perhaps the most important subsidy was the legal printing contract. Key newspapers in each state and territory were paid to reprint the texts of various laws. This plum was handed out strictly along party lines, as a form of political patronage. Scores of influential frontier papers could never have started without their government printing contracts.

Between 1800 and 1830, the American media prospered, but they changed very little in character. Some of the commercial dailies turned partisan, while some of the partisan weeklies went daily—and dozens of new weeklies were founded every year. By 1830, then, there were three kinds of newspapers in America: (1) A handful of strictly commercial dailies; (2) Roughly sixty partisan metropolitan dailies; and (3) Well over a thousand small-town and frontier weeklies, most of them partisan.

Improvements in printing enabled publishers to produce as many as 1,100 impressions an hour. The extra capacity was seldom needed—the average daily still circulated only a thousand copies, and weekly circulation was lower still. The cost of the average newspaper rose to six cents an issue, the same as a pint of whiskey. Headlines improved the appearance of the typical paper, while the use of part-time "correspondents" in Washington and elsewhere improved its quality. But the overall look of the page was still very gray, and most of the content was still essays and commentary.

The magazine and book industries also thrived. Most of the hundred-odd magazines in business in 1830 neglected politics and concentrated on literary and social comment. Typical were the *Port Folio* (founded in 1801), the *North American Review* (1815), and the *Saturday Evening Post* (1821). The *Post,* an immediate success, was made up of fiction and poems, essays, and regular columns on morals and religion. Although most

CHRONOLOGY

1783   The first American daily newspaper, the *Pennsylvania Evening Post and Daily Advertiser,* is published in Philadelphia.

1787   Federalist newspapers print *The Federalist,* a series of essays by Alexander Hamilton and others urging ratification of the Constitution. Republican papers respond with Richard Henry Lee's *Letters from a Federal Farmer.*

1789   *The Triumph of Nature,* the first native American novel, is published.

1791   The First Amendment to the Constitution is ratified, guaranteeing freedom of the press from congressional censorship.

1792   The Post Office Act grants newspapers special low mailing rates.

1798   The Federalist Congress enacts the Sedition Act in an effort to restrain Republican newspapers. The invention of the iron press permits printers to make as many as 250 impressions per hour.

1801   The Jefferson administration allows the Sedition Act to lapse.

1811   Frederick Koenig of Germany invents a steam-driven cylinder press, capable of producing 1,100 impressions per hour.

1821   The *Saturday Evening Post* is founded, the first successful magazine to appeal to women as well as men.

1822   A crude but permanent photograph is produced in France. By 1839 the process will be practical.

1827   The Washington Hand Press is invented; it will cross the continent and give the frontier nearly all its newspapers.

books sold in the United States were still printed in England, by 1820 more than 40,000 titles written and published by Americans had appeared. Among the best sellers were histories (John Marshall's *Life of Washington*), political commentaries (*The Federalist*), and novels (James Fenimore Cooper's *The Spy*).

The American mass media in 1830 were healthy and flourishing, but they were nevertheless the property of the privileged classes. Books, magazines, and newspapers were not designed to appeal to the working class. They were too expensive, for one thing. For another, they were too literate. What did a dock worker in New York care about the price of wheat on the Philadelphia commodity market or the latest antics of a famous novelist? The population of the United States in 1830 was twelve million. The total circulation of all the newspapers in the country was well under two million.

The times were ripe for a newspaper for the masses.

By 1830 the urban working class was the largest potential newspaper audience in America. The papers that emerged to meet the needs of that audience were cheap and readable, stressing human-interest features and objective news over political partisanship. These were the first genuinely mass media in the country, and they quickly became the most influential. Other kinds of newspapers survived (the partisan press, the frontier press, the elite press), but they were clearly secondary in importance.

THE PENNY PRESS

The Industrial Revolution began in America early in the nineteenth century. Thousands of farm children and recent immigrants flooded the cities of the eastern seaboard in search of factory work. This new urban working class soon demanded—and received—the right to vote. The workers used their suffrage

to institute tax-supported public schools, and by 1830 most of them knew how to read. But they couldn't afford the newspapers of the period, nor were they interested in shipping and commercial news.

On September 3, 1833, Benjamin Day published the first issue of the *New York Sun*. He greeted his audience with these words:

> The object of this paper is to lay before the public, at a price within the means of every one, ALL THE NEWS OF THE DAY, and at the same time afford an advantageous medium for advertising. . . .[13]

Day's definition of news was much broader than that of the commercial and political newspapers of his time. It included whatever might entertain the masses—especially human-interest features. The first issue of the *Sun* carried this story on page one:

> *A Whistler.*—A boy in Vermont, accustomed to working alone, was so prone to whistling, that, as soon as he was by himself, he unconsciously commenced. When asleep, the muscles of his mouth, chest, and lungs were so completely concatenated in the association, he whistled with astonishing shrillness. A pale countenance, loss of appetite, and almost total prostration of strength, convinced his mother it would end in death, if not speedily overcome, which was accomplished by placing him in the society of another boy, who had orders to give him a blow as soon as he began to whistle.[14]

Everything in the *Sun* was designed with the urban masses in mind. Day chose a type face nearly twice as large as the opposition's. He cut the paper down to three columns per page, a far more readable format than the customary jumble of five or six columns. More important, Day filled the *Sun* with entertaining features. Perhaps the most entertaining was George Wisner's "Police Office," a daily round-up of local crime news. Wisner was the first police reporter in American journalism. He was one of the first reporters of any kind.

The key to the *Sun's* financial success was marketing. Recognizing that the urban masses could not afford six cents for a newspaper (nor an annual subscription at almost any price), Day sold the *Sun* on the street for a penny a copy. Newsboys bought the paper for 67 cents a hundred, then filled the downtown area with cries of crime and violence— on sale for only a penny. By 1836 the *Sun* had a daily circulation of more than 30,000.

The success of the *Sun* spawned dozens of imitators throughout the East. But the three most important ones were right in New York: the *New York Herald,* the *New York Tribune,* and the *New York Times.*

James Gordon Bennett founded the *Herald* in 1835. He matched the *Sun* crime for crime and sensation for sensation, and then some; in 1836 the *Herald* turned the murder of a local prostitute into a national issue. But Bennett was not content with just the working-class audience. He challenged the middle-class press as well, with up-to-the-minute coverage of commercial, political, and foreign news. Bennett's private pony express carried first-hand reports from Washington, and European news intercepted in Newfoundland. When Samuel Morse's telegraph was perfected in 1844, the *Herald* became one of its biggest customers.

Such newsgathering techniques were costly, and Bennett was forced to charge two cents for his paper. The public was apparently willing to pay the price. The *Herald's* extensive (and expensive) coverage of the Mexican War gave a giant boost to both circulation and advertising. By 1860 the *Herald* was the richest newspaper in America, selling 60,000 copies a day.

Horace Greeley's *New York Tribune,* founded in 1841, proved that a penny newspaper could succeed without sensationalism. Greeley's large editorial staff included correspondents in six American cities, plus Europe, Canada, Mexico, Central America, and Cuba. In place of scandal, the *Tribune* offered solid news coverage and a zesty editorial page. Greeley campaigned against slavery, whiskey, tobacco, debt, and numerous other evils both personal and political. A special weekly edition of the *Tribune* circulated nationwide—200,000 copies a week by 1860.

The *New York Times,* a latecomer to the Penny Press, was founded by Henry J. Raymond in 1851. Almost from the first, the *Times* was the most "elite" of the massmarket newspapers. Its news was wellbalanced and well-edited, and there was plenty of it—with special attention to foreign affairs. The *Times* was not yet the "paper of record" for the United States, but it was on its way.

The Penny Press began with sensationalism and human interest. By mid-century it was the "two-penny" press. The human interest continued unabated, but the sensationalism began to disappear; it was replaced with hard national and international news.

In 1848 six New York newspapers banded together to share the cost of telegraphing national news from Washington and European news from Boston. The organization they formed, the Associated Press of New York, soon became a wire service for the entire nation. Newspapers throughout the country purchased the news reports that AP prepared in Washington and Boston. Since the member papers represented a variety of editorial viewpoints, AP could satisfy them all only by having no viewpoint of its own. Objectivity had come to American journalism.

Now it was left to each newspaper to add its own interpretation or bias to the AP story. Many did just that—but many more didn't bother. Before long, newspapers in Atlanta, Chicago, and New York were carrying identical, unbiased reports. The change was startling. The following wire article on the Supreme Court's Dred Scott decision was carried by the *New York Times* in 1857. It is impossible to tell from the article where the *Times* stood on slavery:

> The opinion of the Supreme Court in the DRED SCOTT case was delivered by Chief Justice TANEY. It was a full and elaborate

1830	*Godey's Lady's Book* is founded, a monthly magazine especially for women.
1830-1833	Englishman David Napier perfects the Koenig steam press, producing thousands of impressions per hour.
1833	Benjamin Day publishes the *New York Sun,* the first of the penny newspapers, designed for the working class.
1835	James Gordon Bennett starts the *New York Herald* with $500. The two-cent paper will appeal to both the workers and the middle class.
1840	A German process for making paper from wood pulp permits truly mass-market publishing.
1841	Horace Greeley's *New York Tribune* stresses hard news and editorials instead of sensationalism.
1844	Samuel F. B. Morse perfects the telegraph.
1846	The rotary or "lightning" press is invented; it costs $25,000—but can produce 20,000 impressions an hour.
1848	Six New York newspapers form the Associated Press of New York to pool telegraph costs. Other papers with varying political views will soon tie onto the AP, forcing it to report the news objectively.
1850	*Harper's Monthly* is founded, with an emphasis on science and travel.
1851	Henry J. Raymond publishes the *New York Times,* with an initial investment of $100,000. Paul Julius Reuter establishes the first commercial wire service in Europe.
1857	*Harper's Weekly* is founded, using dramatic engravings to report national news.
1860	The Government Printing Office is established; partisan newspapers lose the patronage of federal—but not local—government printing.

statement of the views of the Court. They have decided the following important points:

First—Negroes, whether slaves or free, that is, men of the African race, are not citizens of the United States by the Constitution. . . .[15]

The magazine and book industries, meanwhile, followed the same trends as newspapers—appealing to the mass market first through sensationalism and human interest, and later through solid news coverage. *Godey's Lady's Book* (founded in 1830) was one of the first of a host of monthlies for women. *Graham's* (1840) stressed the special interests of men. *Harper's New Monthly Magazine* (1850) concentrated on science, travel, and current events, while the *Atlantic Monthly* (1857) had a more literary flavor. Weekly periodicals like *Gleason's Pictorial*

(1851) and *Leslie's Illustrated Newspaper* (1855) attracted readers with woodblock illustrations of fires, railroad accidents, and the like. *Harper's Weekly* (1857) added dramatic engravings of more important national events.

The fortunes of book publishing rose with the appearance of great American authors. Emerson, Thoreau, Poe, Cooper, and Whitman were read by "everyone." So were scores of sentimental novels—and Harriet Beecher Stowe's blockbuster, *Uncle Tom's Cabin.*

THE CIVIL WAR

The second third of the nineteenth century witnessed the development of several crucial journalistic trends—mass-circulation newspapers and magazines, human-interest stories, and objectivity. But the Partisan Press was by no means dead during this period. It was kept alive first by the issue of Jacksonian Democracy, and later by the even more divisive issue of slavery.

As early as 1837, an abolitionist editor died for his views. He was Elijah Lovejoy, editor of the *St. Louis Observer,* a strident anti-slavery weekly. Lovejoy was forced by public pressure to move his presses across the river to Alton, Illinois. Three times his office was ransacked—but still he refused to moderate his words. Finally, the editor was murdered by an angry mob. The *Liberator,* a Boston abolitionist paper edited by William Lloyd Garrison, headlined the story:

Horrid Tragedy!
BLOOD CRIETH!
Riot and Murder at Alton.

By the outbreak of hostilities in 1861, the American mass media were once more divided. Almost without exception the Southern newspapers supported slavery and secession, while most Northern papers were firmly opposed to both. Once again, there was no middle ground.

The Civil War was covered as no American war had ever been covered before. More than 150 newspaper and magazine reporters scoured the Northern front for news, while the well-organized Press Association of the Confederate States of America served Southern newspapers from the other side of the line.

Freedom of the press is not designed for a nation at war with itself. Civil War censorship was strict. In 1861, Union officials discovered that Confederate spies were masquerading as Northern reporters, sending back military secrets in the form of "news" telegrams. The Union army quickly issued an order forbidding telegraph companies from sending reports on military activity without prior government approval. The rule was almost certainly unconstitutional, but this was wartime, and the Supreme Court declined to rule on the matter.

Military officials used their censorship powers not only to protect military secrets but also to preserve their own reputations. The war between the generals and the reporters was nearly as violent as the war between the North and the South. In 1863, correspondent Thomas W. Knox described the Northern defeat at Vicksburg for the *New York Herald:*

> Throughout the battle the conduct of the general officers was excellent, with a few exceptions. General Sherman was so exceedingly erratic that the discussion of a twelvemonth ago with respect to his sanity was revived with much earnestness. . . . With another brain than that of General Sherman's, we will drop the disappointment at our reverse, and feel certain of victory in the future.[16]

Sherman immediately had Knox court-martialed as a spy. The reporter was found guilty only of ignoring the censorship regulations, and was handed a light sentence. But Sherman succeeded in having him banished from the front lines for the remainder of the conflict.

In 1864, the *New York World* and the *Journal of Commerce* mistakenly published a forged presidential proclamation, ordering the draft of 400,000 men. The government retaliated by closing down both papers for a two-day period. Consistently "Copperhead" (pro-Southern) newspapers, meanwhile, were stormed by mobs and forced to quit publishing. It was the same in the South. The *North Carolina Standard* argued that the war benefited only the wealthy; its office was destroyed by a Georgia regiment. Freedom of the press, it seems, was a concept for peacetime only.

The Civil War was the first American war to be covered by photographers. Photography had already become a practical process by 1839, as a result of the experiments of Frenchmen Joseph Niepce and Louis Daguerre. But subjects had to remain motionless for more than a minute, which effectively limited photography to portrait work and landscapes. In 1855, New York portrait photographer

Mathew Brady experimented successfully with the quicker wet-plate photographic process invented by Frederick Scott Archer. On the eve of the Civil War, Brady put his flourishing business aside and asked President Lincoln's permission to produce a photographic history of the conflict.

Brady and his associates turned wagons into darkrooms and set out to cover the war. In some 3,500 photographs—of generals, common soldiers, and the horrors of battle—they put the Civil War in focus. Though Brady was the nation's first great news photographer, the media of his day were not able to reproduce his photos. Until photoengraving was invented in 1878, newspapers and magazines had to rely on artists' drawings and woodcuts instead. As a result, many newspaper illustrations during the Civil War carried the credit line, "From a photograph by Brady."

The Civil War brought about several major changes in American journalism. For one thing, Washington, D.C. became the most important news center in the country—a role it still plays. Reporters had been covering the Capitol since 1822, and the *New York Herald* had established the first Washington bureau in 1841. But when war came the number of reporters in Washington more than doubled, and for the first time a journalist was assigned to cover the White House.

From the Civil War on, more news came out of Washington than any other American city.

Reporters at the battlefronts, meanwhile, were suspicious of the new telegraph machine. Fearful that their entire dispatch might not get through, they made sure to put the most important information first, leaving details and "color" for later. The rambling, roughly chronological news style of the early 1800s gave way to this tighter structure, which we now call the "inverted pyramid" style.

Telegraph reports from the front were often transmitted in spurts. Instead of waiting for the rest of the story, editors began setting these "bulletins" in headline type while the details were still being written. Such many-decked headlines became characteristic of the mid-nineteenth-century press.

A final result of the war was the development of the feature syndicate. Ansell Kellogg, publisher of a weekly in Baraboo, Wisconsin, was short of printing help in his backshop. So he arranged for the *Wisconsin State Journal* in Madison to send him sheets of war news, ready to fold into his own paper. One side was left blank so that Kellogg could add local copy or advertisements. Seeing a good thing, Kellogg later moved to Chicago and started his own syndicate service. By 1865 he had 53 clients.

CHRONOLOGY

1831 William Lloyd Garrison founds the *Liberator* in Boston, the most influential of the abolitionist newspapers.

1837 Abolitionist editor Elijah Lovejoy is killed by a pro-slavery mob in Alton, Illinois.

1850 Horace Greeley's *New York Tribune* adopts the cause of abolition, the first major daily to do so.

1851 Robert Barnwell Rhett, editor of the *Charleston Mercury*, is elected to the Senate. Rhett will lead the Southern fight for secession.

1852 Harriet Beecher Stowe's *Uncle Tom's Cabin*, formerly serialized in newspapers, becomes a best-selling book, arguing forcefully against slavery.

1861 The Civil War begins. Both sides immediately institute strict military censorship of war correspondents.

1862 The Press Association of the Confederate States of America is founded.

Some of these trends can be seen in the following article from the *New York Times* of April 15, 1865, reported by Associated Press correspondent Lawrence A. Gobright:

AWFUL EVENT

President Lincoln
Shot by an
Assassin

The Deed Done at Ford's
Theatre Last Night

THE ACT OF A DESPERATE REBEL

The President Still Alive at
Last Accounts

No Hope Entertained of His
Recovery

Attempted Assassination of
Secretary Seward

DETAILS OF
THE DREADFUL TRAGEDY

WASHINGTON, Friday, April 14—12:30 A.M. The President was shot in a theatre tonight and is, perhaps, mortally wounded. . . .[17]

TRANSITION

In a sense, the history of the United States starts over again at the end of the Civil War. The last third of the nineteenth century was characterized by three vitally important trends: industrialization, immigration, and urbanization.

Between 1865 and 1900, the national wealth of the country quadrupled, while manufacturing production increased sevenfold. This was the age of steel, oil, railroads, and electricity; the age of expanding factories and a growing labor movement. Meanwhile, the population more than doubled, from 35 million in 1865 to 76 million in 1900. Much of the growth was due to immigration, averaging as many as half a million new residents a year. Most of the immigrants, naturally, remained in the large cities on the East Coast, where jobs were plentiful for the unskilled. In the generation from 1860 to 1900, the population of New York City alone grew from slightly over a million to 3.4 million.

Inevitably, the American mass media changed with these conditions. By 1900, there were 2,326 daily newspapers in the country, roughly six times the number in 1865. More important, newspapers geared themselves more and more for the blue-collar reader, especially the urban immigrant. They were cheap and easy to read, filled with bold headlines, exciting artwork, human-interest stories, and editorials that championed the rights of the working classes. These developments were to culminate in the turn-of-the-century "New Journalism" of Joseph Pulitzer, William Randolph Hearst, and E. W. Scripps.

Of course, not all American publishers were busy cultivating the urban mass market. The frontier press, for example, had no mass market to cultivate. Many Western weeklies survived on circulations of only a few hundred. A few such papers were lucky enough to attract superlative journalists. Mark Twain, for instance, worked for several years as a reporter for the *Territorial Enterprise* of Virginia City, Nevada. But most frontier newspapers made do with more ordinary talent. Their pages were dominated by government proclamations (paid legal advertising) and reports on the activities of local civic groups.

The elite press, meanwhile, pursued the

specialized interests of its readers with little regard for national trends. Every large city supported at least one newspaper devoted to commercial and financial news, plus a second paper that stressed the conservative, business-oriented attitude toward the events of the day. Intellectuals could subscribe to any of hundreds of literary magazines. For political and social commentary they might read *The Nation,* a weekly magazine founded by E. L. Godkin in 1865. *The Nation* consistently lost money (in more than a hundred years of continuous publication, it has never once earned a profit), but it was (and is) a highly influential vehicle for liberal political philosophy.

The elite press and the frontier press were important, but it was the mass-circulation newspaper that was to change the course of American journalism. Industrialization, immigration, and urbanization created the mass market. Publishers did their best to capture it.

They could never have succeeded without the help of dozens of inventors and engineers. The following technological developments all took place between 1860 and 1900, making possible a truly mass-circulation newspaper:

1. The first transatlantic cable is completed, permitting up-to-the-minute news reports from overseas.

2. The telephone is invented, speeding the flow of information from news source to newsroom.

3. The web perfecting press is developed, capable of simultaneously printing both sides of a continuous roll of paper.

4. The electric press and the color press are introduced, increasing production speed to 48,000 12-page papers per hour.

5. Improved paper-making techniques reduce the price of newsprint from $246 a ton in 1870 to $42 a ton in 1900.

6. The development of the electric light bulb makes after-dinner reading possible, stimulating an upsurge in evening newspapers.

7. The typewriter is invented and adopted by the Associated Press and many large newspapers.

8. The linotype machine is patented, immediately tripling the speed of typesetting.

9. Halftone photoengraving is perfected, enabling newspapers and magazines to print photographs in addition to drawings and woodcuts.

All this newfangled equipment cost money—a lot of money. A single high-speed press might cost as much as $80,000; linotype machines, photoengravers, and even typewriters added to the bill. In 1835, James Gordon Bennett had started the *New York Herald* with a capital investment of $500. In 1895, William Randolph Hearst paid $180,000 for the printing plant of the *New York Journal.* And in 1901, *Editor & Publisher* magazine estimated that it would take at least a million dollars to launch a daily newspaper in New York. In order to run a "modern" newspaper, then, the turn-of-the-century publisher *had* to attract a mass audience. A high-speed press is simply too expensive to stand idle; it must be used to capacity, or it loses money.

Metropolitan newspapers need a mass audience to survive, but they seldom earn their profits directly from that audience. The profits come from advertising. It is doubtful that mass-circulation newspapers would have been possible without the invention of the department store.

Until the 1860s, newspaper advertising was mostly of the "classified" variety—brief, solid-type notices of products for sale. Then department stores began to replace neighborhood merchants as the chief source of goods. Besides the convenience of buying everything in one place, they offered fixed prices, credit, and free delivery. They also offered the first standardized, uniform-quality merchandise—the same hat or tin of flour in Boston as in Chicago. Suddenly newspapers were inundated with two new kinds of advertising: ads from the department stores (special on soap flakes at John Wanamaker's), and ads from the manufacturers whose brand names the stores carried (our chewing tobacco is better than their chewing tobacco). By 1880, advertising accounted for nearly half of newspaper gross revenue. By 1910, the figure would be two-thirds.

Most of this advertising was aimed at women—then as now the main customers for consumer goods. This was a boon for the women's magazines of the period (*Ladies' Home Journal, Woman's Home Companion, McCall's*). It also forced the daily newspapers to supply more material of presumed interest to women: fashion, cooking, society, etc. This was not the last time that the American mass media would tailor their content to the needs of advertisers.

A publisher who has sunk a few hundred thousand dollars into a printing plant wants to get as much use out of it as possible. Morning newspapers thus began printing afternoon editions as well. With improvements in home lighting in the 1870s, these became evening editions. By 1890, evening newspapers outnumbered morning ones two to one.

The same logic led to the development of the Sunday edition. Publishers were happy to have another use for their presses, while retailers were eager to reach the reader on a no-work day. Since there was little real news over the weekend, the Sunday papers were filled with features, short fiction, comics, and the like. They soon outstripped their parent dailies in size, circulation—and profit.

By the mid-1880s, industrialization, immigration, and urbanization had progressed to the point where, for the first time, a truly mass market existed for newspapers. By the mid-1880s, also, technological improvements and retail display advertising had developed sufficiently to permit publishers to exploit that market. It was the era of Big Business in American history. And the mass media were about to become a big business themselves.

The period from 1880 to 1910 produced a revolution in American journalism. Joseph Pulitzer and William Randolph Hearst created the nation's first truly mass-circulation newspapers, reaching heights of sensationalism never matched before or since. E. W. Scripps founded the first of the great newspaper chains, helping to transform journalism into a Big Business. Powerful wire services introduced standardization in newspaper content, while magazines like McClure's offered readers their first and finest taste of persistent full-length muckraking.

JOSEPH PULITZER

Joseph Pulitzer came to America from Hungary to fight in the Union army. Instead, he wound up as a newspaper reporter in St. Louis. In 1878, he founded the *St. Louis Post-Dispatch*. The paper was an immediate success, and by 1883 Pulitzer had saved enough money to try the "big time." He moved to New York and bought the *World*—a sober, commercial paper with a circulation of 20,000.

In his very first issue, Pulitzer announced that the *World* would be sober no longer:

> There is room in this great and growing city for a journal that is not only cheap but bright, not only bright but large, not only large but truly democratic—dedicated to the cause of the people rather than to that of the purse potentates—devoted more to the news of the New than the Old World—that will expose all fraud and sham, fight all public evils and abuses—that will battle for the people with earnest sincerity.[18]

Two weeks later, Pulitzer began to fulfill his promise. The Brooklyn Bridge was dedicated, and the *World* launched its first crusade: no tolls. In the months that followed, the paper exposed and denounced the New York Central Railroad, the Standard Oil and Bell Telephone monopolies, political brib-

1863 William Bullock introduces the web perfecting press, which prints both sides of a continuous roll of paper.

1865 E. L. Godkin founds *The Nation,* an elite weekly opinion magazine.

1866 The first successful transatlantic cable is completed.

1868 Charles A. Dana buys the *New York Sun,* and turns it into a lively combination of political activism and feature writing.

1869 The N. W. Ayer & Son advertising agency is founded to help advertisers buy newspaper space.

1871 The *New York Times* and *Harper's Weekly* (through cartoonist Thomas Nast) break the story of Tammany Hall corruption in New York government—an early example of muckraking journalism.

1876 Alexander Graham Bell invents the telephone.

1878 Thomas A. Edison develops the first phonograph. Frederick E. Ives introduces a practical method for halftone photoengraving; the technique will not be widely used for newspaper photography for another twenty years.

1879 Edison invents the incandescent bulb (electric light). John Wanamaker of Philadelphia buys the first full-page newspaper advertisement for his department store.

1885 Ottmar Mergenthaler files a patent for the first linotype machine.

---

ery, tenement housing conditions, inheritance tax loopholes, vote-buying, and civil service corruption—all on the front page.

Pulitzer's *World* also offered solid news coverage—but so did many other newspapers. What was special about the *World* was its exposés, its human-interest stories, and its stunts.

Averaging sixteen pages an issue, the paper was filled with gossip, scandal, and sensational tidbits of all sorts. Headlines were lively, and illustrations were plentiful: crime scenes (X marked the spot), disaster drawings, political cartoons, etc. The *World* promoted itself in every issue, using coupons, contests, and assorted other gimmicks. Pulitzer led the drive to build a pedestal for the Statue of Liberty, and sent an expedition to rescue a pioneer woman from Indian captors. He designed and executed some of the first public opinion polls. He invented the man-in-the-street interview. He sent columnist "Nellie Bly" (Elizabeth Cochran) to improve on Jules Verne by circling the globe in

only seventy-two days. All to build circulation.

In 1884, one year after Pulitzer took over, the *World's* circulation hit 100,000. Ten years later the figure, including both morning and evening editions, topped 400,000. Pulitzer's formula (news + human interest + stunts + editorial crusades) was a resounding success. It would be widely imitated.

WILLIAM RANDOLPH HEARST

While a student at Harvard, William Randolph Hearst was fascinated by the sensationalism of Pulitzer's *World.* He begged his father, owner of the *San Francisco Examiner,* to let him try the same trick. Daddy went along, and the *Examiner* had a new, 24-year-old publisher.

"Wasteful Willie" spent a small fortune transforming the paper into an exciting medium for the masses. He used special trains to get his reporters to the scene first, and hired the finest and most sensational writers he could find, whatever the cost. News for Hearst was defined as anything that made the reader say "Gee whiz"—and the columns of satirist Ambrose Bierce and sob-sister "Annie Laurie" (Winifred Black Bonfils) more than filled the bill. Within a year the *Examiner* had doubled its circulation. In 1893 it overtook the staid *San Francisco Chronicle* to become the most successful newspaper in the West.

Young Hearst was eager to battle Pulitzer on the *World*'s home turf. Financed by the family fortune (earned through precious metals, not newspapers), he purchased the *New York Morning Journal* in 1895. Scandal, gossip, sex, and pseudo-science immediately began to fill the pages of the *Journal*. Hearst spent wildly to acquire an all-star line-up, hiring, among others, most of the staff of the *World*'s Sunday edition. The *Journal*'s circulation rose to 150,000, and several advertisers dropped Pulitzer to take advantage of Hearst's cheaper ad rates.

A few years before, Pulitzer had hired R. F. Outcault to draw the first cartoon comic, "The Yellow Kid of Hogan's Alley," for his Sunday edition. Printed in color, the cartoon was very successful. When Hearst stole Outcault from the *World*, Pulitzer hired himself another artist. Both newspapers now carried "The Yellow Kid." The competition between the two comics came to symbolize the entire Hearst-Pulitzer circulation war, and gave that war a name: yellow journalism.

By 1897, both the *World* and the *Journal* were publishing morning, evening, and Sunday editions. Hearst's daily circulation matched Pulitzer's at 700,000; his Sunday circulation of 600,000 was coming close. In the struggle for readers, no feature was too silly to run. A typical article from the Sunday *World* was headlined "Does Tight Lacing Develop Cruelty?" The story began:

> The wearing of tight corsets will lower the moral character of the most refined woman. It will make her cruel. It will lead to morbid impulses—perhaps to crime. It will wholly destroy in her the naturally gentle and humane impulses of the feminine character.
>
> Tight lacing, we are told, compresses the solar plexus. . . . By reflex action the compression of the corset disturbs the entire nervous system—and the victim proceeds to descend from her lofty mental heights and to grovel in the depths of nervous depression.[19]

Yellow journalism reached its high point as the *World* and the *Journal* (and dozens of imitators across the country) covered the Cuban struggle against Spanish colonial rule. Hearst, in particular, intentionally built up war fever in order to build up circulation—and his competitors played the same game. It is probably unfair to claim that the *Journal* single-handedly started the Spanish-American War, but certainly Hearst did his share.

In 1897, Hearst sent writer Richard Harding Davis and artist Frederic Remington (both nationally famous) to cover the Cuban story first-hand. Nothing much was happening, and Remington cabled Hearst for permission to come home. The publisher is supposed to have replied: "Please remain. You furnish the pictures and I'll furnish the war." And so he did. One issue of the *Journal* carried a Remington sketch of a naked Cuban woman surrounded by leering Spanish officers, supposedly searching her clothes while on board an American ship. The banner headline read: "Does Our Flag Protect Women?" The *World* piously revealed that no such incident had ever happened—and then went out in search of its own atrocity stories.

When the battleship Maine exploded mysteriously in Havana harbor, both papers pulled out all the stops. The *Journal* devoted its whole front page to the story. "Destruction of the war ship Maine was the work of an enemy," it announced—and then went on to offer a $50,000 reward for proof of the claim. The *World* discovered "evidence" that a Spanish mine was responsible. Both newspapers passed the one-million circulation mark. Weeks later the war began.

NEWSPAPER CHAINS

In 1873, James E. and George H. Scripps founded the *Detroit News*. In 1878 Edward Wyllis Scripps started the *Cleveland Press*. During the next twelve years the three brothers added the *Buffalo Evening Telegraph*, the *St. Louis Chronicle*, the *Cincinnati Post*, and the *Kentucky Post*. The first modern newspaper chain was born.

E. W. Scripps quickly proved the most talented of the three brothers. His formula was simple. Find a city with weak newspapers and an editor with strong ideas. Start a new paper from scratch, emphasizing human-interest stories and an occasional crusade, always on behalf of the working class. Pay your top editor $25 a week until the paper shows a profit, then give the editor a huge block of stock. And sit back and wait.

Not every Scripps paper succeeded, but the successes far outweighed the losers. By 1914, the Scripps-McRae League was publisher of 23 newspapers across the country. Scripps himself wrote the editorials for all his papers. The chain was further unified by the United Press Association (a wire service), plus a feature syndicate and a science service. Readers of Scripps papers from coast to coast were offered identical national news and editorials.

E. W. Scripps was not primarily a businessman. He was sincerely dedicated to his crusades for the common people, and so hated pressure from advertisers that he twice experimented with adless papers. Nevertheless, Scripps proved that a large chain of newspapers, run from afar, could earn immense profits for its owner. Later chain publishers were often more interested in the profits than in news and editorial influence.

Until 1900, William Randolph Hearst owned only two newspapers, the *San Francisco Examiner* and the *New York Journal*. Then, obviously impressed by Scripps' suc-

cess, he began to make up for lost time. First came papers in Chicago, Boston, and Atlanta, then two new ones in San Francisco—all before 1917. Between 1917 and 1921, the Hearst chain acquired six properties. Seven more were added in 1922, and sixteen more by 1934.

Even more than Scripps, Hearst preferred power to profit. He built his chain partly to further his political ambitions in the Democratic Party. And he ran his papers with an iron hand. They were as fanatically anti-war and anti-Ally in 1916 as they had been pro-war and pro-Cuban in 1897. Hearst personally directed local crusades for his member papers, and led them on the first great "red hunt" after the Russian Revolution. The chain was united by two wire services—International News Service and Universal Service. Other Hearst subsidiaries included King Features (now the largest feature syndicate in America) and *American Weekly*, a Sunday supplement that was stuffed into every Hearst paper.

Hearst rule was healthy for some newspapers, deadly for others. In search of top-flight staffs and no competition, Hearst often bought out and merged or folded the opposition papers. In Chicago, the *Herald* and *Examiner* became the *Herald-Examiner;* in Boston, the *Daily Advertiser* was merged into Hearst's *Record*. Came the Depression of the 1930s, the Hearst chain found that it had overextended its financial reach, and began killing its own papers in a frantic economy drive. At one time or another, Hearst owned forty-two newspapers. By the time he went into semi-retirement in 1940, the chain was down to seventeen. Seven of the others had been sold. The remaining eighteen were dead.

WIRE SERVICES

The development of mass-circulation daily newspapers greatly increased the importance of the wire service—how else could a paper get the news of the world quickly and cheaply? For thirty-four years after its founding in 1848, the Associated Press was the only wire service in America (aside from the short-lived Confederate group during the Civil War). A loose cooperative of regional services (New England AP, Western AP, etc.), the Associated Press was actually run by the New York AP. It used its power to set rates and news policies that favored the needs of New York newspapers. It also enforced a rule whereby any member newspaper could blackball a competitor from AP membership.

By 1882 the need for a second wire service was obvious. A new group, calling itself the United Press, was organized to meet that need. Soon it had enrolled non-AP papers in nearly every major city. But this was the age of monopoly. Instead of competing with the new service, the Associated Press decided to make a deal. A secret agreement was negotiated; UP promised not to encourage any new papers in AP cities, and both services agreed to share their news reports.

Word of the agreement eventually leaked out to the Western AP members (already unhappy with New York's management), and in 1890 a government investigation was launched. Embarrassed, the New York group bolted to the United Press, leaving the Westerners in charge of the AP. They quickly incorporated as the Associated Press of Illinois.

Melville E. Stone was drafted as general manager of the newly organized AP. Stone managed to work out exclusive news-exchange contracts with the European press services, severely hampering the UP operation. In 1897 the United Press was forced into bankruptcy. Again the country was left with only one national wire service.

In 1900 the Illinois Supreme Court ruled that the AP was not entitled to blackball would-be members. In response, the company left Illinois and incorporated in New York. The membership protest right (blackball) survived until 1945, when the U.S. Supreme Court finally outlawed it.

In the meantime, a newspaper without an AP membership had only two alternatives. It could buy out a member paper, or it could start its own wire service. In 1907, E. W. Scripps founded the United Press Association, and Hearst followed in 1909 with the International News Service. Instead of issuing memberships, these services sold their reports to subscribers. In 1958 they merged. The resulting United Press International has been the major U.S. competition for the Associated Press.

THE MUCKRAKERS

In October of 1902, *McClure's* magazine printed the first of a nineteen-part series on "The Rise of the Standard Oil Company." Written by Ida Tarbell, the series revealed a number of secret agreements—kickbacks, rebates, and the like—between Standard Oil and the railroads. The public was inflamed, and the government brought suit against the oil company under the Sherman Anti-Trust Act. As a result of the first great magazine crusade, Standard Oil was fined $29 million.

That same issue of *McClure's* also carried an article by Lincoln Steffens on "Tweed Days in St. Louis." It was a part of Steffens' "Shame of the Cities" series, which exposed political corruption in Minneapolis, Pittsburgh, Chicago, Philadelphia, and New York, as well as St. Louis.

McClure's was by no means the only crusading magazine of the period. Others included *Cosmopolitan, Everybody's, Pearson's, Hampton's, La Follete's Weekly,* and the *American Magazine. Collier's* magazine was also partial to exposés. In 1911 it began a fifteen-part series by Will Irwin on "The American Newspaper." Highly critical of weak-kneed publishers and strong-armed advertisers, the series is among the earliest and finest examples of journalism exposing journalism.

Theodore Roosevelt, who had complimented the early magazine exposés, later turned against them. He called their writers "muckrakers," claiming that like the Man with the Muckrake in Bunyan's *Pilgrim's Progress,* they ploughed through the filth without ever seeing the positive side of life. In time, the reading public came to agree, and the crusading magazines began losing circulation. By World War I, Americans were more interested in the features and light fiction to be found in publications like *Munsey's* and the *Saturday Evening Post.* The opinion magazines had had their day. Never again would they be so popular or so influential.

Muckraking is a cyclical phenomenon, and it did not disappear for good when World War I began. Some sixty years later, the social disquiet and political scandal of the 1970s would give rise to a similar spurt of investigative journalism, led this time by a few newspapers and newsmagazines. With Watergate as its centerpiece, muckraking in the 1970s would once again stress the themes of industrial greed and government corruption.

What happened to American journalism between 1880 and 1910 may well be the heaviest irony in media history. For the first time, a truly mass-circulation newspaper industry was able to develop—made possible by urbanization, immigration, industrialization, technological improvements, and retail display advertising. And such an industry did develop. Media barons like Hearst and Pulitzer combined the human-interest emphasis of the Penny Press with the crusading zeal of the Partisan Press, and came up with a wholly new kind of journalism: the Yellow Press. What they produced was uniquely suited to the needs and wants of their mass audience.

But yellow journalism was also big-time journalism. By 1897, Pulitzer's *World* had a circulation of more than 700,000 copies a day. The paper was valued at $10 million, employed a staff of 1300, and earned an annual profit of nearly a million dollars. Hearst's *Journal* was just as big. And dozens of smaller newspapers, with circulations hov-

ering around the 100,000 mark, were quite big enough to consider themselves full-fledged businesses.

When a newspaper becomes a business, its owners begin to think like business executives. The bigger the paper gets, the more money it makes, the more it struggles to get still bigger and make still more money.

The heyday of yellow journalism was the late 1890s. By the turn of the century, newspapers were already becoming perceptibly less sensational. They still ran light human-interest stories, but they no longer ballyhooed them with giant headlines. They still planned and led crusades, but they no longer dared to raise new and controversial issues. The change was due partly to public resentment of Hearst, whose passionate invective was accused of inciting the assassination of President McKinley in 1901. But it was far more the result of a growing business orientation on the part of American publishers. The "people's newspapers" were turning middle-class.

Magazines like *McClure's* picked up the cudgels for a while, but soon reverted to features and fiction. The most pressing social issues of the day were already being handled through legislation, and the public's appetite for muckraking was waning.

By 1915, the most typical newspaper article was not a feature or an exposé, but a concise, objective news report supplied by the Associated Press. The most typical newspaper was not the *World* or the *Journal,* but one of the small-city afternoon dailies owned by Scripps—readable, responsible, and immensely profitable. The most prestigious newspaper in the country was, again, not the *World* or the *Journal,* but Adolph S. Ochs' *New York Times*—accurate, voluminous, and dull.

Historians Harry J. Carman and Harold C. Syrett summarize the period this way:

> As the circulation of the large urban dailies reached unprecedented figures, many of them became huge enterprises that in all essential

features were similar to the large corporations of industry and transportation. . . . Despite important exceptions, the increasing financial success of the larger papers often resulted in a corresponding growth of a conservative outlook in their editorial columns. This view was succinctly expressed by Arthur Brisbane, a Hearst employee: "Journalistic success brings money. The editor has become a money man. 'Where your treasure is, there your heart will be also.'" As journalism became more and more a big business, there was also a noticeable develop-

ment toward standardization. The press services supplied the same news to all their customers, and syndicates furnished many papers with the same cartoons, comic strips, photographs, and feature stories. Equally striking evidence of the trend toward standardization was the formation of several newspaper chains that had papers in several cities under a single management. . . .[20]

The era of yellow journalism left a legacy of many characteristics still to be found in today's newspapers: large headlines and pic-

---

CHRONOLOGY

1873	The Scripps family founds the *Detroit News,* the first newspaper in the first great newspaper chain.
1878	Joseph Pulitzer establishes the *St. Louis Post-Dispatch;* a series of popular crusades soon makes it the most popular evening paper in that city. E. W. Scripps starts the *Cleveland Press.*
1882	The United Press is organized to compete with the Associated Press.
1883	Pulitzer buys the *New York World,* adds human interest, gossip, and crusades, and within a year is selling 100,000 copies a day. Cyrus H. K. Curtis begins publishing the *Ladies' Home Journal;* by 1903 its circulation will top the one-million mark.
1887	William Randolph Hearst takes over the *San Francisco Examiner* and begins to transform it into a mass-market newspaper.
1889	The *World* publishes the first regular newspaper comics section.
1890	Western publishers take over the Associated Press; the New York AP joins the United Press.
1895	Hearst buys the *New York Journal* to compete directly with Pulitzer.
1896	Adolph S. Ochs takes over the undistinguished *New York Times;* he will buck the trend by stressing accuracy, objectivity, and depth.
1897	The United Press goes into bankruptcy.
1897-1898	Competition between Pulitzer and Hearst leads to sensational "yellow journalism," culminating in coverage of the Cuban insurrection and the Spanish-American War.
1902	*McClure's* magazine presents the first great magazine exposé, a 19-month attack on Standard Oil. E. W. Scripps founds the first national feature syndicate, the Newspaper Enterprise Association.
1904	Ivy Lee founds the first modern public-relations firm in New York.
1907	Scripps organizes the United Press Association to compete with the Associated Press; two years later Hearst will add a third wire service, the International News Service.
1911	Will Irwin begins a 15-part muckraking series in *Collier's* on "The American Newspaper."
1914	Hearst forms the King Features Syndicate.

tures, Sunday comics, human-interest features, public-service crusades. It also left a tradition of stunts and sensationalism that still influences many editors. But the greatest effect of the yellow journalists was paradoxical: They produced the first Big Newspapers, and thus inevitably turned newspapering into a Big Business. Pulitzer, Hearst, and Scripps might best be described as "crusading press barons." Today we have press barons galore, but few crusaders.

The history of the mass media before the twentieth century is the history of printing—newspapers, magazines, and books. Then came the new media: first film, next radio, and finally television. These upstarts quickly began to compete with the established media, forcing them to change their character in order to retain their influence. Television in particular had—and continues to have—a tremendous effect on all the other media.

NEW MEDIA

The existence of the motion picture rests on the 1824 discovery that the human eye retains an image for a fraction of a second longer than the picture actually appears. If a slightly different picture is substituted during this brief interval, the illusion of motion results.

In 1903, almost eighty years later, Edwin S. Porter produced the first American commercial film with a plot. *The Great Train Robbery* was eight thrilling minutes of stunt-riding and gunfighting. Suddenly film was a realistic medium, a worthy competitor of the legitimate theater.

Until 1912, no American film ran longer than fifteen minutes. This was the decision of the Motion Picture Patents Company, an industry association that apparently felt there was no market for films of more than one reel. The Patents Company also ruled that film actors should not be identified—since a well-known performer might demand higher

wages. And it established the National Board of Censorship to insure that member producers did nothing to offend the moviegoer.

Then, in 1912, Adolf Zukor purchased the American rights to a four-reel production of *Queen Elizabeth,* starring Sarah Bernhardt. The Patents Company refused to distribute the film through normal channels (nickelodeons and store shows), so Zukor persuaded the Lyceum Theatre in New York to run it. The movie later toured the country, and Zukor founded Paramount Pictures with the profits.

Three years later, D. W. Griffith produced *The Birth of a Nation,* incorporating a sympathetic approach to the Ku Klux Klan. It ran twelve reels (nearly three hours), and had a special score performed by a symphony orchestra. Griffith's film gripped its audience as no movie had before, and as few have since. Race riots followed its presentation in several cities; Woodrow Wilson called it "like writing history in lightning."[21] Film was now a force to be reckoned with.

During the next decade, the movie industry moved west to Hollywood, where it found lower taxes and better shooting weather. The Patents Company weakened and dissolved. The feature film replaced the one-reeler, and the "first run" movie theater replaced the nickelodeon. Moviegoers came to idolize certain performers—Mary Pickford, Lillian and Dorothy Gish, Lionel Barrymore, William S. Hart, Fatty Arbuckle, Douglas Fairbanks, Charlie Chaplin. The appearance of any of these stars guaranteed a box-office hit.

By the mid-1920s, movies were Big Business—slick, commercial, and very profitable. But a new competitor was already on the scene: radio.

Radio owes its existence to the "wireless telegraph," invented by Gugliemo Marconi in 1895. The wireless was fine for dots and dashes, but voice transmission was impossible until 1906, when Lee De Forest perfected the vacuum tube. Four years later, De Forest dramatically broadcast the voice of Enrico Caruso from the stage of New York's Metropolitan Opera House.

Experimentation continued during World War I, and in 1919 Westinghouse engineer Frank Conrad began broadcasting music throughout the Pittsburgh area. Listener response was enthusiastic; Westinghouse immediately started advertising its crystal sets "to hear Dr. Conrad's popular broadcasts." In 1920, the station was christened KDKA.

The *Detroit News,* meanwhile, was running what was to become radio station WWJ in order to gain goodwill and help sell newspapers. Publishers in Kansas City, Milwaukee, Chicago, Los Angeles, Louisville, Atlanta, Des Moines, and Dallas soon followed suit. Department stores ran radio stations to promote their goods. So did manufacturers like AT&T, General Electric, and of course Westinghouse.

From the very beginning, news was an important part of broadcasting. KDKA's first transmission was the 1920 election returns. In 1922, the Associated Press decided that radio might soon constitute a major threat to the newspaper business, so it ruled that AP reports could not be carried on radio. Station-owning publishers rebelled against the rule, complaining that their competitors would use the UP or INS reports anyhow. Although AP tried to reserve its 1924 election returns for the print media only, some three million families learned of the victory of Calvin Coolidge via radio. AP soon joined the other wire services in supplying news to broadcast stations.

Meanwhile, New York station WEAF was discovering, rather to its surprise, that radio could earn money. In 1922 the station's owner, AT&T, began selling time to advertisers. Word spread quickly, and the race for broadcast licenses was on. Plans to develop radio as a nonprofit public-service institution were abandoned. In 1921 there had been only 30 commercial radio stations; by 1923 there were more than 500.

Radio networks developed to meet the needs of national advertisers. By 1925, AT&T already operated a chain of 26 stations, stretching from New York to Kansas City.

RCA, Westinghouse, and General Electric (all radio manufacturers) were working together to organize a competing network. In 1926, AT&T agreed to sell out to its rivals in return for a monopoly over all network relays, the lines that connect member stations. The National Broadcasting Company was founded as an RCA subsidiary to run the new operation. The old AT&T network became the NBC "red network," while the original Westinghouse-RCA-GE network was called the "blue network." Coast-to-coast programming began in 1927, under the leadership of NBC head David Sarnoff. Three years later, Westinghouse and GE were forced out of network operation by an antitrust suit, and Sarnoff took over control of RCA.

The competing Columbia Broadcasting System was founded in 1927 by the Columbia phonograph record company. William S. Paley soon became its president, and by 1929 CBS was making money.

In 1927 there were 733 stations in the nation. Many of them found it necessary to skip around from frequency to frequency, searching for a clear one where they could broadcast without interference. Inevitably, the more powerful stations were smothering their weaker rivals. The radio industry and the listening public asked the federal government to clear up the interference problem by assigning each station its own frequency. Congress accepted the responsibility. The Radio Act of 1927 gave a five-person Federal Radio Commission the power to regulate all broadcast transmissions.

The job of the FRC was to grant licenses for the use of specific frequencies renewable every three years. Licensees were expected to act in the "public interest, convenience, or necessity."[22] The implicit power of censorship through license renewal expressed in these standards has been used only rarely (and very hesitantly) by the Commission.

In order to put a stop to signal interference, the FRC eliminated more than a hundred stations, leaving the total number at roughly 600. "Clear channels" were established to allow selected urban stations to reach distant rural areas with no stations of their own. Most of these highly lucrative channels soon fell into network hands.

The film and radio industries both experienced a surge of tremendous growth in the 1920s. What were the print media doing during that decade?

OLD MEDIA

America may have entered World War I reluctantly, but American newspapers entered with enthusiasm. Even the isolationist Hearst chain abandoned its campaign for neutrality after the 1917 declaration of war. Throughout the nineteen months of fight-

---

CHRONOLOGY

1824   Peter Mark Roget discovers the principle of motion pictures—that the human eye retains an image briefly after the picture is gone.

1839   Louis Daguerre and Joseph Niepce develop a practical photographic process.

1877   Eadweard Muybridge and John D. Issacs use 24 cameras in sequence to photograph a race horse in action.

1884   George Eastman introduces roll film, leading in 1888 to the easy-to-operate Kodak camera.

1888   Edison invents the wax-cylinder record.

1889   Edison and William K. L. Dickson develop a sprocket system for motion pictures.

1895   Systems for projecting motion pictures on a screen are developed simultaneously in several countries. Gugliemo Marconi transmits wireless telegraph signals for one mile.

1901   Marconi sends wireless signals across the Atlantic.

1903   *The Great Train Robbery* becomes the first American movie with a plot.

1906   Lee De Forest perfects the vacuum tube, making possible radio voice transmissions.

1912   Adolf Zukor presents the four-reel movie *Queen Elizabeth,* starring Sarah Bernhardt. Congress passes the Radio Act of 1912 to prevent individual ham operators from interfering with government transmissions.

1915   D. W. Griffith produces *The Birth of a Nation,* the longest and most powerful film to date.

1919   Westinghouse engineer Frank Conrad begins broadcasting music throughout the Pittsburgh area.

1920   Westinghouse obtains a license for station KDKA in Pittsburgh.

1922   New York station WEAF begins selling airtime to advertisers. The Associated Press refuses to allow the broadcasting of AP reports. In an effort to avoid government censorship, the movie industry establishes a production code and self-censorship procedures.

1923   The Eveready Battery Company prepares and sponsors its own hour-long show on WEAF; a year later it will produce the show on a national network.

1926   AT&T turns its radio network over to a joint RCA-Westinghouse-GE consortium, leading to the development of the RCA-controlled National Broadcasting Company.

1927   The Columbia Broadcasting System is organized to compete with the NBC network. The Radio Act of 1927 establishes a five-person Federal Radio Commission to license broadcasters and prevent signal interference.

---

ing, anti-German propaganda dominated the press.

The government did what it could to insure that dominance. President Wilson appointed former newsman George Creel to head the Committee on Public Information. The C.P.I. issued over 6,000 patriotic press releases during the course of the war, most of which were faithfully carried by the nation's press. The Creel Committee also established "guidelines for voluntary censorship" on touchy subjects such as troop movements.

In addition, Congress passed a series of laws aimed at putting a stop to "treasonous" publications. These laws culminated in the Espionage Act of 1917 and the Sedition Act of 1918. The latter outlawed, among other things, "any disloyal, profane, scurrilous, or abusive language about the form of government of the United States, or the Constitution, military or naval forces, flag, or the uniform of the army or navy of the United States."[23] No attempt was made to invoke the Sedition Act against mainstream publishers; it was used instead to stifle the socialist and German-language press. Mainstream publishers, after all, minded their manners. When the war was over, *The Nation* magazine was moved to comment:

> During the past two years, we have seen what is practically an official control of the press, not merely by Messrs. Burleson and Gregory [heads of the Post Office and Justice Department] but by the logic of events and the patriotic desire of the press to support the government.[24]

The end of World War I was the start of the Roaring Twenties. It was a sensational decade—jazz and flappers; Prohibition, speakeasies, and gangsters; Mary Pickford and Douglas Fairbanks; Charles Lindbergh and the Prince of Wales; Jack Dempsey, Red Grange, and Babe Ruth; Leopold and Loeb; Sacco and Vanzetti. The Roaring Twenties virtually cried out for a renaissance in yellow journalism.

The cry was answered with a new kind of newspaper: the tabloid. Tabloids may be recognized by their small size (easy to carry on the subway), their small number of columns (seldom more than five), and their extensive use of photography (often the whole front page). The first modern American tabloid was the *New York Daily News,* founded by Joseph M. Patterson in 1919. The *News* offered its readers a steady diet of sex and crime, luridly illustrated and simply written. By 1924 it had the largest daily circulation of any newspaper in America.

Typical of the *News* approach to news was the paper's 1928 front-page photo of the execution of convicted murderer Ruth Snyder. The heavily retouched picture filled the entire page, with the following caption:

> WHEN RUTH PAID HER DEBT TO THE STATE!—The only unofficial photo ever taken within the death chamber, this most remarkable, exclusive picture shows closeup of Ruth Snyder in death chair at Sing Sing as lethal current surged through her body at 11:06 Thursday night. . . . *Story and another electrocution picture on page 3.*[25]

Dozens of tabloids appeared in major cities throughout the country in the 1920s, modeled on the *News* formula of sex and violence. Some died off, but many survive to this day, often with very healthy circulation figures. Though tabloids obviously exert great influence on their readers, they are viewed by journalists and students of journalism almost as a quirk, quite separate from the mainstream of American publishing. The *New York Daily News* still has one of the largest readerships in the United States, and as a *news*paper it has greatly improved since the 1920s—but not one university in a hundred receives and microfilms the paper.

Like the Penny Press and the Yellow Press, the Tabloid Press built its circulation on people who had not regularly read a daily newspaper—immigrants and blue-collar workers. Mainstream newspapers ignored the tabloids, sticking firmly to the standards of accuracy, objectivity, and responsibility established before the war. The finest example of this tradition was the *New York Times,* published by Adolph S. Ochs and edited by Carr V. Van Anda.

The *Times* strove in every issue to be a "newspaper of record," correct, careful, and complete. Its motto was "All the News That's Fit to Print." An unwritten corollary was "and not a *word of* interpretation." According to the *Times* ethic, interpretation was like bias, unworthy of a newspaper that prided itself on straight reporting.

Not every newspaper in the 1920s was a miniature *New York Times,* but except for the tabloids nearly every newspaper secretly wished it was. The wire services helped to point the way. In an effort to please publishers with all sorts of viewpoints, AP, UP, and INS tried to write without any viewpoint. The wire story—an assortment of accurate but uninterpreted facts—became the epitome of good newspaper journalism. Occasionally every paper would lapse into sensationalism or bias or interpretation, and some papers lapsed more than others. But every paper (tabloids aside) tried to lapse as little as possible, to stick as best it could to the straight and narrow path of objectivity.

American journalists now considered themselves members of a full-fledged profession. In 1922, the editors of the major daily newspapers organized the American Society of Newspaper Editors. The group had its first annual meeting in 1923, and immediately adopted a seven-point code of ethics, known as the "Canons of Journalism." The Canons stressed sincerity, truthfulness, accuracy, impartiality, fair play, decency, independence, and fidelity to the public interest. They were extremely general and strictly voluntary. The Canons were an expression, not of what newspapers were, but rather of what newspapers thought they ought to be. They were thus indicative of a major transition in American journalism, from the free-wheeling libertarian theory of the nineteenth century to the more sober "social responsibility" theory of the twentieth.

But the social responsibility of the press, according to the Canons of Journalism, was limited to telling the truth about the news. Nothing was said about interpreting the news, giving it meaning, or making sense of it for the reader. Editors and publishers would soon discover that this limited notion of responsibility was not enough.

As newspapers grew more "responsible," they also diminished in number. Competition

CHRONOLOGY

1917   World War I begins, and American newspapers willingly accept "voluntary" censorship at the hands of the Creel Committee.

1918   Congress passes the Sedition Act and other laws which were used to stifle the socialist and German-language press.

1919   The war ends, and Joseph M. Patterson founds the *New York Daily News,* the first of the sex-and-violence tabloids.

1922   DeWitt Wallace begins publishing *The Reader's Digest,* destined to become the largest general-interest magazine in the world.

1923   The American Society of Newspaper Editors adopts the Canons of Journalism, an expression of the "social responsibility" of the press. Henry R. Luce and Briton Hadden found *Time* magazine, the first of the modern weekly newsmagazines.

1924   H. L. Mencken establishes the *American Mercury,* an outspoken and frequently obstreperous magazine of opinion.

and economic pressures caused the death of many papers. Intentional consolidation at the hands of media barons killed others. Still others died simply because there was no longer any need for them; as newspaper content became more and more standardized, readers cared less and less which paper they read. In 1910, there were 2,200 English-language dailies in the United States, serving 1,207 cities. By 1930 there were only 1,942 dailies serving 1,002 cities. During the same period, the number of American cities with competing daily newspapers plummeted from 689 to 288. These trends would continue in the decades ahead. By 1960, the number of daily newspapers would be stabilized at 1,763; the number of cities with competing dailies would be down to a mere 61 and still decreasing.

The magazine industry, meanwhile, grew less and less concerned with news and public affairs. The muckraking magazines of the turn of the century either folded or reverted to features and fiction. So did most of the serious magazines of opinion that had flourished before the war. They were replaced for a while by H. L. Mencken's *American Mercury*. Founded in 1924, the *Mercury* was outspoken and sensational, the magazine equivalent of a tabloid. Other new entries of the 1920s included *The Reader's Digest* (1922), the *Saturday Review of Literature* (1924), and the *New Yorker* (1925).

The major exception to the retreat of magazines from the real world was *Time*, founded by Henry R. Luce and Briton Hadden in 1923. Both were young men in their twenties; both wanted to publish a weekly magazine that would make sense of the news. "People are uninformed," they argued, "because no publication has adapted itself to the time which busy men are able to spend on simply keeping informed."[26] *Time*'s interpretations of the news were slick, facile, and often misleading—but it *did* interpret the news. It thus satisfied a need that would become increasingly acute in the years ahead.

DEPRESSION AND AFTER

On October 29, 1929, the New York stock market crashed—heralding the Great Depression, the New Deal, and a revolution in American life. Every institution was significantly changed by the events of the 1930s, and the mass media were no exception.

The Depression cut heavily into newspaper revenue, but radio continued to grow and prosper. In 1932, the American Newspaper Publishers Association voted to combat the electronic competition by cutting off its supply of news. ANPA asked the wire services to stop selling news to radio stations, except for brief announcements that would stimulate the sale of newspapers. It also recommended that member papers start treating their radio logs as advertising. The wire services and most major newspapers supported the boycott, and radio was on its own.

CBS immediately set up news bureaus in New York, Washington, Chicago, Los Angeles, and London. Within a few months, daily newscasts by H. V. Kaltenborn and Boake Carter were supplying CBS affiliates with an adequate replacement for the wires. The NBC news service wasn't nearly as good, but many local stations didn't really care—they simply stole their news reports out of the early editions of local newspapers. Several lawsuits by the Associated Press clearly established the illegality of this practice. But AP couldn't afford to sue half the radio stations in the country.

The boycott was a failure. A compromise Press-Radio Plan was worked out in 1934, granting stations the right to ten minutes of wire news a day. It wasn't enough. Radio wanted more, and was willing to pay for it. In 1935, UP and INS agreed to sell complete news reports to stations. AP soon followed suit. Today, both major services have special radio wires. AP services 5,600 U.S. broadcast clients (and only about 1,750 publications), while the UPI wire goes to 3,700 stations (and only about 1,600 publications).

Radio soon became *the* mass medium for spot news. The vacuum tube has a tremendous advantage over the printing press: speed. It warms up faster; it requires no typesetters and no delivery trucks. Radio can have a story on the air minutes after the event; newspapers take hours. By the end of the 1930s, it was obvious to editors that the "scoop" and the "extra" were obsolete. Newspapers could still serve the public by supplying the details of the news, or the significance of the news—but radio was bound to get there first with the news itself.

Thus interpretive journalism was born. It was pioneered in the 1910s and 1920s by columnists like David Lawrence (*New York Evening Post*), Mark Sullivan (*New York Herald Tribune*), and Frank R. Kent (*Baltimore Sun*). It was picked up by the feature syndicates in the early 1930s, making national figures of such pundits as Walter Lippmann, Heywood Broun, and Drew Pearson. All these people did their best to tell newspaper readers "the news behind the news."

Interpretive journalism made it to the front page in 1933, when the United States went off the gold standard. This was far too complex a subject to report "straight." President Roosevelt sent a group of White House economic advisers over to the press room to help reporters understand the meaning of the move. The reporters were grateful, and interpretive news articles (with or without the help of presidential advisers) soon became commonplace.

Consider, for example, this "news lead" from a 1935 issue of the *Buffalo* (N.Y.) *Evening News:*

WASHINGTON, Aug. 15.—A scratch of a pen by the Chief Executive Wednesday extended to approximately a fourth of America's population some measure of federal protection from the vicissitudes of life.

It was the signing by President Roosevelt of the nation's first social security legislation, regarded by the President more than any other action taken during his administration as the heart of the New Deal.[27]

A sidebar to the story began: "Here are some examples of how the new social security program will operate. . . ." This was the kind of reporting that radio didn't do.

What radio *did* do was offer the country a varied diet of news and entertainment. Performers like Amos 'n' Andy, Jack Benny, Rudy Vallee, and Kate Smith entertained millions of Americans throughout the Depression. Kaltenborn's news broadcasts and President Roosevelt's "fireside chats" proved the medium's potential for more than pap. So did live coverage of the Spanish Civil War, and of innumerable sporting events. By the end of the decade, William L. Shirer in London and Edward R. Murrow in Vienna (later in London as well) were reporting the rise of Nazism *as it happened,* to a public that had learned to expect its news instantly.

As radio thrived and newspapers turned more interpretive, the film industry discovered sound. The first full-length talking picture, *The Jazz Singer* starring Al Jolson, was produced by Warner Brothers in 1927. It was an instant success. Sound movies singlehandedly rescued the film industry from the doldrums caused by radio competition. By 1929, nearly half of the nation's 20,000 movie theaters were equipped to handle sound. Paid admissions rose from 60 million a week in 1927 to 110 million a week in 1929. By the early 1930s, the silent film was dead.

Movie magnates had other problems to worry about. Censorship was by far the biggest. The public outcry against "dirty movies" was fed as much by stories of corruption and immorality in Hollywood as it was by the films themselves. In 1922 the major studios had founded the Motion Picture Producers and Distributors of America, headed by Will H. Hays. The "Hays Office" did its best to forestall government censorship by instituting self-censorship instead. The tactic was only partially successful. It stopped the government (by and large), but it didn't stop the Legion of Decency, established by a group of Catholic laypeople in 1934. It wasn't until the late 1950s that movie producers discovered that the public would support a good film (and sometimes a bad film) even if it lacked the Legion's seal of approval.

Newsreels were standard movie theater fare throughout the 1920s and 1930s. Though newsreel news was often two or three weeks old, it had the tremendous advantage of including both pictures and sound. Newsreels remained popular until the advent of television.

The motion picture industry of the 1930s produced movies in waves—musicals, then prison pictures, then screwball comedies, then biographies, etc. As World War II drew near, Hollywood went to war. From the beginning, the Nazis were the villains. When the United States entered the conflict in 1942, war movies were turned into frank propaganda for the Allies.

The biggest development in the magazine world, meanwhile, was the success of *Life* magazine, first published by Henry R. Luce in 1936. Capitalizing on the public taste for big photographs nurtured by the tabloid papers in the 1920s, *Life* was an immediate circulation and advertising success. Alfred Eisenstaedt, Thomas McEvoy, Peter Stackpole, and other photographers filled the pages of the new magazine with a visual record of American lifestyles.

Margaret Bourke-White was probably the greatest photographer on *Life*'s team. A veteran of industrial photography and Luce's business magazine *Fortune,* she produced a nine-page photo essay for the first issue of *Life,* recording the lives of workers who were building the Fort Peck Dam in Montana. In succeeding years she was to travel a million miles for *Life* and *Fortune.* She photographed the Nazi bombing of Moscow, was the first woman photographer accredited by the U.S. armed forces in World War II, and shocked the world with her photographs of Nazi concentration camps. Margaret Bourke-

White captured a whole generation of history in her lens.

World War II was radio's "finest hour." Kaltenborn left CBS to head the NBC news team in Europe, but no one at NBC could match the impact of Edward R. Murrow, broadcasting from London for CBS. "Neutral" Americans listened in awe as Murrow narrated, blow by blow, the Battle of Britain. For newspapers, meanwhile, the war was a repeat of World War I: massive reporting of battles, scant reporting of issues, and voluntary self-censorship of military details.

This, then, is how the American mass media stood at the end of World War II. Radio was fat and sassy, with both the number of stations and the amount of advertising expanding rapidly. It offered listeners a potpourri of news, culture, sports, and lowbrow entertainment. Newspapers were also doing well, the beneficiaries of consolidation, monopoly ownership, and the postwar boom. Most combined their straight news with interpretive stories, features, backgrounders, syndicated columns, and editorials. Magazines were slick and profitable, geared to entertaining the mass market and little more. So were movies. And even the book industry was earning money, especially with its paperback and textbook lines.

Then came television.

———————————

Television had its start in the 1920s, but it didn't begin to develop seriously until after the war. Then, in just a few years, it transformed itself from an experiment into a way of life. In revenue, in circulation, and in the devotion of its audience, television quickly became the mass medium of the mid-twentieth century. All other media have been forced into subordinate roles.

TV DEVELOPS

In 1923, Vladimir Zworykin invented the iconoscope and the kinescope, the basis for television transmission and reception respectively. Philo Farnsworth added the electronic camera, and Allen B. Dumont contributed the receiving tube. General Electric put them all together, and in 1928 founded the first regular television station, WGY, in Schenectady, New York. By 1937, there were seventeen such experimental stations on the air.

The development of the coaxial cable in 1935 enabled these early TV stations to hook up into a primitive "network" in order to broadcast special events. They did so for the opening of the New York World's Fair, for the 1940 nominating conventions, for several football and baseball games, and for at least one speech by President Roosevelt.

In 1939 the *Milwaukee Journal* applied for a commercial TV license. The Federal Communications Commission pondered the no-tion of commercial television for a period, finally approving the license in 1941. Ten commercial stations, including the *Journal's*, appeared within a year, and immediately began soliciting ads. When war broke out in 1942, the FCC put a "freeze" on TV development: no new licenses, no new receivers to be manufactured, and a limited schedule for stations already on the air. Only six of the ten 1941 pioneers lasted through the war.

The influence of government over broadcasting was becoming increasingly important. In 1934 Congress had replaced the five-person Federal Radio Commission with a seven-person Federal Communications Commission, responsible for television, telephone, and telegraph as well as radio. Like the FRC before it, the FCC viewed its job as a maintenance function: dividing up the spectrum and preventing interference. But there were more applicants for radio licenses than there was space on the radio band. The Commission was forced to choose between applicants, to decide which would best serve "the public interest, convenience, and necessity."

It simply wasn't possible for the FCC to confine its duties to technical matters. In 1939, for example, the Mayflower Broadcasting Corporation applied for the license of radio station WAAB, arguing that the frequent editorials of the current WAAB licensee were not in the public interest. After much thought, the Commission agreed. Mayflower was denied the license on other grounds, but WAAB was ordered to stop editorializing. This 1941 "Mayflower decision" outlawing broadcast editorials stood until 1949, when the Commission changed its mind and reversed the ruling. The so-called "fairness doctrine," requiring broadcasters to give fair treatment to all sides in a controversy, developed out of the Mayflower confusion.

Even when it confined itself to technology, the FCC had a vast impact on the future of broadcasting. The Commission spent the war trying to decide what to do about two new media—television and frequency modulation (FM) radio. FM had been invented by Edwin H. Armstrong in 1933; Armstrong's experimental station was on the air in Alpine, N.J., by 1939. Like television, FM boomed in the early 1940s. Like television, it was "frozen" by the FCC during the war.

In 1945 the Commission made its crucial decision. It moved FM "upstairs" to another part of the spectrum (making all existing FM receivers obsolete), and opened up more space for thirteen commercial television channels instead. The move set FM back nearly twenty years. NBC, which had encouraged its affiliates to apply for TV licenses, was elated. CBS was badly hurt; it had put its money on FM instead.

Once a favorable decision had been made, television growth was fast and furious. In 1948 the FCC reassigned Channel 1 for non-

broadcast services, and again ordered a freeze on channel allocations, this time to study the interference problem and the possibility of color television. The Korean War prolonged the freeze until 1952. Nevertheless, some 15 million families purchased TV sets during the freeze in order to watch the 108 stations then on the air. They saw Milton Berle's debut in 1948 on a 13-station NBC network. They saw Ed Sullivan on CBS for the first time that same year. They saw baseball's World Series as it happened. They saw news and public affairs broadcasting, too, notably the Kefauver Committee investigation into organized crime. And they saw some fine theater—"Philco Playhouse," "Goodyear Playhouse," Gian-Carlo Minotti's opera *Amahl and the Night Visitors*. But mostly they saw "I Love Lucy" and "Your Show of Shows"; "Arthur Godfrey's Talent Scouts" and "Kukla, Fran, and Ollie"; "The Web," "The Front Page," "The Big Story," and "The Cisco Kid."

And they saw ads—hour after hour of ads—for cars and appliances, for cigarettes and detergents, for banks and insurance companies, for presidential aspirants Eisenhower and Stevenson.

When the freeze was lifted in 1952, television grew quickly. The development of microwave relays made coast-to-coast hookups practical for the first time, and the networks were quick to employ them. By 1961 there were 548 television stations in the country, broadcasting to 60 million receiving sets (in 89 percent of all American homes). Of these stations, 205 were affiliated with CBS, 187 with NBC, and 127 with ABC; only 29 stations had no connections with any network. The average TV station in 1961 earned a profit of 15 percent. The average TV set was left running for at least five hours a day, 365 days a year.

Television changed little in the 1960s and early 1970s. It grew, of course. By 1975, more than 66 million homes (97 percent) had at least one TV set. And the 1959 quiz show scandals forced the three networks to produce most of their own programs, instead of letting the advertisers do it for them. But aside from that, TV content in 1975 was much the same as TV content in 1965 and 1955: one-tenth news and public affairs, one-tenth drama and culture, and four-fifths ads and light entertainment.

To the extent that TV changed at all in the 1960s and early 1970s, it changed at the hands of the Federal Communications Commission. In the early 1970s, for example, the FCC adopted a series of rules requiring local stations to carry something other than network programming in prime time. The Commission also proposed or enacted several restrictions on radio-TV and print-broadcasting combinations in a single market. These steps were designed to alleviate the two biggest problems of American television today: the bland homogeneity of entertainment programming, and the economic and political danger of monopoly.

Meanwhile, the FCC continued to arbitrate the demands of technological innovations that could revolutionize the broadcast industry. The RCA system for color television got the final go-ahead in 1953; by 1979, 83 percent of all American homes had a color TV set. A huge slice of the spectrum was set aside in 1952 for ultrahigh frequency (UHF) television. UHF developed slowly until 1962, when the FCC asked Congress to require all new TV sets to include UHF receivers. By 1980, 381 out of a total of 997 television stations were UHF. Educational television was also given a boost by the Commission, which set aside special channels for noncommercial use. There were 255 such stations in operation by 1980.

Color, UHF, and educational TV are practical and important developments, but the greatest potential for change is in cable and satellite television. Either one could revolutionize broadcasting—cable by permitting the growth of dozens of new local channels, satellites by permitting the growth of dozens of national and international networks. But revolutionary potential doesn't always lead to revolutionary change. The first substantial cable TV system was set up in 1950, bringing

television to Lansford, Pa. Satellite transmission began twelve years later, with the launching of Telstar in 1962. Yet until the mid-1970s, cable was used mostly to improve TV reception in mountainous rural regions and skyscraper cities, while satellites were used for international viewing of funerals, inaugurations, Olympic Games, and the like.

Why didn't cable and satellites have the revolutionary impact that was predicted for them? Much of the responsibility belonged to the FCC. Throughout the 1960s, the Commission intentionally slowed the development of both innovations, putting its chips instead on the maintenance of network-dominated broadcasting and on the slow but steady growth of UHF.

In the early 1970s, however, the FCC decided to give cable and satellites a better break. In 1972, it adopted new rules to encourage cable while still protecting the economic security of over-the-air broadcasters. In the same year, it broke the monopoly over domestic communications satellites held by Comsat (a semi-public corporation dominated by AT&T), and announced that other companies were free to orbit their own systems.

Still the revolution did not occur. Many independent cable TV companies ran into serious financial problems: the cost of wiring a city for cable proved higher than expected, and urban viewers were less than enthusiastic about the extra channels and clearer reception offered (for a price) by cable. Over-the-air broadcasters continued lobbying to protect their interests at the expense of cable. And the communications industry moved very cautiously into satellites, making sure to protect the current domination of the three networks and the current profitability of the land lines that serve them.

By 1975, cable and satellites were growing —slower than expected and later than expected, but they were growing. And in the last half of the 1970s they finally took off. The communications satellite business, newly opened to competition, proved highly profitable for companies like Western Union;

1923 Vladimir Zworykin invents the iconoscope and the kinescope, the basis for television.

1928 The first experimental TV station, WGY, begins operation in Schenectady, New York.

1933 Edwin H. Armstrong invents FM radio.

1934 Congress passes the Communications Act, establishing a Federal Communications Commission with authority over television as well as radio.

1935 The first coaxial cable is built between New York and Philadelphia, making TV hook-ups possible.

1939 Armstrong begins operating his experimental FM radio station in Alpine, N.J.

1941 The FCC issues the first ten commercial TV licenses. The Mayflower decision outlaws broadcast editorials.

1942 The FCC puts a wartime freeze on TV and FM development.

1945 The freeze ends; the FCC decides to encourage television and downgrade FM radio.

1946 The FCC "Blue Book" obligates broadcasters to include some public affairs programming.

1948 Once again the FCC freezes TV development; this time the delay will last until 1952.

1949 The FCC reverses the Mayflower decision; broadcasters may "editorialize with fairness."

1950 The first commercial cable TV system begins serving the mountainous community of Lansford, Pa. The FCC authorizes experimental "pay TV" and approves the CBS system for color television.

1951 The first transcontinental microwave relay connects TV stations in New York and San Francisco.

1952 The FCC provides for the future development of 70 ultrahigh frequency (UHF) television channels, reserving many of them for nonprofit and educational use.

---

more and more satellites were launched into space, leaving experts in 1980 to worry about a forthcoming satellite "traffic jam." Among their many services to telecommunications, the satellites gave independent stations cheap access to specialized national programming, opening up new sources of profit for them.

Satellites also offered the same cheap programming access to local cable systems. National all-sports, all-news, and all-movie channels evolved quickly, providing cable companies with attractions that over-the-air broadcasters could not duplicate. The biggest lure proved to be all-movie channels—subscribers were even willing to pay an extra monthly fee for a full schedule of movies without commercials. Between 1974 and 1980, the number of cable subscribers more than doubled, to 17 million homes. By 1980, when the FCC eliminated nearly all the remaining rules that had hobbled cable programming, there were already 4,200 cable systems in operation, and cable was at last a paying proposition.

The new television technologies will eventually change the structure and content of American broadcasting. They haven't taken over yet, however. In 1979, roughly 90 percent of the prime-time viewing audience was still glued to the three networks. That

1953   Reversing its earlier decision, the FCC approves the RCA (NBC) color TV system, because it permits noncolor sets to receive color programming in black and white.

1959   The quiz show scandals force the networks to take over all program production from advertisers.

1962   The Telstar satellite makes live international broadcasting possible. A prolonged and inconclusive experiment with pay TV is begun in Hartford, Conn. At the FCC's request, Congress requires UHF receivers on all new television sets, starting in 1964.

1966   The FCC asserts control over cable television and passes restrictive regulations designed to encourage UHF at the expense of cable.

1968   The FCC authorizes commercial pay TV.

1970   The FCC adopts rules to encourage local prime-time programming; these will prove largely unsuccessful.

1972   The FCC adopts new rules governing cable TV, which are designed to encourage cable growth while still protecting over-the-air broadcasters. But financial problems and consumer disinterest slow the growth of cable.

1975   The FCC rules that new newspaper-broadcast combinations in the same market will no longer be approved.

1977   ABC broadcasts "Roots." The 12-hour "miniseries" on the struggles and triumphs of one black family earns the highest ratings in television history, with 130 million viewers. ABC is now fully competitive with the other two networks.

1978   On Nov. 26, for the first time, a news program wins the ratings battle. The CBS show, "60 Minutes," will go on to become the top-rated program of the 1979-80 season.

1979   A UHF independent station in Washington, D.C. sells for $15.5 million, while one in Austin, Texas goes for $13.2 million. For the first time, FM captures over half the radio audience. UHF and FM have come of age.

1980   The FCC drops virtually all the remaining rules that had restricted cable TV. Westinghouse offers $646 million for the Teleprompter Corporation, the nation's largest cable operator. Cable revenues grow to $1.8 billion. Led by pay-TV movie channels, cable begins to threaten network domination of television.

percentage will probably be a good deal lower in 1989.

One truth about television will remain untouched by cable and satellites: it will still be the nation's Number One entertainment medium. In 1979, a TV set was on in the average home for 6 hours and 28 minutes a day. Experts expect *this* figure to grow, not decline, by 1989. A family that resolves to enjoy all the new television technologies—video playback, video games, video computers, cable, satellites, pay-TV, and the traditional network fare—may have little time left for sleeping.

THE OLD MEDIA RESPOND

Television revolutionized American life. Naturally, it revolutionized the other mass media as well.

Part of the revolution was economic. In 1950, the infant TV industry received only 3 percent of all money spent on advertising. Newspapers got 36 percent; magazines, 9 percent; and radio, 11 percent (the other 41 percent went to billboards, direct mailings, and the like). In 1968, by contrast, TV received 18 percent of the advertising dollar. Newspapers were down to 29 percent, magazines to 7 percent; radio to 6 percent. If you eliminate local ads and billboards and the like, the figures are even more impressive. In 1939, national media advertising was almost evenly divided: 38 percent for newspapers, 35 percent for magazines, and 27 percent for radio. In 1968, this was the division: television, 49 percent; magazines, 25 percent; newspapers, 19 percent; radio, 8 percent. Television was rich. Everyone else, at least comparatively, was fading.

But economics are only half the story. Television did (and does) a superlative job of satisfying the public's appetite for spot news and light entertainment. No other medium could possibly compete with TV in those areas. The older communications industries were forced to rebuild their formats along new lines.

Radio was the hardest hit. Audio news programming could not help but suffer as the networks became more and more TV-oriented. Edward R. Murrow's "Hear It Now" turned into "See It Now," and radio documentaries disappeared almost completely. The networks continued to supply stations with hourly spot news reports, but the rest of the news operation was geared for TV and TV alone. Moreover, the melodramas, soap operas, comedy shows, and variety programs that had comprised the bulk of radio time soon became standard fare on television instead. The local station was left with hour after hour to fill on its own—on a dwindling budget and limited advertiser support.

For a while it seemed to some that commercial radio might die. Instead, radio became the "low-key" medium of the 1960s and 1970s, unspectacular but steady. News, sports, and music were the winning combination for thousands of stations. Others chose to specialize: all-rock, all-country-and-western, all-news, or all-talk. Still more specialized stations aimed their shows at one or another minority group—blacks or chicanos, teens or commuters. Whatever the format, it was always low-budget. An engineer, two or

three disc jockeys, and someone to sell ads were all the average station needed.

Radio never regained the "importance" it had had before television, but it did manage to retain its popularity. Between 1950 and 1980, the number of AM radio stations in the country rose from 2,086 to 4,554. The number of radio sets reached an incredible 450 million—two radios for every man, woman, and child. No home, car, or beach blanket was without one.

Because it was less profitable to begin with, FM radio recognized the threat of television a little sooner than AM. By 1950 it was already gearing itself for specialized audiences, offering high-quality reception and highbrow music. During the 1960s the FCC did its best to promote the development of FM. It authorized stations to broadcast in multiplex stereo, and required them to loosen programming ties with AM stations. Aided by these policies, the number of FM stations grew from 753 in 1960 to 4,263 in 1980. Although radio's share of the advertising dollar has remained modest (about 7 percent), by 1980 radio had become a healthy $3-billion industry.

The movie industry had enough problems even before television. A 1949 Supreme Court decision forced film producers to sell off their chains of movie theaters. This solved the antitrust problem of combined production and distribution, but it also cut deeply into Hollywood revenues. The political purges and anti-Communist witch-hunts of the early 1950s added to Hollywood's headaches.

When television came along, the movie companies declared a fight to the finish. Film stars were not allowed to appear on TV, and the studios refused to sell their old films to the rival medium. But it was soon obvious that the public would no longer pay to see Grade B movies when equivalent fare was available on television. One by one, the great studios reversed their positions. They sought windfall profits by selling their old movies to be shown on the tube, and urged their stars to trade TV appearances for plugs. Finally, the large companies agreed to produce programs specifically for the television screen. The major studios were now part of the electronic medium.

Because routine movies wouldn't sell any more, the film industry turned to giant wide screens, stereophonic sound, and multimillion-dollar epics. To save money, these pictures were often produced abroad. And still they lost money. In 1950, there were 474 actors, 147 writers, and 99 directors under contract to the major studios. By 1960 the figures were down to 139 actors, 48 writers, and 24 directors. Three studios (RKO, Republic, and Monogram) stopped production entirely, and some 6,000 movie theaters shut down. Traditional Hollywood was on the ropes. The back lots of some once-prosperous studios were converted into apartment complexes.

Into the struggling movie market came the independent producers, Europeans as well as Americans. Their topical, low-budget films struck a responsive chord in the increasingly youthful theater-going public. They intentionally violated the industry's code of self-censorship, fighting (and winning) their case in court. Taboos about drugs, sex, violence, and language disappeared. While the large studios lost vast sums on spectaculars like *Cleopatra*, independent producers filled movie houses with low-budget films like *Easy Rider*.

In the early 1970s, Hollywood finally derived the formula that would bring a decade of success. It backed young, independent, creative filmmakers, gave them artistic independence but tight budgets, and hoped the results would attract both young moviegoers and their elders. The 1970s produced eight of the top ten all-time moneymakers (and 17 of the top 20), including *The Godfather, The Exorcist, Jaws,* and *Star Wars*. Nearly all appealed simultaneously to young people and their parents, and many were produced on reasonable budgets. But at the end of the 1970s budgets again rose sharply,

leading some observers to predict a repeat of the 1960s disasters. By 1980 the average feature film cost $10 million to make, and breaking even had become Hollywood's pessimistic definition of box-office success.

Such a definition was possible, ironically, only because of television. Throughout the 1970s, the Hollywood studios earned their bread and butter by selling old movies to TV and by producing TV shows and made-for-TV movies. They risked the profits from these activities on theatrical releases. As the 1980s began, cable and other television innovations threatened to erode still further the movie audience—but promised new markets for Hollywood films.

Television hit the magazine business almost as hard as it hit radio and film. Magazines, after all, are largely dependent on national advertising, also the main support for network TV. Moreover, television tended to satisfy the public demand for light entertainment and illustrated news—the two main staples of magazine content.

The result: general-interest magazines began losing money. Soaring production costs and postal rates added to their difficulties, until one by one they folded—*Collier's, Coronet, Look,* the *Saturday Evening Post,* and finally *Life*. Although the *Saturday Evening Post* and *Life* were revived in the 1970s, and the *Reader's Digest* was still going strong, the era of the mass-circulation general-interest magazine was over.

Other kinds of magazines did better. Newsmagazines like *Time* and *Newsweek* offered background and interpretation as well as straight news, and thus survived the rise of television. The "quality" magazines (*National Geographic, New Yorker,* and the like) were little damaged by TV, and the same was true of the women's magazines (*Ladies' Home Journal, McCall's, Good Housekeeping*). All these publications seemed to prosper in the 1960s and 1970s.

By and large, the most successful magazines were the most specialized; television was unable to steal either their audience or their advertisers. Leaders in the specialty fields range from *Playboy* to *Scientific American,* from *Business Week* to *Better Homes and Gardens,* from *Ebony* to *Sports Illustrated,* from *Successful Farming* to *Rolling Stone.* Ironically, the most successful of all the specialized magazines was *TV Guide.*

Television's effect on the book industry was indirect, but powerful. As soon as the first TV station was erected in a city, public library use and bookstore sales began to decline. People simply weren't using as much leisure time for reading; they spent more time with the tube instead.

Broadly speaking, there are three kinds of books. Textbooks are sold directly to primary and secondary schools, or through college bookstores to students. Mass-market paperbacks are sold by the millions through drugstores, supermarkets, and the like. Trade books are sold through ordinary bookstores; they include the majority of the 40,000 new books published every year, both paperbacks and hardcovers, fiction and non-fiction.

Textbooks and mass-market paperbacks are highly profitable. Trade books typically earn much less. Most Americans today read only two kinds of books: what they have to read in school, and the lightest of light fiction and equally light nonfiction.

Although the rise of television affected newspapers, the impact was less than some had feared. TV did cause a precipitous drop

---

CHRONOLOGY

1940   *Newsday* is founded in suburban Long Island; 20 years later it will soar to leadership in both circulation and advertising revenue.

1945   Bernard Kilgore takes over the *Wall Street Journal;* by 1980 it will be the top-circulation daily in America.

1948   Peter Goldmark of CBS invents the long-playing record.

1949   The Supreme Court forces movie companies to sell off their theater holdings. The film audience reaches a peak of 90 million tickets a week; by 1971 it will be down to 18 million a week, climbing slowly to 21 million by the end of the decade.

1950   The Intertype Corporation comes out with its "fotosetter," making offset newspapers feasible.

1951   Edward R. Murrow's documentary "Hear It Now" leaves radio for television, becoming "See It Now."

1953   Twentieth Century Fox produces *The Robe,* the first of the wide-screen Cinemascope spectaculars.

1955   The major film studios begin selling old movies to television. By 1958 they will sell nearly 9,000 of them at bargain prices, but by the late 1970s networks will be paying $3 million and more for the rights to broadcast a single successful movie.

1956   *Collier's* becomes the first of the mass-circulation, general-interest magazines to fold.

1958   United Press and International News Service merge to form United Press International.

1960   The *New York Herald Tribune* leads the trend toward magazine-style newspaper layout. Phonograph record sales total $600 million, more than triple the 1950 figure, thanks to LPs and rock.

1961   The FCC approves multiplex stereo for FM radio.

in the newspaper's share of national advertising, but this was more than balanced by an increase in local ad linage. The growth of "cold type" offset printing helped many smaller papers cut costs, while the industry in general turned to computerized typesetting and other labor-saving devices.

The 1950s and 1960s witnessed a tremendous explosion in suburban living, opening up new markets for new publishers. Suburban newspapers like *Newsday* (on Long Island) built huge circulations in just a few years. Such papers were often among the most profitable in the country. Residents depended on them for neighborhood news (which television couldn't provide), and every new shopping center meant thousands of dollars more in advertising.

The development of regional printing facilities, meanwhile, led to the growth of the country's first truly national newspapers: the *Wall Street Journal* and the *Christian Science Monitor*. The *New York Times* continued as a national paper of sorts. It was the nation's "newspaper of record"—and no legislator, public library, or university could do without it.

In the face of these trends, the metropolitan daily suffered but survived. There were still enough readers and advertisers in the

---

1963 Several metropolitan daily newspapers begin setting type by computer.

1964 The FCC rules that AM-FM radio combinations must run different programs on the two stations at least half the time, signaling the coming growth of FM. With 17-year-olds the biggest single age group in the country, the Beatles top the charts and the record industry thrives.

1966 The *New York Herald Tribune, World-Telegram & Sun,* and *Journal-American* merge; the resulting *World Journal Tribune* will die in 1967, foreshadowing the end of metropolitan newspaper competition. Hollywood begins making movies especially for television, a "sideline" that will soon become the bread and butter of the industry.

1969 *Easy Rider,* a low-budget topical film, is a smash at the box office. In the 1970s the youth subculture and mainstream American culture will merge—at least at the movies.

1971 The Supreme Court permits the *New York Times* and other papers to print the Pentagon Papers. Record and tape sales now total about $2 billion, more than triple the 1960 figure.

1972 The original *Life* magazine dies, while specialized magazines thrive.

1973 The *Washington Post* sticks with the Watergate story, and wins a Pulitzer Prize for its efforts.

1974 Time, Inc. creates *People,* a magazine specializing in celebrity gossip. Within a few years it will rank among the ten most profitable U.S. magazines. The *New York Times* and *Daily News* sign union contracts that permit automation.

1976 The *New York Times* inaugurates weekly sections on sports, science, cooking, decorating, and entertainment, and a daily section on business. New attention to "lifestyles" and business will characterize newspaper journalism in the last half of the 1970s.

1978 The "Saturday Night Fever" record album is on its way to worldwide sales of nearly 30 million copies; the recording industry is on its way to a $4 billion annual gross by the end of the decade.

1979 The Gannett newspaper chain merges with Combined Communications. Chain-owned newspapers account for 74 percent of total circulation.

nation's big cities to support one morning and one evening paper—and by the mid-1960s very few cities had more than that number.

The competition of television brought significant changes in newspaper content, a continuation for the most part of changes already begun in the face of radio news. Now it was television as well as radio that could reach the public with a bulletin before any newspaper had a chance. All the more reason for newspapers to go the way they were already going—interpretive and featurey, the details of the news, the news behind the news, and the "service material" that wasn't news at all. Television greatly intensified the trend. In keeping with their new content, many papers followed the lead of the *New York Herald Tribune* and moved to a simplified, uncluttered, magazine-style layout. And even the wire services backed off the who/what/where/when concept of journalism and began moving some interpretive stories. The growing dominance of service features won the stamp of respectability in 1976, when the august *New York Times* inaugurated weekly sections on sports, science, cooking, decorating, and entertainment.

Many of the most widely read items in today's newspapers have nothing to do with news. They include the weather forecast, the movie listings, the ads, and (of course) the TV logs. Newspapers still supply much more hard news than any other medium. But the average American reads rather little of it. Most of us get most of our news from television.

Something else happened in the 1970s that cannot be traced to the influence of television. The media and the government fought an all-out battle, and the media won. The battle had its beginnings in the events of the late 1960s—especially the war in Vietnam and the antiwar movement at home. Covering the issue of war was a consciousness-raising experience for the media, forcing them to deal seriously with concepts like imperialism, repression, and government

credibility. When the scandals of the Nixon administration began to emerge, the media were prepared to cover them aggressively. The president was prepared to fight just as aggressively against that sort of coverage, and so the battle was joined.

The period from the discovery of the Watergate break-in in 1972 to the resignation of President Nixon in 1974 was fraught with dangers—the danger that the government would succeed in its efforts to intimidate the media, the danger that the media would become permanent and reckless enemies of the government, the danger that the public would lose all its faith in either or both. By 1975 the crisis was over. Press-government relations through the rest of the decade were a healthier—and more typical—blend of cooperation and conflict.

This, then, is how the American mass media stand as of mid-1981. Newspapers are profitable monopolies, moving toward interpretive news but read mostly for their ads and service features. Books have failed to attract a mass audience, except for light paperbacks and required school texts. Magazines are becoming more and more specialized, while most of those that couldn't make the switch have died. Movies are torn between theatrical gambles and the safety of the TV market. Radio has settled on a low-key, diversified, background approach that earns steady profits. And television—television is for viewers a way of life, and for owners (increasingly cable as well as over-the-air) a license to print money.

Notes

1 John Milton, *Paradise Lost and Selected Poetry and Prose,* ed. Northrop Frye (New York: Rinehart & Co., 1951), pp. 486-500.

2 Edwin Emery, ed., *The Story of America* (New York: Simon and Schuster, Inc., 1965), p. 3.

3 James Playsted Wood, *The Story of Advertising* (New York: The Ronald Press Co., 1958), p. 45.

4 Frank Luther Mott, *American Journalism,* 3rd ed. (New York: The Macmillan Co., 1962), p. 25.

5 Emery, *Story of America*, p. 5.

6 Louis L. Snyder, and Robert B. Morris, *A Treasury of Great Reporting* (New York: Simon and Schuster, Inc., 1949), pp. 21-24.

7 Emery, *Story of America*, p. 10.

8 Snyder and Morris, *Treasury of Great Reporting*, pp. 29-30.

9 *The Federalist*, LXXXIV, in Mott, *American Journalism*, p. 145.

10 Paul L. Ford, ed., *The Writings of Thomas Jefferson* (New York: G. P. Putnam's Sons, 1892-99), II, p. 69.

11 *Aurora*, March 6, 1797, in Frederick Hudson, *Journalism in the United States* (New York: Harper & Brothers, 1873), pp. 210-11.

12 Emery, *Story of America*, p. 27.

13 *Ibid.*, p. 44

14 *Ibid.*, p. 44.

15 *Ibid.*, p. 61.

16 Thomas H. Guback, "General Sherman's War on the Press," *Journalism Quarterly*, Spring, 1959, pp. 172-73.

17 Emery, *Story of America*, p. 80.

18 *The World*, May 11, 1883, in Mott, *American Journalism*, p. 434.

19 Emery, *Story of America*, p. 107.

20 Harry J. Carman and Harold C. Syrett, *A History of the American People* (New York: Alfred A. Knopf, Inc., 1958), II, p. 228.

21 Arthur Knight, *The Liveliest Art* (New York: Mentor Books, 1957), p. 35.

22 Radio Act of 1927.

23 Mott, *American Journalism*, pp. 623-24.

24 *Ibid.*, p. 625.

25 Emery, *Story of America*, p. 184.

26 Edwin Emery, *The Press in America*, 2nd ed. (Englewood Cliffs, N.J.: Prentice-Hall, Inc., 1962), p. 645.

27 Emery, *Story of America*, p. 203.

Suggested Readings

BARNOUW, ERIK, *Tube of Plenty*. New York: Oxford University Press, 1975.

EMERY, EDWIN, ed., *The Story of America*. New York: Simon and Schuster, 1965.

———, and MICHAEL EMERY, *The Press in America*, 4th ed. Englewood Cliffs, N.J.: Prentice-Hall, 1978.

HALBERSTAM, DAVID, *The Powers That Be*. New York: Alfred A. Knopf, 1979.

KENDRICK, ALEXANDER, *Prime Time: The Life of Edward R. Murrow*. Boston: Little, Brown & Co., 1969.

KNIGHT, ARTHUR, *The Liveliest Art*, revised ed. New York: Macmillan, 1978.

MOTT, FRANK LUTHER, *American Journalism*, 3rd ed. New York: The Macmillan Co., 1962.

POLLACK, PETER, *The Picture History of Photography*. New York: Harry N. Abrams, Inc., 1969.

SIEBERT, FRED S., THEODORE PETERSON, and WILBUR SCHRAMM, *Four Theories of the Press*. Urbana, Ill.: University of Illinois Press, 1956.

SNYDER, LOUIS L., and RICHARD B. MORRIS, eds., *A Treasury of Great Reporting*. New York: Simon and Schuster, Inc., 1949.

SWANBERG, W. A., *Citizen Hearst*. New York: Bantam Books, Inc., 1961.

———, *Luce and His Empire*. New York: Dell Publishing Co., 1972.

TALESE, GAY, *The Kingdom and the Power*. New York: World Publishing Co., 1969.

PART II
RESPONSIBILITY

The Introduction and first section of this book dealt with the impact and history of the mass media. By this point it should be clear that, if nothing else, the media are important.

We turn now to the question of responsibility. Which individuals, groups, and institutions in this country determine the course of the mass media? Which ones wield its enormous power? Which will decide its future history? If the media themselves are important, then these questions are also important.

In the next seven chapters we will examine the following sorts of control over the media:

1. *Self-control* through professional codes and ethical standards.

2. *Internal control* at various points in the media bureaucracies, from publisher and station manager down to reporter and assignment editor.

3. *Monopoly control* through chains, conglomerates, networks, and other forms of media monopoly.

4. *Advertiser control,* whether directly through pressure from individual advertisers or indirectly through media recognition of broad business needs.

5. *Source control* through secrecy, news manage ment, and other techniques for the manipula tion of media content before it reaches the media.

6. *Government control,* including the massive influence of law and the federal regulatory agencies.

7. *Public control* through letters to the editor, ratings, and many less passive techniques.

Two vital points must be made with respect to the interplay of these seven kinds of control. They are emphasized here because they will be largely ignored in the following chapters, as the forms of media control are treated one at a time.

1. *The dynamics of media control are an ongoing process, and may change dramatically from decade to decade.* Since the 1950s, for example, the techniques of public relations have become more sophisticated and widespread, increasing the significance of source control. Citizen groups of all sorts have begun to apply pressure for media content favorable to their causes, making public control a force to reckon with. During the same period, the media's increasing preoccupation with profit rather than power and the journalist's increasing preoccupation

with ethical standards have lessened the problem of internal control. Changes in the 1980s and 1990s will doubtless yield yet another pattern of media control.

2. *The various forms of media control are in conflict, not balance, and often help keep each other in check.* Consider, for example, the interplay of government and monopoly control. A television network is a dangerous monopoly, an incredible concentration of power in the hands of a few people. Yet only the networks are strong enough to defy the government when it demands—even more dangerously—that newscasters be kinder in their commentary on the misuse of government authority. The power of the federal regulatory agencies, conversely, is frightening when applied to something so delicate as the First Amendment. Yet only the government has the necessary strength to forbid newspapers to own broadcast stations in the same city—an equally disturbing threat to the marketplace of ideas.

Pluralism is central to a democracy. The goal of a social critic or policy-maker should always be to equalize power, to play off one influence against another in the hope that freedom will be the winner. If all seven forms of media control on our list were equally powerful, there would be no danger. It is only when one or two of the seven usurp the power of the others and upset the dynamic tension that we need to worry.

Chapter 2
Self-Control

Like most professions, journalism is greatly influenced by ethical standards. Unlike most professions, however, journalism has avoided codifying its ethics into clear and enforceable rules. The various professional codes of the mass media tend to concentrate on truisms and trivia. When working journalists wrestle with real ethical dilemmas, they may well feel accountable to the public and to their peers—but they are in fact accountable only to their own values and the values of their employers.

In 1976, the National Labor Relations Board was asked to decide an unusual case concerning the status of journalists. Editorial employees at the *San Antonio* (Texas) *Express-News* wanted to join with the paper's mechanical workers in a single bargaining unit, represented by the International Typographical Union. Realizing that single representation would increase the two groups' negotiating power, management opposed the move. Since labor law normally provides that professional and nonprofessional employees should be represented by different unions, the paper's owners asked the NLRB to designate journalism as a profession. In an argument tinged with irony, the American Newspaper Guild (the national union of newspaper journalists) urged the NLRB to rule that journalism is not a profession.[1]

The NLRB decided in the union's favor. Its ruling that journalists are not professionals was influenced by the testimony of Prof. John C. Merrill, then of the University of Missouri School of Journalism. "There is, in journalism, no minimum entrance requirement," Merrill pointed out. "Anybody can be a journalist who can get himself hired—experience or no experience, degree or no degree." Furthermore, said Merrill, "no journalist is required to abide by any professional code of ethics. No journalist is licensed, thereby giving the 'profession' some kind of control over him. There are no professional standards commonly agreed upon, and followed, by journalists."[2]

PROFESSIONALISM OR NOT?

The NLRB case was unusual because each side was arguing what is normally the other side's position. Media owners like to think of reporters and editors as mere employees, subject to the usual arrangement between management and labor in American society: unless there's a negotiated agreement to the contrary, you do what the boss tells you to do or you lose your job. Reporters and editors, on the other hand, like to claim the special prerogatives of professionals. Like medicine and law, they say, journalism has certain standards to which every journalist owes his or her first allegiance, regardless of the boss's orders.

The dispute is important because of what it implies about the accountability of journalists to the public. Consider a profession like law. You cannot become a lawyer unless the Bar Association accepts you—and it won't accept you unless it is convinced that you have the training and character it believes a lawyer should have. Once accepted, you are obligated to follow a detailed legal code of ethics. If you prove unscrupulous or incompetent, the Bar Association can throw you out; it then becomes a crime for you to try to practice law. At least in theory, the Bar Association exercises this power on behalf of the public. If a lawyer deals irresponsibly with a client, the client can complain to the Bar Association—and the lawyer may become an ex-lawyer.

Journalism has no such mechanisms. You become a journalist when you declare that you are one, and you remain a journalist as long as you keep declaring that you are one. It is hard to think of another occupation of comparable importance to society that exercises so little formal control over itself—no entrance requirements, no explicit code of ethics, no system for weeding out the incompetents and the scoundrels.

But the individual journalist does not stand alone in solitary splendor either. A reporter may not be accountable to the public or the journalism profession, but the reporter *is* directly accountable to management—the publisher or station owner. The ethics of American journalism, then, are ultimately in the hands of the people who own

our media. A responsible employer can fire a journalist for behaving unethically. An irresponsible employer can fire a journalist for refusing to behave unethically. In neither case does the community of journalists or the public have a say in the decision.

Perhaps this is just as well. Professional standards often seem to do a better job of protecting the profession than of protecting the public. The Bar Association notwithstanding, incompetent and unethical lawyers are probably as plentiful as incompetent and unethical journalists, but their incomes are higher. Would a powerful journalism profession really improve the ethics of journalists, or would it weed out instead the innovators, the mavericks, the advocates of unpopular viewpoints? There is some consensus in our society about how a good lawyer or a good doctor should behave, so it is possible to set up a code of ethics and enforce it. As we shall see, journalism lacks that consensus. An enforceable journalistic code of ethics might remedy some abuses, but it could easily become a straitjacket for nonconformists.

Most journalists *feel* accountable to the public and their peers already. This feeling shows up in the journalism reviews (see p. 224), in which reporters discuss the defects of their craft. It shows up in the surprisingly high number of reporters and editors who quit their jobs rather than obey an order they consider unethical. It shows up in countless newsroom and lunch-table conversations about how to make news coverage more accurate, complete, and ethical. Few occupations devote as much time and energy to criticizing their own work.

But regardless of how they feel, journalists are in fact accountable only to themselves and to their employers. As you read the rest of this chapter, think about whether you would like to see journalism become more professional. That is, should there be enforceable standards that a journalist must adhere to in order to remain a journalist? If so, what should those standards be?

REPORTER POWER

As an alternative to the American system of media owners who give orders and journalists who take orders, consider the reporter power movement in Europe. At *Le Monde*, *Le Figaro*, *Stern*, and other French and German newspapers, employees collectively own a substantial block of stock. They choose their own editors and are represented on financial and policy issues by elected editorial committees. The national labor contract for journalists in France even includes a "conscience clause," which guarantees French reporters and editors substantial severance benefits if they are fired or feel compelled to quit because of policy differences with management.[3]

In the United States only a handful of newspapers (and no major broadcast stations) share their stock with employees in large enough amounts to affect decision-making. One exception is the *Omaha* (Nebraska) *World-Herald*, where owner Peter Kiewit arranged for control of the paper to pass to its employees when he died. Kiewit specified that full-time employees would own a majority interest in the paper.[4]

While employees do not own the *Minneapolis Star* and *Tribune*, management does meet regularly with committees of reporters to discuss "matters affecting relations between employees and the employer," including issues of professional responsibility, ethics, and news judgment.[5] This is a small step by European standards, but it's a step most American media have yet to take.

For the reporter power movement to take root in the U.S., it will probably have to be achieved through collective bargaining by the nation's journalism unions—the American Newspaper Guild (newspaper writers), the Writer's Guild of America (broadcast writers), and the American Federation of Television and Radio Artists (broadcast on-the-air talent). There is no evidence that this is about to happen. All three unions have historically been interested only in bread-and-butter issues like salary and pension, not in professional issues like ethics and news judgment.

Ethical issues are an important topic at the conventions of the Society of Professional Journalists (Sigma Delta Chi) and in the Society's monthly magazine, *The Quill*. But the Society is entirely a voluntary organization, whose main activity is its monthly chapter dinners. It has no clout with media owners, or even with journalists themselves.

MEDIA CODES

As befits an occupation that thinks of itself as a profession, almost every journalistic organization subscribes to some sort of code of ethics. As befits an occupation that does not meet all the criteria of a profession, none of the codes is binding. Most tend to be very broad collections of platitudes.

The oldest, shortest, and broadest of the codes is the Canons of Journalism, adopted by the American Society of Newspaper Editors in 1923. As revised in 1975, the six "canons" are entitled Responsibility; Freedom of the Press; Independence; Truth and Accuracy; Impartiality; and Fair Play. "Responsibility," for example, reads as follows:

The primary purpose of gathering and distributing news and opinion is to serve the general welfare by informing the people and enabling them to make judgments on the issues of the time. Newspapermen and women who abuse the power of their professional role for selfish motives or unworthy purposes are faithless to that public trust.

The American press was made free not just

to inform or just to serve as a forum for debate but also to bring an independent scrutiny to bear on the forces of power in the society, including the conduct of official power at all levels of government.[6]

There is nothing in the Canons of Journalism that a publisher or editor need fear—but just to be on the safe side journalists are not required to subscribe. And should a newspaper or a reporter "violate" a provision—whatever that might mean—there is no punishment or means of enforcement.

The other four major media codes (for movies, radio, television, and comic books) were all developed in response to public pressure and criticism. They were designed to forestall government regulation by substituting self-regulation instead. As a result, they are negative rather than positive, and more specific than the Canons of Journalism—but only a little.

Consider the Television Code, adopted by the National Association of Broadcasters in 1952. It starts with sections on "Advancement of Education and Culture," "Responsibility Toward Children," and "Community Responsibility"—all very broad and clichéd. Then comes the meat of the code, a list of "special program standards." These are almost exclusively concerned with guaranteeing that nobody is offended by anything on television. They include such items as:

3. Narcotics addiction shall not be presented except as a destructive habit. The use of illegal drugs or the abuse of legal drugs shall not be encouraged or shown as socially acceptable.

6. Special precautions must be taken to avoid demeaning or ridiculing members of the audience who suffer from physical or mental affliction or deformities.

7. Special sensitivity is necessary in the use of material relating to sex, race, color, creed, religious functionaries or rites, or national or ethnic derivation.

9. The presentation of marriage, the family and similarly important human relationships, and

material with sexual connotations, shall not be treated exploitatively or irresponsibly, but with sensitivity. Costuming and movements of all performers shall be handled in a similar fashion.[7]

After the special program standards comes another collection of platitudes, this time on the treatment of news and public events, controversial public issues, political telecasts, and religious programs. The remaining six sections are devoted to advertising standards. They contain the most specific provisions of the code, including items like: "The advertising of hard liquor (distilled spirits) is not acceptable"; and "In prime time on network affiliated stations, non-program material shall not exceed nine minutes 30 seconds in any 60-minute period."[8]

Enforcement of the Television Code is almost nonexistent. The NAB has a Code Review Board that awards a seal of approval to any station that subscribes to the code and obeys it. The seal is customarily flashed, with a brief explanation, at sign-on and sign-off; farmers and insomniacs are thus able to get a quick look at it. The only penalty for a station that does not subscribe to the code or does not follow it is denial of permission to exhibit the seal.

Here's how it works. In 1957 the Code Review Board outlawed TV ads for hemorrhoid remedies. When "enforcement" of the ban began in mid-1959, 148 stations were advertising Preparation H, a hemorrhoid remedy; 84 of them were code subscribers. After two weeks 17 stations resigned from the code rather than drop the ads, and 21 more continued the ads and lost the seal. Only 46 out of 148 stations agreed to conform to the code.[9]

Since so many broadcasters wouldn't follow the code, the code eventually followed the broadcasters. It no longer forbids ads for hemorrhoid remedies, but rather warns: "Because all products of a personal nature create special problems, acceptability of such products should be determined with special emphasis on ethics and the canons of good taste. Such advertising of personal products as is accepted must be presented in a restrained and obviously inoffensive manner."[10] Even feminine hygiene ads are now acceptable on television.

Despite its weak enforcement provision, the code is not without influence. More than three-quarters of all stations in the top 50 markets subscribe to it.[11] And even nonsubscribers look to the code and its voluminous handbook of interpretations for guidance on how to handle touchy matters of taste and policy. Pressure groups like the Gray Panthers and the National Organization for Women have found it worth their while to negotiate their grievances about TV content with the Code Review Board. A new code guideline on how to treat old people or women doesn't change programming overnight, but it does signal broadcasters that increased sensitivity is called for.

Bear in mind that the Television Code is the creation of the National Association of Broadcasters—an organization of media owners, not professional journalists. The same is true of the radio, motion picture, and comic book codes. All are designed to avoid offending the public, and thereby to avoid the threat of government regulation. All are administered by owners, not their employees. And all are minimally enforced, and as a practical matter unenforceable.

By contrast, the most specific and enforceable codes are the in-house standards promulgated by individual publishers and broadcasters. A number of newspapers and stations have elaborate written codes of ethics to which their employees must subscribe. Many more have informal standards, based on tacit

---

POLICING ADVERTISING

In response to increasing government regulation, the advertising industry set up the National Advertising Division of the Council of Better Business Bureaus in 1971. The function of the NAD and its appeals court, the National Advertising Review Board, is to police advertising ethics from the inside.

At first the NAD and NARB were greeted with skepticism by consumer groups and government agencies, but over the years they have won respect from both.[12] They confine their work to factual misrepresentation, not psychological manipulation or social impact (see pp. 377-81), and they tend to enforce accepted ethical standards rather than extending ethical boundaries. But within these self-imposed limits they are considered reasonably effective.

The NAD employs six advertising review specialists who process challenges to national advertising claims. The challenges may come from the public, from other advertisers, or from the NAD's own media monitoring. In all, the NAD investigated 174 advertisements in 1979.[13]

The NAD begins by asking an advertiser to substantiate the disputed claim. If the NAD finds the substantiation inadequate, it then asks the advertiser to change or discontinue the ad. An advertiser that disputes the NAD's finding can appeal to the NARB, which sets up a special panel of three advertisers, an ad agency representative, and a representative of the public. If this panel also rules against the advertiser and the advertiser still refuses to change or drop the ad, the NARB will turn the case over to the Federal Trade Commission for possible action. The NARB has never yet had to do this.[14]

Often, in fact, the NAD doesn't even have to investigate a challenged ad—its announced intention to investigate is frequently enough to persuade the advertiser to drop the ad.

---

newsroom understandings and an occasional warning memo on the bulletin board. In 1976, reporters at the *Madison* (Wisconsin) *Capital Times* objected to management's in-house code, arguing that its provisions should have to be negotiated just as salary and fringe benefits are negotiated. The National Labor Relations Board heard the dispute, and decided that while management was entitled to establish a code of ethics, the disciplinary provisions for enforcing it had to be negotiated with the union.[15]

In-house codes are often useful to reporters, because they clarify the employer's stance on the debatable issues of journalism ethics. They represent a growing sense of responsibility on the part of media owners. But they are not a significant step toward professionalism. Having your employer tell you what to do is not at all the same thing as having your peers tell you what ought to be done. However virtuous they may be, in-house codes are simply instructions from the management, not standards of the profession.

THE DILEMMA OF OBJECTIVITY

The most serious ethical problem confronting reporters and editors is also the most common. It is expressed in questions like these: How do I approach the story? Whom do I interview? What do I ask? What do I lead with in my first paragraph? What do I leave out? What headline do I write? How long do I let the story run? Which stories do I put on the front page? The conventional answer to all these questions is "Be objective"—which is about as useful as telling a batter to hit a home run, please.

Most journalists today aim at objectivity—and often fail. When the home team wins 6-4, it has "thumped" the opposition. When the home team loses 6-4, it has been "edged." That crowd of demonstrators marching on City Hall is "unruly, vicious, and dangerous." The same crowd celebrating a World Series victory is "jubilant, ecstatic, and playful." Words have connotations as well as de-

notations; they imply more than they mean. And reporters have values and attitudes as well as eyes and ears; they must interpret what they see and hear. As long as journalism is produced by people and expressed in words, complete objectivity is impossible.

The former editor of the *New York Times* Sunday magazine, Lester Markel, argues the same point:

> The reporter, the most objective reporter, collects fifty facts. Out of the fifty he selects twelve to include in his story (there is such a thing as space limitation). Thus he discards thirty-eight. This is Judgment Number One.
>
> Then the reporter or editor decides which of the facts shall be the first paragraph of the story, thus emphasizing one fact above the other eleven. This is Judgment Number Two.
>
> Then the editor decides whether the story shall be placed on Page One or Page Twelve; on Page One it will command many times the attention it would on Page Twelve. This is Judgment Number Three.
>
> This so-called factual presentation is thus subjected to three judgments, all of them most humanly and most ungodly made.[16]

Everything Markel says is true. Yet it is still possible for a reporter and an editor to at least try to put aside their prejudices and strive for fair and balanced news. The late Kenneth Stewart, a longtime journalist and journalism educator, wrote: "If you mean by objectivity the absence of convictions, willingness to let nature take its course, uncritical acceptance of things as they are (what Robert Frost calls the 'isness of is'), the hell with it. If you mean by objectivity a healthy respect for the ascertainable truth, a readiness to modify conclusions when new evidence comes in, a refusal to distort deliberately and for ulterior or concealed motives . . . all well and good."[17]

Even in these terms, it can be argued that objectivity is a false god. All too often, objectivity means writing in such a way that the reader or viewer cannot tell where the reporter's sympathies lie. If the reporter does in fact have sympathies and those sympathies are in fact influencing the story, this simply makes the prejudice less obvious. Sociologist Gaye Tuchman argues that journalistic objectivity is essentially a "strategic ritual," designed not to keep the story from being biased but rather to keep the story from seeming biased. Reporters who talk to representatives of both sides in a controversy, who quote and attribute every judgment they use, who start the story with who/what/ where/when and only then go to why, Tuchman argues, are thereby protecting themselves from criticism.[18] The story may be no less misleading for all its objectivity, but it is safer.

Another sociologist, Michael Schudson, agrees with Tuchman. He argues that objective news stories often contain a whole set of political assumptions that are never explicitly acknowledged. The who/what/ where/when/why format of the objective lead, for example, focuses on recent public events, and allows the sources who stage such events to define what is newsworthy. One assumption here is that what "important" people did and said yesterday matters more than the historical, philosophical, or political background of the issues they were addressing. Schudson notes another assumption: that the official viewpoints of government and industry leaders matter more than the views of other people.[19]

Schudson defines objectivity as "a faith in 'facts,' a distrust of 'values,' and a commitment to their segregation."[20] As we have seen, this segregation is extraordinarily difficult to achieve. The desire to achieve it is itself a value—and a debatable one.

Suppose a reporter is somehow successful in keeping his or her values from influencing the story. Is this necessarily good? What is the value of having humane and concerned journalists if they hide their humanity and concern when they set out to cover the news? Was objectivity a good thing in the 1950s, when it forced the media to be "fair" to the incredibly unfair allegations of Senator Joseph McCarthy? Ultimately, why should a conservative reporter be "fair" to the scourge of Communism? Why should a radical reporter be "fair" to the capitalist Establishment?

On the other hand, the notion of objectivity does impose a useful discipline on journalists. Even if it is unattainable and sometimes a bit hypocritical, objectivity as a goal reminds reporters that they are paid to tell us about events, not about their own feelings; that they are obliged to talk to all sides in a dispute before writing their story; that they should resort to volatile language sparingly and only where it is justified. Objectivity is journalism's cautious response to its own power. In limiting the reporter's freedom to guide the audience, objectivity also limits the reporter's freedom to misguide the audience.

Whether or not it is a false god, objectivity is certainly a fairly new one. In the late eighteenth century and well into the nineteenth, most newspapers were openly partisan in their news judgments. It wasn't until the first wire service was born in the 1840s that objectivity became a part of American journalism. And even then it was assumed that a subscribing newspaper would add its own unique bias to the wire reports if it had the time. Often newspapers didn't have the time. Local reporters copied the neutrality of the wires, and objectivity eventually became the defining characteristic of responsible journalism.

Wire-style objectivity dominated the media for decades. But by the 1930s, the world had become too complicated a place for journalists to report it solely in police-blotter facts. In 1933 the United States went off the gold standard, and a confused group of Washington reporters faced the task of telling the nation about it. President Roosevelt sent over some of his economic advisers to help the reporters understand the move, and together they tried to explain it to the country. Some journalism historians point to that day as the birth of interpretive reporting in the U.S.[21]

Interpretive journalism reports not only the facts but also explanation and analysis of the facts. Can objectivity stretch this far? In the 1930s, most editors said no. As late as the mid-1960s, the wire services were still resisting the trend toward interpretive reporting. But journalism professor (and former newspaper editor) Carl E. Lindstrom expresses the more common view today. Lindstrom sees interpretive reporting as simply the addition of new kinds of facts—"historical, circumstantial, biographical, statistical, reflective"[22]—that can throw added light on the events of the day. Though objectivity is often considered more difficult to achieve in interpretive articles than in "straight" writing, interpretation and objectivity are no longer viewed as inconsistent with one another.

While the battle over interpretive reporting was still raging, a new threat to objectivity emerged on the scene. In the late 1950s and early 1960s, a group of journalists, most of them working in New York, began experimenting with fiction techniques in their writing. Trying to report a different sort of "truth" to their readers, these men and women used a number of unconventional devices: narrative, unstructured styles; extensive dialogue; detailed scene-building; strongly evocative adjectives and verbs (including some they made up); playful punctuation; etc. Tom Wolfe has become a principal advocate of this approach, which is most often called the "New Journalism."

Wolfe points to a story about heavyweight boxer Joe Louis, which appeared in *Esquire* in 1962, as a trend-setter for the New Journalism. The author was Gay Talese, who later profiled the *New York Times* in *The Kingdom and the Power*. The beginning of the article sets it apart immediately from much of what was (and still is) typical of American journalism:

"Hi, sweetheart!" Joe Louis called to his wife, spotting her waiting for him at the Los Angeles airport.

She smiled, walked toward him, and was about to stretch up on her toes and kiss him—but suddenly stopped.

"Joe," she said, "where's your tie?"

"Aw, sweetie," he said, shrugging, "I stayed out all night in New York and didn't have time—"

"All *night!*" she cut in. "When you're out here all you do is sleep, sleep, sleep."

"Sweetie," Joe Louis said, with a tired grin, "I'm an ole man."

"Yes," she agreed, "but when you go to New York you try to be young again."[23]

Instead of merely describing the former champ, Talese took his readers behind the scenes, revealing conversations and thoughts, painting pictures, setting scenes. These became the trademarks of the New Journalists, as they tried to penetrate reality by breaking the bonds of objective journalism. Norman Mailer, Murray Kempton, Jack Newfield, Truman Capote, Gail Sheehy, Wolfe, Talese, and many others adopted this approach in their writing. So did Daniel Defoe several centuries ago, in his *Journal of the Plague Year*. The New Journalism is not entirely new. What *is* new is the large number of once-conventional reporters who now try to use some of these novelistic techniques in their daily writing.

The New Journalism is now accepted in magazine writing (though many of the more traditional magazines won't touch it). It still isn't a regular part of most newspapers' reporting, but it does find its way into feature sections and the like. Most editors now view the New Journalism as a valid alternative journalistic technique—one that is often abused but worth trying where appropriate.

Is the New Journalism anti-objective? Many New Journalists happily claim that it is; they applaud the impending death of traditional novels and traditional objective reporting, both to be replaced by the hybrid they have created. Critics of the technique agree that it violates the canons of objectivity. Michael J. Arlen, for example, faults the

REDPANTS AND SUGARMAN

As a narrative vehicle to tell the true story of prostitution and pimping in New York City, journalist Gail Sheehy created two composite characters—Redpants and Sugarman—based on her lengthy interviewing of street people. This is an old and honorable technique, permissible so long as the composites are realistic, quotations are not fabricated, and the reader is told that there is no Redpants or Sugarman.

The article appeared in 1971 in *New York* magazine, home-base of the New Journalism. Sheehy had written a paragraph early in the piece explaining the composite characterization, but her editor, Clay Felker, took it out because he felt it slowed up the narration. Said Felker (later): "I thought it was perfectly apparent one person couldn't do all that. . . . I made a major mistake."[24]

The *Wall Street Journal* brought the oversight to the attention of the public, much to the embarrassment of Sheehy and *New York*. The example has been used to damn all of the New Journalism, which is not really fair. But it does point up the absolute necessity of being honest with the reading or viewing public: Your audience must be told what is fact and what is fiction, what is truth and what is satire, what is exposé and what is fantasy.

New Journalism for its "determination and insistence that we shall see life largely on [the New Journalist's] terms."[25] Arlen prefers to make his own judgments, based on the more dispassionate information provided by objective reporters. Jack Newfield, on the other hand, believes that separating journalism into two factions is a pointless and destructive exercise. "There is only good writing and bad writing," says Newfield, "smart ideas and dumb ideas, hard work and laziness."[26]

In thinking about the complex issue of objectivity, it may help to distinguish among three aspects of the journalistic process—deciding what topics to cover, deciding which information to include, and deciding what language to use.

The objective solution to the first problem is to define news as public events of interest or importance to the audience. Under this view the journalist's job is simply to look at what the sources are doing and saying, then choose the stories the audience seems most likely to want to know about. Morris Janowitz calls this the "gatekeeping" approach to news selection. He contrasts it with the "ad-vocacy" approach, which permits the reporter to seek out news that no source is offering, merely because the reporter feels that the audience will find the information useful.[27] Old-line supporters of objectivity see this as perilously close to "making news." But most journalists today view this sort of "advocacy" as acceptable, even admirable. They may not do enough of it, but they approve of a colleague who sets out to investigate pollution at the local steel mill or police-community relations in the black ghetto—even if no source has staged a press conference on either topic.

When deciding which information to include, however, traditional objectivity remains the dominant standard. Reporters may differ on how rigidly they should enact the rituals of balance—do you have to count paragraphs to make sure each side gets the same number?—but they agree that once a topic is chosen to be covered, it must be covered fairly. Only special-interest publications (for political activists, church leaders, and other ideologues) are comfortable ignoring inconvenient facts in search of a "greater truth." Mainstream journalists try to report the facts, and let the truth fall where it may.

It is on the choice of language that the New Journalism has had its greatest impact. The more novelistic techniques are still considered suspect, but the inverted pyramid structure and carefully neutral, almost bored tone of traditional objectivity are no longer the stylistic straitjackets they once were. TV news must compete with TV entertainment, after all, and newspapers must compete with TV news—and so the descriptive adjective and the narrative anecdote have returned to journalism.

This summary leaves out many of the tougher objectivity debates. It may be okay to go looking for a story that you think the audience should know about, but is it okay to turn down a story that you think the audience shouldn't know about? Suppose a reporter runs across evidence that a political candidate has a child with a criminal record. Believing that this should be irrelevant to the campaign, he or she ignores the story—even though many readers might well consider it worth knowing. Is this objective? Is it right?

Similarly, it sounds fine to say that objective journalists report the facts and let their audience decide where truth lies. But suppose the reporter is fairly sure that the facts are misleading—such as an unsubstantiated charge that a politician is crooked. Is it objective to go with the charge and the politician's inevitably unconvincing denial? Is it objective to refuse to cover the charge without evidence? If the accuser has a reputation for baseless gun-slinging, is it objective to put this into the story? To leave it out? To go looking for someone willing to say it on the record?

However you feel about these issues, one thing is sure: the choice is up to you and your employer. The public and your fellow journalists will have little or no influence on your decision. And if you did try to poll other journalists for advice, it is unlikely that they would agree on much. Objectivity is an important ethical dilemma that serious reporters think about often. But they have reached no consensus on the issue, and have found no way to impose a consensus on their colleagues even if they had one.

In the absence of meaningful and enforceable codes of ethics, journalists must resolve their ethical problems on their own—aided only by their employers. Among the dozens of ethical dilemmas confronting the reporter, consider six that have caused continuing controversy in the nation's newsrooms: (1) Journalistic deception; (2) Invasion of privacy; (3) Withholding information; (4) Checkbook journalism; (5) Conflict of interest; and (6) Junkets and freebies. None of them is easily solved.

JOURNALISTIC DECEPTION

At a 1976 convention of journalists, *Los Angeles Times* investigative reporter Robert Scheer was on a panel on "The Art of the Interview." The discussion turned to the techniques of investigative reporting, and Scheer said: "Politicians try to prevent you from knowing what's going on because that's how they survive. And they have lots of people employed to help them. The journalist's job is to get the story by breaking into their offices, by bribing, by seducing people, by lying, by anything else to break through that palace guard."[28] Scheer's bluntness created an uproar among journalists because he touched a sensitive spot in journalistic ethics: How much deception should be permitted in pursuit of the story?

The key issue is whether reporters are obligated to identify themselves as reporters. Doing so naturally puts people on their guard; often you'd get a better story without your press card. Nonetheless, it is generally accepted that sources have a right to know that they are talking to a reporter.

THE KING OF DECEPTION

Gunter Wallraff, an investigative reporter for the West German newspaper *Bild Zeitung,* has made a career out of deception. In his most famous caper, Wallraff impersonated a member of the German right wing and visited Portugal's ex-President Antonio de Spinola, who was living in exile in Switzerland. Urging an armed effort to regain power in Portugal, Wallraff lured Spinola into making many incriminating statements. When Wallraff's story was published, the Swiss government deported Spinola.

In the course of attacking big industry and government, Wallraff has assumed the identities of an official of the German Interior Ministry, an insurance investigator, a police informer, and a derelict. His justification is straightforward: "The method I adopted was only slightly illegal by comparison with the illegal deceptions and maneuvers which I unmasked."[29]

Few American reporters would go as far as Wallraff, but many would sympathize with his defense of journalistic deception.

But there are plenty of exceptions. A restaurant critic does not announce his or her identity before sitting down to eat. The temptation to the staff to provide special service and unusual dishes would be too great, and the journalistic goal would be defeated. Similarly, a consumer reporter would have a tough time making an accurate appraisal of an auto repair service if the mechanics knew a story was in the works. Most journalists accept this sort of deception because the reporter is simply doing what ordinary citizens do—eating in a restaurant or getting a car fixed—and then evaluating the service received.

But suppose you're a reporter at a private party in a friend's home, and you overhear another guest saying something newsworthy. Must you identify yourself as a journalist and risk having the source clam up? Most reporters would probably say that you must. Many would be willing to use the overheard information as background for later on-the-record interviews, but few reporters would feel comfortable publishing a party conversation on which they had eavesdropped.

Actively posing as someone you are not also raises ethical problems. After Spiro T. Agnew resigned as Vice President of the United States, he put his house up for sale.

A reporter for the *Baltimore Sun* wanted to tour the house, to find out if the government had put in security improvements from which Agnew would now profit. The reporter knew that Agnew and his real estate agent would refuse to show the house to a journalist, so he posed as a potential buyer. Agnew later found out about the deception and complained to the *Sun,* which agreed not to print the story.[30] Should the reporter have tried to get the story "legitimately" by interviewing others who had seen the house? Should the *Sun* have used the story even though it was obtained by deception?

At a public event, as opposed to an interview, a real estate tour, or a party, reporters need not identify themselves in order to watch. It is assumed that participants in the event realize reporters may be present. Gene Roberts, now executive editor of the *Philadelphia Inquirer,* is willing to stretch this standard a bit. In the late 1950s and early 1960s, Roberts covered the civil rights movement in the South. He wore a jacket and tie, and stuffed a thick notebook inside his jacket breast pocket. Roberts knew that the only people on those hot streets wearing ties and jackets with bulges in their pockets were FBI agents, and he felt the disguise protected him from being hassled by segregationists hostile to the media. Roberts calls this "passive posing"—he never *told* anyone he was an FBI man.[31]

Two decades later, an *Inquirer* team under Roberts' direction won a Pulitzer Prize for its coverage of the nuclear accident at Three Mile Island. This time "active" posing played a supporting role in the story. Three Mile Island telephone operators were unwilling to put through calls from journalists to the experts working on the accident, but of course they immediately put through calls from other experts. So *Inquirer* reporters earnestly identified themselves as "so-and-so of PNI"—mimicking the initials by which many high-technology companies are known. "PNI" are the little-used initials of Pennsylvania Newspapers, Inc., corporate owners of the *Inquirer*. Once the experts were on the line, the *Inquirer* reporters identified themselves more fully.

But suppose they hadn't. It is not unusual for a police reporter working in the pressroom, say, of the Los Angeles Police Department to call a police source in another city and say, "Hey, this is Flanagan over at the LAPD"—knowing that the source will assume Flanagan is a policeman, not a journalist.[32] If a cop pulled the same trick on a reporter, calling from the pay phone in a newspaper lobby, most journalists would be outraged. Journalists are usually outraged when government people masquerade as reporters (it happens often, especially at demonstrations and riots). Then what about the reverse?

In 1979, Gary C. Schuster of the *Detroit News* was able to penetrate the supposedly tight security around President Jimmy Carter, Egyptian President Anwar Sadat, and Israeli Prime Minister Menachem Begin to witness the signing of the Camp David accords at the White House. Schuster simply joined the crowd of 290 Senators and Representatives waiting for the bus to the White House, gave the name of a Congressman who he knew had decided not to go, and got on the bus.

Journalists differed in their judgments of Schuster. "You don't go impersonating congressmen or cops," said Watergate reporter Carl Bernstein. But former *New York Times* investigative reporter Seymour Hersh was not so sure. "If the guy was trying to seriously write about White House security, how else is he to do it?"[33]

Walter Anderson, former editor of the *White Plains* (New York) *Reporter Dispatch*, still feels uneasy about a story he broke on inefficiency and cover-up in a police narcotics squad. Anderson had purchased quantities of heroin and methadone himself, and had photographed police work rosters while pretending to take shots of policemen hard at work. The series resulted in arrests of heroin dealers and reform of the county methadone program—but Anderson still isn't sure it was worth it. He proposes four questions that reporters should ask themselves before proceeding with a deception:

> Is the story worth it? It had better be for what you're risking: your career and the integrity of journalism as a whole.
>
> Is your violation—be it a lie or criminal act—absolutely necessary to obtain the story?
>
> Will it work? I'd guess that most reporters ask the first two questions to some degree and really do not give enough thought to the third. How sure are you that your dark act is anything more than fishing?
>
> What are the consequences? If you get your story, be prepared to publish how you got it. Will that make your story less credible? If so, reexamine whether the story is worth it.[34]

At the beginning of this section we quoted Robert Scheer on the extreme pro-deception position: anything to get the story. For the extreme anti-deception position, here is A. M. Rosenthal, executive editor of the *New York Times*: "Reporters should not masquerade. We claim First Amendment rights and privileges, and it's duplicitous of us to then pass ourselves off as something other than reporters. Saying you'll get a better story or per-

Reporters at the *Chicago Sun-Times* wanted to investigate rumors that small businesses in the city were forced to bribe countless government inspectors in order to stay open. After rejecting more traditional investigative techniques, the paper decided to open its own bar, the Mirage, staffed by reporters who would secretly photograph and record the illegal payments demanded.

The ploy worked well. The *Sun-Times* produced a series of stories carefully documenting official corruption, and a number of inspectors were indicted. So they could not be accused of committing illegal acts themselves, the reporters informed the Illinois Department of Law Enforcement each time they paid a bribe. And they made sure not to entrap potential bribe-seekers by offering money before it was requested.

The series was nominated for a Pulitzer Prize in 1979, and the nominating jury voted to give the award to the paper. Deceptive journalistic techniques had won Pulitzers in the past—in 1961 for a *Buffalo Evening News* reporter who posed as a social worker, in 1971 for a *Chicago Tribune* reporter who masqueraded as an ambulance driver.

But this time the Pulitzer Board took issue with the *Sun-Times'* methods, and awarded the prize to another nominee. Benjamin Bradlee, executive editor of the *Washington Post*, asked: "How can newspapers fight for honesty and integrity when they themselves are less than honest in getting a story?" Eugene C. Patterson, editor of the *St. Petersburg (Florida) Times*, agreed. "This story could have been reported without the dissembling that occurred. If the *Sun-Times* had interviewed bar owners, that would have been the *hard* way to get the story."[35] Others outside the Pulitzer Board insisted that that would have been an impossible way to get the story, and praised the *Sun-Times* for its enterprise.

Journalists disagee on the ethics of deceiving sources, but there is no dispute that *inventing* sources (and thus deceiving the audience) is unethical. In 1981, the *Washington Post* was forced to return the 1980 Pulitzer it had won for reporter Janet Cooke's story about an 8-year-old heroin addict (see p. 199). Cooke finally confessed that she had fabricated the entire story.

---

form a valuable public service doesn't change anything. It's still wrong."[36]

And in the pragmatic middle, Robert Sherrill, White House correspondent for *The Nation:* "A little tut-tutting and sermonizing make us feel righteous and purged. But let's not waste too much time on it. Trying to decide in the abstract how far a reporter should go is about as futile as parents trying to decide how far their daughter should go. When the passions are up and the story is tempting, any reporter . . . is likely to do whatever the moment seems to call for."[37]

Of course this is precisely what an abstract code of ethics is for—to provide a basis for judging what reporters do when the passions are up. Journalism lacks such a code. An Indiana University survey of newspaper managing editors found that two-thirds believed reporters should have to identify themselves as reporters, while one-third said they shouldn't.[38] More detailed questions would yield more qualified answers—but no greater consensus.

INVASION OF PRIVACY

Journalist Richard Reeves has profiled more than 50 prominent political figures. On each profile, he says, he has faced a particular personal dread. "I was afraid I would discover one was homosexual. What would I do? What would I write? Could I ignore it and believe I was presenting a complete picture?"[39]

Reeves has a good reason for not wanting to usher a prominent politician involuntarily out of the closet—such a disclosure could ruin the person's career and perhaps his or her life. Yet the fact of homosexuality certainly seems relevant to a thorough profile. The question, then, is this: Where does the public's right to know leave off and the source's right to privacy begin?

The reluctance of reporters to hide their identities is really just a special case of this privacy issue—reporters reveal who they are so that sources can protect their own privacy by not saying things they don't want published.

But the newsgathering process often invades the privacy of a source even when the reporter is properly identified. Broadcaster Robert Schulman recalls his cub reporter days, when he was often sent to the home of a recent widow to pick up a photo of her deceased husband. Once Schulman was the first to arrive, and had to tell the woman her husband was dead before asking for the picture. TV reporter Gabe Pressman was in a New York airport when news arrived of a transoceanic plane crash. Pressman recalls how uncomfortable *he* was watching another TV reporter interview the shocked relatives—capitalizing on their sorrow for the sake of a story.[40]

Reporters can also invade a newsmaker's privacy without talking to the newsmaker. Early in the Watergate story, the *Washington Post's* Carl Bernstein persuaded a "source" at the telephone company to give him a list of the long-distance calls of one of the Watergate burglars; the list included calls to the Committee to Re-Elect the President. Bernstein later expressed doubts about the ethics of this breach of privacy—but Watergate was a big story.

The privacy issue comes up most forcefully not in the newsgathering process but in the decision to publish or not publish what the reporter has found out. Richard Reeves' hypothetical problem can easily become all too real. In 1965, for example, a *New York Times* reporter discovered that a prominent member of the American Nazi Party was of Jewish ancestry. The Nazi made it clear to the reporter that his "career" would be finished if this fact were revealed to the public. The *Times* ran the story anyhow, and the Jewish Nazi committed suicide.[41] Was this a valid intrusion on his private life, or was it unethical?

Journalists are aware of their power to damage people's lives. They try to deal with it by not dealing with it. Their job, they say, is to get the facts and tell the public, not to worry about the consequences. But journalists are people, too, and in reality they do worry about the effects of what they write.

Occasionally these issues turn up in court, when someone sues a reporter for invasion of privacy. But it is very difficult for individuals to win a privacy action against the media, and there has been comparatively little litigation in this area (see pp. 185-86). Privacy remains predominantly an ethical question. Should photographers have chased down a grand jury witness in a gambling probe when the witness was avoiding publicity for fear of mob reprisals? Should reporters have printed the names of police doctors accused of brutality by a student arrested at a demonstration? Should TV stations have run the film of two airline crash victims, still strapped in their seats and still recognizable, floating in the water? Should newspapers have used the names of customers caught in a police raid on a bookie joint?

In 1979 Rod Deckert, managing editor of *The Missoulian* (in Missoula, Montana), was faced with a decision that he says caused him more anguish than anything else in his career. The daughter of a prominent Missoula couple was stabbed to death in Washington, D.C. She had been an honor student in high school, and had won a scholarship to Radcliffe. Obviously the murder was news. The problem was that the young woman had died as a street-walking prostitute.

Deckert knew that he couldn't simply report that she had been murdered and let it go at that. Even if he had wanted to, the *Washington Post* was preparing a long story on how she had become a prostitute, and the story would inevitably find its way back to Missoula. Deckert would then be accused of covering up to protect the family.

He decided to take the same approach as the *Post,* running additional material on how pimps were recruiting women from Missoula to work as East Coast prostitutes. Deckert hoped that the story would save other local women from the same fate.

Before the story was printed, the family's lawyer called Deckert, warning him that publication might drive one family member to suicide. After the story came out, the mother went into shock and had to be treated by a doctor. Journalists "can destroy people," she said, "and they have." The community was outraged—at least 200 readers cancelled their subscriptions and a few advertisers withdrew their ads. The *Missoulian* printed more than 150 letters on the subject, all but a few attacking the paper for invading the family's privacy.

"I remember lying there in bed, after we decided to run the story," recalls Deckert. "I kept saying to myself, 'I wish there'd been an easy way out.' It's never the kind of thing where you feel you can stand up and beat your chest. You can't come away feeling good through and through when you know you have put a family—and your community—through a lot of grief and pain."

Months later, the *Missoulian* published an investigative feature on small-town recruiting for urban prostitutes. The victim's family cooperated with the reporter, and community reaction to the story was generally favorable.[42]

WITHHOLDING INFORMATION

The ethical issue in the previous section was the harm done by publishing information. But what about the harm done by refusing to publish information? When jour-

nalists withhold a story for reasons that have little to do with the mission of journalism, they are vulnerable to the charge that they have defaulted on the reporter's highest ethical obligation: to inform the public.

In 1974, for example, Patricia Hearst was kidnapped by the Symbionese Liberation Army and held for ransom. At the request of the FBI and local police, media in the San Francisco area (including the *San Francisco Examiner,* published by her father) maintained a blackout on the story for $12\frac{1}{2}$ hours. Lou Boccardi, executive editor of the Associated Press, defended the ethics of the blackout. "To have rushed out in a life-be-damned headline splurge would have been, in my view, nothing short of irresponsibility on our part."[43]

Not all editors agreed. One responded: "No editor would want to be responsible for the girl's death, but publicity seldom changes the situation. . . . The police professionally take the gloomiest view. The editor should never withhold simply because the police ask him to."[44] Suppose Patricia Hearst had been killed during the blackout, and a witness later came forward who could have helped the authorities if news of the kidnapping had been published. Or suppose the kidnappers had claimed other victims during the blackout, and their families later charged that the media had failed to warn them of kidnappers on the loose.

Community leaders often argue that publicity makes social problems worse, that the problems might diminish if the media left them alone. The argument sounds reasonable for certain kinds of problems—airline hijackings, for example, tend to feed off the notoriety of previous ones. Assume for a moment that there would be fewer such skyjackings if reporters ignored the ones that did happen. Is that enough reason to justify withholding the story? Is it the reporter's job to prevent skyjackings, or to tell people about them?

And often the argument proves false. In 1974, for example, the *Daily Freeman-Journal* and radio station KQWC in Webster City, Iowa, agreed to a 90-day news blackout on local vandalism. Police statistics showed that vandalism during the three-month experiment actually increased by 36.5 percent over the same period the year before. The *Freeman-Journal* later editorialized: "[I]t is our opinion now, as it was when the moratorium was suggested, that turning one's back on problems with the hope that they will go away rarely, if ever, has the desired effect. . . . An uninformed public often harbors a false sense of self-security. The outcome of the past three months is proof of that."[45]

It is easy to think of convincing reasons why news should not be published. A story on the financial woes of a local corporation might push it into bankruptcy, costing the community many jobs. A story on toxic wastes leaching into the water supply might provoke exaggerated fear among readers or viewers. A story on how teenagers get high on household products might lead other teenagers to try the experience. A story on the deteriorating central business district might deter merchants from opening stores there.

Some of these reasons fall under the heading of "civic boosterism"—the insistence that reporters portray their community in the best possible light. But others may seem at least as legitimate as the story itself, raising difficult ethical problems for the reporter.

In 1979, when Iranian militants seized 53 hostages at the American embassy in Tehran, six other Americans managed to escape to the Canadian embassy nearby. The fact that these Americans were in hiding was known to at least five news organizations: the *New York Times, Time, Newsweek,* CBS, and NBC. None of them published the story until the Americans had been safely spirited

---

RIOTS AND BLACKOUTS

News blackouts of racial unrest have a long history in the U.S. In the early 1960s, for example, one Southern city established an interracial commission to desegregate its lunch counters. An agreement was negotiated under which the media ignored the story, and the sit-ins proceeded without violence. Said one member of the commission: "I am convinced that if these matters had received normal news treatment, the alarm would have sounded among the Ku Klux Klan and the redneck types, and that they would have been there with their baseball bats and ax handles; extremists among the Negroes would have responded in kind."[46]

The argument for a blackout seemed most persuasive during the summer of 1967, when a rash of urban riots appeared to be feeding on each other's publicity. Editors in some cities negotiated secret agreements to keep quiet about ghetto unrest. It may be true that early publicity about a minor incident can help it grow to major proportions— especially if it's based on exaggerated rumors. People hearing on the radio about a scuffle a few blocks away may head for the scene to see what's going on, and pretty soon the scuffle is a riot.

On the other hand, people need to know if the streets are blocked or dangerous, so that they can avoid the trouble. Word-of-mouth rumors are likely to be less accurate than media accounts. And if serious grievances have festered to the point of a riot, the public has a right to know about it.

Otis Chandler of the *Los Angeles Times* has written of "the social value of truth; whether or not truth hurts, whether or not truth is inflammatory."[47] Reporters who withhold a story are flouting this central conviction of journalism.

out of the country nearly three months later. Said Seymour Topping, managing editor of the *Times:* "There was never any conflict in journalistic terms. It wouldn't serve the public interest in any way for us to print that story and it would simply endanger American lives, so we were quite prepared to cooperate."[48]

Few responsible journalists would have risked the lives of six people for a meaningless cloak-and-dagger scoop. But what if the story had seemed genuinely important for the public to know about? Then Topping would have faced a classic ethical dilemma: good reasons to print the story, good reasons to withhold it. Reporters covering international affairs face such dilemmas frequently, especially in the national security area. In Chapter 17 we will look in detail at how they try to resolve the problem.

CHECKBOOK JOURNALISM

The competitive pressures of journalism sometimes lead reporters and editors to pay their sources for information—an exclusive tip, a damaging document, even just a celebrity interview. Like all the ethical issues in this chapter, "checkbook journalism" (as it is often disparagingly termed) provokes sharp disagreement among practitioners. In the Indiana University survey of managing editors, 60 percent opposed it, while 40 percent said it could be justified.[49]

The loudest outcry against the practice came in the wake of the Watergate scandals. H. R. Haldeman, a top aide to ex-President Nixon, was paid $100,000 in 1975 for two CBS interview programs. Then Nixon himself signed a profitable deal with entertainer David Frost for exclusive syndicated TV interviews on his career. A variation on this theme found NBC signing former Secretary of State Henry Kissinger and former President Gerald R. Ford to exclusive contracts after they left office.

The media have been paying for news stories ever since the first circulation wars of the 1800s. In 1908, for example, explorers Robert E. Peary and Frederick A. Cook set out to reach the North Pole. The *New York Times* had its money on Peary; it had arranged for exclusive rights to his story. The rival *New York Herald* was backing Cook. When both explorers claimed to have discovered the North Pole, a lively battle erupted in the New York press, each paper supporting its own man. Peary turned out to be right—but it was not that victory that made the *New York Times* the fine newspaper it is today.

It is well known in the mass media that certain types of public figures give "better answers" in interviews if there's some money in it for them. Professional athletes are often paid for broadcast interviews, and as a matter of course most guests on pregame and postgame shows receive cash or gifts. NBC paid $4,000 to interview former Nazi Baldur Von Schirach when he was released from Spandau Prison. And escaped Chinese violinist Ma Szu-tsung told *Life* magazine all about his experiences in Communist China—for a price.

In 1967, *Life* set a disturbing precedent by offering every U.S. astronaut $6,200 a year for the "personal" story of his involvement in the manned space program. Since the astronauts received all their training and experience at the taxpayer's expense, there was reason to question the ethics of their selling exclusive rights to their story—and reason also to question the ethics of *Life* in making the offer.

There are at least three dangers in paying for the news. First, the less wealthy media may not be able to compete. Second, the cost will inevitably be passed on to the consumer. Third and most important, news sources may be tempted to sensationalize their stories—perhaps even invent them—in order to earn a higher price. In the late 1960s, a group of self-proclaimed revolutionaries asked CBS for $30,000 for the rights to film their invasion of Haiti. It soon became clear to the network that the $30,000 would finance the invasion, or at least a landing on a strip of unpatrolled beach. No money, no invasion. CBS promptly backed out of the deal.[50] A congressional committee later investigated the incident. Its conclusions were highly critical of CBS, but it did not recommend any official action.

JUNKETS AND FREEBIES

The ethical problems we have discussed so far concern how journalists treat their sources—deceiving them, invading their privacy, deferring to their wish for secrecy, or paying for their help. Here the problem is reversed. In an effort to influence news coverage, sources often offer reporters free trips and other gifts—commonly called "junkets" and "freebies." The source's hope, of course, is that these favors will make the journalist feel obliged to write a more positive story. How should the ethical journalist respond?

On its face this ethical problem would seem to have an easy solution: just ban all junkets and freebies. But consider. The travel editor of a small newspaper will be able to check out a lot more vacation spots with some financial help from interested tourist bureaus. The sports department's budget will go a lot further if reporters travel with the team at team expense. Touring a new auto plant a thousand miles away isn't a "must" story, but it's a legitimate story, and it's feasible when the company pays for the trip. And not even purists object to a war correspondent who hitches a free ride to the front with the army.

A case of whiskey at Christmas is a bribe (or at best a "gift") and obviously should be returned—but many junkets and freebies genuinely facilitate news coverage. And many reporters are convinced they can withstand the temptation to repay the source's generosity at the typewriter.

Can they? Apparently PR people don't think so. Most are pleased enough with the publicity resulting from junkets and freebies that they keep arranging more junkets and freebies. As publicist J. E. Schoonover puts it, the story that results from a junket "carries a stamp of objectivity and credibility no paid advertising can match."[51]

Many editors, too, are inclined to doubt that their reporters can stay objective in the face of such generous sources. A 1976 survey asked newspaper editors to respond to a list of junkets and freebies. Below is the percentage who thought each item would affect a reporter's objectivity:

A free trip to a foreign country (77.1%)

A free membership at a local country club (70.9%)

Gifts (Christmas or other) (61.1%)

A free trip outside the community, but not abroad (58.9%)

Free passes or cut-rate fees at a local golf course (56.8%)

Free season tickets in a choice location for college or professional sports (51.8%)

Complimentary drinks or meals (38.9%)

Free samples of foods, toiletries, perfumes, etc. that routinely came to the office (33.6%)

Complimentary tickets to theaters or movie houses (32.7%)[52]

Two conclusions are apparent. The more valuable the gift, the greater editors think its influence will be. And (according to the editors) almost any gift can have a significant influence.

As a result, more papers and stations have firm policies against junkets and freebies than on any other issue of journalistic ethics. And the policies are getting stricter. According to a 1979 survey by the American Society of Newspaper Editors, 62 percent of the responding newspapers now turn down free transportation for industry tours; 64 percent refuse free rides on inaugural airline flights; 74 percent say no to government-sponsored travel; and 80 percent decline free trips to cover sporting events.[53]

SPORTS FREEBIES

In the course of a 1973 investigation into ticket scalping (the illegal sale of tickets above their printed price), the New York State Attorney General's office uncovered a Madison Square Garden "master freebie press list," outlining who was to get how many free tickets to Knicks (basketball) and Rangers (hockey) games. Sports editors of the three New York daily newspapers were receiving from six to a dozen free seats for every home game, with smaller numbers going to the wire services, many broadcast stations, and such super-commentators as Howard Cosell, Dick Schaap, and Bill Mazur. The three papers alone were getting nearly $65,000 a year in free tickets—not counting the gifts that might be sent to the homes of reporters at Christmastime.

While no one suggests that free tickets were enough to make very many writers slant their stories, the practice did provide access for the Garden's PR people when they were trying to drum up publicity for something less popular than a Knicks or Rangers game.

In the words of one Garden PR man, here's how it worked: "I once had this bomb [unpopular] event I was pushing, and since I had been giving seats to one of the sports editors of an unnamed local paper for years, I was able to walk into his office and lay my cards on the table. I told him I really needed a favor. He had to bail me out. . . . He sat there and made me justify his putting it in the paper. But that was okay. That was my job. Once we agreed on an appropriate advance I wrote it and the paper printed it under the editor's byline. It stayed in the paper through all editions, as well. That's why make-up editors and composing room bosses have been on the freebie lists too." Presumably the story sold a few extra seats for the Garden's "bomb."[54]

These figures represent a huge shift from the media's easy acceptance of junkets and freebies in years past. Consider this tolerant article from a 1954 issue of *Editor & Publisher,* the trade journal of the newspaper industry:

Schenley Distributors, Inc. [threw a party] for the first American importation of Canadian OFS, Original Fine Canadian. It seems that the first shipment was due in New York aboard the SS President Monroe. So a special car on a New Haven Railroad train was arranged to take the press representatives from New York to Boston . . . [followed by] an overnight trip on the Monroe to New York. The letter of invitation said: "I know you will thoroughly enjoy it, for we are prepared with sumptuous cuisine and delightful entertainment." An *E&P* staffer noted: "And with a boat load of whiskey, it sounds like a perfect lost weekend."[55]

Junkets and freebies are still a journalistic fact of life. The more profitable and prestigious media may now forbid them, but reporters from the smaller media still attend gala events at least as elaborate as the Schenley boat trip. (See p. 387 for two modern examples.) But they no longer gloat over them in *Editor & Publisher.*

CONFLICT OF INTEREST

In October, 1977, the *Philadelphia Inquirer* published an extraordinary story, spread out over nearly six full pages of the paper, detailing the amorous relationship between a former *Inquirer* political reporter and a Philadelphia politician. During the time Laura Foreman was covering politics for the *Inquirer,* she was living with State Senator Henry Cianfrani. The relationship came to light when Cianfrani was indicted on federal racketeering charges, and the FBI questioned Foreman about his activities. By then Foreman was reporting for the *New*

York Times. She resigned under pressure, claiming that while she may have been "injudicious" in her conduct, she had not done anything wrong.[56] (Foreman and Cianfrani later married.)

No one could prove that Foreman's political coverage was inaccurate or misleading. But she had written about Cianfrani for the *Inquirer*. She had used him as an anonymous source, had written positively about his prospects in the state Democratic hierarchy, and had steered him into leading a well-publicized investigation of conditions at a hospital for the criminally insane. And he had given her some $20,000 in gifts.[57]

Foreman was guilty of a classic conflict of interest: she had become too close to a person she was covering. Foreman's editors and readers had to wonder if she was reporting all she knew about Cianfrani. Was she slanting the news to help his career? Did their relationship affect how she reported other political events? Was Cianfrani using her and the *Inquirer* for his own political purposes?

Reporters are also private individuals, and they are entitled to a personal life and to be

---

"JOURNALISTS ARE NOT SPIES"

For reporters operating in foreign countries, some of the most useful sources have been agents of the Central Intelligence Agency. And for CIA agents, some of the most useful sources have been reporters. The latter raises a conflict-of-interest problem that has worried journalists in recent years.

Since the end of World War II, some 400 American journalists have aided the CIA in its intelligence gathering, according to reporter Carl Bernstein. Some traded their help for CIA information; others offered it out of patriotism or friendship with particular agents. Among the tasks they performed were these: briefing agents on what they had heard or observed; hosting parties to bring together agents and foreign spies; targeting potential spies for the U.S. within foreign governments; planting misinformation in the foreign press; and helping transmit sensitive information back to the U.S. The news organizations that have proved most valuable to the CIA over the years, Bernstein says, are the *New York Times*, CBS, and *Time*.[58]

Until the mid-1960s there was little debate about the propriety of such relationships; many journalists saw themselves as working toward the same goals as the CIA. The Vietnam war challenged that cozy view. In a 1980 editorial entitled "Journalists Are Not Spies," the *New York Times* stated the case against further cooperation:

> American reporters cannot long function abroad if forced to operate under a cloud of suspicion. They need to be what they represent themselves to be: independent seekers of information which they communicate to the public. They may be suspected of national, political or personal bias, but they should never be plausibly suspected of also being CIA operatives.[59]

Journalistic opposition persuaded George Bush, director of the CIA under President Ford, to end existing relationships with reporters and pledge that the CIA would no longer ask journalists for intelligence help. But in 1980 Admiral Stansfield Turner, CIA director under President Carter, said that he had approved using journalists for secret intelligence operations in three instances and that he "wouldn't hesitate" to do so in the future.[60]

Peer pressure probably keeps most reporters today from cooperating with the CIA. But the practice has not disappeared. As the political climate changes, it could become acceptable once again.

involved in community activities. Yet virtually any outside interest on a journalist's part may begin to affect news coverage—or at least raise the suspicion of affecting news coverage. Where do you draw the line? In financial matters, for example, it makes sense to forbid business reporters to take advantage of inside information by cashing in on a tip before reporting it. But to really protect against financial conflicts of interest, we would have to forbid business reporters to own stocks altogether. Is that fair to the reporters?

In 1978 the *Lewiston* (Idaho) *Morning Tribune* decided to discuss its own conflict-of-interest problems with its readers. It listed, among others, a reporter who worked as a Democratic precinct committeeman; an editorial writer who had been press secretary to Idaho Senator Frank Church; a night managing editor who chaired the Governor's Blue Ribbon Committee on Taxation and served on the Idaho Advisory Committee to the U.S. Commission on Civil Rights; and a publisher who was president of the Idaho Board of Education.[61]

Did these outside activities bias the *Morning Tribune*'s coverage? According to the Democratic committeeman, "They're saying I won't give a fair interview to the Republicans because I'm a Democrat precinct committeeman. I'm saying that doesn't make a damn bit of difference." The reporter who covered the state board of education said the publisher never looked over his copy in advance. In fact, he said he gave the publisher *less* attention than he thought he really deserved, bending over backwards to avoid the appearance of bias.[62] Still, the paper acknowledged the possibility of bias in all these situations. Left unresolved was whether Idaho's journalists should remain involved in public affairs, or quit their extra-curricular posts to preserve their neutrality. The risk of the former is conflict of interest; of the latter, isolation and loss of personal freedom.

Most of the media have yet to develop policies on journalistic conflict of interest.

Some forbid their business writers to own stock in the companies they write about. Some refuse to let reporters run for public office, or do PR for politicians. A few prohibit PR of all kinds, even for charities, and require that any outside writing be cleared by management.

And while the rules for reporters and editors are scanty and unclear, the rules for publishers and owners are nonexistent. In 1979 John Cowles, Jr., chairman of the *Minneapolis Star* and *Tribune,* was criticized for leading a campaign to convince the Minnesota legislature to build a sports stadium next door to the newspapers' offices. And in 1978 a group of Florida newspaper and station owners contributed $180,000 to help defeat a referendum to legalize gambling in the state.[63] Such community involvement has traditionally been considered a virtue; it's putting the medium's clout and cash where its editorial policy is. But the result in the Florida case was that the *Miami Herald* vastly overplayed the casino story at the expense of other issues on the ballot, and a *Herald* poll of its readers found that 59 percent felt the paper could not give the issue fair coverage because of the contribution of ownership.[64]

The three television networks and all the stations they own and operate (as well as many newspapers) have a standing rule that prohibits reporters from publicly taking sides on behalf of any political candidate or party. Geraldo Rivera, then a reporter for WABC in New York, was giving speeches on behalf of candidate George McGovern in 1972, and was ordered to stop. William Sheehan, director of TV news for the network, said Rivera's speech-making was "contrary to all our policies governing behavior of news personnel. There are no gray areas in such cases; they're all black and white."[65]

But they are *not* all black and white. The *Lewiston Morning Tribune* points out some of the subtler questions in the gray area. Can a reporter put a bumper sticker on his or her car? Be married to a government official?

Cover the education beat if he or she has a child in school? Managing editor Ladd Hamilton summarizes the problem this way: "You can't say that because you're a newspaperman you have to be a monk and stay in a cell all day. You have to live a relatively normal life and be involved in the community. At the same time you've got to be clear-eyed, and write on the basis of what you see, not what you belong to or where your money might be."[66]

Where do you draw the line? That is the question for every ethical problem confronting the mass media. We have discussed just six of them, seven if you count the broader issue of objectivity. If space permitted, we could easily discuss a dozen more. Two legal issues that also raise ethical dilemmas—protecting the confidentiality of sources, and the conflict between free press and fair trial—are discussed in Chapter 7.

Three points are worth emphasizing. First, none of these ethical problems is obvious or easy to solve. Second, most journalists do their best to solve them, to be as ethical as they know how. Third and most important, working journalists still receive very little help from their peers in setting ethical standards. Journalism likes to think of itself as a profession; if it is, it is a profession without a clear and enforceable code of ethics.

Notes

1 George Kennedy, "Is Journalism a Profession?", Freedom of Information Center Report No. 359, School of Journalism, University of Missouri at Columbia, September, 1976, p. 1.

2 Ibid., p. 4.

3 Charles R. Eisendrath, "Politics and Journalism: The French Connection," Columbia Journalism Review, May/June, 1979, pp. 58-61.

4 "Employees to Have Control of Omaha World-Herald," Editor & Publisher, February 2, 1980, p. 20.

5 Richard Pollak, "The Liebling Ledger Comes Off the Press," More, November, 1973, p. 4.

6 James C. Thompson, Jr., "Journalistic Ethics: Some Probings by a Media Keeper," The Poynter Center, Indiana University at Bloomington, January, 1978, p. 12.

7 Broadcasting Yearbook 1978, p. D-17.

8 Ibid., pp. D-18, D-19.

9 Meyer Weinberg, TV in America (New York: Ballantine, 1962), p. 93.

10 Broadcasting Yearbook 1978, p. D-18.

11 "Another Hand of Government Strikes at NAB TV Code," Broadcasting, June 18, 1979, p. 27.

12 Eric J. Zanot, "The National Advertising Review Board 1971-1976," Journalism Monographs, No. 59, February, 1979, p. 36.

13 Philip H. Dougherty, "Mediator of Disputed Claims," New York Times, January 17, 1980, p. D11.

14 Ibid.

15 "N.L.R.B. Reverses a Ruling on Ethics in Newspaper Case," New York Times, April 9, 1976, p. 42.

16 William L. Rivers, Theodore Peterson, and Jay W. Jensen, The Mass Media and Modern Society, 2nd. ed. (San Francisco: Rinehart Press, 1971), p. 188.

17 Ken Macrorie, "Objectivity: Dead or Alive?", Journalism Quarterly, Spring, 1959, pp. 148-49.

18 Gaye Tuchman, "Objectivity as Strategic Ritual: An Examination of Newsmen's Notions of Objectivity," American Journal of Sociology, January, 1972, pp. 660-79.

19 Michael Schudson, Discovering The News (New York: Basic Books, 1978), pp. 184-85.

20 Ibid., p. 6.

21 William L. Rivers, "The New Confusion," Progressive, December, 1971, p. 26.

22 Carl E. Lindstrom, The Fading American Newspaper (Gloucester, Mass.: Peter Smith, 1964), p. 63.

23 Tom Wolfe, "The Birth of 'The New Journalism'; Eyewitness Report by Tom Wolfe," New York, February 14, 1972, p. 34.

24 A. Kent MacDougall, "Clay Felker's New York," Columbia Journalism Review, March/April, 1974, pp. 36-47.

25 Michael J. Arlen, "Notes on the New Journalism," Atlantic Monthly, May, 1972, p. 47.

26 Jack Newfield, "Of Honest Men and Good Writers," Village Voice, May 18, 1972, p. 7.

27 Morris Janowitz, "Professional Models in Journalism: The Gatekeeper and the Advocate," Journalism Quarterly, Winter, 1975, pp. 618-26, 662.

28 Ken Auletta, "Bribe, Seduce, Lie, Steal: Anything to Get the Story," More, March, 1977, p. 14.

29 Robert Sherrill, "Looking for Mr. Wunderbar,"

Columbia Journalism Review, September/October, 1979, p. 65.

30 Gordon Chaplin and Claudia Cohen, "Eclipse in Baltimore," *More,* March, 1974, p. 8.

31 David Shaw, "Deception—Honest Tool of Reporting?" *Los Angeles Times,* September 20, 1979, p. 1.

32 *Ibid.*

33 Claudia Cohen, "Reporter's Ruse Enrages the Feds," *New York Post,* May 22, 1979, p. 6.

34 Walter Anderson, "The Underhanded Means to an End," *Quill,* November, 1977, pp. 28-29.

35 Steve Robinson, "Pulitzers: Was the Mirage a Deception?", *Columbia Journalism Review,* July/August, 1979, pp. 14, 16.

36 Shaw, "Deception—Honest Tool?" p. 1.

37 Sherrill, "Looking for Mr. Wunderbar," p. 65.

38 Thomas H. Harmening, "The Status of Investigative Reporting in American Daily Newspapers," Research Report No. 1, Center for New Communications, School of Journalism, Indiana University at Bloomington, July 20, 1977, p. 2.

39 Richard Reeves, "The Capital Letter," *New York,* January 19, 1976, p. 8.

40 Gabe Pressman, Robert Lewis Shayon, and Robert Schulman, "The Responsible Reporter," *Television Quarterly,* Spring, 1964, pp. 10, 22.

41 Gay Talese, *The Kingdom and the Power* (New York: Bantam, 1970), pp. 431-48.

42 Jack Hart and Janis Johnson, "Fire Storm in Missoula," *Quill,* May, 1979, pp. 19-24. Jack Hart, "Return to Missoula," *Quill,* February, 1980, pp. 24-26.

43 Joe Shoquist, "Editors Back Decision to Delay AP Kidnaping Story," *APME News,* April, 1974, p. 1.

44 *Ibid.,* p. 4.

45 "So Much for Conventional Wisdom," *New York Times,* March 3, 1974, sec. 4, p. 13E.

46 William L. Rivers, "Jim Crow Journalism," *Seminar,* March, 1968, p. 12.

47 Otis Chandler, "The Greater Responsibility," *Seminar,* March, 1968, p. 7.

48 Deirdre Carmody, "Some News Groups Knew of 6 in Hiding," *New York Times,* January 31, 1980, p. A10.

49 Harmening, "The Status of Investigative Reporting," p. 2.

50 Bill Surface, "Should Reporters Buy News?", *Saturday Review,* May 13, 1967, p. 86.

51 Frederick C. Klein, "Junket Journalism," *Wall Street Journal,* February 14, 1966, pp. 1, 12.

52 Keith P. Sanders and Won H. Chang, "Codes—The Ethical *Free*-For-All," Freedom of Information

Foundation Series, No. 7, Freedom of Information Foundation, Columbia, Missouri, March, 1977, p. 6.

53 "ASNE Poll Reveals Fewer Editors Are Taking Freebies," *Editor & Publisher,* May 5, 1979, p. 12.

54 Nicholas Pileggi, "Freebies—Fringe Benefits of the Sporting Life," *New York,* June 18, 1973, pp. 53-56.

55 Wilbur Schramm, *Responsibility in Mass Communication* (New York: Harper & Brothers, 1957), p. 145.

56 Donald L. Barlett and James B. Steele, "The Full Story of Cianfrani and the Reporter," *Philadelphia Inquirer,* October 16, 1977, sec. F, pp. 1-8.

57 *Ibid.*

58 Carl Bernstein, "The CIA and the Media," *Rolling Stone,* October 20, 1977, pp. 55-56.

59 "Journalists Are Not Spies," *New York Times,* April 14, 1980, p. A18.

60 Deirdre Carmody, "C.I.A. Head Defends Approving Use of Journalists," *New York Times,* April 11, 1980, p. D14.

61 Cassandra Tate, "Let's Come Out Front," *Quill,* June, 1978, pp. 12-16, 39.

62 *Ibid.,* pp. 14, 15.

63 Lawrence Irgrassia, "Owners of Newspapers Stir Debate by Taking a Role in Public Affairs," *Wall Street Journal,* August 24, 1979, p. 1.

64 Austin Wehrwein, "A News Council Cop-out?", *Columbia Journalism Review,* March/April, 1979, pp. 13-15.

65 *New York Times,* October 16, 1972, p. 75.

66 Tate, "Let's Come Out Front," p. 39.

Suggested Readings

ALBERTSON, MIKE, *et al.,* "The Underhanded Means to an End," *The Quill,* November, 1977.

BERNSTEIN, CARL, "The CIA and the Media," *Rolling Stone,* October 20, 1977.

HART, JACK, and JANIS JOHNSON, "Fire Storm in Missoula," *The Quill,* May, 1979.

HULTENG, JOHN, *The Messenger's Motives: Ethical Problems of the News Media.* Englewood Cliffs, N.J.: Prentice-Hall, Inc., 1976.

In The Public Interest—II, A Report by The National News Council, 1975-1978. One Lincoln Plaza, New York, N.Y. 10023: The National News Council, Inc., 1979.

KOCH, KATHARINE, "The Caviar Caper," *Washington Journalism Review,* October, 1980.

ROBINSON, STEVE, "Pulitzers: Was the Mirage a Deception?" *Columbia Journalism Review,* July/August, 1979.

SILVERBERG, JAY, "Big Gamble in Florida," *The Quill,* October, 1978.

SWAIN, BRUCE M., *Reporters' Ethics.* Ames, Iowa: Iowa State University Press, 1978.

TATE, CASSANDRA, "Let's Come Out Front," *The Quill,* June, 1978.

WELLES, CHRIS, "The Short Sellers and the Press," *Institutional Investor,* July, 1977.

WILCOX, WALTER, "The Staged News Photograph and Professional Ethics," *Journalism Quarterly,* Autumn, 1961.

Chapter 3
Internal Control

The main qualification for owning a newspaper, magazine, or broadcast station in this country is enough money to buy it. Besides cash, mass-media owners have one other thing in common: power. By hiring and firing, rewarding and punishing, commanding and forbidding, an owner can control news content as much as he or she wishes. Most media owners use this power sparingly. A few resort to it freely; they view the media as convenient outlets for their own economic aims, personal whims, and ideological convictions.

Horace Greeley launched the *New York Tribune* in 1841. Greeley was greatly taken with the philosophy of French socialist Charles Fourier. For five years he preached Fourierism wherever he went—and so did the *Tribune*. Then he lost interest in the movement, and his paper never mentioned it again. Greeley was a teetotaler; the *Tribune* fought for prohibition. Greeley was opposed to capital punishment; the *Tribune* campaigned for its abolition. Greeley was a bitter enemy of slavery; so was the *Tribune*.

Joseph Medill bought into the *Chicago Tribune* in 1855, and by 1874 owned the majority of its stock. Medill was a firm believer in simplified spelling, so for years the *Tribune* used words like "infinit," "favorit," and "telegrafed." Medill also attributed all natural phenomena to sunspots—until one day he read of the existence of microbes, which he immediately adopted as his new explanation. Soon after, a *Tribune* editor wrote that a plague in Egypt had been caused by sunspots. Medill went through the copy and crossed out each reference to sunspots, substituting "microbes" instead.

Greeley and Medill are typical of nineteenth-century publishers. They viewed their newspapers as extensions of themselves. Greeley knew that many New Yorkers were fond of alcohol—but he wasn't, so his paper wasn't either. Medill knew that most Chicagoans spelled words the way the dictionary did—but he didn't, so his paper didn't either. Both men spent a great deal of time in their respective newsrooms, making sure that reporters and editors covered the news *their* way.

Today's metropolitan publishers belong to a different breed. Whether they own one newspaper or a chain of twenty, they are far more likely to be found in the "front office" than in the newsroom. They look after the financial health of the company, and let their professional employees look after the news.

Yet even today the mass-media owner retains almost absolute power to control news coverage—and sometimes that power is used.

POLICY

In 1967 David Bowers surveyed hundreds of newspaper managing editors throughout the country, asking them to assess the influence of their publishers. Bowers found that the larger the paper, the smaller the role of the publisher in day-to-day news coverage. This is presumably because metropolitan publishers are too busy with corporate affairs to waste much time looking over a reporter's shoulder. Nearly a quarter of the editors told Bowers that their publishers never entered the newsroom.[1]

But media owners are still owners. Armed with the power to hire and fire, reward and punish, they can still set "policy" when they want to. And sometimes they want to.

There are three reasons why a mass-media owner may wish to control news coverage, and each reason dictates its own sort of policy. Thus:

1. The economic interests of the company dictate a "business policy."
2. The individual likes and dislikes of the owner dictate a "personal policy."
3. The ideological convictions of the owner dictate a "political policy."

We will discuss each in turn.

1. Business Policy. Since modern media owners are most concerned with the financial health of their companies, it is scarcely surprising that more news is altered because of business policy than for any other reason. Even the most *laissez faire* publisher, Bowers found, is very interested in any article that might directly or indirectly affect news-

paper revenue. Most such articles have to do with advertisers or potential advertisers. The daughter of a department store owner is charged with drunk driving—should the newspaper report it? A new shopping center would like its grand opening covered on television in exchange for a healthy spot advertising contract—should the station accept? A national magazine is asked to print a twelve-page "news" supplement written by a corporation PR department—is it worth the money? Such decisions are made every day, and usually by the owner or publisher.

Business policy is not a recent invention. In 1911 *Collier's* magazine ran an anonymous article, "The Confessions of a Managing Editor," in which the author unburdened his conscience by revealing the tight policy control of his boss. He told how caustic movie reviews were abandoned because they displeased a theater owner who advertised regularly; a harmless department store fire was reported so as to imply that the stock had been damaged, permitting the store to announce a "fire sale" in the next day's paper; a story on a local electric power monopoly was killed because the chairman of the power company was a major advertiser.[2] If this 1911 article were reprinted in 1981, few informed readers would sense any incongruity—the same abuses are still taking place.

When business policy doesn't concern advertisers, it usually involves investors or the owners themselves. In a 1979 survey, for example, one-third of the editors of chain-owned newspapers said they would be reluctant to publish a story that might damage the chain.[3]

2. Personal Policy. Like everyone else, mass-media owners have friends, and like everyone else they do what they can to help their friends. In the case of the media, this means playing up stories that the friends are proud of (like a society wedding), and playing down or killing stories that the friends find embarrassing (like a divorce or an arrest). The friends of mass-media owners, by the way, tend to be leaders of the local business community. They are often in the news, so the owners have plenty of chances to do them favors.

Media owners are also subject to their own personal whims—and the privilege of indulging them. Walter Annenberg is a good example. Annenberg is owner of Triangle Publications, which publishes *TV Guide;* until 1970 he also owned the *Philadelphia Inquirer* and *News.* In addition, Annenberg is a man with strong likes and dislikes.

Veterans of the *Inquirer* newsroom recall Annenberg's "shit list," a collection of names never to be printed in the paper. Columnist Rose DeWolf once did an article on the Philadelphia-Baltimore Stock Exchange, quoting its president, Elkins Wetherkill, at length.

Told that Wetherkill was on the list, she had to call him back and ask that all his quotes be attributed to an Exchange vice president. The president of the University of Pennsylvania, Gaylord P. Harnwell, was also on Annenberg's list. Each year Harnwell awarded the prestigious Wharton School gold medal to a distinguished alumnus; each year the *Inquirer* ascribed the presentation to an unnamed "university official." Other names banned from all Annenberg publications included Imogene Coca, Zsa Zsa Gabor, and Dinah Shore—a constant challenge for the staff of *TV Guide.* Even the Philadelphia 76ers basketball team was in Annenberg's bad graces. He limited the team to two paragraphs after each win, one paragraph after each loss.[4]

PASSING IT UP

A media owner who tries to change a reporter's copy too often is likely to face a newsroom revolution. Passing up a syndicated cartoon or column, or a network program, is a much safer way to exercise policy influence.

Because of its political content, "Doonesbury" is often skipped for a day or two by publishers or editors who disagree. In 1974, for example, editor Charles Betts of the *Hartford Times* decided not to carry a "Doonesbury" strip that he felt was trying to make fun of an embattled President Nixon.[5] In 1979 at least seven West Coast newspapers refused to use "Doonesbury" strips that satirized California Gov. Edmund (Jerry) Brown Jr. by implying ties with an alleged organized crime figure.[6] And a 1980 "Doonesbury" tour of Ronald Reagan's brain was skipped by many publishers who feared accusations of election bias. Syndicated political columnists, from satirist Art Buchwald to muckraker Jack Anderson, receive similar treatment from time to time when their views conflict with an owner's politics, values, or sensitivities.

On television, such censorship is even more common. Throughout the 1960s, many Southern broadcasters refused to carry network documentaries on the civil rights movement. A 1973 episode of "Maude" in which abortion was sympathetically treated was passed over by dozens of disapproving station owners throughout the country. And in 1977, ABC faced a moral uprising among its affiliates when it introduced "Soap," a slapstick comedy based on "adult themes." Nineteen stations refused to carry the show at all, and 58 delayed it till a later time period. WOWK-TV in Huntington, W.Va., for example, spent $400,000 for "Mary Tyler Moore" reruns to fill the hole caused by its refusal to carry "Soap." The station's general manager, Leo MacCourtney, said the program "attacks basic human moral principles. Young people watching it will think, 'I guess it's okay to sleep around; I guess it's okay to be a transvestite.' I don't think this program should be on television."[7]

The personal predilections of a publisher usually do the reader more harm than good, but sometimes the tables are turned. The late William F. Knowland, former publisher of the *Oakland* (Calif.) *Tribune,* was a strong conservationist. As a result, the *Tribune*—in many ways a mediocre newspaper—was well ahead of other California papers in its coverage of environmental issues. Neighboring publishers were reluctant to mention corporate polluters by name; the *Tribune* seldom hesitated.

3. Political Policy. Many nineteenth-century publishers were ideologues; they purchased newspapers largely in order to advance a particular political or social philosophy. Most modern publishers, by contrast, are strictly business-oriented; they purchase newspapers in order to make money, and they seldom mount the soapbox.

There are exceptions, of course. In 1968 Harold F. Gross, owner of WJIM-TV in Lansing, Michigan, ordered a total blackout on Democratic congressional candidate James A. Harrison. A reporter for the station told Harrison that he had been instructed, "I don't want to see that son-of-a-bitch Harrison on again for the rest of the campaign." The *Detroit Free Press* unearthed a number of similar abuses by Gross, and outraged Lansing citizens put pressure on the FCC to investigate the case.[8] The investigation and FCC hearings went on for more than a decade. As of 1980—twelve years later—Gross remained owner of WJIM-TV.

William Loeb, publisher of the *Manchester Union Leader* in New Hampshire, is notorious for his personal attacks on political candidates. His unfounded accusations against the family of Edmund Muskie in 1972 brought angry tears to the presidential candidate's eyes. Muskie said of Loeb, "That man doesn't walk, he crawls."[9] Eight years later Loeb was still attacking candidates in New Hampshire primaries. He called Edward Kennedy a "hypocrite and cheapskate," and his accusations against Illinois Rep. Philip Crane were

so outrageous that the New Hampshire state legislature passed a resolution calling them "134 inches of totally unsubstantiated allegations."[10]

A challenger to Loeb's reputation for political bias is Rupert Murdock, an international chain owner whose U.S. flagship is the *New York Post.* Murdock's 1977 advocacy of Edward Koch for mayor and Carol Bellamy for city council president included an unlabeled front-page editorial and a profile of Bellamy entitled "Cinderella Carol" that featured eleven family snapshots. In mid-campaign 50 of the *Post*'s 60 reporters signed a petition urging more even-handed political coverage. Murdock responded that any reporter who questioned his integrity should leave the paper.[11]

In 1977 the New York bureau of the Panax newspaper chain distributed a series of derogatory articles about President Carter, accusing him of condoning promiscuity among his staff and grooming his wife for the vice presidency. Chain owner John P. McGoff sent a memo with the articles calling on all editors to run them as soon as possible, preferably on the front page. The memo asked that tear sheets be sent directly back to McGoff. When the editors of two Michigan newspapers refused, McGoff fired them for insubordination.[12] In response, the National News Council (see pp. 222-23) voted to censure McGoff and Panax for "gross disservice to accepted American journalistic standards."[13]

These are damning examples—but they were damned: Gross faced a license challenge, Loeb a legislative rebuke, Murdock a newsroom revolt, McGoff a National News Council censure. Such overt political policy was commonplace and even admired in the nineteenth century; today it is relatively rare, especially on major national and international issues. Thus, although most media owners and most editorial endorsements are Republican, news coverage of presidential campaigns has been remarkably balanced, at least since the 1960s (see p. 425). And when an owner ignores these modern standards of

Time magazine founder and longtime publisher Henry R. Luce exerted a policy control over content that few modern publishers would dare to emulate. In *Luce, His Time, Life, and Fortune,* author John Kobler paints the following picture of *Time's* coverage of Vietnam in the early 1960s:

> Operating in the area of national and foreign affairs like a state within a state, *Time* was seldom content to print news as its correspondents filed it from the scene. Such stories had to be pondered at New York headquarters in the light of Lucean policy decisions. There would be weighty conferences and staff luncheons resembling a convocation of the National Security Council by the President of the United States. Frequently, editors and executives would take quick fact-finding trips like Congressmen. . . . During a visit home in 1963 *Time's* Hong Kong correspondent, Stanley Karnow, was repeatedly asked by the big brass, "What's the alternative to Diem?" They seemed to feel that they ought not to criticize the beleaguered ruler unless they could propose a successor. *Time* should confine itself to reporting the war, said Karnow, instead of trying to make policy. He cut no ice.[14]

Luce was an opponent of "Red China." In an article on the Chinese economy, Karnow wrote that its failures resulted from "successive years of mismanagement, confusion, natural calamities and population pressures—and perhaps the sheer unwieldiness of China itself." Luce noted in the margin of the manuscript: "Too many explanations. The simple answer is Communism." Where Karnow commented that China had "exaggerated" its claims to economic progress, Luce changed the word to "lied." For "official statements," Luce substituted "official lies."

The Luce bias affected the reporting of domestic affairs as well. The week before Roosevelt's easy second win in 1936, an editor asked Luce why *Time* didn't tell its readers that Roosevelt was winning. Luce answered: "Because it might help him win."[15]

---

balance, the public and the community of journalists respond with outrage.

We have detailed three ways that mass-media owners control the news—business policy, personal policy, and political policy. The first is by far the most common. The third is probably the most dangerous. All three are important forms of media control.

SOCIAL CONTROL

In 1967, Lewis Donohew studied coverage of the Medicare issue in 17 Kentucky daily newspapers. He related coverage to three factors: community need for Medicare, community attitudes toward Medicare, and publisher attitudes toward Medicare. His findings were surprising. The correlation be-

tween the attitude of the publisher and the kind of coverage was very high (.73), while the other two factors did not correlate significantly with coverage. In other words, newspapers whose publishers favored Medicare gave the issue favorable treatment and plenty of it—regardless of community attitudes or community needs. Papers with publishers opposed to Medicare, on the other hand, accorded it much less space and handled it much more critically.[16]

The important point here is that Donohew found almost no evidence of overt publisher influence on Medicare coverage. Apparently the Kentucky reporters and editors knew without being told what sort of news play would be most pleasing to their boss. And, without any direct orders, they provided it.

In a landmark essay on "Social Control in

the Newsroom," written in 1955, sociologist Warren Breed reached essentially the same conclusion. Newspaper reporters, Breed argued, learn "by osmosis" which stories involve policy and how they should be handled. It is seldom necessary—and considered rather gauche—for an owner to issue an explicit policy manifesto.[17]

This view is supported by a disturbing experiment conducted on journalism students in 1964. The students were instructed to write news articles (based on fact sheets) for imaginary newspapers. They were told in advance what the editorial policy of "their paper" was toward that particular issue. In the overwhelming majority of cases, the students voluntarily biased their article in the direction of the paper's policy. Students whose own beliefs were farthest from policy made the greatest effort to go along. Those who agreed with the newspaper policy were actually more likely to be fair to the anti-policy view than those who were themselves anti-policy. On the other hand, business students with no training in journalism tended to be much less influenced by the policies of their imaginary publishers.[18]

The more you think about this study the more frightening it is. These were journalism students; today many of them are probably working journalists. Without the slightest hesitation, and largely without noticing what they were doing, they slanted the news the way they thought their employer wanted it slanted. If most reporters are like the subjects in this experiment, then there is really no need for owners to be crass about policy. All they have to do is let it be known how they like their news—and that's how they'll get it.

UNANIMITY

Suppose there are two independent newspapers in a city, and both publishers have a lot to say about how the news is covered. This is a bad enough situation even if the publishers are enemies. But suppose they're friends, suppose they play tennis together every weekend at the club, suppose they agree on almost every issue. Then the situation becomes much more dangerous.

It is a fact of life that mass-media owners are businessmen. Most of the important ones are, by definition, big businessmen. They are overwhelmingly white, upper-middle-class, urban males. Whether high-level corporate executives or self-made entrepreneurs, they inevitably share many of the same attitudes and opinions. To the extent that they influence news coverage, they are likely to influence it in the same direction.

Look at the three sorts of policy we have discussed—business, personal, and political. Media owners are all in the same business, dependent upon the same advertisers. So their business policies are similar. Media owners move in the same circles, with the same kinds of likes and dislikes and the same kinds of friends. So their personal policies are similar. Media owners share the same conservative, capitalistic political orientation. So their political policies are similar. This phenomenon has sometimes been called "country-club journalism."

The influence of policy, in other words, may be a consistent bias in the media—not just in one newspaper here and another TV station there, but in nearly every newspaper and nearly every TV station everywhere.

It is hard to find two mass-media owners today as different from each other as, say, Horace Greeley and Joseph Medill. It is just as hard to find two owners as intimately involved in the day-to-day production of news. Modern publishers and broadcasters intervene only occasionally—but when they do, their policy is predictably and conventionally that of Big Business.

Owners are potentially the most powerful individuals in the mass media, but most use their power sparingly. The vast majority of the impor-

tant day-to-day news decisions are made by the staff—by reporters and editors. Certain positions within media bureaucracies inevitably involve tremendous influence over news content. Many of these are relatively low-level positions, in terms of status and salary. Their occupants are often unaware of their own power.

GATEKEEPERS

Every piece of news passes through many hands between the original source and the final consumer. A corporation, say, mails a press release to a local newspaper. A *mail clerk* opens the envelope, reads the release, and decides that it should go to the financial department. An *assistant financial editor* reads it and judges that it is worth the attention of the *financial editor.* The financial editor assigns the piece to a *reporter,* who goes out in search of more information. The reporter writes the story and submits it to an *assistant city editor,* who decides that it needs more flair, and therefore turns it over to a *rewrite specialist.* The revised article is checked over by the *night editor.* He or she makes a few changes, then gives the article to a *copy editor,* who corrects the grammar, writes a headline, and sends the manuscript to the *typesetter.* A *photographer,* meanwhile, is out taking a picture to accompany the article, and the *layout editor* is busy dummying it into the newspaper. Eventually the story is okayed by the *city editor* and the *managing editor.* Then it is printed.

In this simplified example, thirteen people got a crack at a single corporate release. Most of them had a chance to change the content of the article in significant ways; at least six of them could have ruled it out of the paper entirely.

Communications researchers refer to these thirteen individuals as "gatekeepers." A gatekeeper is any person in the newsgathering process with authority to make decisions affecting the flow of information to the public. The image is precisely that of a turnstile gate-

keeper at a sporting event, who examines the qualifications of the people in line, and decides whether or not to let them in. The difference is that what gets let in or left out is not a person, but a piece of news.

Turnstile gatekeepers have very little room for flexibility. They are under orders to let in anyone with a ticket, and no one without a ticket. Occasionally mass-media gatekeepers are in the same position—the owner decides how a story is to be handled and an editor mechanically does the job. Most of the time, however, the owner remains neutral, so the editorial gatekeepers are left to make the decision. San Francisco journalist Lynn Ludlow puts it this way:

> On the surface the newspaper is organized along strict lines of authority and responsibility. The reporter is responsible to the city editor, who works under the policies of the managing editor, editor and publisher, etc. The insider knows, however, that . . . the man who actually does the work is actually setting his own strategy, tactics and policy a good deal of the time.[19]

We turn now to a few specific examples of mass-media gatekeepers.

THE TELEGRAPH EDITOR

Just about all state, national, and international news reaches the mass media via teletype, sent out by the Associated Press, United Press International, and other wire services. The job of the telegraph editor is to sort through this news and decide what to use.

It's an incredible job. A large metropolitan newspaper may subscribe to as many as 25 wires (including specialized ones like business news and weather). Out of maybe 2,500 separate news items a day, the metro telegraph editor must pick out 200 or so for use in the paper. Working pretty much alone, the telegraph editor must consider questions like: Did we have something about this in the paper yesterday? Is our competition using anything on it? Are we likely to get a better story later in the day, in time for our deadline? Is the story too narrow or technical to interest our readers? Does it need checking for a local angle? Are more important stories likely to come in later? Even if the story is good, do I have room for it?

On the basis of the answers to these questions, the telegraph editor either edits the wire copy for publication or tosses it into a giant wastebasket that waits beside his or her desk. Throughout the day, this editor is busy comparing, figuring, squeezing, and discarding—in short, gatekeeping.

In 1949 researcher David Manning White spent a week with the telegraph editor of a small Midwestern daily newspaper. The editor received a total of 11,910 column inches of copy from three wire services. He was able to use only 1,297 column inches, less than 11 percent. Exactly 1,333 stories were not used. Just under half of them, White reported, were discarded solely because of lack of space. Many of the rest were eliminated because the editor chose to print the same item from another wire service.[20]

Seventeen years later, in 1966, Paul Snider duplicated the White study, using the same telegraph editor. In the intervening time the paper had merged with its opposition and cut down to one wire service. (This is unusual; most newspapers get more wire copy than ever before.) As a result, the editor had only 1,971 column inches available during a five-day period. That was more than enough —he used only 631 inches, less than a third of the total.[21]

Telegraph editors have no universal standards or criteria to apply in deciding which wire stories to use. They invent their own— and each editor makes a different choice. Consider a 1959 study of wire copy in six small Michigan newspapers.[22] During a typical week, 764 wire stories appeared in at least one of the six papers. Only eight stories appeared in all six, and only four were on the front pages of all six. The total number of wire articles used ranged from 122 to 385; the number on the front page ranged from 45 to 105. One newspaper printed almost no international stories; another ran nearly as many foreign datelines as domestic ones. Every newspaper included at least a few articles that none of the other five bothered with.

Clearly, then, the telegraph editor is a gatekeeper of tremendous importance. Working under deadline pressure with little time for careful thought, each telegraph editor determines almost entirely what that paper will publish about the world beyond its own city limits.

OTHER MEDIA GATEKEEPERS

The telegraph editor is only one of dozens of mass-media gatekeepers. An entire book could be filled with gatekeeper studies of the various media. In the pages that follow we will discuss only a few of the more important or less obvious examples.

1. The Wire-Service Editor. Telegraph editors have plenty of news to choose from— but there is lots more they never see. Only a fraction of the stories prepared by AP and UPI reporters are put on the national wire each day. Every article must pass through a succession of local and regional wire-service editors, who decide whether it is important enough to teletype. Any one of these editors can kill the story.

In 1948 the Mississippi state legislature approved the creation of the Mississippi Bureau of Investigation, a special police force with wide discretionary powers. The AP and UPI Southern regional editors decided it was a minor story, so they kept it off the national wires. Press critic A. J. Liebling read about it in a New Orleans newspaper, and disagreed. Liebling's *New Yorker* articles on the M.B.I. started a national controversy. Only then did the wire services carry the story outside the South.[23]

2. The Reporter. No matter how many gatekeepers get their hands on a news item before it reaches the public, the one who influences that item most is the reporter. The reporter decides whom to interview and what questions to ask, where and how to cover an event, which facts to include and which to leave out. Editors can kill the story or cut it to ribbons, but only occasionally do they know enough to add or correct anything. The way a reporter sees an event is almost certain to be the way that event is described by his or her newspaper, magazine, or broadcast station.

But no two reporters see the same event in the same way. Most journalists try hard for objectivity, but they know before they start that they are doomed to failure. It is a fundamental law of psychology that people perceive the same stimulus in different ways, depending on their own attitudes, interests, and biases. If you support a political candidate, your estimate of the crowd at the rally will be larger than the estimates of opponents. If you disapprove of a war, you will see war crimes in actions that less critical observers view as unfortunate accidents. If you distrust college students, you will miss the evidence of legitimate grievances behind campus rebellions. Conscientious reporters do what they can to control these influences—but inevitably their opinions and feelings affect what they write.

3. The Headline Writer. The people who write headlines for newspaper articles tend to be hurried, harried, and often careless. Yet many readers never get further than the headline.

Even those readers who plow through an entire article are greatly influenced by its headline. In 1953, Percy Tannenbaum planted a story about an imaginary murder trial in the *Daily Iowan,* a student newspaper. Tannenbaum used three different headlines. "Admits Ownership of Frat Murder Weapon" was intended to imply that the defendant was guilty. "Many Had Access to Frat Murder Weapon" seemed to imply innocence. And "Approach Final Stage in Frat Murder Trial" was neutral. Each reader saw only one headline, followed by the identical article in every case.

Tannenbaum then asked a sample of students whether they thought the defendant was guilty or innocent. This was their response:

	Guilty	Inno-cent	No Opinion	Total
Guilty headline	44	20	65	129
Innocent headline	29	38	65	132
Neutral headline	35	25	77	137

In all three groups, more people chose the "no opinion" answer then either of the other two. However, among the three groups, the "innocent headline" group was most inclined to feel that the defendant was innocent. And the "guilty headline" group was most inclined to feel he was guilty. Tannenbaum concluded that the headline "has a most definite effect on the interpretation of a story." He added: "The headline writer who recognizes the potentialities of the headline, and who is aware of the reading habits of the public, is certainly in a position to exert a significant influence upon the opinions of his audience."[24]

4. The Assignment Editor. Every mass medium has someone whose job it is to tell the reporters what stories to cover. Whatever the title, the person who makes the assignments is an important gatekeeper. Nothing gets covered unless the assignment editor asks someone to cover it.

William Whitworth offers this description of assignment editor Robert Northshield's role in preparing for the evening NBC network newscast:

Assignments have been made the day before, by Northshield or by the show's producer, Lester Crystal. Correspondents are at work in

LEADING LEADS

Next to the headline, the lead of a news story—the first paragraph or two—is by far the most important part. Few readers get any further. The following excerpts all refer to an anti-war march on the Pentagon in October, 1967. Regardless of the articles that followed, these passages would create very different impressions of that event.

1. *Chicago Tribune,* October 22, 1967, page 1:

HURL BACK PENTAGON MOB

An estimated 4,000 to 5,000 anti-war demonstrators settled down in front of the Pentagon this evening, apparently planning to spend the night.

They were all that were left of an estimated 30,000 to 35,000 protestors who earlier in the day stormed the Pentagon and were hurled back by armed soldiers and club swinging United States marshals. They came close to breaking the doors they considered a symbol of militarism.

2. *Washington Post,* October 22, 1967, page 1:

55,000 RALLY AGAINST WAR;
GIs REPEL PENTAGON CHARGE

More than 55,000 persons demonstrated here against the war in Vietnam yesterday in what started out as a peaceful, youthful rally but erupted into violence at the Pentagon late in the day.

At one point, a surging band of about 20 demonstrators rushed into the Pentagon, only to be thrown out by armed troops.

Dozens of youthful demonstrators were arrested during two brief but angry melees at the Pentagon's Mall Entrance. Several thousand demonstrators surged across boundaries that the Government had prescribed.

3. *Time* magazine, October 27, 1967, page 23:

THE BANNERS OF DISSENT

[Starts with a physical and historical sketch of the Pentagon.] Against that physically and functionally immovable object last week surged a self-proclaimed irresistible force of 35,000 ranting, chanting protestors who are immutably opposed to the U.S. commitment in Vietnam. By the time the demonstration had ended, more than 425 irresistibles had been arrested, 13 more had been injured, and the Pentagon had remained immobile. Within the tide of dissenters swarmed all the elements of American dissent in 1967: hard-eyed revolutionaries and skylarking hippies; ersatz motorcycle gangs and all-too-real college professors; housewives, ministers, and authors; Black Nationalists in African garb—but no real African nationalists; nonviolent pacifists and nonpacific advocates of violence—some of them anti-anti-warriors and American Nazis spoiling for a fight.

4. *London Times,* October 23, 1967, p. 4.

BESIEGE THE PENTAGON

The anti-war demonstration continued outside the Pentagon and elsewhere today after a night of disorder and some violence. About 200 demonstrators marched on the White House this morning, but a strong police guard kept them at a distance.

The vast Defense Department building, which stands on 583 acres of lawn and car parks, was penetrated briefly yesterday by a few dozen youngsters. United States marshals, with clubs swinging, quickly turned their attack into a retreat.

other cities and other countries, and are in touch with Northshield and Crystal off and on all day. . . .

By noon, Northshield has seen some film, discussed story ideas with his producer and with the Washington staff, spoken to a correspondent or two, and read as much wire copy as possible. These chores will occupy him throughout the day. . . . Northshield will begin trying to make a rundown—a list of the stories that will be used on the program, with an estimate of the time to be allotted to each—between three-thirty and four. Perhaps six or eight of these stories will be filmed or taped reports. . . . The twenty or so other stories will be briefer. . . . Shortly before five, Crystal holds a story conference with the writers and gives them their assignments. Each man's is likely to be brief—anywhere from thirty seconds to three minutes of copy.[25]

Assignment editors in network television are seasoned professionals. In radio and local TV, however, they are likely to be comparative newcomers. They receive much lower pay than on-the-air reporters, yet they—not the reporters—determine which stories are to be covered.

5. The Film Editor. The television film editor (or the radio tape editor) takes twenty minutes of an interview or press conference and cuts it down to a minute or less. The film editor's job is to pick the most important, pithy, memorable, and interesting statements of the news source—without distorting the meaning. This is an extremely difficult and vital task. Often it is performed by a trainee fresh out of college.

6. Other Media. When the editors of a small newspaper are unsure how to report a national story, they may well check to see what the big city papers did with it. When a telegraph editor is swamped with copy, he or she looks to see what's on the wire-service list of the day's most important stories. When

a radio disc jockey sits down to prepare the station's hourly five-minute news report, local stories are quietly borrowed from the front page of the nearest newspaper. In these and other ways, the larger and more established news media serve as gatekeepers of a sort for the smaller and less established ones.

Sometimes small media wind up as gatekeepers for the large ones. The *New England Journal of Medicine* is hardly a mass magazine, but it is one of the world's most influential medical publications. The *Journal* receives around 4,000 research papers a year, of which only 10 to 15 percent make it through the review process and into print. By long-standing rule the *Journal* refuses to publish studies whose results have already been announced to the mass media. This policy guarantees that most researchers will stay silent until the medical profession has had a chance to look at their work.[26] It also guarantees that the *New England Journal of Medicine* will continue to be must reading for the nation's medical journalists, who find many newsworthy scoops on its pages.

7. The Censor. The three television networks employ whole departments of gatekeepers with titles like program practices reviewer and standards editor who must screen every show and commercial in advance and approve it for broadcast. TV censors generally apply well-established criteria, such as the Television Code of the National Association of Broadcasters—but sometimes they seem to be making up the rules as they go along.

For example, a Muriel cigar commercial featuring a slinky young woman prowling through a men's locker room was judged acceptable by ABC and NBC, but CBS rejected it as "too sexy."[27] The CBS censors were also offended when the presidential character in its Watergate movie, "Blind Ambition," used "Jesus Christ" in vain, while ABC's censors were unmoved by Woody Allen's use of the same phrase in "Annie Hall." Not that CBS is always the most cautious network. It readily approved the showing of "Flesh and Blood," a TV movie featuring an incestuous relationship between a boxer and his mother.[28]

Local stations and some major metropolitan newspapers employ censors of their own —with similarly unpredictable results. In 1978, for example, the director of broadcast standards at WXYZ in Detroit refused to carry a commercial for "Miss Margarita's Way," a one-woman show starring Estelle Parsons. The commercial had won a prestigious Clio Award the year before, but as far as WXYZ was concerned it was "lewd and sexually suggestive."[29]

8. The Syndicator. Syndicators are companies that purchase features and columns to sell to newspapers, and old network reruns to sell to TV stations. Their main gatekeeping power, of course, is deciding what properties to handle.

But they have other powers. Syndicated reruns, for example, have to be cut by as much as three minutes so that local stations that buy the shows can add extra commercials. Usually the dullest three minutes are the ones to go. In 1977, Viacom Enterprises, a major syndicator, decided to delete the most violent sequences instead, making programs like "Hawaii Five-O" and "The Rookies" more acceptable for family viewing hours.[30]

There are many other gatekeepers in the mass media—from the writer who handles photo captions to the TV camera operator who decides where to point the lens, from the librarian who supplies background for stories to the rewrite specialist who adds sparkle to dreary copy. All of them have two things in common. First, they exercise a tremendous influence over the flow of information to the public. And second, they are largely unaware of their power. From time to time a publisher consciously sets policy. Working journalists unconsciously set policy minute by minute.

UNANIMITY AGAIN

The dangerous thing about mass-media owners is that they are all so much alike. Can the same charge be leveled against media gatekeepers? At least one observer, former Vice President Spiro Agnew, thinks it can:

> A small group of men, numbering perhaps no more than a dozen "anchormen," commentators and executive producers, settle upon the 20 minutes or so of film and commentary that is to reach the public. . . .
>
> We do know that, to a man, these commentators and producers live and work in the geographical and intellectual confines of Washington, D.C., or New York City—the latter of which James Reston terms the "most unrepresentative community in the entire United States." . . . We can deduce that these men thus read the same newspapers, and draw their political and social views from the same sources. . . .
>
> The upshot of all this controversy is that a narrow and distorted picture of America often emerges from the televised news. . . .[31]

Though Agnew's comments here concentrated on television, he made it clear elsewhere that he feels the same way about most newspaper reporters. Media owners, we have charged, tend to be conservatives. Working journalists, Agnew replies, tend to be liberals. Both statements are overgeneralizations, but both are more true than false.

A detailed study of 1300 working journalists, published in 1976, found that most reporters are young, white males from urban, middle-class backgrounds. Forty percent of the staffers viewed themselves as left of center. The same figure for their editors and executives was only 28 percent.[32] It would undoubtedly be lower still for their publishers and station managers.

The above figures intentionally left out reporters and editors for the networks and elite newspapers (*New York Times, Wash-*

ington Post, etc.), because the study found that they were too liberal to be representative. In a 1981 study, Stephen Hess reported that many Washington journalists considered themselves more conservative than their reputations—yet they overwhelmingly agreed that the Washington press corps leans more to the left than to the right.[33] Of course these are precisely the reporters who dominate the tone of national news coverage, especially the political coverage that Agnew was complaining about.

Thus, when George Romney was running for the Republican presidential nomination in 1968, many of the country's most influential political reporters refused to take his candidacy seriously. David S. Broder comments: "I often thought . . . as I saw Romney during his Presidential campaign, surrounded by our circle—men a generation younger than he, many of us with cigarettes in our mouths, drinks in our hands, and cynicism in our hearts—that he must have felt as helpless with us as I would feel if my fate or future as a journalist were being decided by a committee of Romney's colleagues among the elders of the Mormon Church."[34] Broder offers this description of the leading political reporters in Washington:

> Not only is the group small, but its characteristics make it a highly atypical group of Americans. Its members are all Easterners, by residence if not by birth. They are all college graduates. They all enjoy, despite the low-paying reputation of newspapers, incomes well over the national median. Not one of them is a Negro. Only two are women. More of them vote Democratic and fewer of them regularly attend church, I would guess, than in a random sample of the population. None is under 30 and few, except for the columnists, are over 45. . . . I think I have said enough to indicate that they—or we, I should say—represent a narrow and rather peculiar slice of this society.[35]

In his book *The Boys on the Bus,* author Timothy Crouse offers numerous examples of the press corps' fundamental dislike for Nixon and identification with McGovern during the 1972 campaign.[36] Yet when McGovern's running-mate, Thomas Eagleton, was found to have a history of mental disorder, reporters were able to sweep aside their emotional and ideological ties. They wrote the story with enough accuracy and enthusiasm that it may well have played a role in Nixon's large victory.

That is the crucial difference between the bias of reporters and the bias of media owners. Working journalists are presumably trained to overcome their biases and present as balanced and objective a picture of the news as possible. And working journalists are indiscriminately enthusiastic about a big story, no matter whom it helps or hurts. Most mass-media owners have no such training, and no such enthusiasm. When publishers walk into their newsrooms, they generally do so for the express purpose of coloring the news to suit their taste. The gatekeepers who belong in that newsroom, on the other hand, are striving—with some success—not to color the news at all.

Sixty years ago political scientist Curtice N. Hitchcock wrote a review of Upton Sinclair's newspaper critique, *The Brass Check.* In his review, Hitchcock made the following statement:

> Granted an adequate standard of professional journalism—a body of highly trained men competent to weigh news in terms of social significance and to present it adequately—the problem of control becomes one of turning the control over to them.[37]

Journalism has a long way to go yet before it satisfies Hitchcock's premise. But at least it is moving in that direction.

In the final analysis, the difference between owners and gatekeepers is this: Owners set policy (occasionally) in order to achieve their own business, personal, and political goals. Gatekeepers influence the news (constantly) despite their honest efforts to remain objective.

Notes

1 David R. Bowers, "A Report on Activity by Publishers in Directing Newsroom Decisions," *Journalism Quarterly*, Spring, 1967, pp. 44-49.

2 "Confessions of a Managing Editor," *Collier's*, October 28, 1911, p. 19.

3 Jerry Walker, "ASNE Poll Finds Group Editors Have Freedom," *Editor & Publisher*, March 29, 1980, pp. 7, 10, 32.

4 Edward W. Barrett, "Books" (Review of *Annenberg*, Gaeton Fonzi), *Columbia Journalism Review*, Spring, 1970, p. 56.

5 United Press International (file #276A), Hartford, Conn., March 2, 1974.

6 *The Home News*, New Brunswick, N.J., July 12, 1979, p. 3.

7 Brent Stutzman, "Television's 'Soap' Controversy," Freedom of Information Center Report No. 387, School of Journalism, University of Missouri, Columbia, Mo., March, 1978.

8 David Anderson, "Blackout in Lansing," *Columbia Journalism Review*, March/April, 1974, pp. 27-28.

9 "He Won't Be Eaten Alive," *Time*, May 12, 1980, p. 18.

10 Bernard Weinraub, "Loeb Shrugs Off Criticism of His Newspaper Attacks," *New York Times*, February 11, 1980.

11 Carey Winfrey, "50 of 60 Reporters on Post Protest 'Slanted' Coverage of Mayor's Race," *New York Times*, October 5, 1977.

12 "2 Editors Dismissed in Articles Dispute," *New York Times*, June 26, 1977.

13 John L. Hulteng, "The Crux of Panax: The Performance or the Power?" *Quill*, October, 1977, p. 24.

14 John Kobler, *Luce, His Time, Life, and Fortune* (Garden City, N.Y.: Doubleday & Co., 1968), pp. 6-7.

15 *Ibid.*, pp. 151, 177.

16 Lewis Donohew, "Newspaper Gatekeepers and Forces in the News Channel," *Public Opinion Quarterly*, Spring, 1967, pp. 62-66.

17 Warren Breed, "Social Control in the News Room," in *Mass Communications*, ed. Wilbur Schramm (Urbana, Ill.: University of Illinois Press, 1960), p. 182.

18 Jean S. Kerrick, "Balance and the Writer's Attitude in News Stories and Editorials," *Journalism Quarterly*, Spring, 1964, pp. 207-15.

19 Personal communication from Lynn Ludlow of the *San Francisco Examiner* to David M. Rubin, August, 1969.

20 David Manning White, "The 'Gate Keeper': A Case Study in the Selection of News," *Journalism Quarterly*, Autumn, 1950, p. 387.

21 Paul B. Snider, " 'Mr. Gates' Revisited: A 1966 Version of the 1949 Case Study," *Journalism Quarterly*, Autumn, 1967, p. 423.

22 Guido H. Stempel, III, "Uniformity of Wire Content of Six Michigan Dailies," *Journalism Quarterly*, Winter, 1959, p. 48.

23 A. J. Liebling, *The Press* (New York: Ballantine Books, 1961), pp. 126-43.

24 Percy H. Tannenbaum, "The Effect of Headlines on the Interpretation of News Stories," *Journalism Quarterly*, Spring, 1953, pp. 189-97.

25 William Whitworth, "An Accident of Casting," *New Yorker*, August 3, 1968, pp. 48-50.

26 "The Ingelfinger Rule," *Time*, March 3, 1980.

27 John E. Cooney, "Network Censors Screen Commercials for Taste and Accuracy, Giving Admen Severe Headaches," *Wall Street Journal*, October 13, 1978, p. 48.

28 Peter J. Boyer, "Paying Customers Aid 'Flesh & Blood,' " *The Home News*, New Brunswick, N.J., October 10, 1979 (AP).

29 "Detroit TV Station Refuses Ad on Play," *New York Times*, December 3, 1978.

30 Les Brown, "Reruns of TV Series Being Edited to Delete Violence for Syndication," *New York Times*, February 17, 1980.

31 Address of Vice President Spiro T. Agnew before the Midwest Regional Republican Committee, Des Moines, Iowa, November 13, 1969.

32 John W. C. Johnstone, Edward J. Slawski and William W. Bowman, *The News People: A Sociological Portrait of American Journalists and Their Work* (Urbana, Ill.: University of Illinois Press, 1976).

33 Stephen Hess, *The Washington Reporters* (Washington, D.C.: The Brookings Institution, 1981).

34 David S. Broder, "Views of the Press: Political Reporters in Presidential Politics," *Washington Monthly*, February, 1969, p. 28.

35 *Ibid.*, p. 28.

36 Timothy Crouse, *The Boys on the Bus* (New York: Random House, 1972).

37 Curtice N. Hitchcock, "The Brass Check: A Study of American Journalism: By Upton Sinclair," *Journal of Political Economy*, April, 1921, pp. 343-44.

Suggested Readings

ANDERSON, DAVID, "Blackout in Lansing," *Columbia Journalism Review,* March/April, 1974.

BOWERS, DAVID R., "A Report on Activity by Publishers in Directing Newsroom Decisions," *Journalism Quarterly,* Spring, 1967.

BREED, WARREN, "Social Control in the News Room," reprinted in Wilbur Schramm, ed., *Mass Communications.* Urbana, Ill.: University of Illinois Press, 1960.

CARROLL, PATRICK, "Mutiny in Greensburg," *Columbia Journalism Review,* January/February, 1974.

FLEGEL, RUTH, and STEVE CHAFFEE, "Influences of Editors, Readers, and Personal Opinions on Reporters," *Journalism Quarterly,* Winter, 1971.

FONZI, GAETON, *Annenberg.* New York: Weybright and Talley, Inc., 1970.

GANS, HERBERT J., *Deciding What's News.* New York: Pantheon, 1979.

HESS, STEPHEN, *The Washington Reporters.* Washington, D.C.: The Brookings Institution, 1981.

HULTENG, JOHN L., "The Crux of Panax: The Performance or the Power?" *The Quill,* October, 1977.

JOHNSTONE, JOHN W. C., EDWARD J. SLAWSKI, and WILLIAM W. BOWMAN, *The News People: A Sociological Portrait of American Journalists and Their Work.* Urbana, Ill.: University of Illinois Press, 1976.

KOBLER, JOHN, *Luce, His Time, Life, and Fortune.* New York: Doubleday & Co., Inc., 1968.

SILVERBERG, JAY, "Big Gamble in Florida," *The Quill,* October, 1978.

STARK, RODNEY W., "Policy and the Pros: An Organizational Analysis of a Metropolitan Newspaper," *Berkeley Journal of Sociology,* Spring, 1962.

STUTZMAN, BRENT, "Television's 'Soap' Controversy," Freedom of Information Center Report No. 387, School of Journalism, University of Missouri at Columbia, March, 1978.

WHITE, DAVID MANNING, "The 'Gate Keeper': A Case Study in the Selection of News," *Journalism Quarterly,* Fall, 1950.

WITCOVER, JULES, "The Indiana Primary and the Indianapolis Newspaper—A Report in Detail," *Columbia Journalism Review,* Summer, 1968.

Chapter 4
Monopoly Control

Like many other industries in the United States, the American mass media are increasingly dominated by monopolies. But unlike other industries, the media are a crucial source of information and ideas. The growth of local monopolies (cross-media ownerships and joint operating agreements) and national monopolies (chains, networks, and conglomerates) has drastically reduced the diversity of media voices. This concentration of power in the hands of a few media "barons" represents a potential threat to our First Amendment freedoms unanticipated by the Founding Fathers.

Freedom of the press is predicated on the belief that if people have access to a wide range of opinions and information, they will make intelligent decisions. Supreme Court Justice Oliver Wendell Holmes put it this way: "The best test of truth is the power of the thought to get itself accepted in the competition of the market."[1] It follows that the government should not be permitted to regulate the media. Let each paper and station cover the news however it likes, the theory goes, and the people will be able to figure out who's right and who's wrong.

The theory works only so long as Holmes' "market" remains competitive. The fewer the number of independent media outlets in a given location, the weaker the case for freedom becomes. Consider an extreme example. If there were only one newspaper publisher in the entire United States, it would obviously be very dangerous to leave that publisher free to decide how to cover the news. How could the people choose right from wrong if they had only one source of information? Every media combination brings us that much closer to this "one source" situation.

Not that the evidence of harm from media monopolies is very compelling, as we shall see in the second half of this chapter. Individual abuses of monopoly power are easy enough to find, but overall monopoly media seem little different from independently owned media in quality or diversity of content. Opponents must therefore rely on theory and metaphor. Monopolies, they say, are eating away at the First Amendment the way termites eat away at a house—the damage is subtle at first, but the structure is weakening day by day. Today's monopolists may maintain the quality of their outlets and permit them to take differing ideological positions. But unfettered by competition, tomorrow's monopolists may not. Thus, they conclude, all media combinations threaten freedom and diversity of expression.

Media combinations come in many forms, but there are four major varieties:

1. *Chains and networks*—two or more outlets in the same medium (television, newspapers, or whatever), usually in different cities, are owned or controlled by the same person or group.

2. *Cross-media ownership*—two or more outlets in different media, often in the same city, are owned by the same person or group.

3. *Joint operating agreements*—two separately owned newspapers in the same city arrange to combine certain operations, such as printing and advertising, and to split the profits.

4. *Conglomerates*—companies that are not primarily in the communications business own or are owned by mass-media outlets.

We will discuss each briefly in turn.

CHAINS AND NETWORKS

At the end of 1979, there were 1,763 daily newspapers in the United States, with a total circulation of 60.5 million. Chains owned 1,115 of the papers, with a circulation of 45.7 million. A little arithmetic reveals that 63 percent of the papers and 74 percent of the circulation were accounted for by chains.[2]

These were all-time high figures, but they are doubtless higher today. In 1979 alone, 53 dailies changed hands; 48 of them were purchased by chains.[3] In some states more than 80 percent of the newspapers are now chain-owned.

Most newspaper chains consist of only three or four papers—but some are massive. Thirteen chains have combined circulations of more than a million readers each. And as independent newspapers that are for sale become harder to find, the big action in the

1980s will be the purchase of small chains by larger ones. The circulation leader as of 1980 was Knight-Ridder (the result of the 1974 merger of the Knight and Ridder chains), with 3.7 million weekday readers of 34 papers. Tops in total number of outlets was Gannett, with 80 papers (up from 52 in 1973) and 3.4 million readers.[4]

Broadcasting chains are almost as old as broadcasting. But they are limited in size by the Federal Communications Commission, which sets a maximum for each owner of seven television stations, seven AM radio stations, and seven FM radio stations. In 1980 there were 461 companies in the U.S., Canada, and Puerto Rico that owned more than one TV station or more than two radio stations. Among the largest were Metromedia, Westinghouse, Storer, CBS, NBC, and ABC. Such chain ownership is a far bigger problem for television than for radio, because there are nine times as many radio as TV stations in the U.S.

Unburdened by FCC limits, cable television chains are much larger than over-the-air broadcast chains. As of 1980, Teleprompter and American Television and Communications led the pack, each with more than a hundred cable systems operating or under construction. In all, there were 250 cable operators with more than one system.[5]

The chief danger of media chains is, of course, the power they put in the hands of a single owner to manipulate public opinion in scores of cities. As we shall see, most chain owners do not use this power for ideological purposes. The homogeneity they strive for has more to do with profits than with political power. The blandness of many chain-owned media is a problem in itself—but it's the risk of editorial control that most worries the opponents of media chains.

Many people think of broadcast networks as a kind of chain, but there is an important difference. The links in a broadcast chain are all owned by the same person or company, while the links in a network may be separately owned. Nonetheless, networking can

GANNETT GROWS AND GROWS AND GROWS

In 1978, the Gannett newspaper chain merged with a company called Combined Communications. It picked up Combined's two newspapers, the *Cincinnati Enquirer* and the *Oakland* (California) *Tribune*, plus seven TV stations, 13 radio stations, and the nation's largest outdoor advertising agency.[6] Rep. Morris K. Udall of Arizona called the merger "an alarming development . . . a case of a whale swallowing a whale."[7]

Even before the merger, Gannett was the nation's largest and fastest-growing newspaper chain. It usually buys papers that have no competition, in small cities like Battle Creek, Michigan and Santa Fe, New Mexico. Editorial control is left in the hands of local editors, while national headquarters sets profit targets, makes sure the books are kept properly, puts in the latest production equipment, and keeps out the unions.

A writer at the Gannett-owned *Valley News Dispatch* in Tarentum, Pa. comments: "We did lose some of the family atmosphere around here when the big guy moved in. I had my fears about casting my lot with him. But we've been given local autonomy. I think all Gannett does is look at the bottom line. Each of us is like a little gold mine. As long as the golden stuff keeps pouring out, they leave us be."[8]

And the golden stuff keeps pouring out. Under Chairman Allen Neuharth, Gannett has tripled its revenue in the past ten years, and has increased its profits every quarter since the mid-1970s. Neuharth's 1979 salary was $390,000. Not surprisingly, when asked if he fancied himself a businessman or a newspaperman, Neuharth answered "businessman."[9]

Yet there is a certain similarity to the 80 Gannett newspapers. They use a lot of syndicated and wire copy. They play up local features, sports, and photos, rather than crime or investigative reporting. News budgets are usually increased when Gannett buys a paper, but not by much. Explains Neuharth: "Basically we respond to reader studies. Whatever diet the readers want, we custom-tailor the paper for that diet."[10] This is essentially the formula of most newspaper chains. It is a formula calculated to make money safely. Gannett newspapers—and chain newspapers generally—are better than the worst independent papers, but they rarely aspire to the uniqueness of a great newspaper.

---

reduce the diversity of the media every bit as much as chains. If a network-affiliated station invariably takes most of its programming from the network, the fact that it isn't owned by the network makes very little difference to its audience.

Radio networks are not a major problem. More than two-thirds of the radio stations in the U.S.—including many powerful and profitable ones—have no network affiliation at all. And even the network affiliates do most of their own programming, relying on the nets principally for national news.

Television networks are another story. The three TV networks provide their affiliates throughout the country with much of the day's programming. And most TV stations are network affiliates. Of the 741 commercial TV stations in 1980, 241 were affiliated with ABC, 212 with NBC, and 198 with CBS. That left only 90 independent stations—mostly the less profitable UHF stations.[11] Although the FCC allows the three networks to own only seven TV stations apiece, they nonetheless control the nation's television through their affiliates. Like chains, the networks use their control for profits, not political power. Unlike chains, they are beginning to lose their monopoly as cable and pay-TV rise in popularity. But for now at least they remain the dominant force in television.

CROSS-MEDIA OWNERSHIP

Media monopolists see no special reason to confine themselves to a single medium. Most of the big ones prefer to branch out into several media. The result is a continuing upsurge in cross-media ownerships.

In 1979, for example, newspaper companies purchased 50 radio stations and 13 television stations. The *San Francisco Chronicle* bought a TV and AM radio station in Wichita, Kansas; the *Toledo* (Ohio) *Blade* bought a TV station in Lafayette, Indiana; the *Peoria* (Illinois) *Journal Star* bought an AM-FM combination in Albuquerque, New Mexico. These purchases brought the total broadcast holdings of newspaper and magazine interests to 318 AM stations, 258 FM stations, and 225 TV stations.[12] Many of the big newspaper chains, including Gannett and Newhouse, also own broadcast chains.

It works in the other direction too. Capital Cities, which started out as a broadcast chain, now owns Fairchild Publications (a magazine chain), the *Kansas City Star* and *Times,* and smaller newspapers in Texas, Michigan, Pennsylvania, and elsewhere.

Cable companies are also heavily cross-owned. Over 30 percent of all cable systems have ties with broadcast interests; 13 percent have ties with newspaper interests; and 18 percent have ties with program producers, such as movie studios.[13]

Every possible combination has been tried, and most are growing. Some major newspapers own their own feature syndicates. Several newspaper chains and broadcast networks own magazine chains, while some of the larger magazine chains own broadcast stations or newspapers. Nearly half of the major book publishing houses either own or are owned by broadcasting, newspaper, or magazine interests. Even advertising and public relations are getting into the act, with ad agencies buying up many of the large PR consulting firms. In 1978 Foote, Cone & Belding bought Carl Byoir & Associates; in 1979 Young & Rubicam bought Marsteller

Inc. and Benton & Bowles bought Manning, Selvage & Lee; in 1980 J. Walter Thompson bought Hill & Knowlton.[14] It is hard to imagine any field with more interconnections than the communications industry.

These cross-media ownerships are really no different from single-media chains—until they turn up in the same city. Then the unique danger of cross-media ownership becomes visible: its ability to dominate the media diet of a community.

At the close of the 1960s, a single owner controlled at least one television station and one newspaper in 34 of the 50 largest cities in the U.S. Overall, 94 TV stations and about 200 radio stations were owned by newspapers in the same city.[15]

The FCC became worried about these one-city monopolies in the early 1970s, and in 1975 it ruled that no further newspaper-broadcast combinations in the same community would be approved. It even ordered a handful of such combinations to split up, in small communities like Watertown, N.Y. and Bluefield, W. Va., where there was little or no media competition from other owners (see pp. 130-32). Even after the ordered divestitures are completed, cities that will be left with only one newspaper and one radio station under common ownership will include Santa Cruz, Calif.; Coeur D'Alene, Ida.; Alliance, Ohio; Gettysburg, Pa.; Stamford, Conn.; and Bethlehem, Pa. Cities with just one newspaper and one TV station under the same owner will include Fort Smith, Ark.; Akron, Ohio; and Cheyenne, Wyo. Local news management in these cities will be a powerful threat indeed.

And all the big-city cross-ownerships will survive unscathed. Examples of newspaper-television combinations untouched by the decision include San Francisco, where the *Chronicle* owns KRON; Atlanta, where the *Journal* and *Constitution* own WSB; Chicago, where the *Tribune* owns WGN and the *Sun-Times* owns WFLD; Louisville, where the *Courier-Journal* and *Times* own WHAS; Baltimore, where the *Sun* owns

WMAR and the *News-American* owns WBAL; St. Louis, where the *Post-Dispatch* owns KSD and the *Globe-Democrat* owns KTVI; and New York, where the *Daily News* owns WPIX.[16] Most of the TV stations in these cities that are *not* owned by local newspapers are owned instead by chains or networks. In the top 20 markets, in fact, there are a total of 74 commercial VHF stations. All but seven of them are owned by media combinations of one sort or another.

JOINT OPERATING AGREEMENTS

Albuquerque, New Mexico, has only two newspapers, the morning *Journal* and the afternoon *Tribune*. In 1933 the two papers negotiated, in secret, the first newspaper joint operating agreement. They arranged to do all their printing in one plant, and to employ a single business office, circulation department, and advertising department. Commercial expenses were split down the middle. At the end of each year the profits were to be divided according to a set ratio, regardless of either paper's circulation or advertising revenue.

As of 1980, newspapers in twenty-four cities had established joint operating agreements. In the following list, the combinations that involve chain-owned newspapers as well are marked with a bullet:

- *Albuquerque Journal* and *Tribune*
- *Birmingham Post-Herald* and *News*
- *Bristol Herald-Courier* and *Virginia-Tennessean*
- *Charleston Gazette* and *Daily Mail*
  Chattanooga Times and *News-Free Press*
- *Cincinnati Enquirer* and *Post*
- *Columbus Citizen-Journal* and *Dispatch*
- *El Paso Times* and *Herald-Post*
- *Evansville Courier* and *Press*
- *Fort Wayne Journal-Gazette* and *News-Sentinel*
- *Honolulu Advertiser* and *Star-Bulletin*
- *Knoxville Journal* and *News-Sentinel*

- *Lincoln Star* and *Journal*
- *Madison State Journal* and *Capital Times*
- *Miami Herald* and *News*
- *Nashville Tennessean* and *Banner*
  Oil City-Franklin Derrick and *News-Herald*
- *Pittsburgh Post-Gazette* and *Press*
- *St. Louis Globe-Democrat* and *Post-Dispatch*
- *Salt Lake City Tribune* and *Deseret-News*
- *San Francisco Chronicle* and *Examiner*
- *Shreveport Times* and *Journal*
- *Tucson Arizona Star* and *Citizen*
  Tulsa World and *Tribune*.

Some of the advantages of the joint operating agreement are obvious: It reduces the cost of advertising sales, printing, and distribution. As long as the agreement is confined to these points it is harmless, even helpful. But many newspapers have used joint operating agreements as an excuse for manipulating advertising rates in such a way that no third newspaper can possibly develop. And some papers may illegally extend their cooperation to include news and editorials as well as advertising and circulation, posing a clear threat to media diversity.

CONGLOMERATES

A conglomerate is a company that operates in a number of different and unrelated markets. Media conglomerates sometimes start as media companies and then diversify, but more often they start in some other field and then broaden into the media. Here are a few examples:

- RCA manufactures radar, TV sets, and other electronic equipment; owns Banquet Frozen Foods, Hertz Rent-a-Car, and Mar-Jon Carpet Mills; and through its subsidiary NBC operates 13 broadcast stations and a broadcast network.
- Gulf & Western Industries owns Madison Square Garden, Beautyrest mattresses, Dutch Masters cigars, Schrafft candies, Cole swimsuits, and many other companies from tourist resorts

to cement manufacturers. It also owns Paramount Pictures, Paramount Television, and the Simon & Schuster book publishing house.

- Westinghouse makes circuit breakers, transformers, nuclear power plants, refrigerators, and electric ranges—and owns chains of broadcast stations and cable systems.

The special danger of media conglomerates is that they may use their communication outlets to advance the interests of their other operations. In 1979, for example, American Express tried to buy McGraw-Hill, Inc. American Express specializes in credit cards, traveler's checks, and insurance; McGraw-Hill publishes *Business Week* and a number of more specialized business magazines. Naturally, McGraw-Hill writers often have occasion to cover American Express activities.

Business Week's editor-in-chief, Lewis H. Young, circulated a memorandum outlining five reasons for his opposition to the takeover. His concerns were:

That American Express would taboo certain story subjects, such as the troubles in the entertainment credit card business or problems in the casualty insurance industry, because it had major business activity in them.

That, if American Express allowed coverage of such subjects, our readers wouldn't believe what we published, thinking it was biased in favor of the owner of the magazine.

MEDIA INTERLOCKS

A watered-down version of the conglomerate is the interlocking directorate, where top executives or directors of Corporation X also sit on the board of directors of Corporation Y—putting them in an ideal spot to brief each company on the viewpoint of the other. The American corporate system is an intricate network of such interlocks, and media corporations are no exception. The Ford Motor Company, for example, shares directors with the *New York Times*, the *Washington Post*, and the *Los Angeles Times*. All three newspapers have other interlocks with major American corporations; the *Los Angeles Times* has more than two dozen of them.[17]

Media interlocks always involve a potential conflict of interest—but sometimes the media surmount the problem. General Public Utilities, which owns the Three Mile Island nuclear power plant, shares an interlock with Knight-Ridder, which owns the *Philadelphia Inquirer*—yet the *Inquirer* won a Pulitzer Prize for its very tough coverage of the 1979 Three Mile Island accident.

On the other hand, the principal owner of the *Los Angeles Times*, Otis Chandler, served on the board of GeoTek, an oil-drilling company that came under SEC investigation in 1971. The *Times* did not cover the company's troubles until the *Wall Street Journal* did a piece on them. Even then, *Times* media critic David Shaw wrote that the paper's coverage of GeoTek "would have been far more aggressive" if Chandler hadn't been on the GeoTek board.[18]

In Minneapolis, similarly, *Star* and *Tribune* publisher Donald R. Dwight sits on the board of Pillsbury, a company whose activities are often covered by the papers. Lynda McDonnell, a *Tribune* business and labor writer, comments: "The interlock embarrasses me. You have his directorship in the back of your mind if you have to write something about Pillsbury. You probably are more cautious; you probably are going to think twice. I have no doubt that if I write a critical article, Dwight will get a call from Pillsbury because he's a director there."[19]

That American Express wouldn't support the editors after they had written unpopular ideas or critical stories that unleashed corporate or government complaints.

That American Express would use the editorial columns of the magazine to sell its other products and services or to curry favor with government officials to aid its international businesses.

That American Express, because of its financial orientation, wouldn't make the financial resources available for the staff to do the aggressive and comprehensive reporting job our readers expect.[20]

The McGraw-Hill board turned down the American Express offer.

WHY MEDIA CONCENTRATION?

Increasing monopoly control is not, of course, a phenomenon unique to the mass media. Most industries in the U.S. are moving in the same direction. Yet there are several reasons why media monopolies in particular have grown so phenomenally in recent decades.

First and probably most important is the perception that owning a mass medium is just a business, not a "calling" as it was for many newspaper publishers in the eighteenth and nineteenth centuries. When a publisher decides that earning money is more important than advocating a viewpoint, he or she naturally eliminates most of the ideological advocacy from the paper, and cares very little about the advocacy that is left. There is then no reason not to merge with another paper. One publisher is bought out and retires with a tidy profit. The other publisher gains a monopoly and thus increases the paper's profit. And the reader seldom notices the difference.

Second, media properties are extraordinarily profitable. It is difficult for a newspaper with a morning or evening monopoly in its community or a TV station with a network affiliation to avoid making money.

Owners not particularly interested in the quality of the product can make even more money by cutting corners—without risking a customer rebellion. The average business sells for six or seven times its annual earnings—but some newspapers have been going for as much as 50 times earnings, and broadcast stations are not far behind. In 1980, a California chain bought the *Delta Democrat Times* in Mississippi for more than $16 million—about $1,000 per subscriber.[21]

If you want to own a newspaper or broadcast station, it's a lot easier and safer to buy one than to start one from scratch. This is the third reason for the growth of media monopolies. The number of daily newspapers in the U.S. was static throughout the 1970s at roughly 1,760. Anyone who wants to can start a new paper, but the start-up costs are monumental and the chances of success against an existing competitor are slim. And in broadcasting you can't even start a station unless there's an unlicensed spot available on the dial. The only spots available, of course, are the ones that seem unlikely to earn a profit. Other media, like magazines and cable systems, are still expanding, but in the newspaper and broadcast businesses merger is pretty much the only way to grow.

A fourth reason for the growth of media monopolies is the financial pressure on privately owned media. Many family-owned newspapers, for example, sell out to chains when they face the need to buy new presses, video display terminals, or other expensive hardware. Many more sell out when the original owner dies; unlike the owner's children, the chain will not have to pay an inheritance tax. Of course the family paper could sell to another private owner. But a big company can afford to pay top dollar; it can wait longer to recoup its investment and start earning a profit; it has no trouble financing the deal and is likely to pay a larger portion of the purchase price in cash.

For these and other reasons, the American mass media are dominated by monopolies, and will doubtless be still more dominated by monopolies in the years ahead. We have already discussed the theoretical danger of these monopolies—the reduced diversity of media voices available to the public. It is time now to look at the mixed evidence on the actual effects of monopoly on the nation's media.

———————

Though every media monopoly reduces the number of media voices, statistical studies comparing monopoly and non-monopoly media have been indecisive. On balance, media combinations seem modestly worse than independent media in some ways, modestly better in others. We are left with occasional examples of abuse of monopoly power, and the theoretical threat of further abuses as power becomes still more concentrated. In the face of this inconclusive picture, the government has acted to halt the growth of some forms of media monopoly, while leaving others to flourish undisturbed.

EFFECTS OF CONCENTRATION

Because of the FCC's efforts to stop one-city cross-ownerships, research on the effects of media concentration has tended to focus on broadcast/newspaper combinations in the same community. There has been somewhat less research on the effects of media chains, and almost none on joint operating agreements and conglomerates. To complicate the situation still more, researchers have often reached conflicting conclusions. Supporters of monopoly find evidence that monopoly media are better, opponents discover that monopoly media are worse, and each side attacks the methodology of the other side's studies.

To make sense of this confusion, we will look separately at three aspects of the question: (1) Do monopoly and independent media differ in their quality? (2) Do they differ in their strength? (3) Do they differ in their contribution to media diversity?

1. Quality. Traditional capitalist theory holds that competition keeps entrepreneurs on their toes. Competing media should therefore do a better job than monopoly media. But Paul Block Jr., once the publisher of both the *Toledo Blade* and the *Toledo Times,* offered an opposing theory:

> For one thing, a newspaper which isn't competing against a rival can present news in better balance. There is no need to sensationalize. . . .
>
> Competing newspapers live in fear of each other. They may be stampeded into excesses by their fear of losing circulation to a competitor less burdened with conscience. . . .
>
> The unopposed newspaper can give its reader . . . relief from the pressures of time. Deadlines no longer loom like avenging angels. . . . A single ownership newspaper can better afford to take an unpopular stand. It can better absorb the loss of money in support of a principle. . . .[22]

Research provides little evidence for either theory. Comparisons of independent and cross-owned TV stations, for example, have found only unimpressive differences at most. One study concluded that cross-owned stations ran 56 minutes a week more local news than independents.[23] Another reported only tiny differences, except in one-station communities, where cross-owned stations offered 135 minutes a week less local programming than independents.[24] A third discovered that independent stations carried more public affairs in the top ten markets, while newspaper-owned stations carried more in the smaller markets.[25] Most of these studies predicted larger differences than they found. For most of the variables they looked at, the most common finding was no difference at all.

As for chains, back in the 1950s Gerard Borstel examined news coverage in four kinds of newspapers—independent papers with local competition, chain papers with local competition, independent papers without competition, and chain papers without competition. He found absolutely no differences of any sort.[26] More recent comparisons of chain and non-chain broadcast stations have reached similar conclusions.[27]

Only one difference regularly emerges in quality comparisons of monopoly and non-monopoly media: the editorials. The difference argues against monopoly. Ralph Thrift, for example, found that newspaper editorials on local issues become less "vigorous" (less controversial, less argumentative) after the papers are purchased by chains.[28] And William T. Gormley, Jr. found that independent TV stations are twice as likely to editorialize as stations owned by newspapers in the same community.[29]

Should we conclude that aside from the editorials monopoly has little or no effect on media quality? Probably not—but the effects are apparently too subtle or too variable to be picked up by statistical studies. Much undoubtedly depends on the individual monopolist. Some build their properties into prize-winners, while others homogenize them for steady profits. Still more depends on the individual property. When a monopoly acquires a really bad newspaper or station, it pretty much has to improve it with infusions of new money, new staff, and new ideas—if only to protect the investment and the reputation of the parent company. But when a monopoly buys an unusually fine newspaper or station, the uniqueness of the new property may give way to corporate homogeneity.

Monopolies, in short, cultivate mediocre media, the sort that earn steady profits and little attention.

2. Strength. The finding of no difference in quality between monopoly and non-monopoly media is in a sense an anti-monopoly finding—because monopolies certainly have the financial resources to do a better job than most independents. If they don't do a measurably better job, it may be because they prefer to earn a larger profit instead.

The economic advantages of media monopolies have been documented in some detail. Here, for example, are eight of the advantages of newspaper chains: (1) Newsprint, ink, and other supplies can be purchased more cheaply in bulk. (2) One representative can sell national ads for the entire chain. (3) Standardized accounting methods turn up problems in particular papers that can be quickly corrected. (4) Editors and reporters can exchange ideas and criticize one another. (5) Valuable feature material can be obtained for the chain more easily and cheaply. (6) High salaries and employee stock benefits can be maintained more easily, even in hard times. (7) Costs can be cut by centralizing some business functions in chain headquarters. (8) Chain papers can pool their resources to support national or international news bureaus, or to work together on important stories. Many of these advantages—or comparable ones—apply also to cross-media ownerships, joint operating agreements, and conglomerates.

Monopolies, in short, can afford to improve the media they buy—and sometimes they do. When the Gannett chain purchased the *Camden* (New Jersey) *Courier-Post,* for example, it raised the paper's editorial budget by 43 percent. Gil Spencer, editor of the nearby *Philadelphia Daily News,* says the former owners of the *Courier-Post* "just let the town physically deteriorate around them. They were part of the establishment, and they didn't do a damn thing. I don't think the Gannett people would let that happen. The paper keeps an eye on things now."[30] Similarly, the Knight-Ridder chain brought great improvements to the *Philadelphia Inquirer* and the *San Jose* (California) *Mercury* and *News.* Management made it known to the individual editors and publishers that it was willing to sacrifice some short-term profit for quality newspapers.[31]

More often, however, media monopolies use their economic clout to improve earnings rather than performance. Bryant Kearl, in one study, found that monopoly newspapers purchased no more wire services than competitive ones[32]—though wires are among the cheapest and easiest ways to improve a paper.

It is true that media combinations have more economic strength than most independent media, but they do not always use that strength to serve the public.

But what about political strength? During the Watergate period of 1972-1974, virtually all the serious muckraking of the Nixon administration's misbehavior was undertaken by reporters working for powerful media combinations. This is not a coincidence. Such combinations are better able to withstand government (or corporate) intimidation, while independent media may be more easily cowed. Even in calmer times, monopoly strength can be a useful counterweight to government strength. When a judge decides to hold a trial in secret, a monopoly-owned medium has more resources than an independent medium to fight the decision through the appeals courts. When the Supreme Court is considering an important First Amendment issue, friend-of-the-court briefs are more likely to come from chains and networks than from local independents. And when the decision is handed down, media combinations can afford to pay for legal advice on its implications.

But as we shall soon see, the political strength of media monopolies is a two-edged sword. The same power that helps a monopoly fight government interference today may help it manipulate public opinion tomorrow.

3. Diversity. In principle, of course, all media monopolies reduce media diversity, simply by reducing the number of owners responsible for setting policy for the media they own. On the other hand, most monopoly owners aren't very interested in policy. They worry about profits, and let their editorial employees worry about the news. What, then, is the actual effect of monopoly ownership on diversity of content?

For chains and networks, the effect is subtle and undocumented. Both leave local news in the hands of local editors. And as for national and international news, monopoly actually adds to diversity—without a

chain membership or a network affiliation, everyone would be relying exclusively on AP and UPI. But chains and networks create a homogenized "tone" that reduces diversity in subtle ways. When a chain adds a new station or paper to its collection, for example, it naturally tries to spruce up the newcomer's product. Applying the accumulated wisdom of the chain's other members, it quickly buffs away the rough edges—an eccentric column, an idiosyncratic bit of typography, a quirky way of handling station breaks.

The reduction in diversity for one-city cross-ownerships, at least, is well-documented (though, as always, there are contrary studies that show little or no effect). In 1965, for example, Karl Nestvold studied the relationships between 128 newspapers and the radio stations they owned. He found that 25 of the stations were located right within the newspaper building. Over 40 of them used newspaper personnel on the air. And roughly half the stations had access to prepublication carbons of newspaper articles.[33] Regular readers of newspapers in Nestvold's study had little to gain from listening to the radio stations those newspapers owned.

In 1976, William T. Gormley, Jr. repeated Nestvold's study for local newspaper-TV combinations. Controlling for the effects of market size, Gormley found that a TV station owned by a newspaper in the same community averages 16.7 percent more stories that the paper also ran than the same station would have used if it were independently owned. This is not a large difference. "Nevertheless," Gormley concluded, "homogenizing effects of cross-ownership need not be blatant, deliberate, or spectacular to warrant remedial action."[34]

It is true nonetheless that monopoly owners are more likely than independent owners to refrain from meddling in news and editorial content. Here, for example, are some results from a 1980 survey of editors, sponsored by the American Society of Newspaper Editors.[35]

	Chain	Independent
Editor decides national political endorsements without consulting owner.	60%	50%
Editor usually wins in disagreements with owner.	32%	8%
Editor decides how to handle controversial issues without consulting owner.	85%	27%
Editor is free to take editorial positions that conflict with owner's viewpoint.	93%	41%

Similarly, George Litwin found that owners of local newspaper-broadcast combinations were more likely than independent owners to adopt a hands-off policy.[36]

But that isn't really the point. When an independent owner makes a news or editorial decision, the decision affects only one medium. It reduces the freedom of the editor, but not the diversity of media viewpoints. When a monopoly owner sets policy, on the other hand, all the media in the monopoly have to fall into line, and diversity inevitably suffers.

ABUSES OF CONCENTRATION

Where, then, do we stand on the effects of media concentration? Monopoly ownership improves the quality of some media, hurts the quality of others—score it as a dead heat on quality. Monopoly ownership gives the media substantial economic and political strength, but that strength isn't reliably used to benefit the public—another dead heat. And finally, monopoly ownership does reduce media diversity, indirectly through story overlap and directly through occasional policy decisions by management. This adds up to a weak case against media monopolies.

Many would argue that a weak case is enough to justify government regulation of monopolies. As the Federal Communications Commission phrased it: "Centralization of control over the media of mass communications is, like monopolization of economic power, *per se* undesirable."[37]

What makes the case stronger is the undeniable fact that media monopolies do sometimes abuse their power. As you consider the following examples of monopoly news management, remember that owners of independent media also manage the news—but they cannot manage it in several media at once.

Between 1926 and 1937, conservative George Richards acquired an impressive chain of AM radio stations, including major outlets in Detroit, Cleveland, and Hollywood. He left standing orders for all his news staffs to give no favorable coverage to President Roosevelt, but rather to depict the president as a lover of "the Jews and Communists." When Mrs. Roosevelt was in an auto accident in 1946, Richards ordered his stations to make it seem that she had been drinking. Local editors who refused to follow the Richards line were fired.[38]

A less ideological example of news management came to light in 1969, when the FCC began its investigation of KRON-TV, a local station owned and operated by the *San Francisco Chronicle*. Station employees testified that when the *Chronicle* and the afternoon *Examiner* formed a joint operating agreement in 1965, KRON failed to report the story. Returning the favor, the *Chronicle* grossly underplayed the events leading to the FCC hearings on KRON.

And *Chronicle* columnist Charles McCabe testified that a piece he had written deploring violence on television was "killed" by higher-ups at the paper.[39]

In 1967 the International Telephone and Telegraph Company attempted to purchase the ABC network. Despite the fact that ITT was already a giant international conglomerate, the FCC approved the sale. Three commissioners dissented. "We simply cannot find," they wrote, "that the public interest of the American citizenry is served by turning over a major network to an international enterprise whose fortunes are tied to its political relations with the foreign officials whose actions it will be called upon to interpret to the world."

Their fears were borne out by ITT's conduct while the sale was under scrutiny by the FCC and the Justice Department. ITT officials phoned AP and UPI reporters and asked them to make their stories more sympathetic to the company position. A *New York Times* correspondent who had criticized the merger received a call from an ITT senior vice president. The man asked if she was following the price of ABC and ITT stock, and didn't she feel "a responsibility to the shareholders who might lose money as a result" of what she wrote.[40] If ITT was pressuring reporters now, one might ask, what would it do after it owned its own reporters to pressure? Fortunately, the Justice Department balked at the merger, and ITT eventually withdrew the offer.

In 1977, owner John McGoff ordered all 46 editors in his Panax newspaper chain to give prominent display to two articles critical of President Carter, one of which al-

ECONOMIC MANIPULATION

Aside from news management, monopoly power sometimes provides opportunities for unfair economic competition. Consider the *Examiner-Chronicle*-KRON combination in San Francisco. Before 1965 the two newspapers were involved in a bitter circulation war for the morning San Francisco market. *Chronicle* owners used the profits from KRON to win the battle, forcing the *Examiner* to move to the afternoon and sign a joint operating agreement.

Once the agreement was reached, the *Chronicle* doubled its advertising rate, while the weaker *Examiner* raised its rate by about 50 percent. The joint rate for placing the same ad in both papers was set only slightly higher than the *Chronicle's* rate alone. The *Chronicle* had a morning monopoly, so advertisers were forced to pay its doubled rate. It then made sense for them to pay just a little more and get into the *Examiner* as well. The result: suburban afternoon papers that were hoping to compete with the *Examiner* were at a disadvantage. And metropolitan competition was rendered virtually impossible. The weekly *San Francisco Bay Guardian* filed suit against the two papers, alleging that their joint operating agreement was manipulating ad rates in ways that threatened the *Bay Guardian's* survival. The case dragged through the courts for years, and eventually the struggling *Bay Guardian* accepted an out-of-court cash settlement to drop the suit.

Monopoly media also wield increased economic power over employees. In 1979, *New York Times* reporter Fox Butterfield proposed a book entitled *The Chinese*, to be based in part on his experiences as the *Times'* first China correspondent. His agent offered the book first to the *Times'* own publishing company. But Times Books was willing to pay only a $125,000 advance, while Doubleday and Random House both bid $250,000. Butterfield was called in for a chat with *Times* managing editor Seymour Topping—and he quietly signed with Times Books. Topping's explanation: "It's our belief that when a guy is going off on an assignment for us exclusively, through our efforts, then he ought not to get an agent and peddle his book."[41] Of course if the *Times* were not a cross-owner, it wouldn't have had a publishing company with which to whipsaw Butterfield—and Butterfield wouldn't have lost $125,000 in advance money.

leged that the president condoned promiscuity among his staff. Two editors refused to run the stories, which they felt were poor journalism. McGoff fired them both.[42]

What exactly do these anecdotes prove? Supporters of media monopoly argue that they prove nothing—a handful of horror stories don't add up to a national problem, they say, and in any case owners of independent media are also guilty of occasional news management.

True enough. But as we have already pointed out, owners of independent media can manage the news in one medium at most, while media monopolists can manage it wholesale in all their properties. Any newspaper publisher can instruct editors not to offend a supermarket advertiser, but only a cross-owner can make sure the local TV station also avoids supermarket muckraking. Any media owner can decide to promote a favorite senator for president, but only a chain owner can promote the senator in scores of media at once.

And media monopolists may well have more reason to *want* to manage the news. A conglomerate, for example, is by definition involved in several different businesses; what reasonable conglomerate owner wouldn't be tempted to use his or her media business to help out the others? Similarly, cross-owners who live in the community tend to be bigger wheels locally than independent owners. They have their fingers in more pies, and thus may have a personal stake in more of the news. The profit orientation of most monopolists offers some protection against ideological interference, but none at all against interference based on economic self-interest.

Monopoly owners thus possess greater power to manage the news, and face greater temptation to manage the news. Unless they are intrinsically more ethical than independent owners—which seems unlikely—they presumably are responsible for more news management.[43]

But assume this is not the case. Assume monopoly owners are so busy with the business side of their properties that they seldom get around to editorial interference, even when such interference could improve profits. Assume these anecdotes of monopoly news management are isolated exceptions rather than the tip of the iceberg. The power and the temptation would still be there—and so would the danger that one day media monopolists might give in to the temptation and begin to exercise the power. Congressman Morris Udall graphically captures this fear for the future: "I know the folks who run these chains and they're nice people and they love their kids and all, but the day may come when you have some leaders who hunger for political power. The power is there. It's not comforting to know that it isn't being used."[44]

GOVERNMENT REGULATION

From what has been said about the dangers of media monopolies, it should come as no surprise that the federal government has made efforts to contain and restrict them. What is surprising is the weakness of those efforts, at least until the end of the 1960s. Let us examine the extent of government restraint on each of the four forms of media combination.

1. Chains and Networks. Commercial radio was barely out of its infancy when the Federal Communications Commission began to worry about broadcast networks. The big problem was NBC, which owned two of the three existing networks, serving a majority of the strong metropolitan stations. In 1941 the FCC finally acted, ordering that "no license shall be issued to a standard broadcast station affiliated with a network organization which maintains more than one network."[45] This forced NBC to get rid of its so-called Blue Network. Lifesaver king Edward J. Noble bought the holdings; they became the nucleus of what is now ABC.

The Justice Department doesn't worry much about broad-based newspaper chains, but when the chains are local and begin to dominate local advertising, Justice gets interested. In 1968, for example, the department required the afternoon *Cincinnati Post & Times-Star* (a Scripps-Howard chain paper) to divest itself of the morning *Cincinnati Enquirer*, in order to "restore competition between downtown papers."[46] The Gannett chain picked up the *Enquirer*. In 1970, similarly, Justice forced the *Chattanooga* (Tenn.) *Times* to close its sister paper, the *Evening Post*, because the latter was started with the sole intention of driving the competing *Chattanooga News-Free Press* out of business. The *Evening Post* was deliberately published at a loss, Justice claimed, to make it impossible for the *News-Free Press* to compete.[47]

Both stories end with an ironic twist. In 1979, Justice approved a joint operating agreement between the *Post* and the *Enquirer* in Cincinnati. And in 1980 the *Chattanooga Times* and *News-Free Press* received qualified permission for a joint operating agreement of their own.

Satisfied with this one-network-to-a-customer rule, the government took no further action against networks until the early 1970s. FCC and Justice Department efforts since then have tried to chip away at network power, without much effect. For example, networks were forbidden by the FCC to own cable systems anywhere in the country—but in 1980 the FCC was considering letting CBS into cable ownership. And local TV stations were required to carry at least half an hour of non-network content a night during prime time—but in 1979 the FCC's own staff recommended abandoning the policy.

The FCC acted promptly to control the growth of broadcast chains. In the early 1940s it took two actions, known jointly as the Duopoly Rule. First, it ordered that no licensee could operate two stations of the same kind (AM, FM, or TV) in the same community. Second, it put a limit on the number of stations throughout the country that one licensee could own. Today that limit stands at seven AM, seven FM, and seven TV (of which no more than five may be VHF). A more recent rule forbids chains to own more than three TV stations in the top 50 markets—but those that already do are approved under a "grandfather clause."

The FCC, of course, can regulate only broadcasting; the government agency that watches over print monopolies is the Department of Justice, with the help of the Federal Trade Commission. From time to time Justice has opposed a particular newspaper sale or merger, but on the whole it doesn't object to newspaper combinations unless they are within a single city. In 1970, for example, the Justice Department approved the sale of *Newsday*, a large Long Island tabloid, to the Times Mirror Company of Los Angeles. That company already owned the *Los Angeles Times,* the *Dallas Times-Herald,* and assorted other publishing and broadcast properties—but the Justice Department didn't seem to mind. Mused one *Newsday* editor: "The *Times* has the best national reporting in the country for my money. But it's a long way from Long Island."[48]

2. Cross-Media Ownership. For many years, the FCC had no policy concerning the extent to which newspaper publishers should be permitted to operate broadcast stations in the same city. Instead, it decided cross-media applications on a case-by-case basis, and usually approved them.

But in 1968 the Justice Department offered the FCC a legal rationale for moving systematically against cross-media combinations on antitrust grounds. Combined ownerships, it submitted, "may facilitate undesirable competitive practices by which the 'combined' owner seeks to exploit his advantages over the single station owner."[49] Justice urged the FCC to take action against cross-media combinations.

To the shock of many broadcasters, the Commission agreed. In 1969 it refused to renew the license of Boston station WHDH-TV, owned by the *Boston Herald Traveler*. On several grounds, including media diversity, it awarded the license to a committee of local educators and business executives.

That was only the beginning. In 1970, the FCC adopted a rule it had proposed in 1968, providing that henceforth no licensee of a VHF television station could also own an AM or FM radio station in the same market. AM-FM and UHF-radio combinations would be considered on a case-by-case basis. This might have revolutionized broadcast ownership, but a grandfather clause provided that combinations already in existence could remain intact. The ruling thus produced practically no change at all in the major markets.

Also in 1970, the Commission announced a "declaration of proposed rulemaking"—a statement of what it hoped to do in the near future. The terms were severe: (1) Within five years all newspaper owners would be required to get rid of all their broadcast holdings in the same city; (2) After five years no owner of a television station would be permitted to operate a radio station in the same city; and (3) Any broadcaster who purchased a newspaper in the same city would be required to give up the broadcast license. Industry response to the bombshell was immediate. NBC, for example, announced that the FCC "is seeking a rule requiring divestiture (if not forfeiture) in the absence of any showing either of monopoly power or of any restraint of trade."[50]

After five years of intensive lobbying, the FCC finally took action on its proposed rules in 1975. The action was a compromise. Henceforth, the FCC said, no new newspaper-broadcast (or cable-broadcast) combinations would be permitted in the same community. But existing ones could continue as long as there were competing stations serving the same audience. The Commission found only 16 combinations around the country that failed to satisfy this criterion, and ordered them to get rid of either the paper or the station by 1980 (some extensions were later granted). No big-city combinations were listed.[51]

The National Citizens Committee for Broadcasting challenged the ruling, arguing that the FCC ought to split up far more than 16 cross-ownerships. In 1977 the appeals court agreed. Noting that the Commission had required divestiture only where it had evidence that cross-ownership was harmful, the court said: "We believe that precisely the opposite presumption is compelled, and that divestiture is required except in those cases where the evidence clearly discloses that cross-ownership is in the public interest."

This time the National Association of Broadcasters and the American Newspaper Publishers Association appealed—and in 1978 the Supreme Court overruled the appeals court and backed the original FCC order. There are good reasons for avoiding wholesale divestiture, the Court explained, such as the virtues of local management and industry stability. The FCC could reasonably view these virtues as more important than the dangers of cross-ownership in communities where the newspaper-owned station had at least some local competition.

Except for the FCC's 16 victims, then, existing cross-ownerships are legal, but future ones are effectively outlawed.

In 1980 the Commission tentatively reopened the one-city cross-ownership issue, inquiring whether existing broadcast-cable combinations in the same market should be forced to sell one or the other.[52] And several state governments have taken legal action against local newspaper-cable combinations.[53] Combinations involving cable are all relatively new, and thus vulnerable. Long-standing newspaper-broadcast combinations, on the other hand, are still safe. But there will be no new ones.

3. Joint Operating Agreements. In 1965 the Justice Department filed suit against the *Tucson Arizona Star* and *Citizen,* charging that the two newspapers had entered into a joint operating agreement that violated anti-trust laws. The papers were accused of price-fixing, profit-pooling, and creating a total monopoly over the daily newspaper business in Tucson. The U.S. District Court in Arizona agreed, and declared the agreement unlawful. The U.S. Supreme Court upheld the decision. The newspaper joint operating agreement (except for limited arrangements involving papers in genuine danger of folding) was dead.

It was born again in 1967, when Arizona Senator Carl Hayden introduced the Failing Newspaper Act, which explicitly legalized agreements like Tucson's. The act died in committee, but was reintroduced as the Newspaper Preservation Act. In 1970 it passed both houses of Congress and was signed into law.

The act was vigorously lobbied through Congress by the powerful newspaper industry. Proponents argued that only the joint operating agreement could keep weak metropolitan papers from folding, leaving their cities with just a single newspaper. The act, they said, was therefore an attempt to preserve competition and forestall monopoly.

Opponents saw it differently. They pointed out that in most American cities it is the *third* newspaper, not the *second,* that is in imminent danger of folding. And a newspaper that cannot survive as one of two in a big city must be doing something wrong, they said. Perhaps if it were allowed to fold, another paper might take its place and do a better job.

Nevertheless, the Newspaper Preservation Act is now law, and joint operating agree-ments are legal once again. The Justice Department, which must approve new agreements, has so far done so whenever it was asked. But there are still legal challenges to individual joint operating agreements pending in courtrooms in Honolulu and elsewhere. Typically, these lawsuits claim that neither of the newspapers was in genuine danger of bankruptcy, and that they are manipulating advertising rates to force *other* newspapers into bankruptcy (not to mention the extra cost to advertisers).[54] A favorable ruling in any of these cases could reopen the issue.

Interestingly enough, there has not been any rush to form new joint operating agreements in the wake of their legalization. The number of such agreements remained virtually constant from 1970 to 1980. Chains and cross-media ownerships are apparently more attractive to the average publisher than joint operating agreements.

4. Conglomerates. Neither the FCC nor the Justice Department nor any other government agency has a policy restricting the right of conglomerates to get into the media business. As the Justice Department's refusal to approve the proposed ITT-ABC merger demonstrates, the government is likely to balk when a giant conglomerate wants to take over a major media system. But conglomerates buy individual stations, newspapers, and magazines all the time, without any serious objections from the government. As long as a conglomerate builds its media holdings slowly, and doesn't violate the rules governing broadcast chains and cross-media ownership, it is reasonably safe.

CHOOSING AMONG EVILS

We have discussed four forms of media combination—chains and networks, cross-media ownership, joint operating agreements, and conglomerates. It is probably not feasible to outlaw them all. This is the age of Big Business, in communications as in all other industries. Critics of media monopoly must therefore decide which forms to fight, and which to leave alone as the lesser among evils.

The government, too, must make this decision. So far none of the four forms has been outlawed. Still, it is possible to examine the actions of the FCC, the Justice Department, and Congress, and to deduce from them how the government views the problem. The "official government ranking," from most dangerous to least dangerous, would probably look like this:

1. Cross-media ownership (in the same city).
2. Chains and networks.
3. Conglomerates.
4. Joint operating agreements.

As of 1980, in short, new cross-media ownerships within a single community are illegal. Chains are nearly unregulated as long as they stay geographically spread out, and conglomerates are safe as long as they don't try to gobble up too big a piece of the media pie in one bite. Joint operating agreements are protected by law if the Attorney General approves.

All this could change overnight. Congress could pass a law permitting new cross-media ownerships; the Justice Department could start fighting chains more vigorously; the FCC could refuse to let conglomerates buy television stations.

Which form of media monopoly is really the most dangerous? The answer depends on what sort of danger worries you the most. In terms of local diversity, cross-media ownership is the most serious problem, because it limits the number of independent voices within a community, and thus directly threatens the free marketplace of ideas. In terms of national power, chains and networks are the most serious; they enable a single executive to decide what tens of millions of readers and viewers will be told. And in terms of the likelihood of intentional news bias, conglomerates are the most serious; a

conglomerate with media holdings has the rare privilege of reporting about itself. Even joint operating agreements may be viewed by some as the most serious problem, because of their ability to keep sick newspapers alive and prevent the growth of healthy, new ones.

Then there are the advantages of monopolies to consider. The same economic and political strength that makes media combinations dangerous also makes them valuable. Would a small, independent, local broadcast station have the resources to produce top-quality documentaries? Would a small, independent, local newspaper have the courage to resist government intimidation? These are serious questions to ponder before advocating a wholesale attack on media monopoly.

But the strength of America's media has traditionally been their diversity. And media monopoly—*every* form of media monopoly—is antithetical to diversity. Despite new media voices in radio and cable, our media are still too much alike in many ways, offering their audience a painfully narrow range of viewpoints from which to choose. Allowing media ownership to concentrate further in the hands of a few powerful monopolists can only worsen the problem.

Notes

[1] *Abrams v. United States,* 250 U.S. 616, 630 (1919).

[2] "Group Ownership Trend Continues for Dailies; Number of Groups Dips," *Presstime,* November, 1979, p. 22.

[3] "Groups Gain 48 in Sales of 53 Dailies in '79," *Editor & Publisher,* January 5, 1980, p. 28.

[4] "Senate Panel Is Told Why Newspaper Groups Continue to Grow in the U.S.," *Editor & Publisher,* September 1, 1979, p. 9.

[5] *Broadcasting Yearbook 1980.*

[6] N. R. Kleinfield, "Combined Communications Agrees to a $370 Million Gannett Merger," *New York Times,* May 9, 1978, pp. 1, 63.

[7] David Gelman, "Gannett: Chain Reaction," *Newsweek,* May 22, 1978, p. 82.

[8] N. R. Kleinfield, "The Great Press Chain," *New York Times Sunday Magazine,* April 8, 1979, p. 41.

9 David Shaw, "The Chain in Command," *Quill*, December, 1978, p. 12.

10 Kleinfield, "The Great Press Chain," p. 52.

11 *Broadcasting Yearbook 1980*.

12 "Publishers Buy 50 Radio and 13 Video Stations," *Editor & Publisher*, January 5, 1980, pp. 43-45.

13 *Broadcasting Yearbook 1980*, p. G-3.

14 Philip H. Dougherty, "J. Walter Thompson to Acquire Top U.S. Public Relations Firm," *New York Times*, February 12, 1980, p. 1.

15 Federal Communications Commission, "Further Notice of Proposed Rulemaking," 70-311 46096, March 25, 1970, para. 30-31.

16 W. H. Masters, "Media Monopolies: Busting Up a Cozy Marriage," *More*, October, 1977, pp. 12-13.

17 Peter Dreier and Steve Weinberg, "Interlocking Directorates," *Columbia Journalism Review*, November/December, 1979, pp. 51-52.

18 *Ibid.*, p. 53.

19 *Ibid.*, p. 67.

20 James Boylan, "A Fifty Days' War: McGraw-Hill and American Express," *Columbia Journalism Review*, May/June, 1979, pp. 19-20.

21 Robert Lindsey, "Conservative Chain Buys Liberal Mississippi Paper," *New York Times*, February 12, 1980, p. B7.

22 Paul Block Jr., "Facing Up to the 'Monopoly' Charge," *Nieman Reports*, July, 1955, p. 4.

23 Michael O. Wirth and James A. Wollert, "Public Interest Program Performance of Multimedia-Owned TV Stations," *Journalism Quarterly*, Summer, 1976, pp. 223-30. Federal Communications Commission, "Staff Study of 1973 Television Station Annual Programming Reports," Appendix C, Second Report and Order, Docket No. 18110, January 31, 1975.

24 Harvey J. Levin, "Supplementary Comments," Federal Communications Commission Docket No. 18110, May 15, 1974.

25 Michael O. Wirth and James A. Wollert, "Public Interest Programming: FCC Standards and Station Performance," *Journalism Quarterly*, Autumn, 1978, pp. 554-55.

26 Gerard H. Borstel, "Ownership, Competition and Comment in 20 Small Dailies," *Journalism Quarterly*, Spring, 1956, pp. 220-21.

27 Wirth and Wollert, "Public Interest Programming," p. 560.

28 Ralph R. Thrift Jr., "How Chain Ownership Affects Editorial Vigor of Newspapers," *Journalism Quarterly*, Summer, 1977, pp. 327-31.

29 William T. Gormley, Jr., *The Effects of Newspaper-Television Cross-Ownership on News Homogeneity* (Chapel Hill, N.C.: Institute for Research on Social Science, University of North Carolina, 1976).

30 Shaw, "The Chain in Command," p. 12.

31 *Ibid.*, p. 15.

32 Bryant Kearl, "Effects of Newspaper Competition on Press Service Resources," *Journalism Quarterly*, Winter, 1958, p. 64.

33 Karl J. Nestvold, "Local News Cooperation Between Co-Owned Newspapers and Radio Stations," *Journal of Broadcasting*, Spring, 1965, pp. 145-52.

34 Gormley, *Effects of Newspaper-Television Cross-Ownership*.

35 Jerry Walker, "ASNE Poll Finds Group Editors Have Freedom," *Editor & Publisher*, March 29, 1980, pp. 7, 10.

36 George H. Litwin and William H. Wroth, *The Effects of Common Ownership on Media Content and Influence*, National Association of Broadcasters, July, 1969, pp. 5-13.

37 Federal Communications Commission, "First Report and Order," 70-310 46095, para. 17.

38 Erik Barnouw, *The Golden Web* (New York: Oxford University Press, 1968), pp. 221-24.

39 "McCabe Testifies at TV Hearings," *San Francisco Chronicle*, April 15, 1970, p. 6.

40 Nicholas Johnson, "The Media Barons and the Public Interest," *Atlantic*, June, 1968, pp. 44-46.

41 "Times Reporter Mustn't Stray," *New York Post*, April 30, 1979, p. 6.

42 Kleinfield, "The Great Press Chain," p. 49.

43 Peter M. Sandman, "Cross-Ownership on the Scales," *More*, October, 1977, p. 24.

44 Kleinfield, "The Great Press Chain," p. 49.

45 Barnouw, *The Golden Web*, pp. 170-71.

46 Walter B. Kerr, "The Problem of Combinations," *Saturday Review*, October 12, 1968, p. 82.

47 "Antitrust Consent Decree Closes Chattanooga Post," *Editor & Publisher*, February 28, 1970, p. 9.

48 "Thank You, Mr. Smith," *Newsweek*, April 27, 1970, p. 94.

49 Department of Justice Memorandum, August 1, 1968, p. 6.

50 Federal Communications Commission, "Further Notice of Proposed Rulemaking," 70-311 49069, March 25, 1970, para. 19.

51 I. William Hill, "FCC Bars Cross-Ownership, Breaks Up Media in 16 Cities," *Editor & Publisher*, February 1, 1975, p. 9.

52 Tony Schwartz, "F.C.C. Seeks to Split TV and Cable Units," *New York Times*, June 25, 1980, pp. 1, D7.

53 Bill Kirtz, "Mass. to Allow Publishers to Own

Cable TV," *Editor & Publisher*, January 7, 1980, p. 88.

[54] Stephen R. Barnett, "Monopoly Games—Where Failures Win Big," *Columbia Journalism Review*, May/June, 1980, pp. 44-45.

Suggested Readings

BARNETT, STEPHEN R., "Monopoly Games—Where Failures Win Big," *Columbia Journalism Review*, May/June, 1980.

BROWN, LES, "Time Marching On With Video," *The New York Times*, January 2, 1980, p. D1.

COMPAINE, BENJAMIN M., *Who Owns The Media? Concentration of Ownership in the Mass Communications Industry*. White Plains, N.Y.: Knowledge Industry Publications, 1979.

DREIER, PETER, and STEVE WEINBERG, "Interlocking Directorates," *Columbia Journalism Review*, November/December, 1979.

HICKS, RONALD G., and JAMES S. FEATH[...] "Duplication of Newspaper Content in[...] trasting Ownership Situations," *Journa[...] Quarterly*, Autumn, 1978.

PEAGAM, NORMAN, "Like Father, Like Son? No, but All Goes Well In Thomson Empire," *The Wall Street Journal*, May 27, 1980, p. 1.

SCHWEITZER, JOHN C., and ELAINE GOLDMAN, "Does Newspaper Competition Make a Difference to Readers?" *Journalism Quarterly*, Winter, 1975.

SHAW, DAVID, "The Chain in Command," *The Quill*, December, 1978.

SMITH, EDWARD J., and GILBERT L. FOWLER, JR., "The Status of Magazine Group Ownership," *Journalism Quarterly*, Autumn, 1979.

STEMPEL, GUIDO H., III, "Effects on Performance of a Cross-Media Monopoly," *Journalism Monographs*, June, 1973.

THRIFT, RALPH, "How Chain Ownership Affects Editorial Vigor of Newspapers," *Journalism Quarterly*, Summer, 1977.

Chapter 5
Advertiser Control

Most of the money in the mass media comes from advertising. If money means power, then advertisers must have enormous power to control the media. And they do. Surprisingly, they exercise that power only on occasion, and usually for business rather than political reasons. Advertiser control does have an effect on overall media performance, especially in broadcasting, but the effect is usually more subtle than most critics imagine.

Newspaper people are not easy to embarrass, but this time the *Denver Post* offices were filled with red faces. Someone had spirited an interoffice memorandum from the newspaper's files and published it. Addressed to the managing editor, the memo read as follows:

Regarding "editorial" commitment on advertising schedules for Villa Italia Shopping Center. . . .

I'm open to review on figures, based on Hatcher's [retail advertising manager] stated commitment of 25 per cent free space ratio to advertising, but believe this is reasonably accurate. . . .

We have since Feb. 2 . . . published in vari-

ous sections of the *Post* 826 column inches of copy and pictures directly related to Villa Italia, through March 7.

Coverage beyond Monday (three days of grand openings . . . which we can't ignore and must cover with pix and stories) won't come close to the total commitment, but probably would put it over the half-way mark. If we did a picture page each day of the opening . . . we would be providing another 546 column inches and thus be beginning to get close to the commitment figure. . . .[1]

Why is this memo so damning? All it reveals, after all, is that the *Post* had promised the shopping center one inch of free "news stories" for every four inches of paid advertising—and that the paper was having trouble finding the necessary news angles. Such a commercial arrangement is straightforward, legal, and common. It is also typical of the way advertisers influence the content of the mass media. The Villa Italia Shopping Center did not bribe the *Post* to support a particular political candidate, or even to fight for a zoning change it might have wanted. It simply purchased a little free space along with its ads. That seems harmless enough.

Nonetheless, the loss to *Denver Post* readers is clear. For one thing, they were falsely led to believe that the newspaper's editors considered Villa Italia an important news story. Moreover, in just over a month 826 column inches of genuinely important stories (roughly 30,000 words, the equivalent of a short novel) were eased out of the paper to make room for this disguised advertising.

WHO PAYS THE PIPER

Almost all American mass media are commercial. Some, like the book and motion picture industries, earn their revenue directly from the consumer. Most earn it—or at least the bulk of it—from advertising.

Newspapers: Sixty percent of the space in the average newspaper is devoted to ads, which account for three-quarters of the paper's income.

Magazines: A little over half of all magazine income is derived from ads, which fill just about half the available space.

Broadcasting: One-quarter of the nation's air time is reserved for commercial messages, which pay the entire cost of the other three quarters.

In 1979 advertisers spent $14.5 billion on newspapers; $10.2 billion on television; $3.4 billion on radio; and $2.9 billion on magazines. Each year the figures are larger. It is obvious that none of these media could exist in the form we know them without advertising.

Imagine that you are the Vice President for Advertising of Procter & Gamble, which in 1980 spent roughly $486 million on television advertising alone, much of it for daytime serials. Imagine also that the script for one of your serials calls for an episode in which the heroine goes swimming in detergent-polluted water and suffers a psychotic breakdown because of the slime. You would almost certainly feel tempted to ask the producer to skip that part, and you might well feel cheated if he or she refused. As far as we know P&G does not interfere with soap opera plots. But then, as far as we know no soap opera has ever featured the dangers of detergent pollution. With $486 million of Procter & Gamble's money at stake, no soap opera is likely to do so.

Advertisers pay the piper. If they want to, they can more or less call the tune.

IDEOLOGY VERSUS BUSINESS

In the late 1950s, General Motors signed with CBS to sponsor a series of television documentaries. When it was learned that the first program would be entitled "The Vice Presidency: Great American Lottery," the company guessed that the show might attack V.P. Richard Nixon. Nixon was a great favorite of many GM executives, so GM withdrew from the entire series.[2]

This anecdote has been told and retold many times over, and for good reason: It is rare. Advertisers almost never exercise their power, as GM apparently did, purely for ideological reasons. Their goal, after all, is to sell a product, and they pick their outlets on commercial grounds, not political ones. No matter how conservative a company may be, if it wants to sell to young people it will be pleased to have an ad in the middle of "Laverne & Shirley." Wherever the market is, that is where the advertiser hopes to be. In a 1962 speech, conservative business editor Donald I. Rogers described (and criticized) this devotion to circulation:

> When businessmen place their advertising in Washington, where do they place it?
>
> They place 600,000 more lines per month with the liberal, welfare-state loving *Post* than in the *Star*, and the poor old conservative *News* runs a poor—a very poor—third. . . .
>
> The picture is no different here in New York. We find that the greatest amount of ad-

vertising placed by businessmen goes into the liberal *Times*. . . .

The influential conservative New York papers, the *Herald Tribune* and the *World Telegram & Sun,* get very sparse pickings indeed from the American business community which they support so effectively in their editorial policies.[3]

Rogers urged the business establishment to support the papers that support business. He was ignored. As a result, the *Herald Tribune* and the *World Telegram & Sun* are now dead, victims of scanty advertising. The *Washington News* was forced to merge with the *Star,* but the merged paper still lost money, and in 1981 it folded. American advertisers simply will not pay to keep an ideological supporter in business. They pay to reach an audience, period.

Rogers' theme was echoed in a 1979 speech by Leonard S. Matthews, president of the American Association of Advertising Agencies. "Until now, advertisers have made remarkably few attempts to influence editorial content in the media," Matthews said. "To expect private companies to go on supporting a medium that is attacking them is like taking up a collection for money among the Christians to buy more lions."[4]

Rogers and Matthews consider the ideological neutrality of advertisers shortsighted. Perhaps it is. But it is also very fortunate for the independence of the media. Because of this neutrality, a newspaper, magazine, or broadcast station that attacks the business establishment will be kept in business *by* the business establishment, as long as it can attract an adequate audience.

PATTERNS OF ADVERTISER CONTROL

The fact that most advertisers are ideologically neutral does not mean that they ignore the content of the programs they sponsor or the publications they appear in. Some companies, of course, are satisfied to pay for their ads and let it go at that. But many like to have at least a little say over what comes before and after.

There are at least four types of advertiser control over mass-media content:

1. The ads themselves.
2. Connecting the product to nonadvertising content.
3. Making the company and product look good, never bad.
4. Avoiding controversy at all costs.

We will discuss each of these in turn.

1. The Ads Themselves. It may be obvious, but it is worth emphasizing that nearly half the content of the mass media is written directly by advertisers—the ads. The average American adult is exposed to several hundred separate advertising messages each day. Many find their way into the language as symbols of our culture—"Reach Out and Touch Someone," "You Deserve a Break Today," "It's the Real Thing." Besides selling goods, these ads undoubtedly have a cumulative effect on American society. Philosopher Erich Fromm has defined Western Man as *Homo consumens*—Man the Consumer. If the description fits, the institution to blame is advertising.

Legally, a publication or station is free to reject most kinds of ads if it wishes, but as a practical matter only the most egregiously dishonest or offensive specimens are ever turned away. It is a strange paradox that advertisers exercise more power over the content of the media than the media do over the ads.

2. Connecting the Product to Nonadvertising Content. The clearest example of the blurred line between advertising and nonadvertising is the common newspaper custom of trading free "news stories" for paid ads, as in the *Denver Post* case already discussed. A parallel practice in the magazine world is the disguising of advertisements as editorial copy. The May 26, 1980, issue of *New York* magazine was a special summer fun extravaganza, including articles on perfect summer weekends, on jug wines, and on "Guest Bets"—three pages of "gifts for your host, or yourself, to make weekend entertaining manageable, even fun." Filling the magazine's centerfold was another eight-page section called "Summer Specialties." Its format was identical to "Guest Bets"—only the store name "Bloomingdale's" on the bottom corner of each page tipped off the careful reader that *this* section was paid advertising.

Are readers confused by such ads? Not as confused as they are by *New York*'s "Restaurant Directory," an 18-page feature accompanied each week by a tiny note explaining that the feature is really "a list of advertisers plus some of the city's most popular dining establishments" too prominent to leave out.

A 1979 survey of daily newspapers found that 80 percent are willing to position advertising near "appropriate" editorial material.[5] At least some of this editorial material is there only because certain advertisers want to be next to it. Frequent offenders include the real estate section, entertainment page, church page, and travel and dining pages. There is nothing evil about a newspaper deciding to run, say, a weekly ski page. But if the only function of the page is to give skiing advertisers a place to locate—and if the page disappears when the ads fall off—then the editor's news judgment has been replaced by the business manager's. In his book *The Fading American Newspaper,* Carl Lindstrom calls these sorts of articles "revenue-related reading matter."[6] Many newspaper executives use another term: BOMs, or Business Office Musts. The reader, of course, pays the price—a steady diet of pap and puffery.

In broadcasting, the best way to connect paid and unpaid content is to hire the performer to do his or her own ads. It was Dinah Shore herself who sang, at the end of every show, "See the U.S.A. in your Chevrolet." Between monologues and interviews, Johnny Carson tells millions of viewers what to buy.

Almost from the beginning, network television newscasters refused to do commercials, believing that it was unfair and misleading to slide from a review of the day's action on Capitol Hill to a review of the reasons for taking Excedrin. But until recently the networks were a good deal less scrupulous in the morning than in the evening. The hosts on NBC's "Today" show, including Barbara Walters, regularly did their own commercials. In 1974, NBC had trouble finding a replacement for Frank McGee on the show, because several top prospects refused to do the ads. Jim Hartz, a reporter for WNBC in New York, accepted the job and did the commercials.[7] The NBC news department finally adopted a policy against commercials by "anchor" personnel, even in the morning—so Tom Brokaw and Jane Pauley didn't pitch, but Willard Scott and Gene Shalit did.

Morning or evening, many local TV reporters are less conscientious than their network colleagues, and nearly all radio announcers are willing to alternate between news and commercials. In 1978, Robert E. Short, owner of all-news radio station WTTC in Minneapolis, carried this to its logical extreme. He directed his 20 news people to join with the sales staff in an all-out campaign to sell commercials. Short said it was "patently fallacious" to raise the issue of conflict of interest.[8]

Blurring the line between news and advertising is intended to strengthen the credibility of the ads. It may also lessen the credibility of the news.

3. Making the Company and Product Look Good, Never Bad. Advertisers go to a great deal of trouble to look good in their ads; wherever possible, they would like to look good between the ads as well. It is sometimes possible. Then CBS reporter Alexander Kendrick recalled the cigarette sponsor that "dictated that on none of its entertainment programs, whether drama or studio panel game, could any actor or other participant smoke a pipe or cigar, or chew tobacco,

Product plugs can be found on the big screen as well as the tube. In the mid-1970s motion picture "The Late Show," for example, Pepsi-Cola was the beverage of choice; plugs were also worked in for Beringer Wines, Sharp Electronics, Wilson Sporting Goods and Botany 500 suits.

According to product plugger Larry Dorn, it wasn't necessary to pay the producers of "The Late Show" for the publicity. Movie scripts call for everything from cars to calculating machines, and Dorn is employed by manufacturers to make sure their products are the ones on the screen. Dorn supplies the moving van or the beer can free of charge to the producer, collecting from $1,000 to $5,000 per plug from the delighted manufacturer.[9]

---

or even chew gum that might be mistaken for tobacco. Only cigarettes could be smoked, and only king-sized, but no program could show untidy ashtrays, filled with cigarette butts. . . ."[10]

Such policies are less common today, because for the most part advertisers no longer sponsor whole programs. Instead, they buy a minute here and a minute there (see pp. 145-46), which makes it hard for them to exercise the careful control over program content they used to take for granted. But when an advertiser does decide to underwrite an entire show, this kind of control is often part of the package. If Bufferin sponsors a special television drama, the star is unlikely to take plain aspirin for her headache.

In addition, TV producers regularly accept products and services from various companies in exchange for a plug on the show. Chevrolet, for example, provided six free cars for use on "Mannix." The deal stipulated that only sympathetic characters were to drive the Chevys, and that they could not be used in collision scenes. Similarly, "Hawaii Five-O" often needed film of an airplane landing on the island. United Airlines paid the producers a substantial fee, estimated by one CBS source at $25,000 a year, to guarantee that all such shots would feature a United plane, thus plugging the airline's service to Hawaii.[11] Of course if the plot called for an airplane crash, a United plane would not be used.

Nowadays the fact that a fee has been paid for a promotional consideration is flashed on the screen at the end of the program—a welcome piece of candor but also another plug for the obliging company.

When an airplane does crash, newspapers and news broadcasts must report it, and they even mention the name of the airline (though there was a time when they didn't). But if an airline ad is scheduled next to the news show, it is moved to another spot.

The subservience of news to advertising is reflected mostly in small favors. When someone commits suicide in a downtown hotel, many newspapers don't name the hotel. When a bigshot with a big ad account gets married, the story receives big play on the society page; when the bigshot gets divorced the story is often ignored. The names of shoplifters and embezzlers are printed, but whenever possible the names of the stores and businesses they stole from are not. But no advertiser today is powerful enough to make a major news organization kill an important story, just because the story reflects badly on the advertiser.

Advertisers keep trying, of course. In early 1972, the Bumble Bee Tuna people objected to CBS coverage of a congressional investigation of the fishing industry. The company felt that correspondent Daniel Schorr had paid too little attention to industry rebuttals on water pollution, chemical additives, monopoly, etc. So it instructed its ad agency not to buy any Bumble Bee spots on CBS stations in February and March. Richard Salant, then head of CBS News, commented that "I do not recall ever having been faced before with so blunt an attempt by advertisers to influence news handling and to punish a news organization."[12] It didn't do any good. Coverage remained the same, and Bumble Bee returned to CBS in April.

When the General Electric Company learned that a 1979 Barbara Walters special would include an interview with actress Jane Fonda, the company withdrew its sponsorship of the ABC program. Fonda had recently starred in "The China Syndrome," a motion picture about an attempted cover-up of nuclear power plant hazards, and was outspoken about her own anti-nuclear views. G.E. explained that it was "inappropriate" for a company that manufactured nuclear power equipment to sponsor a show containing "material that could cause undue public concern about nuclear power."[13]

"It's not an unusual situation," commented Anthony D. Thomopoulos, president of ABC Entertainment. "It's happened before that an advertiser looked at a program and found that he had a problem with it, and it'll happen again."[14] What's important is that ABC broadcast the program anyhow, as General Electric no doubt expected it would. Two weeks later came Three Mile Island, the worst accident so far in the history of commercial nuclear power.

Smaller media are more vulnerable to advertiser pressure than the networks, especially if the story under fire is a feature or an investigative piece, rather than a hard news story that everyone else is covering too. When the Danbury (Connecticut) News Times published a used car consumer guide in 1979, local used car dealers responded with an advertising boycott. The publisher met apologetically with the dealers, and promised to provide more favorable coverage in the future. Just as things were settling down, an assistant copy editor ran a photograph of a woman picketing an auto dealership. The next day the editor was fired for "a gross lapse in judgment."[15]

In 1977 the Beaumont (Texas) Enterprise and Journal published a comparison of prices in local supermarkets. Executives from the stores with the highest prices complained directly to publisher Gene Cornwell, who promptly fired the editor responsible for the story. "The point was the story could have affected this newspaper financially and I should have known about it," Cornwell explained.[16]

On the other hand, when local car dealers pulled their ads from the Salina (Kansas) Journal because it had editorialized in favor of a city sales tax, publisher Fred Vandegrift refused to back down. He said his stance, which cost the Journal four percent of total revenues, enhanced the paper's reputation for integrity.[17]

In sum, a big medium is more likely to stand up to advertisers than a small one, and all media are more likely to stand up for big stories than for small ones. But whatever the medium and whatever the story, owners want to make this decision themselves, not leave it to reporters and editors.

And rather than negotiate with the boss, reporters and editors may prefer to kill the story on their own. For example, soon after Chevron gasoline started advertising its "anti-pollution" F-310 additive in 1970, a San Jose (California) Mercury reporter attended a respiratory disease convention in San Francisco. Several of the expert participants were highly critical of the additive and advertising claims for its environmental benefits. The reporter wrote the story as a sidebar (a related feature running next to a piece of hard news) to the convention article. What followed, he says, was not typical of the Mercury:

> The city editor at the time held the story for several days. I questioned him about [it] and he finally redlined [banned] it with the astounding comment: "Oh, hell. This isn't all that pertinent, and the firm has a big advertising campaign with us now. Maybe later." I

have done some intensive research on my own on that score and have determined that it was his own second-guessing of management's desires rather than any kind of order from above that prompted his decision.[18]

When the FTC later charged that the F-310 ads were fraudulent, it became a major story, and the *Mercury* covered it well. (The charge was eventually dropped.)

4. Avoiding Controversy at All Costs. A major advertiser of breakfast foods once sent the following memo to the scriptwriters of the television series it sponsored:

In general, the moral code of the characters in our dramas will be more or less synonymous with the moral code of the bulk of the American middle class, as it is commonly understood. There will be no material that will give offense, either directly or by inference, to any organized minority group, lodge or other organizations, institutions, residents of any state or section of the country, or a commercial organization of any sort. . . . We will treat mention of the Civil War carefully, mindful of the sensitiveness of the South on this subject. . . . There will be no material for or against sharply drawn national or regional controversial issues. . . . There will be no material on any of our

programs which could in any way further the concept of business as cold, ruthless and lacking in all sentiment or spiritual motivation.[19]

The goal of this broad coat of whitewash is to give advertisers an antiseptic environment in which to sell their goods—an environment that nobody could possibly find offensive. This is desirable for two reasons. First, advertisers are afraid that offended readers and viewers might project the controversy onto the ads too, and angrily buy their widgets from someone else. Second, advertisers believe that a sales pitch is most likely to be successful if the audience isn't thinking. Anything that wakes you up and makes you think—even if it doesn't offend you—may lessen the impact of the ads.

All this is especially important on television, which caters to a mass audience of millions that tends to view programs and commercials as all part of the same steady stream of stuff.

In 1972, David W. Rintels, a television writer and chairman of the Committee on Censorship of the Writers Guild of America, testified before the Senate Subcommittee on Constitutional Rights. He complained that writers of TV dramas were not allowed to touch certain topics. On medical shows, for example, the taboos included: the political

BITING THE HAND THAT FEEDS

The media today are a lot less subservient to advertisers than they were fifty or even twenty years ago. A good example of this modern independence was an April, 1973, CBS documentary entitled "You and the Commercial." Narrator Charles Kuralt took the viewer behind the scenes of television advertising. He showed market research efforts to make commercials more persuasive, and interviewed philosopher Erich Fromm on the suggestive power and social impact of advertising. He delved into the emotional topic of children's advertising, and noted that the average child sees 25,000 commercials a year and spends more time in front of a TV set than in school. He covered the laxness of government regulation, the luxuriousness of production budgets, and nearly every other aspect of the world of the TV commercial.[20]

Advertisers were unhappy about "You and the Commercial," as CBS knew they would be. It produced the show anyhow.

VIOLENCE, SEX, AND COMMERCIALS

Television violence has been controversial since the 1950s, but until the 1970s the controversy somehow didn't touch advertisers. TV violence would wax and wane with the vagaries of public and government pressure, while advertisers rode out the periods of heavy violence and less heavy violence without much interest.

Two events in 1976 and 1977 brought sponsors into the picture. The J. Walter Thompson advertising agency, one of the biggest, began advising its clients to avoid the most violent shows, partly because the agency felt the shows "desensitized" the public to real-world violence and partly because it felt they endangered the image and sales of the products advertised. And the National Citizens Committee for Broadcasting began commissioning and publicizing research that named not only the most violent networks and programs, but also the advertisers that were footing the bills for all that murder and mayhem.

"We were quite shocked to be on the NCCB list," explained Bruce Wilson of Kodak. "We got a few hundred letters. The company felt strongly that it did not want to be visible on that list or any such list." So Kodak asked J. Walter Thompson to supervise its ad placements to make sure it got off the list.[21] Other companies that adopted anti-violence ad policies included Oscar Mayer, Kraft, Samsonite, Kimberly-Clark, and Colgate-Palmolive.[22]

When TV started stressing sex in the late 1970s, advertisers had another dilemma to wrestle with. Fearful of still more public pressure, many sponsors withdrew from programs like ABC's controversial "Soap."[23] But the shows proved popular, and skittish advertisers paid a high price for their uprightness. "We decided not to advertise on 'Three's Company' when we saw the pilot episode," said Douglas Johnson of Colgate-Palmolive. "But it's been among the top five shows week in, week out. We probably made the right decision, but theoretically we're missing out on a lot of potential viewers and customers."[24]

Even with advertisers playing a hand, the controversies over violence and sex didn't always affect network policy. In 1978, the president of Sears, Roebuck & Company complained that it was hard to find "enough acceptable programs" on which to advertise.[25] But that may be changing. In 1981, the Coalition for Better Television upped the ante by threatening a boycott, to be organized by Moral Majority and other new-right groups, against sponsors of violent and sexy shows. At the last minute, after private meetings with advertisers, the Coalition announced it would postpone naming the boycott targets in order to give them a chance to change their ad policies "voluntarily."

lobbying of the American Medical Association; the quality and cost of hospital care, especially for the poor; medical education and the supply of doctors; and the need for national health insurance. Rintels read into the record a 1959 memo from the head of an ad agency to a CBS executive:

We know that your series is striving mightily to do things that are different and outstanding so as a series it will rise above the general level of TV drama. This is fine, but since the series is a vehicle for commercial advertisers, it must also be extremely sensitive to utilizing anything, however dramatic, however different, however well done, if this will offend viewers. You know that we can never lose sight of the fact that the sole purpose for which an advertiser spends money is to win friends and influence people. . . . Narrow, prejudiced, ignorant, or what you will, though any part of the population may be, as a commercial vehicle the series must be ever alert not to alienate its viewers.[26]

Rintels summarized his point with a quotation from another writer, William Brown Newman (author of the original "Gunsmoke" script): "In television the writer's job is to write about nothing."[27]

THREATS, BRIBES, AND UNDERSTANDINGS

When the average citizen thinks of advertiser influence, two images are likely to come to mind: the sumptuous party at which journalists are wined and dined into the "right" attitude, and the irate merchant who storms into an editor's office and threatens to withdraw all advertising unless. . . . Both images —the bribe and the threat—have some truth to them. There isn't an editor, reporter, or broadcaster of experience who hasn't experienced both at one time or another. But such tactics are too gauche, and so they tend to fail as often as not.

More subtle techniques are more effective, and always have been. During the oil pipeline wars of the 1890s, the Ohio press was highly critical of John D. Rockefeller's Standard Oil Company. The boss assigned his trusted "fixer," Dan O'Day, to sweeten the sour press. O'Day did not threaten anybody, nor did he offer any outright bribes. Instead, he planned a heavy advertising campaign for Mica Axle Grease, a very minor Standard product. Huge ads were purchased on a regular basis in every Ohio newspaper. Editors got the point: Don't bite the hand that feeds. After a year of receiving monthly checks from the axle grease subsidiary, most had quit knocking John D. and the parent corporation. Mica, by the way, became a top seller.[28]

Even this indirect sort of bribe is not often necessary. When cigarette commercials were banned from broadcasting in 1971, many tobacco companies increased their magazine advertising. In 1978, the *Columbia Journal-* *ism Review* published a study of magazine coverage of the tobacco health issue since the broadcast ban. In magazines that accepted cigarette ads, it was unable to find a single article that clearly explained the dangers of smoking. There were a few "how to quit" pieces and glancing references to the risk, but no hard-hitting articles on cigarettes as a major public health hazard. Without any overt pressure from advertisers, editors intuitively understood to avoid such articles. Some leading national magazines, such as *Reader's Digest* and the *New Yorker,* refuse cigarette advertising. Their coverage was much better.[29]

Over the years, editors have come to know what advertisers expect, and at least on minor stories they supply it without questioning. Nobody has to tell the copy editor of a newspaper to cut the brand name of the car out of that traffic accident article. Editors understand without being told that including the name might embarrass the manufacturer. They understand that embarrassing the manufacturer would be in "bad taste" for the newspaper. They understand that that just isn't the sort of thing one business (publishing) does to another business (automotive). Copy editors don't have to be threatened or bribed; such tactics would only offend and bewilder them.

Can you call this advertiser control? Only in the sense that in the back of every editor's mind is the need to keep advertisers happy. The local auto dealer, after all, doesn't even know that the newspaper copy editor is "censoring" the name of the car. Should the name slip in, the dealer would probably take no action at all. At worst, the topic might come up casually when dealer and managing editor met at the country club or the next Chamber of Commerce meeting. Certainly most auto dealers would not threaten to withdraw their ads over such a minor offense; they need the newspaper at least as much as the newspaper needs them. The important point is that this conflict of wills seldom takes place. Copy editors know their job, and so the brand of the car rarely gets into the traffic accident report.

BROADCASTING: A SPECIAL CASE

When radio was invented at the turn of the century, few thought it would ever be a profit-making medium, and fewer still expected it to earn its profit from advertising. Events reversed expectations:

1919: Dr. Frank Conrad begins the first regular entertainment broadcast, offering Pittsburgh crystal set owners a few hours of music each week.

1920: Westinghouse obtains the first commercial radio license, KDKA, also in Pittsburgh.

1921: Thirty commercial stations are in operation throughout the country.

1922: WEAF in New York sells the first radio advertisement.

1923: The Eveready Battery Company produces its own radio program, "The Eveready Hour," on WEAF.

1924: A "network" hook-up is arranged to broadcast "The Eveready Hour" on several stations at the same time.

By 1927, only eight years after the Conrad broadcast, "The Eveready Hour" was a part of a nationwide NBC radio network. It offered a varied diet of concert music, dance music, and drama. Programs were prepared jointly by the station, the company, and its advertising agency. They were submitted to the sponsor three weeks before air time, and if declared unsatisfactory they were revised or abandoned.

There were objections voiced to the delivery of the radio medium into the hands of the advertisers—but they were quickly outshouted by soaring profit curves. Throughout the 1930s and 1940s, advertisers and their agencies closely controlled the content of the programs they sponsored, and sponsored programs made up the bulk of network radio schedules. The job of the station was merely to sell the time and run the transmitter; the sponsor and its ad agency handled everything else. When commercial television was introduced in the late forties, this pattern of advertiser control and advertiser production was accepted from the very start.

By the late 1950s, the cost of even a single prime-time network television show had grown too big for all but the largest advertisers to afford. When the "quiz show scandals" at the end of the decade brought public pressure on the networks to accept responsibility for programming, broadcasters were only too happy to comply. It was good business as well as good politics. ABC set the trend by encouraging sponsors to scatter their ads among several different programs; NBC and CBS soon followed suit. By 1962 it was rare for a sponsor to produce its own show.

HOW MUCH FOR THIRTY SECONDS?

Advertisers pay the networks an incredible sum for the privilege of reaching your living room. In the 1979-80 season, the cost of a 30-second commercial on "Happy Days" was about $140,000. "M*A*S*H" was getting around $135,000, while advertisers paid a mere $90,000 for 30 seconds of choice airtime on NBC, which was behind in the ratings race. These figures all come out to about half a cent per viewer.[30]

The Super Bowl that season went for an astonishing $234,000 per 30-second commercial. Since more than a hundred million viewers were watching, it was a bargain at roughly a quarter-cent per viewer.[31]

Some continued to sponsor particular network-produced programs, while most settled for the ABC "scatter plan" system. This is still the pattern in broadcasting today.

Though the networks took over programming control from advertisers in the early sixties, they did nothing to alter the fundamental nature of the programs. Advertisers no longer write their own shows, but they still decide where to put their ads. A show without advertiser appeal is unlikely to be produced, unlikelier to be broadcast, and unlikeliest to be renewed for a second season.

To most Americans this sounds like a truism, an inevitable result of the free-market system. It isn't. Even within the context of commercial broadcasting, advertisers need not be all-powerful. In England, for example, sponsors are not permitted to choose where in the day's program schedule their advertising spots will be placed. They simply purchase so many minutes of television time, and the station decides which minutes to put where. British advertisers are free to utilize television or not as they like. But they cannot pick their program, and therefore cannot influence programming to any great extent.

American television is designed to attract advertising, and advertising is designed to

---

THE QUIZ SHOW SCANDALS

On June 7, 1955, emcee Hal March posed before the world's first "isolation booth" and announced to a massive CBS network audience: "This is The $64,000 Question." The era of big-money TV quizzes had begun. NBC countered with "Twenty-One," and within a year six similar programs were on the air.

"The $64,000 Question" was the invention of Revlon, Inc., a cosmetics firm, with some assistance from Revlon's ad agency, a few independent producers, and CBS. It was a package product: Revlon and its agency supervised the content of the show as well as the commercials, and paid CBS $80,000 for each half hour of network time. CBS had some say in how the show was run, but not much. The other quiz programs were similarly organized.

Syndicated columnist Steve Scheuer was the first to suggest that the shows were frauds, fixed to allow certain participants to win. Soon a former contestant on NBC's "Twenty-One" told a congressional subcommittee that he had been forced to lose to Charles Van Doren.

As a result, 1959 was a year of television soul-searching. Van Doren admitted that he had been fed the questions and answers for his $129,000 streak on "Twenty-One." The packagers of "The $64,000 Challenge," meanwhile, revealed that Revlon executives had personally decided which contestants to bump and which to keep. Both networks claimed to know nothing, fixing the blame on the sponsors, ad agencies, and producers. In November, 1959, CBS President Frank Stanton told a House subcommittee:

> I want to say here and now that I was completely unaware . . . of any irregularity in the quiz shows on our network. When gossip about quiz shows in general came to my attention, I was assured by our television network people that these shows were completely above criticism of this kind. . . . This has been a bitter pill for us to swallow. . . . We propose to be more certain . . . that it is we and we alone who decide not only what is to appear on the CBS Television Network but how it is to appear.[32]

Stanton kept his promise, as did the other two networks. Broadcasters resumed control of programming content, and the scandals since have been few and far between.

influence the largest possible audience. It follows that the great majority of TV programming must be aimed at the "mass market," at the lowest common denominator of public viewing tastes. The potential audience for an opera may be, say, six million viewers. The potential audience for an adventure drama in the same time slot may be 30 million. Naturally commercial network television will choose the adventure drama, not the opera, to broadcast. The opera will not even be allotted one-fifth as much broadcast time as the adventure drama (though it has one-fifth the potential audience). Ad rates are determined by audience size, after all. Why should a network forfeit four-fifths of its potential profit on even a single hour of programming?

Even when advertisers can be found who are willing to pay premium rates for small-audience shows, stations and networks are reluctant to go along. A single "high-brow" program can force millions of viewers to switch to another channel; once switched, they may stay there for hours or even days. The ratings on adjacent shows are therefore lowered. Other advertisers begin to complain, and profits begin to drop.

Exactly this happened to the Firestone Hour in the early 1960s. Sponsored by the Firestone Tire & Rubber Company, the classical music program had a consistently low rating. Firestone did not mind; it wanted an "elite" audience for its ads. But adjacent mass-market programs were suffering. After moving the show around a few times in an effort to reduce the adjacency problem, the network finally gave up and refused to continue the show. Companies like Bell Telephone and Xerox, which like to sponsor documentaries and cultural programs, have had similar difficulties finding a time slot.

Advertising revenue is at the heart of the debate over the quality of television programming. In the 1959-60 season NBC and CBS tried an experiment, offering several "high-quality" music and drama shows. ABC, then financially weakest of the three networks, refused to go along. Instead, it chose that season to introduce its gory detective series "The Untouchables," plus ten westerns a week. Ratings were excellent and ABC closed the gap on its older rivals. The next season, NBC and CBS followed the ABC lead, with detective and western series galore. The experiment was over.

Comments critic Robert Eck: "In the audience delivery business, you do not have the luxury of setting either your standards or those of your audience. Instead, they are set for you by the relative success of your competitors."[33] This is another way of saying what then NBC President Robert Kintner answered in response to the question "Who is responsible for what appears on network cameras?": "The ultimate responsibility is ours," Kintner replied, "but the ultimate power has to be the sponsor's, because without him you couldn't afford to run a network."[34]

Notes

[1] "News for Advertisers: A Denver Case," *Columbia Journalism Review,* Summer, 1966, p. 10.

[2] William L. Rivers and Wilbur Schramm, *Responsibility in Mass Communication,* 2nd ed. (New York: Harper and Row, 1969), p. 107.

[3] Donald I. Rogers, "Businessmen: Don't Subsidize Your Enemies," *Human Events,* August 11, 1962, pp. 599-600.

[4] Sol J. Paul, "Opening Television's Pandora's Box," *New York Times,* January 2, 1980, p. A23.

[5] Bill Gloede, "Majority of Dailies Fill Ad Positioning Requests," *Editor & Publisher,* March 1, 1980, p. 11.

[6] Carl E. Lindstrom, *The Fading American Newspaper* (Gloucester, Mass.: Peter Smith, 1964).

[7] "NBC Will Replace McGee by July 31," *New York Times,* July 19, 1974, p. 70.

[8] "Comment," *Columbia Journalism Review,* September/October, 1978, p. 27.

[9] Robert Lindsey, "Product Pluggers Find Gold in Silver Screen," *New York Times,* February 25, 1977, pp. D1, D5.

[10] Alexander Kendrick, *Prime Time* (Boston: Little, Brown & Co., 1969), p. 449.

11 Peter Funt, "How TV Producers Sneak in a Few Extra Commercials," *New York Times,* August 11, 1974, section 2, pp. 1, 15.

12 "Why You Won't See Bumble Bee Ads on C.B.S.-TV," *New York Times,* March 7, 1972, p. 79.

13 Les Brown, "G.E. Quits Fonda Show Over Atom-Power Issue," *New York Times,* February 28, 1979, p. C22.

14 *Ibid.*

15 "Comment," *Columbia Journalism Review,* May/June, 1979, p. 28. "Unfinished Business," *Columbia Journalism Review,* July/August, 1979, p. 77.

16 Carla Marie Rupp, "Editor Fired over Story about Supermarket Prices," *Editor & Publisher,* March 12, 1977, p. 9.

17 "Auto Dealers Pull Ads to Protest Endorsement," *Editor & Publisher,* March 29, 1980, p. 11.

18 David M. Rubin and David P. Sachs, *Mass Media and the Environment* (New York: Praeger, 1973), p. 46.

19 Dallas Smyth, "Five Myths of Consumership," *Nation,* January 20, 1969, p. 83.

20 "TV: Those Commercials," *New York Times,* April 26, 1973, p. 87.

21 Peter M. Sandman, "The Fight over Television Violence Ratings," *More,* April, 1978, pp. 35-40.

22 Winifred I. Cook, "Colgate Quits TV Bloodbath," *The Home News,* New Brunswick, N.J., April 28, 1977, p. 32. Philip H. Dougherty, "Screening Out Violence in the Media," *New York Times,* January 19, 1977.

23 Les Brown, "TV Ads Cancelled on ABC's 'Soap,'" *New York Times,* August 26, 1977.

24 Edwin McDowell, "TV Sex Upsetting Sponsors," *New York Times,* May 30, 1978.

25 *Ibid.*

26 David W. Rintels, "Will Marcus Welby Always Make You Well?" *New York Times,* Sunday edition, March 12, 1972, pp. D1, D17.

27 *Ibid.,* p. D17.

28 Will Irwin, "Our Kind of People," *Collier's,* June 17, 1911, pp. 17-18.

29 R. C. Smith, "The Magazines' Smoking Habit," *Columbia Journalism Review,* January/February, 1978, pp. 29-31.

30 Jack Egan, "Network Advertising: The $1.6-Billion Pyramid," *New York,* July 23, 1979, p. 12. "TV Rights Go Up," *The Home News,* New Brunswick, N.J., August 13, 1979 (AP).

31 Stan Isaacs, "The TV Reaction: No Reaction," *Sports Illustrated,* January 28, 1980, p. 25.

32 Fred W. Friendly, *Due to Circumstances Beyond Our Control* (New York: Random House, 1967), pp. 101-102.

33 Robert Eck, "The Real Masters of Television," *Harper's,* March, 1967, p. 49.

34 "The Tarnished Image," *Time,* November 16, 1959, pp. 72-80.

Suggested Readings

BARNOUW, ERIK, *The Sponsor.* New York: Oxford University Press, 1978.

CUNNINGHAM, ANN MARIE, "Sour Grapes," [*MORE*], November, 1974.

ECK, ROBERT, "The Real Masters of Television," *Harper's,* March, 1967.

HAMMITT, HARRY, "Advertising Pressures on Media," Freedom of Information Center Report No. 367, School of Journalism, University of Missouri at Columbia, February, 1977.

MARTIN, TERRENCE L., "Wilting in the Heat," *Columbia Journalism Review,* May/June, 1974.

SMITH, R. C., "The Magazines' Smoking Habit," *Columbia Journalism Review,* January/February, 1978.

Chapter 6
Source Control

Only a small percentage of the news covered by the mass media comes from on-the-scene reporting. The vast majority must be obtained from news sources—often through interviews, even more often through mimeographed press releases and the like. Sources are seldom unbiased. In one way or another they usually try to control the form and content of the news they offer. Such news management on the part of both governmental and private sources has a tremendous effect on the nature of the news reaching the public.

Throughout his eight years in the White House, President Dwight Eisenhower depended heavily on his press secretary, James Hagerty. One of Hagerty's main jobs was covering up for his boss's longish vacations. *Time* magazine described the process:

Hagerty struggled valiantly and, to a point, successfully in stressing work over play. . . . He took with him on trips briefcases full of executive orders, appointments, etc., and parceled them out daily to make news under the Augusta or Gettysburg dateline. He encouraged feature stories on the Army Signal Corps' elab-

orate setup to keep Ike in close touch with Washington. . . . He did anything and everything, in short, to keep the subjects of golf and fishing far down in the daily stories about the President.[1]

If Hagerty had been working for General Motors, say, instead of Eisenhower, his job would presumably have been a little different. In place of diligence, he would have stressed the economic health of the company and the beauty of its new models. In place of vacations, he would have obscured price hikes and auto safety complaints.

But wherever they work, the purpose and technique of press secretaries and public-relations people are the same. The purpose: to protect and advance the good image of the employer. The technique: news management.

In one form or another, news management is probably as old as news. But conscious, full-time, *professional* news management is a relatively recent invention. The first corporate press agent was hired in the 1880s. The first presidential press secretary was hired twenty years later (by Theodore Roosevelt). Today there are more than 100,000 public-relations people working for private companies, plus tens of thousands more in government. The federal government spends about $1 billion a year on public relations and public information.[2] The executive branch alone spends more on publicity and news than the entire combined budgets of the legislative and judicial branches. All together, the cost of federal government PR is greater than the total newsgathering expenses of AP and UPI, the three television networks, and the ten largest American newspapers. News sources, in short, pay more to manage the news than the media pay to collect it.

All this managed news may sound pretty threatening to freedom of the press—and occasionally it is. But the lion's share of "news management" is simply an organization straightforwardly announcing information favorable to itself, making that information cheap and easy for the media to report. Why get upset about a company issuing a press release detailing its quarterly profits, or a candidate holding a news conference proposing his or her solution to inflation? The company's profits and the candidate's views on inflation are news. If reporters were forced to ferret out these stories instead of being handed them on a silver platter, newspapers and newscasts would have to be more expensive or less complete—or both.

"We're here to get information out to the public," explained Ernest Lotito, then public information chief for the Commerce Department (with a 1978 PR budget of $5.6 million). "The news media couldn't survive without us."[3]

The managers of news are thus also the providers of news, and as such they offer an invaluable service. But by its very nature the service is one-sided. That's not a serious problem when the story has only one side, or when skeptical reporters and opposing news managers are busy digging up the other side. When the other side stays hidden, however, news management is something to worry about.

The tools of news management are many and varied, but two workhorses carry most of the load: press releases and pseudo-events. We will discuss each in turn.

PRESS RELEASES

A press release is a piece of news written by the organization whose activities it describes. It is distributed wholesale to the media in the hope that as many as possible will decide to print or broadcast it without further investigation.

Releases are ground out by the bushel. In a single ten-day period, one small country newspaper in Vermont received 149 handouts from 68 different sources, totaling to 950 pages or nearly a quarter of a million words —more than the length of this book. The list included 80 releases from businesses; 16 from philanthropic organizations; 14 from government; 6 from lobbies and pressure groups; 29 from educational institutions; and 4 from political parties.[4] That's for a *small* newspaper. The average metropolitan daily receives well above a hundred releases a day; the average big-city broadcast station gets at least sixty.

Most releases—say around three-fifths—are thrown away. The bulk of the rest are either used as is or rewritten and condensed in the office, usually the latter. Only a few releases (all the staff has time for) are actually investigated by reporters.

Though most releases are never used, those that are used account for an incredible share of the average news hole. In many newspapers more than half the articles printed started as press releases. Some departments are almost entirely dependent on handouts— finance, travel, etc. Even political reporters have time to cover only the most important stories themselves; for much of the day-to-day news of local government they count on the City Hall mimeograph machine. The backbone of every news beat is the press release.

However important releases may be in reporting local news, they are far more vital on the state, national, and international levels. A Washington correspondent covering the White House spends relatively little time chatting with the president, or even the president's aides. Most of his or her effort is devoted to reading and rewriting White House releases. And reporters covering the "minor" executive departments have even less time for in-person digging and interviewing. Instead, they spend a few hours each morning picking up the day's handouts from the various agencies and offices within their assigned departments. The rest of the day they sort through the stack—throwing out most, rewriting many, following up on maybe one or two.

Governments (as well as private organizations) use press releases to announce new policies and procedures, to publicize plans and accomplishments, to reveal facts and research findings, etc. They may also use releases to influence the course of events. The Defense Department, for example, might issue a release on the "tight nuclear race" between the U.S. and the Soviet Union just as the State Department is planning strategy for arms limitation talks. It seems fair to surmise that at least one purpose of the release is to force the negotiators to adopt a tougher stand.

Broadcast stations as well as newspapers receive press releases (which is why canny PR people call them "news releases" instead), but since releases have no film or tape their broadcast use is limited. The real broadcast version of a press release is a film clip or tape provided to stations for use on their news shows. This is an expensive operation for television, but radio tapes can be made available by telephone, cheaply and easily. The

---

CANNED NEWS AND EDITORIALS

Readers of a small weekly newspaper may occasionally run across brightly written features with titles like "Candy Through the Ages" or "How to Keep Your Dog in Condition." Back on the editorial page they may find surprisingly informed editorials on the importance of cotton tariffs or the dangers of labor unions.

Nothing in the newspaper will say so, but these articles and editorials are probably canned. That is, they probably arrived free at the editor's door in the form of mats or plates ready to be inserted into the paper. Their authors work for a company like the U.S. Press Association or the North American Precis Syndicate, whose clients (the candy industry, the nation's veterinarians, the cotton growers, or the Right to Work Committee) paid a fee for the service.

Individual corporations also mail out canned news and editorials, and in the mid-1970s the Mobil Corporation added a new wrinkle: canned cartoons. It sent cartoons supporting the oil industry to 5,000 small papers. Many used them without identifying the source. Explained an editor in Philadelphia: "There is a tendency to discredit anything the corporations put out. Attribution would tend to weaken the point of my editorial."[5]

Most metropolitan dailies refuse to use canned material. But smaller papers may be desperate for content, and the temptation of a well-written, well-researched, free article or editorial is often too great to resist. The typical canned piece is picked up by roughly 200 newspapers. Press critic Ben Bagdikian calculates that the cost of placing advertisements in all 200 papers would run at least ten times as much—and the canned stuff is much more effective than ads.[6]

station simply calls a toll-free number, tapes the recorded message, adds a newscaster's introduction, and airs the result. Since the mid-1970s the technique has been used by an increasing number of corporations, advocacy groups, and state and federal agencies, including the Carter White House (see p. 387).

The danger of press releases is obvious—they put the initial decision as to what is and is not newsworthy in the hands of the source instead of the reporter or editor. Even when the media follow up a release on their own, the questions they ask and those they forget to ask are likely to be determined by what's in the release. And most releases are *not* followed up. The blatant propaganda may be edited out, but the substance is printed—and it is substance that the source, not the reporter, has selected. It is substance designed to help build the image and advance the aims of its source. It is, in short, public relations.

It is also news. If a newspaper were to quit relying on press releases but continued covering all the news it now covers, it would need at least two or three times as many reporters. That would cost money—and how many of us want to pay eighty or ninety cents for our daily paper? And if a paper stopped covering the news it now gets from releases, we would all be a good deal less informed. The less glamorous arms of the federal government would then operate in almost total secrecy; the plans, promotions, and products of business would come and go without notice; graduations, charity drives, and PTA meetings would be nearly invisible to the community.

Journalists are ambivalent about releases. In 1980, the *Columbia Journalism Review* published a critique of press release use in the *Wall Street Journal,* the largest circulation newspaper in the U.S., and one of the finest. In one typical issue of the *Journal,* author Joanne A. Ambrosio found 111 articles that dealt with specific companies. She wrote the companies and asked what they had given the paper. Seventy responded—53 of them with releases that included all the information in the resulting articles. Thirty-two of the articles were virtually verbatim copies of the releases; 20 of them carried the misleading slug "By a WALL STREET JOURNAL Staff Reporter."

That day the *Journal* published a total of 188 articles. Based on these figures, it can be estimated that between 30 and 45 percent of the *Wall Street Journal* came from press releases. Ambrosio's article was sarcastically entitled "It's in the Journal. But this is reporting?". The paper's executive editor, Frederick Taylor, was not embarrassed. "Ninety percent of daily coverage is started by a company making an announcement for the record," he explained. "We're relaying this information to our readers."[7]

Short of an outright ban, what can we do to control press-release abuses? One very sensible suggestion that has often been made is to identify release-based news stories in the same way we now identify wire service stories, with the initials PR (instead of AP or UPI) in parentheses at the start of the story. This would at least warn readers that what was coming had not been checked out by the newspaper's staff. Another proposal would urge reporters to rely on releases only for routine news, not for controversial public issues.

The biggest problem with press releases is not that they are biased, but that their bias is predominantly in one direction. Most releases come from government, industry, or other big organizations with professional PR staffs. Smaller community groups, representing less established perspectives, are far less likely to have the time or skill to write an acceptable release. If all kinds of people with all kinds of viewpoints had equal skill in public relations, news management would be a much less serious threat. The media would still be manipulated, of course, but at least they would be manipulated by everybody.

LEAKS AND TRIAL BALLOONS

When a top public official wants to try out a new policy without committing the government to it, standard procedure is to release the proposal to the press in secret. In late 1956, for example, the Eisenhower administration began formulating a new policy toward the Middle East. Secretary of State John Foster Dulles invited a select group of Washington correspondents to his home and *leaked* to these reporters the nature of the change. The story was published, on Dulles's instructions, with the source identified only as a high, unnamed State Department official. This was the *trial balloon*. Dulles now waited to see how the public, other government officials, and foreign governments reacted to the proposal. The response was favorable, so Dulles formally announced the new "Eisenhower Doctrine" for the Middle East. If the feedback had been discouraging, Dulles was free to change the plan or to disavow it entirely. Similarly, in 1971 Henry Kissinger anonymously told reporters that Soviet support of India in its dispute with Pakistan might endanger the U.S.–Soviet détente. Kissinger's goal was to warn Russia without committing himself.

The leak and the trial balloon are accepted tactics of diplomacy, but they are subject to abuses. Politicians can punish critical reporters by leaking exclusive stories to those who are not so critical. Alternatively, they can force a reporter to write a one-sided article by trading exclusive information for the reporter's promise not to interview anyone else on the subject. Both practices are common in Washington today.

At best, leaks and trial balloons are delicate. They enable government officials to say anonymously what they don't dare to say on the record. Beyond doubt they are a useful tool of diplomacy, and beyond doubt they are here to stay. But they may mislead the public. Conscientious reporters participate in them reluctantly and cautiously.

Hometown news of Congress, for example, is usually dominated by releases from the legislators themselves. But in 1977 the National Republican Congressional Committee started a release service of its own, called "NEWS FROM THE OTHER SIDE." Aimed at the home districts of 110 incumbent Democrats, the releases pointed out facts like "Congressman so-and-so ranks 293rd in attendance." Then Massachusetts Representative Robert F. Drinan cried foul, accusing the *Waltham News-Tribune* of "irresponsible journalism" for running the OTHER SIDE releases. The paper's news editor responded logically that he ran plenty of Drinan's releases, and the critical ones helped balance his coverage.[8]

However, most releases are not countered in this way.

PSEUDO-EVENTS

The cognac industry of France wanted to introduce the product to the American market with a splash, so in the late 1950s it hired a PR man named Bill Kaduson. On President Eisenhower's 67th birthday in 1957, Kaduson offered several bottles of 67-year-old cognac as a gift. He insured the bottles for $10,000, then took them to the city room of the *Washington Daily News* for photos. The cognac was poured into a special keg and conveyed to the White House by two uniformed guards, where secret service agents accepted the gift on behalf of Eisenhower. The stunt received newspaper headlines throughout the country.

Kaduson also arranged for French Premier Pierre Mendes-France to be photographed drinking cognac when he visited the United States in 1954. He got a French chef onto the Jack Paar television show to create on camera the world's biggest crepe suzette, sprinkled with a gallon of cognac. Between 1951 and 1957 cognac sales in the U.S. increased from 150,000 to 400,000 cases a year. Bill Kaduson claimed much of the credit.[10]

The interesting thing about Kaduson's antics is that they took place solely to gain the attention of the mass media. In Daniel Boorstin's terms, they were not real events at all, but rather "pseudo-events," performed in order to be reported.[11] The media are easily manipulated through pseudo-events. By their very nature they feel compelled to cover conventions, demonstrations, dedications, press conferences, stunts, and the like.

Anyone who desires news coverage is therefore wise to arrange a convention, a demonstration, a dedication, a press conference, or —like Kaduson and his cognac—a stunt.

The congressional committee hearing is a perfect example of a government-sponsored pseudo-event. Some hearings, of course, aim at obtaining information on proposed legislation. But many congressional hearings have a different purpose—to provide publicity for the committee, its members, and its predetermined legislative goals. The 1951 hearings of the Senate Crime Investigating Committee were the first ever to be televised, and they catapulted their chairman, Senator Estes Kefauver, to national fame. The chief witness was Frank Costello, an over-the-hill ex-con, with no real power and little inside information. Kefauver knew that Costello's testimony would have great public impact on TV, despite its limited value as a source of new knowledge. And he was right.[12]

Television is uniquely susceptible to manipulation by means of pseudo-events. The chief advantage of TV over the other media is its ability to reproduce talking pictures. Quite naturally, TV news directors strive constantly to make use of this ability, to come up with effective films or videotapes. But most television news departments are severely understaffed. They can seldom afford to let a reporter and camera operator spend a day or two digging into a story the hard way. It is much, much easier to send the team to cover a ready-made story—a press conference, say, or a demonstration.

The typical public controversy gets covered largely through pseudo-events created by advocates on both sides of the issue. The best pseudo-events win the most coverage.

In the late 1970s, for example, New York City was trying to decide whether to let the supersonic Concorde land at Kennedy airport. Anti-Concorde groups staged protest marches, provided pickets, and even organized a "drive-in" that slowed airport traffic to a crawl. Pro-Concorde forces stuck with more sedate pseudo-events, mostly press conferences. The antis seemed to be gaining until New York publicist Richard Aurelio persuaded French President Valery Giscard d'Estaing to fly a Concorde to Houston. Aurelio explains:

> The mayor of Houston not only met the plane with a brass band but gave a speech at the airport in which he said that with the Concorde Houston was the new New York. . . . The *New York Times* carried a front-page story that said: "Mayor of Houston Twits New York." That was a big break. The New York business community became very anxious and nervous.

"I HAVE HERE IN MY HAND. . . ."

Perhaps the greatest news manager of them all was Senator Joseph McCarthy, the Red-baiting Wisconsin Republican. He began as soon as he reached Washington in 1948, treating reporters to Wisconsin cheese and making himself available night and day for comment on any subject.

McCarthy was a master of the pseudo-event. Often he would call a morning press conference solely to announce an afternoon press conference, thus earning headlines in both editions. His lists of Communists in government service were released only minutes before newspaper deadlines. This insured that he could not be questioned closely, and also made it impossible for the accused to reply in the same edition as they were charged. McCarthy made his most damaging allegations from the Senate floor, where he was protected by law from libel suits. He seldom permitted reporters to examine the "documentary evidence" that he habitually carried in his briefcase and frequently waved in his hand.

By 1952, most of the Washington press corps already knew that McCarthy's claims were often fraudulent and always self-serving. Yet they continued to accord him headlines, day after day. They were caught in the mechanics of the pseudo-event: When a famous Senator accuses someone of Communism it's news—even if the charge is without foundation.

Then came the televised Army-McCarthy hearings of 1954. This time the news management was in the Army's hands, and McCarthy could do nothing to halt the pitiless publicity that brought his career in demagoguery to a quick end.

After winning over the business community, Aurelio says he won over the politicians, the courts, and the Port Authority. When the Concorde finally landed in New York, there was only one picket at the airport—and he was pro-Concorde.[13]

As long as all sides know how to create them, there's nothing especially wrong with pseudo-events. They embody complex issues in easy-to-cover happenings, adding drama to what might otherwise be abstract debates. Of course some of the complexity of the debates gets lost in the drama, but that's the price news managers must pay to get the attention of the public.

Reporters, by the way, are enthusiastic about pseudo-events, because they make good copy and good pictures. But reporters hate the word. They like to think they're covering events.

OTHER TECHNIQUES

The essential tools of news management are the press release and the pseudo-event; no public-relations operation could survive for long without them. Here are a few additional tools.

Interviews. When a large municipal water pipe breaks and floods the neighborhood, the appropriate city commissioner is likely to reach the scene nearly as fast as the TV cameras. The commissioner probably can't help the repair crew solve the problem, but he or she can tell reporters how quickly it is being solved, and how much more money for pipe repair would help. Standing at the commissioner's elbow is the public-relations professional who insisted that the official make the trip. The same PR professional sets up office interviews at calmer moments, and answers questions when the commissioner is not available. This is, of course, a service to the media. It is also a way to control what the media say about the water commission.

Sourcing and suggesting. A good reporter knows that PR people have lots of useful information at their fingertips, and often calls them not only for on-the-record interviews, but also for background statistics, off-the-record advice, and even tips on whom to interview and what to ask. This is called sourcing, and a good PR person does it often; it's a way to influence the news without getting into the news. The phone calls go the other way too—PR people call reporters with suggestions for stories they might want to explore.

Junkets, favors, and contests. Some stories are too expensive for reporters to cover without help, so sources who want the stories covered provide the help. Travel writers get free trips to tropical islands, courtesy of the islands' ministries of tourism; environmental reporters get free tours of nuclear power plants, courtesy of the nuclear industry. On a smaller scale, many journalists get free seats for movies, plays, and sporting events. If these gifts have nothing to do with the story—like a case of liquor at Christmas—they may give the appearance of bribes. The ethical question is harder to call when a junket or a favor genuinely makes a story possible—but perhaps colors the story out of gratitude to the source (see pp. 95-96). Similarly, contests that award cash prizes for the best feature on cigars or the best cartoon about population control offer journalists an incentive to seek out and publish news favorable to the contest sponsors.

Publishing. Aside from managing other people's media, sources are free to publish their own media. Virtually every corporation, interest group, and government agency has an inexhaustible supply of pamphlets and brochures; most publish newsletters for customers, employees, stockholders, or members; some make their own movies; a few even own mainstream newspapers and broadcast stations. The granddaddy of source publishing is the U.S. Government Printing

Office. As of 1980 it has 25,000 titles in stock and sells 47 million copies a year.

Direct access. Despite a source's best efforts to manage the news, reporters sometimes write unfavorable stories. A safer course is to avoid journalists entirely and go directly to the public. For corporations and interest groups, this usually means paid advertising, or perhaps a letter to the editor. The president of the United States has an even better way. He asks the TV networks for prime time to make an important address to the nation, and the networks usually (though not always) say yes. The ways recent presidents have used and abused this power are discussed on pp. 407-08.

When people talk about biased reporting, they usually mean the reporter's bias. That is a real problem, of course. But the greatest bias in most news stories is not the reporter's bias, but rather the bias of the source. With the help of news management experts, it is usually possible to get your story into the media pretty much the way you want it, regardless of the reporter's views. Without the help of news management experts, you will more than likely lose the publicity battle.

The moral for would-be sources is obvious: get expert help. The moral for the media audience is more subtle: remember that much of what you learn from the news is what the sources wanted you to learn.

Most cases of news management involve public relations people who want the story told, and told their way. But sometimes the goal of a news source is not publicity, but secrecy. When a government censors a reporter's article, that too is news management. It is news management also when a reporter is forbidden to attend a meeting, examine a record, or interview an official. And it is news management when the media are threat-ened, bribed, or even politely asked to keep an item to themselves. These practices are associated mainly with government—but private companies and associations have their secrets too.

GOVERNMENT SECRECY

The central premise of the democratic process is that government officials are accountable to the public. That accountability is essentially meaningless unless the public is told what the officials are doing. "The people's right to know" is therefore a cardinal principle of democracy. In practice this means the media's right to know—because only the media are capable of keeping tabs on the government and reporting back to the public.

The concept of government secrecy is thus alien to the democratic theory of press-government relations. But the reality is rather different from the theory. Government officials naturally prefer to conduct much of the public's business in private. Often their reasons are self-serving, but at least occasionally government secrecy seems desirable or even necessary. The problem is deciding when secrecy is called for, and when it isn't. In the United States, the government must have a good reason for hiding anything from the public. But what counts as a good reason?

The most frequent answer—and the most frequently abused—is national security. Nearly everyone agrees that wartime information on troop movements, battle plans, and the like should be kept secret. During World War II an American newspaper revealed that U.S. forces had broken the Japanese Navy Code. (The government of Japan somehow missed the article, and thus failed to change the code.) Certainly the Defense Department should have prevented publication of that fact.

But most cases are not so clear. Troop movements are related to national security all right, but what about troop morale?

Which is more important, that the enemy should be misled about the mood of American forces, or that the American people should be fully informed? And how does national security apply to cold wars, to unpopular wars where many people don't consider the "enemy" an enemy, or to internal "wars" against dissident groups? These are not easy questions to answer.

John B. Oakes of the *New York Times* has pointed out that "the natural bureaucratic tendency to hide mistakes or stupidity behind the sheltering cover of 'national security' is almost irresistible."[14] So is the temptation to use national security as an excuse for political expediency. In 1957, Assistant Secretary of Defense Murray Snyder refused to release photographs of the Titan missile—though the missile itself had been

sitting on an open launching pad in Boulder, Colorado, for months. Snyder waited until just before the 1958 elections, then handed the press a picture of President Eisenhower viewing the Titan.[15] Was national security behind the delay, or vote-getting?

In the early 1960s, in such cases as the Bay of Pigs invasion and the Cuban missile crisis, the media voluntarily withheld information from the public, believing it was up to the president to determine what constituted a threat to national security. This practice continued in the early years of the Vietnam war. But as the war grew more and more unpopular, reporters began to substitute their own judgment for the government's as to whether or not it was in the public interest to report a particular piece of news. In November, 1967, the government launched an extensive

---

LOCAL GOVERNMENT SECRECY

City, county, and state authorities are at least as tempted as the federal government to withhold information from the media. But they don't have the excuse of national security. As a result, considerable progress has been made in guaranteeing the people's right to know on the local level.

By 1979, every state in the U.S. had an open-meeting law, and 49 had open-record laws as well. These regulations are binding on every level of government within the state, right down to the neighborhood board of education. They allow some exceptions—for personnel hearings and income tax files, for example—but by and large they insure that a reporter can get access to local news if he or she works at it.

Unfortunately, working at it often means making a fuss, antagonizing local news sources, and going to court. A big story is worth the hassle, but the media often decide a little one isn't. And even when a newspaper does go to court, it doesn't always win. For an investigation of welfare costs, the *Philadelphia Inquirer* sought access to state and city welfare rolls under the Pennsylvania "right to know" law. The state courts ruled against the paper, partly to protect the privacy of welfare recipients, and partly because the *Inquirer* would not be using the information for "noncommercial" and "nonpolitical" purposes as specified in the law. The U.S. Supreme Court upheld the decision.[16]

The philosophy behind the right to know is well expressed in the preamble to the Ralph M. Brown Act, California's open-meeting law:

> The people of the State do not yield their sovereignty to the agencies which serve them. The people, in delegating authority, do not give their public servants the right to decide what is good for the people to know and what is not good for them to know. The people insist on remaining informed so that they may retain control over the instruments they have created.[17]

The 1979 killing of ABC correspondent Bill Stewart at a roadblock in Managua, Nicaragua was not an isolated incident. In a 15-month period in 1977-78, at least 24 journalists around the world were murdered. Thirty-seven more were tortured by police or injured by political extremists; another 20 were kidnapped. In 1978 alone, 280 journalists in 39 countries were imprisoned or disappeared after arrest. Physical violence is the ultimate censorship, and it is regularly practiced by extremists in and out of government.

In Argentina, for example, 35 journalists were killed between 1974 and 1978; 30 more were arrested, and scores left the country after receiving death threats. There is no formal press censorship in Argentina. With journalists regularly disappearing in the middle of the night, there doesn't have to be. Anti-government reporters are visited by the terror squads. Those who are left are pro-government or silent.

Comments the International Press Institute: "Journalism is fast becoming one of the world's riskiest professions."[18]

media campaign to reassure the American people about military progress in Vietnam. Two months later, the Tet offensive against South Vietnam shattered what was left of the media's trust in the official version of the war. Thus, when the government decided to bomb Cambodia in 1969, it could hide this fact from the public only by hiding it from the press as well. (See Chapter 17 for a more detailed discussion of these events.) Reporters were no longer willing to keep the government's secrets for it.

In 1971, a former Defense Department consultant named Daniel Ellsberg delivered to the *New York Times* a copy of a forty-seven-volume top-secret report on Vietnam policy-making in the 1950s and 1960s. Despite the report's security rating and the fact that its release was unauthorized, the *Times* selected huge segments of it for publication. *Times* editors argued that the report revealed nothing that was dangerous to American national security, but much that was significant in understanding the tragic U.S. involvement in Southeast Asia. In particular, the report made clear how consistently the American government had lied to the American people about the war.

As soon as the first two installments were published in the *Times,* the federal government applied for a temporary injunction to forbid any further installments. When the *Washington Post* began reprinting the report, it too was served with an injunction. Other newspapers were also involved, but it soon became clear that the *Times* and *Post* would serve as the test case. The Nixon administration believed that only the government was entitled to release classified information, and planned to prove the point by forcing the papers to cease publication. This exercise of prior restraint of the press—a technique characteristic of authoritarian dictatorships—was unprecedented in modern American history. The government argued that the circumstances were unprecedented as well; never before had a major American newspaper determined to reveal defense secrets to the entire world. The conflict between freedom of the press and national security seemed unresolvable.

If the report had actually contained vital defense secrets, as the government claimed, the resulting court decision would have been a legal landmark. But a federal district court, a federal circuit court, and finally the U.S. Supreme Court all studied the documents in question, and all were unable to find any important secrets. True, the report would embarrass certain government officials, and even the government itself—but embarrassment is not the same as national security. The Supreme Court dissolved both injunctions, and the "Pentagon Papers" (as they came to be called) were widely reprinted. Even the U.S. Government Printing Office came out with an almost complete edition.

A similar case arose in 1979, when the Justice Department won a restraining order preventing the *Progressive* magazine from publishing an article entitled "The H-Bomb Secret: How We Got It, Why We're Telling It." Author Howard Morland had put together a detailed account of hydrogen bomb design using only publicly available sources. The government argued that if any situation justified prior restraint this one did; the *Progressive* argued that no classified documents, and therefore no government secrets, were involved. Once again a definitive ruling on press freedom versus national security seemed to be in the offing. But the furor over the case led other media to publish various H-bomb details, defeating the government's purpose, and the Justice Department dropped the suit.[19]

The government was more successful in the 1970s in its efforts to stop former CIA agents from revealing the agency's secrets (see p. 179). Relying largely on the secrecy pledges CIA agents sign when they start working, the courts ruled that whether or not the government can keep the media from publishing CIA secrets, it can at least keep ex-agents from revealing them.

This is an important distinction in assessing government secrecy. Over the past twenty years the media have shown an increasing unwillingness to censor themselves voluntarily, and the courts have shown no great enthusiasm for letting the government censor them. Except in truly serious national security cases, then, the only way the government can keep the media from publishing its secrets is to keep the media from knowing about them in the first place.

Hence the government's efforts to plug leaks and punish leakers—efforts that except for the ex-CIA agents have not been remarkably successful. Most leakers, after all, demand anonymity, and most reporters will go to jail sooner than disclose the name of an anonymous source. Sometimes they don't know the name. One top Pentagon official says anonymous leaking of defense information is now so brisk that journalists "regularly get unsolicited documents in the mail."[20]

If somebody knows a government secret and wants it public, then, there's not too much the government can do to stop the leaker from revealing it or to stop the media from publishing it. Most major controversies over government policy fall into this category. There's bound to be an official or legislator somewhere who knows what's going on, disapproves, and wants to blow the whistle. On issues like foreign policy and defense, indiscriminate leaking of fragile negotiations is likely to be a more serious problem than secrecy.

But lesser controversies and bureaucratic decisions often lack the all-important leaker. There may well be no one at the Bureau of Indian Affairs interested in disclosing a questionable reservation oil drilling contract, no one at the Securities and Exchange Commission interested in revealing a borderline stock transaction. What right do the media have to demand this sort of information from the government?

FREEDOM OF INFORMATION

Freedom of information (often called simply "FoI") is the peculiarly American notion that the media and the public are entitled to insist that the government reveal a particular secret. Executive privilege is the more traditional notion that the government is entitled to refuse. Executive privilege is a much older concept, and still a stronger one, but freedom of information is gaining fast.

In 1792, a committee of the House of Representatives asked President George Washington to hand over all documents relating to the Indian massacre of Maj. Gen. Arthur St. Clair and his troops. In response, Washington told Congress that the executive branch of government had a right to withhold any information that might injure the public if disclosed. He turned over the documents anyhow, but later presidents used his arguments for withholding them as the basis for a new "legal" principle, now known as the doctrine of executive privilege. It has been used by many presidents since Washington to thwart not only congressional investigations, but inquisitive reporters as well.

In 1946 the concept of executive privilege was formalized into the Administrative Procedure Act. The act provided that all official documents of the federal government were open to the public, with three exceptions:

1. "Any function of the United States requiring secrecy in the public interest."
2. "Any matter relating solely to the internal management of an agency."
3. "Information held confidential for good cause found."[21]

In other words, everything was open to the public except whatever the executive branch wanted to keep secret.

During the Eisenhower administration, the veil of government secrecy was extended even further. In a series of executive orders, Eisenhower established the security classifications of confidential, secret, and top secret, thus forbidding disclosure of defense-related information. He also commanded all executive employees to keep quiet about their internal discussions, debates, and disagreements. So far as Congress and the public were to know, Eisenhower decreed, the executive branch was unanimous on every issue.

Such matters became far removed from national security. In 1959, for example, a reporter for the *Colorado Springs Gazette-Telegraph* was unable to obtain from the Forest Service a list of ranchers with permits to graze in the Pike National Forest. Explained a Forest Service official: "We have

to protect the permittees. We consider their dealings with the Forest Service and their use of Forest Service land strictly a private affair between them and the Forest Service."[22]

Executive privilege, remember, helps the president keep information from Congress as well as from the mass media. In 1955, therefore, the House Subcommittee on Government Information was set up to look into the problem. Under Democrat John E. Moss of California, the committee accumulated thirty-one volumes of testimony. In several cases it forced executive departments to reveal information they had been keeping hidden. In many more cases, it simply documented the need for a stronger federal law protecting the people's right to know.

The Moss Subcommittee was instrumental in drafting the 1966 Federal Public Records Law (also known as the Freedom of Information Act). The bill was designed to put a stop to unnecessary government secrecy—but by the time President Lyndon Johnson signed it into law, nine exemptions had been added. The law thus left plenty of loopholes for government officials who wanted to evade public accountability for their actions.

Still, the Freedom of Information Act was a definite step forward. It put the burden of proof on the government to justify each secret, and it empowered any citizen (or reporter) to sue in federal court for release of a public record. Among the documents that were "sprung" under the law in the late 1960s were: Labor Department lists of corporations violating federal safety standards; Interstate Commerce Commission travel vouchers; Renegotiation Board records on excessive corporate profits from defense contracts; and Federal Aviation Agency handbooks.

In each of these cases, however, someone had to go to court to *force* the government to release the information. The government did not do so willingly. In fact, as consumer advocate Ralph Nader charged in 1970, "Government officials at all levels . . . have violated systematically and routinely both

VARIATION ON A THEME

The National Aeronautics and Space Administration is as secret-prone as most other federal agencies. Yet it frequently boasts that the American space program—unlike Soviet Russia's—is completely open and aboveboard.

How does NASA resolve the conflict? Easy. It simply floods reporters with mountains of technical facts and figures—too much to understand and much too much to publish or broadcast. NASA aides ("public-relations scientists") are available night and day to help reporters figure out what it all means. At the height of the space program, the job of interpreting the handouts kept the press too busy to look into more controversial aspects of the NASA operation—subcontracting deals, excessive costs, safety problems, etc.

the purpose and the specific provisions" of the Freedom of Information Act.[23]

And usually there was no one sufficiently interested in a particular secret to bother to sue for it. During the first four years of the Freedom of Information Act, only 112 cases were filed under it, and most of those came from persons or organizations outside the mass media. The typical reporter with a deadline to meet is not free to kill a few weeks in a federal courthouse.

The Watergate scandals of 1972-1974 gave new importance to the fight against excessive government secrecy, and new meaning to the doctrine of executive privilege. The key issue was the White House tapes, secretly recorded by President Nixon over a period of several years. As soon as the existence of these tapes was revealed at the Senate Watergate hearings of 1973, it became obvious that they could answer at least some of the questions that had been raised about Watergate and related scandals.

In the year that followed, Nixon handed over progressively more transcripts and tapes to the various grand juries, special prosecutors, and House committees investigating Watergate. But he always held some back, arguing that the confidentiality of presidential discussions should be protected, and that his right of executive privilege was absolute and could not be second-guessed by any court.

The case reached the Supreme Court in July, 1974, just as the House Judiciary Committee was moving toward impeachment. A unanimous decision against Nixon was announced on July 24; the president would have to give up the tapes. Chief Justice Warren E. Burger, speaking for the Court, acknowledged the existence of a doctrine of executive privilege rooted in the Constitution, but held that the application of that doctrine could be limited by the courts. Executive privilege, he declared, "must yield to the demonstrated, specific need for evidence in a pending criminal trial."[24] Some of the tapes did indeed reveal that Nixon had lied about his 1972 involvement in the Watergate cover-up. Faced with the virtual certainty of impeachment and conviction, President Nixon resigned on August 9.

Spurred on by Watergate, Congress passed seventeen amendments to the 1966 Freedom of Information Act, closing many of the loopholes in the original law. One of the key amendments called for judicial review of classified information to determine if the executive branch was justified in withholding it. President Ford vetoed the package, arguing that judicial review of classified materials would give federal judges "the initial classification decision in sensitive and complex areas where they have no expertise."[25] Congress overrode the president's veto, and the new Freedom of Information Act went into effect in February, 1975. The amended law enables a reporter—or any citizen—to petition a federal court to decide whether "secret" government information should be released. It also provides strict time limits to keep a government agency from sitting for years on a demand for information. Loopholes still exist, but the amended Freedom of Information Act makes government secrecy harder, and access to government information easier.

William Shawcross used the amended Act to get a look at government files on the secret bombing of Cambodia during the Nixon administration. The Union of Concerned Scientists used it to review the records of 230 nuclear power plant accidents.[26]

But executive privilege is still very much alive. The reporters, scholars, and antiwar activists who sued for transcripts of Henry Kissinger's telephone conversations learned from the lower courts that the Freedom of Information Act does not apply to the president's immediate staff within the executive office. Because of executive privilege, Kissinger was immune for the period he served as national security adviser. But what about Secretary of State Kissinger? While still in office, Kissinger had removed his phone transcripts from the State Department. In 1979, the Supreme Court held that by doing so he had successfully put the transcripts beyond the reach of the Freedom of Information Act.[27] And in 1981, the Reagan administration proposed new amendments designed to weaken the Act and ease the path of government secrecy, especially in the national security area.

CORPORATE SECRECY

Except for the government, Americans are free to keep whatever secrets they want to keep. There are limitations on this freedom; corporations, for example, are required to make public their financial statements and the names of their principal stockholders. And they have to give all sorts of information to various government agencies. But if a company wants to say absolutely nothing to the mass media about its activities, it is within its rights.

Some day the United States may decide that large corporations, like governments, should be held accountable to the public. A huge company like General Motors or Exxon obviously has a very substantial impact on the lives of many Americans. The policy decisions of GM's president, for example, probably affect you more than the policy decisions of all but a handful of government officials. At the moment, you have no right to know what these decisions are. Only the government must have a good reason for hiding information from the public. Corporations may hide—or try to hide—whatever they wish.

To make matters worse, reporters are a lot less persistent about investigating the secrets of industry than they are in pursuing government secrecy. Most journalists believe that politics is the nation's number one news story, and so business reporters are both fewer in number and lower in status than political reporters. And they are much more polite to their sources. While most government reporters would jump at the chance to expose official double-dealing, many business reporters consider this sort of muckraking grossly inappropriate, almost sacrilegious.

When corporate secrets *are* exposed in the media, it is usually because some interest group opposed to the corporation has obtained and leaked the information. In recent years this has happened with greater and greater frequency, as consumer advocates, environmental groups, populist political movements, and the like have discovered how to use public relations to their own advantage. The result is a startling and important change in business reporting. From the very beginning, political reporters could count on opposition forces to supply the information that government officials were hiding. But until recently large corporations had no or- ganized opposition. Today that opposition exists, and it is slowly teaching the media what rocks to look under in their coverage of corporate America.

The move toward aggressive coverage of business is greatly helped by the increasingly public activities of many American corpora- tions. Most big companies today are enmeshed in a complex network of government sub- sidies, government contracts, and govern- ment regulations. Their dealings with gov- ernment provide ample opportunity for po- litical reporters to get a good look at their policies and actions. Those dealings also re- quire a more active corporate PR strategy than was customary a few decades ago. To win the government concessions they want and defeat the government regulations they fear, companies must present their case to the public via the media. The days when corporate PR departments felt free to re- spond to every unpleasant question with a tight-lipped "no comment" are almost over. Today they usually offer an answer of some sort, and thus open the door for other sources to offer quite different answers.

Because of these changes, corporate secrecy today often means manipulating the media, not ignoring them. A good example is the way the Transamerica Corporation lined up press support for construction of its massive, pyramid-shaped headquarters in downtown San Francisco.[28]

The company kept plans for the building secret as long as possible. Finally, in Janu- ary, 1969, Transamerica announced a press conference. The date was chosen to coincide with the annual chamber of commerce ban- quet. The company planned to make this "the day of the pyramid," and so it was. Transamerica filled the morning with brief- ing sessions for key officials and neighbor- hood groups. Next, the company served lunch to the publishers and general man- agers of all the city's newspapers and tele- vision stations. Then came the afternoon press conference, featuring not only company officials, but the mayor and the president of the chamber of commerce as well. The mayor himself helped pull back the drapes to ex- pose a five-foot model of the building. The model was prominently displayed at the ban- quet that evening, and the audience of more than a thousand listened while the chamber of commerce president praised the pyramid.

Press coverage was massive and favorable. The pyramid was front-page news in North- ern California. Both wire services carried pictures of the model and the story appeared in more than 140 American newspapers. Even more important to Transamerica, both San Francisco papers ran editorials support- ing the project.

Despite the press support, various citizen groups and some public officials fought the Transamerica pyramid. Demonstrations were organized by both sides to rally support. John Krizek, Transamerica's public-relations manager, described the company's response

---

GARDEN CLUB NEWS MANAGEMENT

News management can turn up in the most unlikely places. One afternoon in 1964, reporter Alex Dobish of the *Milwaukee Journal* showed up at the Wauwatosa Woman's Club to cover its monthly meeting. The featured speaker was a local attorney, and his topic was "managed news."

No, said club chairwoman Mrs. Cyril Feldhausen, Mr. Dobish could not cover the lecture. "What he says is for us," she vowed, adding that she would "give the papers what is to be said." Before booting Dobish she reminded him that "we are not getting the news from the news media."[29]

to one anti-pyramid demonstration—a model of effective public relations:

> Our strategy was not to lock ourselves up in our corporate fortress, and thereby lend credence to the charges of corporate arrogance and insensitivity. And we did not want to expose our officers to a dialogue with highly emotional demonstrators, in front of the TV cameras. Therefore it was the public relations manager who greeted the leaders of the demonstration, as they came through the door, followed by the TV cameras. After promising to deliver their petition to the chairman of the board, he led a covey of attractive corporate secretaries out on the sidewalk to serve iced tea to the demonstrators, with the news cameras as witnesses.

Within less than a year, Transamerica convinced the necessary city boards to approve the exact design it wanted. To forestall any possible rebirth of the opposition, Transamerica held the groundbreaking ceremony in absolute secrecy.

The point of this anecdote is that big corporations can't always keep their secrets totally secret any more. No doubt Transamerica would have liked to build its pyramid without a word to anyone—but it couldn't. So it kept quiet about what it thought it could hide successfully, and embedded the rest in a facile, professional publicity campaign. And it won.

In July and August of 1973, seven American corporations faced an even tougher secrecy problem. In the wake of the Watergate scandals, they were forced to admit that they had illegally donated almost half a million dollars to President Nixon's 1972 re-election campaign. They couldn't keep their guilt a secret. What they could do—and did do—is control the announcement in such a way as to insure minimal public impact.

Before making its confession public, each of the seven companies sent a lawyer to the office of the Watergate special prosecutor, Archibald Cox, to formally acknowledge the illegal contribution; and then to the office of the Finance Committee to Re-Elect the President, to ask for the money back. Then each company issued its public statement—almost invariably on a late Friday afternoon.

Why late Friday afternoon? On Fridays, especially during the summer, most newspapers and broadcast news departments operate short-handed after about 5 P.M. Any statement released at that time is certainly too late for the Friday papers, and probably too late for the Friday evening network news. Since these releases were very short, a reporter who wanted to make a substantial story out of one of them would have had to go looking for more information—hard to do on a Friday night or a Saturday with only a skeleton crew in the newsroom.

The result for most of the companies was a short article in Saturday's newspaper and a short story on Saturday's newscast. Saturday papers and news programs, of course, have the smallest audience of the week. And by the time Monday rolled around and people were available for comment, the confessions were old news. This strategy did not prevent the bad publicity entirely, but it did help ease the PR blow, maybe a lot. Prof. Raymond D. Horton of the Columbia University School of Business commented: "If a public official had to admit to this kind of thing, he'd be in a hell of a lot of trouble. What amazes me is that there isn't more of an outcry. They seem to be getting away with it."[30]

COOPERATION AND INTIMIDATION

Keeping secrets from the public is the hardest kind of news management to accomplish. It takes a lot more clout to keep news out of the media than to get news into the media. In fact, as we have said, the only sure-fire way to prevent newspapers and broadcast stations from revealing a piece of information is to make certain they never find out about it. But sometimes, inevitably, a reporter stumbles onto the secret. What then?

When the British government is anxious to prevent a certain piece of information from appearing in the British media, it uses what is called the D notice system. A D notice is a formal letter circulated confidentially to the media, warning them that some fact is of secret importance to the government and should not be published. The notice is only advisory, but the implication exists that any item covered in a D notice may also be protected under the British Official Secrets Act. Very few D notices are ever ignored, even when they seem to the media less concerned with national security than with national scandal.

The United States has nothing like the D notice system. But a confidential chat between a reporter and a government official sometimes serves the same purpose, as does a phone call from the president to the publisher. This is called voluntary self-censorship. In wartime it is necessary, and far safer than government-enforced censorship. In peacetime, however, it is a dangerous form of government news management.

President Franklin Roosevelt had a standing request that no pictures be taken of him while in pain from the polio that crippled him for decades. Once, surrounded by dozens of photographers, the president fell full-length on the floor—and not a single picture was snapped. This was very polite of the photographers—but are journalists supposed to be so polite? In May of 1970, a Nixon adviser asked the *New York Times* to skip certain details of the resumption of bombing in North Vietnam, because those details were "embarrassing" to the president.[31] The *Times* printed them anyhow—a blow to politeness, perhaps, but a victory for the people's right to know.

Traditionally, the American media have tended to cooperate with the American government on the matter of keeping secrets, especially when national security was involved. But in recent years—largely because of the government's "credibility gap" in foreign affairs—such cooperation has waned.

The *New York Times* dutifully downplayed the planned Bay of Pigs invasion in 1961, and kept the secret of the Cuban missile crisis in 1962. But by 1971 the *Times* was willingly reprinting top-secret government documents supplied by a former Defense Department consultant. We will return to this issue in Chapter 17.

When cooperation fails as a tool of government news management, intimidation may be tried in its stead. Perhaps because he received so little cooperation from the media, President Richard Nixon relied very heavily on intimidation. In 1969, he appeared on national television to explain, in person, his Vietnam policy. Immediately after the speech, network commentators and their guests began to discuss the president's remarks—analyzing, interpreting, often criticizing.

Ten days later, addressing the Midwest Regional Republican Committee in Des Moines, Vice President Spiro Agnew delivered a stinging attack on network television news. He focused particularly on the "instant analysis" that had followed the Nixon speech, arguing that TV commentators comprised a "tiny and closed fraternity of privileged men." Agnew continued:

> I am not asking for government censorship or any kind of censorship. I am asking whether a form of censorship already exists when the news that forty million Americans receive each night is determined by a handful of men responsible only to their corporate employers and filtered through a handful of commentators who admit to their own set of biases.[32]

There is much truth in what the vice president had to say. That is not the point. The question is, to what extent was President Nixon, through Agnew, trying to cow the media into being less critical of White House policies? And to what extent did he succeed?

Shortly after Agnew's speech, the Federal Communications Commission asked all three networks to submit transcripts of their commentary on the Nixon Vietnam telecast—clearly implying at least the possibility of government interference. White House Director of Communications Herbert Klein made the threat even more explicit. "If you look at the problems you have today," Klein said, "and you fail to continue to examine them, you do invite the government to come in. I would not like to see that happen."[33] As for the effectiveness of the attack, many observers noted that television commentary on the president's later war messages tended to be bland and noncommittal. CBS cut out all "instant analysis" for a while, then reinstated it.

The Nixon administration's efforts to intimidate the media reached a first-term peak as the 1972 election approached. Vice President Agnew told a Republican rally in Palo Alto, California, that "the pundits of the networks and national publications" are "demagogues" who "pander to the worst instincts of the leftist radical mob." Presidential speechwriter Patrick J. Buchanan declared in a television interview that if the networks continued to "freeze out opposing points of view and opposing information . . . you're going to find something done in the area of antitrust-type action, I would think." Sure enough, the Justice Department moved against the networks, accusing them of having "monopolized and restrained trade in prime-time entertainment programming." Bill Monroe, then Washington editor of the NBC "Today" show, called the administration campaign an effort to "maximize government pressure and minimize media independence."[34]

The attacks on the media continued after the election, with the harshest assaults aimed at the *Washington Post*'s Watergate coverage. Nixon allies applied for the licenses of *Post*-owned broadcast stations in Florida, while at the White House the *Post* stories were explicitly denounced as "character assassination" and "the shoddiest type of journalism."[35] But as the Watergate saga unfolded, the tables were turned. By spring,

1973, White House Press Secretary Ron Ziegler was publicly apologizing to the *Post* and declaring the president's previous statements on Watergate "inoperative."

The liberal leaning of many top journalists is real; so is the threat of powerful media monopolies. But when high government officials publicly attack the mass media, there is more at stake than merely whether or not their criticisms are justified. Even the most valid arguments, from that source, constitute a form of news management—an attempt to intimidate the media.

Intimidation is by no means confined to the White House. It seems most frequent, in fact, in the military. During the postwar occupation of Japan, General Douglas MacArthur branded several reporters as Communists, and demanded the removal of others because they were unfair or overly critical. Some correspondents were threatened or interrogated, and one had his home raided by Army investigators. The harassment continued until only friendly reporters were left.

In 1962, Assistant Secretary of Defense Arthur Sylvester directed all Pentagon employees to file a report on "the substance of each interview and telephone conversation with a media representative . . . before the close of business that day."[36] Sylvester also had Public Information Officers sitting in on many of the interviews—effectively terrorizing both the source and the reporter. Hanson Baldwin of the *New York Times* recalls that his fellow military writers were investigated by the FBI, shadowed in the halls of the Pentagon, and subjected to frequent telephone wiretaps—all on stories without any overtones of national security.[37]

In 1970, CBS produced and broadcast a documentary entitled "The Selling of the Pentagon." One of the most admirable (and controversial) programs of the year, the documentary dealt with the public-relations activities of the Defense Department.

The government's response to this exposé of Pentagon news management was more news management. The Defense Department

A STAGED ATROCITY?

Late in 1969, the CBS evening news program broadcast a film of a South Vietnamese soldier stabbing to death a North Vietnamese prisoner. The Pentagon asked CBS to turn over the unused portion of the film for study, and CBS refused. At that point Presidential Assistant Clark Mollenhoff went to work. Mollenhoff decided that CBS had staged the entire episode. He passed along his conclusion to syndicated columnists Jack Anderson and Richard Wilson, who then published versions of the Mollenhoff theory.

On May 21, 1970, CBS responded to the attack. In a seven-minute segment incorporating the original film, the network convincingly demonstrated that it was genuine. CBS correspondents even tracked down the South Vietnamese sergeant who had done the stabbing, and put his cheerful confession on the air. The White House was forced to back down.

Walter Cronkite concluded this unprecedented nationwide rebuttal with the following words:

> We broadcast the original story in the belief it told something about the nature of the war in Vietnam. What has happened since then tells something about the government and its relation with news media which carry stories the government finds disagreeable.

immediately issued a statement claiming that the documentary was biased, that interviews with Pentagon spokesmen were edited out of context to make them appear more damning than they actually were. Some of the specific complaints were indeed justified, but they effectively obscured the main point—that the documentary itself was essentially accurate. When the Defense Department demanded rebuttal time, CBS agreed—and rebutted the rebuttal in the same program. It also rebroadcast the original documentary for those who had missed it the first time.

In the wake of these events, the House Commerce Committee, headed by Harley O. Staggers (D.-W.Va.), decided to investigate the documentary. The committee asked CBS to supply all film used in preparing the program, including film that was not broadcast. Despite a subpoena, CBS President Frank Stanton refused, claiming the protection of freedom of the press. The committee voted 25-13 to cite Stanton for contempt of Congress, but the full House (not anxious to battle a powerful network on a debatable legal point) turned down the recommendation. It is conceivable, of course, that the Staggers Committee actually contemplated some sort of government regulation of broadcast documentaries (though any such regulation would almost certainly be unconstitutional). But most observers agreed that the purpose of the investigation was more probably to intimidate the media, to make broadcasters think twice before planning another documentary critical of the federal government.

Private corporations are also fond of intimidation as a form of news management. Back in the 1950s, syndicated columnist Ray Tucker wrote a scathing account of airline lobbying for the rights to a new route. The day before the column was scheduled to appear, Pan American Airways sent the following telegram to every newspaper that subscribed to the syndicate: "Pan American understands that you may be planning to publish a column by Ray Tucker containing numerous scurrilous references to Pan American. We feel it our duty to tell you that we believe a number of these statements to be libelous. You may also wish to take into consideration the columnist's obvious bias against the airline that has earned for the United States first place in world air transport." Many papers decided not to carry the column.[38] The threat to withdraw advertising if a certain story is published (see Chapter 5) is another common variety of corporate intimidation.

In the final analysis, the best answer to secrecy is an uncompromising attitude on the part of the mass media. Reporters must be willing to dig, to ask embarrassing questions, to play off one source against another, to follow up unpromising leads. Editors must be willing to back up their reporters, to give them the time and freedom they need in tracking down elusive secrets. And owners must be willing to publish or broadcast what the reporters and editors have found, without bowing to polite requests or overt threats.

It can be done. In the 1960s, while columnist Joseph Alsop was complaining about "total news control" by Defense Secretary Robert McNamara, his brother Stewart Alsop was publishing a detailed story on American defense planning, based on unauthorized interviews with forty senior Pentagon officials.

Notes

[1] "Authentic Voice," *Time*, January 27, 1958, pp. 16-20.

[2] "Government Spends $1 Billion on Image," *New York Times*, August 6, 1978, p. 43 (UPI).

[3] *Ibid*.

[4] Evan Hill, "Handouts to the Country Editor," *Nieman Reports*, July, 1954, pp. 8-9.

[5] Mark Green, "How Business Is Misusing the Media," *New York Times*, December 18, 1977.

[6] Ben H. Bagdikian, "Behold the Grass-Roots Press, Alas!" *Harper's*, December, 1964, pp. 102-105.

[7] Joanne A. Ambrosio, "It's in the Journal. But This Is Reporting?", *Columbia Journalism Review*, March/April, 1980, pp. 34-35.

[8] Adam Clymer, "G.O.P. Benefits as Small Papers Publish Press Releases as News," *New York Times*, July 18, 1977, p. 12.

[9] Conversations between David Sachsman and Lorry Lokey, July 26, 1971, and June 3, 1980.

[10] Irwin Ross, *The Image Merchants* (Garden City, N.Y.: Doubleday, 1959), pp. 23-24, 129.

[11] Daniel J. Boorstin, *The Image* (New York: Atheneum, 1962).

[12] Ivan Doig, "Kefauver Versus Crime: Television Boosts a Senator," *Journalism Quarterly*, Autumn, 1962, p. 490.

[13] Nicholas Pileggi, "That New Flack Magic," *New York*, September 3, 1979, pp. 36-41.

[14] John B. Oakes, "The Paper Curtain of Washington," *Nieman Reports*, October, 1958, p. 3.

[15] Samuel J. Archibald, "Secrecy from Peanuts to Pentagon," Freedom of Information Center Publication No. 20, School of Journalism, University of Missouri, Columbia, Missouri, pp. 1-2.

[16] Warren Weaver Jr., "High Court Dismisses Paper's Plea for Access to Welfare Rolls," *New York Times*, March 19, 1974, p. 13.

[17] Ralph M. Brown Act, California Government Code, Sec. 54950.

[18] Andrew Kopkind, "Publish and Perish," *MORE*, April, 1978, p. 13. "The Riskiest Profession," *Editor & Publisher*, January 21, 1978, p. 6. "Some Reporters Called Back from Managua," *Editor & Publisher*, July 7, 1979, p. 17. "Journalists Abroad: Almost 300 Arrested," *The Quill*, February, 1979, p. 6. "Drive on Argentine Leftists Takes Toll of Journalists," *New York Times*, March 12, 1978, p. 22.

[19] "Bomb Article Lures F.B.I. to Magazine," *New York Times*, October 30, 1979 (UPI).

[20] Nicholas M. Horrock, Anthony Mauro, and Richard Burt, "White House Reported Acting To Stem Information Leaks," *New York Times*, May 14, 1978, pp. 1, 24.

[21] "Press-Endorsed Info Act Restrictive, Frustrating," *Editor & Publisher*, November 12, 1966, p. 11.

[22] Archibald, "Secrecy from Peanuts to Pentagon," p. 1.

[23] "Government's Urge to Hide Facts," *San Francisco Sunday Examiner and Chronicle*, "This World," April 12, 1970, p. 21.

[24] Raoul Berger, "Lessons of Watergate," *New York Times*, February 19, 1975, p. 35. Saul Pett, "An American Ordeal," *New Brunswick* (N.J.) *Home News*, April 6, 1975, p. A14.

[25] Martin Arnold, "Congress, the Press and Federal Agencies Are Taking Sides for Battle Over Government's Right to Secrecy," *New York Times*, November 15, 1974, p. 15.

[26] Karen J. Winkler, "FBI Destroys Files, Historians Charge," *The Chronicle of Higher Education*, January 7, 1980, pp. 1, 4.

[27] Linda Greenhouse, "Supreme Court Backs Kissinger on Transcripts," *New York Times*, March 4, 1979, pp. A1, B9.

[28] John Krizek, "How to Build a Pyramid," *Public Relations Journal,* December, 1970, pp. 17-21.

[29] Curtis D. MacDougall, *Reporters Report Reporters* (Ames, Iowa: Iowa State University Press, 1968), pp. 95-96.

[30] Michael C. Jensen, "The Corporate Political Squeeze," *New York Times,* September 16, 1973, pp. F1-F2. "Corporations: Where the Money Went," *Newsweek,* January 13, 1975, p. 66.

[31] Jack Anderson, "A Reminder of McCarthy Era," *San Francisco Chronicle,* May 8, 1970, p. 41.

[32] Address of Vice President Spiro T. Agnew before the Midwest Regional Republican Committee, Des Moines, Iowa, November 13, 1969.

[33] "Beat the Press, Round Two," *Newsweek,* December 1, 1969, p. 25.

[34] Potomacus, "The Word from Washington," *Progressive,* July, 1972, p. 10.

[35] James McCartney, "The Washington 'Post' and Watergate: How Two Davids Slew Goliath," *Columbia Journalism Review,* July/August, 1973, p. 18.

[36] Clark R. Mollenhoff, "News 'Weaponry' and McNamara's Military Muzzle," *Quill,* December, 1962, p. 8.

[37] Hanson W. Baldwin, "Managed News, Our Peacetime Censorship," *Atlantic Monthly,* April, 1963, p. 54.

[38] Wilbur Schramm, *Responsibility in Mass Communication* (New York: Harper & Brothers, 1957), p. 154.

Suggested Readings

"After the Pentagon Papers—Special Section: The First Amendment on Trial," *Columbia Journalism Review,* September/October, 1971.

AMBROSIO, JOANNE A., "It's in the Journal. But This Is Reporting?" *Columbia Journalism Review,* March/April, 1980.

BAGDIKIAN, BEN H., "Behold the Grass-Roots Press, Alas!" *Harper's,* December, 1964.

BERGER, RAOUL, *Executive Privilege.* Cambridge, Mass.: Harvard University Press, 1974.

BOORSTIN, DANIEL J., *The Image.* New York: Atheneum, 1962.

FRIEDMAN, ROBERT, "The United States v. The Progressive," *Columbia Journalism Review,* July/August, 1979.

KIELBOWICZ, RICHARD B., "The Freedom of Information Act and Government's Corporate Information Files," *Journalism Quarterly,* Fall, 1978.

KOPKIND, ANDREW, "Publish and Perish," [MORE], April, 1978.

MORLAND, HOWARD, "The H-Bomb Secret, How We Got It, Why We're Telling It" (and associated articles by Erwin Knoll, John Buell, Samuel H. Day Jr., Ron McCrea, and Ron Carbon), *The Progressive,* November, 1979.

MORRIS, ROGER, "Eight Days in April: The Press Flattens Carter with the Neutron Bomb," *Columbia Journalism Review,* November/December, 1978.

ROSS, IRWIN, *The Image Merchants.* Garden City, N.Y.: Doubleday, 1959.

ROTHMYER, KAREN, "The McGoff Grab," *Columbia Journalism Review,* November/December, 1979.

"Special Section: Watergate and the Press," *Columbia Journalism Review,* November/December, 1973.

WEINSTEIN, ALLEN, "Open Season on 'Open Government,' " *The New York Times Magazine,* June 10, 1979.

Chapter 7
Government Control

The traditional American commitment to free-dom of the press is an unusual idea. Throughout history most governments have controlled their media, and most governments continue to do so today, justified by theories of press-government relations that make as much sense to them as the First Amendment makes to us. Even in the United States, press freedom is far from absolute. New theories and new laws are constantly evolv-ing in pursuit of the proper balance between the rights of the media and the rights of the rest of society.

The First Amendment to the United States Constitution reads in part: "Congress shall make no law . . . abridging the freedom of speech or of the press." This is the earliest and most important statement of the rela-tionship between the U.S. government and the mass media. Because it is part of the Constitution, all other laws and government policies must be consistent with it—otherwise they are unconstitutional and therefore il-legal.

Freedom of the press is not limited to newspapers and magazines. In a series of ju-dicial decisions, the courts have made it clear that the First Amendment applies also (though somewhat differently) to broadcast-ing, film, and the other mass media. Nor is it only Congress that must respect press freedom. The other arms of the federal gov-ernment are equally bound by the First Amendment. By means of the Fourteenth Amendment, the same restrictions are bind-ing on state and local governments as well.

It is fair, then, to rephrase the First Amend-ment as follows: "No arm of any government shall do anything . . . abridging the free-dom of speech or of the media." That is where we start.

Throughout our history, there have been judges on the Supreme Court who believed that the First Amendment meant exactly what it said: "no law." The most recent rep-resentative of this viewpoint was the late Justice Hugo Black, who steadfastly held that anything any government does to regu-late the mass media is unconstitutional. Jus-tice Black was in the minority. His colleagues believed that libel laws are needed to protect individuals from unfair attacks, that obscen-ity laws are needed to protect society from moral corruption, that occasional censorship is needed to protect military secrets from en-emy spies. They believed, in other words, that freedom of the press is not absolute, that it has exceptions.

This chapter—one of the longest in the book—is devoted to the exceptions, to the ways our government permits itself to control our mass media. We will start by examining some alternative theories on the proper relationship between government and the media.

THE AUTHORITARIAN THEORY

The printing press was born in the wholly authoritarian environment of fifteenth-century Europe. The Church and local political leaders exercised their waning power with little thought for the will of the people. Infant nation-states flexed their new-found muscles. Absolute monarchies demanded absolute obedience. It was no time for a small printer with a small hand press to insist on freedom.

The first books to be published, Latin Bibles, posed no particular threat to the Establishment. But before long books and pamphlets began to be printed in the vernacular, and a growing middle class soon learned to read them. Here was an obvious danger to the aristocracy—who could tell what seditious or heretical ideas those books and pamphlets might contain? Every government in Europe recognized the urgent need to regulate the press.

A philosophy of regulation quickly developed. By definition, the ruling classes were right in everything they did and said. Any published statement that supported or benefited the government was therefore "truth." Any statement that questioned or damaged the government obviously had to be "falsehood." Consistently truthful publishers— those who regularly supported the government—were rewarded with permission to print religious texts, commercial newsletters, and other nonpolitical material. Untruthful publishers—dissenters—were denied permission to print anything; many wound up in prison as well. As one scholar has put it, the

function of the mass media in the sixteenth century was to "support and advance the policies of government as determined by the political machinery then in operation."[1] This is the authoritarian theory of the press.

Johann Gutenberg and his successors were not government employees. The printing press was invented well before State Socialism, and for the first 400 years of post-Gutenberg history the presses were privately owned. From the very beginning, private ownership was the major problem of the authoritarian theory: How can the government control the media when it doesn't own them?

The earliest answer was licensing. Each printer was required to obtain a "royal patent" or license to print. Usually the license included vast privileges, often a local monopoly. It was understood that if a printer deviated from the government-defined truth, that printer's license would be revoked. Licensing by itself didn't work very well. Unlicensed printers appeared by the hundreds, and even some licensed ones occasionally published anti-government materials, possibly by accident. For a while precensorship was tried—a government censor for each press, reading every word it printed. But the volume of copy soon made precensorship impossible except for emergencies.

By the end of the seventeenth century, the primary tool of authoritarian governments was postcensorship. Printers could publish anything they liked. Eventually the government got around to reading it—and if the government didn't like what it read, that was the end of that printer. Stiff fines, long jail sentences, and occasionally even death were the penalties for a seditious publication. The mere threat of these punishments was enough to keep most printers in line.

The authoritarian theory is not some dead notion dredged up from seventeenth-century history. Many Asian, African, and South American countries today maintain authoritarian controls reminiscent of Henry VIII. About 60 percent of the world's population today lives in countries whose media are ranked by experts as "controlled" or "partially controlled."[2] This means that journalists in these countries cannot or dare not publish information that their governments would prefer not to see published. In some countries a government censor must approve each story before publication. In others, journalists whose stories displease the government are fired, jailed, beaten, or even murdered. The authoritarian theory is as healthy and popular in the 1980s as it was in the 1680s.

THE SOVIET THEORY

The problem of controlling private owners of the media is solved in the Soviet Union and mainland China through state ownership. Newspapers, magazines, and broadcast stations are all owned and operated by the government itself. It is no mere metaphor in Russia to speak of the media as "the fourth branch of government"; it is a simple statement of fact. The chiefs of *Pravda* and *Izvestia*, for example, are high officials in the Communist Party—rather as if the Vice President ran the *New York Times*.

Under state ownership there is no question of whether the mass media will support or oppose government policy. They are *part* of government policy. The fundamental purpose of the press, states the 1925 Russian Constitution, is "to strengthen the Communist social order." Consider these instructions offered to a broadcasting trainee in the Soviet Union: "The Soviet radio must carry to the widest masses the teachings of Marx-Lenin-Stalin, must raise the cultural-political level of the workers, must daily inform the workers of the success of socialist construction, must spread the word about the class struggle taking place throughout the world."[3]

Professor Fred S. Siebert offers this description of the Soviet theory:

> The function of the press is not to aid in the search for truth since the truth has already been determined by the Communist ideology. No

tampering with the fundamental Marxist system is tolerated. . . . The stakes are too high and the masses too fickle to trust the future of state policies to such bourgeois concepts as "search for truth," "rational man," and "minority rights."[4]

Accustomed to a media system that is part of the government, Soviet authorities are naturally inclined to censor American correspondents as well as their own. In preparation for President Nixon's 1974 trip to the Soviet Union, an uncensored satellite relay system was negotiated for the use of Western journalists. But when the time came, ABC's Harry Reasoner and NBC's John Dancy were cut off in mid-sentence as they tried to transmit interviews with dissident Russian physicist Andrei D. Sakharov. Murray Fromson of CBS was interrupted when he tried to report on a jailed Jewish scientist, and Marvin Kalb of CBS was censored when he tried to mention the blocked transmissions. Moscow simply pulled the plug on New York. Richard S. Salant, then president of CBS News, commented: "There it is—for everyone to see—what happens when a government controls the news."[5]

Paradoxically enough, the Soviet media are free to criticize the government—not the basic dogmas of Communism, of course, but the actions of specific government agencies and officials. Because the media are part of the government, such criticism is considered to be *self*-criticism, and is therefore acceptable. Some years ago *Pravda* ran an article on factory production shortages, headlined: "Bring Parasites To Account!" Undoubtedly, the article was part of a carefully orchestrated government campaign. Nonetheless, such a story could never have appeared in a country with privately owned media governed by the authoritarian theory.

These, then, are the three essential differences between the authoritarian and Soviet theories of the press: (1) The media are privately owned in the authoritarian theory, state-owned in the Soviet theory; (2) Authoritarian control of the media is negative,

Dissident Russians cannot legally publish their ideas inside or outside the Soviet Union. But that hasn't stopped them. In 1962, the so-called "Phoenix Group" began circulating typewritten manuscripts hand to hand. This was the beginning of the Russian underground *samizdat* (self-publication) press. It culminated by the end of the 1960s in a regularly published underground newspaper, *Current Events*, which survived until 1972.

Many of the Phoenix writers and publishers were caught and sent to insane asylums, forced labor camps, or prisons. Others who smuggled their manuscripts out of the country for publication in the West were similarly punished. But some of the leading dissenters, notably novelist Aleksandr I. Solzhenitsyn, were protected from such treatment by their worldwide reputations, and were allowed to voice their protests publicly.

By 1973, Soviet officials had had enough. They seized portions of Solzhenitsyn's book *The Gulag Archipelago,* a searing indictment of the vast network of Soviet prisons and detention centers. Solzhenitsyn then decided to publish the book in the West. Two months after it appeared, he was charged with treason and banished from Russia forever—a fate one of his characters had called "spiritual castration."[6]

Throughout the cycles of tolerance and repression, Russian dissent continues. A story is supposedly making the rounds in Moscow about a Russian a hundred years from now who asks a friend, "Who was Brezhnev?"

"Oh," the friend replies, "he was a politician who lived in the time of Solzhenitsyn."

---

while Soviet control is affirmative; (3) The authoritarian theory permits no criticism of the government, while the Soviet theory allows some criticism but forbids the questioning of ideology. You could sum it up this way. In the authoritarian theory, the government decides what the media should not do, and punishes it. In the Soviet theory, the government decides what the media should do, and does it.

THE LIBERTARIAN THEORY

Apples fall from trees because of gravity, not the whim of some dictator or the dogma of some church. One does not need a dictator or a church to understand the law of gravity; one needs only one's own mind. This was the great insight of the scientific Enlightenment of the seventeenth and eighteenth centuries: People are rational beings, and as such they can discover natural laws on their own.

If it's true of natural laws, reasoned the philosophers of the Enlightenment, it should be true of people's laws as well.

If men were free to inquire about all things, . . . to form opinions on the basis of knowledge and evidence, and to utter their opinions freely, the competition of knowledge and opinion in the market of rational discourse would ultimately banish ignorance and superstition and enable men to shape their conduct and their institutions in conformity with the fundamental and invariable laws of nature and the will of God.[7]

How does this philosophy apply to the mass media? People are rational beings. Offered a choice between truth and falsehood, they will unerringly choose truth—at least in the long run. It follows that the best thing a government can do with the media is to leave them alone, let them publish whatever they want to publish. This is the libertarian theory of the press.

The libertarian theory developed out of

the Enlightenment, out of science, but it is doubtful that it would have done so without the parallel development of democracy. Even if a dictatorship accepted the philosophical premise of libertarianism—that the people can tell truth from falsehood—there would be no reason for it to relax its hold on the mass media. Why should an authoritarian regime want the people to know the truth in the first place? *It* does the governing, not they. It is important for the government to know the truth, perhaps—and for the people to know whatever the government feels like telling them, no more, no less.

In a democracy, on the other hand, the people do the governing. If they are to make the right decisions, they must know the truth. James Madison put it this way: "Nothing could be more irrational than to give the people power, and to withhold from them information without which power is abused. A people who mean to be their own governors must arm themselves with power which knowledge gives. A popular government without popular information or the means of acquiring it is but a prologue to a farce or a tragedy, or perhaps both."[8] Thomas Jefferson was more blunt: "If a nation expects to be both ignorant and free it expects what never was and never will be."[9]

It is no coincidence, then, that the growth of libertarian theory in eighteenth-century England was accompanied by the rising power of Parliament over the king. Nor is it accidental that libertarianism achieved its most nearly ideal form in the democracy of nineteenth-century America. Other countries with a libertarian press include Canada, Australia, New Zealand, Sweden, Norway, Denmark, and Israel—all democracies.

The greatest assets of the libertarian theory, one scholar has said, "are its flexibility, its adaptability to change, and above all its confidence in its ability to advance the interests and welfare of human beings by continuing to place its trust in individual self-direction."[10] There is no doubt about the last point. Libertarianism is almost incredibly optimistic about the rationality of the people. The other two points—flexibility and adaptability—are more debatable. It can be persuasively argued, in fact, that the libertarian theory has failed to keep up with social change, that it is now obsolete and should be discarded.

What are the implicit assumptions of the libertarian theory? The most important one, of course, is that the people are capable of telling truth from falsehood, given a choice between the two. Some of the other assumptions include:

1. That there are enough voices in the mass media to insure that the truth will be well represented.
2. That the owners of the mass media are different enough to include all possible candidates for truth.
3. That the mass media are not under the control of some nongovernmental interest group, such as news sources or advertisers.
4. That it is not difficult for those who wish to do so to start their own newspaper, broadcast station, or other mass-media outlet.

All of these premises were more or less satisfied by conditions in the eighteenth and nineteenth centuries. As we have seen in the last several chapters, all of them are considerably less well-satisfied today. The modern mass media are a vital part of Big Business. Concentration of media ownership increases every year, as does the similarity of the remaining independent voices. Media owners are extremely responsive to the wishes of pressure groups. And starting a new mass medium is difficult and costly.

Even the first premise of libertarian theory—that the people can tell truth from falsehood—may be less valid today than it was three hundred years ago. Life and government are far more complex now than they were then. Decisions are harder to make, harder even to understand. It is no longer so obvious that common sense is enough to solve the problems of the world.

THE SOCIAL RESPONSIBILITY THEORY

The social responsibility theory was first articulated in 1947, by the Hutchins Commission Report on a Free and Responsible Press. This important piece of press criticism from scholars in many fields accepted the basic assumption of libertarian theory. It agreed, in other words, that the way to run a democracy is to expose the people to all kinds of information and all kinds of opinions, and then let them decide for themselves. But the Hutchins Commission questioned whether the libertarian theory was working, whether the people were getting enough information and opinions to give them a fair chance of making the right decision. It therefore proposed five "requirements," designed to guarantee that the media include "all important viewpoints, not merely those with which the publisher or operator agrees."[11] According to the Hutchins Commission, the mass media should:

1. Provide a truthful, comprehensive, and intelligent account of the day's events in a context which gives them meaning.
2. Provide a forum for the exchange of comment and criticism.
3. Provide a representative picture of the constituent groups in society.
4. Be responsible for the presentation and clarification of the goals and values of society.
5. Provide full access to the day's intelligence.[12]

The difference between the libertarian and social responsibility theories is subtle, but vitally important. The libertarian theory holds that if each publication and station does whatever it wants, all will work out for the best. The social responsibility theory disagrees. It *urges* the media to do what the libertarian theory *assumes* they will do—provide a free marketplace of ideas. "A new era of public responsibility for the press has arrived," stated the Hutchins Commission. "The variety of sources of news and opinion is limited. The insistence of the citizen's need

has increased. . . . We suggest the press look upon itself as performing a public service of a professional kind."[13]

The essence of the social responsibility theory is that the media have an obligation to behave in certain ways. If they meet that obligation voluntarily, fine; otherwise the government may be forced to make them meet it. Theodore Peterson interprets the theory this way:

Freedom carries concomitant obligations; and the press, which enjoys a privileged position under our government, is obliged to be responsible to society for carrying out certain essential functions of mass communication in contemporary society. To the extent that the press recognizes its responsibilities and makes them the basis of operational policies, the libertarian system will satisfy the needs of society. To the extent that the press does not assume its responsibilities, some other agency must see that the essential functions of mass communication are carried out.[14]

THEORY AND PRACTICE

The four theories of the press are less concerned with what the media should and should not do than with *who decides* what the media should and should not do. Consider the chart on the next page.

In libertarian theory there is no control over the media. In Soviet theory the state controls everything, while in authoritarian theory the state has only negative controls. In social responsibility theory the "experts" suggest answers; the media carry them out either voluntarily or through state control.

Which theory offers the most freedom? The most obvious answer is the libertarian theory, under which the media are free to do whatever they choose. But that is freedom for the publisher and the broadcaster, not for the private citizen. Soviet philosophers argue that a government-run press is likely to be freer than a press that is controlled by cor-

	Who decides what the media should do?	Who decides what the media should not do?	Who enforces these decisions?
Authoritarian theory	The media	The state	The state
Soviet theory	The state	The state	The state
Libertarian theory	The media	The media	The media
Social responsibility theory	The experts	The experts	Ideally the media; if necessary the state

porations and advertisers, whose special interests seldom mirror those of the general public. Authoritarian theorists assert that the freedom to oppose the government is not freedom, but anarchy. And advocates of social responsibility claim that the people are truly free only when the media are required to inform them properly.

Different theories of the press follow inevitably from different theories of government. Dictators invariably choose the authoritarian model; communism leads naturally to the Soviet model; simple democracies follow the libertarian model; more complex, bureaucratic democracies seem to require the social responsibility model. It is hard to imagine a communist state with a libertarian press, or a democracy with an authoritarian press, or any other mismatched combination of media and government.

Yet it is just as hard to find a pure example of any of the four theories. In practice, everything turns out to be a combination—with one element dominant, perhaps, but with others represented as well. The First Amendment to the U.S. Constitution perfectly embodies the libertarian theory; yet the Constitution itself was debated and passed in secret, and journalists were told only what the Founding Fathers thought they ought to know. This authoritarian strain has persisted throughout the history of our country. Sedition is *the* mass-media crime under authoritarian regimes. It is still a crime in the United States today.

The United States is not, in fact, the most libertarian country in the world as far as

freedom of the press is concerned. The leading contender for that title is probably Sweden, the first nation ever to pass a law guaranteeing press freedom from government control. In Sweden, unlike the United States, reporters have a right to look at nearly every government document and attend nearly every government meeting; they have had that right since the 1766 enactment of the "King-in-Council Ordinance Concerning Freedom of Writing and Publishing." Similarly, Swedish journalists may not be compelled to name their confidential sources of information unless that is absolutely essential to reach a judicial decision. In all other cases it is illegal for a Swedish reporter to reveal the names of informants without their permission.[15]

But even Sweden is not perfectly libertarian. The Swedish law forbidding journalists to reveal their sources is as much an expression of social responsibility theory as the U.S. law requiring journalists to reveal theirs when subpoenaed. The two countries apparently disagree on what is best for the society, but they agree that this decision should not be left in the hands of the media. In much the same vein, Sweden has a long history of press councils—voluntary and nongovernmental, but nonetheless a departure from pure libertarianism.

Swedish television, like American television, is privately owned. But while the U.S. government lets its three networks compete but imposes a complex web of regulatory constraints, the Swedish government appoints a majority of the board members of the country's only network, and then leaves it pretty much alone.[16] Which policy gives the broadcast media more freedom? The question is difficult to answer. Certainly neither policy is libertarian.

No government in the world today has a truly libertarian stance toward broadcasting. The very nature of broadcast technology—the limited number of available channels—makes it necessary for the government to hand out licenses. A few governments, like the U.S., leave the stations in private hands but regulate them and set conditions on their keeping the license. Many more governments, like England, Canada, and Sweden, establish quasi-governmental organizations to run all or some of the broadcast stations in the country. And most governments—even democracies like France—simply own the broadcast media outright.

Despite the apparently absolute protection of press freedom in the First Amendment, many federal and state laws in the United States do limit that freedom. So do the decisions of judges and the rulings of regulatory agencies like the Federal Communications Commission. The existence of this considerable body of law obviously contradicts the libertarian notion that only the media should decide what the media may and may not do. The rest of this chapter will concentrate on that contradiction, on the ways in which a country dedicated at its founding to freedom of the press has found it necessary to limit freedom of the press.

PRIOR RESTRAINT AND NATIONAL SECURITY

If there is an exact opposite to press freedom, it is probably prior restraint—government action that prevents the media from reporting a particular piece of information. A hallmark of authoritarian theory, prior restraint (also called precensorship) aims at keeping information from the public view entirely. A law that permits the government to punish a journalist only after the story is published leaves everyone a little room to maneuver. The journalist may decide to take the risk and go with the story; once it's out, the government may decide it wasn't so harmful after all. If worst comes to worst and the journalist is fined or jailed, at least the story is out. Prior restraint, by contrast, keeps the story secret for all time. This is why authoritarian governments prefer it—and why libertarian governments do not. As the late constitutional lawyer Alexander Bickel once said, "a criminal statute chills [the media], prior restraint freezes."[17]

But if there is ever a case for limiting the media's freedom, it is when publication could endanger the very survival of the government that insures that freedom. Though government officials often shout "national security" to stop a story that merely threatens to embarrass the current administration, like the boy who cried wolf they may sometimes shout "national security" and mean it. What happens, then, when a really good reason for controlling the media, national security, comes up against a really bad type of control, prior restraint?

We start in 1931, with the landmark case of *Near v. Minnesota*. In this case the U.S. Supreme Court overturned a Minnesota law that allowed the state to shut down any publication that was frequently "malicious, scandalous and defamatory." Shutting down a newspaper is obviously a prior restraint, and the Court said the First Amendment forbids prior restraints—except in very special cases. As an example of the exception, the Court offered the case of a newspaper that is about to publish "the sailing dates of transports or the number and location of troops" in wartime.

The *Near* standard rules out prior restraint as a way of protecting lesser interests than national security. In 1974, for example, a manufacturer of baby cribs tried to stop ABC from broadcasting a news report that one of its cribs was not fire-retardant. Though the company did find a local judge to issue a temporary injunction forbidding the broadcast, the injunction was quickly lifted as a violation of ABC's First Amendment rights.[18]

Similarly, the Supreme Court in 1979 overturned a West Virginia law that barred the media from publishing the names of juvenile defendants.[19] If a news story unfairly damages a juvenile or a crib manufacturer, the proper remedy is a lawsuit after the story appears. Prior restraint must be saved for genuine threats to national security.

The government thought it had such a threat in 1971, when the *New York Times,* the *Washington Post,* and other media began to publish the so-called "Pentagon Papers" (see pp. 159-60). Arguing that the top-

---

THE CIA CONTRACT

Before going to work for the Central Intelligence Agency, a recruit must sign a contract agreeing never to reveal any information received while in the Agency's employ. All writing, the contract says, must be approved in advance by CIA censors—a classic form of prior restraint.

The contract was first enforced in 1974 against Victor Marchetti. The Agency cut a number of passages from Marchetti's book *The C.I.A. and the Cult of Intelligence.* Marchetti objected on First Amendment grounds, but a federal appeals court found that the CIA had a right to censor classified information, and the Supreme Court refused to review the case. The court did not make the CIA prove that the deleted passages endangered national security, or even that they were properly classified as secret. It was enough to show that they were indeed classified and that the CIA hadn't approved their publication.[20] By signing the Agency's employment contract, in other words, Marchetti had signed away his First Amendment rights so far as revealing classified intelligence information was concerned.[21]

In 1980 another former agent, Frank Snepp, was severely punished by the Supreme Court for publishing his book *Decent Interval* without first submitting it to CIA censors. An account of the fall of Saigon to the North Vietnamese, *Decent Interval* contained no classified information. But for publishing it without Agency approval, the Court ordered Snepp to forfeit all his earnings from the book (about $125,000), and to submit everything else he might write about the Agency—even fiction—for prior CIA review.[22]

Also in 1980, the CIA finally released some of the deleted passages from Marchetti's book. One sentence read: "There was sharp disagreement within the government on how hard a line the United States should take with the. . . ." Here are the censored words that complete the sentence: ". . . white-minority regimes of South Africa, Rhodesia and the Portuguese colonies in Africa."[23] Other passages that are still secret might involve national security. This one, clearly, does not.

The contract approach cleverly bypasses the First Amendment objection to prior restraint and the tough *Near* standard, allowing the CIA to decide for itself which reminiscences of ex-agents to permit and which to censor. Among the government agencies that now require such employment contracts are the FBI, the State Department, the National Security Agency, and various sections of the Treasury Department, the Department of Energy, the Defense Department, and the Nuclear Regulatory Commission.[24] In the years ahead, other government agencies (and perhaps private employers) may be expected to follow the CIA's lead, seriously limiting the ability of their employees to communicate to the public.

secret documents on Vietnam policy could irreparably damage U.S. national security, the government successfully obtained a temporary injunction forbidding any further publication. When the Supreme Court examined the documents, however, it was unable to find any vital defense secrets, and by a 6-3 vote it therefore dissolved the injunction. Perhaps the newspapers could be prosecuted for publishing classified information, the Court said, but they had to be allowed to publish the information first. Just as in the *Near* case, the Court acknowledged that a *real* threat to national security might justify a prior restraint.

The Pentagon Papers were duly published, and the newspapers that published them were never prosecuted.

In 1979 the issue arose again. *The Progressive* magazine had a draft of an article by freelance writer Howard Morland entitled "The H-Bomb Secret: How We Got It, Why We Are Telling It." Using only unclassified sources and interviews, Morland had managed to write a detailed explanation of the workings of the hydrogen bomb. The purpose of the article was to demystify H-bomb "secrets" and spark a public debate about U.S. nuclear strategy.

Under the Atomic Energy Act of 1954, *The Progressive* could have been prosecuted if it had published such an article. But once the cat was out of the bag, the government probably wouldn't have risked testing the Atomic Energy Act's application to unclassified information. In what proved to be a tactical error, however, the magazine sent Morland's draft to a number of scientists for comment, and it ended up at the Department of Energy. The government wanted to censor the article, editor Erwin Knoll refused, and the government went into court to stop publication.[25]

In March of 1979, Judge Robert W. Warren issued an injunction forbidding *The Progressive* to publish the article. It was the first time ever that a federal judge had ordered a prior restraint against the media in a national security case—not just a temporary restraining order as in the Pentagon Papers case, but a permanent order permanently forbidding publication. Judge Warren was unimpressed by *The Progressive*'s argument that the article used no classified sources; he accepted the government's claim that on nuclear matters even a good guess by a private citizen was "classified at birth" and thus censorable. Publishing the article, he said, "could possibly provide sufficient information to allow a medium-size nation to move faster in developing a hydrogen weapon," a possibility he was not willing to permit.[26]

The case had everything necessary for a landmark Supreme Court decision on prior restraint versus national security. But while *The Progressive*'s appeal was pending, a small newspaper in Madison, Wisconsin (the *Press Connection*) printed a letter-to-the-editor from another nuclear amateur that contained much of the information in Morland's draft. The government decided it would be pointless to pursue the case, and *The Progressive* was permitted to publish the article—nearly a year late and after $250,000 in legal fees.[27]

We are still waiting for a landmark Supreme Court decision balancing the authoritarian tyranny of prior restraint against a genuine threat to national security. If such a test case ever reaches the Court, the Justices will start with a strong democratic bias against prior restraint, and a strong tendency to look twice at national security claims. But it is doubtful that a future Supreme Court would be any more willing than the Supreme Court that decided *Near v. Minnesota* to permit a newspaper to publish "the sailing dates of transports or the number and location of troops." Every right of the media, even the fundamental right to be free from prior restraint, must be balanced against the rights of others.

In our examination of that balancing, we will begin with the conflicts between media rights and individual rights—the laws gov-

Governments naturally tend to think that any criticism of the government may threaten national security. Sedition—the crime of criticizing the government—is therefore one of the oldest crimes in history.

The Sedition Act of 1798, for example, made it illegal to publish "any false, scandalous and malicious writing" that might bring into disrepute the U.S. government, Congress, or the president. Seven editors were convicted under the act; all were opponents of the Federalist Adams administration. When Jefferson (an anti-Federalist) took office in 1801, he pardoned all seven and allowed the Sedition Act to lapse.

A new sedition law was passed in 1901, but this time the definition was narrower, making it a crime only to advocate the violent overthrow of the government. The Supreme Court narrowed the definition still further after World War I, eventually ruling that advocating revolution could be illegal only in circumstances that "create a clear and present danger" to the society.[28] The Smith Act, passed by Congress in 1940, continued to outlaw the advocacy of violent revolution. Interpretations of the "clear and present danger" standard tended to be rather broad after World War II, and the Smith Act became a popular tool for prosecuting Communists during the Cold War.

In 1957 the Supreme Court narrowed the definition still further. It is not sedition, the Court said, to advocate the violent overthrow of the government as an abstract principle. That is protected by the First Amendment. Sedition is confined to advocating the violent overthrow of the government as an incitement to immediate action.[29]

In recent years there have been very few prosecutions for sedition. The "incitement" standard is too tough, and the government has easier ways of dealing with revolutionaries—notably the conspiracy laws. But sedition is still a crime.

The mainstream media don't customarily advocate revolution, so they needn't worry much about sedition laws. But the existence of a crime called sedition illustrates the authoritarian strain in American press law. And the increasingly narrow definition of that crime illustrates the libertarian tradition as well. Where should the balance be struck? In a healthy, free society, should advocating *anything* be a crime?

erning libel, privacy, obscenity, copyright, advertising, antitrust, and coverage of criminal trials (pp. 181-94). Most of these areas focus on what the media may legally publish once they have the information, but in coping with the free press versus fair trial controversy the courts have found a different way to control the media—limitations on the news-gathering process. The following section (pp. 194-200) will therefore look at laws governing the journalist's access to information—whether reporters may insist on reading certain documents and attending certain meetings, whether they may protect their sources and notes, etc. In the final section (pp. 200-13), we will examine the special case of broadcasting, a technologically limited medium whose regulation is dominated by a classic form of prior restraint—licensing.

Freedom of the press must always be balanced against the rights of others. Thus libel law protects the right to a good reputation, privacy law protects the right to be left alone, obscenity law protects the right to live in a sexually uncorrupted society, copyright law protects the right to benefit from one's own work, advertising law protects the right to honest ads, antitrust law protects the right to compete, and the laws covering court reporting protect the right to a fair trial. In each case two important rights conflict, and the courts and legislatures must try to find the best solution.

LIBEL

The most common legal issue confronting journalists on a daily basis is libel. Libel law is also an excellent example of how an essentially libertarian government tries to protect the rights of the individual without abridging the rights of the mass media. We must start with some definitions.

Defamation is any statement about an individual which exposes that individual to hatred, contempt, or ridicule; or which causes the individual to be avoided; or which tends to injure the individual in his or her occupation. Libel is essentially written defamation. The distinction between libel and slander (spoken defamation) was established long before radio and TV came along to confuse the issue. As a rule, scripted broadcasts and films are treated as libel, while live radio and TV ad libs fall under the heading of slander. Since the laws and penalties are pretty much the same, we will ignore the distinction and call them all libel.

With rare exceptions, libel is a civil action, not a crime. A person who believes something has appeared in the media that defames his or her reputation may file a libel suit against the reporter, the editor, the company that owns the medium, or anyone else involved in publishing the libel. The person who files the suit is called the plaintiff. The person sued—and it's customary to sue everyone involved—is the defendant. Both sides hire their own attorneys, and the state provides a judge and jury to settle the dispute. If the plaintiff wins, the reward is usually a sum of money and vindication in open court. If the defendant wins, no money changes

hands and both sides pay their own legal fees. Either way, nobody goes to jail.

If a news medium is doing its job, obviously, it will libel literally dozens of people every week. Reporting the news necessarily involves identifying certain individuals as swindlers or terrorists or liars or incompetents. For the media to function at all, then, some kinds of libel must be permitted. The four basic defenses against a libel suit are truth, privilege, fair comment, and the constitutional defense. If the libel is covered by any of these four defenses, it is permissible and the plaintiff will lose the case.

1. Truth. It wouldn't make much sense to punish a reporter for writing the truth. In almost all cases, therefore, truth is a complete defense, and a medium that can prove its allegations is safe, regardless of any other factor. Literal truth on every point is not required, only on the important ones. If a newspaper says that John Smith was arrested for shoplifting in Detroit, when he was really arrested for shoplifting in a suburb of Detroit, the newspaper is still substantially accurate—and Smith loses his libel suit.

2. Privilege. Certain official documents and proceedings are said to be "privileged." This means that the mass media may quote from them (accurately) without fear of a lawsuit, even if they contain libelous statements. The precise definition of what material is privileged varies from state to state, and it is important to learn the local variation. A police arrest record, a trial, and a Senate speech are all privileged, but an unofficial interview with the police chief, the judge, or the senator is not.

In 1970 the Supreme Court vastly expanded the definition of privilege, ruling that any statement on a public issue made at a public meeting (such as a city council session) is privileged, and may be quoted with impunity.

What is the purpose of the defense of privilege? The authors of the Constitution recognized that legislators would be unable to debate many issues effectively if they had to steer clear of possible libels. So the Constitution includes a clause providing that "for any Speech or Debate in either House, they [senators and representatives] shall not be questioned in any other place." This was quickly expanded to include a variety of other federal, state, and local government officials. How could a judge conduct a trial, or a police officer file an arrest report, if what they said could be held against them in a libel suit?

But the single most important function of the mass media in a democracy is to report on the actions and statements of government officials. Unless governmental privilege were extended to the media, the police report, the trial, and the Senate speech all would be secret. It soon became apparent that the media must be privileged to report everything that government officials are privileged to say. No doubt some individuals are damaged (libeled) in the process. But without the defense of privilege the mass media would be paralyzed.

3. Fair Comment. Statements of opinion that are not malicious and are of legitimate interest to the public are protected against libel charges by the defense of fair comment. A theater review is the most common example. A reviewer who writes that a particular actor gave a rotten, incompetent performance last night cannot be sued for libel. But if the reviewer says the actor was drunk on stage (a statement of fact, not opinion), then a libel suit is possible. Ditto if the reviewer never bothered to attend the play (malice). And a reviewer can certainly be sued for adding that the actor is also a rotten, incompetent golfer (not of legitimate public interest). But as long as the review is simply an honest opinion of the performance, the reviewer is safe from a libel action.

4. The Constitutional Defense. So much for theater reviewers. But what about political reporters? The survival of democracy, after all, depends at least in part on the ability of the mass media to tell the public all

there is to know about government officials and political figures. Wouldn't it be a good idea to extend the defense of fair comment to political reporters, leaving them free to give their honest opinions without fear of a libel suit? Perhaps we should go even further. A newspaper or broadcast station that is afraid to say something untrue will hesitate to say a lot of things that *are* true, for fear it might not be able to prove them. (The defense of truth requires proof.) If we really want the mass media to offer a freewheeling discussion of public officials and public affairs, perhaps we should exempt these topics from libel actions altogether.

So far no court has gone quite so far. But the Supreme Court started a significant trend in this direction in 1964, with the landmark case of *New York Times v. Sullivan.*

The case centered on a protest advertisement placed in the *Times* by a civil rights group in Montgomery, Alabama. The ad accused the Montgomery police of a "wave of terror" against black activists. L. B. Sullivan, Commissioner of Public Affairs for the city (responsible for the police department), sued the *Times* for libel. He had a strong case. Newspapers are, of course, liable for anything they print, including the ads. This particular ad did contain factual errors of a libelous nature; even though Sullivan wasn't named, the ad reflected badly on his department and therefore (to anyone who knew the governmental set-up in Montgomery) on him. None of the three traditional defenses—truth, privilege, and fair comment—could save the *Times.* An Alabama jury awarded Sullivan $500,000, and the Alabama Supreme Court upheld the verdict.

The U.S. Supreme Court reversed it. In order to insure free debate on issues of public importance, the Court said, critics of public officials must be given more leeway than those who write about private individuals:

The constitutional guarantees require, we think, a federal rule that prohibits a public official from recovering damages for a defamatory falsehood relating to his official conduct unless he proves that the statement was made with "actual malice"—that is, with knowledge that it was false or with reckless disregard of whether it was false or not.[30]

After *Times v. Sullivan,* a public official could not hope to win a libel suit without showing that the defendant medium acted with actual malice—in other words, that the defendant knew that the libel was false, or acted with reckless regard for its truth or falsity. This is extremely difficult to prove—not to mention that it would be totally unethical behavior for a journalist in the first place. The constitutional defense is thus a strong deterrent against libel suits by public officials. They would be wasting their money on legal fees.

In the years that followed, the Supreme Court extended the constitutional defense beyond public officials to cover so-called "public figures" as well. The same logic applied. To insure spirited media discussion of people in the public eye, the Court reasoned, the media should be protected from libel suits by such people unless the actual malice standard was met.

The high-water mark of this protection came in 1971, in the case of *Rosenbloom v. Metromedia.*[31] George A. Rosenbloom was a Philadelphia distributor of nudist magazines. When the police arrested Rosenbloom, Metromedia radio station WIP called his business an example of the "smut literature rackets." Rosenbloom was later acquitted on the obscenity charge, and he then sued Metromedia for libel. By a 5-3 margin, the Supreme Court ruled that Rosenbloom had been involved in an issue of public importance, and would have to meet the actual malice standard. Far from being a public official, Rosenbloom was a private citizen who had been involuntarily thrust into a public issue by getting arrested. Private persons involved in newsworthy events, the Court said, could be treated as if they were public figures.

Between 1974 and 1980, however, the Su-

preme Court decided that the balance had swung too far in favor of the media. Almost everyone in the news, after all, is somehow involved in an issue of public importance; under the *Rosenbloom* precedent virtually nobody would be protected from defamatory media attacks. So in four subsequent libel cases to reach the Court, each of the following in turn was held *not* to be a public figure:

• A prominent Chicago lawyer who was representing the family of a youth shot by a Chicago policeman;[32]

• A socially prominent woman in Palm Beach, Florida, who held press conferences during her widely publicized divorce trial;[33]

• A Michigan researcher whose $500,000 government grant to study monkeys under stress was criticized by Senator William Proxmire as "transparently worthless";[34]

• A man who had been found guilty of contempt of court in an espionage case nearly twenty years earlier.[35]

In each case, by ruling that the plaintiff was not a public figure, the Supreme Court made the plaintiff's libel suit much easier to win. This is because a private citizen doesn't have to show actual malice, only some degree of fault by the media. And just what constitutes reportorial fault is a matter for juries to decide—based on how many sources the reporter talked to and the reliability of those sources; whether the person attacked was given a chance to respond; how much deadline pressure the reporter was working under; how the story was edited and what got cut; etc. Since there are few accepted standards for assessing responsibility on these issues, journalists are understandably wary of handing them over to juries to decide.

James C. Goodale, long-time legal counsel to the *New York Times,* comments on the four rulings:

It seems to me the Court's intent is clear. The public figure definition is going to be made more and more narrow until it applies to very

THE NATIONAL ENQUIRER LOSES BIG

When the *National Enquirer* intimated in a 1976 gossip column that actress Carol Burnett had been drunk in a restaurant, Burnett filed suit for libel. Her victory in 1981 broke no new legal ground. Though Burnett was a public figure, she had little trouble convincing the jury that the charge was false and that the *Enquirer* had shown almost no concern over whether it was false or not. The only surprise was the size of the judgment against the *Enquirer*—an astounding $1.6 million in actual and punitive damages.

Even the *National Enquirer,* a highly profitable sex-and-scandal tabloid, can't afford many judgments that big. Although an appeals judge later cut the amount in half, the jury's decision in the Burnett case should force the *Enquirer* and similar publications to exercise a bit more care over what they write. But if the size of libel judgments keeps rising, as seems likely, more reputable publications with more important exposés in mind may also pull back.

---

few cases indeed. The cost of this approach also seems clear: "political speech"—broadly speaking, discourse about public issues—is thus given less and less constitutional protection in the libel area.[36]

The Court's new approach has encouraged people in the news to bring libel suits when attacked, since they now stand a much better chance of winning. This spate of libel suits, in turn, has made the media gun-shy, afraid not only of losing but also of the huge cost of defending a libel suit they could eventually win. Says Neil Skene, assistant city editor of the *St. Petersburg Times,* "We are much more careful, hesitant to put stories in the paper that tend to damage people's reputations."[37] Whether you consider this result good or bad depends on which you value more highly, robust journalism or the right to an undamaged reputation.

The Supreme Court can encourage one only at the expense of the other. Between 1964 and 1971 it leaned toward robust journalism; between 1974 and 1980 it moved partway back toward undamaged reputations. Journalists may still criticize public officials with great freedom. But they must now—again—be wary of what they say about newsmakers who are not officials. As of 1981, no one can be sure just who is a public fig-

ure, and just what constitutes faulty reporting—two issues that will occupy judges and lawyers in the 1980s as libel law continues to change.

PRIVACY

The right to privacy is a comparative newcomer to the law. It was first suggested by two young Boston lawyers, Samuel Warren and Louis D. Brandeis, in an 1890 article in the *Harvard Law Review*. The authors argued that precedent for privacy law already existed in legal areas like defamation and trespass. They urged the courts to expand the notion to include the right to be left alone by the mass media.

The courts refused, so various state legislatures did the job instead. In 1903 New York passed the first specific privacy law, making it illegal to use the name or picture of any person for advertising purposes without permission. Today, most state courts recognize a right of privacy, and six states have enacted privacy statutes.[38]

The law of privacy varies substantially from state to state, but in every state it is just as illegal for a journalist as for anyone else to invade a person's private property without permission. Reporters who trespass or steal personal files in their search for news are operating outside the law. But if some-one else takes the papers and gives them to a reporter, and if the papers are legitimately newsworthy, most courts have ruled that the reporter may legally publish them.

The concept of privacy is much broader than defamation, and a wide variety of com-plaints have been brought under its banner. The four types of privacy suits of special in-terest to the media are discussed briefly be-low, each with its appropriate defense.

Using someone's name or picture for com-mercial gain. Even without a statute like New York's, the courts have held that the right to privacy protects against commercial appropriation of a person's name or picture. A toothpaste company is not entitled to plas-ter your face (or Joe Namath's face or Chris Evert Lloyd's face) on a billboard. The proper defense here is consent, that you gave your permission in return for money or glory.

Intruding on someone's solitude. A news photographer is entitled to take your picture in a public place, but the photographer may not normally invade your livingroom for a picture. Nor does an electronic journalist have a right to film you or tape your voice in the privacy of your home. Once again, the best defense is consent.

Putting someone in a negative false light. These types of cases usually involve exaggera-tions, stories that are not quite defamatory but still misleading. In 1968, for example, the *Cleveland Plain Dealer* published a fea-ture about the family of a man killed in a widely publicized bridge collapse. The re-porter overstated the extent of the widow's poverty, and made up quotes to show how devastated the family had been by the acci-dent. The widow sued for invasion of pri-vacy, and in 1975 the Supreme Court agreed that she could collect. The proper defenses here are newsworthiness and truth. The Court acknowledged that the story was news-worthy, but the phony quotes cost the *Plain Dealer* the case.[39]

Publishing embarrassing personal facts. This category comes closest to the ethical concept of privacy (see pp. 90-92), what readers and viewers are talking about when they complain that the media lack respect for people's privacy. Unlike the previous category, the information published isn't misleading, only personal and embarrassing. Newsworthiness has proved a potent defense against this type of privacy action.

In 1976, for example, a privacy suit was filed against the *Des Moines Register and Tribune* for a story it had published about health care at an Iowa county home. The story named an 18-year-old woman who had been sterilized on a psychiatrist's recommen-dation. The court ruled that the woman's name "contributed constructively to the im-pact of the article" and was therefore news-worthy, especially since the name was ob-tained from public documents.[40] In related rulings, the courts have found that publish-ing the names of rape victims or juvenile offenders (also on the public record) cannot give rise to privacy suits. Although many media voluntarily withhold such names, le-gally the public's right to know takes prece-dence here over the right to privacy.

But if a state legislature wants to push the balance a little more toward the privacy side, the courts have held that it may do so with-out running afoul of the First Amendment. In Massachusetts, for example, the alphabeti-cal criminal court records are closed to the press and public, making it impossible to look up a name to see if that person has a criminal record. The Massachusetts Supreme Court upheld the law in 1979 as a reasonable way to protect the privacy of ex-offenders.[41] Overall, nearly two dozen states now have laws that in some way limit access to crimi-nal records on privacy grounds.[42] Journal-ists, of course, believe such laws are a dan-gerous threat to the public's right to know. Many non-journalists, however, believe there should be more laws to keep the media from prying into people's private affairs. Once again, a balance must be struck.

OBSCENE VIOLENCE

Many people believe that violence on film and television is probably more dangerous to society than sexually explicit material. And many believe that what is most dangerous about sexual content is its heavy component of violence against women, visible in everything from record jackets to hard-core pornography. Social scientists have found some evidence to support both beliefs, though the question is still open to debate.

While no legal definition of obscenity yet contains any reference to violence, that too may come. In 1976 the city of Chicago passed an ordinance banning children under 18 from excessively violent movies.[43] In 1979 the French Ministry of Culture put *The Warriors* (a violent American film about teenage gangs) into the same category as pornographic movies—it could be shown only in certain theaters, could not advertise, and had to pay a special tax.[44] And in recent years some American films received "X" ratings because of violence rather than sexual explicitness.

OBSCENITY

Attitudes toward sexually explicit materials vary not only from individual to individual, but also from generation to generation. Novels that are now studied in college English courses were once banned in the United States on grounds of obscenity. Our grandchildren may one day be shocked that some Americans in the 1980s objected to *Hustler* magazine on our newsstands and *Deep Throat* in our movie theaters. Or they may be shocked that some Americans approved.

Social scientists have studied the effects of pornography—on the number of sex offenders and their behavior, on the sexual attitudes and adjustments of the law-abiding, on sexism and the oppression of women, on social values and the strength of the family, etc. So far their research has generated more heat than light. Those who believe pornography is healthful and liberating can find studies to support their viewpoint. So can those who believe pornography is corrupting and harmful.

Furthermore, the scientific question is not identical with the legal policy question. Even if pornography is harmless, some would still want to regulate it on the grounds that it is offensive to many people; does a prude have a right to walk through Times Square without embarrassment? And even if pornography is harmful, some would still want to leave it unregulated on the grounds of freedom of expression; does a corrupter of moral values have the same First Amendment rights as a political dissident?

Into this confusion of conflicting values come the courts, struggling to draw a line between sexual materials that are legal and sexual materials that are obscene and therefore illegal. Not surprisingly, they have not had much success.

An early definition of obscenity was any material that tends "to deprave and corrupt those whose minds are open to such immoral influences and into whose hands a publication of this sort might fall."[45] If any part of a book or magazine met this test—that is, if any part was thought capable of damaging someone who might see it—then the whole book or magazine was obscene. This broad concept of obscenity dominated judicial reasoning until the 1930s.

Slowly the mood became more tolerant. First judges decided to look at the material as a whole, rather than the most questionable passage. Then they decided to base the standard on ordinary people, rather than unusually vulnerable ones. These trends culminated in the so-called "Roth test," enunciated by the Supreme Court in 1957:

". . . whether to the average person, applying contemporary community standards, the dominant theme of the material taken as a whole appeals to prurient interest."[46] In the 1960s the Supreme Court further refined the Roth test. To be judged obscene in the late sixties, a movie or magazine had to be utterly without "redeeming social value." Just about anything with a plot or a few moralistic sentences could pass muster.

Every decade or so the Court takes another crack at defining obscenity. The key case for the 1970s was *Miller v. California,* decided in 1973. Speaking for the new majority of sexually less tolerant Justices, Chief Justice Warren E. Burger threw out the "redeeming social value" standard. He redefined obscene works as those "which, taken as a whole, appeal to the prurient interest in sex, which portray sexual content in a patently offensive way, and which, taken as a whole, do not have serious literary, artistic, political, or scientific value." Burger went on to rule that national standards are not necessary, that a jury could use its own community standards to decide what constituted "prurient interest" and "patent offensiveness."[47]

Film producers and book and magazine publishers immediately complained that local censorship, enforcing local standards, would cripple their industries. To avoid prosecution a national distributor would have to conform to the standards of the most conservative communities, penalizing audiences in more liberal parts of the country. And how could the distributor know in advance what some community somewhere might find obscene?

But the predicted crackdown never happened. A 1977 survey of prosecutors found that most felt obscenity convictions were harder to get in 1977 than in 1971, and only 13 percent said they were making obscenity a high priority in law enforcement.[48] If the *Miller* decision was trying to stem the tide of pornography, it failed.

It also failed to solve the basic problem in obscenity law—drawing a clear line (wherever it's drawn) between sexual materials that may be published and sexual materials that may not. Supreme Court Justice Stevens sums up the complaint: "In the final analysis the guilt or innocence of a criminal defendant in an obscenity trial is determined primarily by individual jurors' subjective reactions to the materials in question rather than by the predictable application of rules of law."[49]

COPYRIGHT

The Constitution makes no mention of libel, privacy, or obscenity. But the right of an author, poet, filmmaker, composer, or producer to benefit economically from his or her work is there: "The Congress shall have power . . . to promote the Progress of Science and useful Arts by securing for limited Times to Authors and Inventors the exclusive Right to their respective Writings and Discoveries."

Copyright law is an obvious necessity. Without it, no writer or publisher could earn a living, and hence few would bother to try. Yet strictly speaking, copyright law is a violation of the libertarian theory. It is a government-enforced limitation on what the mass media are permitted to publish.

Copyright is a civil, not a criminal, affair. The government doesn't arrest you for it; the owner of the copyright sues you. The amount of money the copyright owner can collect is limited to the amount you profited by stealing the material, plus a little extra to cover the costs of the lawsuit. For newspapers, then, copyright is seldom a serious matter. Very little money is made or lost when one newspaper steals an article from another; unless it becomes a habit, no one is likely to sue. When a national magazine or a college textbook infringes on a copyright, however, the settlement is likely to be several thousand dollars, enough to justify a lawsuit. And when a best-selling novel or a successful movie is involved in copyright litigation, the winner may stand to gain $100,000 or more.

In 1976 President Ford signed the first major revision of copyright law since 1909. Besides changing many provisions of the old law, the new one helped answer questions about some recent copyright problems, such as the use of photocopy machines and the obligations of cable TV systems.

Under the new law, all works are automatically given copyright protection from the moment they are created. The length of protection is the life of the author plus 50 years. An author may, of course, transfer the copyright to someone else, as when a writer sells an article to a magazine. Or the author may choose to retain some rights, such as the right to sell the article to the movies or turn it into a novel.

Copyright covers the style and organization of a work, not its facts or ideas. The doctrine of fair use permits brief quotations without the author's permission. Students, teachers, and librarians may also make a few photocopies of copyrighted material for classroom use without permission—but the wholesale copying of articles, chapters, and books is not permitted.

Cable television companies must now pay a fee to whoever owns the copyright on the programs they rebroadcast. The new law set up a Copyright Royalty Tribunal to regulate such payments. Other provisions of the law cover record royalties, payments from jukebox operators to owners of record copyrights, and a special method whereby an author can renegotiate a copyright after 32 years if he or she made a bad deal the first time around.

Copyright law is a good example of legal balancing—in this case the economic rights of creators versus the society's right to free flow of information. As writers, the authors of this book are naturally pleased that instructors must have our permission to photocopy their favorite chapters for handouts. As teachers, however, we would like the right to photocopy the works of others for our classes. Judges and legislatures experience this dual allegiance to conflicting rights in virtually every area of media law.

ADVERTISING

The First Amendment was written chiefly to protect political speech—that is, to create an open marketplace of ideas about everything related to the process of self-government. As the courts have interpreted it over the years, the First Amendment affords much less protection to non-political content, pornography for example. And it affords the least protection of all to advertising.

The Supreme Court first enunciated this principle in *Valentine v. Chrestensen*, de-

---

PLAGIARISM AND COPYRIGHT

Copyright is a matter of property. The people who create a piece of writing are entitled to control its use, to decide whom they will allow to publish it and what price they will charge for the privilege. Without a copyright law no one could earn a living as a writer.

Plagiarism, on the other hand, is an ethical standard of scholarship, written into the regulations of every college. It obliges students (and their teachers) to give proper credit when they borrow the ideas or words of others.

If you use a few sentences from this book in a term paper, the fair use doctrine says you are not guilty of any copyright infringement—but you *are* guilty of plagiarism unless you footnote the quotation. Conversely, if you mimeograph a whole chapter to hand out to the class, complete with credit, you are innocent of plagiarism but guilty of infringing on our copyright, and Prentice-Hall may sue you if it chooses.

cided in 1942.[50] Chrestensen owned an old Navy submarine, moored in New York City's East River. When he handed out a flyer advertising the sub and the admission price for a tour, the police stopped him for violating the city's Sanitary Code, which permitted only handbills devoted to "information or a public protest." The Supreme Court ruled that this city ordinance was constitutional, that governments are free to limit commercial advertising despite the First Amendment.

This distinction between political and commercial content is the legal basis for the work of the Federal Trade Commission in its regulation of false and misleading advertising (see pp. 377-78). The First Amendment forbids the government to distinguish between "true" and "false" political ideas. All political ideas are protected. But the government is free to outlaw false advertising.

In 1975, however, this neat distinction began to break down. At issue was a Virginia law forbidding ads for abortion services. Abortion was then illegal in Virginia, but legal in New York. When a New York abortion referral service advertised in a Virginia newspaper, the Court ruled that Virginia could not punish the newspaper's editor. This particular ad, the Court said, involved information of clear public interest and thus deserved First Amendment protection.[51]

A year later the Court further weakened the *Chrestensen* precedent when it overturned another Virginia law, this one prohibiting pharmacists from advertising the prices of prescription drugs. Here again the Court decided that the free flow of commercial information contributed to the public's ability to make wise decisions. Pharmacists thus had a First Amendment right to advertise.[52] In 1977 the Court used the same logic to permit lawyers to advertise their services and fees without fear of punishment from state bar associations.[53] Since then other professionals have begun to assert their newfound right to advertise.

This is not to say that commercial content has now achieved the same protection as political content. The FTC and various other agencies may still regulate misleading advertising. Governments may still outlaw ads for illegal acts (such as prostitution) or illegal substances (such as marijuana). Congress may still prohibit advertising for a product that is legal, as it did when it banned cigarette commercials on television. Even New York's prohibition against distributing commercial handbills might still be constitutional. But events of the last few years have made it clear that governments must weigh the First Amendment value of commercial messages before suppressing them.

All this, of course, applies only to governments. Stronger control over advertising is in the hands of the media, which are entitled to reject almost any ad they choose to reject, except some ads from political candidates. The notion that advertisers with an ideological message should have a First Amendment right to buy time and space in the media has attracted considerable support from civil libertarians, but very little support from the courts. As of 1980, the government may not censor ideological advertising, but the media may . . . and sometimes do (see p. 234). This too is a question of conflicting rights—the rights of advertisers versus the rights of the media.

ANTITRUST

The Sherman Act of 1890 provides that "every contract, combination in the form of a trust or otherwise, or conspiracy, in restraint of trade or commerce among the several states, or with foreign nations, is hereby declared illegal." The Clayton Act of 1914 further outlaws all practices that "tend to lessen competition or to create a monopoly in any line of commerce." These two laws are the basis for all antitrust action in federal courts today.

As we have seen (see Chapter 4), the mass media are by no means immune to the twentieth-century trend toward monopoly.

It is not surprising, then, that the Sherman and Clayton Acts have sometimes been invoked against the media—the First Amendment notwithstanding.

The first such case occurred in 1945, when the Supreme Court decided *Associated Press v. United States.* The Justice Department brought suit against the Associated Press, charging that it was a "conspiracy in restraint of trade." At issue were two AP bylaws: One provided that AP members could not sell news to nonmembers, and the other gave each member virtual veto power over the applications of competitors for the service. Together, these two regulations permitted a one-newspaper monopoly of wire news within each city. The Supreme Court agreed that this constituted an illegal news monopoly, and outlawed the two bylaws.

The following are typical of antitrust actions against the mass media since 1945:

- *Lorain Journal Company v. U.S.* A local newspaper refused to accept advertising from any company that advertised on a competing radio station. The court outlawed the practice.
- *Times-Picayune v. U.S.* Two New Orleans newspapers required advertisers to buy ads in both papers or neither. The court permitted the practice so long as it had no deleterious effects on competing media.
- *U.S. v. Kansas City Star.* A morning-evening-Sunday newspaper combination killed its daily competitor by requiring advertisers to buy space in all three at once. The court stopped the practice, and made the company sell its radio and TV outlets.
- *U.S. v. Times Mirror Corporation.* The court refused to allow the *Los Angeles Times* to buy the nearby *San Bernardino Sun,* since the two competed for the same advertising and some of the same readers.
- *U.S. v. Citizen Publishing Company.* The court outlawed a Tucson newspaper joint operating agreement because it involved profit pooling, price fixing, and other monopolistic practices. (Congress later passed a law legalizing such arrangements once again.)

As these five cases indicate, antitrust prosecutions against the mass media have traditionally tended to concentrate on advertising. This is because advertising is more obviously related to "trade" and "commerce" than news or entertainment. To base an antitrust suit on *news* monopoly would weaken the government's case and make First Amendment objections more persuasive.

Yet, as we have seen, it is news monopoly that is the real problem for today's mass media. In recent years, the Federal Communications Commission and the Justice Department have sometimes attacked monopoly in the media without relying on advertising for their rationale (see pp. 129-32). The changes they have achieved are hardly far-reaching— but they still pose a real dilemma for libertarian theorists. Who is the FCC, after all, to tell a newspaper it may not purchase a TV station in the same community? In libertarian theory such interference is evil incarnate. Yet only the government is powerful enough to reverse the trend toward monopoly in the mass media. Is the threat of government control still the greatest danger to freedom of the press, as it was when the First Amendment was written? Or is monopoly now a greater danger? Does the problem of media monopoly justify an increase in government regulation?

FREE PRESS/FAIR TRIAL

The First Amendment to the Constitution guarantees freedom of the press. The Sixth Amendment to the Constitution guarantees the right of every defendant to an impartial jury. When the mass media set out to report a juicy trial, the two amendments come into inevitable conflict. Consider the most extreme case in modern history: the assassination of President John F. Kennedy. After the incredible publicity surrounding the assassination, how could you possibly have found an impartial jury to decide the guilt or innocence of Lee Harvey Oswald (accused of shooting Kennedy) or Jack Ruby (accused of shooting Oswald)?

A number of techniques exist within the judicial system for protecting the rights of defendants. Trials can be moved to distant cities where prospective jurors are less likely to have been influenced by press accounts. The jury panel can be questioned by prosecution and defense lawyers and those showing any bias can be excused from the case. The trial can be postponed until publicity and emotion abate. Jurors can be kept together during the trial and shielded from media coverage. Perhaps most important, judges can ask the jurors to put aside whatever they may have heard about a case and reach a verdict strictly on the facts presented in court.

As a final resort, if publicity may have prejudiced a decision, the conviction can be set aside and a new trial granted. This happened in 1966 when the Supreme Court reviewed the case of Dr. Sam Sheppard, convicted of murder in Cleveland twelve years before. The Court ruled that the newspaper publicity before and during the trial (headlines such as "Sheppard Must Swing!" were common) had denied Sheppard his right to an impartial jury. Because the judge had failed to insulate the jury from this furor, the Supreme Court threw out the conviction.

To avoid such a result, journalists, lawyers, and judges have tried to work out an equitable balancing of First and Sixth Amendment rights. The American Bar Association and some two dozen state press-bar groups have adopted voluntary guidelines for reporters, urging them not to publish such items as the defendant's prior arrests and convictions, references to confessions or the results of lie detector tests, and opinions about the guilt or innocence of the accused.

Just putting lawyers and journalists in the same room to discuss First and Sixth Amendment problems has been an important educational experience for both sides. But voluntary guidelines do not always work. One study of crime news in 29 newspapers showed an average of slightly more than one violation of the ABA guidelines per story. Fully one-third of the stories contained opinions about the character, guilt, or innocence of the accused.[54] Since the mid-1970s, therefore, judges have often resorted to other methods to limit press coverage of criminal proceedings—non-voluntary methods that have posed a significant threat to First Amendment freedoms.

Among the most popular techniques has been the so-called "gag order," in which a judge bars anyone connected with the case from talking to reporters. Lawyers or police officials who violate a gag order run the risk of being found in contempt of court and serving a jail sentence. Some judges have gone even further and aimed gag orders at the media themselves—forbidding them to publish certain information about a case. If this sounds like prior restraint (see pp. 178-81), it is.

The issue of gag orders on the media came to a head in 1976 when the Supreme Court decided *Nebraska Press Association v. Stuart*.[55] Erwin Charles Simants had sexually assaulted and murdered some members of the Kellie family in the small Nebraska town of Sutherland. Reporters from all over the country descended on the community, leading the local judge to fear that widespread publicity would make it impossible for Simants to get a fair trial. So he ordered the media not to report various facts they already knew that were "strongly implicative" of Simants, including the existence of a confession. A number of news media organizations appealed the order.

All nine Supreme Court justices agreed that prior restraint was not an acceptable way to limit pretrial publicity. The press cannot be stopped, the Court said, from publishing what it knows. In addition, the Court found the order too broad, noting that it had been issued without any evidence that other methods (such as moving the trial) were inadequate to protect Simants' rights.

The case was a victory for the media, but

it suggested other strategies to judges. If reporters are free to publish what they learn, many judges reasoned, then why not limit what they learn by issuing gag orders forbidding lawyers and police to talk to them, and by closing pretrial hearings and even trials to press and public. By limiting what reporters were able to find out, judges figured they could avoid prejudicial publicity without gagging the media directly. The *Nebraska* decision did not prohibit these tactics, which became increasingly common in the late 1970s.

Thus in the murder retrial of W. A. Boyle, former president of the United Mine Workers of America, the judge ordered all attorneys and public officials not to discuss the case with the media. When pretrial hearings began, the courtroom was cleared and testimony given in secret. And in the Florida corruption trial of Senator Edward Gurney, the judge did not allow the names of jurors to be released, refused to let reporters see exhibits introduced into evidence, and repeatedly held conferences at the bench out of earshot of the press and public.[56]

The Supreme Court addressed the question of closed courtrooms in 1979 in *Gannett v. DePasquale.* The case concerned the murder of an upstate New York policeman by two young men. At a pretrial hearing three months after the crime, the lawyers for the defendants requested that the public and media be excluded from the hearing because publicity would endanger the possibility of a fair trial. The prosecuting attorney did not object and the hearing was closed. The Gannett newspapers in Rochester, N.Y. appealed.

In a confusing 5-4 decision, the Court said judges could close pretrial proceedings if they found a "reasonable probability" that the attendant publicity would threaten a fair trial. The majority opinion, written by Justice Stewart, reasoned that the right to a public hearing is the defendant's right under the Sixth Amendment, not the public's right, and the defendant is entitled to waive it. Justice Blackmun noted in dissent that some 90 percent of all criminal cases are disposed of before trial. Closing pretrial proceedings would thus close off "the only opportunity the public has to learn about police and prosecutorial conduct, and about allegations that those responsible to the public for the enforcement of laws themselves are breaking it."[57]

Encouraged by the *Gannett* ruling, judges all over the country began to close their courtrooms to media and public—not just pretrial hearings, but sometimes entire criminal trials. In the 12 months after the decision, 266 motions were made to close pre-

---

RESTRICTING BRITISH CRIME COVERAGE

American judges who view contempt of court citations as an appropriate way to insure nonprejudicial coverage of crimes and criminal trials often point to the British model. The British media can be held in contempt for publishing anything that might interfere with a fair trial. They may not use information that would not be admissible as evidence, such as past criminal records; they may not mention the existence of a confession (much less publish the details); they may not conduct their own investigations of crimes or publish their findings. Moreover, the British media are forbidden to question the fairness of judges and court proceedings—a restriction that seems to protect the judicial system more than it does the defendant.

Nevertheless, British popular newspapers provide sensational crime coverage in huge quantities. They shoot for maximum shock value and get their stories across without directly violating specific court restrictions.

indictment, pretrial, trial, and post-trial proceedings.[58] Among the proceedings that were closed was the Richmond, Virginia trial of a man accused of killing a motel operator. The Richmond order was protested by local newspapers and reached the Supreme Court in 1980.

In *Richmond Newspapers v. Virginia*,[59] the Court clarified some of the confusion produced by *Gannett*, ruling 7-1 that the Richmond trial should not have been closed. Chief Justice Burger wrote the opinion: "In guaranteeing freedoms such as those of speech and press, the First Amendment can be read as protecting the right of everyone to attend trials so as to give meaning to those explicit guarantees. . . . A trial courtroom also is a public place where the people generally—and representatives of the media—have a right to be present, and where their presence historically has been thought to enhance the integrity and quality of what takes place." While the Court did not say trials could never be closed, it ruled that judges would have to show an "overriding interest" to justify closing them.

As of 1981, then, there *is* a constitutional right for the public and media to attend criminal trials. Judges cannot close them without evidence of an overriding interest. And the media cannot be gagged from publishing whatever has happened in open court or whatever they have learned from their sources. But some proceedings *can* be closed when necessary to protect the rights of the defendant, and court personnel can be gagged and threatened with contempt if they talk to reporters. And so the quest to balance First and Sixth Amendment rights continues.

This chapter so far has focused on the media's right to publish or broadcast information and how that right is balanced against the rights of others. But unless reporters can gather information, their right to publish it is empty. This is clearest in the free press versus fair trial issue: without the right to attend trials, journalists cannot properly inform the public. Can the First Amendment, then, be interpreted as guaranteeing not only the right to publish, but also the right to find out, the right of access to information?

Until the *Richmond* case, the judicial answer to this question was a resounding "no." Legislatures might decide to grant reporters certain access rights, but the courts refused to say that the First Amendment guaranteed those rights. This is what makes *Richmond*, in the words of Supreme Court Justice Stevens, a "watershed" case:

> Until today the Court has accorded virtually absolute protection to the dissemination of information or ideas, but never before has it squarely held that the acquisition of newsworthy matter is entitled to any constitutional protection whatsoever.
>
> I agree that the First Amendment protects the public and the press from abridgement of their rights of access to information about the operation of their government, including the judicial branch.[60]

In *Richmond* this right was applied only to the issue at hand—a criminal trial. How far the courts will extend it remains to be seen. In the next section we will examine other developments affecting the journalist's "right" of access to information.

The media's right to publish information relies on their ability to acquire it first. But the courts have been reluctant to extend First Amendment protection to the news-gathering process. They have ruled, for example, that reporters have no special right to be where the news is happening, and that governments may disrupt the confidential reporter-source relationship with subpoenas and search warrants. What protection has been granted to the news-gathering process has come from legislatures, through Freedom of Information laws and the like.

FREEDOM OF INFORMATION

During the 1979 accident at the Three Mile Island nuclear power plant, the Nuclear Regulatory Commission in Washington was obliged to tape-record its meetings about how to handle the emergency. Transcribed and released to the public, the tapes provided valuable evidence of the NRC's confusion in the crisis.

The law that required the NRC to reveal its Three Mile Island problems was the "Government in the Sunshine Act," passed by Congress in 1976. This law requires some 50 federal agencies to conduct their business in public. Meetings can be closed only to talk about such matters as national security, trade secrets, and the hiring and firing of staff. All 50 states today have comparable laws, mandating open meetings of state and local public agencies. While these laws vary in scope, most provide specific legal recourse for citizens (or reporters) who think meetings have been held in secret, and many authorize the courts to invalidate any official action taken at an illegally secret meeting.[61]

Companions to these sunshine laws are the so-called "open record" laws, which recognize the public's right of access to government reports, investigative files, and regulatory documents. At the federal level, the Freedom of Information Act was passed in 1966 and tightened up with amendments in 1974 (see pp. 160-63). By 1979 every state except Mississippi and the District of Columbia had a similar open record law.[62]

About 150,000 requests for documents are received each year under the federal Freedom of Information Act alone.[63] Only one percent of these come from the news media, which often find the process too time-consuming for a deadline story. The largest number, 58 percent, come from private businesses seeking information about competitors.[64] Still, the law has yielded some important news stories. The *Daily Oklahoman* used it to get a copy of the Army's report on the 1968 My Lai massacre in Vietnam. The Associated Press used it to piece together a story on top federal officials who used to work for the industries they were now regulating. The *Washington Star* used it to uncover a CIA training program to teach local police departments how to gather intelligence about dissidents.[65]

Both open meeting and open record laws have their critics. They make the process of government less convenient and, some say, less flexible by exposing it to the harsh light of publicity. Open record laws in particular are expensive to administer; the FBI estimated its 1978 cost at $9.1 million.[66] Some officials fear that criminals use the laws to gain access to their FBI files or to documents on how to manufacture illegal drugs.[67] Reporters, on the other hand, complain that the laws give officials too many loopholes to wriggle through, and that some agencies intentionally discourage their use through cumbersome procedures and high fees.

The laws are, of course, a compromise, a balance between the public's right to know and the government's right to protect certain secrets. At worst, they at least acknowledge some right of access to information. Importantly, they are the result of legislative action, not judicial decision. Congress and the state legislatures decided to open government meetings and records to the public; no court ruled that they must. As we shall see, these legislative gifts are virtually the only legal tools a journalist has with which to gather information. For the rest, the reporter must rely on cooperative sources and his or her wits.

NEWSWORTHY LOCATIONS

Unfortunately, much of the news cannot be found in government records or at government meetings. Often the story is behind police lines at the scene of a crime, or inside a prison, or in the locker room of a football

CAMERAS IN THE COURTROOM

The *Richmond* decision broke new ground in guaranteeing reporters the right of access to courtrooms. It did not, however, guarantee that right for their cameras.

Photographers and broadcasters have long faced special restrictions in their coverage of trials. The Supreme Court encouraged such restrictions in 1965, when it reversed the fraud conviction of Billie Sol Estes because his Texas trial had been televised. The TV equipment caused "considerable disruption of the proceedings," the Court said, possibly distracting jurors and witnesses and denying Estes his right to a fair trial.[68] This was not the usual free press versus fair trial issue of prejudicial publicity. The Court didn't object to what the cameras were reporting; it objected to their very presence in the courtroom.

As broadcast technology became less intrusive in the 1970s, broadcasters began pressuring the courts to let the cameras in. The most ambitious experiment was begun in Florida in 1977. The state's Supreme Court ordered all trials open to television, regardless of the objections of judges, attorneys, or witnesses. Among the televised trials, ironically, was that of Ronald Zamora, accused of murdering an 83-year-old woman. His defense was that the killing had been triggered by an episode of "Kojak."

The experiment was a success. The judge in the Zamora case, for example, said he had "no complaints" about television's performance, and the public's response was overwhelmingly favorable.[69] A newspaper reporter at another televised trial, Tony Polk of the *Rocky Mountain News*, commented that far from creating a sensation, the TV cameras actually "diminished the circus-like atmosphere. Reporters didn't have to rush from the court whenever something important happened. And the arrangement all but ended those dehumanizing scenes where cameramen and photographers lie in wait for defendants being led out of court."[70] By early 1980, 26 states had adopted plans to permit televised trials.[71]

In the spring of 1980, however, a Miami jury acquitted four white policemen in the beating death of a black insurance man. The trial had been televised, a fact that some observers blamed for the violence that erupted in Miami's black ghettoes after the verdict was announced. Wrote George Gerbner, dean of the University of Pennsylvania's Annenberg School of Communications: "What happened in Miami is a very high price to pay for a very little gain" from televised trials.[72]

In 1981, the Supreme Court gave the green light to state experiments with cameras in the courtroom. The case was *Chandler v. Florida*, appealing a 1977 murder conviction on the grounds that the trial was televised. Departing from the *Estes* precedent, the Court ruled that the mere presence of TV cameras does not necessarily mean a trial was prejudiced; defendants who appeal their convictions on the basis of TV coverage must show evidence that the cameras influenced their trials. The Court thus steered a middle course, ruling neither that trials must be open to television nor that they must exclude the TV cameras.

---

stadium. Do journalists have any legal right of access to these locations in pursuit of a story?

So far they do not. By custom, police and fire officials usually permit accredited reporters to cross protective barriers to get to the scene of a story. But this permission can be revoked if officials believe the danger is too great or if they are too busy to cope with the media. A journalist who disobeys an official order to leave risks arrest for hampering the investigation. And a journalist who enters private property without the owner's permission risks arrest for trespass or suit for invasion of privacy. Like everyone else, in other words, reporters may go only where officials or property owners permit them to go.

Much of the legal action in this area has concerned access to prisons and prisoners. In a number of cases beginning in 1974, the courts have ruled that the Federal Bureau of Prisons may prevent the interviewing of specific inmates,[73] that Utah may exclude the press and public from an execution,[74] and that California may restrict media access to prisons to the same limited rights as the average citizen.[75] Reporters argue that they are the eyes and ears of the public, and must therefore be free to find out what's going on in the prisons and to interview any prisoner willing to be interviewed. So far they have not won that right.

The only media victory in this area has been the guarantee that individual reporters may not be singled out and punished by denying them access to an event that is open to other reporters. The Tennessee State Senate, for example, was forbidden to ban a particular reporter from the Senate floor and press galleries.[76] And the New York Yankees were told they couldn't keep women reporters out of the locker room unless they also shut the doors to men.[77]

The bottom line is that reporters have no special rights of access to newsworthy places. But this may change. The *Richmond* decision interpreted the First Amendment as entitling the public and press to attend criminal trials. Future cases may well broaden this right, for journalists, to include prisons, airports, schools, and even the Yankees locker room.

CONFIDENTIALITY

Even without much legal protection for the news-gathering process, reporters have proved remarkably skilled at digging out the information they need. One way they have managed to do this is by promising to protect the identities of sources who provide information in confidence. The ability to keep this promise is often essential to good investigative news coverage. Max Frankel of the *New York Times* explains why:

In private dealings with persons who figure in the news, reporters obtain not only on-the-record comments but also confidential judgments and facts that they then use to appraise the accuracy and meaning of other men's words and deeds. Without the access and without such confidential relationships, much important information would have to be gathered by remote means and much could never be subjected to cross-examination. Politicians who weigh their words, officials who fear their superiors, citizens who fear persecution or prosecution would refuse to talk with reporters or admit them to their circles if they felt that confidences would be betrayed at the behest of the Government.[78]

There are many relationships in this country that are considered "privileged"—which means that the government is not permitted to pry into them in search of information. Among these are lawyer-client, doctor-patient, priest-parishioner, and husband-wife; in some states the list also includes social worker-client, accountant-client, and psychologist-patient. The question is whether journalists and their sources should also have this "privilege" in order to protect the flow of information to the media, and from there to the public.

There is no ethical debate here. Once a reporter has promised to protect the identity of a source, that promise *must not* be broken. This is one of the few ethical rules on which virtually all journalists agree. But honoring the rule can put journalists in conflict with grand juries, judges, and attorneys, all of whom may want information to further criminal investigations.

The most important Supreme Court statement on this question came in 1972 in the case of *Branzburg v. Hayes.* The Court consolidated three separate cases concerning journalistic privilege into one ruling. Paul Branzburg, a *Louisville Courier-Journal* reporter, had written an inside story on the illegal drug trade, which made him privy to the identities of those involved. Paul Pappas of WTEV-TV in New Bedford, Mass., and Earl Caldwell of the *New York Times* had both reported on the activities of the Black Panthers, a black political group often the target of grand jury probes in the 1970s. All three had received subpoenas demanding confidential information and the names of confidential sources. All three had refused, and faced court orders to change their minds or go to jail.

The Court ruled that there was no First Amendment right on which these reporters could rely to protect confidential sources and information. Unless an investigative body is intentionally harassing the media and not acting in good faith, the Court said, reporters like other citizens must answer its questions. The Court added that while there was no privilege for reporters in the First Amendment, Congress and the various state legislatures were free to enact such a privilege if they liked by passing so-called "shield laws."[79]

By the beginning of 1980, 26 states had adopted such laws,[80] and the voters of California had passed a measure to incorporate the journalist's right to protect confidential sources into the state constitution.[81] Some of these shield laws grant absolute protection; others qualify it in some way, typically permitting demands for confidential information only if it is crucial and unavailable from other sources. In 24 states and the federal system, there is no shield law at all.

The argument for laws permitting report-ers to keep their promises of confidentiality is persuasive—without this right some sources will refuse to talk and some information will be held back. But so is the argument for making reporters help the legal system when they have information of value. Information, not secrecy, is the business of journalism, and it is easy to understand the frustration of judges and lawyers when a reporter insists on withholding facts that could convict or acquit a criminal defendant. Once again, two legitimate rights are in conflict, and balancing them is not simple.

Consider a 1978 case in New Jersey, a state with a strong but qualified shield law. Myron Farber, an investigative reporter for the *New York Times,* had uncovered new evidence concerning 13 mysterious deaths at a New Jersey hospital. Prompted by Farber's articles, state law enforcement officials conducted an investigation that led to the indictment of Dr. Mario Jascalevich for murder.

The defense argued that Farber and the prosecution were collaborating against Jascalevich, and that a knowledge of Farber's sources and information (beyond what was published in the *Times*) was therefore essential. The defense first called Farber as a witness, but he refused to answer questions that might reveal confidential sources or information. He was then subpoenaed to turn over virtually his entire file on the murders. The *Times* asked the trial judge to throw out the subpoenas on the grounds that Farber was protected by both the First Amendment and New Jersey's shield law.

Instead, the judge ordered Farber to turn over the materials so he could examine them in his chambers and determine if they were really necessary to Jascalevich's defense. Farber refused, arguing that even this would endanger his confidential sources. The court then found Farber and the *Times* in contempt. Farber spent 40 days in jail and the paper paid $286,000 in fines, but they did not yield. The murder trial continued without Farber's help, and Jascalevich was ac-

SHIELDING NONEXISTENT SOURCES

Opponents of shield laws often argue that requiring journalists to reveal their sources is the only way to make sure they *have* sources, to prevent them from fabricating quotations or even whole stories. The argument took on new strength in 1981, when the *Washington Post* was forced to return a Pulitzer Prize it had won because reporter Janet Cooke admitted inventing the prize-winning story. Cooke had written about an 8-year-old heroin addict who was allegedly being forced to take the drug by an adult. She did not name the boy or the adults involved, telling her editors and readers that she had promised anonymity. The *Post* backed her in this stand, even when the municipal government said it wanted the names so the boy could be helped. But Cooke's refusal to name names had nothing to do with honoring a promise to her sources. She had no sources, no boy, no story. She had hidden behind confidentiality to hoodwink her editors and readers.

Other abuses of confidentiality are less starkly unethical—and far more common. Political reporters, for example, sometimes know more about what is happening than they can find sources willing to say, even anonymously. The temptation is great to fill the gap with an invented quotation, attributed to "a source close to" the president or the mayor. If anyone demands to know who the well-placed source is, the reporter can always reply that he or she promised not to tell.

None of this contradicts the fact that there are real sources who will tell what they know only if the reporter can promise anonymity and make the promise stick. But confidentiality should be used as a last resort, not an easy way out. As much as possible, the public deserves to know where the reporter's information is coming from.

---

quitted.[82] After the acquittal the court had no further use for the files, so Farber was freed.

In retrospect, it is easy to say the defense didn't really need to infringe on Farber's confidentiality. But suppose Jascalevich had been convicted. And suppose there was information in Farber's files that might have led the jury to acquit instead. When a reporter's need to protect a confidence comes into conflict with the genuine needs of the judicial system—of the defense *or* the prosecution—it is difficult to say which should take precedence.

One thing is certain—subpoenas like Farber's do have a chilling effect on media performance. One survey of investigative reporters found that 35 percent believe they have lost stories or sources because they could not legally guarantee that they would protect anonymity.[83] Between 100 and 125 cases contesting subpoenas of journalists' confidential information occur each year.[84] And that's just the tip of the iceberg. Often news organizations simply don't fight such subpoenas, because they don't have the money or they think it's futile. In 1980, for example, television stations in Greensboro, North Carolina turned over footage not aired of a rally at which five members of the Communist Workers Party were killed by members of the Ku Klux Klan. The film was shown to the jury at the murder trial of the Klansmen.[85]

SEARCH WARRANTS

When a journalist is served with a subpoena demanding that confidential information be turned over to an investigative body, he or she can at least appear before a judge first to argue that the subpoena should not be enforced. In 1971, however, police in Palo Alto, California chose a quicker route. Officials had reason to believe that the *Stanford Daily*, Stanford University's student newspaper, had pictures of a demonstration at which nine policemen were injured. They wanted the pictures to identify those responsible. Rather than resort to a subpoena, the police obtained a search warrant, walked into the newspaper office, and rummaged through the files. Had they found the pictures they would have taken them. (The paper had a policy of not keeping unpublished photographic evidence that might incriminate people, so the negatives had been destroyed.)[86]

The search outraged reporters and editors across the country. It showed how easily the media could be converted into an investigative arm of the government. It swept aside possible protection from a shield law or a First Amendment argument. It enabled police to examine material not covered by the warrant, thereby opening up other confidential information to government scrutiny. And it made it likely that some individuals would refuse to be photographed or filmed, chilling press freedom and the ability to gather information. Backed by many national media groups, the students appealed to the courts.

In 1978 they lost. The Supreme Court ruled that police may search *any* premises (be it a newsroom, a doctor's office, or a private home) if they have reason to believe they will find evidence of some crime. Neither the Fourth Amendment (which guards against unreasonable searches and seizures) nor the First Amendment protects the media from such searches.[87]

The use of a search warrant against the media is hardly routine; police and journalists are usually more cooperative than antagonistic. But the *Stanford Daily* case was not unique. In 1974, Los Angeles police searched radio station KPFK for a letter mailed to it by the New World Liberation Front. In 1977, police in Coventry, Rhode Island searched for film of a picket-line fight that they believed was in the possession of television station WJAR.[88] And in 1980, police searched a Boise, Idaho TV station for film of a prison riot.[89]

Finding no help in the courts, journalists have turned to Congress and their state legislatures for protection. In the year after the Supreme Court ruled on the *Stanford Daily* case, 25 states started the process to consider laws protecting newsrooms from such searches. Six states—California, Connecticut, Illinois, Nebraska, Oregon, and Texas—actually passed such laws. All six protect only the news media, not other third parties thought to possess evidence of someone else's crime. California's is absolute; the others permit searches only if journalists are themselves suspected of a crime or if there is reason to believe the material being sought will be destroyed or moved.[90] In 1980, Congress passed a similarly limited law protecting newsrooms and authors.[91]

Newsroom searches do provide useful evidence from time to time, occasionally even crucial evidence. Against this genuine law-enforcement value, weigh the threat to journalistic freedom. In hindsight, there was probably nothing to stop the Justice Department from raiding the files of *Washington Post* reporters Woodward and Bernstein in 1973, in order to learn their source for much of the damaging information they were publishing about the Watergate scandal. If that confidential source—"Deep Throat"—had been unmasked, how likely is it that continuing disclosures would have finally forced the resignation of President Nixon?

The authority of the government over radio and television is far greater than government control of the print media. In theory, at least, any broadcast license may be revoked by the government if the station fails to fulfill its obligation to the public. In practice, however, government regulation tends to concentrate on the pettier aspects of broadcasting. Though the fear of government intervention often motivates the behavior of broadcasters, the government has done little to justify that fear.

WHY BROADCASTING?

Government regulation of radio began in 1910, when Congress ratified a treaty providing that ships at sea and shore stations must answer each other's emergency radio messages. Two years later came the Radio Act, another common-sense law. It required private broadcasters to steer clear of the wavelengths used for government transmissions. The Secretary of Commerce was given the job of administering the law. Each station was awarded its own radio "license," which authorized it to broadcast whatever it wanted, wherever it wanted, whenever it wanted, on whatever frequency it wanted— as long as it avoided the government-used wavelengths.

By 1927, there were 733 private radio stations in the country. Most were concentrated in the big cities. They spent much of their time jumping from point to point on the radio dial, trying to avoid interference—but the stronger stations still managed to smother the weaker ones. The situation was intolerable. Radio manufacturers, the National Association of Broadcasters, and the listening public all called on the federal government to do something about it. The air waves belong to the public, they argued. Since the airwaves were a mess, it was the government's job to clean the mess up.

Thus was born the Radio Act of 1927. A five-person Federal Radio Commission was given the power to license broadcasters for three-year periods, allotting each one a specific frequency in a specific location. If there were more license applicants than available frequencies (as there were bound to be), the Commission was to favor those applicants most likely to serve "the public interest, convenience, or necessity." The same standard

was to be used in judging whether a licensee deserved to keep the license at the end of the three years. And in case new problems came up, the Commission was empowered to "make such regulations not inconsistent with law as it may deem necessary to prevent interference between stations and to carry out the provisions of this Act."

Seven years later, Congress passed the Communications Act of 1934. Besides radio, the Commission was given authority over telephone, telegraph, and television as well. It was expanded to seven members and renamed the Federal Communications Commission. The other provisions were essentially the same as those of the Radio Act. They are still essentially the same today.

The government began broadcast regulation by popular request, in order to allocate frequencies. But there were more would-be station owners than available wavelengths. At that point the government *could* have assigned licenses by picking numbers out of a hat, or by raffling them off to the highest bidder. But it decided instead to judge program content, to award the license to the most "deserving" applicant, not the luckiest or the richest.

If this sounds like censorship to you, it did to some broadcasters too. The 1927 Radio Act provided:

> Nothing in this Act shall be understood or construed to give the licensing authority the power of censorship . . . and no regulation or condition shall be promulgated or fixed by the licensing authority which shall interfere with the right of free speech by means of radio communications.

The Communications Act of 1934 included a nearly identical provision.

Its meaning was tested in 1931, when the Federal Radio Commission refused to renew the license of station KFKB, because the owner used a daily medical program to plug his own patent medicines. The station took the case to court—and lost. The court ruled:

In considering the question whether the public interest, convenience, or necessity will be served by a renewal of appellant's license, the commission has merely exercised its undoubted right to take note of appellant's past conduct, which is not censorship.[92]

It is fruitless to debate the point. Licensing has traditionally been a tool of authoritarian governments, which used it as a form of censorship. The power to license a broadcast station is—beyond doubt—the power to control what it broadcasts. Yet licensing of radio and televison is inevitable—because there are not enough channels to go around and because stations will interfere with each other's signals if they are not properly separated in the broadcast spectrum. Every libertarian government has faced this dilemma. The only ones that didn't wind up licensing their broadcast stations wound up owning them instead—an even more authoritarian solution.

The First Amendment does apply to broadcasting—but not in the same way it applies to newspapers and magazines. As the Federal Court of Appeals put it in 1966: "A newspaper can be operated at the whim or caprice of its owner; a broadcasting station cannot. After nearly five decades of operation, the broadcasting industry does not seem to have grasped the simple fact that a broadcast license is a public trust subject to termination for breach of duty."[93]

LICENSING

The fundamental power of the Federal Communications Commission is its power to grant and renew broadcast licenses. The standard to be used in this operation is, of course, the "public interest, convenience, and necessity." Over the years, the FCC has expanded this notion to include many different criteria, such as financial qualifications and broadcast experience. In deciding between competing applicants for an open frequency, the FCC actually uses these criteria. But this

happens only on occasion. Most of the desirable frequencies are already taken—which is why the government got into broadcast regulation in the first place. In practice, then, the FCC spends most of its time considering license *renewal* applications. And that's another story entirely.

Between 1934 and 1980, the FCC refused to renew the licenses of a grand total of 102 radio and TV stations; it revoked licenses or permits from 39 more.[94] That's 141 No votes over nearly five decades, compared to more than 70,000 licenses that were granted or renewed during the same period. And most of the stations that did lose the precious license lost it by default—they failed to operate the station, refused to stay on the assigned frequency, or transmitted with unauthorized power. It would seem that the average broadcaster has very little to worry about.

The FCC is severely limited in the penalties it is allowed to impose on errant broadcast stations. It can assess a small fine, which for a profitable station is a wrist-slap of no particular importance. It can renew the license for a probationary period of one year, which merely prolongs the agony. Or it can take the license away altogether. The FCC is rather like a judge with only two sentences to choose between: five minutes in jail or the gas chamber. The judge knows the first sentence is too light to be effective, but the other one is far too severe. Loss of the license is the gas chamber for a radio or TV station. Understandably, the FCC imposes that penalty only on the most egregiously irresponsible broadcasters. A station that falsifies its records or tries to bribe the Commission stands a good chance of losing its license. A station that merely does a poor job is reasonably safe.

In 1980 the FCC reminded the industry of its regulatory power by stripping RKO General, Inc. of its licenses to operate television stations in Boston, Los Angeles, and New York. It was the strongest such action in the Commission's history. RKO's parent corporation, General Tire, had been caught bribing officials of foreign governments and making illegal campaign contributions; it had also tried to pressure companies into placing advertising with RKO stations as a condition of doing business with General Tire. On the open market, the three stations were worth about $270 million.[95] But without the licenses to operate they became almost worthless, mere assortments of used equipment. As the *New York Times* reported, the decision sent "shockwaves" through the broadcast industry.[96]

A more typically cautious approach is illustrated by the WLBT-TV case. In 1964, Dr. Everett Parker of the United Church of Christ led a drive by local blacks to deny the Jackson (Mississippi) station its license renewal, on the grounds that it had made no effort to serve the black population. At first the Commission simply dismissed the complaint, claiming that a citizen group had no standing in a license hearing. Dr. Parker went to court and had the ruling overturned. Then the Commission decided that there wasn't enough proof of discrimination by the station to justify taking away the license. Dr. Parker went to court again, and won the right to still a third hearing. Said Judge Warren Burger:

> The intervenors [Dr. Parker and his colleagues], who were performing a public service under the mandate of this court, were entitled to a more hospitable reception in the performance of that function. As we view the record, the examiner [for the FCC] tended to impede the exploration of the very issues which we would reasonably expect the commission itself would have initiated; an ally was regarded as an opponent.[97]

In an unprecedented move, the court *itself* revoked the license of WLBT. It instructed the FCC to consider the matter from scratch, reviewing all applications for the license—including the original licensee's—as if it had never seen them before. Reluctantly, the Commission obeyed. While the FCC pondered the case, WLBT was run on a non-profit basis by a biracial caretaker group.[98] In 1979 the Commission finally awarded the license to TV3, a local Jackson group that is 51 percent black-owned.[99]

The fact that it took 15 years and pressure from the courts to bring about this change in the WLBT licensee might be expected to reassure broadcasters that the FCC is squarely on their side. But broadcasters were not reassured. WLBT did finally change hands—and any time any broadcast company loses its license for whatever reason, the entire industry shudders in fear.

It is important to understand the paranoia of the broadcast industry. Broadcasters know that the FCC still renews nearly every license it considers. They know that the Commission hasn't got the staff, the time, or the money to give a typical renewal application searching consideration. They know that the Commission usually rubber-stamps renewals unless a competing applicant or a citizen group stirs up a huge political and legal fuss, and that even then it bends over backwards to favor the current licensee. And they know that all this will continue to be true for the foreseeable future.

But then there are those exceptions, unexpected, seemingly almost random: WLBT . . . RKO. . . . Lurking in the back of every broadcaster's mind is this fear: Maybe *my* license will be the next exception. However unjustified, this fear makes radio and television somewhat more responsive to the public (and much more responsive to the federal government) than they would otherwise be.

PROGRAMMING

The Communications Act of 1934 forbids the FCC to abridge the First Amendment rights of broadcasters by interfering directly with program content. Common sense suggests that the power to award and deny licenses is inevitably the power to control content by deciding who gets the license. But the FCC tries hard to keep its influence on programming as indirect as possible.

The Commission's efforts to regulate media monopoly are a good case in point (see pp. 129-32). A TV-newspaper cross-ownership in the same city, for example, is a source of concern because shared ownership makes it more likely that the two media will cover the same news and express the same editorial opinions. Monopoly ownership, in other words, threatens diversity of *content*. The easiest way to eliminate the threat would presumably be for the FCC to order cross-owned broadcast stations to stop borrowing news and editorials from the newspaper down the hall. But that would be regulating content. So instead the FCC has tried to stop the cross-ownerships themselves, regulating ownership directly and content only indirectly.

Despite its commitment to avoiding direct content regulation, sometimes the FCC has no choice. Three areas of broadcast law put the FCC squarely into programming: the equal time law for political candidates, the regulation of broadcast obscenity, and the fairness doctrine. We will consider each in turn.

1. Equal Time. The equal time law, Section 315 of the Communications Act, requires any station that provides time for a political candidate to provide the same amount of time, on the same terms, for every other candidate for that office. Section 312 of the Act requires broadcasters to *sell* "reasonable amounts" of airtime to candidates for federal office; the Supreme Court ruled this provision constitutional in 1981. Thus, if a Senate candidate wants to buy a prime-time

---

SWITCHING FORMATS

For nearly 50 years, radio station WEFM in Chicago was a prime source of classical music on the FM dial. Then in 1972 the Zenith Radio Corporation sold the station to General Cinema, which announced plans to switch to a rock format. Normally the FCC would have rubber-stamped the sale without even considering the format change—format is content, after all, and content is what the FCC is supposed to avoid regulating. But a Citizens Committee to Save WEFM organized to fight the sale, arguing that Chicago could not afford to lose one of its three classical music stations and that the FCC should hold hearings to determine if the format switch was detrimental to the public interest.

In New York City, meanwhile, WNCN radio decided to abandon its own classical music format. This time the station was not to be sold, but again a citizens group was formed to stop the format change, and of course the group pressured the FCC to help.

The FCC is understandably reluctant to get involved in these sorts of content issues. If it can order a station to program classical music instead of rock, then what's to keep it from ruling that punk rock, say, is not in the public interest, or that what Chicago or New York really needs is a station devoted to fundamentalist preaching or conservative politics or military marches? Arguing that the marketplace, not the government, should control the kinds of programs offered to the public, the FCC refused to rule on radio formats.

The WEFM and WNCN disputes were ultimately settled privately. WEFM's new owner agreed to donate money and albums to support classical formats on two other Chicago FM stations.[100] And the owners of WNCN sold the station to another company willing to retain the classical format.

In 1979 the U.S. Court of Appeals ordered the FCC to hold hearings if a unique radio format was in danger of being changed.[101] But in 1981 the Supreme Court overruled the decision. Market forces, not the FCC, should determine radio formats, it said.[102]

minute, the station must say yes (312), and then every other Senate candidate is entitled to a prime-time minute at the same price (315). Regularly scheduled newscasts and interviews, on-the-spot stories, and documentaries are exempt. No station may censor or edit the equal time remarks of a political candidate.

The purpose of the equal time law is, of course, to make sure that broadcasters do not use their power to influence political campaigns by freezing out one candidate and plugging another. But the law raises almost as many problems as it solves. Suppose there are twenty-seven declared candidates for mayor of some city. A local station may wish to schedule half-hour interviews with the two or three top contenders. It knows that if it does so, the other two dozen (Vegetarian, Prohibitionist, Communist) candidates will all be entitled to a free half-hour apiece. So it drops the interview idea entirely.

The flexibility of broadcasters increased somewhat in 1975, when the Commission ruled that candidates' news conferences and political debates are exempt from equal time requirements as bona fide news events. At the presidential level this meant that whereas the Kennedy-Nixon debates of 1960 took place only because Congress temporarily suspended the equal time law, the Carter-Ford debates of 1976 required no Congressional action. This explains why the League of Women Voters sponsored the 1976 and 1980 Presidential debates. If the networks sponsored them, the FCC said, they would be media creations and not bona fide news events, and the equal time law would apply. The myth that the debates were events that would have happened even without TV enabled the FCC to permit them despite the equal time law—at the expense, of course, of those "minor party" candidates who were not invited to participate.

2. Obscenity. Federal law specifically forbids "obscene, indecent, or profane language" in broadcasting. Control of broadcast obscenity is far more stringent than the comparable rules for the print media, presumably because broadcasting reaches into every living room. Stations have been fined simply for letting a single "dirty word" slip out over the airwaves. Poems and plays that were manifestly legal in print and on stage have become suddenly illegal when repeated over radio or television.

The most significant test of broadcast obscenity law came in the 1978 case of *FCC v. Pacifica Foundation*.[103] One fall afternoon in 1973, radio station WBAI in New York City broadcast a recording of a 12-minute monologue by comedian George Carlin, in which Carlin had some fun discussing seven dirty words "that will curve your spine, grow hair on your hands" . . . and likely be banned from the airwaves. Sure enough, a listener complained to the FCC. After the Commission ruled against the station, the case eventually reached the Supreme Court.

The Court found that while the words were not obscene (because they had no prurient appeal), they *were* indecent and therefore covered by the federal statute. And the statute, the Court said, was not unconstitutional. "Patently offensive, indecent material presented over the airwaves," wrote Justice Stevens, "confronts the citizen not only in public, but also in the privacy of the home, where the individual's right to be let alone plainly outweighs the First Amendment rights of an intruder." This is especially true, Justice Stevens noted, in the afternoon when children can be expected to be listening.

As a result of *Pacifica,* broadcasters know that they can be punished for airing indecent words in mid-afternoon. What about indecent pictures? The question hasn't been answered yet, because broadcasters usually censor themselves and do not air potentially offensive films of nudity and sex acts. But this is changing, particularly in cable and pay television. It is only a matter of time before the courts will define the limits of indecent video expression. These limits are certain to be stricter than those affecting theater and film.

3. Fairness Doctrine. From the very beginning of radio, the government has held that broadcasters must not present only one side of controversial issues. As early as 1929, the Federal Radio Commission revoked a station's license for bias, insisting that "the public interest requires ample play for the free and fair competition of opposing views."[104] Over the years, on a case-by-case basis, this notion has evolved into the fairness doctrine.

Between 1929 and 1941, several stations lost their licenses for "unfair" treatment of controversial issues. And in 1941, radio station WAAB nearly lost its license simply for running editorials on various issues. The FCC finally decided to give the station another chance, but it firmly declared that "the broadcaster cannot be an advocate."[105] These decisions badly frightened most broadcast executives. They not only dropped their editorials; they dropped just about all their controversial programming. As long as they didn't talk about anything important, broadcasters reasoned, they couldn't possibly be unfair about anything important.

This was not what the FCC had intended. In the late 1940s the Commission reconsidered the whole fairness problem, and in 1949 it announced its conclusions. Although it has changed over the years, the fairness doctrine today retains the following major provisions:

1. Licensees must devote a reasonable amount of broadcast time to controversial public issues.

2. In doing so, they must encourage the presentation of all sides of those issues.

3. Licensees are encouraged to editorialize so long as the end result is balanced programming on public controversies.

4. Whenever a licensee broadcasts a specific attack against a person or group, the victim must be offered comparable free time in which to reply. Newscasts, news interviews, and on-the-spot news coverage are exempt.

5. Licensees have an "affirmative obligation" to

seek out representatives of opposing viewpoints.

6. Those who reply to earlier broadcasts under the fairness doctrine have no obligation to pay for the time; the licensee must provide it without charge.

7. If licensees endorse a candidate for political office, they must permit spokespersons for all other candidates for that office to reply to the endorsement.

It is important to stress what the fairness doctrine is *not*. First, it is not a guarantee that individuals and groups will have access to the broadcast media. Aside from two narrow provisions (4 and 7 above), the fairness doctrine doesn't grant anyone a right to time on radio or television. Rather, it grants listeners and viewers the right to be exposed to both sides of controversial issues. The broadcaster decides whether a particular issue is controversial, whether the station has covered all sides adequately, and who shall present any additional viewpoints that might be needed for balance. An interest group that believes its viewpoint has been ignored may complain to the station, and to the FCC if it's not satisfied with the station's response. As a practical matter stations often settle fairness doctrine complaints by offering the complaining group a chance to appear (see pp. 228-29). But they don't have to. Even if the FCC ultimately decides against them—months or even years later—they can still choose any way they like to cover the neglected viewpoint.

Second, the fairness doctrine is not a guarantee of "equal time" for opposing positions on public controversies. The equal time law applies only to political candidates; the fairness doctrine is much broader but much looser, requiring only a "reasonable balance" of conflicting positions. The FCC has often held that a reasonable balance was achieved when one side had five or six times as much coverage as the other, or when one side was represented by dozens of advocacy

THE RIGHT OF REPLY?

The equal time law and the personal attack provision of the fairness doctrine both require broadcasters to provide airtime to certain individuals—candidates whose opponents have been on the air, and people who have been attacked on the air. Supporters of a "right of access" to the media have argued that these provisions should be extended to the print media as well. By way of example, they have sometimes cited an obscure 1913 Florida law requiring newspapers to print the reply of a candidate attacked in the paper "in as conspicuous a place and in the same kind of type as the matter that calls for such reply."[106]

The law was tested in 1972, when the *Miami Herald* accused Pat L. Tornillo, Jr., a candidate for the Florida legislature, of being a "labor czar" who took part in "shakedown statesmanship." Tornillo wrote a reply to the attack, the *Herald* refused to print it, and the case went to court. The Florida Supreme Court declared that the right-of-reply statute "enhances rather than abridges freedom of speech and press," and ruled that the law was constitutional.[107]

In 1974, the U.S. Supreme Court unanimously reversed the decision. Wrote Chief Justice Warren E. Burger: "The choice of material to go into a newspaper, and the decisions made as to limitations on the size of the paper and content and treatment of public issues and public officials—whether fair or unfair—constitutes the exercise of editorial control and judgment." The state, he said, is prevented by the Constitution from interfering with that judgment.[108]

The equal time law and the fairness doctrine are still constitutional. The courts have repeatedly stressed that this is because the limited number of broadcast frequencies justifies government interference to insure fairness. But as far as the print media are concerned, the right of reply is an unconstitutional concept. And the right of access remains more an ethical theory than a legal one.

---

ads throughout the day while the other had only a single long interview at an unpopular time. Recent FCC decisions have been moving toward a more even balance, but they are still far from requiring equal time.

Third, the fairness doctrine is not primarily a tool to insure public exposure to extreme viewpoints. In fact, the FCC has often ruled that very unpopular positions (atheism, communism, fascism) were too far out to deserve fairness doctrine protection. When the public is more or less evenly divided on an issue, the fairness doctrine requires stations to pay attention to both sides. When extremists control a station, the fairness doctrine requires them to acknowledge more conventional viewpoints. But a station that covers the full range of moderate opinions is not obliged to cover the extremes as well.

Add to these limitations the fact that fairness doctrine complaints are time-consuming, expensive, and slow, and it is easy to see why many critics are dissatisfied with the doctrine as a way to insure balanced broadcasting. Yet it does work sometimes. Scores of FCC decisions under the fairness doctrine have obligated stations to provide more balanced coverage. Hundreds of fairness complaints to broadcasters have forced more balanced coverage without recourse to the FCC. And every day the programming decisions of broadcasters are influenced by their knowledge that the fairness doctrine exists.

Many broadcasters and civil libertarians, in fact, argue that the fairness doctrine is *too* effective, that it gives the government too much control over broadcast content. Though the Supreme Court has ruled that the doctrine does not violate the First Amendment,[109] it certainly does involve the government in the editorial process in ways that would be unconstitutional for the print media. Consider an award-winning NBC documentary entitled "Pensions: The Broken Promise," which aired in 1973. Acting on a complaint from the conservative citizens group Accuracy in Media, the FCC voted 5-0 that the program violated the fairness doctrine by paying too little attention to good pension plans.

NBC could have ended the matter by broadcasting something complimentary about pension plans, but instead it announced that it would appeal the decision. The government, it contended, had no right to use the fairness doctrine as a basis for second-guessing the news judgment of broadcast journalists. In 1974 a three-judge panel of the Court of Appeals endorsed the NBC position, ruling that when a broadcaster exercises news judgment in good faith, the fairness doctrine does not provide a vehicle for the FCC to substitute its own news judgment instead. The full nine-judge Court of Appeals considered the case in 1975. But the FCC suggested that the conflict was now irrelevant, since Congress had passed a pension reform law and pensions were no longer a controversial issue. The court agreed, and let the panel's decision stand.

Although NBC did not have to air additional material, the case left unresolved the question of how much FCC interference in broadcast content is acceptable to the First Amendment under the fairness doctrine.

This case illustrates another issue as well. NBC could have avoided the whole problem simply by deciding not to do an exposé on pension plans in the first place. It is impossible to tell just how often broadcasters avoid controversial issues in order to avoid fairness doctrine complaints. But certainly the doctrine does discourage hard-hitting programming; mealy-mouthed programming is a lot safer. The first provision of the fairness doctrine, requiring broadcasters to pay some attention to controversial issues, was designed to avoid this pitfall—but it is seldom enforced. Stations often get into trouble for treating controversy one-sidedly, but rarely for ignoring it altogether.

The results are most visible in the area of advocacy advertising. Throughout the 1970s, citizens groups were highly successful in winning fairness doctrine complaints against paid issue advertising. In 1977, for example, the FCC ordered WTOP-TV in Washington to find a way to balance 53 Texaco ads opposing breakup of the oil companies into smaller units; a group called Energy Action wound up with 30 free spots of its own.[110] And in 1978 KTTV in Los Angeles sold time to a group opposing a ballot measure that would have restricted smoking in public places; the FCC ordered the station to provide free time to those supporting the measure.[111]

How can a station avoid the costly obligation to balance paid advocacy ads with unpaid spots? By turning down the ads. Today the networks and many local stations refuse to sell prime time for issue advertising. The courts have upheld their right to reject such advertising. Broadcasters thus wind up presenting neither side of the controversy instead of both. This is an unintended—and many would say unfortunate—effect of the fairness doctrine.

Under attack from all sides, the fairness doctrine may not survive the next few years. The most likely change would end case-by-case application of the doctrine. Instead, a station would be judged on its overall performance at license-renewal time, to see if it had generally adhered to the spirit of fairness on controversial issues.[112] A monumentally and consistently unfair station might thus lose its license, but occasional bias would be the station's right, as it is now the print media's right. Such a change would get the FCC out of the day-to-day editorial business and perhaps encourage more controversial broadcasting—both highly desirable results. They would come at the expense of those whose points of view on particular issues are ignored by broadcasters.

TECHNOLOGY

The FCC began its career by allocating frequencies in order to eliminate interference. As befits this beginning, the Commission is always very preoccupied with technology. The vast majority of FCC regulations are technical—they concern the height of the transmitter, the precise wavelength of the signal, the number of "dots" per square inch on the TV screen, etc.

Government regulation of broadcast technology is important not only to technicians, but to anyone who cares about the role of broadcasting in American society. Past FCC decisions about which technologies to encourage and which to ignore have largely determined what we hear on the radio and see on TV today. Current decisions will largely determine what we hear and see tomorrow.

In 1945, for example, the FCC was considering two infant technologies—FM radio and television. It decided to encourage TV and let FM sit for a while. As a result, FM made little progress until 1961, when the Commission authorized FM stereophonic broadcasting, a unique service especially attractive to music lovers and hi-fi fans. In 1964, the FCC adopted rules limiting AM-FM simulcasting, thus encouraging separate FM programs specifically aimed at FM audiences. At last, FM began to grow.

Like FM radio, UHF television has been around for several decades. But throughout the 1950s, the FCC chose to concentrate on the VHF channels instead, preferring to build the economic base of the TV industry rather than working for a larger number of less powerful stations. Only after VHF television was firmly entrenched did the Com-

mission adopt a series of rules aimed at encouraging the growth of UHF. These culminated in a 1962 law that required every new television set made in 1964 or later to include a UHF receiver and antenna. Today, nearly all TVs can receive UHF—but VHF had an enormous head start.

Satellite television is another technology whose time has come belatedly as a result of government policy. In 1962 Congress created Comsat, a semi-public corporation charged with developing satellite communications. AT&T is Comsat's largest stockholder. But AT&T also owns the profitable land lines that connect American TV networks with their local stations. Comsat understandably decided not to develop a domestic satellite television system. Despite proposals and recommendations from a number of companies, foundations, and even government commissions, the FCC made no move to encourage Comsat or anyone else to take action on satellites. The Nixon administration forced the issue in 1969, urging the FCC to give the go-ahead to any company willing to build a domestic satellite system. Pressured by the White House Office of Telecommunications Policy, the Commission formally adopted this "open-sky" approach in 1972, ending the domination of Comsat and finally opening the way for satellite communications in the United States.

FM, UHF, and satellites are all important now. Other technologies, such as fiber optics, show promise of becoming important in the future. FCC decisions today will determine whether and how that promise is realized.

Perhaps the clearest example of FCC control over the development of a new technology is the history of cable television. Cable brings a TV signal into the home through a wire, rather than over the air. The carrying capacity of the wire can be more than fifty channels on some of the newer systems, much more than is possible on the crowded over-the-air broadcast spectrum. When cable systems carry local channels, the picture quality is usually substantially improved. And cable operations can bring distant channels to an audience that was previously out of range. Cable companies can also originate their own programming, or carry special pay-television channels offering first-run movies, sporting events, and special-interest programming. Finally, a cable system can be turned into a two-way communication network, permitting such science-fiction possibilities as home plebiscites and shopping by television (see pp. 321-25).

All this is understandably threatening to traditional broadcasters, who see their mass audience being broken up and siphoned away by the abundance of cable. Beginning in 1966, and continuing over the next dozen years, the FCC moved to protect over-the-air broadcasters by passing a number of rules to hobble the growth of cable. For example:

- Cable systems were required to carry the signals of all VHF and UHF stations within a 35-mile radius.
- Cable systems were limited in the number of distant signals they could import from other markets. Systems in the major markets, for example, were allowed no imported signals in the 1960s, a maximum of two in the early 1970s.
- Cable systems were forbidden to show local sporting events that had been blacked out from over-the-air broadcasting by the league.
- Cable systems were required to set aside channels to be used free of charge by the public, local government, and local schools.
- Cable systems were forbidden to carry syndicated programs also being aired by a local station.

These rules successfully slowed the growth of cable, but they didn't stop it. By the end of the 1970s, about 20 percent of all television homes were on the cable, many of the remaining 80 percent were anxiously awaiting the arrival of a local cable system, and the cable industry was becoming powerful enough to lobby effectively for less restrictive rules. The lobbying came at a time when "deregulation" was coming into vogue as a government policy. And so, despite the protests of traditional broadcasters, it found a receptive audience at the FCC.

The Supreme Court took the first step in 1979, when it ruled that the Commission had overstepped its authority in ordering cable systems to set aside channels for public access.[113] Then in 1980 the FCC decided that cable systems could import as many distant signals as they wanted to, and that they could carry syndicated programs even if a local station was broadcasting the same show.[114] By the end of 1980 the only major rules left standing were the obligations to carry all local signals and to obey local sports blackouts.

Just as restrictive regulations hampered cable's growth in the 1970s, deregulation is bound to foster its growth in the 1980s. The National Association of Broadcasters naturally complained that cable deregulation constituted unfair competition and threatened the survival of traditional broadcasting; the NAB was especially annoyed that the new copyright law required cablecasters to pay only a small royalty to broadcasters for the programs they retransmitted. Many citizens groups complained too, regretting the loss of mandatory access channels and other regulations that had forced cable to be more responsive than over-the-air broadcasting to minority viewpoints. Charles Ferris, then FCC chairman, dismissed both sets of complaints. Deregulation, he said, "removed the regulatory debris of a previous decade. We have thus expanded the choices that consumers will have in the future."[115]

The FCC, in short, abandoned cable regulation—and the battle between cablecasting and broadcasting—to the decisions of the marketplace. Television will be more competitive in the 1980s than it has been in the past. The results are sure to benefit the cable industry, sure to damage (at least a little) the broadcasting industry. How they will affect the viewing public remains to be seen. Much will depend on what performance standards local communities write into the thousands

RULES AND MORE RULES

Every year *Broadcasting Yearbook* includes twenty pages or so of fine print listing specific FCC regulations pertaining to the broadcast media. We have already covered the important ones. But it is the "unimportant" ones—hundreds and hundreds of them—that keep the FCC always on the mind of every broadcaster. The following is a sample of ten, selected more or less at random.[116]

1. No station may move its main studio across any state or municipal boundary without first receiving a permit from the FCC.
2. Every station must remain on the air at least two-thirds the number of hours per day that it is permitted to be on the air, except Sundays.
3. Every station must employ at least one fulltime radiotelephone operator with a first-class FCC license.
4. No station may sign a contract obligating it to broadcast programs supplied by a network.
5. Every station with five or more full-time employees must file an employment report by May 31 of each year on FCC Form 395.
6. Before recording a telephone conversation for broadcast, every station must make sure the person on the line knows the conversation is being recorded and may be broadcast.
7. Every station must identify its call letters and location on the air at the beginning and end of each hour of operation.
8. No station may rebroadcast Voice of America programs except by special arrangement.
9. Every station must identify in advance any taped, filmed, or prerecorded material that might otherwise seem to be a live broadcast.
10. No station may broadcast an advertisement for a lottery except state-run lotteries under certain circumstances.

Remember, these are only ten rules. We could list hundreds—and a broadcaster must know and obey them all.

---

of cable franchise agreements that will be negotiated over the next decade.

DEREGULATION

One of the goals of Jimmy Carter's presidency was to decrease federal regulation of business, relying more on market forces instead. Under Chairman Charles Ferris, a Carter appointee, the FCC considered dismantling some of the regulations that bind the broadcasting industry. We have already looked at one result of this policy, the deregulation of cable. But the FCC's strongest moves away from regulation came in another area—radio.

In 1979, the Commission voted unanimously to propose new rules for radio that would substitute a "market forces" philosophy for the traditional "public interest" standard. Instead of forcing radio stations to serve their audience, in other words, the FCC proposed to let the audience do that by listening or not listening.

The proposed changes were sweeping. Licensees would no longer have to identify community needs and specify how they were meeting those needs. The FCC would no longer make stations keep logs of what programs they had broadcast, and would no longer judge this record at license-renewal time to see if the stations carried enough news, public affairs, and public service programming. There would no longer be a limit on the number of commercial minutes per hour a station was permitted to broadcast.[117] If the experiment was successful, the Commission added, other rules (like the fairness doctrine) would be next to go, and eventually television too would be deregulated.

To support this radical break with the past, the FCC noted that regulation of broadcasting has always been a reluctant governmental intrusion on media freedom, justified by the scarcity of broadcast channels. In 1934, for example, there were only 583 stations on the air. But by 1980 there were more than 8,600 stations in operation, greatly weakening the case for regulation.[118] Furthermore, the Commission said, most stations exceed many FCC requirements already; for example, they broadcast more news than required

and fewer commercials than permitted.[119] Where market forces are working so well, why clutter them up with unnecessary regulations?

The FCC set aside more than six months for public comments on the new proposals, and many were not complimentary. Dr. Everett C. Parker, a longtime broadcast critic as director of the Office of Communication of the United Church of Christ, said the FCC was "trying to deprive the people of rights that have been guaranteed them, the rights to the air the public owns. The FCC has no proof that its plan will benefit anyone, not even the broadcasters."[120] Theodore Jones, president of radio station WCRB in Boston, agreed. "Too many broadcasters," he told the FCC, "are interested in the dollar at the expense of local rights, needs and program-

---

DEREGULATION IN CONGRESS

Enthusiasm for broadcast deregulation is not limited to the FCC. In the late 1970s, Congress began an effort to rewrite the 1934 Communications Act, spearheaded by California Democrat Lionel Van Deerlin, then chairman of the House Communications Subcommittee. Van Deerlin shared with then FCC Chairman Ferris the conviction that deregulation would foster competition, growth, and responsiveness to the public in broadcasting.

The bill Van Deerlin introduced in 1978 was too radical a departure from past practice to suit either the broadcasting industry or the public-interest movement. After nearly two years of complex maneuvering, it died in committee. Nevertheless, some of its provisions show what Congress will be considering in coming sessions:

- Suspension of all radio regulations, including the fairness doctrine and the equal time law.
- Granting of radio licenses (and eventually television licenses) for an indefinite term instead of the current three years.
- Formal congressional declaration that regulation is appropriate only "to the extent marketplace forces are deficient."
- Prohibition of all federal rules restricting cable television.
- Establishment of large fees for radio and television licenses, the money to be used to support public broadcasting, minority ownership of stations, rural telecommunications systems, and other projects.[121]

As of mid-1981 Congress has declined to act on these provisions, and the FCC is still at the forefront of broadcast deregulation. But at some point in the coming decade Congress may well rewrite the Communications Act of 1934 in the spirit of deregulation.

ming. . . . Please don't deregulate. We need you. The public needs you."[122]

Despite substantial opposition, the FCC passed the radio deregulation package in 1981.

Is deregulation a trend to applaud or to bemoan? The answer depends on your judgment about three issues—how well broadcasting serves the public, how effectively government regulation insures such public service, and how effectively market forces could do the same job without regulation. Nobody favors unnecessary rules, and nobody wants to abandon necessary ones. The problem is deciding which are which.

This is precisely the same problem we face in all areas of government control of the media. The less the government interferes with media freedom, the better—this is our heritage from libertarian theory, embodied in the First Amendment to the Constitution. Government control is tolerable only to the extent that it is genuinely needed to insure a free marketplace of ideas or to protect the rights of others—of audiences, of advocates of unpopular viewpoints, of persons defamed by media content, of defendants in criminal trials, of all whose lives are affected by what the media do. As always, the task is to balance the rights of the media against the competing rights of others.

The search for the proper balance is a never-ending process. As we write this chapter, regulation of broadcasting is on the decline. The legal trend is also in the media's favor in such areas as invasion of privacy and access to newsworthy locations. On the other hand, things are getting tougher for the media in areas like libel law and protection of confidential sources. Ten years ago the pattern was quite different, and ten years from now it will be different again. Only one thing never changes: the need to find a balance, to protect the rights of the media without denying the rights of everyone else.

Notes

1 Frederick S. Siebert, "The Historical Pattern of Press Freedom," *Nieman Reports,* July, 1953, p. 43.

2 Marna Perry, "Gauging World Press Freedom," *Presstime,* April, 1980, pp. 6-11.

3 Fred S. Siebert, Theodore Peterson, and Wilbur Schramm, *Four Theories of the Press* (Urbana: University of Illinois Press, 1963), p. 135.

4 Siebert, "The Historical Pattern of Press Freedom," p. 44.

5 "U.S. TV Screens Go Blank as Russians Block News," *New Brunswick* (N.J.) *Home News,* July 3, 1974, p. 2.

6 "The Exile: A Tale of Repression," *Newsweek,* February 25, 1974, p. 36.

7 Carl Becker, *Freedom and Responsibility in the American Way of Life* (New York: Vintage Books, 1945), p. 34.

8 Alvin E. Austin, "Codes, Documents, Declarations Affecting the Press," Department of Journalism, University of North Dakota, August, 1964, p. 55.

9 *Ibid.,* p. 56.

10 Siebert, Peterson, and Schramm, *Four Theories of the Press,* p. 71.

11 *Ibid.,* p. 90.

12 *Ibid.,* pp. 87-92.

13 *A Free and Responsible Press* (Chicago: University of Chicago Press, 1947), p. 92.

14 Siebert, Peterson, and Schramm, *Four Theories of the Press,* p. 74.

15 John C. Merrill, Carter R. Bryan, and Marvin Alisky, *The Foreign Press* (Baton Rouge: Louisiana State University Press, 1970), pp. 128-29.

16 *Ibid.,* p. 131.

17 James C. Goodale, "Tit-for-Tat Court Rulings May Be Unworthy of Justices' Attention," *National Law Journal,* July 16, 1979.

18 "Indiana High Court Rules for ABC-TV on Airing Crib Seg," *Variety,* June 19, 1974, p. 30.

19 *Smith v. Daily Mail,* 5 Media L. Rptr. 1305.

20 Warren Weaver Jr., "Justices Let Stand Censorship Order Over a C.I.A. Book," *New York Times,* May 28, 1975, pp. 1, 17.

21 Taylor Branch, "The Censors of Bumbledom," *Harper's,* January, 1974, pp. 62-63.

22 *Snepp v. U.S.,* 100 S.Ct. 763 (1980).

23 Anthony Lewis, "The Mind of the Censor," *New York Times,* April 7, 1980, p. A19.

24 "Judge Rules Snepp Violated Contract and Must

Forfeit Profits on Book," *New York Times,* July 8, 1978, p. 8.

25 Ben H. Bagdikian, "A Most Insidious Case," *Quill,* June, 1979, p. 22.

26 *Ibid.,* p. 29. "Progressive Case Ended," *The News & The Law,* November/December, 1979, p. 52.

27 Philip Taubman, "U.S. Drops Efforts to Bar Publication of H-Bomb Articles," *New York Times,* September 18, 1979, pp. 1, C7. "Bomb Article Lures F.B.I. to Magazine," *New York Times,* October 31, 1979, p. A16.

28 *Schenck v. U.S.,* 249 U.S. 47, 39 S.Ct. 247 (1919).

29 *Yates v. U.S.,* 354 U.S. 298, 77 S.Ct. 1064 (1957).

30 *New York Times Co. v. Sullivan,* 376 U.S. 254, 279-80, 84 S.Ct. 710 (1964).

31 *Rosenbloom v. Metromedia,* 403 U.S. 29, 91 S.Ct. 1811 (1971).

32 *Gertz v. Robert Welch Inc.,* 418 U.S. 323, 94 S.Ct. 2997 (1974).

33 *Time Inc. v. Firestone,* 424 U.S. 448, 96 S.Ct. 958 (1976).

34 *Ronald R. Hutchinson v. William Proxmire and Morton Schwartz,* 61 L.Ed.2d. 411, 99 S.Ct. (1979).

35 *Wolston v. Reader's Digest,* 61 L.Ed.2d. 450, 99 S.Ct. (1979).

36 Goodale, "Tit-for-Tat Court Rulings."

37 James J. Cramer, "Acts of Malice?" *Columbia Journalism Review,* July/August, 1980, p. 17.

38 Donald M. Gillmor and Jerome A. Barron, *Mass Communication Law,* 3d. ed. (St. Paul, Minn.: West Publishing Co., 1979), p. 315.

39 Martin Arnold, "Privacy vs. the Press: The Issue Remains," *New York Times,* March 6, 1975, p. 12. Warren Weaver Jr., "Court Backs Invasion-of-Privacy Award," *New York Times,* December 19, 1974, p. 39. I. William Hill, "Newspaper Must Pay Award for Invasion of Privacy," *Editor & Publisher,* December 28, 1974, p. 13.

40 *Howard v. Des Moines Register, The News & The Law,* June/July, 1980, p. 29.

41 "State Supreme Court Upholds Sealing of Court Records," *The News & The Law,* August/September, 1979, p. 35.

42 "Courts Divided on Criminal History Files," *The News & The Law,* August/September, 1979, p. 34.

43 "Chi Ord Shields Kids From Brutal Pix," *Variety,* June 2, 1976, p. 7.

44 "French Rate 'Warriors' as Pornographic Film," *New York Times,* August 9, 1979, p. C19.

45 *Regina v. Hicklin,* L.R. 3, Q.B. 360, 370 (1868).

46 *U.S. v. Roth,* 354 U.S. 476, 77 S.Ct. 1064 (1957).

47 Harold L. Nelson and Dwight L. Teeter, Jr., *Law*

of *Mass Communications,* 2nd ed. (Mineola, N.Y.: Foundation Press, 1973), pp. 424-28.

48 Tom Goldstein, "Survey Finds High Court Decision Fails to Spur Convictions on Smut," *New York Times,* March 20, 1977, p. 57.

49 *Smith v. U.S.,* 97 S.Ct. 1771 (1977).

50 *Valentine v. Chrestensen,* 62 S.Ct. 920 (1942).

51 *Bigelow v. Virginia,* 95 S.Ct. 2222 (1975).

52 *Virginia State Board of Pharmacy v. Virginia Citizens Consumer Council,* 96 S.Ct. 1817 (1976).

53 *Bates v. State Bar of Arizona,* 97 S.Ct. 2691 (1977).

54 James W. Tankard, Jr., Kent Middleton, and Tony Rimmer, "Compliance with American Bar Association Fair Trial—Free Press Guidelines," *Journalism Quarterly,* Autumn, 1979, pp. 464-68.

55 *Nebraska Press Association v. Stuart,* 427 U.S. 539, 96 S.Ct. 279 (1976).

56 Deirdre Carmody, "Ways of Curbing Press at Trials Pose Tricky Questions," *New York Times,* November 26, 1977, p. 14.

57 *Gannett v. DePasquale,* 99 S.Ct. 2898, 61 L.Ed.2d. 608 (1979).

58 *Presstime,* August, 1980, p. 13.

59 "Public's Access to Trials Is Upheld," *New York Times,* July 3, 1980, pp. 1, D15-16.

60 *Ibid.*

61 Wayne Overbeck, "Toward State and Local Government in the Sunshine," presented to the Association for Education in Journalism, Boston, Mass., August 11, 1980.

62 Gillmor and Barron, *Mass Communication Law,* p. 466.

63 William V. Thomas, "Freedom of Information Act: A Reappraisal," *Editorial Research Reports,* February 16, 1979, p. 127.

64 Jacquelyn Jackson, "FOIA Spirit Sagging as Government Chips Away," *Presstime,* June, 1980, p. 9.

65 Thomas, "Freedom of Information Act: A Reappraisal," p. 130.

66 Dorothea Wood, "Diverse Legislative Efforts to Amend the FOIA Increase," *FoI Digest,* January/February, 1980, p. 4.

67 Thomas, "Freedom of Information Act: A Reappraisal," p. 130.

68 *Estes v. Texas,* 85 S.Ct. 1628 (1965).

69 Terry Ann Knopf, "Camera Coverage on Trial," *Quill,* November, 1977, pp. 23, 30.

70 Mark Pinsky, "The Bundy Case: Fair Trial *and* Free Press," *Columbia Journalism Review,* September/October, 1979, p. 8.

71 Don White, "Florida's Bold Experiment," Freedom of Information Report No. 422, School of Journal-

ism, University of Missouri at Columbia, June, 1980, p. 6.

72 Mary Voboril, "Cameras on Trial," *Columbia Journalism Review*, September/October, 1980, pp. 9, 12.

73 *Saxbe v. Washington Post*, 417 U.S. 843 (1974).

74 *Kearns Tribune v. Utah Board of Corrections*, 2 Media L. Rptr. 1353 (1977).

75 *Houchins v. KQED*, 98 S.Ct. 2888 (1978).

76 *Kovach v. Maddox*, 238 F.Supp. 835 (1965).

77 *Ludtke v. Kuhn*, 4 Media L. Rptr. 1625 (1978).

78 "Passing Comment," *Columbia Journalism Review*, Spring, 1970, p. 3.

79 *Branzburg v. Hayes*, 92 S.Ct. 2646 (1972).

80 *National Law Journal*, December 24, 1979, p. 14.

81 "Californians Vote to Include a Newsman's Shield in the State Constitution," *Quill*, July/August, 1980, p. 9.

82 Lesley Oelsner, "Jersey Judge Jails Times Reporter for Refusal to Yield Notes in Trial," *New York Times*, July 25, 1978, p. 1. Lesley Oelsner, "Times Reporter Jailed as Marshall Refuses to Extend Stay of Penalties," *New York Times*, August 5, 1978, p. 1.

83 *Columbia Journalism Review*, September/October, 1979, p. 93.

84 Deirdre Carmody, "Subpoenas of Notes of Reporters Grow," *New York Times*, November 11, 1978, p. 38.

85 "Klan Trial Jurors See a News Film Showing Shootings and Arrests," *New York Times*, August 13, 1980, p. A20.

86 Halina J. Czerniejewski, "Your Newsroom May Be Searched," *Quill*, July/August, 1978, p. 21.

87 *Zurcher v. Stanford Daily*, 98 S.Ct. 1970 (1978).

88 Czerniejewski, "Your Newsroom May Be Searched," p. 23.

89 Wayne King, "TV Tapes Are Seized in an Idaho Inquiry on Prison Uprising," *New York Times*, July 27, 1980, p. 1.

90 "Newsroom Search Decision Stirs State Actions," *Presstime*, November, 1979, p. 30.

91 "Newsroom Search Limit Becomes Law," *New York Times*, October 15, 1980, p. 28.

92 *KFKB Broadcasting Association v. FRC*, 47 F.2d. 670, 60 App.D.C. 79 (1931).

93 *Office of Communication of United Church of Christ v. FCC*, 359 F.2d. 994, 1003 (1966).

94 *1977 FCC Annual Report*, pp. 131-32. Telephone interviews with William Silva and Konrad Herling, Federal Communications Commission, August 13, 1980.

95 "FCC Lifts Three RKO Licenses; 13 Others Are Now in Jeopardy," *Broadcasting*, January 28, 1980, pp. 27-28.

96 Les Brown, "Broadcast License Battles," *New York Times*, January 26, 1980, p. 44.

97 Marvin Barrett, ed., *Survey of Broadcast Journalism 1968-1969* (New York: Grosset & Dunlap, 1969), p. 32.

98 Les Brown, "Behind the Scenes at WLBT in Jackson," *New York Times*, February 24, 1977, p. 70.

99 "Black Group Is Awarded License for Television Station in Mississippi," *New York Times*, December 7, 1979, p. A26.

100 Morry Roth, "A Rocky Road to Conversion of WEFM," *Variety*, November 9, 1977, p. 35.

101 Ernest Holsendolph, "Court Tells F.C.C. to Study Radio Formats in Sales," *New York Times*, July 3, 1979, p. C13.

102 "Rock or Bach? Radio Formats Not FCC's Turf," *The News & The Law*, June/July, 1981, pp. 43-44.

103 *FCC v. Pacifica Foundation*, 98 S.Ct. 3026 (1978).

104 *Great Lakes Broadcasting Co.*, 3 F.R.C. 32 (1929).

105 *Mayflower Broadcasting Corp.*, 8 F.C.C. 333 (1941).

106 Tom Wicker, "The Press: Who Shall Edit It?" *New York Times*, January 22, 1974, p. 39.

107 *Ibid*. Arthur S. Miller, "The Right of Reply," *New York Times*, April 24, 1974, p. 41.

108 "Right-to-Reply Demand Rejected," *New Brunswick* (N.J.) *Home News*, June 25, 1974, p. 2 (AP).

109 *Red Lion Broadcasting Co. v. FCC* in Barrett, *Survey of Broadcast Journalism 1968-1969*, p. 39.

110 "WTOP-TV Won't Fight FCC on Texaco Ads, Slates 30 Free Spots," *Variety*, April 27, 1977, p. 43.

111 "Now Here's the News," *Washington Post*, October 24, 1978, p. C8.

112 Les Brown, "Diversity Advocate Heads New Broadcast Agency," *New York Times*, July 18, 1978, p. C17.

113 "U.S. Supreme Court Voids Forced Access to Cable TV," *The News & The Law*, March/April, 1980, pp. 41-42.

114 A. O. Sulzberger, Jr., "FCC Restrictions on Cable TV Eased in a Broad Ruling," *New York Times*, July 23, 1980, pp. 1, C22.

115 *Ibid.*, p. 1.

116 *1980 Broadcasting Yearbook*, pp. A19-32.

117 "FCC Takes Initial Step Toward Setting Radio Free," *Broadcasting*, September 10, 1979, p. 27.

118 Les Brown, "Issue and Debate: FCC's Move to Drop Some Radio Rules," *New York Times*, March 13, 1980, p. C22.

119 *Ibid.*

120 *Ibid.*
121 Ernest Holsendolph, "Plan Seeks to Lessen FCC Role," *New York Times,* June 8, 1978, pp. D1, D6.
122 *Access,* April 7, 1980, p. 4.

Suggested Readings

BAGDIKIAN, BEN H., "A Most Insidious Case," *The Quill,* June, 1979.

COLE, BARRY, and MAL OETTINGER, *Reluctant Regulators: The FCC and the Broadcast Audience.* Reading, Mass.: Addison-Wesley Publishing Co., 1978.

FRANKLIN, MARC A., *The First Amendment and the Fourth Estate.* Mineola, N.Y.: The Foundation Press, Inc., 1977.

A Free and Responsible Press. Chicago: University of Chicago Press, 1947.

GERBNER, GEORGE, "Trial by Television: Are We at the Point of No Return?" *Judicature,* April, 1980.

GILLMOR, DONALD M., and JEROME A. BARRON, *Mass Communication Law* (3rd ed.). St. Paul, Minn.: West Publishing Co., 1979.

LEDUC, DON L., *Cable Television and the FCC: A Crisis in Media Control.* Philadelphia: Temple University Press, 1973.

LEVY, LEONARD W., *Freedom of Speech and Press in Early American History: Legacy of Suppression.* New York: Harper Torchbooks, 1963.

McCARTHY, WILLIAM O., "How State Courts Have Responded to Gertz in Setting Standards of Fault," *Journalism Quarterly,* Autumn, 1979.

NELSON, HAROLD L., and DWIGHT L. TEETER, JR., *Law of Mass Communications* (3rd ed.). Mineola, N.Y.: Foundation Press, 1978.

PEMBER, DON R., *Mass Media Law.* Dubuque, Iowa: William C. Brown, 1981.

RUBIN, DAVID M., "Reporters, Keep Out," *Columbia Journalism Review,* March/April, 1979.

SIEBERT, FRED S., THEODORE PETERSON, and WILBUR SCHRAMM, *Four Theories of the Press.* Urbana: University of Illinois Press, 1956.

SIMMONS, STEVEN J., *The Fairness Doctrine and the Media.* Berkeley: University of California Press, 1978.

SMITH, JO ANNE, *Mass Communications Law Casebook.* Reynoldsburg, Ohio: Advocate Publishing Group, 1979.

TANKARD, JAMES W., ET AL., "Compliance with ABA Fair-Trial-Free-Press Guidelines," *Journalism Quarterly,* Autumn, 1979.

UNGAR, SANFORD J., *The Papers and the Papers.* New York: Dutton, 1972.

Chapter 8
Public Control

A democracy works only if its important institutions are somehow responsive and responsible to the public. The mass media are a vital democratic institution. Since media executives are not elected, other means must be found to guarantee that public opinion will play a role in determining media content. Despite the growth of some mechanisms for internal accountability and external pressure, the main vehicle for public control of the media today is still the mass marketplace.

When producer George Lucas brought out the film *The Empire Strikes Back* in 1980 as a sequel to the smash hit *Star Wars,* he guessed rightly that the public had not had its fill of the adventures of Luke Skywalker, R2-D2, and Darth Vader. The public rewarded him with record box office grosses at theaters around the country, insuring a continued flow of similar science fiction epics.

This is public control in a capitalist economy, and it works. The profit-making media must continue making profits to survive, and those profits must come from the public, either directly through sales or indirectly through advertising. A novel won't get pub-

lished unless the publisher predicts enough people will buy it to earn money; it won't stay in print unless the prediction proves correct. A television drama won't get produced unless the network predicts enough people will watch it to attract mass advertisers and thus earn money; it won't stay on the air unless the prediction proves correct. The novel needs five or ten thousand readers committed enough to invest $12.95 apiece, while the drama needs tens of millions of barely interested viewers. Despite differences in scale, both are subject to the same public control of the marketplace.

Why, then, is public control a problem? Suppose the novel is racist or pornographic. Millions of people may be convinced that it endangers American society—but as long as it has its five to ten thousand purchasers there's not much they can do about it. Suppose the TV drama is a police show, identical to dozens of other police shows. Millions of people may prefer something different, say an opera or a circus, but if tens of millions will fit one more police show into their viewing there's not much the minority can do about it. Or suppose the novel or the drama makes a point you disagree with. You may want to respond, to tell the media audience what *you* think about that issue—but there's not much you can do about it.

The marketplace aside, when we talk about public control of the mass media we are really talking about feedback. We are talking about the power of the public to respond effectively —to complain about content it disapproves of, to ask for something different, or to present a differing opinion. As we have seen, media owners, advertisers, sources, and many others possess this power to influence media content. What about the audience?

RATINGS

A broadcast rating is simply a count of the number of radio or television sets tuned to a given program at a specific time, based on a sample of preselected homes. Movie and book companies get comparable information from gross receipts; newspapers and magazines get it from paid circulation. Since over-the-air broadcasting has no box office and no paid circulation, it relies on the ratings.

At its simplest level, the ratings system is a pricing tool. Advertisers will naturally pay more for thirty seconds on a top-rated show than for the same thirty seconds on a bomb with a smaller audience, so the networks use the ratings to set their ad rates for each program. To make this calculation more sophisticated, ratings companies also collect background data on listeners and viewers—their age, sex, income, etc. Advertisers use this information to place their ads (you don't insert a beer commercial in a program watched primarily by children), while the networks use it to adjust their rates (many will pay more for a wealthier audience).

So far, so good—no one objects to the ratings as a pricing tool. But look at the inevitable next step. If program A has a larger audience than program B, and therefore earns more money for the network, why not eliminate B altogether and find a replacement that's more like A? Why not indeed, reason the networks—and the pricing tool becomes instantaneously a popularity contest. In today's hotly competitive TV market, every program struggles to attract around a third of the viewers watching at that time. Expressed in percentages, this is called a 33 share. A show with less than a 25 share is in trouble. A show with a 20 share is doomed.

If, say, 80 million people are watching television tonight, a 20 share (one-fifth of the audience) would come out to 16 million people. That's a good deal more than the circulation of *any* newspaper, but it's not enough to survive on network television. Says Margita White, a former FCC Commissioner: "The present rating system—by encouraging imitation rather than innovation, by over-emphasizing 'the numbers' at the expense of quality and by encouraging bland programming to the lowest common denominator—may be the single major obstacle to better quality programming."[1]

Ratings people seldom deny that the system leads to bland, homogeneous broadcasting. They simply insist that bland, homogeneous broadcasting is what democracy demands. Arthur C. Nielsen, founder of the nation's largest ratings company, put it this way in 1966:

> After all, what is a rating? In the final analysis, it is simply a counting of the votes, . . . a system of determining the types of programs that people prefer to watch or hear. Those who attack this concept of counting the votes—or the decisions made in response to the voting results—are saying, in effect: "Never mind what the people want. Give them something else."[2]

But ratings are not the perfect feedback device that Nielsen describes. They do not probe *how much* people like a show, or what they like or dislike about it. They do not determine if a program is being tuned in because it is the best of a bad lot at a given time or because someone actually wants to watch it. They do not identify what sorts of shows the audience might like even better.

MEDIA BOYCOTTS

In theory, people who are unhappy with a particular mass medium's performance can make their unhappiness felt in the marketplace by boycotting the medium until it shapes up. In practice, the direct boycott as a tool of public control is almost always futile.

Virtually all local newspapers today are morning or evening monopolies; readers need the papers too much to cancel their subscriptions over a policy dispute. National boycotts are almost impossible to organize in numbers large enough to make a difference. Magazines can take a handful of cancellations in stride, and networks won't notice the difference until millions of viewers tune away. Local broadcast boycotts generally fail when viewers return to their favorite programs before their defection has had time to show up in the ratings. (Secondary boycotts aimed at advertisers can sometimes work—see p. 143.)

Of all the mass media, only the film industry is genuinely vulnerable to consumer boycotts. In 1934 a group of Catholic laypeople founded the Legion of Decency. By granting or withholding its seal of approval, mostly on grounds of sexual content, the Legion influenced the filmgoing habits of millions. In the 1960s the industry came up with its own rating system (G, PG, R, and X) to counter the influence of outside groups like the Legion. But film boycotts persist into the 1980s, usually organized around dramatic picket lines at local theaters.

The film *Life of Brian* came under attack by church groups in 1979 for the way it satirized Christianity. Early protest led the producers to change the name of the film from *Brian of Nazareth*. Theater owners in Brunswick, Maine, New Orleans, and elsewhere replaced the movie after a few days of picketing. In Memphis, petitions were circulated in opposition to the film, though one theater owner said the attack drew publicity that helped more than it hurt.[3]

Cruising, a 1979 film dealing with violence in New York City's homosexual community, was picketed during production by members of the National Gay Task Force and the Gay Activist Alliance. Some scenes had to be moved off the streets into a studio. Gays also picketed the film after it was released, although poor reviews probably had more to do with its lack of success than the surrounding controversy.[4]

They do not indicate if people are paying attention.

To solve some of these problems, critics have suggested a diary-rating system that would permit viewers to record their subjective reactions to programs. Dubbed the "Quality Index" by its developers, this alternative hasn't made much headway with the broadcast establishment.[5] It would be more expensive and less statistically reliable, and it might drive down ad rates for some shows by showing advertisers that the audience, though large, wasn't very interested.[6] More fundamentally, the Quality Index would undercut broadcasting's assumption that a good

program is purely and simply a program with a lot of sets tuned to it.

Two companies do most of the gathering and processing of ratings data: Arbitron and the A. C. Nielsen Company. To measure the network TV audience, for example, Nielsen puts a machine called a Storage Instantaneous Audimeter into 1,200 randomly selected homes across the country. Out of sight in a closet or cabinet, the audimeter automatically records viewing at one-minute intervals, and transmits the information twice daily to Nielsen's computer in Florida. Households selected as part of the sample are paid $25 to start and $25 a year, plus half their TV repair bills. They usually stay in the sample for five years.

This constant national sample is enough for the networks, but it's too small to help local TV stations assess their audience and set their ad rates. So four times a year Nielsen sends diaries to an additional one million homes, and asks the recipients to record precisely what they watch for a week.

These are called "sweep weeks." You can tell you're in one because networks and local stations load up with their most dazzling programs. On one celebrated Sunday in February, 1979, for example, the three networks went head-to-head with $13 million worth of sweep week specials—*Gone with the Wind* on CBS, *One Flew Over the Cuckoo's Nest* on NBC, and a biography of Elvis Presley on ABC.[7] Sweep weeks frustrate viewers by forcing them to choose among unusually attractive programs. The networks then revert to more pedestrian fare for the rest of the season. The alternative, measuring local audiences every week, would cost about $50 million more a year, and so far the industry is unwilling to foot the bill.[8]

Nielsen's Florida computer can tell the networks how their programs are doing na-tionally the morning after they have been aired. The technological marvel of instantaneous ratings leads network executives to remake their program schedules continually, each feverishly seeking a slight edge on the competition. Programs that are faring poorly are now killed more quickly. New shows must prove their audience appeal immediately, with no time to experiment or build a following. The financial stakes are too high to risk a bomb.

How high are the stakes? A booklet published by the Broadcast Rating Council puts it this way: "Ratings largely determine what programs live or die, where advertisers place commercials, what rates will be charged, the market value of broadcast stations, which network is in the ascendency or descendency, and the career fate of broadcast executives. When evaluating industry stocks, Wall Street analysts watch ratings trends more closely than earnings statements because profits follow ratings."[9] It is estimated that a single rating point—one percent of the homes tuning in—is worth $35 million a year to a network.[10]

With that kind of money at stake, you can hardly blame broadcasters for enslaving

---

RATINGS IN EUROPE

In France television ratings are gathered weekly by a government agency, the Centre d'Etudes d'Opinions (CEO). The 1,400 viewers sampled each week are asked not only what they watched, but also why they watched it and whether they liked it. But the findings are *not* made available to the three French TV stations each week. Instead, CEO publishes annual figures on total audience size for each channel, and what the audience thinks of program quality on each channel. Because they don't have the figures for specific shows (and because French advertisers aren't allowed to pick their show), French TV programmers are under much less ratings pressure than their American counterparts. CEO director Philippe Ragueneau explains that "we don't want channel presidents running after the big audiences. They do it anyway, of course, but we strive for the highest quality within the limited context of three channels."[11]

Britain's TV ratings are less secret than France's, but they do measure quality as well as quantity. The BBC gathers qualitative "Reaction Indices," while commercial television compiles "appreciation indices" by mailing questionnaires to viewers asking them to rate the programs they have recently watched.[12]

themselves to the ratings. The result is public control of a sort. The programs that win are the programs most people are watching. But if you're part of a minority that wants to watch something else, or part of a majority that watches what you're offered but might prefer something else, or part of a pressure group that disapproves or disagrees, don't expect much help from the ratings.

All this is true of other marketplace mechanisms as well; television with its mass audience is only the most extreme case. The fact that the American media must earn a profit guarantees that they must genuinely meet the needs of some audience. Only a subsidized media system, such as that in authoritarian countries, can afford to keep selling something the public doesn't want to buy. Unwieldy and unsubtle though it is as a tool of public control, the marketplace does work. The American media are responsive to mass publics because that's how they earn their profits.

The problem is media responsiveness to smaller publics, to individuals and groups who feel the media are ignoring their needs and viewpoints. To deal with this problem, various mechanisms have developed within the media, while pressure groups have developed on the outside. How successful is each of these?

MEDIA ACCOUNTABILITY

The notion that the American media should provide some vehicle for audience complaints about media behavior dates back at least to the development of the social responsibility theory in the late 1940s. The media began to take the idea seriously in the 1960s. They began to do something about it in the 1970s, responding largely to public concern over their apparent power to end a war and topple a president.

Three institutions have developed to help ventilate public criticisms of the media. They are ombudspeople, press councils, and pro-

fessional media critics. We will examine each in turn.

1. Ombudspeople. "Ombudsman" is an old Scandinavian word for an official who investigates citizens' complaints against the government. Its application to the media came in an article in the New York Times by reporter A. H. Raskin in June, 1967. Raskin suggested that each newspaper set up a Department of Internal Criticism to check on the fairness and accuracy of its coverage. "The department head ought to be given enough independence in the paper to serve as an Ombudsman for the readers," Raskin wrote, "armed with authority to get something done about valid complaints and to propose methods for more effective performance of all the paper's services to the community."[13]

Though the Times did not follow Raskin's suggestion, the Louisville Courier-Journal and Times appointed John Herchenroeder to such a position that same month. In his first decade on the job, Herchenroeder fielded 20,000 inquiries and complaints from readers. He was given the authority to ask questions of reporters as well as their news sources. Each day he sent a written report to the papers' editors and executives, listing the day's complaints and his findings. The reports were also posted on the newsroom bulletin board for reporters to read.[14] When appropriate, Herchenroeder published apologies under the standing headline "Beg Your Pardon," along with more general columns explaining the inner workings of the two newspapers.[15]

A 1978 survey of newspapers with circulations of 50,000 or more found 24 papers with ombudspersons on their staffs.[16] Some went further. The St. Petersburg Times, for example, has a complete "Communications with Readers" program, including a telephone hotline for complaints, a regular column reporting on the hotline calls, and a corrections policy that not only corrects errors on the front page of the section in which they appeared, but also removes them from the paper's library so they won't be unwittingly repeated. When a St. Petersburg reader cancels a subscription, the ombudsperson calls to learn if news coverage had anything to do with the decision; if it did, an investigation and a personal letter from the executive editor follow.[17]

Besides righting specific wrongs, ombudspersons have won a number of policy changes at various newspapers—adding more local sports news, eliminating ads for pornographic movies, expanding headlines to allow for more qualifiers, banning the publication of the addresses of witnesses to crimes, etc.[18] All these changes came at the behest of readers.

Wherever they have been appointed, ombudspersons have become lightning rods for citizen reaction. At the *St. Louis Post-Dispatch* the late William Bransted received 50 calls and letters a day;[19] the *Sacramento Bee* logged 3,900 responses in the first year;[20] the *St. Petersburg Times* averages 650 to 850 letters a month.[21] But only a comparative handful of newspapers—and even fewer broadcast stations—employ an ombudsperson. Most media still handle complaints haphazardly, and most readers and viewers still feel they have no one to complain to.

2. Press Councils. A more ambitious mechanism for media responsiveness to the public is the press council. Typically, a press council is a voluntary group of distinguished citizens, journalists, media owners, and laypeople who hear and investigate complaints about media performance. Usually press councils have no formal power to enforce their findings and recommendations. They must rely on their own prestige and the power of publicity to change media performance. Many of the world's industrial democracies have had national press councils for decades. In the U.S., the National News Council was founded in 1973. It is still young and weak, but it may grow.

The British Press Council is the principal

model for the American experiment. It was first recommended by a royal commission appointed by Parliament in 1946 to explore ways of making the press more accurate. The British media were not happy about the idea, but bowed to the inevitable, and the council held its first meeting in 1953. At first its members were all journalists and publishers; outsiders were added in 1963, improving the prestige of the council with media and public alike.[22]

In each case brought before the council, the injured party is first asked to work things out with the local editor. If that fails, the council will act as a mediator between the two. Only as a last resort does the council investigate a complaint and issue a public statement. When that happens the council's decision is given wide publicity, almost always including the newspaper involved.

The Press Council doesn't only criticize the media; it praises them when appropriate and serves as an important buffer against government regulation. These actions have helped it gain acceptance among the media. In 1966 the council published a Declaration of Principle, aimed at establishing ethical standards for British journalism. Every important newspaper editor in the United Kingdom endorsed the document.

"In England the Press Council today is a force to be reckoned with," says Phillip Levy. "The days when it was described by an irate editor as 'a vague and powerless body' have been left far behind. In a recent report by a government committee it was said to be 'feared, respected and obeyed.' "[23]

The U.S. National News Council cannot yet be described in these terms. In 1947, while Britain's royal commission was still pondering its findings, the nongovernment Commission on Freedom of the Press in this country issued its own report. Among its recommendations was the establishment of a voluntary council to monitor media performance in the U.S. But the idea was not well received. In the 1950s and 1960s a few local newspapers—mostly small ones—experimented with community news councils. The first statewide council was founded in Minnesota in 1971. As of 1980, it is still the nation's only statewide council.

The National News Council began operations in 1973. So far, at least, it has limited its scope to news reporting in the truly national media—wire services, syndicated columns, network newscasts, national newsmagazines, and such leading newspapers as the *New York Times* and the *Wall Street Journal.* The council will consider complaints against local media only if they raise issues of national significance.[24] It will not consider complaints about advertising or entertainment at all.

Like its predecessors, the National News Council is wholly voluntary, and has no power other than its own credibility with the media and the public. In its first seven years the council has had little impact on American journalism, mostly because it still lacks this all-important credibility.

The main problem is media distrust. Many of the national media, most notably the *New York Times,* are actively hostile to the council. They decline to cooperate with its investigations, ignore its decisions, and give its activities little or no publicity. As a result few people know that the council exists, and that its New York staff will investigate any complaint about national news coverage. From August 1, 1973 to December 31, 1978, the council decided only 163 complaints, an average of 30 a year. Only 39 of these were found warranted.[25]

The problem is circular. Without the media's cooperation, the council can't get the publicity it needs to attract more complaints. Without meaty complaints, it can't get much attention to its work or build a track record of fairness to win over the media. And the council has been unwilling to pursue cases on its own initiative without a citizen complaint, largely for fear of further alienating the media whose cooperation it needs.

To help break this cycle, the council emphasizes its Committee on Freedom of the Press, which has issued statements on such subjects as the use of journalists by the CIA and the right to cover courtroom activities.[26] In this work, unlike its complaint investigations, the council is obviously an ally of the media. The *New York Times* has not yet relented, but as of 1979 some 31 media organizations were contributing funds to the council, including such giants as CBS, the Gannett Newspaper Foundation, and the Reader's Digest Foundation.[27]

Given time, the National News Council may become, like the British council, "a force to be reckoned with." Even so, press councils have some intrinsic limitations built into their quasi-judicial structure. They are concerned almost exclusively with sins of commission, things the media shouldn't have done; not with sins of omission, things the media might do to serve the public better. They concentrate on specific instances of wrongdoing, departures from journalistic tradition; they are not prepared for complaints that there may be something wrong with the tradition itself, with the media system as a whole.

This is not a criticism of press councils. We need institutions like press councils and ombudspersons to respond to specific complaints and remedy specific abuses. We need them to be stronger and more widespread than they are today. But we also need institutions to grapple with the broader problems of media performance. Professional media critics can play this role.

3. Media Critics. Public media criticism has a distinguished history in the United States. In 1911, for example, Will Irwin wrote a long series of perceptive articles about the press for *Collier's* magazine. Many of Irwin's charges are still valid today, and the old articles have been collected by Clifford F. Weigle and David G. Clark for The Iowa State University Press under the title *The American Newspaper.* Irwin's spiritual successor was the late A. J. Liebling, who wrote a regular *New Yorker* column called

"The Wayward Press" from 1944 to 1963. Liebling's best columns are available in *The Press,* published by Ballantine. Following Liebling at the *New Yorker* was Michael J. Arlen, whose essays on television have been collected in several books. A number of other magazines also run commentaries on media performance as part of their regular offerings—including the *Washington Monthly,* the *Atlantic,* and the *New York Times Magazine.* The bylines of Nora Ephron, Edward Jay Epstein, Tom Bethell, Ben Bagdikian, and Edwin Diamond appear often over magazine articles of media criticism.

Unfortunately, most members of the media audience don't read these magazines. They read daily newspapers, listen to the radio, and watch television. And serious media criticism is a good deal scarcer in these media.

Newspapers have employed movie review-ers for decades. Television reviewers began to emerge at the largest papers in the 1960s, and by the 1970s they were expanding their role to include commentary on the broadcasting industry, its regulation and its impact. Ironically, Chicago rather than New York or Los Angeles became the center of newspaper coverage of broadcasting, with Ron Powers, Frank Swertlow, and Gary Deeb earning top reputations at their respective papers. Les Brown and John O'Connor performed the same role at the *New York Times* until Brown left in 1980 to begin work on *Channels,* a new magazine about television funded by the Markle Foundation.

But newspapers have proved much less willing to cover their own industry. Except for David Shaw of the *Los Angeles Times,* whose paper gives him plenty of space for the job, the media critics working at newspapers today point their guns at the broadcast competition, not at themselves. And

---

THE JOURNALISM REVIEWS

Though journalists often seem reluctant to tell the general public about journalism's problems and failings, they do tell each other, most notably in the journalism reviews.

The first major publication devoted to media criticism—and still the largest and best known—is the *Columbia Journalism Review.* It was founded in 1961 "to assess the performance of journalism in all its forms, to call attention to its shortcomings and strengths, and to help define—or redefine—standards of honest, responsible service." Publishing six times a year, the magazine has achieved a circulation of about 35,000. At the beginning of 1980 it was earning a slight profit.[28]

Beginning in the late 1960s, local journalism reviews were founded in a number of cities, including Chicago, St. Louis, Cleveland, Houston, and Honolulu. In 1971 a second national review, *[MORE],* was started to compete with the *Columbia Journalism Review.* All faced serious money problems. After seven years in the red, *[MORE]* folded in 1978; by then most of the city-based reviews were already dead. But soon after, the *Washington Journalism Review* was begun, also focusing mostly on the national media. To the surprise of many, it survived its first birthday, and in 1980 seemed to be growing.

The media industry also has more than its share of trade publications. These do not generally raise broad issues of media criticism, but they do cover them when they are raised by others. Key magazines to watch are *Variety* (film and broadcasting), *Broadcasting, Editor & Publisher* (newspapers), *Publisher's Weekly* (books), *Folio* (magazines), and *Advertising Age.*

even in their TV coverage, only about a third of the critics' time goes into reporting on the industry. The other two-thirds is devoted to reviews.

As for broadcasting, it has shown virtually no interest in serious commentary on any of the media, either itself *or* the print media. The only strong broadcast effort at media criticism, "Behind the Lines" on public television, died in 1976 because of a lack of station support.

Media critics can make an important contribution to public control of the media by raising issues of media performance for the public and the profession to consider. They can raise broader issues than ombudspersons and press councils are prepared to deal with, and they can educate the public so that the complaints to ombudspersons and press councils become more focused and more sophisticated. All this is happening already in elite magazines. It needs to happen in the more popular media as well.

PRESSURE GROUPS

The ombudsperson, the press council, and the media critic work closely with the media, trying to make them more responsive to their audience. Pressure groups *are* the audience, at least part of the audience. They work on the outside, bargaining with the media for a resolution to their grievances.

Usually they focus on television. TV is the dominant medium in American culture, the one most people think of first when they worry about biased news, manipulative advertising, or similar problems. And TV is regulated by the Federal Communications Commission, and is therefore vulnerable to legal pressures to which the print media are immune.

Not that the print media have been entirely ignored by pressure groups. From the late 1960s on, national organizations concerned with a wide range of issues—feminists and church groups, racial minorities and trade associations—have made it their business to lobby the newspaper industry for greater sensitivity to their needs and viewpoints. Local groups, meanwhile, have conducted similar negotiations with individual newspapers. But broad-gauged organizations dedicated full-time to pushing for newspaper reform have not yet emerged. In 1978, urging the development of such groups, Ralph Nader published a 90-page report on how the public could evaluate daily newspapers. "Newspapers are a privileged and lucrative industry," Nader said. "The only way to insure that they become more accountable to the people they serve is through active appraisal by the public."[29] The effort produced no tangible results.

Television, on the other hand, is the focus of many activist groups. To see how such groups work, we will look at two of the most effective in recent years, the National Citizens Committee for Broadcasting (NCCB) and Action for Children's Television (ACT).

The National Citizens Committee for Broadcasting was founded in 1966 to support the development of public broadcasting as an alternative to the commercial networks.[30] Its agenda was broadened considerably in 1974, when Nicholas Johnson became chairman. A former maverick FCC commissioner, Johnson had earned a national reputation as an advocate of broadcast reform. In 1978 the NCCB had money problems. Ralph Nader replaced Johnson as chairman and integrated the group into his network of consumer-advocacy organizations. It operates out of Washington, D.C. on a budget of about $100,000 a year.[31]

In its own words, the NCCB's goal is to "make media diverse and more responsive to the public interest rather than to government, advertiser or corporate dominance."[32] Its staff participates actively in dozens of FCC proceedings, on issues ranging from deregulation of radio to requirements for public service advertising, from new FCC appointments to new communications technologies. Its filings help balance those from the broadcast industry, which usually (though not always) argue the other side.

Through a newsletter and its biweekly magazine *access,* the NCCB encourages other groups and individuals to get involved in the regulatory process. Readers are told how to file comments with the FCC and are kept abreast of all legislative and regulatory developments affecting broadcasting. When Congress was considering a massive rewrite of the 1934 Communications Act in 1978-79, *access* provided thorough coverage from a consumer perspective.

The NCCB considers itself largely a clearinghouse for other media reform groups, local and national. Its directory of such groups, published in 1977 (with supplements in 1979 and 1980), carries the names of nearly 500 organizations, ranging from Feminists for Media Rights in Lancaster, Pennsylvania to the Alaska Public Interest Research Group in Anchorage. When these groups encounter a legal or regulatory problem, their first telephone call for advice is often to the National Citizens Committee for Broadcasting.

Perhaps the most successful NCCB effort to date focused on television violence. In 1976, with money raised from the American Medical Association, the NCCB commissioned a research firm to determine which advertisers were sponsoring the most violent shows. When the names of the companies were announced, many switched to sponsoring less violent programs to avoid the unfavorable publicity.[33] The Parent Teachers Association distributed the NCCB findings to its 6,500,000 members, increasing the pressure. The networks themselves have since given credit to this NCCB-PTA campaign for reducing TV violence.[34]

Action for Children's Television, founded in Boston in 1968, has a narrower focus: the quality of children's TV programming and the effects of TV advertising aimed at chil-

dren. On both issues ACT has become a powerful national force for change.

In 1971, ACT helped persuade the FCC to begin a formal investigation of children's programming. The investigation ended in 1974 with an FCC policy statement urging broadcasters to pay more attention to preschool children and weekday programming.[35] In 1979 the FCC's Task Force on Children's Television completed a second look at the problem. Its report agreed with ACT that the industry had not complied with the 1974 requests. This time the task force proposed more specific standards—five hours a week of educational programming for preschoolers, half that for school-age children, all on weekdays.[36] As of mid-1981 the FCC had not yet acted on the recommendations.

While it works for policy change at the FCC, ACT also pressures individual stations for better children's shows. In 1973, for example, it joined with the National Association for Better Broadcasting and several other groups to persuade Los Angeles station KTTV to ban the use of 42 violent cartoon series. The station also promised to preface an additional 81 noncartoon series with a "caution to parents" if it used them. The coalition had threatened to challenge the station's license unless it agreed.[37]

Throughout the 1970s, ACT's members worried at least as much about children's TV advertising as they did about the programs between the ads. The average child watches a minimum of 20,000 commercials by age 12.[38] Researchers aren't sure just what effects these 20,000 commercials have on the child's mind. But a much-told story about a Connecticut teacher rings true to most parents. When she asked her third-graders how to spell "relief," more than half of them replied "R-O-L-A-I-D-S."[39]

In the early 1970s, ACT pressured both the Federal Communications Commission and the Federal Trade Commission to do something about the ads. Soon after the FCC agreed to look into the problem, the Na-

Among the feistiest of the media reform groups is Accuracy in Media, founded in 1969 by Reed J. Irvine, an economist with the Federal Reserve Board. AIM is funded mostly by conservative organizations, and works to balance what Irvine considers the liberal bias of the media. Unlike most media pressure groups, AIM monitors the print media as well as broadcasting.

One of AIM's most famous cases concerned the NBC documentary "Pensions: The Broken Promise," aired in 1972. AIM argued that the program violated the fairness doctrine by not paying enough attention to the positive aspects of corporate pension plans. The FCC supported the claim, but a federal court overturned the decision and the FCC decided not to appeal the case further. Nonetheless, NBC was clearly put on notice that it was being watched for signs of anti-business bias.

Another AIM target has been syndicated columnist Jack Anderson, whose reports on U.S. intervention in Chilean politics were brought by AIM to the National News Council. AIM is in fact one of the council's biggest customers, and the council not infrequently supports AIM's complaints. Anderson calls Irvine a media manipulator and "a dangerously plausible man." But Charles Seib, the former ombudsman of the *Washington Post*, praises him as "a gadfly in the true sense."[40]

Many journalists like to give the impression that they view Irvine as a crank. Few editors publish the free column AIM distributes to newspapers around the country. But many of them read it.

---

tional Association of Broadcasters reduced its recommended maximum number of minutes per hour for children's commercials, and came out against commercials by program hosts. Soon after the FTC's chairman called for stricter regulations, the NAB cut the recommended maximum still further, and opposed children's vitamin ads. No broad new regulations came out of ACT's arm-twisting—but the industry's "voluntary" improvements were big victories for the fledgling group.

In late 1977 ACT went after snack foods. Joined by the Center for Science in the Public Interest, it petitioned the Federal Trade Commission to ban certain snack food commercials entirely, and to require a disclaimer in others about the health dangers of too much sugar.[41] The FTC's Bureau of Consumer Protection not only liked the petition, it went further—recommending that the Commission ban all ads aimed at children under eight (because they can't understand the nature of advertising) and all ads for sugared products posing dental health risks for children between eight and eleven. The remaining ads for sugared products would have to be balanced by nutritional public service spots paid for by the snack food advertisers themselves.[42]

These truly revolutionary proposals became symbolic of what many felt was the FTC's tendency to over-regulate American business. In 1979 and 1980 the FTC itself came under attack by Congress, and the snack food inquiry was quietly dropped. But ACT's work was not in vain. Public-service nutrition announcements began to appear during Saturday morning cartoon shows, and the National Association of Broadcasters added a requirement that cereal commercials indicate that the product should be eaten as part of a balanced breakfast.[43]

And of course ACT is still on the job, pressuring both government and industry for further reforms.

The list of pressure groups working for change in the media is long and growing. Instead of the NCCB and ACT, we could have focused on the Public Media Center, which plans, produces, and distributes public service spots for advocacy groups; or the New Jersey Coalition for Fair Broadcasting, which pushes for better coverage of New Jersey on New York and Philadelphia stations and ultimately for New Jersey's first VHF station of its own; or the Media Access Project, which files fairness doctrine complaints for local citizen groups; or the Alternative Media Center; or the American Council for Better Broadcasts; or the National Black Media Coalition; or the Coalition for Better Television.

Groups not usually concerned with media reform have also discovered the importance of trying to influence media policy. In 1980 the International Association of Machinists and Aerospace Workers put up $100,000 to fund a study of the treatment of unions and workers in TV news and entertainment. Union members did most of the monitoring, and union leaders used the results to put pressure on networks and stations for improved program content.[44] The union thus joins such established media pressure groups as the Gray Panther Media Watch, the National Organization for Women Media Project, and the Office of Communications of the United Church of Christ.

LEGAL PRESSURE POINTS

When pressure groups work for change in the print media, their only real tools are publicity and negotiation. Thanks to the FCC, broadcasting is vulnerable to legal pressure as well. Fighting for a new FCC policy to apply to all stations requires years of work by a national organization, though local groups can and do play a role. But if you're unhappy with a single station's performance, you don't

need a new policy. The FCC already has two policies you may be able to use to bring the station to heel. These are the fairness doctrine and the right to challenge the renewal of a broadcast license. We will discuss each in turn.

1. The Fairness Doctrine. Strictly speaking, the Federal Communications Commission's fairness doctrine is not a form of public control of the mass media. Rather, it is an example of government control exercised on behalf of the public. Among other provisions, the fairness doctrine requires of broadcasters: (1) They must include some discussion of controversial issues in their programming; (2) When discussing controversies, they must make a reasonable effort to provide a balance of conflicting viewpoints; and (3) If in discussing a controversial issue they personally attack an individual by name, they must offer that person a chance to reply on the air without charge.

It's the second requirement that provides the greatest opportunity for public control. A viewer or listener who feels that a station has treated a particular controversy in an unbalanced way may complain to the station involved, and then to the FCC if the station doesn't offer a satisfactory solution. Though it almost never happens, a station *can* lose its license because of flagrant or continued violations. More likely, the FCC may require the station to cover the neglected viewpoints. And still more likely, the station may cover these viewpoints "voluntarily" in order to avoid an FCC investigation and possible rebuke.

In the mid-1960s, lawyer John Banzhaf founded Action on Smoking and Health (ASH), which contended that cigarette smoking was a controversial issue of public importance, and therefore subject to the fairness doctrine. ASH singled out WCBS-TV in New York for a test case. Banzhaf asked the FCC to order WCBS to broadcast information on the hazards of smoking, to balance its steady diet of cigarette commercials.

The FCC agreed in 1967, and the broadcast industry was forced to give millions of dollars worth of free time to such groups as the American Cancer Society. This decision was a prelude to the removal of all cigarette ads from the broadcast media in 1971.

The fairness doctrine is often used as a way of gaining access to the media. If a station agrees that it has neglected a particular viewpoint, it may decide to remedy the situation by offering free time to the person or group that filed the fairness complaint in the first place. But it doesn't have to; John Banzhaf never made it onto WCBS. As far as the FCC is concerned, the fairness doctrine is designed to protect the media consumer, not the would-be advocate. It doesn't grant you the right to appear on television. Instead, it imposes on the station an obligation to tell you something about all sides in a public controversy.

In the years since the ASH decision, the FCC has taken an increasingly narrow view of the fairness doctrine, especially as applied to advertising. The Commission has now said that it will not consider fairness claims against product ads because such ads do not present viewpoints on controversial issues of public importance. A station manager can reject other fairness claims by saying that the issue is not controversial enough, or by showing that somewhere in its smorgasbord of programming the station has already presented the opposing view. While a member of the public can appeal this to the FCC, winning the case and gaining access for a specific idea takes a substantial amount of time, energy, money, and luck.

But you don't have to win in order to succeed. Merely mentioning the fairness doctrine to a local station may be enough to convince the station's management that it had better pay more attention to alternative viewpoints. Or the threat of a fairness complaint may persuade the station to cut back the one-sided content on which the objection is based. Of course the fairness doctrine is a limited weapon. It is useful only against broadcasters, and only in response to unbalanced content of a controversial nature. But when you feel that a radio or television station is not telling you the whole story, the fairness doctrine is the best tool you have for making it pay attention to the other side.

2. License Challenges. Every three years a broadcast station is required to apply to the FCC for renewal of its license. In the past, renewal procedures have been simple and straightforward, with no embarrassing questions asked. Most renewals still are. But in recent years a number of citizen groups have made use of license-renewal time to question the performance of established stations—not because they wanted the license themselves, but because they wanted it to go to someone who would meet their needs more responsibly.

The change began in 1964, when black leaders in Jackson, Mississippi, challenged the license of Jackson television station WLBT. Aided by Dr. Everett Parker, head of the Office of Communications of the United Church of Christ, they charged that WLBT had systematically promoted segregationist views in its editorials and news coverage.

The FCC dismissed the challenge, asserting that the public had no "standing" before the Commission—no right, that is, to help decide whether a licensed broadcaster has earned the privilege of keeping the license. The Jackson citizens appealed this decision to the federal courts, and in 1966 the FCC was ordered to hold a hearing and let them testify. It did so, then renewed WLBT's license anyhow, claiming that racial discrimination had not been proved. So Dr. Parker and the citizens of Jackson went back to the courts.

In 1969, appeals court judge Warren Burger (now Chief Justice on the U.S. Supreme Court) announced his decision. The FCC was rebuked for shifting the burden of proof from the licensee to the challenger, and was ordered to consider new applications for the WLBT license. Two years later, the FCC gave a temporary license to an interim group called Communications Improvement, Inc., which immediately integrated its staff and added some black programming. Not until 1979—15 years after the initial complaint was filed—did the FCC finally settle on a new licensee for the station—a consortium of representatives from the many groups competing for the license. The consortium is 51 percent black-controlled.[45]

Though it took 15 years to settle, the WLBT case established that media consumers have a right to challenge a station's license without wanting the license for themselves, and that it is possible to get the FCC to take away the license of a station that is ignoring the needs of its audience.

The license-renewal challenge is not a cure-all. Like the fairness doctrine, it applies only to broadcasting. and only to those cases where the challenging group has a significant grievance against the station. License challenges take even more time, energy, money, and commitment than fairness doctrine complaints. And most challenges still fail. Former FCC Commissioner Kenneth A. Cox warns that "possession is nine points of the law. FCC will not put a license holder out of business if he has even a halfway decent record."[46]

But like a fairness doctrine complaint, a license challenge doesn't have to be legally successful in order to achieve the goals of the challengers. Many groups have been able to win important concessions from station managements with just the threat of a challenge.

Actually filing the license challenge wins still more concessions, even if the station knows it will probably get to keep its license in the end. Defending a license challenge costs even more time and money than filing one, and no station can be sold while its license is in dispute. Management often finds it easier and cheaper to settle.

In 1969, for example, station KTAL-TV in Texarkana, Texas, received its license renewal only after it signed a 13-point contract with local citizen groups, promising to improve its performance. Twelve local black groups had challenged the license, charging that the station failed to meet the needs of the black community. They agreed to withdraw the challenge on condition that the station sign the contract. Among other points, it required KTAL to hire a minimum of two full-time black reporters; to preempt network programs only after consultation with minority groups; and to run public service announcements prepared by the groups.[47]

In 1976, similarly, the Atlanta NAACP asked the FCC to deny renewal of the licenses of Atlanta stations WSB-TV, AM, and FM, all owned by the Cox Broadcasting Company. It charged that the stations discriminated against minorities in employment and programming. Cox very much wanted to settle the complaint, because it was considering a merger with General Electric. A settlement was reached in 1979, providing that WSB-TV would hire more minorities, that the FM station would be sold to a black group, and that the new GE broadcast company would include a black, a woman, and a third public representative on its ten-member board.[48] In 1980 the merger fell through, so GE is off the hook. But Cox will have to live up to its promises or face another challenge.

For a moment at least, consider the plight of the station, urged from every side to meet the needs of an infinity of conflicting constituencies, threatened with costly fairness doctrine complaints and license renewal challenges if it fails to comply. Little wonder the media sometimes cry out to be left alone to do their job as they think best, without pressure from anyone.

But of course that is not about to happen. As we have seen, the media are controlled by many forces—owners and gatekeepers, advertisers and sources, government officials and professional codes. There is every reason why the public—all kinds of publics—should play a role in the pressures and cross-pressures that determine media content. Because of organized pressure groups on the outside and ombudspeople, press councils, and media critics on the inside, public control of the media has made modest progress in recent decades. But these mechanisms are still weak—much weaker than the mechanisms available to sources, advertisers, owners, and other forces.

The dynamics of the marketplace guarantee that media content stays responsive to the mass audience. But audience groups with narrower interests—and without the power of the purse—must still fight hard for what little influence they have on the media.

The most direct way to influence media content is to provide the content you feel is missing, to become a source, a producer, or a publisher. The notion that unpopular viewpoints have a right of access to the media is attractive to many critics, but it has made little legal headway. Existing mechanisms for access to the established media are weak, but changes in media technology offer new opportunities to start a medium of one's own.

THE "RIGHT" OF ACCESS

The first half of this chapter has dealt with attempts to influence media content through public criticism and organized action. Another way for the public to influence media content is to control it more directly; that is, to gain access to the media to present one's message in one's own words.

The problem of access to the media has been ignored for many years, but it is not being ignored today. Dozens of special-interest groups—ghetto blacks and middleclass whites, young people and senior citizens, radicals and rightists—have come to recognize that access to the media plays a vital role in the fulfillment of their goals. As Hazel Henderson has put it:

The realization is now dawning on groups espousing . . . new ideas, that in a mass, tech-

nologically complex society, freedom of speech is only a technicality if it cannot be hooked up to the amplification system that only the mass media can provide. When our founding fathers talked of freedom of speech, they did not mean freedom to talk to oneself. They meant freedom to talk to the whole community. A mimeograph machine can't get the message across anymore.[49]

In 1967 the *Harvard Law Review* published an article by Jerome A. Barron, entitled "Access to the Press—A New First Amendment Right." The article argued that the entire mass-communications industry "uses the free speech and free press guarantees to avoid opinions instead of acting as a sounding board for their expression."[50] This denial of media access, Barron said, was devastating to the proponents of a new viewpoint, and thus also to the public that might benefit from that viewpoint. Barron therefore urged a new interpretation of the First Amendment, which would recognize the obligation of all the media to afford access to a wide range of opinions, especially unpopular ones. A newspaper publisher, for example, might be required to print at least a representative sample of letters replying to earlier articles or editorials in the paper.

Opposition to the Barron theory stems from an understandable fear of any increased government control of the press. Someone would have to determine, on a day-to-day basis, which representatives of which views were offered time and space. That someone would probably be the government—a cure that many feel would be even worse than the disease. Dennis E. Brown and John C. Merrill wrote for the University of Missouri's Freedom of Information Center that Barron's theory will take root "only when our society has proceeded much further along the road toward Orwell's 1984, wherein a paternalistic and omnipotent Power Structure makes our individual decisions for us."[51]

In the late 1960s and early 1970s, the right-of-access notion seemed to be making legal headway. A federal court, for example, ruled that members of the Students for a Democratic Society must be permitted to advertise their antiwar views in New York's public bus and subway stations. And in the "Red Lion" decision upholding the constitutionality of the fairness doctrine, the Supreme Court noted with apparent approval the emerging concept of a right of access, at least for broadcasting. But the trend came to a grinding halt in 1974.

At issue was a seldom-used Florida law requiring every newspaper to publish, without charge, any reply a political candidate submitted in response to criticism in that paper. Pat L. Tornillo, a candidate for the Florida House of Representatives, cited the law when he asked the *Miami Herald* to print his answer to a *Herald* editorial against him. The paper refused so Tornillo took the case to court. Eventually it reached the U.S. Supreme Court, which declared the Florida law unconstitutional.[52] For now, at least, this decision established that the print media

---

ACCESS OR ELSE

In Buenos Aires six members of a left-wing group called the People's Revolutionary Army kidnapped the owner of an Argentine newspaper and held him until his paper printed their political statement. Hector Ricardo Garcia was released unharmed six hours after his paper published a complete rundown on the kidnappers' ideology.[53]

In Paris an armed revolutionary broke into a radio station and forced the announcer to read an anti-government statement over the air. He then threatened to blow up the place with a grenade unless he was granted half an hour on French television. Four hours later he surrendered to police.[54]

In the U.S. too, terrorists have sometimes made access to the media a key point in their negotiations with authorities. Shortly after the 1974 kidnapping of Patricia Hearst by the Symbionese Liberation Army, Harvard Law Professor Roger Fisher proposed that the attorney general be authorized to offer political kidnappers up to half an hour of television time in exchange for release of their hostages.[55]

Even when media access isn't a bargaining point, it may be an underlying goal of the terrorism. Advocates of extreme and unpopular ideologies are usually convinced that the media are ignoring their viewpoint. Frustrated at the failure of more traditional methods to gain access, some resort to violence as the only way they know to command the media's attention. (We will return to this issue in Chapter 17.)

Terrorism thus creates a serious dilemma for the media. On the one hand, reporters and editors certainly want to inform their audience about the violence itself—and may feel that the ideology behind it deserves more attention than it has received. On the other hand, they don't want to submit to extortion, to become a captive vehicle for extremist propaganda.

The most troubling example of this dilemma in recent years was the seizure of the U.S. embassy in Teheran by militant supporters of the Ayatollah Khomeini. For more than a year after the November, 1979 seizure, the American hostages dominated the nation's newspapers and newscasts.

Whatever else they achieved by seizing the hostages, the Iranian militants did manage to gain access to millions of Americans for their charges of U.S. complicity in the crimes of Iran's former Shah. Without the terrorist incident as a news peg, it is inconceivable that the American media would have told their audience so much about Iran, Islam, the Ayatollah, the Shah, and the debate over U.S. imperialism.

have no legal obligation to provide access to any viewpoint, even one they have opposed in earlier content.

In broadcast law, the situation is almost the same. As we have seen, the fairness doctrine does entitle someone who has been attacked by name on the air to reply on the air. It also requires broadcasters to provide some reasonable balance of viewpoints on controversial issues. And the equal time law protects political candidates. With these minimal exceptions, broadcasters, like publishers, are free to decide what and whom to put on the air.

GETTING ACCESS

The easiest way to get meaningful access to the media is to seem newsworthy to the people who control the media. Reporters cover an event—or an opinion—because it is important, unusual, timely, local, interesting, amusing, violent, traditional, etc. An event or opinion that appears to possess several of these characteristics is likely to be well covered. An event or opinion that appears to possess none of them is likely to be ignored. The trick, then, is to embed your viewpoint in a series of events and "pseudo-events" that will oblige the media to cover it, regardless of their own viewpoints. The craft of doing this effectively is, of course, public relations.

Apart from PR, access to the established media is available through letters to the editor, through talk shows, and through advertisements. How useful are these access mechanisms?

Letters and Talk Shows. Probably the most common method of expressing one's viewpoint through the media is the letter to the editor. It is also the oldest; the *New York Times* published its first letter in 1851, four days after the newspaper was founded. In 1931 a special page was set aside for the letters. Today the *Times* receives more than 40,000 letters a year, of which 2,000 are printed. Letters are edited for grammar, style, and length, but not for content.

Most newspapers today print about twenty column inches of letters a day, usually on the page opposite the editorial page. With some exceptions, most editors are scrupulously careful to use letters that are critical of the newspaper and its editorial stand.

Numerous researchers have found that letter-writers are able to "blow off steam"[56] and "get something off their chest"[57] by writing the editor their thoughts. Letter-writers tend to be educationally well above average, definitely not cranks or crackpots. They are usually well-read and highly individualistic; they are also predominantly male, white, and members of business and professional groups.

Letters to the editor are among the best-read parts of the newspaper. Letter-writing is therefore an excellent device for those who write persuasively to communicate with those who read critically. For individuals who are less literate, or who want to reach audiences other than the elite, the letter to the editor is of limited value.

Though radio and television stations do not usually broadcast letters to the station manager, many have instituted phone-in "talk shows" instead. These programs give the public an opportunity to converse with moderators and their expert guests on almost any topic of interest. Callers are limited to once every three or four days, and the calls are screened to weed out drunks, young children, and crackpots. The talk show format has proved to be immensely popular, and it's a cheap way for broadcasters to fill time. The value of the talk show in providing public access to the media is obvious. Its limitations are equally apparent—no caller stays on for more than a few minutes, and many callers never get through at all.

Advertisements. During the battle over Prohibition, both the Brewers Association and the Prohibitionists attempted to lobby public officials by taking out newspaper ads supporting their positions. It wasn't until the mid-1960s, however, that the tactic gained much popularity with private citizens and citizen groups. Then ads began to appear in metropolitan dailies condemning everything from the bombing of North Vietnam to the massacre of baby seals in Canada. Between 1955 and 1960, fewer than two protest advertisements per month were placed in the *New York Times* (ads for political candidates were not counted). By the first years of the Kennedy administration the average was 4.2 protest ads per month, and the first years of the Johnson administration saw the average rise to 5.7 per month. Nonprotest ads that take a stand on some issue have also increased dramatically in number.

The popularity of the protest advertisement does not seem to be based on any conviction that it works. In a study of one antiwar ad placed by a hundred professors at a New England college, J. David Colfax found that only 20 percent of all readers recalled having seen the ad. More than 90 percent disagreed with it, and no readers said they were heeding the ad's call to write Congress and protest the war. On the other hand, more than half the sponsors of the ad admitted that they expected it to have no effect—though 70 percent said they would sponsor another such ad anyhow.[58] If the Colfax study is typical, then access to the media through protest advertising may not be a very useful solution.

But advertising can be a potent tool in the hands of a citizen group that understands its uses. It is least useful, probably, in the case of a hot national issue on which people have already made up their minds. But when the issue is local and little-known, advertising is a good way to generate interest and concern. And when the issue is one for which potential support already exists, advertising is a good way to arouse these supporters to action. In the late 1960s, for example, Friends of the Earth and other environmental groups on the West Coast successfully used newspaper ads to channel the growing environmental concern of the public into concerted action to save particular parks, landscapes, and urban amenities.

The problem is that controversial groups

are not always permitted to advertise, even if they have the money to buy the ads. A few newspapers, most broadcast stations, and all three networks have policies discouraging controversial advertising. Broadcasters say they are afraid the fairness doctrine would oblige them to carry free answers to a controversial paid ad, so they'd rather not take the ad in the first place. This is true as far as it goes, but there's a more basic reason for closing the airwaves to controversial advertisements. Such ads might shatter the tranquil broadcast environment so crucial to selling toothpaste, detergent, and beer.

In 1970 both the Democratic National Committee and an ad hoc group called Business Executives Move For Vietnam Peace were turned down when they tried to buy airtime from the three networks. The Supreme Court upheld the networks' right to reject the ads.[59] And it wasn't just liberal groups that ran afoul of this broadcast policy. In 1974 the Mobil Oil Corporation wanted to run an ad on all three TV networks soliciting viewers' opinions on whether Mobil should be allowed to drill for oil and gas beneath the continental shelves. Only NBC would accept the ad. Even after Mobil offered to pay for counter-advertising, thus avoiding the fairness doctrine objection, CBS and ABC said no. According to Walter A. Schwartz, president of ABC Television, the Mobil proposal would "open a Pandora's box" of controversial commercials.[60]

In the late 1970s the networks continued, even hardened, their stand against controversial advertising. Led by the oil industry, especially Mobil, a strange coalition evolved between the nation's largest corporations (who wanted to buy airtime to express their views on policy issues) and anti-corporate pressure groups (who wanted to respond to the ads under the fairness doctrine). Both attacked the networks for squelching the debate—and in 1981 ABC announced an experimental plan to permit some issue ads in late-night programming.

Less controversial ads stand a better chance of acceptance. Some, in fact, may be accepted

BIG BUSINESS VERSUS BIG TELEVISION

When it comes to gaining access to broadcasting, giant corporations aren't much better off than tiny citizen groups.

In an advertisement in a 1980 issue of the *New York Times,* the Kaiser Aluminum and Chemical Corporation defended itself against an attack on ABC's newsmagazine show "20/20." The program had claimed that Kaiser marketed aluminum house wiring it knew to be unsafe. Kaiser's full-page ad called the charge "blatantly wrong." It criticized ABC for not letting the company respond in an unedited interview. All network news departments insist on retaining the right to edit—but Kaiser said the ABC producer had made up his mind about the company's guilt, and therefore could not be trusted to edit its reply.

Accusing ABC of "Trial by Television," Kaiser closed the ad with a plea that goes to the heart of the public control issue: "Unfortunately, not all victims of 'Trial by Television' have the resources to defend themselves, as we are trying to do. Their only defense is you. . . . America was conceived to prevent tyranny by providing checks on the power of any institution. Today, a new power is dispensing its own brand of justice—television. There's only one check against it. You."[61]

ABC eventually granted Kaiser reply time on a new show called "Viewpoint," which examines complaints about television news.[62]

---

without charge. As a service to the community, most broadcast stations and some newspapers and magazines accept a limited number of unpaid advertisements from citizen groups. Known as public service announcements (PSAs), these ads urge the audience to help prevent forest fires, support the Scouts or the Red Cross, register to vote, drive safely, etc. The media have plenty of PSAs to choose from, and they naturally prefer the noncontroversial ones. But free publicity in your own words isn't to be sneezed at, even if you have to avoid controversy to qualify.

COMPETITION

If letters to the editor, talk shows, and advertisements don't prove satisfactory, you might want to consider the ultimate mechanism for access to the media: own your own medium. Ownership guarantees that your newspaper, magazine, or station will run what you want it to run. But what are your chances of success, or even survival?

When Daniel C. Birdsell founded the *Hartford* (Connecticut) *Telegram* in 1883,

he became the fifth newspaper publisher in that city. On an investment of under $10,000, he was able to compete successfully from the very start. The first issue of the *Telegram* sold 2,000 copies, as opposed to 10,000 copies a day for the established *Courant* and *Times.* Within months Birdsell's *Telegram* was also considered an established newspaper, and a sixth publisher was no doubt preparing to enter the fray.[63]

Modern-day Birdsells are hard to find. The high cost of newsprint and the complexities of distribution in a metropolitan area conspire to make start-up costs very high. The *New York Times* estimated as long ago as 1968 that an investment of $60 million would be necessary to start an afternoon paper in New York. Today it might cost nearly that much to start a paper in Hartford.

Ideologically, too, there is less room for competitive daily newspapers. The era when a city like Hartford could support six dailies with different political leanings is over. Most metropolitan dailies today have no identifiable political bias; their objective reporting appeals equally to readers of all political persuasions. This makes it difficult for a newcomer to find an audience not served by the existing papers. And even if an audience can be found, few metropolitan areas have enough advertising revenue to support more than one or two mainstream daily newspapers.

These factors have combined to produce a near-monopoly situation in daily newspaper journalism. There is much buying and selling of existing dailies, but few efforts to start new ones. And those few efforts are usually doomed; a new daily that tried to make it in New York—*The Trib*—folded after three months in 1978. Since the early 1970s, in fact, the total number of daily newspapers in the United States has stayed at about 1,760. The number seems unlikely to increase in the future.

The magazine industry is a bit more open to newcomers. Of the 200 to 350 new magazines announced each year, perhaps one in ten survives. Roughly $1 million is required to fully launch a national magazine, but $75,000 will pay for a test mailing to a quarter of a million readers.[64] The results of the mailing will determine if there is sufficient interest to continue.

Successful new magazines are almost invariably specialized (see pp. 283-85). They earn their money from readers who are passionately interested in the magazine's topic, and from advertisers who are passionately interested in reaching just those readers. For a talented entrepreneur with a good idea, a gambler's disposition, and a substantial nest egg, starting a magazine isn't out of the question. But for an advocacy group that wants to reach a broad audience with its viewpoint on public issues, magazine publishing is not the answer.

Neither is broadcasting. Unlike the newspaper and magazine businesses, where an outsider with enough money has at least a long-shot chance to compete, broadcasting is limited by technology as well as economics. The electronic spectrum has room for only so many radio and so many television stations. Once they are all gone, no amount of money can make space for more.

The Federal Communications Commission is responsible for dividing the spectrum and handing out broadcast licenses. In most parts of the country, all the AM and FM radio and VHF television licenses are gone. So are the UHF television licenses in cities large enough to support a profitable UHF station. For the most part, the licenses that are left are the ones no one wants—say an FM station in central Montana.

In 1980 the FCC managed to open the spectrum for 125 new AM radio stations around the country. It did this by abolishing the special privileges of 25 so-called "clear channel" AM stations, which had been given exclusive use of their frequencies after dark so their signals could be heard over a wide area. Listeners will now have a new local station instead of these distant super-stations. The Commission estimated that some 2,000 applications would be filed for the 125 licenses, with up to 25 competing applications for the licenses in choice areas.[65] Also in 1980, the FCC began accepting applications for "low-power" television stations, which will serve neighborhoods rather than whole metropolitan areas.

Those who can't get a license might consider broadcasting without one. In the New York City area alone, the FCC has shut down about two dozen of these "pirate" radio stations in the past few years, but new ones turn up all the time. One of those knocked off the air in 1979 was WFAT ("Fat is where it's at"), operated at 1620 on the dial from a bedroom in Brooklyn, N.Y. Using an army surplus transmitter, the two young men who ran the station were able to reach an audience as far away as West Virginia and Ontario. They were broadcasting rock-and-roll music to compete with the disco and canned formats of the licensed New York stations. WFAT managed to stay on the air for 16 months. "We believe the government should open the airwaves for people like us," said

"PUBLIC" TELEVISION

From its name if nothing else, one might suppose that "public television" was an important enclave of consumer control of the mass media. In truth, the public has no more control over the content of public television than it does over the content of commercial television.

Public television consists of some 240 TV stations around the country that are not permitted to accept commercial advertisements. Instead, they are supported—barely—by Congress, corporate donors, private foundations, and the contributions of viewers. Not surprisingly, public television is responsive less to the will of the people than to the wishes of the government and corporate powers that keep it alive.

Most public stations are operated by educational institutions, government agencies, or boards of directors composed of political and social "heavies" in the community. In no way are these boards representative of the entire spectrum of public opinion. Programming also tends to over-represent the interests of the middle- and upper-class audience, and under-represent the interests of minority and blue-collar viewers. Even the most rudimentary mechanism for audience control over broadcasting, the ratings, is not an important factor in public television. It is a rare show that attracts more than one or two percent of the viewing audience.

Critics on both political extremes agree about the elitist nature of public broadcasting. In 1972, conservative radio commentator Jeffrey St. John wrote:

> There is the quaint fiction that it truly serves the "public." In reality it serves an elitist audience of students, academics, intellectuals, professionals and politicians. . . . No programs representing millions whom we have come to regard as "middle America" have been produced.[66]

The Network Project, a liberal group of communications researchers working out of Columbia University, essentially agreed:

> The term "public broadcasting" implies to many people a truly democratic alternative to the commercial television empires—a communications system that is more responsive to the broad range of popular needs and wishes and more accessible to bold ideas and innovations than are the well-established and entrenched commercial networks. Such assumptions could not be further from the truth; those who control "public" broadcasting are as small and, by the unity of their purpose and the exclusiveness of their interests, as private a group as those who manage the commercial television networks.[67]

---

one of the operators, 21-year-old Perry Cavalieri. "It's a matter of free speech."[68] When pirate operators get caught, it's a matter of a $10,000 fine and a year in prison.

The final option—really the only option—is to purchase an existing station from its current owner, then ask the FCC to transfer the license. A successful urban radio station should cost about $5 million. The price tag on a TV station will be $25 million or more.

As a practical matter, it is a rare citizen group indeed that can afford to start its own daily newspaper, national magazine, or broadcast station. If competing with the established media is to provide access of any meaningful sort, the competition must be on a much smaller scale. Ironically, as the mainstream media have become bigger and more expensive, small-scale alternatives have begun to flourish. We will look first at the print alternatives, then at some emerging alternatives in broadcasting.

Welcome to the world of offset printing. The offset process, also known as cold-type printing or photolithography, reduces the cost of small-scale publishing to a level that is within the reach of nearly everyone. Using fairly inexpensive typesetting equipment, or even an ordinary electric typewriter, would-be publishers can turn out neat and attractive copy in their basements. Joblot printers can then produce thousands of copies at a cost of about $50 a page. Some printers handle literally dozens of such publications a month—neighborhood newspapers, advertising mailers, ideological tracts, special-interest newsletters, and more.

In one form or another the alternative press has been around as long as the establishment press, but it was most visible in the decade from the mid-1960s to the mid-1970s, the heyday of the underground newspaper. Such papers as the *Great Speckled Bird* in Atlanta, the *Berkeley Barb* in California, and the *East Village Other* in New York City were tabloid packages of psychedelic exultation, sexual titillation, social revolution, and traditional muckraking. They were termed "underground" not because they had to publish secretly, but because they published the views of leftist revolutionaries and countercultural hippies who did not have access to more established newspapers. Though they were often harassed by local police, usually on grounds of obscenity, they attracted a combined audience in the millions.

The constituency of the undergrounds faded with the end of the Vietnam war, and most of the papers died. Some of the iconoclast journalists they nurtured moved on to more traditional media, bringing with them a taste for muckraking and a subjective "New Journalism" style of writing. Others turned to specialized publications, aimed at a like-minded audience of feminists, environmentalists, or other advocates of social change. And a new generation of alternative newspapers took the place of the undergrounds.

Typical of this new generation is the *Ann Arbor* (Michigan) *Observer,* founded by Mary and Don Hunt in 1976 with only $1,500. The Hunts began attracting attention when they printed an article about a local drug dealer, explaining why Ann Arbor had become a major narcotics distribution center. They followed this with a 5,000-word piece on the trial of two Filipino nurses charged with murder at a nearby Veterans Hospital. The Hunts had no journalism experience when they began the *Observer,* but they produced a weekly paper that the mayor of Ann Arbor called "a meaty little newspaper that fills the void created when the [daily] *Ann Arbor News* grew regional in scope and superficial in local coverage."[69] After three years the *Observer* had a free circulation of 33,000 and $17,000 a month in advertising—and the Hunts were able to pay themselves a combined annual salary of $16,800.[70]

Like the *Ann Arbor Observer,* the new alternative newspapers usually concentrate on detailed local coverage. The recipe for success seems to be a combination of neighborhood news too parochial for the local dailies, hard-hitting investigation too controversial for the local dailies, and lifestyle features too leisurely for the local dailies (a Chicago alternative called the *Reader* once devoted 19,000 words to beekeeping in the Chicago area[71]). Part of the recipe, too, is a tireless founder willing to struggle on a shoestring for months or years while building a loyal readership and an advertising base.

A recent study for the American Society of Newspaper Editors showed that readers were dissatisfied with the "aloofness" and "remoteness" of their daily newspapers. They wanted news that would help them control their lives, news of their neighbors and of themselves.[72] This is the hole the weekly alternative press tries to fill. For those who succeed, like Mary and Don Hunt, the reward is meaningful access and a real influence on local events.

BROADCAST ALTERNATIVES

What the offset process is to print, cable can be to broadcasting: a chance for ordinary people to play a hand.

In cable television the TV signal comes into the home through a wire, rather than over the air to a rooftop antenna. This has two important advantages. First, the television picture is clearer because the signal is no longer affected by weather conditions, mountains, or tall buildings. Second, the number of channels is no longer limited by the broadcast spectrum. A receiver without cable pulls in at most a half-dozen VHF stations and another half-dozen UHF. Modern cable systems make available from 36 to 52 channels, and one company has proposed to build a system with 125 channels.[73]

The question is what to do with all those channels. Naturally some of them are used to carry regular over-the-air programming from the three networks, the local independents and noncommercial stations. Most cable companies also import a number of out-of-town signals, thus offering subscribers programs they couldn't normally watch in exchange for their $10 to $15 monthly fee. For an extra fee, many also offer sporting events and first-run movies without commercials. That still leaves plenty of unused channels—which is where the public comes in.

In 1972, the FCC adopted rules requiring every cable system in the hundred largest markets to make available a "public access channel," to be used without charge by people wishing to tape and broadcast their own programs. In 1976, the Commission extended the requirement to all cable systems with 3,500 or more subscribers. The Supreme Court ruled in 1979 that these regulations violated the cable operator's right to edi-

torial control. But local governments can still require public access channels as part of the franchise agreement that permits a cable company to wire a city. Many will presumably do so. Without the FCC's authority, however, the future of public access cable does not look nearly as rosy as it did in the mid-1970s.

Where it survives, this is media access in its purest form. Individuals can—and do—use the public access channel to present political statements, host phone-in talk shows, conduct interviews, air their homemade soft-core pornography, sing, dance, and juggle. Programs can last a minute or an hour. Studio appearances are usually free, and portable videotape equipment is available either free or for a small rental charge. Airtime is apportioned according to demand on a first-come first-served basis.

There is only one problem: Who's watching? As of 1980, 17 million U.S. television households subscribe to cable systems, more than double the 1974 figure. But most cable subscribers are not watching the public access channel. The technical quality of public access shows is usually amateurish. You wouldn't want to watch unless you were particularly interested in a certain show. And even then you'd have to find out about the show from a friend—few if any newspaper TV logs list the schedule for cable's public access channel. The exact size of the public access audience is unknown, since there are no ratings for it. But everyone agrees it is tiny.

Cable's potential to revolutionize public control of broadcasting extends far beyond the public access channel. Consider Reading, Pennsylvania. In the early 1970s, Reading developed what was widely acknowledged as one of the most successful public access systems anywhere. Community groups ranging from the Ku Klux Klan to the NAACP, from the John Birch Society to the Che-Lumumba-Jackson Collective, happily produced their own shows without censorship. So did many less ideological groups. But still the public access channel seldom managed to attract more than a few hundred of Reading's 32,000 cable subscribers.[74]

So cable in Reading went two-way. Three neighborhood communication centers were equipped with cameras and monitors so they could see and talk to each other; viewers at home could call in to participate in the interaction.

In one successful experiment, Reading officials and a research team from New York University invited the community's senior citizens to design programs for the interactive system. One of the shows that resulted put nursing home operators and funeral home directors in the studio for questions about their services and rates. Another offered peer group counseling on such issues as sexual activity, insomnia, and the dangers of driving. A third made elected officials available for weekly questioning on services to the aging and other public issues.

When the senior citizens were asked if the programming helped them feel better about themselves and other old people, 84 percent of those who participated at the communication centers and 91 percent of those who participated or watched at home said yes. Eighty percent of home viewers said the cable system was a major improvement in their lives, reducing isolation and providing human contact along with the information.[75]

The Reading experiment was supported by public funds. Whether it is repeated elsewhere will depend on finding a way to pay for it. But the potential is there for genuine two-way television via cable, for programming produced by citizens in the studio that actively involves other citizens at home.

Other experiments with two-way cable have added computer technology, enabling many viewers at once to talk back to their sets. The most celebrated venture so far is called QUBE, operated by Warner Communications, Inc., in Columbus, Ohio.

The heart of the QUBE system is a black box about a foot and a half long, six inches wide, and four inches deep. Each cable subscriber receives one, and each box is connected to the computer in QUBE's headquarters. Using the black box, subscribers can instantaneously answer simple yes-no or multiple-choice questions shown on the screen. They can indicate how much they liked a particular show, agree or disagree with a guest, support or oppose a proposed program, or take a test to see what they learned from a speaker. In a program similar to "The Gong Show," QUBE viewers vote on whether an amateur act should be allowed to continue or be pulled off the stage.[76]

Another experiment called "viewdata" permits home viewers to do a lot more than vote. They can actually request particular information from the computer, and the information will appear instantly on their screen and their screen alone. The Knight-Ridder newspaper chain is currently testing a viewdata system in Coral Gables, Florida. Subscribers ask for what they want by pressing buttons on what looks like a pocket calculator. They can "call up" on demand such information as current news, sports scores, the weather forecast, movie listings, airline schedules, and classified advertising.[77] The *Wall Street Journal* is testing another system that offers up-to-the-minute stock listings, as well as past stock performance and news of the business community. Users can even ask the computer to calculate the current value of their portfolio.

Eventually, computers can offer the home cable viewer everything now available in a newspaper and more—plus the all-important ability to *ask* for what you want instead of settling for what you're given. Add a mechanism to put new information into the computer for others to retrieve if they're interested, and computer cable could become the perfect vehicle for citizen access and audience control of the media.

Edwin Parker, a West Coast consultant on communications technology, describes what may be the "home information utility" of the future:

Imagine yourself sitting down at the breakfast table with a display screen in front of you. You touch a key and the latest headlines appear on the screen. Not the headlines that were written last night—or even those of six or seven hours ago. But headlines that may have been rewritten and updated five minutes or just 50 microseconds before you see them on the screen. You type another key or poke a light pen at the appropriate headline and the whole story appears on the screen. . . .

Are you interested in something that hasn't made the major headlines? Like a bill on education being considered in Congress. . . . Perhaps there's something you missed yesterday or the day before that's not front-page news today; the computer has it stored for you. You can have the latest information whether it's on today's or yesterday's story. . . .

There's a person in the news you'd like to know more about. Ask your computer for a biographical sketch. You don't understand the economics of the gold market. Request a tutorial program on the subject. You want the comics? Press the right button. Catch up on the strips you missed while you were on vacation.[78]

All this was technologically feasible when Parker wrote about it in the mid-1960s. By 1980 it was being test-marketed. By 1990, you might have it in your home.

If computer cable becomes an important medium of the future, it will raise as many problems as it solves. Who will control which information and opinion gets onto the computer? Will audiences use their power of selection to choose sports and entertainment instead of news and information? How will we protect the "information rights" of those who cannot afford to pay? What will happen to social interactions if the system expands to replace banking and shopping, public meetings and even public schools?

The answers to these questions are not clear. What is clear is this. The existing mass media are largely closed to citizen input, offering few mechanisms for access and public control. New mechanisms are needed, and new technologies may be needed to provide them.

Notes

1 Carolyn E. Setlow, "TV Ratings—There Just Might Be a Better Way," *New York Times*, December 31, 1978, p. D23.

2 Arthur C. Nielsen, Jr., "If Not the People . . . Who?" Address to the Oklahoma City Advertising Club, July 20, 1966, p. 5.

3 Cliff Froelich, "Pressure Groups v. The Movies," Freedom of Information Center Report, no. 419, School of Journalism, University of Missouri at Columbia, April, 1980, p. 3.

4 *Ibid.*, pp. 4-5.

5 "Alternative Rating Systems—Something More than Just Head Counts," *Access*, January 15, 1979, pp. 1, 3.

6 Setlow, "TV Rating—There Just Might Be a Better Way," p. D24.

7 Les Brown, "New Method Sought for TV Rating System," *New York Times*, March 8, 1979, p. C20.

8 *Ibid.*, p. C20.

9 Joel Swerdlow, "The Ratings Game," *Washington Journalism Review*, September/October, 1979, p. 38.

10 *Ibid.*, p. 38.

11 Joan Dupont, "Life in a Country Without Overnights," *Variety*, March 28, 1979, pp. 51, 76.

12 Setlow, "TV Ratings—There Just Might Be a Better Way," p. D23.

13 John Herchenroeder, "A Newspaper's Lightning Rod," in *An Open Press* (New York: National News Council, 1977), p. 12.

14 *Ibid.*, p. 9.

15 "How Newspapers Hold Themselves Accountable," *Editor & Publisher*, December 1, 1973, p. 16.

16 Suraj Kapoor and Ralph Smith, "The Newspaper Ombudsman—A Progress Report," *Journalism Quarterly*, Autumn, 1979, v. 56, no. 3, pp. 628-29. Herchenroeder, "A Newspaper's Lightning Rod," p. 13.

17 Stan Witwer, "St. Petersburg Times Communications with Readers Program," in *An Open Press*, pp. 21-23.

18 Kapoor and Smith, "The Newspaper Ombudsman—A Progress Report," p. 630.

19 William E. Bransted, "St. Louis Readers Find an Advocate at the Post-Dispatch," in *An Open Press*, p. 27.

20 Thor Severson, "A New Shibboleth for the Sacramento Bee," in *An Open Press*, p. 16.

21 Witwer, "St. Petersburg Times Communications with Readers Program," p. 22.

22 Phillip Levy, "British Press Council a Force to Be Reckoned With," *IPI Report,* September/October, 1973, p. 13.

23 *Ibid.,* p. 15.

24 "The Council's Rules of Procedure," in *In The Public Interest—II* (New York: National News Council, 1979), p. 423.

25 *Ibid.,* p. 11.

26 *Ibid.,* pp. 326-66.

27 *Ibid.,* pp. 423-24.

28 Edward W. Barrett, "CJR Status Report," *Columbia Journalism Review,* November/December, 1979, p. 24.

29 "Nader Urges Newspapers to Heed Public Criticism," *New York Times,* April 10, 1978, p. A19.

30 Anne W. Branscomb and Maria Savage, "The Broadcast Reform Movement: At the Crossroads," *Journal of Communication,* v. 28, no. 4, Autumn, 1978, p. 26.

31 *Access,* no. 59, October 23, 1978, p. 1.

32 *Citizens Media Directory Update* (Washington: National Citizens Committee for Broadcasting, 1979), p. 2.

33 Peter M. Sandman, "The Fight over Television Violence Ratings," [*MORE*], April, 1978, p. 39.

34 Branscomb and Savage, "The Broadcast Reform Movement," p. 33.

35 David Burnham, "FCC Approves Policy on Children's TV," *New York Times,* October 25, 1974, p. 1.

36 "Children: Task Force Reports," *Access,* Nov. 19, 1979, p. 4.

37 "KTTV Yields to Arm-Twisting by NABB on Kidvid Violence," *Variety,* October 3, 1973, p. 20.

38 "Federal Trade Commission Staff Report on TV Advertising to Children," *Advertising Age,* February 27, 1978, p. 74.

39 Alexander MacKie, "The Children's Advertising Battle," Freedom of Information Center Report no. 398, School of Journalism, University of Missouri at Columbia, January, 1979, p. 1.

40 Ed Hein, "Accuracy in Media: Another Look," Freedom of Information Center Report no. 360, School of Journalism, University of Missouri at Columbia, September, 1976, p. 6.

41 MacKie, "The Children's Advertising Battle," p. 1.

42 "Federal Trade Commission Staff Report," p. 74.

43 MacKie, "The Children's Advertising Battle," p. 4.

44 Seth Kupferberg, "Union Monitors Static in Labor's TV Image," *Columbia Journalism Review,* May/June, 1980, pp. 13-14.

45 "WLBT—15 Years Later," *Access,* October 22, 1979, no. 83, p. 4.

46 *Access to the Air,* Report on a Conference at the Graduate School of Journalism, Columbia University, New York, N.Y., September 28-29, 1968, p. 25.

47 Marvin Barrett, ed., *Survey of Broadcast Journalism 1968-69* (New York: Grosset & Dunlap, 1969), pp. 14, 122-24.

48 "GE Broadcasting Pact to Help Minorities," *Civil Liberties,* September, 1979, p. 2.

49 Hazel Henderson, "Access to the Media: A Problem in Democracy," *Columbia Journalism Review,* Spring, 1969, p. 6.

50 Jerome A. Barron, "Access to the Press—A New First Amendment Right," *Harvard Law Review,* 1967, pp. 1646-47.

51 Dennis E. Brown and John C. Merrill, "Regulatory Pluralism in the Press," Freedom of Information Center Report no. 005, School of Journalism, University of Missouri at Columbia, p. 4.

52 "Justices Void Florida Law on Right to Reply in Press," *New York Times,* June 26, 1974, pp. 1, 18.

53 "Argentine Rebels Seize a Publisher," *New York Times,* March 9, 1973, p. 12.

54 "Gunman Takes Over Paris Radio Station," *New York Times,* February 10, 1974, p. 7.

55 Roger Fisher, "Preventing Kidnapping," *New York Times,* March 13, 1974, p. 41.

56 Sidney A. Forsythe, "An Exploratory Study of Letters to the Editor and Their Contributors," *Public Opinion Quarterly,* 1950, p. 144.

57 William D. Tarrant, "Who Writes Letters to the Editor?" *Journalism Quarterly,* Fall, 1957, p. 502.

58 J. David Colfax, "How Effective Is the Protest Advertisement?" *Journalism Quarterly,* Winter, 1966, pp. 697-702.

59 "Court Backs TV and Radio Refusal of Political Ads," *New York Times,* May 30, 1973, p. 79.

60 "Networks Reject Mobil Equal-Ad Plan," *New York Times,* March 16, 1974, p. 1.

61 *New York Times,* April 29, 1980, p. A17.

62 "Kaiser Aluminum Drops Complaint Against ABC," *Wall Street Journal,* July 30, 1981, p. 33.

63 Carl E. Lindstrom, *The Fading American Newspaper* (Gloucester, Mass.: Peter Smith, 1964), pp. 82-83.

64 N. R. Kleinfield, "The Itch to Start a Magazine," *New York Times,* December 2, 1979, sec. 3, pp. 1, 10.

65 Tom Goldsmith, "125 New Nighttime AM Stations on the Way," *Variety,* June 4, 1980, p. 45.

66 Jeffrey St. John, "Does Public TV Have a Future? Should It Have? Nay!" *New York Times,* July 21, 1972, p. 31.

67 *The Fourth Network* (New York: The Network Project, Columbia University, 1971), p. 3.

68 Francis X. Clines, "About New York: The Sound of Silence on WFAT, Pirate Radio," *New York Times*, April 21, 1979, p. 27.

69 Charles R. Eisendrath, "Back to the People with the Mom-and-Pop Press," *Columbia Journalism Review*, November/December, 1979, pp. 72-73.

70 *Ibid.*, p. 73.

71 Calvin Trillin, "U.S. Journal: Seattle, Wash.," *New Yorker*, April 10, 1978, p. 118.

72 Eisendrath, "Back to the People," p. 74.

73 Les Brown, "From the Air, Programs By Satellite and Cable," *New York Times*, February 17, 1980, p. F1.

74 Tom Shales, "One Town Tries TV Of, By and For the People," *Washington Post*, March 24, 1974, pp. L1, L5.

75 Mitchell L. Moss, "Reading, Pa.: Research on Community Uses," *Journal of Communication*, v. 28, no. 2, Spring, 1978, pp. 163-66.

76 John Wicklein, "Wired City, U.S.A.: The Charms and Dangers of Two-Way TV," *Atlantic*, February, 1979, pp. 38-39.

77 Harry F. Waters, "TV Turns to Print," *Newsweek*, July 30, 1979, pp. 73-75.

78 William L. Rivers and Wilbur Schramm, *Responsibility in Mass Communication* (New York: Harper & Row, 1969), pp. 9-10.

Suggested Readings

BARRON, JEROME A., "Access to the Press—A New First Amendment Right," *Harvard Law Review*, 1967.

BERTRAND, CLAUDE-JEAN, "Press Councils Around the World: Unraveling a Definitional Dilemma," *Journalism Quarterly*, Summer, 1978.

BRANSCOMB, ANNE W., and MARIA SAVAGE, "The Broadcast Reform Movement: At the Crossroads," *Journal of Communication*, Autumn, 1978.

DENNIS, EVERETTE E., and WILLIAM L. RIVERS, *Other Voices*. San Francisco: Canfield Press, 1974.

EISENDRATH, CHARLES R., "Back to the People with the Mom-and-Pop Press," *Columbia Journalism Review*, November/December, 1979.

FROELICH, CLIFF, "Pressure Groups v. The Movies," Freedom of Information Center Report No. 419, School of Journalism, University of Missouri at Columbia, April, 1980.

GORDON, DOUGLAS, "The Great Speckled Bird: Harassment of an Underground Newspaper," *Journalism Quarterly*, Summer, 1979.

HEIN, ED, "Accuracy in Media: Another Look," Freedom of Information Center Report No. 360, School of Journalism, University of Missouri at Columbia, September, 1976.

HENDERSON, HAZEL, "Access to the Media: A Problem in Democracy," *Columbia Journalism Review*, Spring, 1969.

KAPOOR, SURAJ, and RALPH SMITH, "The Newspaper Ombudsman—A Progress Report," *Journalism Quarterly*, Autumn, 1979.

KLEINFIELD, N. R., "The Itch to Start a Magazine," *The New York Times*, December 2, 1979, Sec. 3, p. 1.

MACKIE, ALEXANDER, "The Children's Advertising Battle," Freedom of Information Center Report No. 398, School of Journalism, University of Missouri at Columbia, January, 1979.

RIVERS, WILLIAM L., WILLIAM B. BLANKENBERG, KENNETH STARCK, and EARL REEVES, *Backtalk*. San Francisco: Canfield Press, 1972.

SWERDLOW, JOEL, "The Ratings Game," *Washington Journalism Review*, September/October, 1979.

TRILLIN, CALVIN, "U.S. Journal: Seattle, Wash.," *The New Yorker*, April 10, 1978.

PART III
MEDIA

So far in this book we have discussed the functions and impact of the mass media, their history, and their control by various groups and institutions. By and large, our discussion has treated the media as a whole, not stressing the differences from one medium to another. But those differences are extremely important. It is impossible to understand the mass media without, at some point, considering them one by one.

We have now reached that point. Our discussion will begin with the wire services—the "common denominators" that determine much of the content of the major media. Next will come newspapers, traditionally the most prototypic of the media. Then we will turn our attention to two less news-oriented print media, magazines and books. The following chapter is devoted to broadcasting, which has replaced the print media as the public's main source of news and entertainment. After broadcasting, we will look briefly at two more specialized entertainment media, film and recordings. The final chapter in this section will consider two activities closely related to the mass media that are, in the long run, perhaps the most influential of all: advertising and public relations.

We will discuss a grand total of eight different media: wire services, newspapers, magazines, books, television, radio, film, and recordings; plus advertising and public relations. It is important to recognize that these are by no means the only mass media in existence. Consider the following list:

Comic books
Matchbooks
Posters
Buttons
Plays
Nightclubs
Lectures
Operas
Concerts
Billboards
Graffiti
Paintings
Sculptures
Museums
Boxtops
Postcards
Window displays

All of these—and many more—are in some sense mass media.

The mass media differ from each other in many ways. The most important ways tend to be the most obvious as well. You will find very little to surprise you in the next two pages, but much that is worth keeping in mind as we examine the media one by one. Remember also that only a few of these differences are essential characteristics of the media themselves: most could be otherwise if the people who ran the media wanted them otherwise.

1. Speed. The first medium to find out about an event is almost always the nearest newspaper. The wire services get the story from the paper, and everyone else gets it from the wires. Speed in reaching the public is another matter. Radio is usually first, followed by television. Newspapers come next, then magazines, and finally books.

2. Depth. Depth is inversely proportional to speed. The slowest media, books and movies, are (at least potentially) the deepest. Magazines are next in line. Of the faster media, newspapers are the most likely to treat a subject in depth. Television and the wire services seldom do, and radio almost never does. Advertising could, but doesn't.

3. Breadth. The broadest range of subjects and interests is covered by books and magazines. By comparison, the rest of the media are appallingly narrow.

4. Ubiquity. Virtually every American has access to both a radio receiver and a television set—and spends at least a few hours a day with each. Newspapers reach more than 90 percent of the homes in the country, but seldom get more than a half hour's attention from any reader. Two-thirds of all American families subscribe to at least one magazine; roughly half of the adult population sees at least one movie a month. By contrast, less than one-tenth of the adult population reads a book a month. Every Ameri-

can, of course, is exposed to advertising on a daily—if not hourly—basis.

5. Permanence. Books and recordings are the most permanent of the mass media. Magazines are next, followed by newspapers. Feature films and television shows can be saved on tape. Only ad agencies save ads, and nobody saves wire-service copy.

6. Locality. Newspapers are the only purely local medium. Radio is mostly local; advertising, public relations, wire services, and television are both local and national. Magazines, books, recordings, and movies are almost entirely national.

7. Sensory Involvement. Books appeal only to the eye, usually in black and white and without pictures. In sensory terms, they are the dullest of the mass media. Newspapers have pictures, and magazines have pictures and color—but they are still designed only for the eye. Radio and recordings, on the other hand, reach only the ear. Television and film (and much advertising) appeal to both the eye and the ear, with moving pictures and often in color.

8. Credibility. The print media have traditionally been considered more believable than broadcasting or film. But recent surveys have found that most people believe television more readily than newspapers or magazines. Public relations often masquerades as news and thus gains credibility, while advertising is by far the least credible.

In the Introduction (see pp. 9-12), we listed four functions of the mass media in modern society—to serve the economic system, to entertain, to inform, and to influence. How do the different media compare according to these four criteria?

The "medium" that most directly serves the economic system is of course advertising, with public relations close behind. The rest of the media make their contributions to the economy principally as vehicles for those two. In terms of profits, on the other hand, one can safely say that television is by all counts the most profitable medium. The advertising and PR industries come second, followed by recordings, newspapers, magazines, and radio—probably in that order. Book publishing earns a small but steady profit; films alternately earn huge sums and lose huge sums. And the wire services are losing money.

Although the purest entertainment media are undoubtedly film and recordings, television is close behind—with by far the largest audience. Entertainment is also the principal purpose of most radio stations, and of many magazines and books. Just about every newspaper sugar-coats its information with a heavy dose of entertainment. Even advertising and public relations try hard to entertain, and often succeed.

The United States, unlike many other countries, has no purely informational mass media. Books probably come closest, since far more non-fiction is published every year than fiction. Newspapers (which get most of their information from public relations and from the wire services) are split about evenly, news versus advertising. So are magazines. Though television and radio do less than they should to inform the public, they are the main source of information for most people. Film, recordings, and advertising are least intended to inform—but even they teach us something about our world and ourselves.

The principal purpose of advertising and public relations is to influence people. Both are remarkably successful. By contrast, newspapers usually confine their efforts at outright influence to the editorial page. Many books (but not most) are written with influence in mind; some magazines and a few films have the same purpose. Television, radio, and recordings make little if any conscious attempt to influence our society; their influence is of course enormous, but it is unplanned. The wire services are the most objective and least influence-conscious of the mass media.

The purpose of these oversimplified comparisons is to set the stage for the medium-by-medium discussion that follows. As you read the next six chapters, keep in mind the following questions: How is this medium different from the others? Why is it different in those particular ways? What role does it play in the "media mix" of American society? What role should it play? How could the change be accomplished?

Chapter 9
Wire Services

Most of the nonlocal information in the American mass media comes from the wire services and feature syndicates, especially the Associated Press and United Press International. These two services tell us almost everything we know about events in other states and other countries. Working with skeleton staffs at breakneck speeds, the wire services often provide less than adequate coverage—but without them we would have little coverage at all.

"There are," said Mark Twain, "only two forces that can carry light to all corners of the globe—the sun in the heavens and the Associated Press." While we could get along a good deal easier without the Associated Press than without the sun, there are not many newspaper publishers or broadcast station managers who would like to try.

The Associated Press (AP) is one of the two major American wire services. The other one is United Press International (UPI); it is smaller and younger than AP, but almost as influential. Many other countries have their own wire services—Reuters in Britain, Agence France-Presse in France, Tass in the Soviet Union, etc. But AP and UPI are not only the most important wire services in the United States; they are the most important in the world.

Nearly a billion people a day read or hear the news courtesy of the Associated Press. Each day AP churns out roughly three million words, the equivalent of 10 books the size of this one.[1] UPI produces about the same amount of copy, and reaches nearly as many people. Within the United States, just under 1,300 of the nation's 1,760 or so daily newspapers subscribe to AP. Almost all the remaining 460-odd papers subscribe to UPI, and over 500 papers subscribe to them both. In addition, AP serves some 5,600 U.S. broadcast stations, while UPI serves more than 3,700—and both are beginning to build up a sizable clientele among cable television systems.

What do the wire services do? By means of electronic terminals and teletypes hooked up to long-distance telephone lines and satellites, they disseminate news from everywhere in the world to everywhere in the world. They thus serve as the eyes and ears for thousands of news organizations that cannot afford to send a reporter to another county, much less another continent. Even the largest and most self-sufficient news operations in this country—the *New York Times,* the *Washington Post,* the three networks, etc.— rely on the wire services for much of their day-to-day coverage. The typical daily newspaper or broadcast station simply could not cover nonlocal news without the wire services.

EVERYTHING FOR EVERYBODY

The goal of the wire services is to get the news as quickly as possible, as objectively as possible, and as cheaply as possible. These three characteristics—speed, objectivity, and cost-consciousness—account for both the strengths and the weaknesses of the wires. All three result from the central fact that the wire services must meet the needs of thousands of clients with different schedules and different ideologies, but with a unanimous desire to keep costs down. We will consider each characteristic in turn.

Speed. Every minute of every day, somewhere in the world, a wire-service client has reached its deadline. As a result, wire reporters are always under pressure to get the story now. As one Midwest editor put it: "AP covers the news in a hell of a hurry, and this is what we expect of it."[2] Wire reporters are the last of a dying breed of journalists, immortalized in countless old movies, who sprint for the nearest telephone to dictate a quick, breathless bulletin to the super-calm rewrite specialist back at the office.

Speed has its drawbacks, of course, and one of them is mistakes. On the night of September 30, 1962, the AP office in Atlanta was the focal point for the hottest news story of the day—James Meredith, a Negro, was enrolling at the University of Mississippi. Reporter Van Savell was on the phone from the

MORE AND FASTER

The biggest limitation on the speed of the wire services has always been the speed of the teletype machines that reproduce wire copy in the world's newsrooms. But AP has a solution. With its new "DataStream" system, copy moves at 1,050 words per minute, about sixteen times as fast as the old method.

"Faster delivery of copy," says AP, "smoothes out the flow" of news. "Immediate availability of copy enables news editors to effect better assembly of the news, in contrast to standard speed wires which may deliver important sidebars long after the central story has been cleared. In DataStream, even with the same amount of intervening copy, the sidebars reach the desk at almost the same moment as the main lead."[3]

DataStream and similar innovations have two possible effects—they can get the news to the client faster, and they can get more news to the client. The second effect could turn out to be the more important one. Even major AP and UPI stories seldom run over 500 words, and many minor ones don't make the national wire at all—there simply isn't enough time to transmit long stories or lots of stories. With a faster delivery system, the wire services can begin to carry longer stories or more stories or both.

But what would the typical telegraph editor do with it all? Most newspapers and broadcast stations today use less than one-tenth of the news they get over the wires. If AP or UPI sent them sixteen times as much, they'd have trouble even reading it all, much less deciding what to use. Probably DataStream won't change the nature of wire news after all—just move it faster.

campus. Retired Army General Edwin A. Walker, he dictated, had just taken command of the violent crowd, and had personally led a charge against federal marshals. Savell's dispatch sped over the AP wire to clients from Manhattan to Manilla. But in the heat of the moment, Savell had made a mistake. General Walker sued for libel and won.

The Supreme Court overturned the decision for an interesting reason. "The dispatch which concerns us," it said, "was news which required immediate dissemination. . . . Considering the necessity for rapid dissemination, nothing in this series of events gives the slightest hint of a severe departure from accepted publishing standards."[4] In other words, the wire services have to work so fast they're bound (and allowed) to make mistakes.

Several years later, on a lonely protest walk through the rural South, Meredith was shot. The wire reporters covering the event didn't dare wait to find out how badly he was hurt; they mistakenly reported that he was dead. Of course they soon filed updated stories correcting the error—but many papers and stations had already used the earlier reports.

AP and UPI struggle valiantly to minimize the number of errors caused by their quest for speed. They avoid errors by relying on established sources of information, by attributing as many statements as possible to witnesses or authorities, and by trying to stay cautious about the distinction between what is known and what is merely supposed or predicted. These tactics can cause problems of their own, as we shall see, but they do work. In the media accuracy sweepstakes, the wire services can cite at least as many success stories as horror stories.

Consider the Attica Prison uprising of 1971, for example. While other media, including the *New York Times,* accepted official claims that most of the violence was perpetrated by the prisoners, the Associated Press

carefully reported that it didn't know who was doing the shooting or who was responsible for the death of the hostages.[5] Eventually it was proved that most of the killing was done by the army of police and soldiers sent to break the siege—and AP looked pretty good.

A decade later, presidential Press Secretary James Brady was undergoing brain surgery to remove a bullet intended for President Ronald Reagan. In the chaos that followed the assassination attempt, some officials confided that Brady was dead. AP (and all three networks) used the story. UPI held off, awaiting confirmation. Brady survived and UPI looked pretty good.

Apart from mistakes, the stress on speed has another drawback—it inevitably results in superficial coverage. During a typical hour-long presidential press conference, AP and UPI may produce as many as five different leads each, continually updating the story to meet their clients' deadlines. Half a dozen reporters are kept busy rewriting the story again and again, devising new leads and adding paragraphs on later questions and answers. The result is an up-to-the-minute report for every client—but no attention at all to what the president isn't saying or what the press isn't asking.

Objectivity. The political biases of wire-service clients run the gamut from the far left to the far right. To keep everybody happy, the wires must have no biases of their own. "We can't crusade because we have papers of every complexion under the sun," noted Wes Gallagher, general manager of AP. "A crusade that pleases one is an anathema to another."[6] Hence the traditional wire-service "cult of objectivity." During the early 1970s, when media credibility was under heavy attack by the government, AP and UPI were seldom criticized.

But objectivity, like speed, has its drawbacks. Often the facts alone are not enough to make the meaning of a story clear. Sometimes the facts are simply misleading. One longtime Washington staffer recalls: "You said what Joe McCarthy said and you couldn't say it was a goddamn lie."[7] This is still a big problem for wire-service reporters. They are encouraged to present both sides of the story whenever possible—but not to tell which side they believe is right. Some client somewhere would be bound to disagree.

The growth of interpretive journalism hasn't bypassed the wire services entirely. AP, for example, has a special editor in charge of "enterprise" reporting. But enterprise is not the wire services' strong suit. One critic estimates that AP and UPI together employ no more than a hundred reporters who are regularly freed for investigative or interpretive assignments.[8] The rest cover routine stories. They are urged to get the facts as quickly as possible, and report them as succinctly as possible. News analysis takes time and space, both of which are in short supply. And besides, some client somewhere would surely disagree.

To insure their objectivity, the wire services try to attribute every debatable statement to the most authoritative available source. This practice, according to conventional wisdom, makes the statement less likely to be false—and even if it is false, at least the wire service quoted it accurately. The result, of course, is a bias in favor of what reputable people are doing and saying. When covering a demonstration, for example, wire-service reporters rely heavily on the police for information, rather than seeking out the viewpoint of the demonstrators. A typical AP story about a minor disturbance in Chattanooga ran eleven paragraphs; information was attributed to the police and public officials ten times, while the demonstrators were quoted once.[9]

In a sense, objectivity is itself a bias (see pp. 83-87). Typically, reporters who are struggling to be objective refuse to decide for themselves what is important or what is true. They let other people and institutions make the news, and then they cover it. The news that gets covered, then, is the news that is created by someone with enough power to make news. It almost requires an activist reporter to find out what is happening to powerless people. Wire-service reporters—the most objective and hence the most passive of all—cover mostly the powerful.

Cost-Consciousness. The Associated Press was founded in 1848 by six New York newspapers. To this day it remains a newspaper cooperative; broadcast stations may subscribe but may not join. The member papers elect a 23-person governing board, which tells the operating staff what to do. Costs are split up among the member papers and client stations. Like most cooperatives, AP is under heavy pressure to keep those costs low.

United Press International, on the other hand, is a private business. It is the product of a 1958 merger of the United Press (founded by E. W. Scripps in 1907) and the International News Service (founded by William Randolph Hearst in 1909). UPI has no members, only customers.

Today, UPI is in serious financial trouble. It lost $3.5 million in 1979, bringing its total losses since 1961 to $17 million. In early 1980, Scripps and Hearst tried to turn UPI into a sort of cooperative by selling 90 percent of it to other media companies, but the offering was withdrawn because there were too few takers.[10]

Most editors consider UPI inferior to AP. Between February 1979 and July 1980, 29 daily newspapers that had subscribed to both services dropped UPI. Competition also comes from the supplementary news services established by the *New York Times,* the *Washington Post* jointly with the *Los Angeles Times,* etc.[11] But the main problem is the fierce rivalry with AP. "I don't know of two outfits more destructively devoted to the American principle of free-enterprise competition than AP and UPI," said top UPI reporter Louis Cassels in 1969. "Competition in news gathering drives expenses up, and competition in selling drives income down."[12]

Some of the competition seems pretty pointless, for example the race to be first with Supreme Court decisions. But the fact that AP and UPI cover the same news, that there are two versions of national and international events circulating instead of one, seems almost essential to the survival of media freedom. If UPI is unable to solve its money problems and Scripps and Hearst grow tired of the annual red ink, AP may soon be left without any major U.S. competition. The dangerous possibilities of such a monopoly range from bias to laziness.

Ironically, a possible solution is being pioneered by AP. By using satellites instead of telephone lines, AP estimates that it will save $3.2 million by the end of 1982. Negotiations are under way to share the system with UPI and other news services.[13]

As of 1980, AP and UPI each employed about 1,200 people in the U.S., two-thirds of them directly involved with news. They were spread among 118 domestic bureaus for AP, and an even hundred for UPI. Each service also employed about 80 full-time people overseas, as well as hundreds of part-time "stringers" in other cities here and abroad. If that sounds like a small army of journalists, it is—but the army is too small for the job it must do. The vast majority of wire-service bureaus have only a couple of reporters and editors on duty at any time, and many bureaus have a staff of one reporter-editor, period. This overworked individual seldom ventures out of the office to report the news in person. Instead, he or she reads the early editions of the local newspapers, picks out the major stories, summarizes them in wire-service style, and sends them on their way. The rest of the day is spent rewriting press releases and updating the most important stories by phone.

Given the nature of the job, it is hardly surprising that the wire services can't hold on to their best reporters. They don't really try. Experienced investigative journalists demand high salaries and a chance to practice their craft. They get neither at AP and UPI, and soon leave for newspaper work or free-lancing.

There are exceptions, of course. The pride of the wire services is their Washington bureaus, each with more than 80 editorial employees. Even that isn't enough, as Jules Witcover, then of the Newhouse National News Service, explained. Here's how congressional committees are often covered:

> Overworked AP and UPI staffs routinely make collection runs, visiting a number of committee hearings on any given morning, dutifully collecting witnesses' speech texts, and going back to the House or Senate press gallery to dictate or to grind out several stories. Far from its being digging reporting, it is not even routine reporting. It is skimming. . . .[14]

Both AP and UPI offer a variety of services to their clients. At AP, for example, the most important national and international news is carried on the A wire. The B wire is a secondary national wire that catches the overflow from A and prints the complete text of important speeches and documents. The world service wire is designed to meet the needs of foreign clients. Each region of the U.S. has its own regional wire, while the more populous states have state wires as well. There is a financial wire, a sports wire, a racing wire, a weather wire, a special high-speed wire for the stock prices, and of course the wirephoto for pictures. Additional broadcast wires transmit pretimed five-minute newscasts, ready for a disc jockey to rip and read. And an audio service for radio stations is available with taped interviews that can be played as needed.[15]

Convenience is the key. The broadcast wires don't contain much news, but they don't require much work from the disc jockey either. Similarly, both AP and UPI offer their major services on perforated tape or video display terminal, geared for automatic typesetting machines.

How much does the client pay for these

services? Rates are based on what the individual client decides to subscribe to, and also on where it is located; media in big cities are charged more for the same package of services than media in small towns. The *New York Times,* which subscribes to just about everything AP offers, pays more than $750,000 a year. A small daily paper that settles for the A wire, one regional wire, and the stock quotations may have an annual bill of less than $5,000.[16]

Whatever the cost, the wire services are a lot cheaper than hiring your own reporters to cover the world. In fact, they're cheaper than hiring your own reporters to cover the city. For most newspapers and broadcast stations, wire-service news is the least expensive news they can get, a lot cheaper than local reporting. They aim to keep it that way. Noted Norman E. Isaacs, longtime editor of the *Louisville Courier-Journal:* "Most small papers don't seem to give a damn about the quality of wire service copy—as long as the price is kept low and they can get it delivered on tapes."[17]

THE POWER OF THE WIRES

Take any issue of your local newspaper and count up the total number of news stories. Then go back and count the number of stories designated "AP," "UPI," or "Combined Services." Add in any stories you find from the supplemental wires (see box). If your newspaper is typical, you will discover that between half and three-quarters of the news in the paper came from the wires. This is the power of the wire services.

The structure of AP and UPI resembles a

SUPPLEMENTAL SERVICES

AP and UPI have no real competition in the United States. Nobody else covers both the U.S. and the world in enough detail to meet the needs of American media. But there are other sources of nonlocal news, and many newspapers (and some broadcast stations) make substantial use of them.

Some of the nation's most distinguished newspapers—notably the *New York Times,* the *Chicago Tribune,* and the *Washington Post* and *Los Angeles Times* in combination—sell their newsgathering abilities and reputations to papers in other cities. For a fee that varies with the subscriber's circulation, they will put a teletype in any client's newsroom, over which they transmit selections from each day's paper. These supplemental services concentrate on political commentary, investigative reporting, and hard news exclusives—content not available from AP or UPI. It is thus possible for newspaper readers in Cleveland or Seattle to encounter a Tom Wicker column from the *New York Times* or a White House exposé from the *Washington Post.*

A number of newspaper chains, including Copley, Gannett, Knight-Ridder, and Newhouse, offer similar services. They are designed mainly to serve newspapers owned by the chains, but are available for a fee to nonmember papers as well. Both kinds of services are growing. The *New York Times* wire, for example, has 500 clients worldwide, up from 109 in 1971.

Then there are the foreign wire services—Reuters, Agence France-Presse, etc. None of these covers the United States in enough detail to replace AP and UPI, but several of them offer excellent coverage of Europe and the Third World. And their non-American perspective provides a useful alternative, especially on diplomatic and war stories. Though the American media make much less use of foreign wire services than the foreign media make of AP and UPI, a few U.S. papers do subscribe. In addition, several Euro-

tree, with crucial news judgments made at every branch. Suppose the mayor of Green Bay, Wisconsin, fires the police chief. First, a wire-service stringer in Green Bay decides whether to file the story with the nearest bureau. If the decision is no, that's it—you'll never know what happened in Green Bay unless you live there. If the decision is yes, then the bureau chief decides whether to transmit the story to the capital bureau in Madison. The capital bureau staff, in turn, decides whether to put it on the state wire, and also whether to telegraph it to the regional office in Chicago. If the story makes it to Chicago, that office decides whether to include it on the regional wire, and also whether to send it on to New York. New York can put the story on the national wire, or transmit it to the other regions for possible use on their regional wires, or kill it. Most wire stories, of course, never make it

to New York; of those that do, fewer than half get onto the national wire.

If the Green Bay story is dropped at any stage in this process, it might just as well not have happened as far as the rest of the world is concerned. Conversely, if the story makes the national wire, hundreds of clients are bound to pick it up, and millions of people will become aware of it.

A truly important story, of course, will inevitably find its way to the national wire (unless someone, somewhere along the line thinks otherwise). Then it's up to the local paper or station to decide whether to use the story. But what the story says is still up to the wire services.

The city of Pittsburgh learned this the hard way one year the Pirates won the pennant. On the night of October 17, 1971, Pirate fans celebrated in their city, some of them a bit too boisterously. AP bureau chief

---

pean newspapers, such as the *London Daily Express,* offer their own supplemental wires to U.S. subscribers.

Finally, there are over a hundred more specialized services that sell news to subscribing newspapers and broadcast stations—everything from the giant Dow Jones financial service to the National Black News Service to the Chinese Information Service. For almost any social issue or special interest you can name, from women's liberation to stamps and coins, from environmental quality to movie stars, there is a supplemental news service to keep interested clients up to date.

A recent development is the regional news wire, which competes head-to-head with the AP and UPI regional wires. In California, for example, Richard Fogel started the Bay City News Service in 1979. He has 20 clients (including most of Northern California's major newspapers) and 21 reporters. For a fee ranging from $5,200 to $20,000 a year, subscribers get round-the-clock regional news coverage, a mid-day news roundup, features, consumer items, and an events calendar. Editors who subscribe use BCN mostly for its news of local governments, complaining that AP and UPI focus too much on easy-to-cover police beat items instead. After 16 months BCN was breaking even.[18]

Most of the supplemental services provide only printed copy, which limits their usefulness to radio and television. AP and UPI do offer broadcast feeds for radio stations, as well as their printed broadcast wires. To spruce up the local TV news, network affiliates have access to the network "outtakes"—the film that didn't get used on the network news. Independent TV stations, meanwhile, have an exchange arrangement to borrow each other's film on important breaking news. Several schemes to sell supplemental news services to broadcast stations failed in the 1970s. One that survived is the National Black Network, which transmits black-oriented five-minute radio newscasts to 92 affiliates in the U.S.

Pat Minarcin saw cars overturned, windows smashed, and stores looted. He called it a riot—and so did millions of people around the country who read his story. Pittsburgh Police Superintendent Robert E. Colville disagreed. He accused AP of "gross distortion," and pointed out that UPI had reported only "minor looting" and some horn-blowing. But for all those who read the AP version, Pittsburgh had had a riot.[19]

Local media have no choice but to use the wires for national and international news—but what about state news? To find out, researchers looked at every article about the governor of Connecticut in every Connecticut daily newspaper for three months in 1967, and again in 1976. The largest papers, like the *Hartford Courant* and the *New Haven Register,* relied very little on the wires for news of the governor, they found. But

some smaller papers, such as the *Milford Citizen* and the *Torrington Register,* got literally all their news of their state's governor from AP and UPI. Overall, the wires supplied 55 percent of these stories in 1967, and the figure rose to 71 percent in 1976.[20]

Or consider the power of AP's and UPI's Spanish wires. Spanish-language media in the U.S. rely on them almost exclusively for news of Latin America and the large Hispanic communities in many U.S. cities. Latin American newspapers also use them extensively for news from beyond their own borders. UPI's own survey of the content of its Spanish wire shows the dangers of this reliance: 40-50 percent fast-breaking political news, 20 percent violence and war, 5-10 percent economics, and the rest features and miscellany.[21]

The wire services exercise their greatest

CRIB SHEET FOR EDITORS

Below is a portion of the AP daybook of events scheduled for Thursday, July 24, 1980, in and around New York City, as sent to New York area clients on Wednesday, July 23. As you read the list, bear in mind two things—how easy it must have been for New York editors to plan Thursday's coverage, and how contrived and PR-inspired many of the items seem to be.

Mayor Koch on the Bob Grant WMCA radio show, 888 Seventh Avenue, 9 a.m.

Brooklyn Borough President Howard Golden, Sanitation Commissioner Norman Steisel and Councilman Sam Horowitz walk along Brighton Beach Avenue to point out litter problems created by beachgoers, from Ocean and Brighton Beach Avenues to Ocean Parkway, 9 a.m.

New York City Financial Control Board meets, 21st floor, 270 Broadway, 10 a.m.

Open house at the neonatal intensive care unit and semi-acute nursery of Babies Hospital, where premature infants and their families participate in special physical fitness programs, Columbia Presbyterian Medical Center, 12th floor, Broadway and 166th St., 10 a.m.

Guardian Angels announce they will rid Times Square area of crime, starting with Bryant Park, at law office of Schwartz, Marriarino and Schlanger, 26th floor, 295 Madison Ave., 10 a.m.

Representatives of the North American Afghan Foundation, Afghan Freedom Front and others hold news conference to disclose secret Soviet action in Afghanistan, News World, 401 Fifth Ave., 10 a.m.

Assembly Minority Leader James Emery, Assemblyman Peter Toner and former Congressman Bruce Caputo discuss pollution of the Saw Mill River and clean-up plan, along the bank of the river near Morgan Street off Route 9A in Elmsford, 10 a.m.

Elected officials from the Hartford area discuss problems of solid waste and sludge disposal, headquarters of Metropolitan District Commission, Main Street, Hartford, 10 a.m.

Special events for spouses of delegates to the Democratic Convention are announced by Citizens Committee for the Democratic National Convention, aboard the Peking, Pier 16, South Street Seaport Museum, 10:30 a.m.

influence on radio. Most radio stations (and some TV stations) subscribe to the AP or UPI broadcast wire, which offers five-minute newscasts that a disc jockey can simply rip off the wire and read on the air. These stations exercise no news judgment at all, except perhaps to decide what local stories to crib from the nearest newspaper. On thousands of radio stations across the country, the hourly news is identical word for word. The wire services wrote it.

Newspaper editors must at least decide which wire stories to run—but the wire services help with that too. Every morning and evening, AP and UPI transmit lists of what they believe are the most important stories of the day. Editors who are afraid to trust their own judgment may put together their newscast or front page from the wire-service lists. Hundreds of editors make use of this service, offering their readers, listeners, and viewers news that is not only written by the wire services, but chosen by the wire services as well.

The wires even help decide what stories local reporters will cover. Every day, each major wire bureau compiles a list of local events scheduled for the next day. This "daybook," as it is called, is transmitted over the wires as a service to editors. Since the daybook is made up entirely of pre-scheduled events, it is dominated by things that wouldn't have happened at all except for the media—press conferences, celebrity

---

U.S. Helsinki Watch Committee news conference to welcome Yuri Yarrym-Agayev, member of the Moscow Helsinki Watch Committee, who was forced to emigrate as part of Soviet pre-Olympic campaign to remove dissidents, Harper & Row, 2nd floor, 10 East 53rd St., 10:30 a.m.

Psychiatrists for Equal Rights Amendment, national committee of doctors, protests American Psychiatric Association plans to hold its 1981 convention in Louisiana, where ERA has not been ratified, YMCA, 53rd St. and Lexington Ave., 10:30 a.m.

Communist Workers Party news conference to discuss demonstration yesterday at office of Alcohol, Tobacco and Firearms Bureau, 1 East Broadway, second floor, 10:30 a.m.

Mayor Koch and Democratic Party committee members tour Madison Square Garden to inspect preparations for Democratic National Convention, press assembles at ticket booths in main lobby on Seventh Avenue, 10:45 a.m.

Democratic Senate aspirant Bess Myerson receives endorsements of Teamsters Union locals, at Local 804, 41–50 22nd St., Long Island City, Queens, 11 a.m.

Opening of teenage roller disco roller ice rink, managed by two teenaged boys, Waterside Plaza, 23rd St. and the East River, noon.

Mayor Koch news conference on recent vandalism in Far Rockaway churches, Blue Room, City Hall, 12:30 p.m.

Attorney General John Degnan and Newark Mayor Kenneth Gibson announce $417,000 State Law Enforcement Planning Agency grant to fight street crime and violent robberies, Mayor's office, City Hall, Newark, 1 p.m.

New York City Council meets, City Hall, 1:30 p.m.

Battery Park City Authority meets, 52nd floor, 1515 Broadway, 2 p.m.

Frank Mercurio, Labor Department regional administrator, holds news conference on year-long probe of undocumented alien workers in Northern New Jersey, Federal Building, 970 Broad St., Newark, 3 p.m.

Mayor Koch holds Town Hall meeting, Thomas Jefferson High School, 400 Pennsylvania Ave., Brooklyn, 7:30 p.m.

The New York Grand Opera Company continues series of free presentations with its performance of Verdi's La Traviata, Mall at 72nd St., Central Park, 8:30 p.m.

Lorna Luft, returning from recent tour of Midwest in musical Grease, hosts party for cast and friends, including her sister Liza Minnelli, rock guitarist Rick Derringer and others, New York disco, 33 West 52nd St., 9 p.m.

appearances, store promotions, and the like. Because of the convenience of advance planning, editors often give these "pseudo-events" (see pp. 153-56) more attention than they would otherwise deserve. Television and radio stations are especially dependent on the daybook; it insures usable film or tape, and efficient use of the limited supply of film crews and engineers. As an added help, the wire services frequently indicate which of the listed pseudo-events they won't bother to cover, so local papers and stations can be sure to be there themselves.

AP and UPI, then, are not merely the nonlocal eyes and ears of the news business. They are the mouth too. They don't just decide what stories to cover and how to cover them. By putting or not putting a particular story on a particular wire, they determine who gets it. By including or not including the story in the predigested broadcast wire and the day's list of important news, they influence who uses it. And by means of the daybook, they even have a say in what the local media will do with their own reporters. In all, they are beyond doubt the most powerful media institutions in the country, the common denominators of American news.

THE WIRES OVERSEAS

AP and UPI are, of course, the U.S. media's chief source of foreign news, with AP reporters and stringers in 110 countries and UPI representatives in 90 countries. What we tend to forget is that AP and UPI are also major sources of international news for the media of other countries. Some 3,200 news organizations in 63 foreign countries subscribe to AP, while UPI serves some 2,200 media in 90 countries overseas. They are two of the four major international news services. The other two are Reuters (the British news service), with subscribers in 155 countries, and Agence France-Presse (the French news service) with subscribers in 80 countries.[22]

Four news organizations, in short, each from a highly developed Western democracy, dominate the flow of information around the world. They tell the West what is going on in the rest of the world; they tell the rest of the world what is going on in the West. They even tell the rest of the world what is going on in the rest of the world. Audiences in Malaysia, say, get the lion's share of their news about Argentina or Zaire from American, British, and French news stories. Aside from the Communist Bloc, the entire world relies on "the big four" Western news organizations for its international news.

Are the four unbiased? Of course not, argues Mustapha Masmoudi, chairman of the Intergovernmental Council for the Coordination of Information in the Non-Aligned Countries. In an article entitled "A Call to Broaden the News," Masmoudi asserts that the big four cover the third world with cultural blinders, eternally preoccupied with revolution, disaster, and scandal. "They elect to draw from the facts only their 'big-event' aspects, to enlarge, emotionalize, and shock, missing the real meaning and significance of the situation. Some don't even attempt to hide their bias," Masmoudi continues. "Any item of news not fitting in with their preconceived ideas, and perhaps ideologies, is pushed aside and ignored."[23]

Debates over whether the Western viewpoint of the Western news agencies deserves to be called "bias" are essentially pointless. Certainly the Western agencies *have* a Western viewpoint (see p. 454). It would be shocking if they didn't; they are staffed predominantly by Westerners, writing for an audience that is predominantly Western. The question is what can be done about it.

For years third world leaders confined themselves to criticism, but recently they have tried to correct the imbalance through action. One result was the formation in 1976 of a non-aligned news pool to compete with the big four. Organized by the Yugoslav news agency Tanjug, it includes news organizations from about 50 countries, including Algeria, Cuba, Libya, North Korea, Cambodia,

Iraq, and Morocco. Most of the member countries have authoritarian press systems, so most of the dispatches they contribute are written or approved by government officials.

In 1978, British journalist Michael Dobbs analyzed a week's worth of stories from the Tanjug pool. He found that 40 percent of them reported the activities and policies of the governments involved; 25 percent dealt with trade, aid, or development; 10 percent concerned the work of international organizations like the United Nations; 7 percent focused on liberation movements. Only two percent of the stories had to do with crimes, coups, famines, natural disasters, and the like. Dobbs concluded that the stories projected "a different picture of life in non-aligned countries from that presented in the West—but whether it is a more accurate one is seriously open to question."[24]

Western editors tend to view the pool as a propaganda vehicle for the governments involved, so they don't use it very often. But of course it isn't designed for them. Pool stories do de-emphasize conflict and emphasize guidance on how to cope with the problems of development. Whether that emphasis is a "worse" bias than the Western viewpoint is another pointless debate.

A second initiative to diminish the power of the big four was a commission set up by the United Nations Educational, Scientific and Cultural Organization (UNESCO) to report on the establishment of "a new world information order." The commission issued its report in February, 1980. It called for control over the flow of news from the big four within the borders of non-aligned nations; training of all foreign correspondents in the language and culture of their assigned country; restrictions on media concentration and ownership; a ban on using journalists as spies; and official U.N. encouragement of noncommercial (government-funded) rather than commercial forms of mass communication.[25]

The report stopped short of calling for a code of ethics spelling out the rights and responsibilities of journalists, fearing that such a code could be used by governments as a tool of censorship. And it did urge all countries to let foreign correspondents in and give them access to the entire spectrum of opinion.[26] Nevertheless, Western media executives found the UNESCO report disturbing. Gannett chairman Allen Neuharth said the recommendations "strike directly at a free, unfettered press" and "would virtually deliver the free media of the world into the hands of various governments, either national or international."[27]

The big four do report news that their host governments would rather see unreported. This single virtue makes them indispensable to many, including the governments themselves, which often subscribe to a few wire services to get an unofficial view of what's going on in other countries.[28] But of course these governments do not want an unofficial view of their own country circulated throughout the world. It is virtually impossible to disentangle the legitimate grievance over Western cultural bias from the daily battle over freedom versus censorship—if only because most authoritarian governments view press freedom itself as a Western cultural bias.

Meanwhile, the existence of a non-aligned news pool and the threat of UNESCO restrictions may force the big four to become more sensitive to the sorts of information they transmit into and out of third world countries. And that increased sensitivity may ease the situation a little—and perhaps even improve the international news provided to Western audiences.

FEATURE SYNDICATES

If it wants to, a newspaper can easily fill all its nonadvertising space with wire-service copy, plus a dash of local reporting. But a steady diet of hard news is unappetizing to today's newspaper readers. They want columns, comics, puzzles, recipes, and the like as well. Most papers buy this material from outside sources known as feature syndicates.

The first feature syndicates were organized during the Civil War, but they were small-time affairs until the 1880s, when Samuel S. McClure got into the act. McClure signed contracts with some of the most famous writers of the day, including Robert Louis Stevenson, Rudyard Kipling, Jack London, and Sir Arthur Conan Doyle, and sold their serialized work to newspapers at a bargain price. McClure's rationale for syndication makes as much sense now as it did then:

> A dozen, or twenty, or fifty newspapers— selected so as to avoid conflict in circulation— can thus secure a story for a sum which will be very small for each paper but which will in the aggregate be sufficiently large to secure the best work by the best authors.[29]

The 1980 *Editor & Publisher Yearbook* lists some 390 feature syndicates. Some are tiny and offer the work of only one individual. Others, such as King Features, North American Newspaper Alliance, and Newspaper Enterprise Association, are huge. The United Feature Syndicate, one of the biggest, offers nine different puzzles and word games; twenty-eight comics (including "Peanuts"); five editorial cartoonists; eight political columnists (including Jack Anderson); three humorists; fifteen TV and film writers; and specialized columnists on business, consumer affairs, health, food, beauty, decorating, sewing, fashion, astrology, and a host of other topics.

Big or little, nearly all the feature syndicates follow McClure's model. They offer newspapers exclusive local rights to a particular comic or column, in exchange for a fee that may range from $5 a week or less to $150 a week or more, depending on the popularity of the feature and the circulation of the paper. The combined fees from newspapers all over the country are split by the author and the syndicate. If the feature is popular, both earn substantial incomes— while each subscribing paper gets a local monopoly at a fraction of the cost of hiring its own staff.

Comics are the mainstays of most syndicates, their biggest moneymakers and their most attractive offerings. But don't underestimate the substantive value of the feature syndicates to American journalism. They offer readers a higher caliber of political commentary, humor, advice, and specialized reporting than the staffs of most local papers could possibly produce. And they do it at a price that makes even the most cost-conscious publisher smile.

Yet most syndicated features are light entertainment, the frosting on the newspaper cake. Even the serious columns deal with national and international issues, not the local problems and concerns of readers. When a newspaper replaces a local commentator with a syndicated national one, it lessens its ability to help readers deal with events close to home. And when a newspaper replaces hard news (local or otherwise) with a syndicated comic or a column on astrology, it lessens its ability to inform its readers about events that affect their lives. Because syndicated features are both cheap and popular, publishers are tempted to go overboard. One critic estimates that between 20 and 35 percent of the nonadvertising space in the average newspaper is devoted to syndicated material.[30] That is probably too much of a good thing.

The feature syndicates have at least one advantage over the wire services—diversity. To some extent, of course, nationally syndicated features contribute to the standardization of media content—the same column or comic may appear in Los Angeles and New York, Duluth and Miami. But at least there are lots of columns and comics to choose from, and papers in the same area necessarily make different choices. AP and UPI, on the other hand, are the only available full-scale American wire services. If newspapers and newscasts in this country all seem pretty much the same, the blame and the credit go principally to the wire services. When the wires do a good job, so do the nation's news media. When the wires do a bad job, it is literally impossible for the media to do a good one.

Notes

1 Fred Powledge, "New York—The Associated Press, according to official sources, may have problems communicating with its own people, but it is not out of touch with reality, as some critics have charged. . . ." *New York*, November 15, 1971, p. 55.

2 A. Kent MacDougall, "Grinding It Out, AP, UPI Fight Fiercely for Front Page Space," *Wall Street Journal*, January 28, 1969, pp. 1, 16.

3 *AP Log*, August 12, 1974, pp. 1, 4.

4 *Associated Press v. Walker*, 388 U.S. 130, 87 S.Ct. 1975 (1967).

5 Powledge, "New York—The Associated Press," p. 56.

6 MacDougall, "Grinding It Out," pp. 1, 16.

7 Jules Witcover, "Washington: The Workhorse Wire Services," *Columbia Journalism Review*, Summer, 1969, p. 10.

8 Madeline Nelson, draft article for [*MORE*] on the Associated Press.

9 Powledge, "New York—The Associated Press," p. 56.

10 Deirdre Carmody, "Plan of News Agency to Set Up Partnership Has Ended in Failure," *New York Times*, February 1, 1980, p. D15.

11 Daniel Machalaba, "U.P.I. Struggles as It Loses Ground to AP, Other News Services," *Wall Street Journal*, July 11, 1979, p. 1.

12 MacDougall, "Grinding It Out," pp. 1, 16.

13 "Associated Press Plans to Expand Satellite Distribution Network," *Wall Street Journal*, April 22, 1980, p. 20.

14 Witcover, "Washington: The Workhorse Wire Services," p. 11.

15 "AP Will Supply News for Radio," *New York Times*, June 1, 1974, p. 59.

16 Nelson, draft article.

17 MacDougall, "Grinding It Out," pp. 1, 16.

18 "First Regional Wire Is 16 Months Old," *Feed/back*, Spring, 1980, p. 43.

19 "What Riot?" *Newsweek*, November 1, 1971, p. 82.

20 Thomas R. Donohue and Theodore L. Glasser, "Homogeneity in Coverage of Connecticut Newspapers," *Journalism Quarterly*, Autumn, 1978, pp. 592-96.

21 Michael Massing, "Inside the Wires' Banana Republics," *Columbia Journalism Review*, November/December, 1979, pp. 45-49.

22 Françoise Giroud, "Third World Revolt Against Media Domination," *Manchester Guardian Weekly*, November 19, 1978, p. 11.

23 Mustapha Masmoudi, "A Call to Broaden the News," *New York Times*, July 31, 1978, p. A15.

24 Michael Dobbs, " 'And Now, Here Is the Good News,' " *Manchester Guardian Weekly*, November 26, 1978, p. 8.

25 Osama A. Sebaei, "The Non-Aligned News Agency Pool," Freedom of Information Center Report no. 421, School of Journalism, University of Missouri at Columbia, May, 1980, p. 3.

26 "High Noon at UNESCO," *Columbia Journalism Review*, July/August, 1980, pp. 24-25.

27 *Ibid.*, p. 24.

28 Dobbs, " 'And Now, Here Is the Good News,' " p. 8.

29 Ben H. Bagdikian, "Journalism's Wholesalers," *Columbia Journalism Review*, Fall, 1965, p. 28.

30 *Ibid.*, p. 28.

Suggested Readings

BAGDIKIAN, BEN H., "Journalism's Wholesalers," *Columbia Journalism Review*, Fall, 1965.

DOBBS, MICHAEL, " 'And Now, Here Is the Good News,' " *The Manchester Guardian Weekly*, November 26, 1978.

DONOHUE, THOMAS R., and THEODORE L. GLASSER, "Homogeneity in Coverage of Connecticut Newspapers," *Journalism Quarterly*, Autumn, 1978.

GIROUD, FRANÇOISE, "Third World Revolt Against Media Domination," *The Manchester Guardian Weekly*, November 19, 1978.

LEWIS, PAUL, "U.N. Parley Adopts Principles On News," *The New York Times*, October 26, 1980, p. A14.

MACHALABA, DANIEL, "U.P.I. Struggles as It Loses Ground to AP, Other News Services," *The Wall Street Journal*, July 11, 1979, p. 1.

MASSING, MICHAEL, "Inside the Wires' Banana Republics," *Columbia Journalism Review*, November/December, 1979.

POWLEDGE, FRED, "New York—The Associated Press, according to official sources, may have problems communicating with its own people, but it is not out of touch with reality, as some critics have charged," *New York*, November 15, 1971.

SEBAEI, OSAMA A., "The Non-Aligned News Agency Pool," Freedom of Information Center Report no. 421, School of Journalism, University of Missouri at Columbia, May, 1980.

SUSSMAN, LEONARD R., "A Story of 2 Belgrades,"

The New York Times, October 23, 1980, p. A27.

WITCOVER, JULES, "Washington: The Workhorse Wire Services," *Columbia Journalism Review,* Summer, 1969.

Chapter 10
Newspapers

The newspaper is the oldest and traditionally the most important source of current information. The average daily paper still contains far more news than is available elsewhere, but today its traditional role is threatened, as audiences turn increasingly to television for their news, demanding newspapers that are lighter and more entertaining. The change leaves newspaper reporters frustrated and even more cynical than in the past, despite greatly improved salaries. Newspaper publishers can adjust more happily to the trend, and technological changes have kept profits high. But the diminishing pool of young readers and potential competition from new technologies are ominous clouds on the horizon.

A newspaper is an unbound, printed publication, issued at regular intervals, which presents information in words, often supplemented with pictures.

Don't memorize that definition. It is accurate, but not very useful. Perhaps more useful is this rough breakdown of the content of a typical daily newspaper in 1979:[1]

64% Advertising

16% Entertainment, sports, and opinion

8% Data and listings (stocks, TV, etc.)

8% Wire news (foreign and national)

4% Local hard news

The breakdown tells you some important things about newspapers: that nearly two-thirds of their content isn't news at all, but advertising; that over half of the remainder is really features and specialized departments; that the bulk of what's left is written by wire-service reporters dozens, hundreds, or thousands of miles away; that only a tiny fraction of each paper is local hard news.

That is what a newspaper is. What should it be? Most observers agree that the main function of the daily newspaper is to tell readers what's happening in the world, the country, the state, and the city. It should strive to report significant political and social developments, to include news of special relevance to particular groups of readers, to scrutinize the actions of local government, and to act as a forum for various community viewpoints.

Students of journalism and political science are agreed that this is the role of the daily newspaper. Readers, reporters, and publishers, however, have somewhat different notions of the purpose of the paper. And it is their views (not ours) that control what actually happens.

THE NEWSPAPER READER

The total morning and evening circulation of U.S. newspapers in 1979 was 62.2 million. This is almost exactly the same figure as newspaper circulation in 1971; it's a scant 3.3 million ahead of total circulation in 1960. The U.S. adult population, meanwhile, rose 19 percent in the 1970s, and the number of U.S. households rose 25 percent.[2] Obviously, newspaper circulation is not keeping up.

Among older Americans, newspaper reading is still a firmly entrenched habit. More people read a paper every day than drink coffee, go to work, or drive a car. And newspaper readers are higher in education and income than nonreaders, making them an attractive audience for advertisers.

But younger Americans don't seem to be picking up the habit. In 1957, 78 percent of those aged 50-59 and 75 percent of those aged 20-29 said they read a paper on a daily basis; newspaper reading then had nothing to do with age. In 1967, readership in the 50-59 age group was still 78 percent, but readership for those aged 20-29 had dropped to 64 percent. And in 1977, a healthy 76 percent of the 50-59 group were regular readers, while the figure for the 20-29 group had plummeted to 42 percent.[3] Will the members of this new generation start reading newspapers as they get older? If they don't, the newspaper business is in serious trouble. Even if they do, newspaper reading may soon become predominantly an activity of the middle-aged and older.

Most observers attribute these trends to the coming of age of the first generation born with television.[4] If they're right, the effect is so far confined to newspapers. Along with reading fewer papers, young people today spend less time with the papers they do read, and enjoy them less. But readership and enjoyment of books and magazines have actually *increased* among the "television generation."[5]

Researcher Leo Bogart suggests a different explanation for the declining newspaper audience. Newspapers, he points out, depend mostly on home delivery for stable circulation; the average daily paper home-delivers 87 percent of its copies. But living patterns among the young have changed. Households are increasingly made up of singles and unrelated persons, whose irregular schedules are not conducive to home delivery.[6]

Whatever the explanation, editors and publishers are searching hard for the kind of content that will attract younger nonreaders. In 1979 the American Society of Newspaper Editors released the results of a major study on this question. The study found that young people in particular want a newspaper that is "more attentive to their personal needs, more caring, more warmly human, less anonymous." Besides traditional information on major events, they want help with their own problems—advice on what to buy, where to play, how to cope. And they want that advice from journalists they feel they know. "Instead of faceless editors and reporters—traditional symbols of objectivity—they want real people to relate to."[7]

This demand for lighter, more personal newspaper content is not really so different from the traditional preferences of newspaper readers. Here, for example, are the results of a 1955 study of the percentage of the audience reading each type of news.[8]

Picture pages	74.3%
Comic pages	42.6
Front page	34.3
Solid news-feature pages	24.0
Editorial pages	23.1
Amusement	21.3
Split news-advertising pages	18.2
Solid advertising pages	15.7

Society and women's pages	15.5
Sports pages	13.9
Financial pages	5.4

The readership pattern is clear. Most people turn to the least taxing, most entertaining sections first, glance at the front page, and then stop. Nearly twice as many read the comics as the editorials. Almost as many read solid ad pages as inside news pages. It is figures like these that feed the cynicism of journalists, that prompted one city editor of the 1920s to say: "You and I aren't hired to make the world a better place to live in, or to fight and die for noble causes, or even to tell the truth about this particular main street. We're hired to feed human animals the kind of mental garbage they want. We don't have to eat it. I don't read our paper for instruction or even for fun. I just read it for errors and to see if we're handing out regularly what the boobs like for breakfast."[9]

Boobs or not, most newspaper readers are not very interested in news. When a strike deprives them of their daily paper, what do they miss most? They miss the ads, the "news" of supermarket sales, apartments for rent, and new movies in town. And they miss the service announcements; weddings go uncongratulated, funerals unmourned, and the weather unprepared for. Above all, they miss the habit of reading the paper. But newspaper *news* they can do without—there's always television.

Television is, in fact, the preferred source of news for most Americans today. In 1959, Roper Research Associates asked a sample of Americans where they got their news. Newspapers were mentioned by 57 percent of the respondents; television by 51 percent; radio by 34 percent; and magazines by 8 percent (multiple answers were accepted). In 1978, Roper repeated the survey. This time, 67 percent mentioned television; newspapers were down to 49 percent, radio to 20 percent, and magazines to 5 percent.

The decline in newspaper credibility at the expense of television is even more dramatic. When Roper asked its sample which medium is most believable, this is what it found.[10]

	1959	1978
Television	29%	47%
Newspapers	32	23
Magazines	10	9
Radio	12	9
No answer	17	12

Students of journalism believe that the newspaper is the best available daily source of news. But many newspaper readers prefer to get their news from television. They rely on the paper (if they read it at all) for entertainment and service, for comics, crosswords, and classifieds.

THE NEWSPAPER REPORTER

For reporters, newspapering is first and foremost a job. Traditionally, it has been a job that didn't pay very well. Newspaper reporters still earn less than their on-the-air colleagues in television, and less than many of the backshop employees who print the paper. But throughout the 1960s and 1970s, newspaper reporting salaries climbed steadily, and it is now possible to earn a decent living as a reporter for a metropolitan newspaper.

As of 1980, starting salaries for reporters at unionized newspapers ranged from $29,000 a year at the *New York Times* to $7,000 a year at the *Monessen Valley* (Pa.) *Independent,* with the average for most metropolitan papers in the $13,000 to $16,000 range. The union minimums for veteran reporters (with two to six years' experience) averaged about $21,000 a year, ranging from $30,500 down to $10,000. These are minimums, guaranteed by collective bargaining. Many papers pay their better reporters more than the minimum.

Salaries at nonunion newspapers are generally lower, but only because nonunion papers are generally smaller. A nonunion newspaper must remain competitive with union papers of equal size, or it risks losing its best reporters to union shops. Reputedly the cushiest of all newspaper employers is the nonunion *Los Angeles Times,* which pays many of its reporters over $40,000 a year.

Though newspaper salaries are now adequate, newspaper working conditions—in the view of many reporters—are not. Beginning reporters, and even veterans, are expected to take unconventional shifts and unexpected overtime in stride; missed meals, missed dates, and angry spouses often seem to come with the job. Add to these the low status of newspaper journalism, the whims of publishers, the hostility of sources and would-be sources, and the tedium of covering press conference after press conference after press conference. It's a lot to take (even for an adequate salary) unless you love it.

Newspaper reporters tend to move around a lot in search of a better job. A typical study asked editors of Texas daily papers to describe what happened to their staffs between 1972 and 1976. Two-thirds of the editors said they lost half or more of their reporters during this four-year period; six papers didn't hold onto a single individual from 1972 to 1976. Only about one-fifth of the reporters had stayed with their papers for ten years or more. Overall, the annual turnover rate was 28 percent—twice the national rate for accountants and public school teachers, five times the national rate for college professors.[11]

Much of this movement, inevitably, is out of newspaper journalism altogether. One study, for example, traced the careers of 35 outstanding journalism students. Only 19 of them (just over half) went into newspaper work after graduating. Ten years later, only eight of them were still holding down newspaper jobs. The rest had quit for public relations, advertising, broadcasting, insurance, or whatever.[12]

Who's left after this winnowing process? Two prototypes seem to predominate, both exaggerated but both with more than a germ of truth. First is the young journalist, who loves newspaper work for its excitement, its variety, its sense of power and being where the action is. A graduate of journalism school, the young journalist expects to take the world by storm, to write about important events in ways that will influence those events, and to be reasonably well paid for the work. If these expectations are satisfied— and sometimes they are—the young reporter may become a star reporter. If they are not satisfied, if the reporter is stuck writing fluff or if the reporter's serious writing doesn't seem to lead to serious results, disillusionment may set in. At that point the young reporter may leave the field, or may merge into the second prototype—the cynical veteran.

Today's cynical veteran is usually a white male (because yesterday's young reporter was). He's been in the newspaper business for half his life, and though he doesn't find it especially exciting any more, he doesn't intend to leave either. He has a college diploma, a wife, and a mortgage. He still believes in the mystique of journalism, and will occasionally remark that he has "ink in his veins." But he no longer expects to change the course of history.

The experienced reporter, in other words, is something of a pessimist. He has seen the worst in life and been unable to report it, or has reported it and been unable to change it. Theodore Dreiser put it this way:

> One can always talk to a newspaper man, I think, with the full confidence that one is talking to a man who is at least free of moralistic mush. Nearly everything in connection with those trashy romances of justice, truth, mercy, patriotism, public profession of all sorts, is already and forever gone if they have been in the business for any length of time.[13]

The cynicism of the journalist is largely the result of frustration—the frustration of a would-be participant forced to play the role of an observer. What city hall reporter has not wished to be an Ed Koch? What science writer hasn't dreamed of becoming a Carl Sagan? What sports columnist hasn't imagined a job switch with Reggie Jackson? Many journalists pick newspaper work, it seems to us, in order to change the world. They soon discover that they *can't* change the world, that the most they can do (when

---

INFLUENCE AND THE REPORTER

In the ideology of most newspaper reporters, nothing is more sacrosanct than the claim that they are not trying to advance any particular social goal. In 1973, while many observers were congratulating or condemning the media for pursuing the Watergate scandals, political reporter Richard Reeves offered the following demurrer:

> I am a reporter. In twenty minutes, with a telephone and typewriter, I can write a coherent and substantially accurate 700-word story of a subway accident or the fall of a government. With a rumor, two facts, and an inch-high stack of clippings, I can put together a scandalous account of what's being done with your tax dollar. I can fake my way through a probing conversation with a foreign minister or a mobster. I have knocked on strange doors at 4 A.M. to say, "I'm sorry your son was just killed, do you have a picture of him and could you tell me what kind of kid he was?" I am, according to the New York Newspaper Guild, worth a minimum of $365 a week.
>
> I love it, even if I know it's a kind of prolonged adolescence. That doesn't mean I don't take it seriously—I do, I think it's very, very important, but I'm glad it's fun. . . .
>
> I just wanted to cover good stories, write them well, give the people kind enough to read them a sense of what's going on. I want to be accurate, fair, perceptive and, when I'm lucky, incisive. If I'm interested in influence, it's influence with other reporters. More than anything I want the respect of the men and women in my peer group. . . .
>
> I have met few editors and fewer reporters with ambitions greater than getting better stories —getting stories, not Presidents, whatever the incumbent thinks.[14]

What Reeves says is accurate, but it is misleading nonetheless. It is true that most reporters have no particular policy goals behind their journalism, no hidden bias for which they write consistent propaganda. But it is also true that most reporters have strong opinions about the events and issues they cover, and a strong desire that their coverage should influence the way decisions are made. Yes, reporters set out to get the Watergate story, not to get President Nixon. But as the Watergate saga unfolded, reporters came to expect that the story itself would "get" the president—and their faith in journalism would have been profoundly shaken if it had not done so.

It is no accident that the period immediately after Watergate witnessed a substantial increase in the number of college journalism majors around the country.[15] These novice reporters, attracted to journalism for its power, will also try to cover the news fairly. And they will expect governments to fall, policies to change, and readers to be aroused as a result of their coverage.

Richard Reeves, by the way, is a "New Journalist" and political columnist; for an example of his very personal, very opinionated approach to the news, see pp. 277-78. The typical newspaper reporter works under much stricter constraints than those confronting Reeves. Such a reporter may find newspaper work somewhat less satisfying than Reeves does. When governments don't fall, policies don't change, and readers are not aroused, the result may be disillusionment and cynicism.

there isn't a light feature that requires their attention) is to report the world-changing decisions of others. And so the activist reporter becomes a passive writer of articles. After work he or she adjourns to the neighborhood bar to tell other reporters what the mayor *should* have done.

Perhaps this is an exaggerated view of newspaper work. No doubt there are reporters around who exult with editor Walter Humphrey that "every human activity is on my beat and I am interested in everything that happens in the world, for everything is my concern."[16] No doubt there are other reporters who simply do their job, and do it well, with a minimum of frustration or cynicism. But the typical reporter, we maintain, is a disillusioned idealist.

THE NEWSPAPER PUBLISHER

For publishers the newspaper is a business, and like all business executives the publisher wants the paper to earn a profit. By and large, it does.

Newspaper financial statements are hard to come by. Publishers have traditionally claimed that the wolf was halfway in the newsroom door, treating any inquiry into profits as a direct assault on freedom of the press. The *New York Times* is one of the few newspapers in the country that publicly report their profits. In 1979, the New York Times Company earned $27.4 million on revenues of $394 million from the *Times* itself; the company's 14 small newspapers contributed another $9.7 million on revenues of $41.4 million. Proportionately, the small papers did much better than the *Times*—but both did very well indeed.

Here are some hypothetical 1978 data from *Editor & Publisher* for a composite seven-day newspaper with a circulation of 35,000. The paper's total operating revenue was $5.9 million, with the largest chunks coming from local advertising ($2.2 million), classifieds ($1.0 million), and circulation income ($1.7 million). Operating expenses were just over $4 million, mostly for the editorial department and salaries ($1.7 million), newsprint ($830,000), administration ($497,000) and circulation ($401,000). That left a net profit before taxes of $1,847,000—$960,000 after taxes.[17]

The American Newspaper Publishers Association predicted in 1973 that total newspaper advertising revenue would rise from just over $7 billion then to more than $10 billion by 1980.[18] In 1979 the figure actually hit $14.5 billion.[19]

All this is not meant to imply that starting a new newspaper is a wise investment. It isn't. The initial capital requirements are huge, and it takes years to establish a new paper to the point where it attracts enough readers and advertisers to earn a profit. In fact, there isn't much of a market for new daily papers. Most communities large enough to support one already have one. And very few communities, apparently, are large enough to support more than one. *Editor & Publisher*'s hypothetical newspaper, like the vast majority of the nation's 1,763 dailies, has a local monopoly. Competing papers, by contrast, are a vanishing species; many of the handful that are left are in financial hot water.

Expanding newspaper chains, understandably, do not try starting new papers. They buy existing monopoly papers—an investment so risk-free that they are willing to pay more than 30 times the paper's annual profit. The hypothetical daily discussed above, if it is not already chain-owned, may soon sell to a chain for $30 million or so.

Throughout the 1960s and into the 1970s, one storm cloud threatened this rosy financial picture: the battle over automation.

The oldest of the mass media, newspapering was for many years also the most old-fashioned. As long as the profits were satisfactory, many publishers were content to leave it that way. In an age dedicated to speed, cleanliness, and efficiency, there was a certain thumb-your-nose pleasure in slow, dirty, inefficient newspaper work. Group ownership and increased costs eventually overcame that pleasure. The heads of conglomerates and media chains were not very attracted to the ink-in-your-veins traditions of journalism. Their god was profit. Independent owners of smaller newspapers, meanwhile, were faced with steadily rising costs; for them streamlining was a matter of survival.

It was a matter of survival, too, for the unions of backshop employees who typeset the conventional newspaper. At stake was the manual "hot-type" system with a linotype machine at its center. In this traditional set-up, a piece of newspaper copy is first sent to the linotype operator, who sets the story in strips of hot, molten lead. As each separate line of type is added to the previous one, the story takes shape on a metal tray or galley. The type is then taken from the galleys and fastened into page forms, which tightly hold hundreds of individual lines together to make up a page of the newspaper. The page form then goes to a stereotyper, who turns the unwieldy columns of lead into a curved plate that fits onto the printing press.

In a "cold-type" operation, by contrast, the linotype machine is replaced by a much cheaper device resembling an ordinary typewriter. When the story comes out of this machine (on paper, not in lead), it is carefully cut up and pasted into a "mechanical," along with all the other stories, headlines, and ads that belong on that page. The mechanical goes to a photoengraver, who takes a picture of the entire page, and makes the plate for printing out of that. The cold-type system is neater and cleaner than hot type, and since it uses simpler equipment and fewer (and less highly trained) employees, it's a lot cheaper.

Most important, cold type lends itself ideally to automation. Reporters write and edit their stories on a video display terminal connected to a computer. Editors go over each story on their own terminals, proofreading, cutting, adding the headline. Then the complete story is "sent" electronically to a phototypesetting machine, which automatically sets the story to the editor's specifications, hyphenating and justifying margins as it goes. The story comes out on a strip of photosensitive paper, ready to be pasted onto the mechanical. Result: no typesetters, and a paperless newspaper except for the reporter's notes at the beginning and the published newspaper at the end. The next step will be electronic pagination. Finished page nega-

---

THE PUBLISHER PRODUCES

One person—if he or she happens to be publisher—can change the face of a newspaper. In 1960, for example, the *Los Angeles Times* was "best represented by a middle-aged lady in a mink shrug on her way to a Republican tea."[20] It had three reporters in its Washington bureau, a total news staff of 220, and an annual editorial budget of $3 million. Then Otis Chandler took over as publisher. By the mid-1970s, the *Times* had 18 reporters in Washington, a news staff of more than 500, and an operating budget of $12 million a year. And it was one of the most aggressive, respected—and profitable—newspapers in America. By 1980 the paper had 600 people in its editorial department and 30 bureaus, including 18 overseas—and in national prestige it was right up there with the *New York Times* and the *Washington Post*.

It works the other way too. Under Colonel William Rockhill Nelson, the *Kansas City Star* was once ranked among the top papers in the country. Today, under chain management, it is just another metropolitan daily.

tives, complete with headlines and photos, will be provided by the computer, ready to be made into plates for printing.

Reporters and editors at many newspapers resisted these changes for a while, but they were won over by the obvious advantages: reduced costs, some of which went into the editorial budget; increased speed, postponing final copy deadlines by an hour or more; and elimination of backshop changes and errors that have traditionally annoyed journalists. Automation did alter the mechanics of reporting and editing, but not their essence—which is still asking questions and making sense of the answers.

But automation threatened doom to typesetters and related backshop employees, whose highly skilled work would be done mostly by computers. They fought the inevitable for more than a decade, and they lost.

In 1974, following a precedent set in San Francisco the previous year, the *New York Times* and the *New York Daily News* reached an important agreement with the typographers. In return for lifetime job security for all backshop personnel, the union agreed to give the two papers a free hand to automate as they saw fit. In essence, the union was willing to die out slowly so that its current members could be assured of their jobs for as long as they wanted them.[21]

In 1979, only 21 percent of the nation's 420,700 newspaper employees were unionized, and most unions were simply trying to hold the line rather than recruit new members. The International Typographical Union—once the most active opponent of automation—had declined from 50,000 newspaper members in 1970 to under 34,000 in 1979.[22] And only ten strikes were begun against newspapers in 1979, the lowest total since 1961.[23] Not coincidentally, by 1979 *Editor & Publisher* was able to report that backshop costs had declined for five straight years—thanks to automation.[24]

Roughly half the daily newspapers in the U.S. were automated as of 1979, with reporters and editors doing their work on video display terminals and with computers setting the type.[25] And one study estimated that every daily in Utah, Wyoming, Montana, and Idaho would be using such a system by 1984.[26] Backshop unions may delay some metropolitan newspapers for a few more years. But by the end of the 1980s, virtually every daily newspaper in the country will have installed a computerized cold-type system.

With automation problems eliminated, publishers should be sailing into clear financial waters for the 1980s—at least the vast majority of publishers with local newspaper monopolies. But two new issues are troubling the waters. One we have already discussed—the decline in newspaper readership, especially among the young. The other, ironically, is a new electronic technology, videotext.

Videotext is essentially a televised newspaper, delivered by broadcasting, by cablecasting, or by a telephone line connected to a home computer and screen. Regardless of the delivery system, videotext permits the "reader" to choose which parts of the newspaper he or she wishes to see, then puts those parts on the screen. Robert G. Marbut, chairman of the Telecommunications Committee of the American Newspaper Publishers Association, describes the threat: "The newspaper is really just a bundle of information, and the new technology is making it possible to unbundle some of that information and deliver it electronically on demand, as opposed to delivering it in print *en masse.*"[27]

So far there is no strong market demand for such a system. And there may never be—a similar innovation called facsimile newspapers failed in the 1940s for lack of a market.[28] But publishers aren't taking any chances. Says William J. Keating of the *Cincinnati Enquirer:* "Unless we explore this whole area, we could be left at the starting gate."[29] One major concern is that videotext could take over the highly profitable classified advertising business, using computer links to offer subscribers ads from all across the country.[30]

Videotext experiments are now underway in Britain, France, Japan, and Canada. In the U.S., the Knight-Ridder newspaper chain is experimenting with a videotext system in Coral Gables, Florida, and a company called CompuServe (a subsidiary of H&R Block) is trying one in Columbus, Ohio. Some 225 CompuServe subscribers in Columbus now have the entire contents of the *Columbus Dispatch* available on their home computer terminals. Agreements are being negotiated with other papers, including the *New York Times,* the *Washington Post,* and the *Los Angeles Times,* to make their contents available to CompuServe clients as well.[31] For now the price is prohibitive for most people— around $1,000 for the equipment plus 8⅓ cents a minute to tap into the computer.[32] But if videotext catches on, costs will decline.

Why should people pay for videotext when they can get the whole newspaper for a quarter a day? Jim Batten, Knight-Ridder's vice president for news, offers a possible rationale:

> The guy who wants to check the Red Sox score [must go] . . . through a newspaper that is trying to tell him about Jimmy Carter, the Middle East and Three Mile Island. . . . I think there are a lot of people out there who do not want to be bothered with public issues and public affairs, and what is intriguing about these systems is that they will let people do that. A guy who wants the box scores, three stock prices and the weather in Minneapolis can get that small sliver of information very effectively and quickly. He can cut through all those concerns that we've traditionally figured people in a democracy ought to care about.[33]

Most of the trends affecting the newspaper industry today can be seen as consistent with the wishes of both readers and publishers. Light feature material, for example, appeals to readers and saves money for publishers, while mergers avoid costly competition for publishers without denying readers anything they truly value. But reporters have won some significant victories of their own, most notably the rise of specialized and interpretive reporting.

THE READER-PUBLISHER COALITION

The content of a newspaper is the product of the conflicting goals of the reader (to be entertained), the reporter (to change the world), and the publisher (to make money). In this conflict the reporter usually loses. For one thing, the reader and the publisher have most of the power; for another, their goals are highly compatible. The reporter represents a minority viewpoint.

The decline of the newspaper editorial is a perfect example of the reader-publisher coalition at work. Until the Penny Press era the unsigned editorials were the most important part of most newspapers. But today's readers find the editorial page too heavy for their taste. That's okay with most publishers. They use the editorial page to praise the weather, pontificate on the latest news from Afghanistan, and urge everyone to vote in the next election. There are relatively few newspapers left in the country that regularly publish strong editorials on local controversies, thus risking the reader's anger.

A second example is the growing ascendancy of advertising over news copy. In 1941, the average newspaper was 52 percent news, 48 percent advertising. Today a respectable ratio is 64 percent advertising and 36 percent news. (In all fairness, the size of the typical newspaper has also increased, leaving a bigger news hole by absolute measures than ever before.) Reporters and editors fight for every column-inch of news they can get. But publishers prefer to print ads. And readers often would just as soon read ads.

Three other examples of the impact of

the reader-publisher coalition go to the heart of current newspaper trends, and therefore deserve more extensive discussion. These are the dominance of light entertainment, the decline of competition, and the pursuit of the affluent audience. We will consider each in turn.

1. Entertainment. Several decades ago, publishers discovered that the cheapest and most successful way to fill the space between advertisements was to rely heavily on syndicated features—comic strips, advice columns, and the like. By the mid-1970s, syndicated material comprised as much as one-third the editorial content of many newspapers. A cost-conscious publisher could use the syndicates to fill 35 percent of the paper's news hole for only 10 percent of its editorial budget. And far from objecting to the cut-rate content, readers appreciated it, showing a marked preference for fluff over hard news.

The trend intensified in the last half of the 1970s, with many papers beefing up their local feature staffs to supplement the syndicates. Even the *New York Times*—historically the most somber of major American newspapers—joined enthusiastically in the switch from hard news to features, inaugurating special weekly sections (one a day) on sports, home furnishings, entertainment, food, and science/health. *Miami News* executive Bernie Oelze openly acknowledged one purpose of such sections: to create a newspaper that "people can read while watching the tube."[35]

Readers clearly approved of the change. When asked in audience surveys, they told their papers to shift even further in the direction of service features. In 1980, for example, the *Hammond* (Indiana) *Times* asked its readers what sorts of information they would like more of. Here are the results, in order of preference:[36]

1. Crafts/do-it-yourself
2. Hometown government
3. Home repairs
4. Consumer news
5. Health/doctors
6. Hometown politics
7. Home decoration/furniture
8. Shopping/prices
9. Gardening
10. Recipes/homemaking
11. State government
12. Where to go
13. Hometown sports
14. Hometown schools
15. Where to dine
16. Police/crime

National and international news didn't even make the list.

With enormous appeal to both readers and advertisers, the new feature sections quickly earned their keep. The *St. Louis Post-Dispatch,* for example, introduced its Tuesday consumer supplement, "Dollar/ Sense," in 1977. Circulation for the Tuesday paper immediately climbed by 3,000 copies, making it second only to the Wednesday paper with its special food section chock full of supermarket ads.[37]

There is nothing intrinsically wrong with service features, of course (see pp. 493-94). At their best, they bring important issues home to the reader by casting those issues in a context directly relevant to the reader's life. But all too often the feature explosion has merely replaced hard news with trivia, distracting the attention of reader and reporter alike. When a political reporter can't get five extra inches for a campaign story while the home section is running 50 inches on wicker furniture, it becomes a little hard to take the newspaper seriously. Unfortunately, that's the whole point—many publishers and readers don't want to take the newspaper seriously.

2. Competition. In 1980 there were 1,763 daily newspapers in the United States, exactly the same number as in 1960. The papers were published in more than 1,550 cities. Only 181 cities had two or more newspapers. And most of the two-newspaper cities were still one-publisher cities, with a single owner controlling both a morning and an afternoon paper.

True newspaper competition—two publishers going head-to-head in the same community and the same time slot—is virtually dead in the U.S. Even indirect competition— one publisher in the morning, a different publisher in the afternoon—is a vanishing phenomenon. There were only 35 two-publisher cities in 1978, compared to 51 in 1963, 109 in 1948, 502 in 1923.[38]

We have already discussed the reasons for the growth of media monopolies, and the effects of monopoly ownership on media content (see Chapter 4). For purposes of this chapter, it is enough to say that publishers are always pleased to own the only newspaper (or the only newspapers) in town; without competition, costs are lower and income from advertising and circulation is higher. And as long as the survivor picks up the dead paper's columns, comics, and features, readers seldom object to the loss of a newspaper.

Reporters object, of course. Every time a newspaper folds, a roomful of journalists must start looking for new jobs. And beyond the economic motive, most reporters like the challenge of competition, believing that it keeps them on their toes and produces better journalism. But there is little reporters can do to halt the inexorable trend toward one-newspaper cities.

Now that most of the two-publisher cities are gone, the merger trend continues in one-publisher cities with two papers. The most common scenario is for the afternoon newspaper to quit publishing, joining the morning paper in a so-called "all-day newspaper" that publishes updated afternoon editions. In 1979 alone, six a.m.-p.m. combinations went to a single all-day paper with emphasis on the morning.[39]

Most afternoon metropolitan papers, in fact, are in trouble. Many of those that aren't folding (yet) are adding morning editions in an effort to improve circulation—including such venerable afternoon papers as the *Detroit News,* the *Oakland Tribune,* the *Philadelphia Bulletin,* and the *Dallas Times Herald.*[40] And ten afternoon dailies shifted entirely to the morning in 1979 alone.[41]

What's killing the big-city p.m. paper? To begin with, most breaking news happens too late in the day for an afternoon newspaper to report it properly; the next morning's paper, put together that night, has a better crack at the day's news. Second, the popular-

In 1979, there were 7,954 weekly newspapers in the United States, more than four times the number of dailies. True, the list of weeklies is shorter today than the 1963 all-time high of 8,158. But it's on the way back up. Perhaps more important, weekly circulation, unlike daily circulation, is still climbing. And weeklies are far less vulnerable than dailies to the triple threat of light entertainment, diminished competition, and the pursuit of wealthy readers.

The typical small-town weekly is no longer a mom-and-pop operation, published on an antique press held together with spit and baling wire. That kind of weekly still exists too, but it is quickly giving way to more up-to-date technology, complete with electronic typesetting. The oversupply of journalism graduates in the 1970s provided many weeklies with their first professionally trained reporters. But even without these new staffers, weekly papers have a long tradition of combining folksy community togetherness with hard-hitting local muckraking.

Despite low salaries and long hours, weeklies offer an excellent opportunity for young journalists to sink their teeth into important stories, take pictures, do layout, and learn the newspaper business. Many weeklies employ just two or three reporters, plus the editor/owner. One staffer can have a significant impact. Attracted by this potential, some veterans have even reversed the usual career path, leaving their jobs at big-city papers to edit a local weekly—or even own one.

---

ity of radio news during the afternoon drive time and local TV news in the early evening has cut deeply into the demand for afternoon papers. Third, fewer young people than a generation ago regularly spend their evenings at home; modern lifestyles are more conducive to a morning newspaper habit than an evening one. Fourth, afternoon delivery through rush-hour traffic is much slower and tougher than morning delivery in the uncrowded dawn hours. Fifth, the switch from blue-collar to white-collar work may mean more people staying late at the office or bringing work home, with no time to read an evening paper. And finally, many readers now live in the suburbs, whose local afternoon papers have captured much of the readership and advertising that used to belong to metropolitan p.m. papers.[42]

As newspaper competition continues to dwindle, look for more big-city afternoon newspapers to fold or move to the morning.

3. The Affluent Audience. Metropolitan newspaper journalism had its heyday in the late nineteenth and early twentieth century, as waves of immigrants built the first truly mass circulations the newspaper industry had ever known. Turn-of-the-century newspapers earned their profits partly from readers, but mostly from advertising aimed at this new mass audience.

Starting in the 1950s, two developments substantially changed this picture. The first was television, which could reach a far larger mass audience than any newspaper, and reach it at a far lower cost per reader or viewer. And the second was suburbanization, which saw increasing numbers of middle-class people—and the stores that served them—moving out of the center cities. With television the preferred choice for national product advertising, metropolitan newspapers needed to attract more specialized advertising aimed at more affluent readers. But the affluent readers were moving to the suburbs.

The main beneficiary of these trends was, of course, the suburban newspaper. In terms of return on investment or percentage profits, the most successful newspapers in the U.S.

today are suburban papers. Some are little more than collections of ads from neighborhood stores and shopping centers, with just a sprinkling of local news. The least newsy are often distributed free and are called, appropriately enough, "shoppers." But some suburban newspapers carry almost as much national and international news as their big-city cousins, justifying the claim that readers don't really need to buy another paper as well. Long Island's *Newsday* is often cited as one of the best papers to profit from the middle-class flight to the suburbs; its prize-winning staff frequently outdoes even the nearby *New York Times*. Most suburban papers, of course, fall somewhere in the middle—and nearly all are earning good profits.

In the late 1960s and throughout the 1970s, big-city papers struggled to attract and hold affluent readers by beefing up their suburban coverage. The *New York Times* and the *New York Daily News* added special New Jersey sections; the *Philadelphia Inquirer* focused more on news of southern New Jersey and Delaware; the *St. Louis Post-Dispatch* published a supplement for outlying St. Charles County; the *Washington Post* and the (now dead) *Washington Star* gave more coverage to Maryland and Virginia.[43] Many also hedged their bets by buying a few suburban papers of their own.

This shift in emphasis came, of course, at the expense of the people left in the inner city. The problems of urban people and urban government are certainly no less urgent today than they were two decades ago, but the effort to cultivate suburban readers and advertisers inevitably diminishes newspaper attention to those problems. So does the effort to cultivate affluent readers in the city itself, along with the advertisers who cater to their needs. Consider the service features we discussed earlier. A column on wines serves a very different audience than one on used clothing stores; a how-to piece on refinishing antiques aims at very different readers than one on exterminating roaches. Wines and antiques fill far more newspaper column inches today than used clothing and roaches.

The habit of catering to affluent readers comes naturally to most publishers, who are affluent themselves. In the days when newspapers presumably aimed at a mass audience, this tendency of publishers to focus their papers on upper-class interests was called "country-club journalism." William Allen White had this to say about it back in 1939:

> If he is a smart go-getting up-and-coming publisher in a town of 100,000 to 1,000,000 people, the publisher associates on terms of

---

GOOD-BYE TO GOOD NEWS

A complaint that newspaper editors hear from the public again and again is this one: "Why do you print so much bad news? Why don't you ever print anything good?"

Rather than fall back on the usual response—that good news is seldom a change from the ordinary or expected, and thus is not news at all—Californian Bill Bailey decided to start his own weekly tabloid, *The Good News Paper*. Bailey printed only the listings for stocks that went up. He frequently reported that five million college students had not participated in a particular campus demonstration, or that more than 200 million citizens did not use illegal drugs.

Bailey's paper attracted readers in fifty states and ten foreign countries, and he managed to survive for some sixteen months. In April 1972, he went broke. True to its credo, the paper did not print a notice of its own death. That was left to the carriers of "bad" news in the rest of the profession.[44]

equality with the bankers, the merchant princes, the manufacturers, and the investing brokers. His friends unconsciously color his opinion. If he lives with them on any kind of social terms in the City club or the Country club or the Yacht club or the Racquet club, he must more or less merge his views into the common views of the other capitalists. . . .

So it often happens, alas too often, that a newspaper publisher, reflecting this unconscious class arrogance of the consciously rich, thinks he is printing news when he is doctoring it innocently enough. He thinks he is purveying the truth when much that he offers seems poison to hundreds of thousands of his readers who don't move in his social and economic stratosphere. . . .[45]

The risk that wealthy owners may impose their class biases on content afflicts all media, broadcasting no less than print. But today's media owners are much more interested in profits than in power, so they keep their biases in check. Since television caters to mass-market advertising, it must appeal to a mass audience. Newspapers, by contrast, earn their profits from middle-class audiences and the advertisers that serve them. The middle class wants to read about wines and antiques, not urban problems.

The dynamic has changed, in other words, but not the results. Newspaper news today is more geared than ever to the interests of the well-to-do.

THE REPORTER FIGHTS BACK

In the last section we discussed three newspaper trends that are approved (or at least tolerated) by most publishers and readers, but resented by many reporters: the emphasis on light entertainment, the decline of competition, and the focus on the interests of affluent readers. The inability of reporters to halt these developments has contributed substantially to newsroom cynicism.

Even though reporters lose most of their battles with the publisher-reader coalition,

they are bound to win a few. Two such victories have had a significant effect on the quality of today's newspaper—specialized reporting and interpretive reporting.

Specialized reporting is not a recent invention. The *New York Sun* had its own police reporter back in the 1830s. But except for a few areas (sports, society, business), specialization didn't begin to take hold until the 1950s. A study of fifty-two metropolitan dailies revealed that in 1945 only ten of them had specialized education writers. By 1955 there were twenty-three such writers; by 1960 the number was up to forty. In 1966, only three of the fifty-two papers still had no education reporter on their staffs.[46]

In 1974 the *Milwaukee Journal* (a better-than-average metropolitan daily) listed the following specialized departments and beats: art, auto, aviation, boating, business/financial, education, environment, farm, fashion, food, garden, home furnishings, labor, medicine, men's, motion pictures, music, outdoor, politics, radio/television, real estate, religion, science, society, sports, theater, travel, urban affairs, women's. In addition, a number of the paper's "general assignment" reporters consistently covered certain areas—city hall, police, etc.

Many publishers dislike specialized reporting because it costs more than the all-purpose sort. Specialized reporters need more training, command higher salaries, and grind out fewer words to fit between the ads. Readers don't seem to care much either way. Specialized reporting has grown only because reporters and editors have insisted that specialization is essential to good journalism.

There is little doubt that specialized reporters can do a better job than those on general assignment. A specialist gets to know both the subject and the sources, and develops the background necessary to interpret the story for readers.

But specialization is of little value unless reporters are free to include their expertise in their articles. The traditional who/what/where/when/how/why kind of journalism allows almost no leeway for this sort of interpretation. A complicated political or economic story written in the traditional style can be almost completely incomprehensible. It is not enough for reporters to understand the issues they are writing about; they must be permitted to explain the issues in a way that readers can follow, comprehend, and enjoy.

Hence the rebirth of interpretive reporting. Newspapers in the eighteenth and nineteenth centuries habitually interpreted the news for their readers. But then came the wire services, and just-the-facts objectivity became a hallmark of good journalism. That standard lasted until the Depression of the 1930s, when reporters discovered that neither they nor their readers could make sense of New Deal legislation without plenty of background explanation. At first, interpretation was saved for really big or really complicated stories. But by the mid-1960s, interpretive news articles were becoming more and more common—and more and more outspoken—every day.

The boundary between hard news and interpretive reporting is difficult to define. And there's another boundary that's even harder to draw—between interpretive reporting and a still more subjective, more personal kind of writing that proponents have hailed as the New Journalism. By way of example, consider the six excerpts that follow. The first five are from the *Philadelphia Inquirer* of August 10, 1974, the morning after President Richard Nixon resigned under fire and Gerald Ford was sworn in as the next president. The sixth excerpt also concerns this transition, but represents a kind of writing that the *Inquirer* and most other establishment newspapers would consider unacceptable.

1. Hard News Story. The lead story on the front page, under the byline of Clark Hoyt of the *Inquirer* Washington Bureau, begins:

> Washington—Gerald Rudolph Ford, declaring that "our long national nightmare is over," was sworn in Friday as 38th President of the United States.

> As Richard Nixon flew across the continent and into history after a tear-choked White House farewell, Ford, 61, took the oath of office in a simple, moving ceremony presided over by Chief Justice Warren Burger.

> In a short, eloquent address to the overflow crowd of more than 300 in the White House's East Room and a national television audience, the new President called for healing and reconciliation. . . .

Hoyt's article follows the traditional summary lead pattern, with the who, what, where, when, and why of the story packed into the first few paragraphs. Less important information comes later. A majority of newspaper articles are written according to this formula; they are the meat and potatoes, if not the relish, of the business. Hard news writers are expected to work quickly, to write clearly and dispassionately, to get their facts straight, and to keep their opinions totally out of the story. Because of the importance of this particular event, Hoyt was allowed slightly more latitude than is usual in hard news; phrases like "moving ceremony" and "eloquent address" would probably be cut from an article on a less monumental topic.

2. News Feature. "Portrait Removed in U.S. Offices," by Dominic Sama of the *Inquirer* staff, begins on the lefthand side of the front page, below the fold:

> When President Richard M. Nixon's resignation became effective at noon Friday, his framed picture was stripped from the walls in thousands of Federal offices, but there was nothing to take its place.

> "I know it's a ritualistic thing to do during an election, but the significance of it escapes me at the moment," said a postal worker at the Media Post Office in Delaware County.

> "Mr. Nixon's picture has been removed, but I'm quite sure no one had the foresight to have a picture of President Gerald Ford printed. . . ."

News features are intended to throw additional light on a hard news event (in which case they are often called "sidebars"), or to deal with less weighty topics. Sama is expected to be not only accurate, but entertaining as well, and he is permitted greater stylistic freedom than Hoyt in organizing and writing his article. Such techniques as humor, suspense, and irony are appropriate. But language must remain within the conventional boundaries of the newspaper, and Sama's own views are still no part of the story.

3. News Analysis. "All-New Ballgame In Politics," by Loye Miller, Jr. of the *Inquirer* Washington Bureau, begins below the fold on page one:

> Washington—With the departure of Richard M. Nixon, it looks like a brand new ballgame in American politics.
>
> From Maine to California, Republicans who were fearfully anticipating that Watergate would bring down massive defeat on the GOP next November are taking new hope.
>
> Their new optimism may prove ill founded, but there is widespread belief that the Nixon resignation will remove the Watergate monkey from the backs of Republican candidates. . . .

Also called an interpretive story, the news analysis helps the reader deal with complex issues by explaining their origin and likely impact. Such stories almost always appear as companions to major hard-news articles. Miller is expected to bring his professional knowledge and judgment to bear on the issue; the reader must thus judge the story in the context of Miller's special expertise. Unlike Hoyt and Sama, Miller is entitled to draw conclusions—but they must be based on the facts (which he also reports) and his interpretations of them. He is not to be a cheerleader for any particular ideology, and he is expected to modify his conclusions when new facts arise. Like Sama, he has some freedom in language and organization, but is still bound by the conventions of the paper.

4. Signed Column. Appearing on the editorial page is this column by William Raspberry of the *Washington Post* syndicated service:

> Mr. Nixon finally was driven to confess at least a little of what we knew all along. . . .
>
> The system works: That is the lesson of Watergate. The system works. . . .
>
> The thing that keeps haunting me is how much the vindication of the system is the result of two freak accidents: Frank Wills' discovery of the Watergate burglars and the President's decision to bug his own office. . . .
>
> If he hadn't tape recorded himself and his fellow conspirators, or if he had taken the tapes to the furnace room as soon as their existence became public knowledge, we would have suspected much but known very little, and Mr. Nixon would still be firmly in charge of the government. . . .

The column is a personal statement by the individual who writes it, and readership is limited to those who care what he or she thinks. Readers come to know the personal bias of each columnist—liberal, conservative, hawk, dove, or whatever—and pick the people they want to read. Raspberry, like all columnists, filters facts from hard news and features through his own particular ideology, and emerges with the sort of thought-provoking synthesis that would seldom be permitted on the news pages. Style, language, and organization are all up to the individual columnist, and vary from the conventional to the counter-cultural.

5. Editorial. Appearing on the lefthand side of the editorial page, this statement from the *Inquirer*'s management carries the headline, "It's President Ford Now—And He Begins Well":

> . . . Gerald Ford has never been known as an orator, and he described his own remarks following his inauguration as "just a little straight talk among friends."

The *Dubuque* (Iowa) *Telegraph-Herald* interviewed a random sample of physicians in its circulation area to draw a detailed picture of the local health-care system. The *Philadelphia Inquirer* sampled 1,034 criminal cases to test the claim of the prosecutor's office that lenient judges were putting criminals back on the streets to commit more crimes. The *Roanoke* (Va.) *Times & World-News* analyzed campaign contributions to trace the path of money in politics. The *Miami Herald* interviewed samples of Latins and non-Latins to study the process of cultural diffusion since Cuban refugees started arriving in Miami in the early 1960s.[47]

All these are examples of precision journalism, in which reporters borrow the techniques of social science and market research in order to report accurately and conclusively stories that traditional approaches leave vague and undocumented. Precision journalism demands new skills like sampling, standardized interviewing, and statistics—skills that some recent journalism graduates possess and that some mid-career journalists are going back to school to acquire.

Many publishers and readers are not especially enthusiastic about precision journalism. It costs more than conventional reporting, and it makes for tougher reading. Even some reporters prefer to stick with quotable quotes, unencumbered by statistical methodology. But an increasing number of reporters are convinced that getting a percentage right is just as important as getting a source's name right. Precision journalism is on the upswing.

But there was eloquence in the simplicity with which he spoke, and after too long a period in which it has been a scarce commodity at the highest level of our government straight talk is welcome.

The shattered trust of the American people in our political process will not be restored overnight, but Mr. Ford has made a prompt and persuasive beginning. . . .

The editorial is usually unsigned; it is where the newspaper speaks—with one voice —to its readers. Good editorials have a strong point of view, and attempt to persuade the reader that they are right, based on facts, logic, and sometimes even emotion. Of course the paper should have covered the same topic in its news columns, so that readers can make up their own minds whether to accept or reject the paper's position. Language and style are entirely up to the editorial writer, but traditionally tend to be dignified, perhaps even pompous.

6. New Journalism. Here is a sixth approach to the same subject. This one most definitely did not appear in the *Inquirer,* but rather in the May 6, 1974, issue of *New York* magazine. The author is political reporter Richard Reeves:

I have seen the future and it scares the hell out of me.

I have seen Gerald Rudolph Ford in Troy, Michigan, bringing up busing sixteen times in a seventeen-minute press conference when none of the questions were about busing. . . . I have heard him at Harvard talking about "that great Russian writer" because he can't pronounce Solzhenitsyn. . . . I have seen him, from a chartered airplane, playing golf in the Xanadu isolation of the guarded Annenberg fortress in Palm Springs—choosing to spend his time with the rich, the trying-to-get-rich, and a personal staff that can most charitably be described as being in over their collective heads. . . .

Even more than the typical columnist, Reeves is a very visible part of his article. He uses the forbidden "I," and a richness of language that would make a newspaper copy editor blanch. Much of what he writes is fact (hyped a bit to involve the reader). Much is opinion. Sometimes it is hard to tell which is which. But for those readers who have come to trust Reeves, this style of reporting has many rewards—it is entertaining; it successfully communicates mood as well as information; it can cut through the pomposity and doubletalk to the core of the matter. Of course for readers who don't trust Reeves, this sort of journalism is totally unreliable. And for readers who don't know whom to trust, who tend to trust everything they read in the papers, the New Journalism is a dizzying, disorienting, and potentially misleading experience.

The New Journalism isn't new. The colonial press was intensely personal; so was the Penny Press in the 1830s and the Yellow Press in the 1890s. It can be argued, in fact, that newspaper "objectivity" was nothing but a passing fad that is already on its way out. Perhaps by 1990 newspaper reporters will write as personally and subjectively as newspaper publishers and editors wrote in the early history of American journalism.

But probably not. Many publishers and even many reporters object to the New Journalism, because they fear it will open the door to biased reporting, and because New Journalists tend to be more liberal than their objective colleagues, their readers, or their publishers. H. Lang Rogers of the *Joplin* (Missouri) *Globe* put the objection this way: "We find fewer of the young journalists with the basic honesty and integrity to seek to write entirely objectively and to bend over backwards to keep their own beliefs from slanting their writings."[48]

The problem of biased reporters is a serious one (see pp. 113-15). Heavily personal newswriting in the style of Richard Reeves probably shouldn't become the mainstay of daily journalism. But somewhere between this New Journalism and just-the-facts ob-

jectivity lies the future of newspapers: interpretive reporting. In their efforts to do something broadcasting can't do, publishers are getting used to it. In their rediscovered pleasure at the art of expository writing, readers are getting used to it. And the best of the new crop of young reporters are insisting on it.

The typical publisher, after all, wants only to make money. The typical reader wants only to be entertained. But reporters—especially the under-30 reporters—want to change the world. Perhaps we should give them a chance to try.

But regardless of the future of the New Journalism, newspaper reporting will never be predominantly a world-changing enterprise. And it shouldn't be. The essence of newspaper journalism is telling people what happened, especially telling people what happened at a routine event that isn't photogenic enough to make the TV newscasts, but is nonetheless important to some readers, who rely on newspapers to tell them about it. The most successful reporters, the ones who wind up covering world-changing events, usually enjoy covering routine events as well. They just like to tell people what happened.

How would you summarize the typical daily newspaper as of 1981? It is mildly entertaining, though not as entertaining as many readers apparently want it to be. It is reasonably profitable, though static circulations and new technologies give publishers ample reason to worry about future profits. And it is moderately informative, though reporters justly complain that hard news is losing ground to service features for the affluent. What will the typical daily newspaper be like in 1991? The conflicting wishes of readers, publishers, and reporters will determine the answer.

Notes

1 N. R. Kleinfield, "The Great Press Chain," *New York Times Magazine,* April 8, 1979, p. 50.

2 Leo Bogart, "The '80s: Readership," *Presstime,* January, 1980, pp. 24-25.

3 John P. Robinson, "The Changing Reading Habits of the American Public," *Journal of Communication*, Winter, 1980, pp. 141-52.

4 John P. Robinson and Leo W. Jeffres, "The Changing Role of Newspapers in the Age of Television," *Journalism Monographs*, September, 1979, p. 23.

5 Robinson, "The Changing Reading Habits of the American Public," pp. 141-52.

6 Bogart, "The '80s: Readership," pp. 24-25.

7 Ruth Clark, *Changing Needs of Changing Readers* (New York: Yankelovich, Skelly & White, Inc., May, 1979), pp. 2-6.

8 Charles E. Swanson, "What They Read in 130 Daily Newspapers," *Journalism Quarterly*, Fall, 1955, p. 414.

9 "Sell the Papers!" *Harper's Monthly*, June, 1925, p. 5.

10 "Public Perceptions of Television and Other Mass Media," Television Information Office, 1979 (pamphlet).

11 Marquita Moss, "Reporter Turnover on Texas Daily Newspapers," *Journalism Quarterly*, Summer, 1978, pp. 354-56.

12 Chilton R. Bush, *News Research for Better Newspapers* (New York: American Newspaper Publishers Association Foundation, 1968), III, pp. 80-82.

13 Theodore Dreiser, *A Book About Myself* (New York: Boni and Liveright, 1922), p. 396.

14 Richard Reeves, "A Media Monster—Who, Me?" *New York*, November 26, 1973, pp. 37-38.

15 William A. Sievert, "Watergate Floods the J-Schools," *Chronicle of Higher Education*, September 3, 1974.

16 Alvin E. Austin, "Codes, Documents, Declarations Affecting the Press," Department of Journalism, University of North Dakota, August, 1964, p. 17.

17 "Annual Cost and Revenue Figures for 34,470-Circ. Daily," *Editor & Publisher*, May 12, 1979, p. 15.

18 "Advertising: The Name Is News," *New York Times*, April 25, 1973, p. 55.

19 "Facts About 1980 Newspapers," American Newspaper Publishers Association, 1980, pp. 9-10 (pamphlet).

20 John Corry, "The Los Angeles *Times*," *Harper's Magazine*, December, 1969, pp. 75-81.

21 "Coast Papers Get Automation Pact," *New York Times*, January 21, 1973, p. 46. "Kheel Gives Details on Innovative Pact of Papers and Union," *New York Times*, May 25, 1974, p. 1. "City Papers on Threshold of Future As Result of 11-Year Automation Pact," *New York Times*, July 29, 1974, p. 12.

22 Clark Newsome, "Newspapers, Labor Enter 'New Era,' " *Presstime*, August, 1980, pp. 4-7.

23 *Ibid.*, p. 4.

24 "Annual Cost and Revenue Figures for 34,470-Circ. Daily," p. 15.

25 Emily Yoffee, "Guild Discovers Site for Sore Eyes," *Washington Journalism Review*, July/August, 1980, p. 12.

26 Larry D. Kurtz, "The Electronic Editor," *Journal of Communication*, Summer, 1980, p. 57.

27 Margaret Genovese, "Videotext: Information at the Push of a Button," *Presstime*, June, 1980, p. 18.

28 William D. Rinehart, "The Past Is Littered with Electronic Flops," *Presstime*, June, 1980, p. 21.

29 Cindy Ris, "Electronic Newspapers Could Alter Shape of the $4.6 Billion Classified Ad Market," *Wall Street Journal*, August 11, 1980, p. 15.

30 *Ibid.*, p. 15.

31 Cindy Ris, "Electronic Newspaper Makes a Debut; High Cost of Service Is Key Problem," *Wall Street Journal*, July 8, 1980, p. 14.

32 *Ibid.*, p. 14.

33 Bill Kelly, "All The News That's Fit to Compute," *Washington Journalism Review*, April, 1980, pp. 19-20.

34 A. J. Liebling, *The Press* (New York: Ballantine Books, 1961), p. 23.

35 Cary B. Ziter, "What Do We Have Here, the Daily Paper or the Supermarket Weekly?" *Quill*, December, 1979, p. 29.

36 Hugh Morgan, "Special Section Craze Sweeping the Country," *Editor & Publisher*, March 29, 1980, p. 31.

37 *Ibid.*, p. 31.

38 James N. Rosse, "The Decline of Direct Newspaper Competition," *Journal of Communication*, Spring, 1980, pp. 65-66.

39 "Morning Becomes Elective in Circulation Switches," *Editor & Publisher*, January 5, 1980, p. 14.

40 "All-Day Dailies," *Time*, January 15, 1979, p. 57.

41 "Morning Becomes Elective in Circulation Switches," p. 14.

42 "Morning Paper Pitfalls and Benefits Disclosed," *Editor & Publisher*, January 5, 1979, pp. 11, 14.

43 "Big-City Newspapers Stepping Up Their Coverage of News in Suburbs," *New York Times*, April 23, 1973, p. 36.

44 *New York Times*, April 5, 1972, p. 52.

45 George L. Bird and Frederic E. Merwin, eds., *The Press and Society* (Englewood Cliffs, N.J.: Prentice-Hall, 1951), p. 74.

46 Charles T. Duncan, "The 'Education Beat' on 52 Major Newspapers," *Journalism Quarterly*, Summer, 1966, pp. 336-38.

47 Philip Meyer, "Precision Journalism in the United States," *Media Reporter*, December, 1979, p. 15.

48 "Newspapers Blamed for Loss of Image," *Editor & Publisher*, April 5, 1969, p. 12.

Suggested Readings

ARGYRIS, CHRIS, *Behind The Front Page*. San Francisco: Jossey-Bass Publishers, 1974.

BAGDIKIAN, BEN H., "Fat Newspapers and Slim Coverage," *Columbia Journalism Review*, September/October, 1973.

———, "The Little Old Lady of Dubuque," *The New York Times Magazine*, February 3, 1974.

BOGART, LEO, "Urban Papers Under Pressure," *Columbia Journalism Review*, September/October, 1974.

CLARK, RUTH, "Changing Needs of Changing Readers, A Qualitative Study of the New Social Contract Between Newspaper Editors and Readers," Commissioned by the American Society of Newspaper Editors as part of the Newspaper Readership Project. Reston, Virginia: American Newspaper Publishers Association, 1979.

GENOVESE, MARGARET, "Videotext: Information at the Push of a Button," *Presstime*, June, 1980.

ISMACH, ARNOLD H., and EVERETTE E. DENNIS, "A Profile of Newspaper and Television Reporters in a Metropolitan Setting," *Journalism Quarterly*, Winter, 1978.

KLEINFIELD, N. R., "The Great Press Chain," *The New York Times Magazine*, April 8, 1979.

LIEBLING, A. J., *The Press*. New York: Ballantine Books, 1961.

OGAN, CHRISTINE L., and DAVID H. WEAVER, "Job Satisfaction in Selected U.S. Daily Newspapers: A Study of Male and Female Top-Level Managers," *Mass Comm Review*, Winter, 1978/1979.

ROBINSON, JOHN P., and LEO W. JEFFRES, "The Changing Role of Newspapers in the Age of Television," *Journalism Monographs*, September, 1979.

ROSSE, JAMES N., "The Decline of Direct Newspaper Competition," *Journal of Communication*, Spring, 1980.

SALISBURY, HARRISON E., *Without Fear or Favor, An Uncompromising Look at The New York Times*. New York: Times Books, 1980.

SCHUDSON, MICHAEL, *Discovering the News*. New York: Basic Books, 1978.

TALESE, GAY, *The Kingdom and the Power*. New York: World Publishing Co., 1969.

TUCHMAN, GAYE, *Making News: A Study in the Construction of Reality*. New York: Free Press, 1978.

UDELL, JON G., *The Economics of the American Newspaper*. New York: Hastings House, 1978.

WOLFE, TOM, *The New Journalism*. New York: Harper & Row, 1973.

Chapter 11
Magazines and Books

The typical magazine of the past was a potpourri of features and fiction, aimed at a general audience. Television has now usurped that role, and most successful magazines today are highly specialized. They are run by an editor and staff who know precisely who their readers and advertisers are. While some of these specialized magazines can still claim "mass" circulations, the future of the magazine industry clearly lies in providing a unique service to specialized audiences.

Caskie Stinnett, former editor of *Holiday* magazine, tells this story which he says "sums up the magazine business today." Stinnett was on a travel junket to Portugal with a number of other writers, including *Holiday* contributor Marc Connelly. At a reception for the mayor of Lisbon the visiting journalists were asked to stand and identify their magazines. Connelly announced that he represented *Popular Wading,* a journal for enthusiasts of shallow-water sports. It specialized, said Connelly, in medical articles, particularly the ravages of "immersion foot."

Comments Stinnett: "It was hilarious, and we were all howling. But you know, I don't think anyone would laugh today. In fact, I'll almost bet that somewhere out there, you could find a special-audience magazine for waders."[1]

GENERAL MAGAZINES

The term "magazine" comes from the French word *magasin,* meaning "storehouse." The earliest magazines were literally storehouses of sketches, poems, essays, and assorted other content. Their incredible diversity led journalism historian Frank Luther Mott to offer this definition of the magazine: "A bound pamphlet issued more or less regularly and containing a variety of reading matter."[2]

For more than two hundred years, the most general magazines were invariably the most popular, and the most profitable. The mass-circulation leaders in the late 1800s were the *Saturday Evening Post, Collier's, Leslie's* and *Harper's Weekly. Collier's* and the *Post* continued into the twentieth century, and were joined by *McCall's, Life, Look,* and the *Reader's Digest.* All these magazines earned substantial profits from subscriptions and newsstand sales. Except for the *Digest,* they earned even more from advertising.

In 1929, the nation's 365 leading magazines

had an average circulation of 94,836. By 1950, the 567 top magazines were averaging 223,581 readers apiece.[3] Magazine circulation—and magazine revenue—was at an all-time high.

Then came television. TV did comparatively little damage to the public's appetite for general magazines. But it devastated their appeal to advertisers. The largest magazines could offer a readership of merely a few million; a run-of-the-mill network series offered tens of millions of viewers. And television ads cost less too. In 1970, a minute of time on NBC's "Laugh-In" (with 17 million viewers) sold for $3.82 per thousand households. A full-page four-color ad in *Look* (with 7 million readers) ran $7.16 per thousand households. Nearly three times as many people watched NFL football as read *Life* magazine—yet both ads sold for the same amount, $64,200. Naturally, advertisers preferred "Laugh-In" to *Look,* NFL football to *Life.*

The mass magazines responded to the challenge of television by trying to build TV-size circulations. In the dozen years after 1950, both *McCall's* and *Look* doubled their readership. In 1960, the *Saturday Evening Post, Life, Look,* and the *Reader's Digest* proudly noted that a single ad in each of the four magazines would reach every other American 2.3 times.[4]

The technique for building circulation

DEATH (AND REBIRTH) OF THE POST

For 72 years the *Saturday Evening Post* was the flagship of the Curtis Publishing Company empire. It had a circulation of 6.8 million satisfied readers in 1968—and it was in serious trouble.

When Martin Ackerman became president of Curtis in 1968, the *Post* was deep in debt. Advertisers, it seems, simply were not interested in the *Post's* rural readership and middle-American appeal. Ackerman's battle plan was simple and straightforward: stop fighting for circulation, cut back to three million readers, and turn the *Post* into "a high-class magazine for a class audience." The subscribers to be retained were those living in designated Nielsen A and B counties. These are television rating terms for the most affluent counties in America—the ones advertisers are most eager to reach.

Of the *Post's* 6.8 million subscribers, 4.5 million lived in the Nielsen A and B areas. Ackerman instructed his computer to drop not only the 2.3 million C and D area people, but 1.5 million from the B areas as well—leaving him with a circulation of three million big spenders. *Life* agreed to purchase the extra B subscriptions. But no one was interested in the small-town C and D folks. Form letters went out, telling subscribers that the *Post* no longer wanted them. Among those so informed were Arkansas Governor Winthrop Rockefeller, former *Post* editor Ben Hibbs, and small-town boy Martin Ackerman.

In an effort to impress Madison Avenue, Ackerman spent a lot of money advertising the "new" *Post.* He prepared four dummy issues of the magazine to show off the planned "classy" approach. But advertisers were unconvinced. They doubted the magazine could slough off its rural image so easily. The *Post* earned millions of enemies in 1968, but very few new advertisers. It continued to lose upwards of $400,000 a month. Ackerman finally admitted defeat, and in 1969 the *Saturday Evening Post* folded.[5]

It emerged under new management a few years later as a quarterly magazine for nostalgia fans, and found success on a smaller scale. By 1980 the *Post* had 666,000 readers, each willing to spend $1.50 an issue (or $9.95 for a nine-issue subscription) for the *Post's* new blend of traditional fiction, articles, and nostalgia. Associate Publisher Robert Silvers calls it "a specialized family magazine."[6]

was simple: offer cut-rate subscriptions at a price so low that it would be silly not to subscribe. Newsstand sales, naturally, declined. During World War II, *Life* and *Look* sold 55 percent of their copies at the newsstand price. By the mid-1960s, the number of newsstand sales had dropped to less than 10 percent. As the subscription price went down, production and distribution costs rose steadily. Some time in the late 1950s the two passed each other. It was now possible to subscribe to a magazine for less than the cost of printing it. Advertisers, of course, were expected to make up the difference.

They didn't. Take *Life,* for example. In 1969, the magazine sold for an average of 12 cents per copy. But it cost 41 cents per copy to edit, print, and distribute. For *Life* to break even, advertisers had to cough up the remaining 29 cents per copy. At the start of 1970, ad revenues amounted to only 27 cents per copy. Every week *Life* was actually losing two cents on each copy sold.[7]

Over the next three years the situation went from bad to worse. Because of its low circulation rates, *Life* was forced to charge very high advertising rates—more than twice as much per household as TV (or *TV Guide*). Advertisers were unwilling to pay the premium, and so gross ad revenue dropped from its high of nearly $170 million in 1966 to $91 million in 1971.[8] Meanwhile, production and distribution costs were skyrocketing. Newsprint was a particularly big expense for the oversized magazine, and scheduled postal rate hikes would raise the cost of mailing by as much as 170 percent in five years.[9]

On December 29, 1972, *Life* published its last weekly issue. The magazine that had pioneered a new style of journalism—a combination of tight writing and huge, effective photographs—could not compete with television.

But that is not the end of the story. Time, Inc. kept the image of *Life* alive with a series of special editions, whose success at $1.50 to $2.00 per issue led the company to reintroduce *Life* in 1978 as a monthly "specialized" magazine, with an initial press run

of 700,000 at $1.50 a copy.[10] The new *Life* was designed for "high-quality consumer readers . . . willing to pay top prices," explained Andrew Heiskell, chairman of Time, Inc.[11] It was an instant success.

It took twenty years for the magazine industry to learn that it could not beat television at the numbers game. In the process many magazines died, including such giants as *Collier's, Women's Home Companion,* and *Look*. *Life* and the *Saturday Evening Post* returned, not as the circulation leaders they had been, but as more specialized magazines, aimed at smaller audiences willing to pay higher prices. Their publishers at last understood that while magazines can no longer profitably offer advertisers a huge audience, they can offer something nearly as valuable: a specialized audience.

SPECIALIZED MAGAZINES

The special-interest magazine is nothing new. When film stars first captured the public's imagination, *Photoplay* was founded to cater to that interest. A new hobby in the 1930s gave rise to *Model Railroader;* a labor shortage in the 1940s led to *Jobs;* a sudden craze of the 1950s gave birth to *Skin Diver*. But the number of specialized magazines has increased dramatically in the past decade. *Writer's Market* is an annual magazine directory for free-lance writers; the 1980 edition listed more than 3,000 publications, including:

28 Animal magazines
14 Art magazines
14 Astrology and psychic magazines
39 Automotive and motorcycle magazines
12 Aviation magazines
 9 Black magazines
30 Business and finance magazines
19 Confession magazines
15 Consumer service magazines

Writer's Market, of course, covers only the major magazines that regularly commission free-lance articles. The 1979-80 edition of the *Standard Periodical Directory* lists 68,720 periodicals in the U.S.—including roughly 4,000 college and alumni publications, another 4,000 corporate house organs, some 3,500 religious magazines, another 3,500 education journals, etc. Name any special interest and you will likely find a magazine devoted to it—even wading.

The specialized magazine is a perfect vehicle for advertising. It offers advertisers a chance at a hand-picked audience. Suppose, for example, that you were a manufacturer of low-calorie foods. If you could afford it, you'd probably advertise on television and in the newspapers. But despite the higher cost per thousand readers, you certainly wouldn't miss a chance to take out an ad in *Weight Watchers Magazine*. The average reader of that publication is far more likely to be interested in your product (and hence your ad) than the average newspaper reader or TV viewer.

Some magazines earn so much money from advertising that they don't even need to sell copies; they give them away instead. This is most common among trade journals. A magazine for plastics manufacturers, for example, is well-advised to send a free copy to every plastics manufacturer in the country. That makes it a superlative advertising vehicle for companies that produce the sorts of supplies and equipment plastics manufacturers use. Aside from trade publications, free-circulation magazines include the *American Legion Magazine, Scouting, Today's Education, Signature* (for Diner's Club members), and *TWA Ambassador*.

THE FIRST MS. DECADE

A publication devoted to the concerns of 52 percent of the American people shouldn't really be called a "special-interest magazine." But *Ms.* isn't for all women, only for those who want to read a monthly about feminist issues and feminist culture. When the magazine was founded in 1971, many male publishers predicted it wouldn't find enough readers of that sort to survive. They were wrong.

Support came slowly—but it came. Katherine Graham, publisher of the *Washington Post*, invested $20,000 to start the ball rolling. Warner Communications offered $1 million in exchange for 25 percent of the stock; the women who ran the magazine accepted the financing but retained a majority interest. By September of 1973, after only sixteen monthly issues, *Ms.* had built a paid circulation of 350,000, with a phenomenal subscription renewal rate of 70 percent. Readers were bombarding its offices in New York City with hundreds of telephone calls a day, a thousand letters a week, and 1,500 unsolicited manuscripts a month.[12] *Ms.* had become a national clearinghouse for feminist information.

Ms. readers are relatively high in education and income, and are thus attractive to advertisers—even though the magazine refuses all ads that portray a clichéd or belittling stereotype of women. In October, 1972, *Ms.* earned $47,600 in ad revenue; one year later the month's figure was $99,000.[13] By 1980, *Ms.* was grossing as much as $300,000 a month from its ads, with a paid circulation of over 500,000.

Despite this success, the magazine never really made money. After operating at a loss for six of its first seven years, the owners sold *Ms.* to the Ms. Foundation, which they had originally created to finance feminist causes from the magazine's hoped-for profits. Nonprofit status qualified *Ms.* for lower postal rates and other advantages, and thus insured the magazine's survival.[14]

Free-circulation magazines almost always have a "controlled" readership; only certain people are permitted to receive them. Sometimes the readership is made up of members of an organization. Sometimes it is a captive audience like airplane passengers. But usually the major common ground of a free magazine's readers is that they are a ready market for some specialized group of advertisers. Sometimes the editorial content of such a magazine is quite weak. It is read for its ads.

But specialized magazines don't appeal to advertisers alone. They attract readers as well—readers who are willing to pay high subscription prices for just the right magazine. Martin Gross, then editor and publisher of the *Intellectual Digest,* predicted in 1970 that in the next decade "you'll see more and more magazines supported almost totally by circulation. This has to come with the trend toward specialized reading and a stronger reader commitment."[15]

The most specialized reader-supported magazines are probably the paid newsletters, which now number more than 6,000. They range in circulation from a few dozen to the 430,000 readers served by the *Kiplinger Washington Letter.*[16] Some of the smaller ones are among the most successful—with no ads at all. If you're in the energy business, for example, you can choose from several monthly, weekly, and even daily newsletters on federal government energy activities—policies announced, grants awarded, etc. Subscriptions run as high as $800 a year—a bargain if you really need the information. Many branches of the federal Department of Energy subscribe to find out what the other branches are up to.

Or consider *The Corporate Director,* founded in 1980 with a subscription rate of $890 for six bi-monthly issues. Subscribers receive enough copies for all their board members. The initial list included 75 major corporations, but publisher Stanley Greenfield has an ambitious circulation goal: 350. It won't be easy—he's competing against two already established magazines in the very same specialized field.[17]

There are thus two ways for a specialized magazine to earn a profit. By offering advertisers just the right market for their products and services, it can justify high advertising rates. By offering readers editorial content that is tailored to match their interests, it can justify high subscription rates. Many of the most successful specialized magazines are able to make money from both advertisers and readers.

MASS MAGAZINES FIGHT BACK

General-interest magazines face enormous difficulties in the television age. But the death of the original *Life* did not signal that all successful magazines of the future would be modeled on *The Corporate Director.* Today there are more than 50 American magazines with circulations over a million. Here are the top ten.[18]

TV Guide	19.5 million
Reader's Digest	18.1 million
National Geographic	10.2 million
Better Homes & Gardens	8.0 million
Family Circle	7.6 million
Women's Day	7.5 million
McCall's	6.5 million
Ladies' Home Journal	5.6 million
Playboy	5.5 million
Good Housekeeping	5.2 million

Six of these ten also rank in the top ten in total revenues.[19] Though their expenses are high in proportion to their circulations, all ten (except the non-profit *National Geographic*) are earning healthy profits as well.

What do mass-circulation magazines do to survive and prosper in an age of magazine specialization? First of all, they specialize too. The specialization is obvious for *TV Guide, National Geographic,* and *Playboy.* The *Reader's Digest,* though broader in scope, specializes in a treatment and style aimed at the busy middle class; *Digest* editors joke that the magazine is written to be read on the commuter train. The other six magazines in the top ten are all expressly for women— but they are for somewhat different groups of women. Each magazine attempts to carve out its own unique appeal. Instead of trying to be minimally interesting to just about everyone, it struggles to be absolutely essential to a particular group. The appropriate readers will thus pay more for the magazine, and the appropriate advertisers will pay more to reach those readers. Most of the other magazines over a million are more specialized still—*Cosmopolitan* (2.8 million) for the urban single woman, *Field and Stream* (2.1 million) for the hunting and fishing enthusiast, etc.

Even the new so-called general-interest magazines, *People* (2.5 million) and *Us* (1.0 million) are far more specialized than the original *Life*. When Time, Inc. launched *People* in 1974, some cynics within the company referred to it as *"Life* with a lobotomy." In fact, *People* specializes in personalities. It is the magazine of celebrity gossip. It is also the magazine success story of the 1970s, ranking in the top ten in both revenues and profits.[20] The carbon-copy *Us* started three years later, and has been far less successful. In 1980, after losing both money and prestige on the magazine, the New York Times Company sold it to an affiliate of the Macfadden Group, which also publishes *True Story* and *True Confessions*.[21]

Mass-circulation magazines can specialize in another way as well—by dividing their readers into demographic categories and selling ads by the category. To attract advertisers of luxury products, for example, *Mc-Call's* and *Better Homes & Gardens* publish special zip-coded editions for high-income areas. *Time* has a college student edition, a doctor's edition, an educator's edition, etc., for advertisers interested in reaching these particular audiences. When the *Reader's Digest* started its special edition for high-income

readers, it charged $11.25 per thousand copies for an ad, versus $3.33 per thousand for the *Digest's* regular edition. Editorial content in these demographic editions is usually identical; only the ads are different.

This tactic can earn a mass magazine a good deal of extra income. But in the long run, it does nothing to rid the magazine of its unwealthy, unspecialized readers—the ones advertisers would rather reach on television, not in print. The only real solution is to force these readers to pay the full cost of the magazine. And so cut-rate subscriptions have pretty much disappeared, and annual subscription costs have soared. Inevitably the less rich and less interested readers drop their subscriptions. This leaves the publisher with a smaller number of readers who are paying more for the magazine, and who—since they have more money—are more attractive to advertisers as well.

For many comparatively general magazines, the move away from cut-rate subscriptions has meant a move away from subscriptions altogether. As the gap between the subscription price and the newsstand price has narrowed, more and more readers have chosen to buy their favorite magazines —when they feel like it—at the store. For such magazines as *TV Guide,* the *Reader's Digest, Family Circle,* and *Woman's Day,* supermarket and drugstore sales have proved even more successful than newsstands. The stores like this trend because the commissions are high—20 percent, or eight cents on each 40-cent *TV Guide.* And the publishers like it because they save on overhead and simplify distribution. In the 1970s, roughly 60 percent of all retail magazine sales were at chain stores.

As postal rates continue to climb, magazine circulation will inevitably move from the mails to the chain-store racks. Highly specialized magazines will still have to rely on mail subscriptions, but the more general ones may well abandon the postal system just as they have abandoned the cut-rate subscription.

THE COST OF MAILING

Though general magazines may manage to trade their subscriptions for over-the-counter sales, specialized publications can't. Newsstands and supermarkets value their shelf space too highly to handle a magazine with only a dozen interested readers in town. Such a magazine *must* use the mails.

In the past, the government has always indirectly subsidized the magazine and newspaper industries by means of the inexpensive second-class mailing rate. But since its reorganization in 1971, the U.S. Postal Service has tried to reduce its deficit by making all mailers—including magazines—pay the real cost of delivery. In 1972, the Postal Service proposed a series of rate hikes that would nearly double the postage bills of many magazines over a five-year period.[22]

In response, many magazines reduced their page size or switched to a lighter paper (since second-class rates are based on weight). Many more joined an industrywide lobbying campaign to convince Congress that it should roll back the proposed increases. Particular attention was focused on the plight of the money-losing political journals, such as the *New Republic* and *National Review.*

In 1974, Congress agreed to spread the increase out over a greater number of years than the Postal Service had proposed. That lessened the immediate burden, but not the long-term problem. By 1979, *Newsweek,* for example, had an annual postal bill of $15.1 million, compared to $6.2 million in 1972.[23] The days of bargain postal rates are over for the magazine industry.

The problem is so serious that many magazines have experimented with alternative delivery systems. In 1979, *Better Homes & Gardens* used private carriers in 20 cities, and *Reader's Digest, Time,* and *Newsweek* had their own small-scale experiments.[24] But the magazines that are hardest hit by the new postal rates are the highly specialized ones, whose circulations are too small and too spread out to rely on retail sales or private carriers. Their only distribution possibility is the mail. Either subscribers will agree to pay the added cost or these magazines will fold.

THE STAFF

Once upon a time, a strong-willed would-be editor started a newspaper. Today, he or she is far more likely to start a magazine.

Why? For one thing, the magazine industry is extremely fluid. Of the 20 most profitable magazines in 1927, half were gone by 1950. Of the top 20 magazines in 1962, 15 were not yet founded in 1920.[25] It is possible, in other words, to start a magazine today and be an instant success tomorrow. It is also possible to be an instant flop. Of the 200 to 350 new magazines announced every year, many collapse without ever producing a single issue because of poor test results or inadequate financing. A majority die within a couple of years. "The chances of making it are brutally grim," says one longtime magazine investor. "It's like making movies. I'd say the odds are ten to one. It depends on who's starting it. If Time has a child, the odds are much shorter, maybe two to one. But every damn fool thinks he has an idea for a new magazine."[26]

The specialization of magazines allows plenty of running room for editors with unusual ideas. One newspaper is pretty much like another; it has to try to appeal to all the readers in town. A magazine, on the other hand, can aim at attracting a small, devoted readership of people who think like the editor.

Magazines, notes Clay Felker (himself founder of the highly successful *New York* magazine), are "peculiarly and stubbornly personal products."[28] *Time, Life,* and *Fortune* were the visions of Henry R. Luce. *Playboy* is Hugh Hefner. Arnold Gingrich guided *Esquire* to popularity; Helen Gurley Brown made a winner of *Cosmopolitan;* Robert Peterson did the same with *Hot Rod.* Most of the outstanding specialized magazines—the ones that attract and hold readers who are willing to pay for what they get—are the work of a single mind.

They almost have to be. The editor of a typical monthly trade magazine has a staff of only five or six—a managing editor, an art director, and a few subeditors, period. The editor can give personal attention to every word in the magazine.

Magazines are written by staff writers, free-lance writers, or some combination of the two. Staff writers, of course, work on salary. Free-lancers are paid by the article, at rates ranging from $25 an article all the way up to $10,000 an article. While there are as many as 100,000 people in the country who consider themselves free-lance writers, most work only part-time. And the median annual income of the 500 established free-lancers in the American Society of Journalists and Authors was a dismal $10,000 in the late 1970s. A hard core of about a hundred free-lancers monopolizes most of the writing for the top-paying magazines—and only a handful of these earn more than $40,000 a year. Laments

Catherine Breslin, a now-established free-lance writer who earned only $800 in 1975: "A free-lancer lives at the end of a sawed-off limb."[29]

Each article begins with an assignment. Free-lancers usually think up their own topics, then "query" various magazines to see who's interested. Staff writers, of course, are often told what to write. Either way, one editor is always responsible for approving the topic, the research approach, and the finished manuscript. On most magazines the top editor does this for every article. Some of the larger and more decentralized magazines have department editors for the job. *Better Homes & Gardens,* for example, has twelve of them: residential building, foods, furnishings and decorations, gardens and landscaping, kitchens and equipment, money management, family cars, home entertainment, family health, travel, sewing and crafts, and education.

Once a manuscript is approved, it goes to a copy editor for the finishing touches. At the same time, a copy is sent to the art department, which begins work on drawings, photographs, and other illustrations. The art director and the managing editor rough out an approximate layout, then tell the production editor to prepare the article for the printer. The printer sends back galley proofs. A proofreader checks these for errors, while the production editor cuts and pastes them into a "dummy" of the magazine. The printer uses the dummies to prepare a set of page proofs, a one-color version of the magazine. After final adjustments are made on the page proofs, color proofs are prepared and checked. Finally, the magazine is okayed for printing.

All this takes time. When necessary (as for a weekly magazine), the entire process is squeezed into a single week of frenzied activity. The average monthly, though, takes about ninety days to process an article from accepted manuscript to printed copies. And still the activity can be frenzied.

THE NEWSMAGAZINES

The most influential magazines in the United States are probably the three news-weeklies: *Time, Newsweek,* and *U.S. News & World Report.* Publishing 11.3 million copies a week, these three magazines are a

---

THE WORLD'S NEWSMAGAZINES

The success of American newsmagazines has spawned a raft of imitators around the world—*Tiempo* in Mexico, *Akis* in Turkey, *L'Express* in France, *Shukan Asahi* in Japan, *Elseviers Weekblad* in the Netherlands, *Link* in India, etc. Probably the most controversial of the world's newsmagazines is *Der Spiegel,* published in Hamburg, West Germany, by Rudolf Augstein.

Founded in 1946 under a different title, *Der Spiegel* is obviously patterned after *Time;* it uses the same format, the same editorial style, and the same departmentalized structure. But its content is a great deal spicier, "deliberately aggressive" in the words of one former editor.[30] This aggressiveness is one source of *Der Spiegel's* success, but it's also a source of frequent controversy. In 1962, for example, the magazine accused West German Defense Minister Franz Josef Strauss of inefficiency, and published some allegedly classified documents to bolster the charge. In retaliation, the government raided the magazine's office and arrested publisher Augstein on suspicion of treason. The public outcry that followed led to Strauss's resignation. And *Der Spiegel* continued its editorial policy of picking a fight whenever possible.

---

vital source of news for more than 40 million Americans, and nearly 10 million people overseas. They share three important characteristics: (1) Brevity—the week's news is compressed into as few pages as possible; (2) Subjectivity—fact, opinion, and colorful adjectives are blended together into a slick, highly readable puree; and (3) Group journalism—dozens of researchers, writers, and editors collaborate on each major article.

The oldest and most successful of the three newsweeklies is *Time,* founded by Henry R. Luce in 1923. *Newsweek* has offered increasingly stiff competition since it was purchased by the Washington Post Company in 1961. Both magazines tend to ignore the financially weaker and stylistically stodgier *U.S. News & World Report,* but they compete strenuously with each other.

In 1978, for example, both were planning cover stories on jockey Steve Cauthen. *Time* managing editor Ray Cave was so intent on beating *Newsweek* to the punch that he scheduled the story to run right after the Preakness, instead of waiting two weeks to see if Cauthen and Affirmed would win the Triple Crown. In case Affirmed lost the Preakness, Cave prepared an alternate cover as well. "I sent them both to the printers. It cost us an extra $15,000 to do that, but then I could watch the race on television that Saturday with the telephone right next to me, and as soon as Affirmed won, I called the printer and said, 'Go with Cauthen.' "[31]

The editor, not the reporter, is the key person at a newsmagazine. David Shaw explains:

> A newsmagazine reporter seldom writes a story; he writes a "file"—a long, detailed, fact-filled narrative—which is sent to New York to be fact-checked by a researcher, completely re-written by a writer, then edited by a senior editor, edited again by a top-ranking editor, then—often—edited yet again by the top editor himself.
>
> Too frequently, the story that is ultimately

published bears little resemblance to the reporter's original file.

> This is especially true when reporters in several bureaus submit files for a regional, national, or international roundup story on a broad subject (the impact of inflation, for example). Each reporter on such a story may send in a 20-page file, and when all the files are woven into one story in New York, a given reporter may be represented by only one line. Or one statistic. Or nothing.[32]

Newsmagazine reporters quickly learn that the writers and editors in New York prize revealing anecdotes, startling quotations, and scene-setting facts more than the who/what/where/when/why of traditional journalism. "As the diplomat strolled down the elm-lined avenue, a blonde neighbor muttered. . . ." To produce this typical newsmagazine sentence, a reporter must not only listen to the mutterings of bystanders, but also note their hair color, the trees' species, and the diplomat's walking speed.

This, then, is newsmagazine journalism: reporters supply the raw material, editors pick what they like, and writers package the choice in seamless prose. At its worst, the method results in subtle but systematic distortion, editorial bias through adjectives and anecdotes. At its best, the method produces authoritative, detailed, genuinely interesting interpretations of the news, sometimes extending over 20 pages or more for a major story. More than 50 million people around the world absorb the worst and the best every week, with equal trust.

IMPACT

There is no doubt that magazines have far less impact on American society than either broadcasting or newspapers. It wasn't always that way. Throughout the eighteenth and nineteenth centuries, magazines were the nation's most important entertainment medium. Nearly all the great American authors published their novels in serial form first. And the muckraking magazines of the early twentieth century did much to revolutionize our system of government. The January, 1903 issue of *McClure's*, for example, contained three articles of lasting importance: Ida Tarbell on "The History of the Standard Oil Company," Lincoln Steffens on "The Shame of Minneapolis," and Ray Stannard Baker on "The Right to Work." These articles dealt with serious issues—monopoly, corruption, labor.

Today, the market for magazine fiction is reduced to a dozen major publications and a host of tiny literary quarterlies. As for magazine muckraking, despite a comeback in the 1970s it is still found most frequently in unprofitable magazines with small circulations and little influence on the general public.

Yet magazines are not unimportant. They offer three unique services:

First, magazines are the only mass medium that is both timely and permanent, quick and deep. Television and newspapers take only hours to report a story, but they can report it only briefly. And neither is customarily saved or savored. Books, of course, offer the maximum depth and permanence—but books take years to produce and seldom circulate more than a few thousand copies. Magazines are the ideal compromise.

Second, most magazines are national. So is television, of course—but television is sketchy, impermanent, and devoted almost entirely to light entertainment. The "American perspective" on everything from theater to politics to underarm deodorants is molded largely by magazines. When a serious writer wants to say something, and wants to say it to the whole country, he or she says it in a magazine.

Third, magazines are specialized. If you want to know what's on television, you read *TV Guide*. If you want to know what explorers and anthropologists are doing, you read the *National Geographic*. If you want

help repairing your car or building a stereo, you read *Popular Mechanics*. If you want to know where it's at in rock music, you read *Rolling Stone*. It is only in magazines that writers and advertisers can reach precisely those readers most interested in what they have to say.

The demise of magazines has been predicted many times—in the 1910s with the automobile, in the 1920s with radio, in the 1930s with movies, in the 1950s with television. Each time the prediction proved wrong. Magazines have changed greatly over the years, but they have survived, even flourished. They will continue to change, and survive, and flourish.

As a mass medium, the book is a failure. Once they finish their schooling, most Americans have very little to do with books, and even less to do with "serious" books. Yet the book industry is surprisingly prosperous. In the past two decades it has even become glamorous, prompting serious readers and writers to wonder if the furor over bestsellers and movie rights will eventually endanger more conventional publishing.

BREAKDOWN

The book is the basis for our system of education and the repository of our culture. It is through books that the young learn what they have to learn and the wise teach what they have to teach. To those who are literate, books offer a permanent record of the best and worst in American civilization—and all other civilizations.

The offer is often ignored. Statistics say that the "average" American buys about seven books a year. Actually, 25 percent of us read ten books or more per year, including most of the hardbacks; 30 percent read one to nine books a year, mainly light paperback entertainment; and the other 45 percent read no books at all.[33] Of course there are books that have changed the world—Harriet Beecher Stowe's *Uncle Tom's Cabin,* for example, or Charles Darwin's *Origin of the Species.* But they did it indirectly. Fewer people have read these two since they were published than the number who watched network television last night. In the long run, books may well be the most important of the mass media. But in the everyday life of the average citizen, they are by far the least influential.

The best way to understand book publishing is to look at the kinds of books people buy. The following table shows U.S. consumer expenditures on books in 1978.[34]

Educational Books

College textbooks	$ 830 million
Primary and secondary textbooks	808 million
Professional and technical books	777 million
Subscription reference books	327 million
University press books	67 million

General Books

Mass-market paperbacks	$ 959 million
Trade hardbacks	866 million
Mail-order books	453 million
Book club books	452 million
Religious books	425 million
Trade paperbacks	329 million
Juvenile books	246 million
Total	$6,537 million

Some of these categories deserve amplification.

Educational Books. It is obvious from the table that educational books—especially textbooks—are one of the biggest segments of the book publishing industry. Textbooks alone account for 25 percent of sales dollars, and other types of educational books bring the total up to 43 percent. Of course educational books have always been an important part of the publishing business, but they came to dominate the business in the 1950s and 1960s, as post-war babies reached school age and higher education expanded enor-

mously. In the mid-1970s their dominance started a slow decline, mirroring the decrease in elementary and secondary school enrollments and the budget-cutting of public school systems. The book industry is bracing for a comparable slowdown in college text sales in the 1980s. But educational publishing will doubtless remain a mainstay of the industry.

As purchasers of this text know better than most, educational books are expensive—they account for 43 percent of sales dollars but only 25 percent of total copies sold. Their readers, of course, are a narrow slice of the American public, mostly students and specialists. If you are interested in the effects of books on the average American adult, you must forget about this category.

Paperbacks. Two-thirds of all books sold in the U.S. today are bound with paper. Nearly half of these are mass-market paperbacks, while the rest are paperback textbooks, book club paperbacks, religious paperbacks, juvenile paperbacks, professional paperbacks, even university press paperbacks. Fewer than nine percent are trade paperbacks.

The main difference between mass-market paperbacks and trade paperbacks is quantity. Trade paperbacks are printed in lots of ten to thirty thousand. They are usually about the same size as hardcover books, and are sold mostly through the nation's 4,000 bookstores and 8,000 variety stores with book departments. The average price for a trade paperback is now more than seven dollars. Mass-market paperbacks, on the other hand, are printed in lots of 200,000-plus—often more than a million for a bestseller. They are usually pocket-size, and sell for $1.95 to $3.50 in drugstores, supermarkets, and airports—roughly 150,000 outlets throughout the United States.

Predictions that mass-market paperbacks would soon dominate book publishing have been common ever since 1939, when Robert F. deGraff decided to market his Pocket Book series through newsstands and chain stores instead of bookstores. That year he published 34 titles, sold 1.5 million copies, and created the mass-market paperback. In one sense the predictions have come true. The average nonstudent who reads books at all reads mostly mass-market paperbacks.

But the situation for publishers is much more complicated. Compared to other sorts of books, mass-market paperbacks are cheap. They account for nearly a third of all book copies sold but less than 15 percent of total sales dollars. Yet they are not cheap for publishers to produce. Reprint rights to a potential bestseller can cost millions of dollars; advertising adds hundreds of thousands more; wholesalers and retailers get their percentage off the top: hundreds of thousands of copies languish on the racks and are never sold (an astounding 45 percent of all mass-market paperbacks are eventually returned to wholesalers to be shredded[35]). In short, mass-market paperbacks are very risky, and not always very profitable. As we shall soon see, they are the most glamorous part of the book business, and have exerted a tremendous influence on the "tone" of publishing. Their influence on the profits of publishing is much more debatable.

Book-Club Books. The Book-of-the-Month Club was founded in 1926. Members were notified of each month's selection a few weeks in advance; they had the option of turning it down or buying it by default. In nearly sixty years of operation, the system hasn't changed a bit. The only difference is the number of clubs. Today one may join travel book clubs, mystery book clubs, psychology book clubs, feminism book clubs, environment book clubs, and even pornographic book clubs. The 1978 gross income of all the clubs was $452 million, up 61 percent (and 37 million books) from 1974.

Publishers initially feared that book clubs would hurt bookstore sales. They had the same fear about mail-order books and mass-market paperbacks—but none has proved justified. Cass Canfield notes that "club mail-order operations have created hundreds of thousands of new book-buyers in areas where booksellers are scarce or nonexistent."[36]

Trade Hardbacks. When most people hear the word "book," they immediately think of the trade hardback—the kind of book you find in libraries and bookstores. More than half of the roughly 40,000 new titles published in the United States every year are trade hardbacks. Aside from some 3,000 to 4,000 works of fiction, most trade hardbacks are devoted to information—agriculture, art, biography, business, etc.

Trade hardbacks offer a wealth of culture, information, and entertainment to those who read them. Very few people read them. Fewer than 5 percent of all trade hardbacks sell more than 5,000 copies before they go out of print. Americans buy 123 million hardcover trade books a year. That's less than one book for every adult in the country.

PUBLISHERS

Despite the limited appetite of most readers, book publishing is a profitable industry. Total consumer expenditures on books rose from $4 billion in 1974 to $6.5 billion in 1978, and up to $7.2 billion in 1979.[37] The total number of books in print (and selling well enough to stay in print) climbed from around 400,000 in 1974 to almost 500,000 by the end of 1980.[38] The number of new titles published each year remained level at 40,000 throughout the 1970s, while the price of the average book soared 44 percent from 1974 to 1978.[39]

In the 1970s many of the "name" publishing houses—Macmillan, Random House, Doubleday, Simon & Schuster, etc.—acquired new subsidiaries or were themselves acquired by conglomerates, or both. By the end of the decade the merger trend had become a flood, with 65 major publishing mergers in 1978 alone. Roger W. Straus Jr., president of the still-independent Farrar, Straus & Giroux publishing firm, expressed the misgivings of many when he commented in 1979: "I think that a lot of publishing houses are being run by accountants, businessmen and lawyers who have very little concern for books. They could just as well be selling string, spaghetti or rugs."[40]

Big-time glamor came as something of a surprise to the publishing business, which has traditionally been extremely conservative. Even today, the "typical" book is still a trade hardback without Hollywood appeal or Wall Street numbers. An editor reads the manuscript and guesses that it might sell 8,000 copies or so, at $8 a copy to booksellers. Adding up the expenses of printing, distribution, and overhead, the editor calculates that 8,000 sales will mean a net of around $16,000 (on a gross of $64,000). On the basis of these figures, the publisher offers the author a contract—a 12 percent royalty, say, with a guaranteed advance of $5,000.

A year or more later (publishers work slowly) the book comes out. If it sells the expected 8,000 copies, the author earns back the $5,000 advance plus an additional $2,280 in royalties; the company keeps the remaining $8,720 as its profit. If the book sells only 2,000 copies (to most of the bigger libraries and all of the author's good friends), the author gets to keep the advance and the publisher loses about $10,000. And if by some miracle the book sells a few hundred thousand copies, the author gets rich and the

---

THE MAKING OF A BESTSELLER

Blockbuster bestsellers are important to publishers not just for the profits they earn but also for the prestige they bring. In order to attract the sorts of authors whose books are likely to sell well, publishers need a reputation for knowing how to turn a run-of-the-mill good book into a bestseller. The formula for accomplishing this task is complex, elusive, and ever-changing. But it can be done.

One book for which it *was* done is *Jaws,* a first novel by Peter Benchley about a great white shark that terrorizes a small Long Island town. The book is fun to read. But Doubleday, its publisher, built it into a million-dollar 1974 bestseller through skill and promotion. In an article in the *New York Times Sunday Magazine,* veteran free-lance journalist Ted Morgan described how.[41]

Tom Congdon, then a Doubleday senior editor, had admired some magazine pieces by Benchley and invited him to lunch to discuss possible book ideas. Congdon asked him if he had considered writing fiction. Benchley, an expert on the habits of sharks, said he had been toying with the idea of a story about a shark that attacks a resort town. Congdon liked the idea because it combined two important elements of a bestseller—the public's fascination with the mysterious (in this case, sharks) and the concept of a community trying to cope with disaster. He asked Benchley to prepare a one-page outline.

Congdon whipped up some enthusiasm for the project at Doubleday, and wangled permission to give Benchley a $1,000 advance on the first four chapters. When the chapters came, Congdon was a little disappointed. He and others at Doubleday liked the shark scenes and the sense of menace in the opening pages, but they thought that Benchley's characters were weak and his plot was too predictable. Scores of suggestions were made for tinkering with the incomplete novel. Unlike many authors in similar positions, Benchley willingly accepted most of them.

Nine months after that first lunch, Doubleday offered Benchley a $7,500 advance on the book.

Once the manuscript was completed, the search for a title began. Some 237 different ones were tried, including *The Summer of the Shark* and *The Jaws of the Leviathan.*

publisher gets richer. But miracles don't happen often. Most books either earn a few thousand dollars or lose a few thousand dollars. It's a slow way to get rich.

Too slow, perhaps, for the giant corporations that now own many of the major publishing houses. A decade ago, a publisher might have been willing to take a chance on a book with a potential market of only four or five thousand copies. In those days a trade book could be manufactured for just a dollar a copy, and even 4,000 sales might earn a small profit. Today it costs more than two dollars a copy just to print and bind the book, and overhead expenses—such as the cost of keeping sales people on the road—can be staggering. The result: many major publishers are steering away from small-and-risky books, such as first novels and serious nonfiction. Instead, they focus on small-but-safe books, like reference works aimed at a captive audience of specialists, or on big-but-risky books, like bestsellers. Any book that isn't a sure thing, today's publishers figure, should at least be a potential gold mine.

Paperback publishers take more than their share of the risks. In the late 1970s, for example, Judith Krantz sold her outline for the book that was to become *Princess Daisy* to Crown, a hardback publisher. Crown paid

---

Benchley himself suggested *Jaws*—simple and powerful and frightening, and attractive on a book jacket. The jacket was also troublesome; should they put a shark on the cover, or just a pair of jaws, or a shark plus a swimmer, or a shark plus a town, or what? Doubleday wanted to be sure readers would know that the book was about a menacing monster of a fish, not dentistry or deep-sea fishing.

Meanwhile, the subsidiary rights department at Doubleday sent the manuscript out to paperback publishers for bids. Bantam was the first to respond, bidding $200,000 (of which Benchley would get half) for the paperback rights. This was more than Doubleday had expected, but instead of accepting the offer, it sent the manuscript around to some other paperback houses, and then held an "auction." Bantam was given a chance to top the highest bid, which it did—paying $575,000 for the rights. With that start, Doubleday was able to get $150,000 more for the movie rights, plus $85,000 from book clubs.

Even before *Jaws* was published, in other words, Benchley and Doubleday were guaranteed a successful book. But it was still important to make the hardcover edition a bestseller—to keep the paperback and movie people happy, to make Benchley a "name" so that his second and third books would also succeed, and of course to make some extra money from hardcover sales. To this end, Congdon worked to convince Doubleday's sales staff of the marketability of the book. This was essential and by no means automatic. Doubleday publishes 700 trade books a year, and a salesperson can push only so many titles at the bookstores.

To aid in the effort, Doubleday publicists mentioned the book enthusiastically to reviewers over lunch. (Congdon thought about sending a free shark's tooth to each reviewer, but the teeth proved too scarce.) Blurbs—admiring quotes about the book—were secured from other Doubleday authors for use in the advertising campaign, on which Doubleday spent more than $50,000—a huge sum for a book. Benchley toured the country plugging *Jaws* in every city, and was fortunate enough to get an invitation to NBC's "Today" show, a prime showcase for authors.

It all paid off. *Jaws* quickly sold 40,000 of its first 75,000 copies and landed on the *New York Times* bestseller list, where it remained for many weeks. Benchley estimated that his total earnings from the book would come to more than $600,000, enough to permit him to write for many years without worrying about money.

Krantz an advance of $400,000—a lot of money for a book that hadn't been written yet. But three months before the book's March 1980 publication date, Bantam bought the paperback rights for $3.2 million—$960,000 for Crown and $2,240,000 for Krantz. Regardless of sales, Krantz and Crown were now in good shape, even if Hollywood were to decide not to buy the movie rights. Bantam, on the other hand, would have to sell four to six million paperbacks just to break even.[42]

Twenty years ago, paperback houses exerted little influence on the course of publishing. They merely reprinted cheap editions of successful hardcover books, plus a smattering of original titles. But in the late 1960s and early 1970s, paperback sales came to dominate the bestseller piece of the publishing business. Mario Puzo's *The Godfather* sold 13,225,000 copies in paper, compared to 292,765 in hardcover; Erich Segal's *Love Story* sold 9,778,000 in paper versus 431,976 in hardcover.[43] For some houses, selling paperback reprint rights became a significant source of profits.

So paperback publishers began signing their own authors. William Peter Blatty's *The Exorcist* was first signed by Bantam, which then sold the hardback rights, standing the traditional process on its head. *The Exorcist* went on to sell 205,265 copies in hardback and a whopping 11,948,000 in paperback.[44] Some of the biggest money-makers are the paperback houses like Avon Books and Harlequin Romances that have built stables of authors whose books never appear in hardcover at all. Harlequin alone now accounts for nearly 20 percent of the entire mass paperback publishing industry in North America. Publishing twelve new titles every month, Harlequin sells more than 159 million books a year to readers in 80 countries.[45] Twenty of the 83 books that made the *New York Times* paperback bestseller list in 1979 were paperback originals.[46]

These trends are obviously good for the authors and readers of bestsellers, but not necessarily for the authors and readers of less glamorous books. In recent years, groups like P.E.N. (Poets, Playwrights, Editors, Essayists, and Novelists) and the Authors League have repeatedly warned that the vast sums spent on the bestseller sweepstakes might leave less money to be spent on more solid sorts of books.[47]

Will the emphasis on bestsellers damage the fortunes of book publishers and the sales of more ordinary books? So far it hasn't happened. Between 1974 and 1978, consumers purchased more of almost every kind of book. Mass-market paperbacks jumped 94 percent in sales dollars, 12 percent in copies sold. Trade paperbacks climbed 93 percent in dollars, 14 percent in copies. Trade hardbacks increased only 61 percent in dollars, but an impressive 29 percent in copies.[48] There is no evidence here that mass-market bestsellers are squeezing out the trade books. Most of the money is still made on textbooks, children's books, reference books, and run-of-the-mill trade books and paperbacks. The

---

DIVERSITY IN PUBLISHING

Though huge corporations increasingly control the nation's best-known publishing houses, they do not control publishing. With 66,000 people employed by 1,750 "major" publishing houses and roughly 8,000 small ones, no one can control publishing.[49]

True, the 350 biggest companies that publish the great majority of all titles tend to concentrate on known authors and sure-thing topics—sex and romance, running and cooking, suspense and adventure. But that leaves some 9,400 smaller publishers who might be interested in something a bit innovative.

Book Industry Study Group reported in 1979 that mass-market sales had already reached saturation. Future growth, it said, would come from trade books, juvenile books, and mail-order books.[50]

Ironically, it may be the bestseller part of the business that's heading for trouble. "The whole industry has changed," says Victor Temkin, an experienced paperback executive who is now president of Berkley/Jove. "Fifteen years ago, it was very hard to lose money on a book. Then it got to the point where seven out of ten books were mistakes. But that was all right. The three winners would make up for the seven losers. That won't work anymore. The margins are worse, the competition is tougher. You have to make less mistakes. This business has gotten to be like Hollywood, with the glamor of Hollywood and the big money being paid like Hollywood. The trouble is, it's not a Hollywood type of business."[51]

Notes

[1] "The Hot Magazines Aim at Special Targets," *Business Week*, May 2, 1970, p. 64.

[2] Roland E. Wolseley, *The Magazine World* (Englewood Cliffs, N.J.: Prentice-Hall, 1951), p. 8.

[3] Theodore Peterson, *Magazines in the Twentieth Century* (Urbana, Ill.: University of Illinois Press, 1964), p. 59.

[4] *Ibid.*, pp. 60-61.

[5] Otto Friedrich, "I am Marty Ackerman. I am Thirty-Six Years Old and I am Very Rich. I hope to Make the Curtis Publishing Company Rich Again," *Harper's Magazine*, December, 1969, pp. 95-118.

[6] Telephone interview, July 10, 1980.

[7] "The Hot Magazines Aim at Special Targets," p. 68.

[8] "Advertising: Life Magazine's Post-Mortem," *New York Times*, December 11, 1972, p. 67.

[9] "Dated Publishing Strategy Linked to Downfall of Life," *New York Times*, December 9, 1972, p. 16.

[10] Betsy Carter with Nancy Stadtman, "As Big As LIFE," *Newsweek*, October 2, 1978, p. 83.

[11] "Time Inc. To Revive Life as a Monthly," *New York Times*, April 25, 1978.

[12] "Ms. Magazine, a Success After 16 Issues, Now Tries Other Business Ventures," *New York Times*, September 21, 1973, p. 38.

[13] *Ibid.*

[14] "Harper's Comes Back from the Brink," *New York Times*, July 13, 1980, p. F19.

[15] "The Hot Magazines Aim at Special Targets," p. 72.

[16] "The Kitchen-Table Entrepreneurs," *Time*, May 30, 1977, p. 46.

[17] N. R. Kleinfield, "Magazine for Directors Seeks to Keep Them Well Informed," *New York Times*, January 15, 1980.

[18] *The World Almanac and Book of Facts 1980* (New York: Newspaper Enterprise Association, 1979), p. 427.

[19] Philip H. Dougherty, "Advertising," *New York Times*, November 7, 1979.

[20] Robert Friedman, "'Life,' 'Look,' and the Pursuit of the Perfect Picture Layout," *New York*, September 25, 1978, p. 91.

[21] "Times Co. Sells Us Magazine," *New York Times*, March 7, 1980.

[22] Charles Marler, "Magazines and Postal Rates," Freedom of Information Center Report No. 306, School of Journalism, University of Missouri at Columbia, July, 1973, p. 6.

[23] N. R. Kleinfield, "Newsweek Set to Vault Ahead," *New York Times*, July 13, 1979, p. D6.

[24] N. R. Kleinfield, "Seeking a Postal Alternative," *New York Times*, July 20, 1978, pp. D1-2.

[25] John Tebbel, "Magazines—New, Changing, Growing," *Saturday Review*, February 8, 1969, p. 55.

[26] N. R. Kleinfield, "The Itch to Start a Magazine," *New York Times*, December 2, 1979, p. F1.

[27] Anna Quindlen, "New Owners Find Magazines Costly 'Fun,'" *New York Times*, March 21, 1977, pp. 29, 47. N. R. Kleinfield, "Thought Magazines in Change," *New York Times*, May 5, 1980, pp. D1, D4. Deirdre Carmody, "Nation Magazine Sold to Group Led by Hamilton Fish," *New York Times*, December 23, 1977. "New Cash for an Old Bostonian," *Time*, March 17, 1980, pp. 97-98. "Harper's Hears The Angels Calling," *New York Times*, July 13, 1980, p. E7.

[28] Clay S. Felker, "Life Cycles in the Age of Magazines," *Antioch Review*, Spring, 1969, p. 7.

[29] "Grub Street Revisited," *Time*, April 10, 1978, pp. 75, 77.

[30] John C. Merrill, Carter R. Bryan, and Marvin Alisky, *The Foreign Press* (Baton Rouge: Louisiana State University Press, 1970), p. 142.

[31] David Shaw, "Men at Top Are Key to Time, Newsweek Battle," *Los Angeles Times*, May 3, 1980.

[32] *Ibid.*

33 Ray Walters, "Who Reads What and Why," *New York Times Book Review*, November 19, 1978.

34 Book Industry Study Group, "Book Industry Trends, 1979," in Filomena Simora, ed., *The Bowker Annual of Library & Book Trade Information*, 25th ed. (New York: R. R. Bowker Company, 1980), p. 474.

35 Ray Walters, "Paperback Talk," *New York Times Book Review*, July 6, 1980.

36 Cass Canfield, *The Publishing Experience* (Philadelphia: University of Pennsylvania Press, 1969), p. 60.

37 Herbert Mitgang, "Book Ends," *New York Times Book Review*, January 27, 1980, p. 39.

38 Herbert Mitgang, "After Rough 6 Months, Book Industry Anticipates Fall Upswing," *New York Times*, June 11, 1980, p. C28.

39 John P. Dessauer, Paul D. Doebler, J. Kendrick Noble, Jr., and E. Wayne Nordberg, *Book Industry Trends 1979* (Darien, Conn.: Book Industry Study Group, 1979), p. 247.

40 Herbert Mitgang, "Mergers in the Book World; Still an Unfinished Chapter," *New York Times*, August 19, 1979.

41 Ted Morgan, "Sharks," *New York Times Magazine*, April 21, 1974, pp. 10-11, 85-96.

42 Natalie Gittelson, "The Packaging of Judith Krantz," *New York Times Magazine*, March 2, 1980, pp. 22, 26.

43 Ray Walters, "Ten Years of Best Sellers," *New York Times Book Review*, December 30, 1979, p. 11.

44 *Ibid.*

45 Philip H. Dougherty, "Selling Books Like Tide," *New York Times*, February 26, 1980.

46 Ray Walters, "Paperback Talk," *New York Times Book Review*, January 6, 1980, p. 31.

47 "Future of Books Debated," *New York Times*, February 1, 1980, p. C28.

48 Dessauer, *et al., Book Industry Trends 1979*, pp. 246-72.

49 Mitgang, "After Rough 6 Months," p. C28.

50 Dessauer, *et al., Book Industry Trends 1979*, pp. 246-47.

51 N. R. Kleinfield, "The Problems at Bantam Books," *New York Times Book Review*, May 4, 1980, p. 7.

Suggested Readings

BRAUDY, SUSAN, "Paperback Auction: What Price a 'Hot' Book?" *New York Times Magazine*, May 21, 1978.

BROHAUGH, WILLIAM, ed., *1980 Writer's Market*. Cincinnati: Writer's Digest Books, 1979.

DESSAUER, JOHN P., PAUL D. DOEBLER, J. KENDRICK NOBLE, JR., and E. WAYNE NORDBERG, *Book Industry Trends 1979*. Darien, Conn.: Book Industry Study Group, 1979.

FRIEDMAN, ROBERT, " 'Life,' 'Look,' and the Pursuit of the Perfect Picture Layout," *New York*, September 25, 1978.

GELMAN, DAVID, with JANET HUCK, "Bestsellers," *Newsweek*, August 28, 1978.

GITTELSON, NATALIE, "The Packaging of Judith Krantz," *New York Times Magazine*, March 2, 1980.

HALBERSTAM, DAVID, *The Powers That Be*. New York: Alfred A. Knopf, 1979.

"The Hot Magazines Aim at Special Targets," *Business Week*, May 2, 1970.

MORGAN, TED, "Sharks," *New York Times Magazine*, April 21, 1974.

SIMORA, FILOMENA, ed., *The Bowker Annual of Library & Book Trade Information 1980*, 25th ed. New York: R. R. Bowker Company, 1980.

SWANBERG, W. A., *Luce and His Empire*. New York: Dell, 1972.

TURNER, ALICE K., "The Tempestuous, Tumultuous, Turbulent, Torrid, and Terribly Profitable World of Paperback Passion," *New York*, February 13, 1978.

Chapter 12
Broadcasting

Television is by far the most powerful and pervasive of the mass media. Yet it is used almost exclusively for entertainment. TV entertainment programming has been attacked by some for inculcating false values, by others for degrading American culture, by still others for corrupting the nation's morals. Many critics argue that it is at best a waste of the viewer's time and the medium's potential. The public watches anyhow.

Television is everywhere. Roughly 98 percent of American homes have at least one TV set. More families own televisions than bathtubs. And they use them more. The average in 1979 was 6 hours and 28 minutes per home per day—that's more than 45 hours a week, more than 2,350 hours a year.[1] According to a 1979 *Washington Post* poll, the average American adult watches three hours of TV a day during the week, three and a half hours a day on weekends. Two-thirds of those polled said they watched some TV every day; 95 percent said they watched at least two days a week.[2]

On a typical winter evening, 60 percent of the television sets in the U.S. are turned on, and 128 million Americans are watching

them. About 90 percent of this audience is watching one of the three commercial networks—a total of 115 million people divided among just three programs.[3] These last figures will probably decline in the 1980s, as cable TV, pay TV, and other innovations begin making inroads on the network monopoly. But the other figures are unlikely to decline. Television viewing is a firmly fixed American habit. It occupies fully one-third of all the leisure time in the country, ranking behind only sleep and work as a consumer of time.[4]

Though nearly everyone watches television, we don't all watch the same amount. One-third of the viewers now account for two-thirds of the viewing, and this polarization is on the increase.[5] The committed hard core of TV addicts, in other words, is surrounded by a majority of more selective viewers who watch only a couple of hours a day. The hard core includes disproportionate numbers of the old, the poor, the unemployed, and others who spend a lot of time home alone. College students tend to watch less television than the average, largely because many have no TV sets in their dorm rooms and most have other activities (movies, parties, even homework) to occupy their evening hours. Five years after graduation the typical college student will watch considerably more TV than he or she does today.

Are TV viewers happy with what they watch? In survey after survey, many claim they are not. A 1979 *TV Guide* study, for example, found that 44 percent of the population was dissatisfied with television. The dissatisfaction was greatest among the better-educated, more affluent viewers. Their main gripes were too much violence, too much sex, and too much programming that insulted their intelligence.[6] A similar survey commissioned by the Public Broadcasting Service found that television ranked below magazines, automobiles, clothing, and popular music in consumer satisfaction.[7]

Both surveys reported that many people were cutting back on their TV viewing. But this is not borne out by the ratings, which show a small increase in average viewing time during the 1970s. For decades, in fact, TV viewers have been telling survey researchers that they wanted less pap and more intellect on television—but for decades they've been watching the pap and avoiding the intellect. It seems fair to conclude that the surveys reflect what people think they ought to want on television, rather than what they actually choose to watch. Judging from the ratings, Americans are quite satisfied with TV content. They may not be ecstatic or excited, but they are content to spend hour after hour with the tube. This is all any broadcaster or advertiser could ask.

Radio, by the way, is as pervasive as television. Americans own more than 450 million radio sets, about 5.7 sets per household. The weekly radio audience is 169 million adults, listening an average of three and a half hours per day—an increase of an hour a day since 1968.[8] Radio lacks television's visual appeal; people are more likely to be doing something else while listening to radio than while watching TV; radio programming is far less dominated by national networks; the local audience is segmented among many

more stations. For all these reasons, most critics pay less attention to radio's power than to television's—but it is powerful nonetheless.

Any activity that takes up so much of the time of so many people is bound to exert a tremendous influence on society. Harry J. Boyle of the Canadian Radio-Television Commission was not exaggerating when he stated that "the license to broadcast is almost the heaviest obligation society can allow individuals to bear."[9]

ENTERTAINMENT

How do broadcasters respond to this obligation? As we have emphasized before, they respond with entertainment—hour after hour after hour of entertainment. They respond with soap operas and situation comedies, with variety shows and detective thrillers, with sporting events and music. The vast majority of all radio and television content is meant strictly to entertain.

Americans are so accustomed to the entertainment role of broadcasting that it is necessary to stress what should be an obvious fact: Television and radio are not *inherently* entertainment media. In the developing countries of Asia, Africa, and South America, broadcasting is used primarily for education and information. Even in Western Europe, news and public affairs fill a substantial part of the broadcast day. American broadcasting is entertainment-centered because American broadcasters want it that way. They want it that way because they believe (rightly or wrongly) that that is what the public and the advertisers want. But broadcast advertising isn't inevitable either; there are many countries without it. And it is at least possible to give the public what someone decrees it *should* want instead of what it does want.

We are not arguing that American broadcasting should be turned into a government-controlled education monopoly—though that has been argued. In the face of the daily grind of living, Americans need to relax and unwind. Broadcast entertainment serves this need admirably. But there *are* alternatives to the American system of broadcasting.

Most observers have long been critical of broadcasting's emphasis on entertainment. In 1961, former FCC Commissioner Newton Minow told the National Association of Broadcasters: "When television is bad, nothing is worse. I invite you to sit down in front of your television set when your station goes on the air and stay there without [anything] to distract you—and keep your eyes glued to that set until the station signs off. I can assure you that you will observe a vast wasteland."[10] Robert M. Hutchins of the Center for the Study of Democratic Institutions made the point even more stringently:

> We have triumphantly invented, perfected, and distributed to the humblest cottage throughout the land one of the greatest technical marvels in history, television, and have used it for what? To bring Coney Island into every home. It is as though movable type had been devoted exclusively since Gutenberg's time to the publication of comic books.[11]

Read these two quotations carefully. Minow and Hutchins are criticizing more than just the *fact* of broadcast entertainment. They are criticizing the *quality* of that entertainment. Although there are some entertainment shows on television (symphony concerts and Shakespearean dramas, for example) that simply do not fit Minow's image of a vast wasteland or Hutchins' analogy to comic books, the majority of TV programming does fit.

Of course the majority of printed material is also low-quality—comic books, pulp fiction, and so on. But Minow and Hutchins could choose what they wanted to read, reaching back hundreds of years if they liked for a literary masterpiece. On television, by contrast, we have to settle for whatever broadcasters are offering today. *Average* quality is thus a much more important issue for broadcasting than for print, and Minow and

Hutchins are arguing that the average quality of broadcast entertainment is too low.

Judging the quality of entertainment is a thorny problem. Broadcast executives assert that the proper standard is ratings. If people watch a show then they must like it, and if they like it then by definition it must be good entertainment. Critics of television are not satisfied with this standard. They judge programming according to their own criteria—ideological, esthetic, or moralistic. The ideological critics argue that broadcast entertainment is destroying American values. The esthetic critics claim that it is degrading American culture. And the moralistic critics insist that it is corrupting American morals. Let us examine each argument in turn.

ENTERTAINMENT AND VALUES

To say that American broadcasting is mostly entertainment is not to say that it has little or no effect on American society. No doubt our country would be different without televised moon landings and election results, assassinations and battles. But it would also be different without TV coverage of the World Series and the Academy Awards. Cop shows, soap operas, and the rest of television entertainment teach us things. They reflect and reinforce certain characteristic national traits—competition and aggression, materialism and racism, humor and openness, faith and ambition. It is as entertainers that the broadcast media have their greatest impact on American society. And that in itself says something about the American character.

As we pointed out in the Introduction (see pp. 17-20), the mass media are far better at reinforcing existing values than at inculcating new ones. In this sense the impact of all the media, including broadcast entertainment, is inherently conservative. Yet values do change, and television plays an important role in that change by mirroring the world as seen through the eyes of the people who write for TV.

SPORTS ON THE TUBE

Once upon a time spectator sports were something you journeyed to the stadium or arena to see. Today you stay home and watch them on television. During football season, for example, at least two professional games are televised in major markets every Sunday, with a third on Monday night and a college game or two on Saturday. Major-league baseball now offers one or two nationally televised games each week, plus broadcasts of local teams. And many cable TV systems boast an all-sports channel that brings even minor sporting events to television.

TV has affected sports in other ways as well:

Tennis. Balls are now yellow instead of white, and competitors must wear snappy colors and matching outfits for doubles play. To insure that singles matches don't last too long, sets tied at six games each are ended with a tie-breaker thirteenth game, and the traditional five-set match is down to three. Court composition has been changed to slow the ball, encouraging longer rallies and more exciting points.

Baseball. The World Series and the All-Star Game are now routinely scheduled at night to catch the prime-time audience. The minor leagues, meanwhile, deteriorated rapidly once the TV habit caught on; yearly attendance declined from 42 million in 1950 to 10 million in 1970.[12] Why watch the minors when the majors are on TV?

Boxing. Television first destroyed boxing through overexposure in the 1950s, then built up heavyweight boxing (but not the rest of the sport) in the 1970s. The money in boxing now comes almost entirely from home TV and pay TV, so bouts are scheduled for TV's convenience. The 1974 fight between George Foreman and Muhammad Ali, for example, was held in Zaire at 3 a.m.—which just happens to be 10 p.m. in New York. When a network sports department decides it likes a particular fighter—as ABC did with Sugar Ray Leonard—it promotes him by televising his fights even if they aren't title bouts, becoming every bit as important to the fighter's career as his manager or his trainer.

For example, much of what people know (or think they know) about the practices of doctors, police, lawyers, soldiers, teachers, and blue-collar workers comes from observing their behavior in television dramas. If TV doctors are unfailingly fatherly, taking time out to help patients cope with their personal lives, then why shouldn't our doctors behave in the same way? If TV cops heroically catch criminals by ignoring both the rules of police procedure and the constitutional rights of suspects, then why shouldn't real-world cops do it too?

Stereotypes in television entertainment have been the subject of much research and even more debate. "All in the Family," for example, has been widely praised for its frank treatment of social issues and working-class problems. But researcher Lynn Berk argues that the Archie Bunker character actually feeds middle-class prejudices about blue-collar workers. According to Berk, Archie's malapropisms ("detergent to crime," "misconscrued ideas") show him to be a boob. He exhibits race prejudice that television would never permit in a middle-class character, suggesting that such bigotry is a part of the blue-collar mentality. Real working-class people, says Berk, are invisible on television.[15]

In a more quantitative fashion, George Gerbner systematically studied TV's depiction of the elderly. Old people, he found, are far less common in TV shows than in

Football. Texas and Arkansas opened the 1980 season on September 1—a bit early for college football—to accommodate ABC, which wanted a game that Monday night. The professional National Football League is so flush with TV revenue that most franchises could make money without ever drawing a single fan to the park. Not surprisingly, football officials call timeouts when broadcasters say they need a commercial break, thus dragging out the average contest to three hours.

Hockey. Simply because it does not have a network television agreement, hockey has become a "minor" sport in serious financial trouble.

In nearly all professional sports, television has helped force elaborate playoff systems that guarantee dozens of "big" games after the season, which can be sold to advertisers at fat rates. Cameras and commentators have turned up in post-game locker rooms and baseball bullpens. And the most famous figure in sports today may well be ABC's caustic Howard Cosell, who never played a professional sport.

Television controls many aspects of athletics because it pays the bills. NBC paid $2.9 million for the right to broadcast the 1980 Rose Bowl (and earned a profit of $1.3 million on that single game). It paid $3.3 million for the 1980 AFC championship game between Houston and Pittsburgh, $1.3 million for baseball's 1979 All-Star Game, and $2.5 million for a 13-game package during the regular baseball season. Wimbledon in 1979 went for $600,000. A top college basketball game goes for over $300,000, a major golf tournament for as much as $600,000.[13] On the local level, the Philadelphia Phillies were able to sign free agent Pete Rose to an $800,000-a-year contract only because the TV station with the right to broadcast Phillies games guaranteed part of Rose's salary. Why? Because the station felt his presence on the team would lead to better ratings and more advertising profit.[14] It was a good bet—in 1980 the Phillies won the National League pennant and the World Series for the first time in 30 years.

The sports world, in short, is hooked on television; much of it would collapse without TV.

---

the real world. Older women, especially, are disproportionately cast in roles that make them appear unsuccessful and unattractive. The elderly are used more for comic relief than in serious roles; they are more often treated with disrespect on TV shows than any other age group; they frequently appear as stubborn, foolish, and eccentric nuisances. In his studies of public attitudes toward the elderly, furthermore, Gerbner found that heavy TV viewers are less likely than lighter viewers to see old people as adaptable, alert, and able to get things done.[16] The TV stereotype thus takes its toll.

Many other groups have complained similarly that television inculcates false values about them. The grievances of racial minorities and women will be discussed in Chapter 18. The grievances of white ethnics, teenagers, and a wide range of other groups can be imagined by anyone who watches television carefully. Even upper-middle-class WASP males could legitimately complain that their lives are very different from the placidly self-satisfied TV stereotype.

Nor are television's values limited to its depictions of groups of people. TV also tells us about behavior, about how to act on a date, when to get angry in a conversation, what to do in a crisis. Consider an everyday behavior like eating. Lois Kaufman has studied how people eat in prime-time programs. She found that junk foods dominated the shows even more than the commercials; that TV characters ate primarily for social and emotional reasons; that friendly and hurried snacking were far more common than genuine meals. People who eat that way tend to get fat—but TV characters manage to stay slim and attractive (except for minorities and older people, who are more often shown as overweight or obese). Kaufman concludes that "television presents viewers with two sets of conflicting messages. One suggests that we eat in ways almost guaranteed to make us fat; the other suggests that we strive to remain slim."[17]

Of course the values and information in television entertainment often serve the public instead of misleading it. Every time a TV soap opera features a cancer case, thousands of viewers go for checkups, and dozens of cancers are diagnosed and treated. Many experts in family planning claim that the liberalization in public attitudes toward abortion in the early 1970s was a direct result of television programs in which sympathetic characters considered, obtained, or advocated abortions. And just as TV entertainment has often reinforced the stereotype of witless, dependent women, so too TV entertainment is at last beginning to reflect the existence of women who work, think, and control their own lives.

With occasional exceptions, none of this is planned or intentional. The values and information embedded in broadcast entertainment are the values and information in the heads of the people who write and produce the shows—generally white, male, middle-class, urban, liberal people. Without especially trying to, these people are constantly bombarding the rest of the country with *their* sense of reality. Little wonder the radical left, the reactionary right, and much of "middle America" are displeased with the values in television entertainment.

MASS CULTURE

Some time in the not too distant future, one of the networks may announce a new half-hour series called "Hawthorne Place,"

based loosely on Nathaniel Hawthorne's novel *The Scarlet Letter*. It will be billed as a sort of Calvinist "Peyton Place," with the role of the fallen woman, Hester Prynne, played by Bo Derek. In keeping with the All-American spirit of the show, its theme song will be drawn from the works of Aaron Copland, arranged for jazz sextet.

Guardians of the sacred flame of Culture will no doubt greet "Hawthorne Place"—if they stoop to greet it at all—with cries of dismay. The mass media, they will say, are again raping and debasing our culture in pursuit of profit. In the face of such irreverence it is impossible to be a serious artist or critic in America. The series is just one more proof of the old saying that everything television touches turns to tripe. That's what they'll say.

What is culture? Edward A. Shils supplies this definition: "Superior or refined culture is distinguished by the seriousness of its subject matter, i.e., the centrality of the problems with which it deals, the acute penetration and coherence of its perceptions, the subtlety and wealth of its expressed feeling."[18] This is High Culture. Twentieth-century examples include the music of Stravinsky and Berg, the novels of Conrad and Hesse, the paintings of Picasso and Wyeth, and like works of esthetic and intellectual refinement. High Culture has traditionally been the province of the upper classes.

Before the Industrial Revolution, the only competitor with High Culture was Folk Art—the culture of the common people. Folk Art, says critic Dwight Macdonald, was "the people's own institution, their private little garden walled off from the great formal park of their masters' High Culture."[19] It was expressed in craftsmanship, dance, music, and poetry.

Then came the Industrial Revolution, the burgeoning middle class, and the mass media. With them came Mass Culture—also known as Masscult, Low Culture, Pop Culture, and *Kitsch* (the German word for mass culture). Unlike Folk Art, Mass Culture borrows from the basic content of High Culture. But unlike High Culture, it is designed to be popular, to "sell" to a mass audience. Alexis de Tocqueville described the difference as long ago as 1835:

In aristocratic ages the object of the arts is . . . to manufacture as well as possible, not with the greatest speed or at the lowest cost. . . . In democracies there is always a multitude of persons whose wants are above their means and who are very willing to take up with imperfect satisfaction rather than abandon the object of their desires altogether. . . .

In aristocracies a few great pictures are produced; in democratic countries a vast number of insignificant ones. In the former statues are raised of bronze; in the latter, they are modeled in plaster.[20]

America is by all counts the world's greatest producer of Mass Culture. And television is by all counts America's greatest producer.

Broadcasting is a mass medium in the literal sense of the word. In order to attract advertisers, networks must attract an audience of millions, not thousands or even hundreds of thousands. There is no conspiracy at work here. If broadcasters were convinced that the public appetite for ballet was enormous, they would gladly program hour after hour of ballet. But since there is little demand for televised ballet, there is almost no ballet on television. Of course it is hard to generate a massive demand for ballet when most people have never *seen* one. Television could probably teach the public to enjoy ballet in the same way it has taught the public to enjoy doctor shows and situation comedies. But broadcasters are not in the business of breaking vicious circles. As long as viewers are satisfied with Mass Culture, there is no reason to bother training them to appreciate High Culture.

Critics like Dwight Macdonald not only deplore the public's satisfaction with Mass-

CULTURAL IMPERIALISM

Among many other products, the United States exports television programs. American TV shows, especially detective series, are staples in many foreign broadcast schedules. Much of what people in other countries learn about the U.S. comes from our television entertainment programs.

For the countries on the receiving end, this practice has two unfortunate effects. First, it discourages the development of their own broadcast programming industries. And second, it bombards them with an endless barrage of American popular culture, resulting in a sort of "cultural imperialism" that can overwhelm or distort their own customs and standards.

Overseas sales of U.S. television programming add up to about $300 million a year. Rates depend on the size of the market; a half-hour of "Gunsmoke" or "The Streets of San Francisco" can cost $8,500 to $18,000 in West Germany, $1,000 to $1,500 in Argentina or Belgium, $30 to $100 in Syria or Kenya.[21] This is not a plot to brainwash foreign audiences. It's a business—and for broadcast systems in many countries the U.S. has proved an excellent source of inexpensive programming in huge quantities. The result is cultural imperialism nonetheless.

One country that has worried about this for some time is Canada, which passed regulations in the early 1970s requiring Canadian broadcasters to carry more Canadian programming. Concerned about fostering their own cultural values (and their own broadcast industries), other countries are beginning to follow suit.

cult. They fear it. Macdonald puts the point this way: "Bad stuff drives out the good, since it is more easily understood and enjoyed. . . . When to this ease of consumption is added *Kitsch*'s ease of production because of its standardized nature, its prolific growth is easy to understand. It threatens High Culture by its sheer pervasiveness, its brutal, overwhelming *quantity*."[22]

Macdonald fears that television may destroy High Culture in America. Shils is more optimistic:

> There is much ridicule of *Kitsch*, and it *is* ridiculous. Yet it represents aesthetic sensibility and aesthetic aspiration, untutored, rude, and deformed. The very growth of *Kitsch*, and of the demand which has generated the industry for the production of *Kitsch*, is an indication of a crude aesthetic awakening in classes which previously accepted what was handed down to them or who had practically no aesthetic expression and reception.[23]

Only history can settle this dispute—but it is worth noting that television is becoming a vehicle for High Culture as well as for *Kitsch*. Public television offers a wide range of "cultural" programming for elites that prefer their soap operas elevated by a British accent. Video playback units permit the wealthier culture fanatics to purchase their own tapes or disks to watch when they please. And pay TV provides a "culture channel" in some major markets, available via cable or satellite. As High Culture increasingly shares the TV medium with Masscult, the results could downgrade its quality or expand its appeal . . . or both.

Whatever its effects—and no one really knows what they are—the dominance of *Kitsch* is a genuine cultural phenomenon. National leaders have historically been reared on High Culture; that was a big part of what made them different, what made them elites. Today's national leaders, for the most part, watch the same TV shows as everybody else. For better or for worse, that's a difference that probably *makes* a difference.

BROADCAST CORRUPTION

Sex, profanity, violence . . . our children are in danger! Such is the cry of many critics of the broadcast media.

While the fight against Mass Culture is confined to a few universities and literary magazines, the fight against broadcast corruption is out in the open—in Congress, in the FCC, in outraged letters to networks and stations and advertisers. Broadcasters have more or less ignored their esthetic critics. But they have been forced to make major concessions to their moralistic ones.

Sex is doubtless the big moral issue of our society. But broadcasting has traditionally been so sexless that the critics found little to complain about until the mid-1970s. True, television advertisers have always implied all sorts of sexual advantages to their products—but late-night talk shows used to supply handkerchiefs to women whose clothes might otherwise show a hint of cleavage. TV serials have always relied on sex as a principal motivation for many characters—but when CBS broadcast the movie *Elmer Gantry* it cut out a scene between Gantry and a prostitute. Off-color insinuations have always been a staple of TV comedy routines—but the costumes for a female "genie" in a popular series of the 1960s were carefully designed to cover her navel.

TV's indirect, sometimes leering approach to sex was so tame compared to the raunchy explicitness of the other media that it escaped the critics' notice. TV violence, on the other hand, was anything but tame, and it came under attack early.

American television has been exceedingly violent almost since the birth of the medium. In a single week of Los Angeles TV in 1960, there were 144 murders, 11 murder attempts, 13 kidnappings, 7 torture scenes, 4 lynchings, and hundreds upon hundreds of fights.[24] According to communications researcher George Gerbner, more than three-quarters of all network dramatic shows from 1967 to 1971 contained elements of violence.[25] Nor was the mayhem limited to prime time. The average Saturday morning cartoon hour in 1967 included three times as many violent episodes as the average adult dramatic hour. By 1969 there was a violent episode every two minutes in Saturday morning's cartoon programming.[26]

While violence is obviously good for the ratings, politicians, parents, and behavioral scientists have often wondered how good it is for the impressionable minds of young people. Dozens of studies throughout the 1960s produced mixed results. Generally, they tended to confirm that children learn techniques of violence from the media and imitate those techniques in their play. But on the crucial question of whether this imitation actually makes children more violent the studies were inconclusive. Broadcasters found plenty of ammunition in the data with which to fight off any effort to change the content of TV programs.

Then, in the late 1960s, the Senate Subcommittee on Communications, chaired by John O. Pastore (D.-R.I.), began investigating television violence. In an effort to stave off congressional interference, the networks declared 1969 "the year of anti-violence." The superhero cartoons were eliminated, and so was most of the on-camera killing in adult programs. Commented TV critic John Stanley, "It was the year that if you shot anybody on 'Bonanza' he was only wounded. (If you shot him off-camera, it didn't matter—he could live or die.)"[27]

Despite this progress, the Pastore Committee decided to commission a thorough study of television violence. Appointed in 1969, the Surgeon General's Scientific Advisory Committee on Television and Social Behavior emerged in 1972 with a report entitled *Television and Growing Up: The Impact of Televised Violence*. The report concluded that violence on television can be dangerous.

Media violence seems to have two kinds of effects on children (and possibly on adults). The Surgeon General's Committee called them "imitation" and "instigation."

Imitation is the effect that had already been documented in the 1960s. Children do copy the styles of violence they see on TV—and not only when they're playing. In Los Angeles in the 1950s, for example, a 7-year-old was caught sprinkling ground glass into his family's stew in hopes that the method would work as well as it had on television. Two Chicago boys tried to extort $500 from a neighbor through a bomb threat, a scheme they had watched succeed on TV.[28] And in 1972, after the movie *West Side Story* was televised, children at P.S. 108 in New York's East Harlem spent their play time dividing into gangs of Jets and Sharks, threatening "rumbles," and pulling knives on each other.[29] TV probably didn't create these children's aggressive feelings, but it did teach them more destructive ways to express those feelings. Thanks to television, just about every American youngster knows how to shoot a gun. For an angry child, shooting at baby sister may be the emotional equivalent of yelling at her—but if the gun is real and loaded, the effect on baby sister can be tragic.

Closely related to imitation is the media's ability to teach the audience that violence is an acceptable, even a fashionable way to cope with problems. This is a difficult effect to prove; violence is so thoroughly embedded in our culture that it is hard to isolate the influence of the media. But experimenters have found that children exposed to violent films are more likely to view violence as a solution to their own conflicts than children exposed to films depicting other ways of handling the situation. And of course a small child who has not yet learned to distinguish fact from fantasy may well assume that violence in life will have as few consequences as it has in a "Roadrunner" cartoon.

If imitation is dangerous, instigation is doubly so. Under some circumstances, media violence can actually arouse aggressive feelings (or good feelings about aggression), and thus directly stimulate violent behavior. One 1971 experiment paired preschool children who watched the same amount of TV at home, monitoring the extent of aggression in their play. Then one member of each pair was exposed to a violent Saturday-morning cartoon, while the other watched a nonviolent program. A second play session followed. The researchers found that "the two groups had departed significantly from one another in terms of the frequency of interpersonal aggression. In fact, for every pair, the child who observed aggressive television programming had become more aggressive than his mate who watched neutral fare."[30]

Most of the research on media violence, by the way, has concentrated on the sort of violence the media like best—sanitized. Some psychologists have suggested that this may be the most dangerous sort of violence of all, because it stresses the action and ignores the evil results. Though it is unhealthy to watch a private eye beating up a suspect on TV, perhaps it would be healthy to contemplate the victim's bleeding face. If so, American television is very unhealthy indeed. It has a great deal of violence, but very little pain or suffering.

Soon after the Surgeon General's committee report was published, the networks announced a series of concessions. Most violent cartoon shows were replaced with nonviolent children's programs (though the old ones lived on for years in daytime reruns on local stations). The early evening period from 8 to 9 was declared to be "family viewing time," with programs unsuitable for children saved till later. And even the adult shows saw their violence toned down another notch or two.

But plenty of nightly mayhem remained, and so the pressure continued. In 1974, NBC aired the made-for-TV movie "Born Innocent," which depicted the rape of a young girl by other girls using a broom handle. Shortly after the broadcast, the scene was re-enacted for real on a beach in California, leading to a celebrated (but ultimately unsuccessful) lawsuit by the young victim's parents against the network, claiming NBC was responsible for the attack.[31] Several similar incidents in the first half of the 1970s fueled the flames of public anger, as did the annual publication of George Gerbner's TV violence ratings, reporting continued high levels despite the protests.

A 1977 survey of 7-to-11-year-olds revealed another aspect of television violence: fear. Nearly a quarter of the children said they were afraid of TV programs on which people fought and fired guns, and a disproportionate number of heavy viewers said they feared "real world" violence as well.[32] Gerbner soon reached similar findings about adult TV viewers, especially the elderly—that heavy viewers were more fearful than lighter viewers. TV violence, Gerbner asserted, teaches us that the world is a dangerous place. And through fear, he added, TV persuades us of our powerlessness, makes us docile and apathetic, ripens us for fascism.[33]

Despite mounting pressure, the networks stood firm. As NBC programming executive Paul Klein said, "Nobody gets fired for bad taste. They get fired for losing money. The day violence isn't profitable, it will stop."[34]

TV violence began to become unprofitable in 1977, when citizen groups started attacking the advertisers who sponsored violent shows (see p. 226). The mammoth J. Walter Thompson advertising agency was among the first to respond, advising all its clients to avoid programs with excessive violence.[35] Bristol-Myers, Schlitz, Kodak, and a variety of other national advertisers moved to less violent shows. Such mainstream organizations as the national PTA and the American Medical Association joined in the battle against the sponsors of violent TV. Even the House Subcommittee on Communications went on record as finding television violence a "cause for serious concern and remedial action."[36]

And beginning in the 1977-78 season, network programming became less violent.

Replacing much of the violence for the rest of the decade, ironically, was an increasing emphasis on sex. Network prime-time shows like "Charlie's Angels," "Three's Company," "Love Boat," and "Dallas" began featuring braless women who somehow managed to get soaked in some body of water on almost every episode. Sex scenes still fell far short of the explicitness of X-rated movies, but they were getting spicier—and R-rated movies started running on TV with fewer strategic cuts at the sexy parts. On daytime television, meanwhile, syndicated hits like "The Newlywed Game" made sexual innuendo their stock-in-trade. Reaction peaked in 1981 with a threatened boycott against sponsors of sexy shows (see p. 143). Some advertisers promised to reform, but it is too soon to tell whether the networks will reform as well.

The big test of TV sexuality will not involve the networks, which still fall far to the right side of even soft-core pornography, and intend to remain there. The test will come with the networks' new competitors—pay-cable, video disks, and satellites—all of which expect to bring explicit sex to the home screen in the 1980s. The issue of broadcast corruption will not go away.

The vast majority of what Americans watch on television each evening comes to us courtesy of three companies—CBS, NBC, and ABC. Although many critics fear network power and regret network-imposed standardization of content, the network system developed inevitably because it benefits everyone. Stations earn higher profits, advertisers gain easier access to a national market, and viewers get better (or at least more expensive) programs. Public television coexists with the network system without seriously threatening its monopoly, while the structure of American radio remains predominantly local.

THE NETWORK STRUCTURE

The 1980s are going to be a time of rapid change for the American system of broadcasting. Four relatively new broadcast tech-

nologies—cable TV, subscription TV, satellite communication, and video playback—are beginning to assert their growing power. Competition from these newcomers will inevitably weaken the monopoly and change the character of traditional broadcasting. Before examining these new technologies and their probable effects, however, it is essential to understand the traditional system they will try to change. The rudiments of that system date back to the 1920s, before the invention of television. It is a system dominated by broadcast networks.

A network is a collection of stations tied to a programming source through some combination of cables, microwave relay stations, and satellites. This hook-up permits the programming source to send the same show to all its affiliated stations at the same time. The three major U.S. networks are all headquartered within a six-block area of New York City. The typical network-affiliated television station relies on CBS, NBC, or ABC for about 60 percent of its programming, and for almost all of its crucial prime-time entertainment programming.

In most television markets, one station is affiliated with each network. The two companies sign a contract in which the network promises to offer all its programs to the affiliated station first; in return, the affiliate promises to base most of its programming on that network's offerings. The network cannot force its affiliate to accept a particular program, so as an incentive it pays the station a fee for each program it carries. At first glance this may seem a little backwards; you might expect that the station would pay the network for the privilege of using its programs. Not so. The network pays to insure that as many stations as possible will carry a given program (give the program "clearance"), so that the ads within that program will reach the largest possible audience.

This is necessary because the networks earn nearly all their profits by keeping the revenue from national advertising. Only the local ad revenue goes to the stations—and the networks kindly leave a couple of ad minutes in each program open for the affiliated stations to fill with these local ads.

The business of the networks, then, is to sell the combined audience of local stations across the country to advertisers interested in a national market. To keep the advertisers happy, each network needs an affiliate in every major city and as many minor ones as possible. To keep the affiliates happy, each network needs popular programming that will successfully attract local viewers and thus local advertisers. The number of stations affiliated with each network varies some from year to year, currently ranging between 190 and 220 stations per network. All three networks earn huge profits.

For a local station, the choice is a simple one. If it accepts a network affiliation, it gains two new sources of income—the fees paid by the network for each program given clearance, and the local advertising lured by a chance to "sponsor" a popular network show. At the same time, the station solves its problem of what to do with most of its 18 to 20 empty hours of airtime a day. Of course the *potential* profit is higher without a network affiliation—but only if the station can manage to produce local programs that outdraw the network shows, and only if it can find enough local advertisers to fill all those minutes of ad time. It is a rare station indeed that meets these requirements. The vast majority find it more profitable to turn on the network spigot.

Nearly all independent stations—those without a network affiliation—are independent by necessity, not by choice. Since there are only three television networks, in a city with more than three commercial TV stations the rest have to be independent. As a rule, independent stations carry only a little more local programming than the network affiliates. Instead of the network shows, they run old movies, reruns of former network programs that are no longer being produced, and whatever else they can buy cheaply enough from the TV syndicates.

Like the print media's feature syndicates, broadcast syndicates sell their shows to stations around the country, offering the same incentive of exclusive local rights. Besides reruns and old movies, the syndicates have some original material for sale. Network affiliates can buy syndicated programs too; they use them to fill the hours when the network offers nothing, or to replace the least popular network programs (if they can sell enough local ads to pay for the show). But for the network affiliates, syndicates are just a minor alternative programming source; syndicates are the lifeblood of the independent stations.

Besides the network affiliates and independents, there is a third category of broadcast stations—those owned and operated by the networks themselves. Like any other corporation, a network is entitled to apply for a broadcast license. It is limited only by the FCC rules that restrict each licensee to a maximum of seven AM radio stations; seven FM radio stations; and seven TV stations, no more than five of which can be VHF. All three of the networks own their full complement of VHF television stations, and they own them in the biggest markets—New York, Los Angeles, Chicago, San Francisco, Cleveland, etc. This is no coincidence. The networks were among the first to recognize the profit potential of television, and they moved early to secure the most attractive licenses. Among broadcasters, these stations are referred to as "o-and-o's"; that is, stations owned and operated by a network. Naturally, they carry the full network line-up, thus guaranteeing each network an audience in the largest markets.

Occasionally a network and one of its affiliates (not an o-and-o) will come to a parting of the ways. Once in a while the network initiates the split because the station is preempting too many network shows, replacing them with popular local offerings. But this is a rare event. Affiliates do frequently refuse to clear such low-rated public-service programs as "Meet the Press" or "Face the Na-

UHF STRUGGLES UPWARD

Ultrahigh frequency television (UHF) is a different area of the spectrum from ordinary very high frequency (VHF) television. In terms of channels, VHF is 2 through 13, UHF is 14 through 83. Obviously, UHF opens up a lot more spectrum space for a lot more TV stations, making it possible (in theory, at least) to diversify broadcast programming.

UHF dates back before World War II, but for two decades the FCC actively opposed its development, preferring to nurse along the infant VHF industry first. It wasn't until 1962 that the FCC asked Congress to require UHF receivers on new television sets, making UHF broadcasting economically feasible.

By then, all the network affiliations in major markets had already been snapped up by VHF stations. Some of the new UHF channels were allocated to smaller markets that didn't have any VHF allocations, and these quickly became network affiliates. Big-city UHF stations had no choice but to go independent. As of 1980, there were 226 commercial UHF stations in the country, compared to 516 commercial VHF stations. The V's tend to be big-city network affiliates; the U's are mostly small-city network affiliates or big-city independents.

The poor showing of UHF independents kept the UHF industry unprofitable until the mid-1970s. But by the late seventies profits were climbing at a rate of 30 percent a year. In 1979, a UHF independent station in Washington, D.C. sold for $15.5 million, while one in Austin, Texas went for $13.2 million.[37] Nobody spends that kind of money on a station without profit potential.

Why the turnaround? For one thing, TV advertising time became scarce in the 1970s; would-be advertisers who couldn't find or couldn't afford a slot on the network-affiliated V's turned to the independent U's. More important, perhaps, was the piggyback effect of other new technologies. Cable systems enabled subscribers to receive UHF with the same ease and clarity as VHF. Satellites aided in the formation of ad-hoc "networks" (see pp. 326-27) for specialized programming of various sorts, giving the U's something better to offer than old movies and off-network reruns. Subscription television permitted many UHF stations to send a scrambled signal for part of the broadcast day, charging viewers for the device that unscrambles the signal into first-run movies and sporting events, and thus competing with pay-cable systems.

None of this has been enough to pose a serious threat to network domination of broadcasting. Nor has it hiked the profits of UHF independent stations to anything like the levels of the typical network affiliate. Virtually any independent station would jump at a network affiliation if one were offered. But at least the U's are beginning to make money. Many of the remaining UHF channel allocations, unclaimed for decades, are now hotly contested. (The FCC is giving special preference to minority applicants, since minorities own practically no VHF licenses.) There is even talk of uniting the U's into a fourth network.

Meanwhile, UHF stations add genuinely, if modestly, to the diversity of American television. Some independent U's specialize in Spanish-language programming, or black programming, or news. Even the ones that rely mostly on syndicates and reruns try to compete by offering something slightly different. Says Gene Jacobson of KHTV in Houston: "When they [the networks] go for adults, we go for kids, and in prime time when we all go for adults we play features and counter them as much as we can."[38]

tion." Documentaries often run into trouble, late-night talk shows are sometimes pre-empted by a more profitable non-network movie, and the occasional controversial episode of a network series may be denied clearance. But affiliates almost always clear the popular game shows, soap operas, and prime-time dramas and comedies. Overall, the average affiliate clears 95 percent of prime-time programs and 87 percent of off-peak programs.[39]

More often a split will come about because a station dumps its network for a more successful one, forcing the network to pick up a less successful station (if one is available in that market). ABC long was the weakest of the three networks, settling for the weakest affiliate in three-station markets and no affiliate at all in smaller markets. But in 1976 ABC became number one in the ratings, and in the next few years many stations defected to it. In 1979, for example, ABC scored a coup by luring KSTP—number one in Minneapolis—away from NBC. ABC wanted KSTP because its top-rated local news show would provide a strong lead-in to ABC's national news and the rest of the prime-time line-up. KSTP wanted ABC because its more popular programs would lure 100,000 additional local viewers and an estimated $1.5 million in extra local ad revenue.[40]

As of 1980, NBC had the lowest ratings. If it therefore wound up with the weakest local affiliates in all of its 200 or so markets, that alone could drop its ratings an estimated 20 percent more.[41] And since advertising rates, and therefore profits, are based on the ratings, losing its best affiliates would cost NBC a big chunk of money. Conversely, staying with NBC while its ratings dropped would cost every affiliate a big chunk of money. And so the jockeying continues.

The network system dominates American television because it works. It offers local stations the maximum possible profit with the minimum possible risk. It offers advertisers the greatest convenience in reaching whatever audiences they want to reach, local or national. And it offers viewers the most elaborate, most expensive, most standardized entertainment in the world. Almost anywhere you may be in the United States, tonight and every night, you can watch the same national shows starring the same national personalities. Almost anywhere you may be, you will find that the three strongest stations in town are carrying whatever CBS, NBC, and ABC have offered them. Most broadcasters, advertisers, and viewers can't imagine a better system.

PROGRAMMING AND THE NETWORKS

In the early years of broadcasting, program production was often in the hands of advertisers. But after the quiz show scandals of 1959 (see p. 146), the networks promised to oversee programming themselves. Today, most TV programs come from independent producers, who put together a series "package," and then try to sell it to one of the networks.

But the networks still maintain a heavy (and, some say, heavy-handed) economic interest in program production. Network-owned facilities, for example, are often rented to the producers of programs to be carried by that network. The networks produce some of their own specials and made-for-TV movies. And all three networks habitually put up the money to finance the "pilots" of new series in which they are interested.

Furthermore, independent producers know the rules of the game. They know what types of shows the networks are likely to purchase for distribution. They know which plot lines are acceptable, and which are not. Above all, they know that the market for their wares is very slim—the networks or a few scattered independents, cable systems, and syndicates, period. Without any direct financial interest whatever, the three networks could still dictate the content of TV programming.

So what are the rules of the game? What standards do network executives use to determine which series pilots to buy and which to let die?

The most important rule is to aim at the "lowest common denominator" of the viewing audience. The networks, remember, earn their profits almost entirely from national advertising. And what national advertisers appreciate most about television is its efficiency, its ability to reach huge numbers of people—not just a few hundred thousand or even a few million, but up to 50 million at once. Network ad rates are determined by the size of the audience; the more people who are watching a particular show, the more an advertiser will pay for 30 seconds in the middle of it. So the networks naturally strive for the biggest possible audience. They therefore pick programs with the broadest possible appeal—nothing too highbrow or too lowbrow, too controversial or too boring, nothing too anything.

What do rich people and poor people, dumb people and smart people, tired people and alert people, white people and black people, urban people and suburban people all have in common? Whatever it is, that's what the networks want to appeal to in every program. In their search for the lowest common denominator of American television viewers, the networks have so far come up with game shows, situation comedies, melodramas, and sports. They are quite willing to substitute something else, once they're convinced that just about everyone will enjoy watching it.

Suppose a national advertiser doesn't want this sort of huge, random audience, but rather prefers a smaller and more homogeneous collection of viewers. To some small extent, such "demographic selection" is possible even on network TV. Sports events are aimed mostly at men, afternoon soap operas at women; children and their grandparents

like westerns the best, while the generation in the middle prefers police shows; "One Day at a Time" is popular in urban areas, "Dukes of Hazzard" in rural ones. But if the advertiser's demographic choices are any narrower than that, network television inevitably fails. By their very nature, the networks are a poor medium for selling, say, computers—too many people are bound to be watching who don't buy computers. An ad in a data-processing magazine would be a much wiser choice.

Despite these realities, national advertisers occasionally want to sponsor a "highbrow" program aimed at an elite audience. If it's a once-in-a-while special, a network will readily agree; it has to do that sort of thing from time to time anyhow to keep the FCC happy. But a highbrow *series* will provoke nothing but frowns from network executives, even if the sponsors are lined up and ready to go. Why? For one thing, the smaller audience for such a program will force a lower advertising rate, while production costs remain as high as ever, and profits therefore decrease. Second, local ad minutes for the unpopular program will be hard to sell, which will greatly displease the network's affiliates. And third, viewers may well dislike the show so much that they'll actually get up and switch channels, killing the network's ratings for the rest of the night as well.

The lowest common denominator strategy thus reigns supreme. No program with a potential audience of fewer than ten million viewers can make it onto the networks in prime time.

Even within this framework, network programmers hate to experiment. Instead of guessing at what sort of show might attract a large audience, they use the successes of this season as a guide for planning next season. A hit program about doctors this year insures half a dozen doctor programs next year. When it was first proposed, "All In The Family" was bounced from network to network until it finally found a home. But once it earned a high rating—bigots liked it too—a flock of imitators were hustled into the network line-ups.

Next to choosing new programs and renewing old ones, the networks' biggest headache is deciding what goes where in the schedule. The three networks compete, mostly with each other, for the largest share of the viewing audience. Each network tries to attract a third or more of all the people watching TV at any given moment. If a particular show is chosen by only a fifth of the viewers, it's doomed. Scheduling obviously plays a crucial role in this competition.

The main rule used to guide scheduling decisions is "the theory of the least objectionable program."[42] Network officials are convinced that most of the television audience is there to watch television, rather than any specific program. We are addicted to the medium, not its message. It is a rare viewer, the networks reason, who carefully selects an evening's TV diet—first that drama on CBS, then to ABC for that comedy, then to NBC for that movie, etc. Instead, the typical viewer just turns on the set and watches—until something comes on that he or she doesn't like. Then the viewer reluctantly switches channels, settles back, and watches some more—until another objectionable program turns up. The goal of scheduling, then, is to have the least objectionable programs, especially in the early evening when viewers are picking the night's channel.

In order to steal a portion of the audience from the opposition, a network may try another strategy—counter-programming. If CBS and NBC are both running comedies in a particular time slot, for example, ABC may schedule a western or detective series. If both competitors are showing programs aimed at the older generation, ABC may counter with something for young marrieds. But counter-programming is never allowed to interfere with the "least objectionable program" principle. Stealing new viewers is nice, but keeping your own is essential. Thus, every program must have mass appeal.

STANDARDIZATION

CBS, NBC, and ABC control American television. It's as simple as that. By giving local stations, national advertisers, and the vast majority of viewers exactly what they want, the three networks have achieved dominion over the most powerful mass medium yet discovered.

There are as many criticisms of network performance as there are critics, and lots of them are justified. The networks incorporate too much sex in their shows. They carry too many commercials. They are dominated by a white, male, urban, liberal perspective. They don't hire enough women and minorities. But none of these failings—nor the dozens of others that could be listed—results from the peculiar nature of networks. Much local programming is just as sexy, just as commercial, and just as white, male, urban, and liberal. Reducing the influence of the networks would not automatically cure all the evils of television.

What would it cure? Maybe nothing. If the networks were somehow abolished tomorrow, would local station owners feel any less compelled to make every program attract the biggest possible audience? Would they simply purchase network-type shows from independent producers and syndicates, or would they follow the example of radio and cultivate more specialized audiences? Would the result be greater diversity or just more of the same? Nobody knows. It seems reasonable to predict that a host of independent stations would offer a wider range of programming than three carbon-copy networks—but maybe not.

At a minimum, any lessening in network influence would reassure those who fear the sheer fact of network power, who worry that the minds of millions of Americans are molded every day by a handful of executives in New York.

Of course we'd lose something in the process. It is hard to imagine a more efficient system than the network system for bringing skillfully produced information and entertainment into millions of homes across thousands of miles. The networks help establish the common goals, habits, perceptions, attitudes, and experiences that unite the country. They confer celebrity and status, and they take it away. They are the principal source of current information for many, and the principal leisure-time activity for most. They are nearly indispensable to hundreds of companies that depend on them for selling goods and services. They have the power to confront government and industry when they want to, and the wealth to support unprofitable programming when they need to. They offer us escapist entertainment of incredibly high quality, plus a modest dose of news and public affairs—and except for the cost of the receiver and the hidden cost of advertising, they do it for free.

For decades, critics have urged the Federal Communications Commission to do something about the overwhelming power of the networks—to no avail. We have already discussed government regulation of broadcasting in some detail (see pp. 200-13). Very little of this regulation has anything to do with networks. The FCC's modest restrictions on program content—the fairness doctrine, the obscenity rules, the equal time law—don't significantly affect network freedom to produce hour after hour of bland entertainment. The FCC's efforts to encourage diversity concentrate on ownership of stations; they seriously restrict the number of o-and-o's, but do nothing to keep an independently owned station from contracting with a network for most of its programs. And the FCC's licensing power doesn't even apply to networks; only stations need licenses.

Of course FCC power over broadcasting—however seldom it is exercised—does serve to keep broadcasters cautious, and that caution is passed along to the networks as well. No network is likely to schedule a program that would get its affiliates in trouble with the FCC. But the cozy network-affiliate relationship itself goes essentially unregulated.

And when the government has tried to chip away at network influence, it has not met with resounding success. In 1970, for example, the FCC passed a rule requiring local stations to carry non-network programming for one prime-time hour a night. The Commission hoped stations would use much of the time for documentaries or local-interest shows, something that would add a little diversity to evening television. Most stations didn't,[43] preferring to program game shows and similar light entertainment, purchased from independent producers (who did benefit from the policy). In 1979, the FCC staff recommended abandoning the rule.

Ironically, the FCC's principal impact on networks has been to protect their programming monopoly by slowing the growth of competitors such as cable and satellites (see pp. 209-10). Only in the late 1970s were these new technologies finally permitted to compete unfettered. The results in the 1980s may threaten network domination of television for the first time since the medium was invented.

Before examining these newcomers, we must look briefly at the rest of the traditional structure of American broadcasting—public television and radio.

PUBLIC TELEVISION

As of mid-1980, just over a quarter of all television stations in the U.S. were non-commercial—100 on the VHF band (compared to 516 commercial VHF stations) and 155 on UHF (compared to 226 commercial U's). These "public television" stations are operated by colleges and universities, state and local governments, and various nonprofit civic groups. Some are strictly educational. Others go far beyond the classroom to program political, social, and cultural events of interest, along with specialized entertainment of various sorts. Whatever their content, public television stations accept no advertising. They are supported entirely by donations from individuals and grants from foundations, corporations, and the government.

The goals and activities of any institution are affected by where that institution's money comes from. For network television, advertisers are the funding source, and slick, light, mass entertainment is the result. For public television, Congress, foundations, corporations, and viewers themselves are the main sources of money. The result is a mixture of educational children's programs ("Sesame Street," "Mister Rogers' Neighborhood") and elite entertainment ("Masterpiece Theater" and its many spinoffs). The result is *not* controversial public-affairs programming.

President Richard Nixon was especially averse to public-affairs programs on public television, because he detected a liberal political tilt that would tend to be critical of his policies. To undermine this tendency, the Nixon administration channeled public-affairs money to local stations, leaving the national Public Broadcasting Service (PBS) to concentrate on cultural and educational shows.

A 1971 memo to the president from Clay Whitehead, director of the White House Office of Telecommunications Policy, spelled out the strategy:

> We stand to gain substantially from an increase in the relative power of the local stations. They are generally less liberal and more concerned with education than with controversial national affairs. Further, a decentralized system would have far less influence and be far less attractive to social activists. . . . [Such a policy] provides an opportunity to further our philosophical and political objectives for public broadcasting without appearing to be politically motivated.[44]

Nixon's localism strategy worked, and succeeding presidents have been content to leave public television as nonpolitical as possible. As of 1980, the federal government supplied $175 million a year to public televi-

sion. The rest of public television's $650 million budget came from foundations, viewers, and corporations, in that order (though the corporate share is rising fast, led by the oil companies).[45] None of these funders much likes political controversy either. Between 1970 and 1978, public-affairs programming decreased 37 percent on public television.[46]

This total budget of $650 million, by the way, is only about five percent of the revenues of American commercial broadcasting— a drop in the bucket.[47]

Public television's share of the viewing audience is also a drop in the bucket. In 1980 noncommercial television reached about 35 million homes during the average week, a little under half of all TV homes in the country. This represented an impressive 39 percent increase over the 1975 figures.[48] But the fact that public television must still measure its audience in terms of *weekly* exposure instead of nightly ratings is a telling admission of weakness. Public television captures only about three percent of all prime-time viewing.[49] CBS, NBC and ABC are not quaking in their boots at the loss of three percent.

Public TV's audience is not only small; it is also higher in education, income, and social class than the audience for commercial television. This is understandably attractive to corporate donors, who curry favor with "decision-makers" by underwriting elite entertainment on public television. But public TV was never meant to provide a more convenient cultural life for the rich and well-educated (see p. 237). Neither was it meant to duplicate the network shows. The perennial problem is figuring out what it *was* meant to do.

"Quality programming" is the usual answer, but the question that noncommercial broadcasting has never been able to answer convincingly is this: What does "quality programming" mean for a mass audience that is quite satisfied with commercial offerings? Traditional educational broadcasters have an answer that makes sense; they reach mil-

Critics of noncommercial broadcasting in the U.S. often point wistfully to the British Broadcasting Corporation as the ideal model to follow. And indeed the BBC, which was founded in 1922, is in some ways an excellent example for the U.S. Its long-term funding is assured by an annual license fee for TV sets. It is partially insulated from government control by a parliamentary charter renewed every five years. And it has managed to produce programming that is at once reasonably popular and "culturally elevated." Its exports to the United States, including the dramas shown here as "Masterpiece Theater," have been the most successful adult programs on American public television.

But the BBC has problems too. Political criticism is not unknown, and has been especially sharp in recent years from both the Labour and the Conservative parties, no doubt because of the strains caused by rebellion in Northern Ireland and the deteriorating British economy. A National Viewers and Listeners Association has sprung up to battle sex and violence in BBC shows. And competition from commercial stations is taking its toll. Along with its historical, literary, and educational endeavors, the BBC now offers sports, rock music, and other competitive entertainment.

---

lions of people in and out of schools who are watching or listening for information, not entertainment. Children's programs such as "Sesame Street" and "Mister Rogers' Neighborhood" have an equally sound rationale; kids enjoy the shows at least as much as the network ones, and parents and educators like them a lot more. An argument could be made that political documentaries were a kind of programming with at least the potential for mass appeal, but this particular alternative to network entertainment is anathema to the people who pay the bills. Some stations have tried special-interest shows for minority cultural, ethnic, or interest groups, but the result is usually a low rating and a collective yawn that neither raises money from the public nor justifies money from the government. What is left besides highbrow culture for elites or a pale, underfinanced imitation of the networks?

Public television's solution has been a compromise—programming that is just a little higher-quality (that is, higher-brow) than the stuff on the networks, but not so elevated as to reduce ratings to the vanishing point and fuel charges of runaway elitism. And even this solution, ironically, is threatened by the growth of cable, pay TV, satellites, and video playback. Critic Don Agostino explains why:

> [T]he specialty productions and targeting of small audiences characteristic of the new media invade what had been the exclusive province of public TV. By the late eighties public TV may be one of a dozen sources of specialty programming. Programs are needed to fill the schedules of the new media, and so producers of specialty material such as live music, nature, science and documentary programs, accustomed to the lean public TV market, will be invited to the feast of the new distribution systems. This will result in rising costs for programs of this type, forcing public TV to offer fewer of its traditional kinds of programs. Second, the public TV audience for these programs will be siphoned away to the other media. This shift will challenge the status and rationale of public TV as the principal "alternative" to real-time commercial broadcast programming.[50]

As if to confirm these predictions, the BBC announced in late 1980 that it was signing an exclusive ten-year contract for American rights to BBC programs—with a commercial cable company.

It is possible that public television will survive financially by selling its own best programming efforts to pay-cable or video disk promoters. But how will this sit with Congress and the public, whose tax money built the public television system?

Public television, in short, faces three huge problems—where to get its money, how to keep itself free from political control by its funding sources, and what to do with the money and freedom once they're gained. None of these problems will be rendered any easier by the growth of new commercial alternatives.

RADIO

In 1980, there were 8,817 licensed radio stations in the U.S.—4,554 AM stations (all but a handful of them commercial); 3,214 commercial FM stations; and 1,049 educational FM stations.

Before the invention of television, radio was fat and sassy, the number one news and entertainment medium in the country. But in 1951, for the first time, the networks earned more money from TV than from radio. In 1952, for the first time, A. C. Nielsen reported that there were more TV sets than radio sets in use every evening. And by 1956 radio's share of the advertising dollar was down to a meager 5.7 percent. That figure has since inched its way up almost to 7 percent, third behind newspapers and television.

To survive in the television era, radio stations have been forced to adopt one or another formula—usually music. Of the 500 top-rated U.S. stations in 1980, about 40 percent were devoted to middle-of-the-road and contemporary music; 15 percent concentrated on rock; 10 percent programmed country-and-western music; 7.5 percent had news or talk-show formats; 4 percent stressed blues or jazz for black audiences. The rest were devoted to disco, classical music, religious or foreign-language formats, etc.[51]

For the most part, today's radio programming is designed for background, not for concentration:

Radio is the one medium that cannot seize the eye. It is therefore the one mass medium that can serve an active audience: getting up, bathing, eating, doing housework, shopping, commuting, picnicking, camping, cooking, going to bed. Radio became a symbol of the competitive determination of the mass media to occupy any remaining fragment of audience attention. Radio's role became that of a constant companion.[52]

As we said at the start of this chapter, the average American listens to the radio for three and a half hours a day—most of it while doing other things. Radio is nowhere near as profitable as television, and never will be. But thanks to its symbiotic relationship with the recorded music industry (see pp. 361-62), it is in no danger of extinction.

Unlike television, radio is a highly fragmented medium. Each station has its loyal audience; rock fans seldom listen to the all-news station, country-and-western fans pay no attention to the easy-listening station. This audience segmentation is made possible by the huge number of radio stations in the country (nearly nine times the number of TV stations), and by the weakness of radio networks. Most stations have no network affiliation at all, and even the affiliates do most of their own programming, relying on the networks mainly for national news, news features, and special events. They provide the music themselves.

The biggest change in radio in the past decade has been the astounding growth of FM. In 1973, only 28 percent of the radio audience was listening to FM, 72 percent to AM.[53] By 1979, FM had captured just over half the radio audience.[54] AM collectively is still more profitable, with $2 billion in ad revenues for 1979 compared to FM's $900 million. But FM is at last in the black, and rising fast.[55]

What did the trick? The fact that three-quarters of all radios manufactured today (including most car radios) can receive FM as well as AM certainly helped. So did a 1961 FCC rule that permitted FM stations to broadcast in stereo, and a 1968 rule that forced co-owned AM and FM stations to carry different programming. FM's scarcity of advertisers enabled it to interrupt the music with commercials less often than AM, increasing its appeal to listeners (which has ironically led to more advertisers and thus more commercial interruptions). Perhaps most important, FM was first to experiment with new formats such as hard rock and disco that appeal to young listeners.

FM's arrival as a strong force in radio has further fragmented the already fragmented radio market. The top station in a big city could once command up to 20 percent of the listening audience; today, 6 or 7 percent is a good (and profitable) share. (By contrast, a television network affiliate expects around 30 percent.) These percentages will get smaller still if the FCC makes good on its late-1970s promise to squeeze in another 125 to 700 AM stations around the country.[56] By 1990, the leading radio stations in town may each command as little as one-twentieth of the total radio audience.

In sum, radio has found a secure niche for itself. Radio is local, while TV is dominated by national networks. Radio offers specialized musical formats aimed at small slices of the total audience, while TV tries to attract everybody with "lowest common denominator" programming. Radio provides background for active people, while TV provides something to do at home. Network television no longer threatens the survival of radio, and radio can never threaten the TV networks. They coexist in peace.

MONEY

Television is one of the most profitable businesses in the United States. Precise figures are hard to come by, but many stations in 1980 returned a profit of 50 to 60 percent of their gross revenues[57]—an astounding figure that dwarfs the percentage profits of even the oil industry, a favorite target of TV news.

Virtually every network-affiliated VHF station earns a sizable profit every year, as do the three networks themselves. In 1978 the average VHF station earned $1.2 million before taxes, while the average UHF station had a pre-tax profit of $300,000.[58] A network affiliate in Dayton, Ohio sold for $40 million in 1980; one in Norfolk, Virginia went for $48.3 million; the price of a Sacramento, California station in 1979 was $65 million.[59] The purchasers naturally expected a good return on their investments, and undoubtedly got one. No wonder television is sometimes called "a license to print money."

Radio is riskier. Lacking the network crutch, some radio stations do lose money. The leading stations earn profits—but on a far smaller scale than television. NBC radio, for example, grossed $40 million in 1979; NBC television takes in that much in two weeks.[60]

For the TV networks, every successful show is a financial bonanza. In 1980, for example, each episode of "Little House on the Prairie" earned $400,000 on gross revenues of $775,000; each segment of "Saturday Night Live" earned $160,000 on a gross of $455,000; each night's Johnny Carson show was worth $131,000 in profit on revenues of $190,000.[61] The Carson show alone was responsible for more than $17 million in pretax profit for NBC—a fact that helps explain why Carson himself was the highest paid television performer of 1980.[62]

Such figures also help explain why the networks are reluctant to schedule cultural programs that cannot attract a mass audience. NBC's special "Live from Studio 8-H," featuring Zubin Mehta and the New York Philharmonic, lost $339,000 in 1980—not to mention what the network could have made had it aired something more commercial.[63]

What fuels all these profits is of course advertising. A single 30-second spot on a prime-time show like "Mork & Mindy" sold in 1980 for $116,000. By 1990 experts estimate that such a spot will cost $342,000.[65] Already network television has priced itself beyond the budgets of many companies. In an era when Procter & Gamble spends $486 million a year on television advertising alone, a company with a $3 million ad budget can't make a dent.[66] So the smaller companies spill over into local television, and into radio, which is cheaper yet. Overall, 30 seconds on network television costs about $4.50 per thousand viewers. A 60-second spot on local radio, on the other hand, goes for $1.50 to $3 per thousand listeners.[67] And since radio has fewer listeners to begin with, the price may run as low as $20 for a minute on a not-too-popular local radio station—a far cry from the "Mork & Mindy" rate of $116,000 for 30 seconds.

Virtually unchanged for three decades, the structure of broadcasting is now on the verge of revolution. New technologies like cable and satellites are not really new, but their growth was restrained for years by FCC restrictions and their own inability to attract a market. Today, in combination with pay-TV and video playback, they are just beginning to influence the nation's television diet. In the coming decade that influence will surely increase, significantly eroding the dominance of the three networks.

CHANGES

Back in 1959, FCC Chairman John Doerfer apologized for broadcasting in the following words: "It is an infant industry and it is going through growing pains, the same as the printing press had to do over a period of years. It is a stage."[68] In Doerfer's metaphor, broadcasting had a prolonged childhood—it changed little in the next twenty years. But it is changing today, and the principal agents of that change are cable television, pay television, satellite communications, and video playback.

These innovations are working their magic (wreaking their havoc, the networks would say) more in combination than independently. This is especially true of the first three. The single greatest profit center for cable systems is pay-cable operations such as Home Box Office, which offer first-run movies without commercials for a monthly fee over and above the cost of the cable hook-up itself. And many cable features reach the cable system via satellite, permitting not only the importation of distant "super-stations" but also the creation of specialized cable networks for news, sports, black programming, and the like. Independent over-the-air stations also use satellites to connect themselves into ad-hoc networks. Other independents program first-run movies, scrambling the signal and charging a monthly fee for the home unscrambler. Even video playback is part of the mix; it permits viewers to record this new wealth of programming, creating a permanent library of TV shows to be watched at the viewer's convenience.

Broadcasting, in short, is about to become like the magazine industry. All sorts of special audiences—from news addicts to sports fans to opera lovers—will be able to pick their favorite TV content, to watch now or record for later. Control over video will thus shift significantly to the consumer.

And *away* from the networks. On a typical evening in the late 1970s, roughly 56 percent of the U.S. population could be found watching the three networks. Another 6 percent was watching independent television or public television, and the other 38 percent was doing something else that night. The coming revolution will doubtless increase total viewing time, but it will doubtless also steal some viewers from the networks. No one knows yet how large either effect will be, but for a typical evening in the late 1980s most experts are guessing something like this: 40 percent watching the networks, 30 percent watching non-network TV, and 30 percent not watching.

It's not yet time to start bleeding for the networks. Because some of the new technologies may not be advertising vehicles, the networks should still be attractive to national advertisers, even if they fall to the 40 percent figure—and they may not. And just to be on the safe side, the networks are investing heavily in the new technologies themselves (just as newspaper people bought into radio, and newspaper and radio people bought into television). In 1980, CBS earmarked $15 million to develop a unit that will make pro-

grams for cable.[69] ABC is marketing video cassettes on such events as the 1980 Winter Olympics and the U.S. visit of Pope John Paul II, and also plans to sell theater, opera, and ballet videotapes.[70] RCA, which owns NBC, is one of the leaders in satellite communications, and is already marketing feature films on video disks.[71]

As corporations, the networks will make out all right. But as the pre-eminent force in American broadcasting, their days may be numbered. And watching television in 1990 may be a very different experience from what it has always been before.

CABLE TELEVISION

Cable television is a system for transmitting the TV signal via a wire or cable, instead of over the air. It was first developed in the mid-1930s. For more than a decade, cable was used mainly to connect stations into networks. By the 1950s it was used also to improve TV reception in rural areas, mountainous terrain, and skyscraper cities. The subscriber usually paid a hook-up fee of $10 and a monthly rate of $5, in return for a guaranteed perfect picture. The broadcast industry was delighted.

Then, early in the 1960s, a few cable operators began to import signals from other cities for their clients. Suddenly local broadcasters were no longer delighted; the cable outfits threatened to steal part of their audience. And distant broadcasters complained that the cable companies were using their programs without payment.

Enter the FCC. In 1965, under pressure from the broadcast industry, the Commission declared that it had the right to regulate cable TV. A year later it established a complete set of highly restrictive rules. Among other things, cable systems in the top hundred markets were forbidden to import distant signals unless they could prove that no damage would be done to existing stations.

The proponents of cable quickly organized

their own lobbying effort. They pointed out the incredible advantages of the new medium:

- Cable can easily carry 20 channels; technically, its capacity extends to 84 channels or more. Yet cable "stations" take up no space on the overcrowded electromagnetic spectrum.

- Cable can "broadcast" as selectively as needed. Specialized news and advertising can be programmed for each city, town, neighborhood, or block—even for particular racial or political groups.

- Cable picture quality is uniformly excellent, especially in color.

- Cable is far cheaper than over-the-air broadcasting, sometimes running as little as $5 an hour for an entire channel. This is well within the grasp of school systems, local political candidates, and even ordinary citizens wishing to communicate with their neighbors.

- Cable paves the way for a two-way communications network. It can transmit a facsimile newspaper or a library reference service. It can replace the post office and the telephone. The possibilities are endless.

This is not just propaganda: The possibilities *are* endless. Once an entire country is wired for two-way telecommunications, anything is feasible—from instant political referendums to stay-at-home shopping centers. It all starts with cable.

In early 1972, the FCC adopted a more permissive series of rules governing cable development. The new regulations required the larger cable systems to produce some of their own programming; made all cable operations set aside channels for city government, education, and public access; and permitted cable companies in the top hundred markets to import two distant signals apiece. Cable's boosters predicted that the new rules would quickly force cable to realize some of its potential, to take its place as an important medium of communication.

In the next three years very little happened, and in 1975 the goal of a "wired nation" seemed as far away as ever. Cable operators were unable to convince city dwellers that their service was worth from $6 to $10 a month. The government channels were unused; the programs on the public-access channels were amateurish and uninteresting to middle-class viewers; the programs originated by the cable systems themselves were mostly old movies and sporting events. In 1974, 8 million homes were on cable, about 12 percent of the viewing audience—but only a quarter of these were in the top hundred metropolitan areas.[72] In Manhattan, the two existing cable companies were able to attract only 120,000 subscribers between them, less than 20 percent of the potential; both were losing money.[73] In Boston and Kansas City, public officials decided not to permit any cable development at all for the time being. In Dayton and Birmingham, San Antonio and Newark, owners of cable franchises refused to build the systems until (and unless) they could figure out a way to make them earn a profit.[74]

Alfred R. Stern, chairman of Warner Cable, summed up the situation: "We have hit a plateau, as other developing industries have done before us. Everyone in the cable business is treading water until we find the services that will make people in the cities want cable. We need help from others. We can't do it ourselves. We're not a real communication industry at the moment."[75]

But in the last half of the 1970s, cable finally took off. By 1980 it had become a $1.8-billion-a-year industry, with more than 4,200 cable systems in operation and 17 million homes already connected (more than double the 1974 figure). Even more important, the big cities were at last beginning to catch up with the small towns and suburban areas. Only seven of the nation's twenty largest cities were even partially wired in 1980, but Dallas was on the verge of granting a cable franchise, and Baltimore, Cleveland, Washington, Detroit, and Chicago were close behind. Cable was expanding at a rate of 10 to 20 percent a year, and the cable industry had the fever of a gold rush.[76]

In 1980, the cable division of Time, Inc., owner of Home Box Office, became the company's biggest profit-producer, out-performing the famous magazine.[77] Storer Broadcasting sold its radio chain to get into cable.[78] Westinghouse announced its intention to buy the Teleprompter cable chain. And the Management Analysis Center confidently predicted that total cable penetration would reach 35 percent of all television homes by 1985.[79]

What fueled this sudden take-off? The FCC's new mood of deregulation certainly helped. As of 1980 the Commission had eliminated virtually all the remaining rules that had restricted cable programming for so long (see p. 210). But even without regulation, cable still needed a profitable market. What provided that market, more than anything else, was satellites and pay TV.

By means of satellites, a programming source can "bounce" its signal simultaneously (and cheaply) to local cable systems all across the country. Cable's first use of this technol-

CABLE NEWS NETWORK

Among the most talked-about of the new cable services transmitted by satellite is the Cable News Network, inaugurated by Ted Turner on June 1, 1980. The all-news channel began with 400 subscribing cable systems, each of which pays Turner 15¢ to 20¢ per subscriber per month for the service. These fees add up to a good deal less than Turner's first-year investment of $30 million—which sounds like a princely sum, but isn't all that much to produce 24 hours of news a day; a network spends four times as much annually to produce only two to three hours of news a day. To make up the difference, Turner does what the networks do: he sells ads. CNN's initial roster of 60 national advertisers included Atlantic Richfield, General Foods, Buick, Holiday Inns, and Procter & Gamble, all lured by the affluent audience likely to watch an all-news channel. As an additional enticement to cable operators, Turner leaves them two empty ad minutes each hour to sell locally.[80]

CNN is a huge financial gamble. To succeed, it must attract enough new cable subscribers to justify the fee the cable system pays, then keep them watching enough to justify the rate the advertiser pays. "You need a pretty deep wallet and very strong convictions," comments Nick Nicholas of Home Box Office.[81] TV consultant Jim Yergin adds: "What I don't know is if CNN can build enough audience over the long haul. On all-news radio you find out the temperature, traffic reports, the local news that affects you. I'm not sure people are eager to get other kinds of news all day long."[82] Somewhere down the road, Turner hopes to solve the problem by encouraging cable systems to cut away for a few minutes of local news each hour—but so far few cable operators have shown any inclination to develop their own news departments.

Meanwhile, CNN is produced by a national staff of 300 journalists, including former CBS reporter Daniel Schorr. Special commentators in the first few months included Ralph Nader, Dr. Joyce Brothers, Rowland Evans and Robert Novak. On most days the format closely resembles the network news, except that it keeps recycling all day long and is constantly updated. But when a breaking story justifies the switch, CNN can cut away to blanket coverage. For example, it carried all 27 minutes of Edmund Muskie's inaugural speech as President Carter's second secretary of state.[83]

Will people watch enough of this sort of programming to turn the Cable News Network into a profitable enterprise? Turner is betting they will: "Whenever you're pioneering a company, you have to stick your neck out. I love competition. All my life I've reveled in it. . . . It's the American way."[84]

ogy was to pick up distant stations with attractive programs. Some stations were picked up by cable systems all across the country; among the earliest of these so-called "superstations" was WTBS in Atlanta, owned by Ted Turner. But with thousands of cable systems as potential customers, a program source in search of an audience doesn't need to broadcast its shows over the air at all. By the end of the 1970s, specialized programming was being sold to cable systems and distributed via satellite for audiences of blacks (Black Cable Network), Hispanics (Galavision), the elderly (Prime Time Network), children (Nickelodeon), sports fans (Entertainment and Sports Programming Network), and public-affairs addicts (C-SPAN).[85] Each of these programming sources gives a cable system something to offer its potential customers that the networks and local over-the-air stations cannot duplicate.

Pay-television channels such as Home Box Office also provide a powerful incentive to subscribe to cable—for an extra fee of $5 to $15 a month, subscribers get a full schedule of movies without commercials. But pay-cable helps in another way as well. The biggest expense in running a cable system is laying the network of wires that carry the signals all over town; the biggest problem in the 1970s was that too few customers wanted to subscribe to cover that initial cost. Because pay-cable is a high-profit extra, it greatly reduces the percentage of homes in a neighborhood that must subscribe for the cable system to break even. Before pay-cable, signing up one-third of the homes in a city meant a net loss. But if most of that one-third also subscribes to the pay-cable channel, the whole enterprise suddenly becomes very profitable.[86]

Thanks to satellites and pay TV, cable is finally profitable. But what happened to all those science-fiction promises of the early 1970s? What happened to the neighborhood programming, the instant political referendums, the public-access channels? Here and there, in experimental or subsidized formats,

they are surviving (see pp. 239-40). But for the most part, the reality of cable television in the 1980s doesn't much resemble the dreams of cable television in the 1960s and 1970s.

Until the late 1970s, just about everybody assumed that cable would function as a local common carrier. Just as anyone can use the telephone lines—AT&T doesn't care what you say as long as you pay your bill—local individuals and organizations and governments would be able to lease time on a cable channel, to present whatever message they liked to whoever chose to watch. The cable system would earn its profits from subscribers, and the fee for access would be modest; perhaps there would be no fee at all. Cable was to be a liberating medium, robust, diverse, and almost entirely local.

It didn't work out that way. Cable operators are demanding—and getting—a cut of everything they carry. And cable operators are deciding for themselves what to carry, picking the programming they think will lure the most subscribers. Nearly all of what they pick comes from national programming sources who offer entertainment for profit, not from local interest groups or government agencies. Cable entertainment is still bound to be a lot more diverse than network entertainment; with 35 channels you have room for a children's channel and a black channel and a High Culture channel. But it's a long way from City Council meetings and the opinions of local activists.

And remember, a cable system is by necessity a local monopoly. Like the telephone company and the electric company, only one cable company can be permitted to wire a given area. If the company is also permitted to decide what goes out over all of its channels, it gains a monopoly not only on the hardware, but also on the content of local television. This is an incredible concentration of power, undreamed of by over-the-air broadcasters and networks. The possible abuses of that power boggle the mind.

At least they boggled the mind of Henry

Geller, communications adviser to President Carter. Before Carter left office, Geller recommended legislation that would force cable operators to revert to common-carrier status, at least for most of their channels.[87] It was already clear by then that the selling point of cable was to be specialized national entertainment, brought to the viewer via satellite or pay TV. But when Reagan replaced Carter in 1981, three huge issues remained unresolved: Will subscribers or government exercise some control over cable content, or will the local cable company remain free to dictate which programs are and are not available? Will cable become a vehicle for local programming, or will its programs be provided exclusively by national entrepreneurs? And will public access survive as at least a minor part of the cable package, or will cable television be as much a closed shop as the networks?

PAY TELEVISION

Pay TV earns its profits directly from the viewer, not through advertising. In theory, it is therefore immune to the "mass market" syndrome; any show can be profitable if those who want to see it are willing to pay enough for the privilege. Since the early 1950s, broadcasters and movie theater owners have been convinced of pay TV's revolutionary potential, and have waged an aggressive battle against it. Until the mid-1970s they were winning, and pay TV went nowhere. The FCC helped retard its development by authorizing only small-scale experiments. But even the experiments were discouraging; most people apparently didn't want to pay extra for a medium they were accustomed to getting free.

The catalyst for pay TV growth was cable. In order to attract more subscribers, some cable systems in the early 1970s decided to sweeten the pot by offering pay TV as part of the package. For an extra monthly fee on top of the cable fee itself, subscribers would receive an unending supply of movies and special events, without commercials. In 1973, pay-cable had only 16,000 subscribers nationwide. By 1980 it had 4 million, with new ones signing on at a rate of 100,000 a month.[88] In some cities, Home Box Office (the giant of the pay-cable suppliers) was occasionally earning a higher rating than any of the three networks[89]—a victory that would have been unthinkable in the 1970s.

As pay-cable began to catch on, independent TV stations in cities not yet wired for cable saw a chance to cash in. Several applied for FCC permission to carry a scrambled signal for part of the broadcast day, charging subscribers a monthly fee for the equipment to unscramble the signal back into first-run movies. By 1980, this over-the-air subscription television service was available from about a dozen UHF stations with a combined audience of half a million, and 40 more stations were awaiting FCC approval to make the switch.[90]

Experts estimate that by 1990 one-third of all U.S. television households will receive either over-the-air subscription television or pay-cable.[91] Both services will get a shot in the arm when the technology for a pay-as-you-go system is perfected. Once viewers are paying only for what they watch, instead of a monthly fee, special-interest programming of all sorts should flourish.

Network executives have been watching these developments with understandable dismay. But so far the evidence is that pay TV increases total viewing time more than it decreases network viewing time.[92] No doubt pay TV will eat into network audiences to some extent—but the industry that really needs to worry is the movie business. The cost of one visit to a movie theater for a family of four will pay for an entire month's movies and other events on Home Box Office. Look for a decline in movie theater attendance, thanks to pay TV.

And once the pay-as-you-go system is in place, look for pay TV to take over some of the most popular content you now find in movie theaters and on network television. By 1990, why shouldn't a Hollywood studio try releasing a hot film directly through pay TV at two dollars a home, grossing a quick $40 million or so without needing to print hundreds of copies of the movie, distribute them to theaters around the country, and advertise them in local newspapers? And why shouldn't the National Football League move the Super Bowl to pay television, at two or three dollars per household? Once pay TV is firmly entrenched, networks and movie theaters will have to bid against it for such blockbuster attractions—and they may not win the bidding.

SATELLITE COMMUNICATION

In 1962, AT&T launched the first experimental communications satellite. Later that year, Congress created Comsat, a semi-public corporation charged with developing communications satellites. Intelsat, an international consortium with the same purpose, was organized in 1964. And in 1965 the Early Bird satellite made live trans-Atlantic television possible for the first time.

In 1980, there were 80 satellites in geostationary orbit 22,300 miles above the earth's surface, and experts were predicting a "traffic jam" of 50 more by 1985.[93] Satellites have become such a crucial part of the world's communications system that any disruption in their service—by war or natural disaster—would reduce our ability to communicate to World War II levels.[94]

Satellites solve the dilemma of all telecommunications: electrons travel in straight lines, but the surface of the earth is curved. A wireless signal can reach only as far as the horizon before it must defer to the earth's curvature. But a satellite is high enough that *its* "horizon" encompasses half the globe. By bouncing the signal off a satellite, you can send your telephone or television message from New York to Los Angeles or London instan-

taneously, without wires. Add a couple of other satellites, and you can send your message from anywhere to anywhere, still instantaneously and still without wires.

And satellite communication is a lot cheaper than the cheapest ground communication systems (usually a combination of wires and microwave relays). In 1980, a hypothetical network linking just nine television stations around the country would have paid $9,239 a day for land connections—or $1,944 a day for satellite time.[95] The cost of a nationwide satellite hook-up (including Alaska and Puerto Rico) for an hour was no greater than the cost of only 175 miles of land lines.[96]

At some point in the next decade, CBS, NBC, and ABC will probably start beaming programs direct to affiliates via satellite, cutting transmission costs considerably. (The Public Broadcasting System, leading the pack for a change, switched to this satellite distribution method in 1979.) In the meantime, the laggard networks make only limited use of satellites—to transmit foreign news from reporters in the field back to network headquarters, and to beam network programming to central locations in the Midwest and on the West Coast for retransmission to affiliates via land lines (see box on next page).

But if the networks have been slow to adopt satellite technology, local stations have not. Attracted by the low transmission costs, ad-hoc "networks" of independent stations have sprouted like mushrooms:

- Independent Network News, a collection of some 40 non-network stations around the country that carry a half-hour news show produced at WPIX in New York and viewed by about 1.4 million homes each night.[97]
- The Spanish International Network, beaming programs from Latin America and Spain to Hispanic communities in Miami, New York, and the Southwest.[98]
- The National Black Network, which delivers five-minute black-oriented newscasts on the hour to 90 affiliates and about 300,000 radio listeners.[99]

Though the three networks have used satellite communication less than other broadcasters, they still rely on it for international news coverage. Writing in the *Washington Journalism Review*, Raymond M. Lane described the progress of a news report on the Iran hostage crisis of 1980 from Teheran to you.[100]

First, the news crew makes a film or videotape of the day's events in Teheran. The story is taken to the Iranian national studios in Teheran, which transmit it by microwave to Iran's satellite antenna in Asadabad. The antenna is Iran's small piece of the Intelsat satellite network, which interlinks some 123 nations; without it, Iran would be cut off almost entirely from friends and foes alike.

From Asadabad the report is beamed to an Intelsat satellite over the Atlantic, which bounces the signal back to one of two ground receiving stations on the U.S. east coast, located in Maine and West Virginia. Intelsat charges a minimum of $175 for 20 minutes of satellite time; Comsat operates the receiving stations and charges another $168 for 10 minutes of receiving time.

The signal then travels by land lines from either Maine or West Virginia to the network in New York. This is handled by a consortium of AT&T, ITT, RCA, and Western Union. The charge for 10 minutes of television is $485.

The segment is edited into the network news show, which must then be sent to affiliates around the country. Those on the East Coast get it by microwave. The rest get it in two steps—first by domestic satellite to ground receivers in Illinois and California, then by microwave or land lines to the individual stations. They either tape it for delayed broadcast or air it live. Your roof antenna (or your cable system's antenna) picks the signal out of the air and transmits it by wire to your TV, which turns it back into pictures and sounds—the same pictures and sounds the news crew recorded in Teheran.

Similarly, satellites have facilitated the creation of one-time-only networks for particular programs. In 1979, for example, Mobil Oil transmitted its serial "Edward and Mrs. Simpson" (along with its advertisements) to interested stations via satellite. Of course such programming is particularly attractive to the independent stations, but some network affiliates also used "Edward and Mrs. Simpson," much to the consternation of their networks.[101]

To receive all this specialized satellite programming, you need a ground station. By 1980, most independents and many network affiliates either had one or were building one. For independents, satellites mean easy access to more enticing programs than their former diet of syndicated reruns. For affiliates, satellites mean a real alternative to clearing everything the networks choose to offer. For the networks, obviously, satellites mean trouble.

Satellites are also essential to cable television and pay television. They beam superstations in Atlanta, Oakland, New York, and Chicago to cable audiences throughout the country. They distribute national cable programming such as Nickelodeon and Cable News Network. They carry the movies and sports events that dominate pay-cable and over-the-air subscription television. All of these services would be *possible* via land lines, but they would be far more expensive—too expensive, probably, to earn a profit. Satellite communication makes them feasible.

If local stations and cable systems can gain access to all this programming simply by installing a ground receiver, why can't you? You can. Already a few hobbyists have purchased their own 13-foot satellite-receiving dishes—for $5,000 and up—and are picking out of the air all the television signals raining down from space. A viewer in California can thus watch the New York Knicks play basketball on an independent station in New York; a viewer in Miami can watch the 1980 Summer Olympics from Russia, which were not telecast in the U.S. at all; a viewer anywhere can watch the feeds of overseas correspondents to the three network news organizations.[102]

By the mid-1980s, you may not need $5,000 and a flair for engineering to receive direct satellite-to-home broadcasts. In 1979, Comsat announced plans to develop such a system, using a small, inexpensive antenna that will fit very nicely on the roof or in the attic. Offering the now-familiar mix of films, sports, and occasional cultural events, the Comsat service is planned to compete directly with pay-cable—with no need for local companies and no need to wire the community. But there is nothing to stop Comsat from competing with the three networks as well, earning its profits from advertising instead of monthly subscriptions. Some experts now envision a future of 30 or more satellite-to-home broadcasting networks, enough for mass entertainment plus every kind of special-interest programming. Such a development could destroy not only the conventional networks, but cable as well. It could also destroy local broadcasting, the historic heart of the American telecommunications system.

VIDEO PLAYBACK

One of the givens of broadcast technology has always been that the viewer cannot save programs to play at his or her leisure. Print audiences were free to decide what to read when, but for television audiences the timing was in the hands of the medium.

Video playback has changed all that. Two types of equipment are on the market. Videotape units enable the viewer to tape shows off the air for later viewing, or to purchase prerecorded tapes of films, concerts, educational materials, etc. Video disk units work like a phonograph instead of a tape recorder; the viewer can play only prerecorded content. According to industry estimates, 15 to 20 per-

---

INTERNATIONAL SATELLITE PROPAGANDA?

An interesting international political debate is shaping up over the possible use of satellites for communication from the government or broadcast industry of one country to the people of another. Satellites are already used extensively for international broadcasting, courtesy of Intelsat, but the procedure is carefully controlled: Foreign correspondents can beam their reports back to their own stations; networks can transmit live overseas programs to the home office; a station in one country can agree by prearrangement to pick up a signal from a station in another country. But what would happen if NBC decided to use satellites to carry its shows directly to TV sets in the Soviet Union, or if a Soviet-made broadcast suddenly turned up on channel 4 in the U.S.?

Concerned about such possibilities, the Soviet government has asked the United Nations to establish the principle that no country may beam TV programs into another without the consent of the recipient country. The U.S. opposes the agreement on the grounds that it would contradict the libertarian notion of a free marketplace of ideas.[103] One critic is Dr. Frank Stanton, former vice chairman of CBS, who said the Russian proposal "would make censorship a principle of international law." According to Stanton, "You don't negotiate free speech."[104]

cent of all U.S. television households will have one or both systems by 1985.[105]

Videotape is the older and more established technology. And because it permits viewers to tape off the air and watch when they like, its potential impact on broadcasting is substantial. The ratings companies may no longer be able to tell programmers and advertisers who is watching what when. Networks may no longer be able to rely on carefully constructed schedules (lead-ins, carry-over audiences, counter-programming) to build viewership. Perhaps most important, video recorders make it relatively easy to blip out the commercials; advertisers may begin to ask if the audience they're paying to reach is really watching their spots.

A 1979 study of 700 videotape users found that fewer than half had ever bought a pre-recorded tape. Most were using the system to tape off the air, period. As of 1980, only a million prerecorded tapes were being sold each year—many of them X-rated movies—compared to some six million blank tapes.[106]

The new video disk industry thus has its work cut out for it—to build a market for prerecorded television. If it succeeds, TV viewers in 1990 may not only be recording what's available to watch at their leisure; they may be picking their programs as well. And the television business may move from over-the-air to over-the-counter.

As we have seen, the new television technologies—cable, pay TV, satellites, and video playback—compete with each other as well as with the established broadcast networks. It is impossible to predict with certainty which will flourish, which will merely survive, and which if any will die out altogether. But it is safe to predict that the three conventional networks will lose ground. All this is just about to happen. In structure and in content, television in 1980 was little different from television in 1960. But television in 1990 will be very different indeed.

The broadcast media have incredible potential for the dissemination of news and information. To some extent this potential is realized; certainly broadcast news has contributed greatly to the political awareness of the American public. But the non-entertainment programming on television and radio is often disappointing. In some ways broadcast news is limited by the nature of the medium; in many ways it is limited by the audience-pleasing policies of broadcasters.

NETWORK NEWS

On a typical evening about 40 percent of all U.S. television homes are tuned to one of the three network newscasts. This translates into a nightly audience of some 56 million people, making the networks by far the most powerful news media in the nation. More people watch network news than read newspaper front pages. And according to survey data (see p. 263), Americans trust the network news more than their newspapers. We especially trust the network anchorpeople, who come into our livingrooms every evening to tell us the way it is.

If there were no network news, some of those 56 million people might pay more attention to newspapers—a fact that leads many print journalists to resent the broadcast competition. But a good portion of the television news audience would have simply gone without news in a pre-broadcast era. This "inadvertent audience," as it is sometimes called, doesn't tune in to find out about world events. It "catches" the news—because it's reasonably entertaining to watch and because that's what's on in the early evening. Informing the inadvertent audience is probably the most valuable service network news performs.

Not that the inadvertent audience learns all that much. In a telephone interview poll of network news viewers, half the respondents couldn't remember the topic of a single story they had seen.[107] But even without paying attention they must have learned *something*—

which is more than they would have learned without TV news.

The chief virtue of the network newscasts is almost universally acknowledged. In a thoroughly professional, sober, and responsible manner, they touch on the principal points of the dozen or so most important events each day, even managing to squeeze into their allotted 22 minutes an occasional light feature or a 90-second "in-depth" backgrounder. The chief drawback of the network newscasts is equally obvious. Twenty-two minutes isn't much time to do justice to national and world problems, especially while striving to keep the audience entertained as well. Given these constraints—a 22-minute limit and a priority on entertainment—few of television's critics could do a better job than CBS, NBC, and ABC.

Why not change the constraints? The 22-minute figure is already a network victory, achieved in 1963 when network news moved from 15 minutes to half an hour. Since the early 1970s the networks have been pushing for an hour-long newscast, but affiliates have resisted; they can earn more money from local news or entertainment in the extra half-hour. The resistance may be weakening, however. "ABC News Nightline" now airs from 11:30 to 12:00 weeknights. It began in 1979 as a special show on the hostage crisis in Iran, then converted to a regular newscast in March, 1980. The ratings have been good, frequently edging out Johnny Carson, and so affiliate response has been good too. The 1980s may well see an hour-long newscast on all three networks.

The other constraint, entertainment, will not change. Television is first and foremost an entertainment medium. The inadvertent audience spells the difference between profit and loss for network news—and the inadvertent audience wants to be entertained.

The result is the familiar litany of complaints about broadcast news: action shots are stressed to avoid the tedium of "talking heads"; segments longer than two minutes are taboo because they might bore casual viewers; issues are simplified and compressed into almost mythic tales of good and evil. It seems a bit churlish to criticize the networks for these defects, since network journalists have resisted the pressure to entertain far more successfully than most local newscasters. Still, as critic Ed Diamond points out, even the networks are "locked into a rigid kabuki form." Diamond continues: "They're heavy on Washington because that's where the newsmen are; big on Midwestern tornadoes because the film footage is great. Then, for closers, they all go to California for some wacky, nuts and fruits story. It all marches along in 90-second steps."[108]

A lot of money is at stake, making experimentation risky. The 1980 budget for ABC's "World News Tonight," for example, was $1 million *a week*.[109] Top network newspeople earn as much as top network entertainers— $500,000 a year for ABC's Barbara Walters (plus more for specials); $250,000 to $500,000 a year for CBS' Harry Reasoner, Morley Safer, and Mike Wallace; an $8-million multi-year package for CBS' Dan Rather to replace Walter Cronkite as anchor.[110] To pay these kinds of salaries, network news must be profitable. And it is; ABC News projects it will bill $200 million to advertisers in 1984.[111] Even the profits of prime-time entertainment depend to some extent on the news, because the audience for a successful newscast tends to stay tuned to the same channel for the rest of the evening line-up.

As cable, satellites, and other new technologies begin eating into the audience for network entertainment, news is likely to become even more important in the network profit picture. This is another reason to expect a 60-minute network newscast before too long. But don't expect any change in the format of that newscast. The networks found their formula, their compromise between journalism and entertainment, years ago. It works, and they are unlikely to tinker much with it.

They probably shouldn't. Network news does about as good a job as can be done of

"60 MINUTES"

On November 26, 1978, "60 Minutes" became the top-rated program on television, the first time in television history that a newscast or regularly scheduled documentary had come in first in prime-time ratings. The CBS news-magazine show repeated the trick often enough to become the highest-rated program of the 1979-80 television season, drawing an audience of 40 to 50 million Americans every Sunday evening.

Scheduling is part of the success of "60 Minutes." After a rocky start in 1968, the show found an ideal slot Sundays at 7 p.m., following the National Football League telecasts in the fall and winter and opposed on the other networks by children's programs. But other public-affairs shows have bombed in similar slots. Producer Don Hewitt attributes his program's success to audience identification with its celebrated reporters, such as Mike Wallace, Dan Rather, Morley Safer, Ed Bradley, and Harry Reasoner. Viewers send in a thousand story tips a week, which Hewitt says are often followed up. "We have become America's ombudsman."[112]

The most popular parts of the show are when a reporter—usually Mike Wallace—exposes an individual or company preying on the defenseless: phony diploma mills, doctors who perform useless surgery, insurance executives who cheat the poor. The quartet specialize in nailing the culprit on camera, in what one observer calls a "ritual bloodletting, a journalistic Grand-Guignol."[113]

The 20-minute segments have such impact that the targets have often gone to great lengths to defend themselves. After the Illinois Power Company was criticized by Reasoner in 1979 for nuclear power plant cost and safety problems, the company released its own film documentary, incorporating videotapes of the original Reasoner interviews to document what it saw as a distorted hatchet job.[114] In 1980, former Secretary of State Henry Kissinger publicly refused to cooperate with a Dan Rather segment on connections between Kissinger and the Shah of Iran.[115] Others have criticized "60 Minutes" for selecting easy targets, for picking on "bad apples" instead of bad institutions.

Such periodic controversy has not hurt profits. A one-hour show costs about $235,000 to produce, half the cost of an hour-long situation comedy. Advertising sells for $175,000 per 30-second spot, leaving "60 Minutes" with an estimated profit of some $25 million per season.[116] Not surprisingly, the show has spawned copies at NBC, ABC, and various local stations.

One other "60 Minutes" claim to fame—it was the first news program to broadcast reruns in the summer. Like "Perry Mason" shows from the 1950s, the confrontations on "60 Minutes" are entertaining even when they're no longer news.

---

informing the inadvertent audience. The rest of us can always supplement our viewing with a good newspaper.

LOCAL NEWS

The average commercial television station devotes 9.2 percent of its time to news and 4.2 percent to public affairs.[117] These are not big percentages, but they are bigger than they were in the 1960s, when the typical station offered 15 minutes of local news a night. Today the standard is an hour each evening, while the ABC affiliate in Los Angeles programs three solid hours of news from 4 to 7 p.m.

The news department has become a profit center at many local stations. In major markets, especially, local news can account for up to 40 percent of station profits.[118] Anchorpeople in such markets routinely earn six-digit salaries, and are as ardently courted by station managers as rock stars. Even in a medium-sized market like Columbus, Ohio, a difference of a single percentage point in the news ratings can add up to $250,000 in revenues. In a large market like New York or Los Angeles, a one-percent rise or fall in the ratings means $1 million in advertising income.[119]

The predictable result is a product that is long on entertainment values, short on journalistic ones. Perhaps the most lucrative local news operation in the country is WABC-TV in New York, returning an annual profit of $40 million on a newscast that stresses personality and "happy talk," not journalistic depth.

The qualities that lead to stardom in local television news can be rather different from those associated with eminence in journalism, a point well documented by *Los Angeles Times* reporter Robert Scheer in his devastating profile of Joan Lunden. A reporter and anchor for both WABC and the ABC network's "Good Morning America," Lunden started as a model in Sacramento, California. The charm school she ran was going broke, when she happened to tell an ad salesman for a local station that she was thinking of leaving the area. He convinced her that her appearance and poise justified a try at TV news.

"I was not an avid newspaper reader," Lunden told Scheer, "and I was bad at keeping up with current events." But she moved quickly from weather and consumer reporting to the anchor slot. Her only real training came from TV consultant Frank Magid, who worked on her delivery. There was no effort to teach her to write, report, or deal with current events.

Magid sent her audition tape to other stations, and soon she had an offer to join WABC in New York. With no real experience as a reporter, Lunden found herself re-porting—and later anchoring—for the most popular newscast in the largest market in the country. Scheer is not critical of Lunden, only of television: "It indicated something of the limits of television journalism that she was quite literally thrown into news stories and acquitted herself in ways that were consistent with the work of her colleagues."[120]

The point is not that Lunden was unqualified, but rather that being qualified was not especially important for local TV news. Complains one disillusioned reporter: "First you are sent to a court hearing on busing, then a fashion press conference, suddenly an auto accident, and finally they expect live coverage of the mayor's statement on the budget. You don't have time to formulate questions, let alone read any of the background material."[121]

When a local newscast sags in the ratings, stations call in a "show doctor" like Magid. The advice tendered by these consultants is depressingly consistent, and even more depressingly successful. Hire anchormen and anchorwomen with distinct but pleasing on-the-air personalities. Pace the show faster, with lots of very short stories instead of a few longer ones and with as much action footage as possible. Try for something shocking—violence or sex—near the start of the show, and something amusing—a human-interest feature—near the end. Encourage the news "team" to exchange friendly banter during the program. Promote the news heavily in prime-time station breaks. Jazz up the graphics, the set, the clothing worn by newscasters. . . .

Local TV news does have its share of dedicated broadcast journalists, and they produce their share of solid news stories. But they work within constraints that would make a newspaper reporter, or even a network newscaster, howl with rage. Entertainment comes first.

The late 1970s saw the adoption of three innovations that could potentially improve local television news. News helicopters get reporters to events more quickly and provide a unique perspective for filming or taping. Satellite communication permits local stations to send reporters out of town for same-day coverage of events of special interest to the home-town audience. Perhaps most important, electronic newsgathering (ENG) equipment enables reporters to broadcast live from the scene, eliminating the delay required by film and even videotape.

Some stations have begun using these technologies in promising ways. KOIN in Portland broadcast live from the scene of the Mount St. Helens eruption. KARD in Wichita sent a news crew to Washington to interview the Kansas congressional delegation about problems at a Titan missile silo near Wichita, then aired the interviews via satellite on the same day. KGBT in Harlingen, Texas covered live from a helicopter an oil well blowout that polluted the Gulf of Mexico. KOMO in Seattle sent a crew with then Governor Dixie Lee Ray when she visited China, beaming back daily reports via satellite.[122]

But the technology is most often used to produce highly visual coverage of unimportant stories—traffic jams, car wrecks, and fires.

No less a broadcast journalist than Walter Cronkite has summed up the indictment of local TV news. This is what Cronkite told a group of CBS affiliates:

There is no newsman worth his salt who does not know that advisers who dictate that no item should run more than 45 seconds, that there must be a film story within the first 30 seconds of the newscast, and that it must have action in it—a barn burning or a jack-knifed tractor-trailer will do—that calls a 90-second film piece a "minidocumentary," that advises against covering city hall because it is dull, that says the anchorman or woman must do all voiceovers for "identity"—any real newsman knows that sort of stuff is balderdash. It's cosmetic—pretty packaging—not substance.[123]

But it's local television news.

TV VERSUS NEWSPAPERS

Television and radio news differ from newspaper news in scores of ways. Some of these differences are inevitable results of the nature of broadcasting—but most of them are not.

1. Sensory Involvement. The power of television rests in its capacity to combine voices and moving pictures. Yet that very capacity often turns out to be a disadvantage. TV reporters are trained to think in terms of good film footage. They avoid at all costs the "stand-upper" or the "talking head"—a reporter simply reading the story without audiovisual aids. The assumption that the viewer wants to see action may or may not be justified, but it is nearly universal. The parallel assumption in radio is that voice actualities are a must. "Get the s.o.b. on the phone" is the motto of most radio news departments.

But how do you get good films or tapes on the new city budget? Or on the president's decision to veto a housing act? Or on the discovery of a new treatment for arthritis? Because of its preoccupation with audio-visuals, broadcasting is forced to underplay such stories as these. At best, the newscaster will emphasize some filmable aspect of the event—the political repercussions of the decision instead of the decision itself. Many important stories never get covered on TV because they cannot be effectively photographed.

2. Pseudo-events. Broadcasting's undying allegiance to film footage encourages it to concentrate on pseudo-events (see pp. 153-56). Press conferences, grand openings, conventions, and such may not offer much real news. But they guarantee that something filmable will happen, that the crew will not return empty-handed. By the time a station has covered all these ready-made stories, it has very little time or staff left for anything else.

Newspapers report events. Television and radio, by and large, report staged interviews about events. Michael Arlen of the *New Yorker* carries this to its logical extreme:

I have this picture of the last great interview: The polar icecaps are melting. The San Andreas Fault has swallowed up half of California. Tonga has dropped the big egg on Mauritius. The cities of the plain are leveled. We switch from Walter Cronkite in End-of-the-World Central to Buzz Joplin, who is standing on a piece of rock south of the Galapagos with the last man on earth, the water rising now just above their chins. Joplin strains himself on tiptoe, lifts his microphone out of the water, and, with a last desperate gallant effort—the culmination of all his years as a TV newsman—places it in front of the survivor's mouth. "How do you feel, sir?" he asks. "I mean, being the last man on earth and so forth. Would you give us your personal reaction?"

The last survivor adopts that helpless vacant look, the water already beginning to trickle into his mouth. "Well, Buzz," he says, gazing wildly into the middle distance, "I feel real good."[124]

3. Speed. Television and radio can get the news to the public much faster than newspapers. The bulk of your evening newspaper is written in the morning; the evening newscast includes stories that won't be printed until tomorrow morning. This makes broadcasting the ideal vehicle for spot news. Radio is far superior to television in this respect, because TV executives are reluctant to interrupt profitable entertainment programming with a news bulletin. After all, who sponsors a news bulletin?

4. Impermanence. Newspapers can be saved. You can read them at your leisure, clip them, show them to your friends, or post them on your wall. But unless you own a home videotape machine, broadcasting is a now-or-never proposition. The impermanence of broadcast news probably contributes to its frivolity. Why kill yourself researching a story that will be dead and gone thirty seconds after it starts?

5. Intrusiveness. Broadcasting is intrusive. Even a tape-recorder makes many news sources self-conscious and careful. A camera, a microphone, and a bunch of klieg lights are much, much worse. The appearance of a TV crew alters the nature of any event, from a press conference to a riot. In comparison with broadcasters, print reporters are almost invisible.

Part of the intrusiveness of broadcasting is the fame of many broadcast journalists. Few people know what James Reston looks like—but everyone can recognize Walter Cronkite. "During the 1964 campaign," recalls Robert MacNeil, "David Brinkley [then an NBC anchorman] went to a shopping center in California to watch Nelson Rockefeller on the stump. There was a sizeable crowd around Rockefeller but, when Brinkley was spotted, it melted and massed around the bigger attraction, the TV commentator."[125] The same thing can happen to a local "star" newscaster.

6. Time Limitations. Although some stations have experimented with news shows as long as three hours, the typical TV newscast runs half an hour or an hour. In a half-hour program there is room for perhaps 20 stories at the most, some of which will get no more than 30 seconds. If you were to set the text of a half-hour newscast in type, it would fill less than half of a newspaper front page.

On big news days, a newspaper can add a few pages to make room. Television can't—a highly profitable show is scheduled right after the news. It takes a major cataclysm (an election or an assassination) to make a TV station add more news. When it does so, it usually loses money.

7. Story-Telling. The fact that a TV newscast is much shorter than a newspaper is sometimes summarized as meaning that television is "just a headline service." This is true enough for the briefest news items, the three-sentence summaries more "for the record" than for the audience. But most television news stories, even though they are shorter than newspaper articles, are not less interpretive. They are only less detailed.

In fact, TV news is typically far more interpretive than the average newspaper article. Most newspaper stories are written in "inverted pyramid" style, the facts in diminishing order of importance. Television stories are far more likely to be *stories,* complete with seductive introductions, suspenseful developments, and rousing climaxes. TV news usually gets the facts right, but it tends to encase the facts in a myth-like story-telling structure—David versus Goliath, or rags-to-riches, or evil in high places, etc. TV viewers don't know as much as newspaper readers about what actually happened, but they are told far more directly how to interpret what happened.

8. Indexability. Newspapers can be indexed. For reporters, this means they can be clipped, filed, and used later as background for a story. For readers, it means they can be browsed through. Nobody reads a newspaper cover to cover. You turn to the sections that interest you, check the headlines, and read only what you want.

None of this is possible in broadcasting. Radio and TV newscasts can be taped and stored, but they cannot be indexed for easy access. Unless a station builds a morgue of newspaper clippings (and very few do), it starts fresh with every story. As for the viewers, they have no choice but to watch the show "cover to cover." That's great for advertisers—it takes effort to skip the commercials. But it is a substantial barrier to lengthening newscasts, and to running long stories within newscasts. How much news that you don't want to see are you willing to sit through while waiting for the stories that interest you?

9. Competition. One thing you can safely say about radio and TV news: Both are highly competitive. A typical big city today has only two newspapers, but it has at least three TV stations and dozens of radio stations. Competition for ratings may not produce the best journalism, but it does keep reporters and editors on their toes.

10. Generalism. Except for the weather and sports people, broadcasting has very few news specialists, far fewer than newspapers. The typical station prefers to spend its money on helicopters and new sets, not on specialized science or labor reporters. The broadcast journalist covers everything.

11. Local News. Most television stations are located in big cities—but their signals reach dozens of smaller cities and towns. The local news of these smaller communities is almost never covered on TV. If you live more than 20 miles from the nearest TV station, you will have to subscribe to a newspaper to get any local news. And for national and international news you will be relying on the networks and the wire services. Very few stations cover anything but their own cities.

12. Entertainment. For the record, this is doubtless the most important of the dozen differences. There is sugar-coating in newspapers too, but television news is entertainment first and foremost.

We have detailed twelve major differences between broadcast news and newspaper news —mostly to the disadvantage of broadcasting. Some of these differences are inevitable; others can be changed. It is up to broadcasters—and viewers—to determine whether they ought to be changed, and if so how they ought to be changed.

It is probably unfair to judge television news by the same standards applied to newspapers. The media *are* different. Certainly television does a better job of covering the news than radio or movie newsreels did before it. Judged by two of the most traditional criteria for assessing journalism, speed and accuracy, television stands up quite well against newspapers. If it sacrifices comprehensiveness and overstresses entertainment, that is perhaps the price we must pay for attracting and holding the inadvertent audience.

RADIO NEWS

Throughout the 1940s, radio was the most important news medium in America. It nurtured such renowned journalists as Edward R. Murrow, William L. Shirer, and H. V. Kaltenborn, who covered World War II with honor and distinction. Then came television, and radio was forced to adapt, becoming the nation's number one source of background music. Formula radio may well have saved the medium from near-extinction.

But it had a devastating effect on news quality. The typical radio station styles its news coverage to fit its formula. A hard rock station will adopt a frantic pace, with wire service teletypes pecking away in the background. A classical music station will present a sedate, underplayed, two-minute report every hour. Both newscasts are prepared and read by disc jockeys, not trained journalists.

The typical radio station subscribes to only one wire service—the special UPI or AP broadcast wire, which moves the news in neat five-minute packages, ready to read. Every hour the disc jockey rips the copy from the wire and reads it over the air. Local news is pirated from local papers. Larger metropolitan stations may have a news staff of four or five reporters. But even there the emphasis is on the headlines, the notable and quotable. Even the major radio networks (ABC, CBS, NBC, and Mutual) carry little more than headlines and features.

In entertainment programming, the nation's radio stations are reasonably diverse. In news programming they are incredibly similar. Melvin Mencher of the Columbia University School of Journalism made these observations on a cross-country auto trip:

A station in a town thirty miles ahead came in, and for the fifth time that day I heard the same state news that had been ripped from the wires most of the day. The first item was the number of traffic fatalities in the state for the year, with a description of the latest death; next an endless rundown on bids on state highway construction; then the weather—temperature, wind velocity, barometric readings for every section of the state.

It was like this from Canada through the midwest into the southwest. Local stations sounded alike. Traffic accidents, arrests, judicial actions, deaths—courtesy of the local mortuary—statements by the mayor, the governor, a senator. All of it from the record, as dry and as concealing as dust on the highway. . . .[126]

Despite this performance, radio news is an important source of information. Many listeners presumably handle the hourly news the way they do the commercials; they listen casually until the music comes back on—and what they hear may be all the news they get that day. More than half the adult population, furthermore, gets its first news in the morning from radio, waiting until later for TV news or a newspaper.

The best available radio news comes from the stations with all-news or news-and-talk formats. There are 37 such stations in the 50 largest markets, and in big cities they usually do fairly well in the ratings. They have to. Because of personnel and wire service costs, all-news radio costs 60 percent more than DJ/music formats and many times more than computerized music formats.[127] Despite the expense, the CBS Radio Group, the Group W (Westinghouse) chain, and some independents have managed to make money on all-news radio.

Even these stations don't carry all that much news. They generally run news in one-hour cycles, repeating the old stories and adding a few new ones each hour. With only a handful of reporters on duty at any time, all-news radio stations rely heavily on the wire services, special audio services, local newspapers, and such pseudo-events as press conferences and airport arrivals. But at least a quick, up-to-date rundown on the news is available when you want it. And during elections, disasters, important government hearings, and the like, all-news radio offers the most comprehensive news to be found anywhere.

The most widely praised radio news show, by the way, is "All Things Considered," fed by National Public Radio to some 210 non-commercial radio stations around the country. "All Things Considered" is also the most successful program on public radio—but that doesn't make it successful. Its ratings add up to 1.1 percent of the listening audience.[128]

LIVE COVERAGE AND DOCUMENTARIES

The strongest moments in television are its on-the-spot reports of important events. The Kefauver crime investigation . . . the Army-McCarthy hearings . . . the assassination and funeral of President Kennedy . . . the first man on the moon . . . the Nixon resignation . . . the U.S. visit of Pope John Paul II . . . the space shuttle landing. These are the programs one remembers and talks about for years afterward.

The power of television was first widely recognized in 1951, with the Kefauver Crime Investigation Committee hearings in New York. *Daily News* reporter Lowell Limpus described the public's response to the televised hearings:

They're still trying to figure out just how many people dropped everything to camp in front of the TV screens for an entire week or more. They packed bar-rooms and restaurants to watch Virginia Hill. Suburban housewives entertained swarms of neighbors who studied Frank Costello with bated breath. Big department stores set up TV sets for customers who wouldn't buy anything while former Mayor O'Dwyer was on the stand.[129]

The televised Army-McCarthy hearings a couple of years later are widely credited

with having put a stop to the demagogic career of Senator Joe McCarthy. The public was able to judge the man and his methods for itself. In four years, newspapers had not been able to demolish McCarthy. Television did it in a few weeks.

When John Hinckley Jr. nearly took the life of President Reagan in 1981, much of the U.S. population gathered nervously around radios and TV sets. To meet the public's insatiable need for information, the three networks abandoned regular programming and carried the unfolding story live for the afternoon and early evening. Desperate for information themselves, reporters aired virtually everything they had, including misinformation about the identity and background of the would-be assassin and the condition of the president and his press secretary, James Brady. At one point viewers watched an impromptu press conference given by reporter Ross Simpson of the Mutual Broadcasting System, in which Simpson shared the second-hand rumors he had picked up wandering the halls of the hospital where Reagan and Brady were being treated. But despite the almost inevitable inaccuracies, broadcasting did give the nation the information it needed at a moment of crisis. By the time newspapers could reach the streets with the story hours later, most of the country knew the facts.

Why does it take an event as earth-shattering as the shooting of a president to force television to use its unique ability to cover important events as they happen? Because television is a commercial medium, and extended live coverage loses money.

Ordinary documentaries also lose money—even the ones that are prepared in advance and don't have to preempt scheduled shows. TV stations run them because they are prestige-builders, and because they earn credit in the eyes of the FCC. Most stations use as few documentaries as they think they can get away with.

Television excels in noncontroversial documentaries. Underwater photography, African wildlife, the treasures of our art museums —these and hundreds of similar topics have been magnificently handled by one or another network in the last few years. Controversial documentaries are something else.

Almost always they turn out wishy-washy.

Part of this is the government's fault. The fairness doctrine requires broadcasters to present every side of any controversy they touch at all. Though the fairness doctrine

---

WATERGATE ON TV

TV coverage of the Watergate scandals demonstrated once again that television is best when it is live and spontaneous.

For the first year of its unfolding, Watergate was the sort of story television journalism inevitably botches. It was complex, and TV news does not have the time for complexity. It involved leaks and anonymous sources, and such people do not like to be captured on film. It required dogged persistence to unravel, and television correspondents seldom have that luxury. At one point NBC's Carl Stern scooped the print media on the fact that presidential counsel John Dean had cautioned dirty-trickster Donald Segretti not to discuss his campaign manipulations—but the story never got on the air because it would have required too much explanation.[130] As ABC News vice president William Sheean put it: "This kind of story is not our strength."[131] Throughout 1972 and the first half of 1973, the newspapers and newsmagazines essentially owned the Watergate story.

Television came into its own when the focus shifted to public events—the Senate Watergate Committee hearings under Sam Ervin in the summer of 1973, then a year later the House impeachment inquiry under Peter Rodino, the resignation of President Nixon and the swearing in of President Ford. The ratings companies estimated that 70 million Americans watched some portion of the impeachment debates on TV.[132] More than 45 million U.S. TV sets were tuned in when President Nixon announced his resignation on August 8, 1974.[133]

Characteristically, when television was at its best it was losing money. Many advertisers don't want to "sponsor" an event as controversial as an impeachment hearing, and TV journalists are understandably reluctant to cut away for ads during such a hearing. For economic reasons, the three networks rotated daytime coverage of the Ervin Committee hearings, and decided not to broadcast the last few days of the hearings at all. They carried the six-day House impeachment inquiry in full—at a loss of $3.4 million.[134] A three-hour NBC special the night of the Nixon resignation cost the network $900,000 in canceled ads.[135]

Free from advertising worries, public television taped both proceedings in full and replayed them each night. Noncommercial TV devoted more than 250 prime-time hours to the Ervin hearings alone, earning its largest audience to date and greatly increasing its popularity, visibility, and fund-raising potential.[136] In the process, the American public learned not only about the Watergate cover-up but also about the principles and realities of due process, executive privilege, and separation of powers—and about how the American system of government responds to the crisis of corruption in high places. Television proved once again how powerful a force it can be when its energies are focused on a single event, when it is not preoccupied with cartoons, situation comedies, and earning money.

says nothing about presenting all sides "equally" in the same program, many broadcast executives are afraid to produce a hard-hitting documentary. Robert MacNeil tells the story of an NBC documentary on gun control. The first version examined the problem in some detail, then closed with strong support for gun-control legislation. After viewing this version, NBC executives ordered that an interview with Frank Orth (head of the National Rifle Association) be added at the end to "balance" the presentation. Mac-Neil feels that what was finally aired had no guts, no spirit, and no point of view.[137]

Any topic that's worth a documentary is bound to involve some powerful people and institutions. If the documentary is hard-hitting, someone is likely to resent it—and television doesn't like to make enemies. The fairness doctrine is sometimes a reason for avoiding controversy; more often it is an excuse. In the late 1960s, CBS planned a program on the role of organized religion in the war on poverty. The producers found that many Protestant churches were reluctant to accept federal anti-poverty money for fear they might endanger the traditional separation of church and state. At the request of several Protestant groups the documentary was canceled. How did these groups know what CBS was up to? CBS had asked them—routinely—if they had any objections to the proposed documentary.[138]

The attitude of many television executives toward documentaries was well expressed by Richard Behrendt, program manager of KRON-TV in San Francisco. A documentary, complained Behrendt, "takes up a great deal of time and money . . . and may hold people up to ridicule."[139]

When television does undertake a controversial documentary, the results can be magnificent. Undoubtedly one of broadcasting's finest moments in 1970 was the CBS documentary "The Selling of the Pentagon." The power of this exposé of Defense Department news management is indicated by the mag-

nitude of the response it produced. The government protested bitterly; the Pentagon demanded and received rebuttal time; a congressional committee investigated the documentary for bias (see pp. 167-68) and ordered CBS to turn over its unused film so that its editing procedure could be examined. CBS refused this last demand, and eventually the storm blew over. But it did have an effect. Soon afterward, CBS circulated a long memo to its staff on how to edit questions and answers together on film.

CBS undoubtedly knew in advance that "The Selling of the Pentagon" would stir up a hornet's nest of denials and recriminations. In broadcasting the show, and rebroadcasting it in the midst of the furor, the network showed great (and unaccustomed) courage.

More typical of the network approach to documentaries was the creation in the 1970s of the "docu-drama." Modeled on Truman Capote's "nonfiction novel," the docu-drama uses fiction techniques (made-up dialogue, made-up motivations, even made-up characters and events) to tell a "real" story. Examples of the genre include "The Ordeal of Patty Hearst," "The Amazing Howard Hughes," "Tail-Gunner Joe" (about the life of Senator Joseph McCarthy), "Blind Ambition" (based on John Dean's recollections of Watergate), and "Collision Course" (President Truman's confrontation with General Douglas MacArthur). Such programs attract an audience for history or current events that might well skip a more traditional documentary. But critics of the docu-drama worry that it mixes fact and fiction without giving the viewer any way to distinguish one from the other.[140]

EDITORIALS

In 1941, the Federal Communications Commission outlawed broadcast editorials, ruling that "the broadcaster cannot be an advocate."

The Commission changed its mind in 1949—but there was no mad rush to take advantage of the right to editorialize. A 1977 study found that only 61 percent of all commercial TV stations editorialize ever, and only 31 percent editorialize daily—standard practice at even the poorest newspapers.[141]

When broadcasters do editorialize, they usually stick to noncontroversial topics—"Support Your Local Red Cross" and such. Why? The history of FCC disapproval is part of the answer. So is current government regulation. The fairness doctrine encourages a "yes, but on the other hand" approach in editorials. And the personal attack rule requires stations to give free time to any individual or group criticized in their editorials. Broadcasters who endorse a political candidate must give free reply time to the candidate's opponents. These are significant hindrances to a strong editorial policy.

But they are not the real reason most broadcasters lack such a policy. The real reason is much simpler. Strong editorials make enemies, and broadcasters will do nearly anything to avoid making enemies.

Perhaps this is just as well. Given the immense influence of television, a broadcaster who systematically sought power through everything from entertainment to news to editorials would soon acquire far too much of it. Even the growing segmentation of the TV audience, thanks to cable and satellites, would not adequately protect us from power-hungry broadcasters.

What protects us is that there are very few power-hungry broadcasters. The people who control television are not intentionally the tools of any ideology. Rather, they are the tools of corporations whose only serious goal is profit. For better or for worse, television fritters away much of its power in exchange for money.

How do you maximize profit in nonentertainment programming? You make the news light and action-packed. You keep live coverage infrequent, and documentaries non-controversial. And you don't editorialize much.

Notes

1 Neil Hickey, "Goodbye '70s, Hello '80s," *TV Guide,* January 5, 1980, p. 13.

2 "Poll Shows Less TV Viewing; America Eases to New TV Forms," *Access,* March 12, 1979, p. 1.

3 Hickey, "Goodbye '70s, Hello '80s," p. 13.

4 George Comstock, "The Impact of Television on American Institutions," *Journal of Communication,* Spring, 1978, p. 20.

5 Hickey, "Goodbye '70s, Hello '80s," p. 13.

6 Myles Callum, "What Viewers Love/Hate about Television," *TV Guide,* May 12, 1979, pp. 6-11.

7 Les Brown, "Viewers' Dissatisfaction with TV Programs Found," *New York Times,* January 3, 1980, p. C18.

8 Dennis John Lewis, "Morning Glory: Radio's Prime Time," *Washington Journalism Review,* September/October, 1979, p. 49. *1968 Broadcasting Yearbook,* pp. 22, 24.

9 *San Francisco Chronicle,* May 9, 1970.

10 Newton N. Minow, *Equal Time, the Private Broadcaster and the Public Interest* (New York: Atheneum, 1964), ch. 1.

11 Gary A. Steiner, *The People Look at Television* (New York: Alfred A. Knopf, 1963), p. 235.

12 Comstock, "The Impact of Television on American Institutions," p. 21.

13 Jack Loftus, "NBC-TV Sports Profits: The $$ from the Shows," *Variety,* May 28, 1980, pp. 51, 60.

14 William Oscar Johnson, "The Greenbacking of Pete Rose," *Sports Illustrated,* January 22, 1979, p. 38.

15 Lynn M. Berk, "The Great Middle American Dream Machine," *Journal of Communication,* Summer, 1977, pp. 27-31.

16 George Gerbner, *et al.,* "Aging with Television: Images on Television Drama and Conceptions of Social Reality," *Journal of Communication,* Winter, 1980, pp. 37-47.

17 Lois Kaufman, "Prime-Time Nutrition," *Journal of Communication,* Summer, 1980, pp. 37-46.

18 Norman Jacobs, ed., *Culture for the Millions* (New York: Van Nostrand Reinhold, 1961), p. 508.

19 Bernard Rosenberg and David Manning White, eds., *Mass Culture: The Popular Arts in America* (New York: The Free Press, 1957), p. 60.

20 Alexis de Tocqueville, *Democracy in America* (New York: Vintage Books, 1945), II, pp. 50-54.

21 "Global Prices for TV Films," *Variety*, April 16, 1980, p. 60.

22 Rosenberg and White, *Mass Culture*, p. 61.

23 Jacobs, *Culture for the Millions*, p. 510.

24 Robert M. Liebert, John M. Neale, and Emily S. Davidson, *The Early Window: Effects of Television on Children and Youth* (Elmsford, N.Y.: Pergamon Press, 1973), p. 23.

25 *Ibid.*, p. 25.

26 *Ibid.*, p. 24.

27 John Stanley, "The Year Many a Villain Was Worded to Death," *San Francisco Sunday Examiner and Chronicle, Datebook,* January 4, 1970, p. 12.

28 Liebert, Neale, and Davidson, *The Early Window,* pp. 2-3.

29 "Was 'West Side Story' Bad for East Harlem?" *New York Times,* April 2, 1972, p. D15.

30 F. B. Steuer, J. M. Applefield, and R. Smith, "Televised Aggression and the Interpersonal Aggression of Preschool Children," *Journal of Experimental Child Psychology,* 11, 1971, 442-47.

31 Linda Greenhouse, "Lawsuit Dismissed Against NBC-TV," *New York Times,* August 9, 1978, p. A8.

32 Richard Flaste, "Survey Finds that Most Children Are Happy at Home But Fear World," *New York Times,* March 2, 1977, p. 12.

33 Peter M. Sandman, "The Fight over Television Violence Ratings," *More,* April, 1978, pp. 37-38.

34 Jack Schicht, "Religious Groups v. TV's Sex, Violence," Freedom of Information Center Report No. 416, School of Journalism, University of Missouri at Columbia, January, 1980, p. 7.

35 Deborah Harris, "Advertisers Attack TV Violence," *Access,* June 28, 1976, p. 17.

36 Schicht, "Religious Groups v. TV's Sex, Violence," p. 4.

37 Les Brown, "Picture Turns Bright for UHF," *New York Times,* December 20, 1979, p. D6.

38 Rufus Crater, "UHF: Out of the Traffic and Heading for the Open Road," *Broadcasting,* June 10, 1974, p. 38.

39 Ernest Holsendolph, "FCC Staff Calls Agency Powerless Against TV," *New York Times,* October 17, 1979, p. C26.

40 Betsy Carter, "ABC Goes A-Hunting," *Newsweek,* January 8, 1979, p. 71.

41 Les Brown, "NBC's Slippage in Ratings Spurs Defection by Affiliates to ABC," *New York Times,* May 8, 1979, p. C21.

42 Paul Klein, "The Men Who Run TV Aren't That Stupid . . . They Know Us Better Than You Think," *New York,* January 25, 1971, pp. 20-29.

43 *Variety,* December 26, 1973, p. 24.

44 Les Brown, "Files of Nixon White House Show Bid to Control Public Broadcasting," *New York Times,* February 24, 1979, pp. 1, 9.

45 Willard D. Rowland, Jr., "The Federal Regulatory and Policymaking Process," *Journal of Communication,* Summer, 1980, p. 140. James Roman, "Programming for Public Television," *Journal of Communication,* Summer, 1980, p. 131.

46 Richard Bunce, "The New Economics of Public TV," *Access,* July 28, 1980, p. 2.

47 Rowland, "The Federal Regulatory and Policymaking Process," p. 140.

48 "PTV's Fancy Figures," *Variety,* June 4, 1980, p. 59.

49 David J. LeRoy, "Public Broadcasting/Who Watches Public Television?" *Journal of Communication,* Summer, 1980, pp. 161-2.

50 Don Agostino, "New Technologies: Problem or Solution?" *Journal of Communication,* Summer, 1980, p. 200.

51 "The Fortunate 501," *Broadcasting,* August 25, 1980, p. 62.

52 Richard L. Worsnop, "Competing Media," *Editorial Research Reports,* II, No. 3, July 18, 1969, p. 542.

53 "Radio Listening Is Stable, But FM Climbs, AM Drops," *Variety,* May 22, 1974, p. 52.

54 "The Changing Game," *Broadcast Management/ Engineering,* February, 1980, p. 40.

55 N. R. Kleinfield, "FM's Success Is Loud and Clear," *New York Times,* October 26, 1979, pp. D1, D6.

56 Ernest Holsendolph, "FCC Offers a Plan to Add 125 Stations to AM Radio Bands," *New York Times,* December 20, 1978, pp. 1, D3.

57 Desmond Smith, "Television Enters The 80's," *New York Times Magazine,* August 19, 1979, p. 20.

58 Ernest Holsendolph, "UHF's Broadcasting Struggles," *New York Times,* January 1, 1979, p. 29.

59 "Hearst To Buy WDTN Dayton for $40-Million," *Variety,* May 21, 1980, p. 47. "Knight-Ridder Will Pay $48.3 Million to Buy Virginia TV Station," *Wall Street Journal,* October 22, 1980, p. 12. Remarks of Gene F. Jankowski, President, CBS Broadcast Group, to the Academy of Television Arts and Sciences, Los Angeles, November 29, 1979, p. 9.

60 Roger Piantadosi, "The Resurgence of Radio," *Washington Journalism Review,* October, 1980, p. 26.

61 Jack Loftus, "NBC's Primetime Profits: The $$ From the Shows," *Variety,* April 30, 1980, p. 151.

Jack Loftus, "NBC's Day-Night Profits: The $$ From the Shows," *Variety*, May 14, 1980, p. 88.

62 John E. Cooney, "Johnny Carson Calls This Man 'Bombastic' All the Way to the Bank," *Wall Street Journal*, June 4, 1980, p. 14.

63 Jack Loftus, "NBC-TV Specials & Movies: The $$ From the Shows," *Variety*, June 4, 1980, p. 44.

64 Telephone interview with Robert Higgins of CBS, August 6, 1981.

65 Bill Abrams, "Firms Fret over Rising Costs of TV Spots; Some Raise Budgets and Stress Prime Time," *Wall Street Journal*, April 4, 1980, p. 30.

66 *Ibid.*

67 Lewis, "Morning Glory: Radio's Prime Time," p. 49.

68 Meyer Weinberg, *TV in America* (New York: Ballantine Books, 1962), p. i.

69 Jack Loftus, "CBS Bets $15-Mil on New Cable Unit," *Variety*, May 21, 1980, p. 39.

70 Peter Funt, "Broadcasters Are Switching to 'Narrowcasting,'" *New York Times*, December 16, 1979, p. D43.

71 *Ibid.*

72 "Cable TV, Overextended, Is in Retreat in Cities," *New York Times*, March 9, 1974, pp. 1, 59.

73 David M. Rubin, "Short Circuit in the Wired Nation," *More*, September, 1973, pp. 16-18.

74 "Cable TV, Overextended," pp. 1, 59.

75 *Ibid.*, p. 59.

76 Charles Paul Freund, "Cable TV: The Progress," *Washington Journalism Review*, May, 1980, p. 16.

77 "Progress Report," First Manhattan Co., July 1, 1980, p. 4.

78 Freund, "Cable TV: The Progress," p. 16.

79 "Five-Year Predictions," *Broadcasting*, February 18, 1980, p. 98.

80 Cable News Network advertisement, *Variety*, October 29, 1980, p. 69. Philip H. Dougherty, "Arco Joins Cable News Ad Roster," *New York Times*, July 23, 1980, p. D15. Tony Schwartz, "The TV News, Starring Ted Turner," *New York Times*, May 25, 1980, sec. 3, pp. 4, 5.

81 Schwartz, "The TV News, Starring Ted Turner," pp. 4, 5.

82 *Ibid.*

83 *Ibid.*

84 *Ibid.*

85 Freund, "Cable TV: The Progress," p. 17.

86 "The Gold Rush of 1980," *Broadcasting*, March 31, 1980, p. 35.

87 "Cable TV: The Promise," *Washington Journalism Review*, May, 1980, p. 31. Remarks by Henry Geller to the Communications Media Committee of the American Civil Liberties Union, New York, N.Y., September 25, 1980.

88 Smith, "Television Enters the 80's," p. 17.

89 "Nielsen Gets First Good Grip on Cable and Viewing Levels," *Broadcasting*, August 4, 1980, p. 28.

90 "STV: Scratching Out Its Place in the New-Video Universe," *Broadcasting*, April 7, 1980, p. 46. Les Brown, "Pay-TV, with 12 Stations Approved, Makes Gains," *New York Times*, March 27, 1979, p. C12.

91 Brown, "Pay-TV, with 12 Stations Approved, Makes Gains," p. C12.

92 "Nielsen Gets First Good Grip," p. 27. "Pay Television Isn't Hurting Networks, Ad Agency Reports," *Wall Street Journal*, July 9, 1980, p. 30.

93 John Noble Wilford, "A 'Traffic Jam' in Outer Space," *New York Times*, March 24, 1980, p. D1.

94 Raymond M. Lane, "Satellite Fever," *Washington Journalism Review*, March, 1980, p. 22.

95 "Satellite-to-Homes TV Transmissions Seen Growing Fast," *Wall Street Journal*, April 12, 1980, p. 12.

96 "Special TV Networks for Special Audiences," *New York Times*, April 8, 1980, p. C9.

97 "Indie News Web Nets 36 Stations," *Variety*, September 10, 1980, p. 55.

98 "Special TV Networks for Special Audiences," p. C9.

99 N. R. Kleinfield, "Black Radio Network Expands," *New York Times*, August 1, 1980, p. D1.

100 Lane, "Satellite Fever," pp. 18-19.

101 Les Brown, "Ad Hoc TV Networks Planning Assaults on the 3 Majors," *New York Times*, November 24, 1979, p. 46.

102 Arlie Schardt, "How to Dish Up a Skyful of TV," *Newsweek*, October 27, 1980, p. 101.

103 "U.S. Opposes Soviet Draft of a Satellite TV Treaty," *New York Times*, October 13, 1972, p. 2.

104 "Stanton Hits Proposed Curb on TV Satellite Use," *New York Times*, October 5, 1972, p. 94.

105 Les Brown, "Videotapes for Homes," *New York Times*, June 13, 1979, p. C24.

106 Peter J. Schuyten, "The TV: More to View with Tapes and Disks," *New York Times*, February 17, 1980, pp. F1, F11.

107 James David Barber, "Not *The New York Times*: What Network News Should Be," *Washington Monthly*, September, 1979, p. 14.

108 Frank Greve, "The Nets: When You've Seen One, Have You Seen 'em All?" *New York Daily News*, June 18, 1980, p. 37.

109 Desmond Smith, "The Wide World of Roone

Arledge," *New York Times Magazine*, February 24, 1980, p. 39.

110 *Ibid.*, p. 38.

111 *Ibid.*

112 Harry Stein, "How '60 Minutes' Makes News," *New York Times Magazine*, May 6, 1979, p. 76.

113 Thomas J. Bray, " '60 Minutes' vs. Henry Kissinger," *Wall Street Journal*, June 6, 1980, p. 16.

114 "Fighting Fire with Fire, Television Style," *Broadcasting*, July 14, 1980, p. 58.

115 Bray, " '60 Minutes' vs. Henry Kissinger," p. 16.

116 David Shaw, " '60 Minutes': A TV Habit, Flaws and All," *Los Angeles Times*, June 10, 1980. Tony Schwartz, "Reruns on '60 Minutes' Spur Debate," *New York Times*, May 15, 1980, p. C26.

117 "Programming Status Quo," *Broadcasting*, July 16, 1979, p. 36.

118 Robert Scheer, "Crisis in TV News: Show-Biz Invasion," *Los Angeles Times*, May 29, 1977.

119 Ginnia Woods and Ernest Volkman, "Coming to You Live . . . From Potholes and Trash Baskets," *Panorama*, October, 1980, pp. 46, 48.

120 Robert Scheer, "The Rise of Joan Lunden: News Sense Unimportant," *Los Angeles Times*, May 29, 1977.

121 Robert Scheer, "The Selling of Local TV News Shows," *Los Angeles Times*, June 6, 1977.

122 "Local TV News Takes Wing," *Broadcasting*, July 28, 1980, pp. 33-54.

123 Scheer, "The Selling of Local TV News Shows."

124 Michael J. Arlen, *Living-Room War* (New York: Viking Press, 1969), pp. 194-95.

125 Robert MacNeil, "The News on TV and How It Is Unmade," *Harper's Magazine*, October, 1968, p. 75.

126 Melvin Mencher, "The Roving Listener," *Columbia Journalism Review*, Fall, 1966, pp. 45-46.

127 "The Fortunate 501," p. 62. Eugene F. Shaw and Daniel Riffe, "NIS and Radio's All-News Predicament," *Journalism Monographs*, August, 1980, p. 4.

128 Donald P. Mullally, "Public Broadcasting/Radio: The Other Medium," *Journal of Communication*, Summer, 1980, pp. 190-92.

129 Lowell Limpus, "Television News Comes of Age," *Nieman Reports*, July, 1951, p. 11.

130 "Watergate on Camera," *Newsweek*, May 28, 1973, p. 113.

131 *Ibid.*

132 "Nixon's Days in Court Are TV's, Too; Impeachment Coverage Makes History," *Broadcasting*, August 5, 1974, p. 18.

133 "Almost 47-Mil U.S. Homes Saw Nixon-Ford Switch," *Variety*, August 28, 1974, p. 2.

134 "Nixon's Days in Court," p. 18.

135 "Record TV Audience Attends Nixon Resignation," *Broadcasting*, August 12, 1974, p. 6.

136 "Watergate Spurs Journalism on TV," *New York Times*, December 9, 1973, p. 51.

137 Robert MacNeil, *The People Machine* (New York: Harper & Row, 1968), ch. 11.

138 Richard Severo, "What's News at CBS?" *New Republic*, March 12, 1966, p. 33.

139 "FCC's KRON-TV Quiz: 2 Views," *Variety*, April 22, 1970, p. 35.

140 David W. Rintels, "In Defense of the Television 'Docu-Drama,' " *New York Times*, April 22, 1979, sec. 2, pp. 1, 20.

141 Milan D. Meeske, "Editorial Practices of Television Stations," *Journalism Quarterly*, Winter, 1978, pp. 750-54.

Suggested Readings

Adler, Richard, *All In The Family, A Critical Appraisal*. New York: Praeger Special Studies and the Aspen Institute for Humanistic Studies, 1979.

Arlen, Michael J., *Living-Room War*. New York: Viking Press, 1969.

Barnouw, Erik, *Tube of Plenty, The Evolution of American Television*. New York: Oxford University Press, Galaxy Paperback, 1975.

Berk, Lynn M., "The Great Middle American Dream Machine," *Journal of Communication*, Summer, 1977.

Bower, Robert T., *Television and the Public*. New York: Holt, Rinehart and Winston, 1973.

Brown, Les, *Television—The Business Behind the Box*. New York: Harcourt Brace Jovanovich, 1971.

Comstock, George, et al., *Television and Human Behavior*. New York: Columbia University Press, 1978.

———, "The Impact of Television on American Institutions," *Journal of Communication*, Spring, 1978.

Epstein, Edward J., *News From Nowhere*. New York: Vintage Books, 1974.

Freund, Charles Paul, "Cable TV: The Progress," *Washington Journalism Review*, May, 1980.

GANS, HERBERT J., *Deciding What's News*. New York: Pantheon, 1979.

GERBNER, GEORGE, *et al.*, "Aging with Television: Images on Television Drama and Conceptions of Social Reality," *Journal of Communication*, Winter, 1980.

"The Gold Rush of 1980, Prospecting for Cable Franchises," *Broadcasting*, March 31, 1980.

JACKSON-BEECK, MARILYN, "The Nonviewers: Who Are They?" *Journal of Communication*, Summer, 1977.

LANE, RAYMOND M., "Satellite Fever," *Washington Journalism Review*, March, 1980.

LITMAN, BARRY R., "Is Network Ownership in the Public Interest," *Journal of Communication*, Spring, 1978.

MANKIEWICZ, FRANK, and JOEL SWERDLOW, *Remote Control, Television and the Manipulation of American Life*. New York: Ballantine Books, 1978.

McGILL, WILLIAM J., *et al.*, *A Public Trust: The Landmark Report of the Carnegie Commission on the Future of Public Broadcasting*. New York: Bantam Books, 1979.

POWERS, RON, *The Newscasters: The News Business as Show Business*. New York: St. Martin's Press, 1977.

RINTELS, DAVID W., "In Defense of the Television 'Docu-Drama'," *The New York Times*, April 22, 1979, Section 2, p. 1.

SCHILLER, HERBERT I., *Mass Communications and American Empire*. New York: Augustus M. Kelley, 1969.

SCHWARTZ, TONY, "Some Say This Is America's Best TV Station," *The New York Times*, February 15, 1981, Section 2, p. 1.

SMITH, DESMOND, "Television Enters the 80's," *The New York Times Magazine*, August 19, 1979.

STEIN, HARRY, "How '60 Minutes' Makes News," *The New York Times Magazine*, May 6, 1979.

STERLING, CHRISTOPHER H., and JOHN M. KITTROSS, *Stay Tuned: A Concise History of American Broadcasting*. Belmont, Calif.: Wadsworth Publishing Co., 1978.

SURGEON GENERAL'S SCIENTIFIC ADVISORY COMMITTEE ON TELEVISION AND SOCIAL BEHAVIOR, *Television and Growing Up: The Impact of Televised Violence*. Washington, D.C.: U.S. Government Printing Office, 1972.

WIGAND, ROLF T., "The Direct Satellite Connection: Definitions and Prospects," *Journal of Communication*, Spring, 1980.

WOLLERT, JAMES A., and MICHAEL O. WIRTH, "UHF Television Program Performance: Continuing Questions on Spectrum Use," *Journalism Quarterly*, Summer, 1979.

Chapter 13
Film and Recordings

Feature filmmaking is a game of chance where a dozen winners take home all the money and a hundred others lose money. It wasn't always that way. Before television, everyone went to the movies almost every week, and most feature films made money. Today the film industry earns its bread and butter from television, and risks its profits on theatrical releases. Enough of these risks proved successful in the 1970s to keep the motion picture industry solvent. However, the industry still faces charges of discrimination, stereotyping, and pornography.

In 1947, more than 85 million people in the U.S. visited a movie theater each week. By the mid-1950s, the movie audience had dropped to about 45 million per week. And by 1971 the figure was down around 18 million, a base from which it climbed slowly to just over 21 million by the end of the 1970s—almost exactly a quarter of 1947 attendance. Many factors contributed to the decline, but television was by far the most important. The recent history of the film industry is the history of its response to television.

At first, the major Hollywood studios responded to the competition of TV by pro-ducing fewer but more spectacular feature films. Movie theaters moved to the suburbs with the expanding middle class, and rocking-chair seats, wide screens, and stereophonic sound created a film experience that could not be duplicated on the home television set. Throughout the 1950s and well into the 1960s, Hollywood hoped that big-budget blockbusters would save it from television.

Sometimes the tactic worked. *The Ten Commandments* (1956) and *Ben-Hur* (1959) grossed $40 million each in domestic theaters, did well on the international market, and were eventually sold to television. *The Sound of Music* (1965), which cost $7.6 million to produce, was the biggest moneymaker of the 1960s, earning $72 million in the United States and Canada and perhaps as much as $60 million more internationally. *Doctor Zhivago* (1965), *Funny Girl* (1968), and *2001: A Space Odyssey* (1968) were other big pictures that made money.

But the losers outnumbered the winners. A more typical spectacular was *Doctor Doolittle,* on which Twentieth Century Fox took a loss of $18 million. The end of the 1960s saw a string of such blockbuster flops, including *Sweet Charity, Star, Ice Station Ze-*

bra, and *Chitty Chitty Bang Bang.* The failure of so many spectaculars led to some spectacular failures; in 1969 five of the major studios reported net losses totaling $110 million. In the 1960s and early 1970s, a number of Hollywood studios were forced to fold or merge, while others drastically curtailed their activities. Magazine articles on the "death of Hollywood" were plentiful.

Rising costs were part of the problem. "I wish *The Sound of Music* had never been made," remarked one studio production chief. "The industry lost sight of reality and thought that budgets didn't require a ceiling."[1] Star performers were demanding as much as a million dollars a film, and the studios paid the price, unable to believe that an Elizabeth Taylor or a Julie Andrews no longer guaranteed a hit. Many films in the 1960s cost as much as $20 million to make. To earn a profit after the movie theater owners have taken their percentage off the top, a $20-million motion picture must gross about $50 million in box-office receipts. Most movies simply didn't earn that much.

Even a $20-million spectacular, of course, could make money if enough people wanted to see it. The big mistake of the film industry was to underestimate the public's satisfaction with television. The Hollywood studios of the 1960s were like two-headed monsters with no communication between the heads. One part was busy producing big-budget films for theatrical distribution. The other part was busy selling old movies (and some not-so-old ones) to television, and producing TV programs for the networks. Even while they were selling their souls to television, the studios steadfastly misjudged the success of the electronic medium.

Today, theatrical films and made-for-TV movies comprise much of prime-time network programming, while the products of the film studios dominate many non-network stations and nearly all pay-cable operations. Movie magnates should have seen this coming. They should have realized that faced with the choice of a movie on TV (for free) or a movie in town (at $3 a seat), most Americans would rather stay home in their easy chairs. Instead, the major studios ignored their own increasing contributions to the success of television, pointed to the *Sound of Music* bonanza, and plunged full steam ahead into the disasters of the late 1960s.

ART AND THE YOUTH MARKET

Throughout the 1960s and 1970s, the Motion Picture Association of America commissioned a series of surveys to find out what sorts of people were still going to the movies. The findings were consistent:[2]

1. More than three-quarters of all moviegoers are under 30.
2. Nearly half are between 12 and 20.
3. Roughly a third are under 15.
4. Adults over 50 seldom go.

Despite these facts, the major studios for years paid very little attention to teenagers and young adults. Instead, they aimed their films at a middle-class, middle-aged "family" audience—hoping that if box-office receipts didn't justify that emphasis, sales to television and foreign markets would.

In the late 1950s and early 1960s, the studios did try to attract the youth market with a series of beach-party and Elvis Presley movies. But these films were several years behind the musical pulse of America's teenagers. In choosing between a Presley movie and a Beatles record, young people bought the record—and had their own beach party.

It took Hollywood until the late 1960s to figure out how to appeal to the younger generation. But even before this was accomplished, young people made up an increasingly large percentage of the moviegoing audience. Why?

For one thing, movies were an essential part of the American dating game. While many middle-aged people came to think of films as an unnecessary inconvenience and expense, the younger generation saw them

MAKING MONEY OFF THE KIDS

At least one film company understood early that there was money to be earned from the youth market. Founded in 1954, American International Pictures concentrated on cheap movies and managed to stay one jump ahead of its youth audience for 25 years. AIP consistently made money in even the darkest days of Hollywood. Its alumni include such now-famous actors, writers, and directors as Peter Fonda, Dennis Hopper, Willard Huyck, Jack Nicholson, Bruce Dern, Martin Scorsese, John Milius, Roger Corman, and Woody Allen.

At the beginning, AIP decided to specialize in horror films for the teenage audience at the nation's growing number of drive-in theaters. While the major studios were making big-budget features like *The Robe*, AIP produced black-and-white cheapies such as *The Beast with 1,000,000 Eyes* (made in eight days for $35,000) and *I Was a Teenage Werewolf* (a $123,000 film that grossed $2 million). Between 1954 and 1960, not one AIP movie lost money.

Faced with imitators, and sensing that its audience would no longer buy black-and-white double features, AIP went to color in 1960, and upped its typical budget to $400,000. Edgar Allan Poe stories were in the public domain and Hollywood horror stars were underpriced, so the company released *The Fall of the House of Usher* starring Vincent Price. A string of seven more Poe films followed.

The company continued to demonstrate an uncanny ability to read its young audience's interests in advance. In the mid-1960s, it switched to motorcycle movies, scoring a huge success in 1968 with *Wild in the Streets* (featuring Christopher Jones as a young president who puts his mother in a concentration camp). By the 1970s, AIP was busy making movies about black supermen and superwomen (*Slaughter, Foxy Brown*), as well as a special line of black horror films (*Blacula*). When Kung Fu became the rage, AIP distributed at least a dozen films with titles like *Shanghai Killers* and *Deep Thrust;* by the time the fad was over, AIP had long since moved on to other things.

Horror films continued to be AIP's meat and potatoes, but declining profits in the mid-1970s forced company head Samuel Z. Arkoff to re-examine the genre. Faced with competition from television suspense shows and from major studio productions like *The Exorcist*, Arkoff decided it was time to step up to bigger-budget films. And so AIP spent $5 million on *The Amityville Horror*. Released in 1979, *Amityville* grossed $75 million in the U.S. alone. Also in 1979, Filmways bought AIP for $30 million, making Arkoff its largest shareholder. By the end of the year Arkoff had resigned to return to independent film production, but the spirit of AIP lived on in Filmways' first big movie, Brian De Palma's *Dressed to Kill*, a 1980 shocker that did well both in the reviews and at the box office.[3]

In 25 years, AIP produced about 500 films, most of which were called "trash" by the critics when originally released. Today they are considered prime examples of American popular culture. In 1979 they were actually the subject of a film retrospective at New York's Museum of Modern Art. Art or schlock, the films made money. For 25 years, Sam Arkoff gave movie audiences what they wanted.[4]

Given his track record, Arkoff's prescription for success is worth listening to: "There's no way to sell the young today that's as clearcut as in the past. I don't think our audience is the same audience any more for any two different pictures. Each picture must be attractive to some segment of youth, to some part of the audience under 30."[5]

as an escape from the prying eyes of parents and other adults, as a place to be "alone" with a friend or a date.

But the enthusiasm that young people have shown for film goes beyond the pleasures of popcorn and a dark room. Significant numbers of Americans, most of them under 30 and almost all of them under 45, take movies seriously as an art form. Writing in 1966, film critic Stanley Kauffmann put it this way:

[T]here exists a Film Generation: the first generation that has matured in a culture in which the film has been of accepted serious relevance, however that seriousness is defined. Before 1935 films were proportionately more popular than they are now, but for the huge majority of film-goers they represented a regular weekly or semiweekly bath of escapism. Such an escapist audience still exists in large number, but another audience, most of them born since 1935, exists along with it. This group, this Film Generation, is certainly not exclusively grim, but it is essentially serious. Even its appreciations of sheer entertainment films reflect an over-all serious view.[6]

Kauffmann went on to list five reasons for the emergence of a film generation. First, in an age of technology, film is a heavily technological enterprise, yet it uses that technology to celebrate the human being. Second, film offers a new opportunity to apply artistic sensibility to the world of physical details; "it manages to make poetry out of doorknobs, breakfasts, furniture." Third, the film form is especially appropriate for dealing with many of the pressing issues of modern times, especially the relationship between inner states (tension, doubt, apathy) and external reality. Fourth, a film is instantly available to the entire world without translation, vividly recreating foreign settings and situations. And fifth, film is a young medium whose potential has not yet been explored, much less exhausted.[7]

While Hollywood was very slow to appreciate the artistic potential of movies, European filmmakers were not. The innovative films of the European masters—Truffaut, Godard, Fellini, Antonioni, etc.—were imported to the U.S. and shown through an informal network of small "art" movie theaters. The audience, of course, was mostly college students and recent graduates.

Some of the young people in the audience were also amateur filmmakers themselves. And a few of them were good enough, and dedicated enough, to try to carve out a career in motion pictures. "It was frustrating," one young filmmaker explained. "For one reason or another, the industry was unresponsive to personal films. The industry was controlled and dominated by a business industrial mentality."[8] Some of these young filmmakers sought jobs with the major studios anyway. Others joined independent film companies—and a few founded their own.

The success of *The Graduate* and *Bonnie and Clyde* in 1968 shook the big studios badly. Both movies were produced on incredibly low budgets by Hollywood standards, and both earned phenomenal profits. Speaking personally to the under-30 audience, *The Graduate* told the sentimental story of a young man's struggle with the adult establishment; it earned $43 million in the domestic market alone. Independently produced by its star, Warren Beatty, *Bonnie and Clyde* celebrated random violence as a kind of cultural revolution against stodgy values and lifestyles; it earned $22 million in U.S. theaters.

A year later came *Midnight Cowboy, Easy Rider,* and *Alice's Restaurant.* All three earned huge profits. And Hollywood began to get the message—big-budget films were dangerous, and the movies that returned the highest percentage profits were independent, low-budget productions aimed specifically at a young audience.

Strangely enough, it was the independent filmmakers who helped sustain the Hollywood studios during this crucial period. Even a low-budget movie can easily cost several million dollars to produce. Success requires not just filmmaking skill, but also expertise in financing and distribution. More often than not, the independents wound up depending on Hollywood for these services—and when their films proved successful, the big studios reaped much of the profit. If film-maker Haskell Wexler could bring in *Medium Cool* for under a million dollars for Paramount release, why should Paramount risk over $20 million on a possible bomb like *Paint Your Wagon?* By the end of the 1960s, the major studios were in the bankrolling business, betting on independent low-budget productions and the American youth market.

THE FORMULA FOR THE 1970S

In 1970, the Hollywood studios produced a number of "youth movies" of their own. Most of them failed at the box office; young people sensed the attempt to exploit their ideological and artistic leanings and stayed away in droves. In the same year, Robert Altman's *M*A*S*H* was an immense success. Twentieth Century Fox was able to capitalize on that success by turning the film into a highly rated—and highly profitable—television series. The studios learned several lessons from the year's experience. First, aiming a movie at young people doesn't guarantee a profit. Second, youth movies are most likely to succeed when the power and money are handed over to a filmmaker (young or old) who understands and sympathizes with the young audience. And third, a movie that appeals to young people may appeal to older moviegoers and television viewers as well.

Thus Hollywood derived its formula for success in the seventies: Find a creative film-maker, give him or her a tight budget and a lot of artistic independence, and hope that the result will have box-office appeal to both young people and their elders.

As the 1970s progressed, the formula proved itself. In 1971, for example, Warner Brothers spent a mere $1.5 million on *Summer of '42,* and earned $20 million in return. Elliot Witt, treasurer of M.C.A. Inc. (the talent agency that owns Universal Pictures), ex-plained his company's 1973 strategy this way: "We hope we can average $2 million a film [in expenses] on our 15 to 17 pictures a year. This year we have *American Graffiti* at less than $1 million."[9] *American Graffiti*, of course, turned out to be a bonanza. Naturally, not every low-budget movie has a happy ending at the box office, but one *American Graffiti* can balance a half-dozen low-budget losers.

Notice that the very concept of a "youth movie" has taken on a new meaning in the Hollywood formula. In the late 1960s, it meant a movie whose revolutionary content or counter-cultural tone or artistic style appealed only to young people. But since 1971, it has meant a movie aimed simultaneously at young people and the middle-aged, with a youngish (under 50) filmmaker at the helm. The youth subculture and mainstream American culture moved closer together in the early 1970s, at least on the surface. Young people are still the principal audience for feature films. But with only occasional exceptions, the movies they choose are the same ones their parents pick—for a night on the town now or an evening's television several years later.

For most of the 1970s, Hollywood stuck to its formula, and was rewarded with solid profits. Although fewer American feature films were made in the 1970s than in earlier decades, the list included an unusually high number of blockbusters. By the end of 1979, eight of the top ten all-time money-makers (and 17 of the top 20) were films from the 1970s. Nearly all aimed simultaneously at young people and their parents, and most were produced on modest budgets, in the $5-million to $10-million range. But in the last years of the decade budgets rose steeply, and some observers saw signs of a repeat of the 1960s disasters.

The biggest hit of 1972, for example, was Francis Ford Coppola's *The Godfather,* an almost sympathetic portrait of the Mafia that appealed to a cross-section of Americans, including the all-important youth market. Produced for $6.2 million, *The Godfather*

INDEPENDENTS AND THE STUDIOS

The watchwords of the new filmmakers are independence and artistic control. To avoid interference, many become "hyphenates"—producer-writer-directors—and start their own companies. Typical is Robert Altman (*M*A*S*H, McCabe and Mrs. Miller, California Split, Nashville, Popeye*), who says he became a producer-writer-director to avoid the "group think and group opinion" that prevail at the studios. "Everything I decide to make originates in my own Westwood office," Altman maintains. He doesn't even use studio editing facilities. "When you're around a studio, you're easily persuaded into making a 'type' of picture that seems to be the current fad. I don't want those attitudes to rub off on me."[10]

This sort of distrust may offend the studios' pride, but not their pocketbooks. The big studios can afford to wait until an independent motion picture has been completed, then —if they like it—offer a deal for distribution rights. Columbia Pictures, for example, specializes in this sort of arrangement, spending an average of $2 million per film for prints, advertising, and distribution in return for up to half the profits.[11] This way the filmmaker absorbs most of the risk in return for his or her artistic independence. If the movie does badly, the studio's loss is limited to the distribution costs. And if no studio picks it up in the first place, the movie usually dies unscreened. It is just barely possible to distribute a film without studio help, peddling it theater-by-theater to exhibitors who are not bound to a national distributor. *Hots*, the sorority version of *Animal House*, earned $1.4 million the hard way in 1979, after the studios had all turned thumbs down.[12] But independent distribution is even riskier than independent production. Most filmmakers seek studio distribution, and develop new ulcers if they're turned down.

Nowadays about 65 percent of all films are independently produced, but not all of them are made completely without studio help. Several deals are possible.

Direct financing. The studio buys in early, lock, stock and barrel. Universal Pictures, for example, likes to take credit for *American Graffiti*, but the film was produced by Francis Ford Coppola and directed by George Lucas—neither of whom was an employee

grossed $82 million in its first nine months, and went on to become the biggest money-maker of all time. It held this title for about a year. It was replaced in 1974 by *The Exorcist*, which was replaced in 1975 by *Jaws*, which was replaced in 1977 by *Star Wars*. All three hits appealed simultaneously to young people and their parents. But budgets were starting to go up again.

In 1979 Coppola's *Apocalypse Now* made it to the screen. Years earlier—in saner days—United Artists had put up $7 million for the Vietnam film, and foreign distributors had chipped in another $7 million. When Coppola began going way over budget, UA wisely balked at investing any more, so Coppola put up everything he owned to guaran-

tee a $17.5-million bank loan and finish his $31.5-million epic. He eventually paid about $10 million in interest on the loan, making the picture's break-even point a frightening $95 million in box-office receipts. *Apocalypse Now* did well in the U.S.—but not that well. Coppola would need foreign sales and television just to break even.[15] Far more profitable in 1979 were youth-market movies made on rational budgets—films like *Rocky II, Alien, The Amityville Horror,* and *The Muppet Movie.*

In 1978 the typical American feature film was produced on a budget of $5.5 million. By 1980 the figure was up to $10 million, a greater increase than inflation can account for—with marketing and distribution costs

of Universal. Lucas commissioned the script, and Coppola sold the package (Lucas plus the script) to Universal. By the time the movie began shooting, it was Universal's money that Lucas and Coppola were spending.

Negative pickup deal. The studio agrees in advance to buy the film and distribute it, but no money changes hands until after the shooting is done and the negative is completed. Backed by the studio guarantee, the filmmaker raises production costs elsewhere. Robert Altman used a negative pickup deal for *California Split.* "Columbia read the script, approved the cast and approved me. Then we formed our own company, Won World Productions, and went to the bank ourselves."[13]

Co-financing. The studio covers part of the production costs itself, but asks the filmmaker to raise the rest of the budget somewhere else. Twentieth Century Fox co-financed *Star Wars* with producer George Lucas and several partners. The independents earned enough from their share of *Star Wars* to finance most of *The Empire Strikes Back* themselves, offering Fox a smaller percentage of the profits to print, advertise, and distribute the sequel for them.[14]

Financial arrangements with theater owners also vary, depending on the strength of the movie. Traditionally, distributors take half the gross box-office receipts. But a studio with a blockbuster hit can insist on a guarantee of 70 percent of the gross or 90 percent of the profits (after the theater's expenses are covered)—whichever is higher. An independent filmmaker with a speculative property, on the other hand, may have to resort to "four-walling"—renting the theater for a flat fee that guarantees its owner a profit, and keeping all the box-office receipts. Four-walling can be immensely profitable if the movie catches on, but it's by far the riskiest distribution system.

For the major studios, then, the big issue is how, when, and to what extent to support independent filmmakers. And for the independents, the big issue is how much studio support to accept, and how to function without the support they don't want or can't get. The way this studio-filmmaker relationship is resolved will have a lot to do with the future of the film industry.

---

up even more sharply than production. Thirty-million-dollar budgets were no longer unusual, and studios and investors were once again paying outrageous prices for big-name talent. Paramount President Michael Eisner called the competition "a shark-feeding frenzy."[16] It was the late 1960s all over again.

The big movie of the 1980 winter season was *Star Trek*, a $40-million space extravaganza. Hyped by $10 million in advertising, it sold well, but still needed foreign sales just to break even. George Lucas did far better in the summer season with *The Empire Strikes Back*, a *Star Wars* sequel that was the most profitable movie of 1980 despite its $24-million budget.

But 1980 saw far too many big-budget flops. The list was led by Steven Spielberg's *1941*, which cost $36 million for production plus millions more for advertising and distribution. Its failure even hurt theater owners, who had laid out $15 million in nonrefundable guarantees. John Belushi and Dan Aykroyd's *The Blues Brothers* did good business, but at a cost of more than $30 million it was fighting to break even. *Tom Horn* with Steve McQueen, *Bronco Billy* with Clint Eastwood, and *Rough Cut* with Burt Reynolds were all expensive flops.[17]

Although 1980 had its share of winners, it was the year the studios and investors finally had to pay the price for their "shark-feeding frenzy." Only time will tell whether they return to the formula of sensibly budgeted movies aimed at young people and their parents—movies like *Airplane!,* a 1980 money-maker that broke even in its first two weeks.

DEALING WITH TELEVISION

Feature filmmaking is a highly speculative business. An independent director or producer may manage a string of seven or eight hits, with only a couple of flops along the way, and wind up very far ahead of the game. But a major studio has to involve itself in at least twenty movies a year just to keep its employees and equipment busy. The result may be huge profits one year and huge losses the next. The modest but steady earnings that most investors seek come only over the long haul, if then. It's an ulcer-producing business.

To pay the rent year in and year out, the studios rely on television. They sell feature films to the networks and to pay TV, and they produce movies and other programs especially for television.

The TV sale of a feature film often brings millions, and almost every movie is sold within a few years of its theater run. Fierce competition among the networks has driven the price up. The $3 million ABC paid for *The Poseidon Adventure* in 1974 now seems like petty cash. Even the $7.5 million CBS paid in 1976 for three showings of *Rocky* looks reasonable compared to more recent prices. ABC paid $16.5 million for multiple showings of *The Sting,* $18.5 million for *Close Encounters of the Third Kind,* and $25 million for *Jaws* and *Jaws II.* NBC paid an incredible $19 million for five runs of *King Kong,* only to see it bumped off in the ratings by an ABC made-for-TV movie. And CBS laid out $35 million for the rights to *Gone With The Wind* over the next twenty years.[18]

Television is even more important for the average motion picture, where it often spells the difference between red ink and black. In 1978, for example, Twentieth Century Fox sold CBS the rights to twelve films, including *Silver Streak* and *Lucky Lady,* for a package price of $40 million, while NBC picked up eight Fox films, highlighted by *Julia* and *The Omen,* for $21.5 million. The networks are so hungry for movies that they sometimes buy them before they're made. CBS, for example, bought just such a package of nine forthcoming Universal films, including *The Wiz,* for $22 million in 1979.[19]

A comparatively new market for movies is pay TV, which offers the films to subscribers before they are shown by the networks. As more and more people subscribe to Home Box Office and similar pay-TV services, the potential profits could be enormous.

Besides selling old movies to television, the Hollywood studios also produce their own made-for-TV films. In 1973, for example, Universal Studios turned out more than eighty full-length motion pictures—but over two-thirds of them never saw the inside of an American movie theater. They were sold directly to television, which had commissioned them in the first place. These TV movies are often run interchangeably with old theatrical films.

The original made-for-TV movies of the late 1960s were grade-C films, budgeted at $400,000 apiece. By the mid-1970s, made-for-TV movies still cost less than $1 million, and accounted for only 15 percent of the films shown by CBS, and 28 percent of those on NBC. Even so, companies like Universal were doing fine in the made-for-TV business. Then ABC threw away the financial rulebook and coughed up millions for the multipart TV movie "Roots." The results of the phenomenal success of "Roots" were a spate of TV mini-series and a surge in made-for-TV films. By the end of the decade 37 percent of all CBS movies and 56 percent of all NBC movies were made for television. In 1979, CBS alone spent $70 million for 50 TV films.[20]

Finally, Hollywood is heavily involved in

the production of ordinary half-hour and one-hour television series. In 1974, Universal alone supplied the networks with thirteen hours of prime-time programming a week. Strangely enough, these network sales are not very profitable. The big money comes after the networks have finished running a successful series, when the studio can begin selling it overseas and syndicating it to non-network stations. Of course an unsuccessful series that is canceled after one season may never be syndicated or sold on the international market. The TV series business is thus almost as speculative as the feature film business.

Nonetheless, television production has proved to be Hollywood's bread and butter. Some companies have even made the "backwards" transition from TV shows to feature films. Lorimar Productions, for example, created 15 TV series in the 1970s, including "The Waltons," "Eight Is Enough," and "Dallas." By 1980 it had a feature film budget of $150 million.[21]

Because the movie business—even the television movie business—is so speculative, many of the companies that keep at it are in other, safer businesses as well. Walt Disney Productions, one of the more successful movie studios, nevertheless makes most of its money from Disneyland and Disneyworld. Universal is a part of M.C.A. Inc., which is deeply into real estate, retailing, a talent agency, recording companies, and a savings and loan association. Gulf & Western, an industrial conglomerate, owns Paramount. Nearly every major Hollywood studio today is the most speculative arm of an otherwise stable conglomerate.

STEREOTYPING:
BLACKS AND WOMEN

In Edwin S. Porter's 1903 film production of *Uncle Tom's Cabin,* a white actor in blackface played Uncle Tom. Eleven years later, Sam Lucas became the first black to perform a leading role in a major motion picture; he starred in William Robert Daly's *Uncle Tom's Cabin,* the fourth film version of that classic. With the coming of talking pictures, the number of parts for blacks greatly increased. *Hearts in Dixie* and *Hallelujah,* both released in 1929, were the first two in a long line of all-black spectacles, including such films as *Green Pastures* in 1936 and *Porgy and Bess* in 1959.

Although they employed black performers, these movies were produced and directed by whites for studios owned by whites, and the audience they tried to attract was predominantly white. Lincoln Motion Pictures was founded in 1916 to produce films that were by blacks and for blacks. Other black companies joined in the competition, and by the late 1920s the nation's 700 movie theaters in black neighborhoods were offering a steady diet of black-made films. The switch to talking pictures, the impact of the big Hollywood studios, and the hardships of the Depression forced most of these companies out of business. A few independent filmmakers continued making movies explicitly for a black audience—but nearly all the filmmakers themselves were white. By the end of World War II Hollywood was too strong for these independent competitors, and they too were forced to fold. Black moviegoers were left with no choice but to watch whatever the big studios produced.

The 1950s and 1960s were the era of Sidney Poitier, whose portrayals of integrationist heroes were acceptable to both blacks and whites. But as early as 1958, some segments of the black community had become disenchanted with the Poitier image. Black film historian Donald Bogle reports that ghetto theater audiences jeered when Poitier saved Tony Curtis in *The Defiant Ones.*[22]

While mainstream moviegoers watched Poitier triumph again and again, patrons of the "art" movie theaters were offered a less upbeat picture of the black experience. This white liberal audience applauded films such as John Cassavetes' *Shadows* (1961), Frederick Wiseman's *The Cool World* (1963), Sam Weston and Larry Peerce's *One Potato, Two Potato* (1964), and Michael Roemer's *Nothing But a Man* (1964). Though the work of whites, these movies at least tried to deal seriously with race relations and the real world of black Americans. They paved the way for watered-down Hollywood treatments of the same themes, such as *A Patch of Blue* in 1965 and *Guess Who's Coming to Dinner* (starring Sidney Poitier) in 1967.

Photographer and author Gordon Parks was the first black to direct a major movie for a Hollywood studio. *The Learning Tree,* based on Parks' autobiographical novel, was released in 1969. That year saw several other black films, including *Uptight, Slaves, The Lost Man,* and *Putney Swope.* These movies criticized the white establishment, often militantly. Perhaps more important, most of them featured black artists behind the scenes as well as before the cameras.

In the 1970s filmmakers rediscovered the black audience. While Ossie Davis' *Cotton Comes to Harlem* (1970) was designed to please both white and black moviegoers, Melvin Van Peeble's *Sweet Sweetback's Bad-asssss Song* (1971) was aimed explicitly at blacks. Twelve percent of the American movie audience is black, and *Sweetback* proved that an independent black filmmaker could gross more than $10 million by serving that audience. Gordon Parks' *Shaft* (1971), an MGM release, also scored at black theaters. Advertised as "Hotter than Bond, Cooler than Bullitt," *Shaft* grossed $13 million, and demonstrated that Hollywood could make money bankrolling movies by and for blacks.

The result was an avalanche of black films. Among those released in 1972 were *Super Fly, Sounder, Buck and the Preacher, Slaughter, The Legend of Nigger Charley, Lady Sings the Blues, Melinda, Trouble Man, Blacula,* and *Blackenstein.* Some of these movies appealed to both black and white audiences, but most were strictly black. *Super Fly,* directed by Gordon Parks, Jr., was independently financed by a group of black business executives; it told the story of a ghetto cocaine dealer who beat the system, with plenty of raw violence and sex along the way.

Many critics, both white and black, did not think very much of films like *Super Fly* that glorified black criminals. They even had a name for the trend—"blaxploitation." Junius Green, president of the Hollywood branch of the NAACP, complained that "these films are taking our money while feeding us a forced diet of violence, murder, drugs and rape." But Gordon Parks (who directed *Shaft* and whose son directed *Super Fly*) responded: "The most important thing to me is that young blacks can now, if they work hard enough, enter an industry that has been closed to them for so long."[23]

Blacks did enter the industry, but the early 1970s turned out to be the highpoint for black films. By the middle of the decade, only one black director, Sidney Poitier, was still working regularly on feature films. Poitier's *Uptown Saturday Night, Let's Do It Again,* and *A Piece of the Action* notwithstanding, only a handful of black feature films are made each year—and most of them, like *The Wiz,* are produced by whites. The 1,300 blacks in the Screen Actors Guild and the hundreds of black behind-the-scenes professionals do find the movie business more open to them in the 1980s than it was in the 1960s. But many claim that they are "struggling for crumbs," and the people doing the hiring are again almost exclusively white.[24]

Women in the movies face their own problems. Hollywood has always treated women from a male point of view. Three female stereotypes were prominent—sex object, earth mother, and amusing idiot. There were exceptions, of course, films that depicted women as real, complex people with goals and problems and abilities. For the most part, however, women in film were interesting not for what they did, but for what men did because of them.

At least there *were* women in film. Six of

GLORIFYING VIOLENCE

"The way to get a picture started at United Artists or MGM," commented an executive at another studio, "is to go and say you can make an 'action-adventurer' for $1,200,-000."[25] Violence has always been an accepted part of the movie business, but it has never been rawer—or more profitable—than in the past decade. Despite mounting evidence that media violence can be harmful (see pp. 306–309), many American filmmakers not only utilize violence; they celebrate it.

Under the old Motion Picture Code, films were forced to punish their criminals. But after the code collapsed in 1966, movie crooks were at last allowed to get away with the loot. Some filmmakers used their new freedom to explore the realities of a violent society, but many chose to glorify murder and mayhem instead. In the 1970s, Hollywood celebrated the skills and lifestyles of professional assassins (*The Mechanic*), overzealous cops (*Dirty Harry, The French Connection*), narcotics peddlers (*Super Fly*), and of course the Mafia (*The Godfather, Godfather II*).[26]

An especially popular—and dangerous—theme was the pleasure of violent revenge, which provided the motivation of *High Plains Drifter, The Cowboys,* and most notoriously *Death Wish,* a 1974 release. Many audiences roared with delight whenever Charles Bronson, as an architect-turned-vigilante, slaughtered a mugger. "If we had more people like Bronson, we would have less crime," one satisfied moviegoer told the *New York Times.* Another said, "I think what Bronson did is right—no one else is doing *anything.*" The critics jumped on *Death Wish* for glorifying crime and violence, but Bronson replied simply: "We don't make movies for critics, since they don't pay to see them anyhow."[27]

Not surprisingly, the revenge theme appealed as much to anti-establishment audiences as to establishment ones. *The Trial of Billy Jack* billed itself as a pacifist movie, but its youthful audience broke into applause whenever Billy Jack used his karate to destroy an authority figure.

As the decade progressed, the violence grew increasingly bizarre. The protagonist of *Taxi Driver* went on a bloody rampage; *Marathon Man* featured dental torture; *The Deerhunter* hinged on an explicit scene of Russian roulette. The sexual component of movie violence also became more overt. Erotic violence has been around at least since Hitchcock's *Psycho,* but by the time *Dressed to Kill* was released in 1980, every imaginable fantasy of sexual brutality had become fair game for the wide screen. Feminist activists joined more traditional opponents of movie sex and violence in protests against the trend, but their boycotts and demonstrations made little headway against the box-office appeal of sex-tinged blood.

the top ten box-office stars in 1934 were women—Janet Gaynor, Joan Crawford, Mae West, Marie Dressler, Norma Shearer, and Shirley Temple. In the mid-1970s, Barbra Streisand was the only woman in the top ten, and the ratio of men's roles to women's roles was an incredible twelve to one. Famous film couples have always been an integral part of the movie business—Spencer Tracy and Kath-erine Hepburn, Rock Hudson and Doris Day, etc. In the 1970s the most popular movie couple was Paul Newman and Robert Redford.

And the roles that were left for women were as stereotyped as ever—the sex object was "liberated," the earth mother became a "victim," and the amusing idiot was still going strong. "I'm sick and tired of seeing women being empty-headed," said Marsha Mason, who played the trampy mother in *Cinderella Liberty*. "In the scripts I get," noted actor Susan Anspach, "the woman is either a neurotic, a slut, a whore or somebody's daughter. Or else there are the feminist films about women who hate men. There's never just a real person with real drives—sexual drives and life drives."[28]

For a short period in the late 1970s, a new age of serious women's pictures appeared to be dawning. Films like *Julia, The Turning Point, An Unmarried Woman,* and *Norma Rae* not only offered challenging female roles but actually depicted women as complex, whole people. But most of the movies that proved successful in 1979 and 1980—*Superman, 10, The Empire Strikes Back, Airplane!*—treated women as foreground stereotypes or background props, leaving observers wondering whether the progress of the late 1970s was just a passing fad.

Still, the statistical change is hardly a passing fad. By 1980 there were 89 women in the Directors Guild—well under five percent of the Guild's membership, but nearly quadruple the 1974 figure. A quarter of Hollywood's associate directors, stage managers, and production assistants were women. Sherry Lansing had become president of Twentieth Century Fox, and a dozen other women were rising to top positions in studio managements.[29] Their influence will presumably be felt on the movies of the 1980s.

SEX AND SUCH

The film revolution of the late 1960s and early 1970s depended very heavily on the freedom of the movie business to say and show whatever it pleased. *Midnight Cowboy* featured a male prostitute, and the huge financial success of *I Am Curious (Yellow)* was directly attributable to its explicit sex scenes.

In 1952, the U.S. Supreme Court ruled that movies are protected by the First Amendment. Films could be censored and banned, but only under specific laws within constitutional limitations. Throughout the 1950s and 1960s these limitations expanded. By the end of the 1960s, just about anything could safely be displayed on the screen, as long as the film had some "redeeming social value." Some local governments continued to harass "dirty" movies, but they were seldom able to stop them.

Under pressure from citizen groups like the Legion of Decency, the Motion Picture Producers and Distributors of America had long ago passed the Motion Picture Code. This "voluntary code of self-regulation" prohibited sex, vulgarity, obscenity, and profanity, as well as certain controversial topics. It didn't begin to relax until the mid-1950s. *The Man with the Golden Arm* was refused an MPPDA seal because it depicted narcotics addiction. The film received such praise from the critics that in 1956 the code was amended to allow discussion of drugs. By 1961, the code also permitted "restrained, discreet treatment of sexual aberration in movies."[30]

Foreign filmmakers and American independents ignored even the liberalized code. And the filmgoing public (mostly young people) seemed unconcerned that their favorite movies sometimes lacked the MPPDA seal. The major studios, desperate for a piece of the action, were forced to adopt a new code. In 1968, the Production Code and Rating Administration was established by the Motion Picture Association of America. This board took on the job of assigning each movie one of four classifications. The 1970 revised ratings are:

G All ages admitted. General audiences.

PG All ages admitted. Parental guidance suggested.

R Restricted. Under 17 requires accompanying parent or adult guardian.

X No one under 17 admitted.

In effect, the rating system took the film industry off the self-censorship hook. Henceforth, the industry would simply announce which movies were "clean" and which were "dirty." The rest was up to the public.

But the rating system had some strange side effects. At the beginning, several studios actually tried for an X rating, as a come-on for fans of "adult" fare. Hard-core movies, meanwhile, came out in the open; encouraged by increasingly permissive Supreme Court decisions, they proudly rated themselves XXX. Then the reaction set in. Local governments and civic groups began putting pressure on theater owners to carry only G and PG movies. In 1970, 47 percent of the members of the National Association of Theater Owners had a standing policy of no X-rated films.[31]

While the porno factories continued to crank out ultra-frank sex films (like *Deep Throat* and *The Devil in Miss Jones*) for the growing number of theaters specializing in hard-core fare, mainstream film producers started censoring their own movies. Many struggled desperately for an R instead of an X, or a PG instead of an R, trying to insure that the films would be acceptable to most theater owners, and that the all-important teenage audience would be allowed in. To accommodate these needs, the code administration relaxed its standards. In 1969 *Midnight Cowboy* was rated X; in 1970 it was re-rated R.

By the end of the 1970s the entire rating system was breaking down. Theater owners were regularly filling their seats with unaccompanied teenagers for R-rated movies—and with a few cuts here and there (as suggested by the ratings board), almost anything could earn an R. *Cruising* won an R rating even though some theater chains refused to show it in 1980 because of its stress on homosexual sadomasochism. And *Dressed to Kill* received an R despite its theme of erotic violence. The typical teenage couple out on a date may take all this for granted, but they are seeing things on the screen never dreamed of by Walt Disney.[32]

The rating system, by the way, focuses almost exclusively on sex. In 1974 the code administration awarded its first X for extreme violence to *The Street Fighter,* a precedent it usually ignored in the years that followed. The big issue for the ratings is still which parts of the body appear on the screen. Nobody has yet explained exactly what this has to do with the impact or morality of a film—which may explain why theater owners and moviegoers tend to ignore the ratings and make their own moral judgments.

THE REST OF THE BUSINESS

To most people, "film" means entertainment, movies shown in movie theaters. Yet fewer than 200 feature films are produced in the United States each year. By contrast, more than 13,000 nonfictional and nontheatrical films are produced in the U.S. annually. This figure does not include TV programs or commercials. It does include documentaries, as well as educational and industrial movies.

Although *Woodstock* in 1970 demonstrated that a rock-music documentary could gross $14.5 million on the theater circuit, most documentarists today either settle for a small, select audience or work for television. Frederick Wiseman, probably the greatest living documentary filmmaker in the U.S., made the switch to TV in 1971. In the 1960s, Wiseman's films had sensitively explored the horrors of a prison for the criminally insane (*Titicut Follies*), the regimentation of the educational system (*High School*), the successes and failures of emergency medical treatment (*Hospital*), and other American institutions. His work won critical acclaim and many awards, but very few theater bookings. Wiseman's "Basic Training" made its debut in 1971 on more than 200 public television stations, linked by the Public Broadcasting Service. "The reason for doing all these films," he explained, "is to share what you learn with other people."[33] Through television, Wiseman and other documentarists share their learning with millions.

The largest category of nonfiction films is

the educational and industrial movie. Producers of such nontheatrical motion pictures include government agencies, schools and colleges, religious groups, and corporations—over a thousand nontheatrical film companies, including independents and those housed within other organizations. The films are collected and distributed by some 2,600 American film libraries. Their total budget is more than a billion dollars a year.

Today, an institutional movie about dairy farms in Wisconsin or careers in banking, the promise of nuclear power or the joys of motor-boating, stands a good chance of reaching an audience of millions. Depending on its topic, such a film may be accepted by movie theaters as a short, run by TV stations as a documentary, borrowed by clubs as an entertainment, used by schools as an educational aid—or even all four of these. Of course there are many strictly educational films that don't try to grind any particular ax; these are usually sold or rented to their users. But the biggest-budget institutional films are often the ones that are distributed free. Their goal is to create a favorable image of the organization or issue discussed—in other words to indoctrinate the viewer. Film has proved itself an ideal medium for this purpose.

The mainstays of the motion picture industry today are educational and industrial films, movies made expressly for television, and old movies sold to TV after they have finished their theater run. Theatrical feature films are the most glamorous and most speculative part of the business, but they are not what keeps it alive.

Once upon a time, records were America's number one leisure time activity. That was in 1921, before the heyday of radio, before the invention of television. Today, the recording industry is the second largest entertainment business in America. Like the movie industry, it relies mainly on young people—under 35, anyway—to buy its product, predominantly rock music. And just as

Hollywood is closely intertwined with television, the record business could not exist in the form we know it without radio.

THE RECORD AUDIENCE

Sixty years ago records were a vital source of entertainment for nearly every American. Old as well as young hovered over their Gramophones and Victrolas the way they were soon to group themselves around the radio set, the way they now stare at the TV. But the recent history of the recording industry is the history of its response to young people. The odds are good that many of the readers of this book are listening to a record or tape as they read. Nearly all of them have larger music collections than their parents.

The second boom in records began in the 1950s thanks to two innovations: the high-fidelity long-playing record, and rock-'n'-roll. LPs had been invented in 1948 by Dr. Peter Goldmark of CBS. Rock music also dated back to the 1940s, when it was recorded on 78s by black rhythm and blues artists. In the early 1950s, white singers began recording the black music, and by 1956 when Elvis Presley's "Heartbreak Hotel" hit number one, it was clear that rock-'n'-roll was here to stay. Overall, record sales more than tripled in the fifties, from $189 million in 1950 to about $600 million in 1960—thanks to LPs and rock.[34]

Sales tripled again in the sixties, up to about $2 billion in records and tapes by the early 1970s—more than the box-office receipts of the movie industry. Stereo helped; it completed the transition from the 45-rpm single to the LP stereo album. The post-war baby boom helped even more. In 1964, 17-year-olds were the biggest single age group in the country. The songs they listened to (in stereo) were dominated by the Beatles, whose worldwide sales totaled more than $150 million between 1963 and 1968. By the early 1970s, 80 percent of all record sales were for rock music.[35]

The boom continued through the seventies, pushing the recording industry up to $4 billion in sales by the end of the decade. If the 1950s were the decade of the "gold" single, selling more than a million copies, and the 1960s were the decade of the "platinum" album, breaking the one-million mark at a much higher price, the 1970s were the decade of the "gorilla"—the album with domestic sales of six million or more. The movie soundtracks of "Saturday Night Fever" and "Grease" topped the list of gorilla hits, a list that also included albums by Carole King, Stevie Wonder, Peter Frampton, The Eagles, and Fleetwood Mac. "Saturday Night Fever" eventually posted worldwide sales of almost 30 million copies, earning much more as a recording than as a motion picture.[36]

Popular music diversified in the 1970s—disco, country, hard rock, punk rock, etc. But the dominant variety is probably the mellow

ROCK, RACE, AND VIOLENCE

Rock was originally black music—urbanized rhythm and blues—but whites called it "race music" and wouldn't buy it. They were uncomfortable not only with its blackness, but also with its sexual and aggressive energy, its undercurrent of rebellion. When white teenagers responded ecstatically to Elvis in the mid-1950s, their parents thus had more than one reason to feel outraged. Frank Sinatra's appeal in the 1940s had been sexual too (and parents had objected even then), but Sinatra and his music were clearly non-aggressive, middle-class, and white. Elvis was white, but . . . different.

The segregation of rock seemed to end in the 1960s, when whites as well as blacks bought the Motown sound and turned The Supremes into a number one group. And the tranquility of the Woodstock open-air concert, attended by 400,000 young people, made the age of Aquarius seem loving and nonviolent. But the horror of the Rolling Stones concert at Altamont, where Hell's Angels hired as guards lashed out at the front ranks of the crowd and a black man was killed, again made rock appear the music of violence. Altamont was a reminder that the rock revolution had an unpleasant cutting edge.

The 1970s saw a return to segregation. As the decade progressed, concerts featuring black artists increasingly were attended by predominantly black audiences. Whites still bought black music, but complaints of black-white violence in and around concert halls kept audiences segregated. And then whites stopped buying black music. In 1975, 42 percent of the top-forty singles featured black artists. The figure was 20 percent in 1976, down to 12.5 percent in 1977.[37] The rise of disco put some black artists back on top of the charts, but it also set rock fans against disco fans in confrontations with racial implications.

The issue of rock and violence was much discussed after the 1979 Who concert in Cincinnati. When the doors opened, the crowd rushed in to get the best seats. Eleven young people were smothered or crushed to death by the surging mob. The tragedy forced the popular music world to begin taking crowd control seriously. And it forced some of that world's more thoughtful members, like New York Times critic John Rockwell, to raise a fundamental question: Is rock the music of violence? Rockwell's answer is unlikely to satisfy rock's detractors, much less the parents of eleven dead Cincinnati teenagers. "Yes, there is something inherently violent about rock music. Moreover, there are groups that pander to such violence. But the best groups, while seeming to plunge more deeply into the heart of violence, seek to transform it into an artistic or even a religious experience."[38]

sound of "soft rock." This is due in part to the musical tastes of young teenagers and the preteen set. Though they don't buy as many records as young people in their twenties, their tastes are more consistent. In the 1950s they listened to Fabian, Bobby Rydell, and Frankie Avalon; in the 1960s and early 1970s it was products of television, like The Monkees, David Cassidy, and The Archies; later in the 1970s it was Shaun Cassidy, Debby Boone, and Andy Gibb. Names for this sort of music come and go—"bubblegum rock," "pubescent rock"—but the attraction remains constant: a soft sexuality in sharp contrast with the rebelliousness of hard rock.[39]

What about classical music? Today it accounts for only five percent of total sales, compared to 25 percent in the pre-rock era. But five percent of $4 billion compares quite favorably to 25 percent of $200 million, even considering three decades of inflation. Ever since rock took over the recording business, articles have been written on the "crisis" in classical records. But the nation's major record stores still carry a wide variety of classical recordings.[40] The same can be said for jazz, religious music, and other pre-rock genres. At least as far as recordings are concerned, rock music has not supplanted its predecessors. It has simply grown huge around them, catering to a young audience that knows precisely what it wants.

THE RECORD BUSINESS

A half-dozen giant entertainment conglomerates produce 85 percent of the recordings sold in the United States. The executives of CBS, Warner Communications, Polygram, RCA, MCA, and Capitol-EMI control dozens of labels featuring all kinds of music. Independent recording companies are a creative force, and some, like Motown Records, have become large, multi-faceted corporations themselves. But most of the business is in the hands of the giants.[41]

In 1979, the typical album listed for $8.98.

It cost $2.63 to produce, and was wholesaled to stores for about $4.00—leaving the record company with a healthy $1.37 profit and the store with a whopping $4.98. But it's not that simple. As you know if you buy records, an album that lists for $8.98 seldom sells for $8.98. The discount price usually runs from $5.98 to $6.98, or even less after a year. Discount pricing and stiff competition keep store profits down.

As for record company profits, that $1.37 figure assumes a successful record. If the stores turn an album down, or later return it unsold, the company can be left with a hundred thousand individually wrapped pieces of used vinyl, at a loss of $2.63 apiece.[42]

And that $2.63 in production costs is hardly a firm figure. The biggest item is the performer's royalty. For the typical successful recording artist, the royalty averages $1.45 per album, out of which the artist pays 12¢ or so in studio costs. But some top groups insist on guarantees of as much as $1.50 per album, and make the company cover the studio costs—which can be massive.

To these production costs tack on promotion and advertising, amounting to nearly ten percent of the industry's expenses. Concert tours are underwritten to promote new albums, and a $400,000 advertising budget is not unusual for a potential hit. And don't forget the under-the-table promotion costs. One rock critic in the late 1970s noted—anonymously—that he spent every Christmas turning down gifts of luggage, stereo systems, and the like. He had open offers to travel free with any rock group in concert anywhere in the country, and he was invited to dozens of record company parties. He received every album free along with countless promotional tee shirts and other gimmicks. And, of course, he and a guest had free tickets to every concert and club date. Sitting next to him at the concerts, clubs, and parties were the radio disc jockeys. He often wondered how many of them refused the Christmas gifts.

Now figure in the other expenses—the

"artists and repertoire" people who specialize in finding, signing, and placating the talent and matching them up with the right material; the people who design the cover art, an increasingly significant factor in record sales; and of course the costs of manufacturing, sales, and distribution.

Finally, allow for substantial losses because of the pirates. It doesn't take high technology to produce a counterfeit record, and tapes are even easier. Roughly one out of every ten records and one out of every five tapes in the marketplace today is a pirate production, stealing sales from the recording company and royalties from the artist. Even some of the largest record stores have been caught buying pirated recordings at bargain prices. Unauthorized duplication costs the industry an estimated $400 million a year.[43]

Despite these expenses and problems, the recording industry remains profitable—more profitable than movies on about the same gross income. But the high living and rapid expansion of the past three decades seem likely to falter in the 1980s.[44] "I can remember when I was a kid, a 10-inch LP cost $4.98," not much less than the selling price today, says Columbia Records President Bruce G. Lundvall. "The record business has been the last to raise its prices." Despite rising costs, the record companies have been afraid that price hikes might encourage still more piracy and home duplication (people making their own tapes off the radio or from a friend's collection). Now they have no choice. As prices rise and pirates flourish, sales will probably level off—and so may profits, for the first time in decades.[45]

ROCK AND RADIO

There are about 450 million radio sets in the United States today—at least one radio in 99 percent of American homes and 95 percent of American cars. And the vast majority of the 8,800 or so radio stations in the country program music, music, and more music. Nearly all of it, of course, is recorded.

The most fundamental axiom in the recording industry is that people buy the music they hear on radio. Although exceptions can be found to even this most basic rule, record promoters have been known to do almost anything to get their music on the air. Aside from minor ethical problems like free tickets and Christmas gifts, a 1960 Congressional investigation found evidence of direct cash payments to disc jockeys and other radio personnel ("payola"), chart-rigging by means of purchased radio plays, and kickbacks at all levels of the record business. The investigation led to major shakeups in the radio and recording industries, but it did not completely clean up the business. Payola and kickback scandals continue to surface from time to time.[46]

Ever since the birth of rock in the 1950s, record promoters have pinned their hopes to the "top 40" AM radio stations. The most important stations are the 200 or so with successful top-40 formats in the industry's "primary" and "secondary" record sales markets. The 51 "primary" stations, for example, can be found in 24 cities, which together account for more than half of all record and tape sales. In the bad old days, these stations were what payola was all about—a disc jockey would add a record to the playlist if the price was right. Today top-40 stations actually play as few as fifteen singles over and over again. And the playlists are generally a matter of station policy. Program directors usually rely on the charts, such as the *Billboard* "Hot 100 Singles," and on tipsheets like Kal Rudman's "Friday Morning Quarterback." Some top-40 stations now buy syndicated programs, replacing local disc jockeys with automated tape formats. The most popular syndicated top-40 shows are carried by as many as 400 stations each week.[47]

In the 1970s, FM airplay became increasingly important to the record companies. The number of FM receivers doubled in the late 1970s to more than 200 million sets, 95 percent of all American homes. And FM offered listeners stereo sound and fewer commercial interruptions. By the end of the decade, more people were listening to music on FM than on AM, though AM was still on top in advertising revenue and in the vital car listenership.

FM made its mark through counter-programming, playing albums instead of singles and hard rock instead of the bubblegum type. This format made it an ideal vehicle for promoting album sales. But handy cassette recorders also came into common use in the 1970s, and the FM format made it easy to tape whole albums off the air instead of buying them. By the end of the decade, record companies were urging FM stations to adjust their formats to make home taping more difficult, and the stations in the RKO-General chain had stopped playing albums uninterrupted.[48]

Radio and the recording industry are locked in a symbiotic relationship. The record companies supply the music, and the radio stations attract the audience that goes out and buys the records and tapes. Since the coming of rock in the 1950s, both industries have thrived. And both are betting on the future of rock, whatever its offspring from punk to disco. Ahmet Ertegun, chairman of Atlantic Records, explains that "the people buying records now are not like the ones who bought Benny Goodman records during the Swing craze or the ones who bought Perry Como records eight years later. Rock-'n'-roll is the sensibility of an American generation. It's at once their poetry, their entertainment and their means of expression. These people don't stop buying records just because they've turned 30." Walter Yetnikoff, president of the CBS Records Group, agrees. "Records are no longer a luxury. What's happened is that music—pop music—has become an integral part of people's lives."[49]

Notes

1 "The Old Hollywood: They Lost It at the Movies," *Newsweek*, February 2, 1970, p. 66.

2 Theodore Peterson, Jay W. Jensen, and William L. Rivers, *The Mass Media and Modern Society* (New York: Holt, Rinehart and Winston, 1965), p. 128. Richard F. Shepard, "Effect of TV on Movie-going Is Examined," *New York Times*, November 24, 1971, p. 20. Tom Buckley, "At the Movies," *New York Times*, Nov. 23, 1979, p. C12.

3 Pamela G. Hollie, "Arkoff, Noted Producer, Quits Post at Filmways," *New York Times*, December 6, 1979, pp. D1, D11.

4 Aljean Harmetz, "Museum Celebrates 'Drive-In' Movies," *New York Times*, July 27, 1979, pp. C1, C5.

5 Aljean Harmetz, "The Dime-Store Way to Make Movies—and Money," *New York Times Magazine*, August 4, 1974, pp. 32-33.

6 Stanley Kauffmann, "The Film Generation: Celebration and Concern," in William M. Hammel, ed., *The Popular Arts in America* (New York: Harcourt Brace Jovanovich, 1972), pp. 45-46.

7 *Ibid.*, pp. 46-49.

8 Richard Houdek, "The New Hollywood," *Performing Arts*, January, 1970, p. 6.

9 Robert A. Wright, "Hollywood's Happy Ending: A Profitable Twist," *New York Times*, November 4, 1973, p. F3.

10 Paul Gardner, "Hyphenates Seek Unified Film Approach," *New York Times*, February 25, 1974, p. 19.

11 Aljean Harmetz, "Studios Pick Up More Outside Films," *New York Times*, June 26, 1978, p. C18.

12 Karen Stabiner, "A Look at Filmmaking on the Cheap," *New York Times*, February 11, 1979, p. D15.

13 Stephen Farber, "So You Make a Movie—Will the Public Ever See It?" *New York Times*, February 24, 1974, p. D14.

14 David Lewin, "Can the Makers of 'Star Wars' Do It Again?" *New York Times*, December 2, 1979, p. D17.

15 Aljean Harmetz, "Coppola: Will He Break Even?" *New York Times*, March 18, 1980.

16 Jack Egan, "Wall Street Turns Sour on Hollywood," *New York*, July 21, 1980, pp. 12-13.

17 Aljean Harmetz, "After 2 Good Summers, Film Business Lags," *New York Times*, June 26, 1980, p. C14.

18 D. C. Pringle, "Stalking the Big Movies—with Cash and Cunning," *TV Guide*, March 31, 1979, pp. 49-52.

19 *Ibid.*, p. 52.

20 Kirk Honeycott, "Made-for-TV Films—Hollywood's Stepchild Comes of Age," *New York Times*, August 19, 1979, sec. 2, pp. 1, 27. "TV Update: More TV-Movies on the Way; They Cost Less, Draw More," *TV Guide*, March 31, 1979, p. A-1.

21 Pamela G. Hollie, "Lorimar—A Hollywood Hit," *New York Times,* March 8, 1980, pp. L1, L30.

22 Donald Bogle, *Toms, Coons, Mullatoes, Mammies, and Bucks* (New York: Viking Press, 1973), p. 182.

23 "Black Movie Boom—Good or Bad?" *New York Times,* December 17, 1972, p. D3.

24 Aljean Harmetz, "Black Actors: 'Struggling for Crumbs'?" *New York Times,* April 10, 1980.

25 Aljean Harmetz, "How Do You Pick a Winner in Hollywood? You Don't," *New York Times,* April 29, 1973, p. D11.

26 Stephen Farber, "Isn't It Enough to Show Murder —Must We Celebrate It?" *New York Times,* October 21, 1973, p. D13.

27 Judy Klemesrud, "What Do They See in 'Death Wish'?" *New York Times,* September 1, 1974, pp. D1, D9.

28 Maureen Orth, "How to Succeed: Fail, Lose, Die," *Newsweek,* March 4, 1974, pp. 50-51.

29 Jane Wilson, "Hollywood Flirts with the New Woman," *New York Times,* May 29, 1977, sec. 2, pp. 1, 11. Aljean Harmetz, "Report Shows a Bleak Outlook for Female Directors," *New York Times,* June 20, 1980, p. C31. Aljean Harmetz, "Women in Film Industry: Room at the Top," *New York Times,* January 28, 1980, p. D10.

30 Harold L. Nelson and Dwight L. Teeter, *Law of Mass Communications,* 2nd ed. (Mineola, N.Y.: Foundation Press, 1973), pp. 444-45.

31 Vincent Canby, "Will a Censor Get the Teenybopper?" *San Francisco Sunday Examiner and Chronicle, Datebook,* March 29, 1970, p. 30.

32 Peter Wood, " 'Dressed to Kill'—How a Film Changes from 'X' to 'R'," *New York Times,* July 20, 1980, pp. D13, D19. Aljean Harmetz, "Cheap and Profitable Horror Films Are Multiplying," *New York Times,* October 24, 1979, p. C21.

33 "Public Documents," *Newsweek,* October 4, 1971, p. 99.

34 Steve Chapple and Reebee Garofalo, *Rock'n'Roll Is Here To Pay* (Chicago: Nelson-Hall, 1977), pp. 1, 13-14, 20, 42-43.

35 *Ibid.,* pp. 70-71.

36 "Records: The Gorillas Are Coming," *Forbes,* July 10, 1978. Jack Egan, "Breaking Records in the Record Business," *New York,* March 26, 1979, p. 41.

37 John Rockwell, "Is Segregation Coming to the Rock World?" *New York Times,* January 13, 1978, p. C14.

38 John Rockwell, "Is Rock the Music of Violence?" *New York Times,* December 16, 1979, pp. D1, D26.

39 Rick Cohen, "Pube Rock: Kiddie Music Is Big Business," *New York,* November 20, 1978, pp. 67-77.

40 "Records: The Gorillas Are Coming." Peter G. Davis, "Classical Records: The Sounds of Crisis," *New York Times,* January 13, 1980, pp. D1, D22.

41 Egan, "Breaking Records in the Record Business," p. 41.

42 *Ibid.,* p. 41.

43 Pamela G. Hollie, "Piracy Costly Plague in Record Industry," *New York Times,* March 10, 1980, pp. D1, D5.

44 Egan, "Breaking Records in the Record Business," p. 41. Jack Egan, "The Record Industry: Meltdown in the Wax Factories," *New York,* August 13-20, 1979, p. 10. Steve Ditlea, "Why Record Prices Are Climbing," *New York Times,* February 18, 1979.

45 John Rockwell, "Record Industry's Sales Slowing After 25 Years of Steady Growth," *New York Times,* August 8, 1979, pp. 1, C23. "Music to Beat Inflation By," *New York Times,* July 27, 1980.

46 Chapple and Garofalo, *Rock'n'Roll Is Here To Pay,* pp. 61-63, 226-27.

47 *Ibid.,* pp. 101-102.

48 "Grim Outlook As Disk Boom Slows," *Variety,* January 9, 1980, p. 64.

49 Steve Ditlea, "The Bullish Boom in the Record World," *New York Times,* June 5, 1977, p. D22.

Suggested Readings

BARSAM, RICHARD MERAN, *Nonfiction Film.* New York: E. P. Dutton, 1973.

BOGLE, DONALD, *Toms, Coons, Mullatoes, Mammies, and Bucks.* New York: Viking Press, 1973.

BREITROSE, HENRY S., "Film as Communication," in Ithiel de Sola Pool, Wilbur Schramm, Frederick W. Frey, Nathan Maccoby, and Edwin B. Parker, eds., *Handbook of Communication.* Chicago: Rand McNally, 1973.

CHAPPLE, STEVE, and REEBEE GAROFALO, *Rock'n' Roll Is Here To Pay.* Chicago: Nelson-Hall, 1977.

COHEN, RICK, "Pube Rock: Kiddie Music Is Big Business," *New York,* November 20, 1978.

COPPOLA, ELEANOR, "Diary of a Director's Wife," *New York Times Magazine,* August 5, 1979.

DENBY, DAVID, *Awake In The Dark.* New York: Vintage Books, 1977.

EGAN, JACK, "Breaking Records in the Record Business," *New York,* March 26, 1979.

———, "The Record Industry: Meltdown in the Wax Factories," *New York,* August 13-20, 1979.

KAEL, PAULINE, "Why Are Movies So Bad? or, The Numbers," *The New Yorker,* June 23, 1980.

KAUFFMANN, STANLEY, "The Film Generation: Celebration and Concern," in William M. Hammel, ed., *The Popular Arts in America.* New York: Harcourt Brace Jovanovich, 1972.

KNIGHT, ARTHUR, *The Liveliest Art,* 2nd ed. New York: Macmillan, 1978.

LINDSEY, ROBERT, "The New Wave of Film Makers," *New York Times Magazine,* May 28, 1978.

SCHULBERG, BUDD, "What Makes Hollywood Run Now," *New York Times Magazine,* April 27, 1980.

SKLAR, ROBERT, *Movie-Made America.* New York: Vintage Books, 1975.

TUNSTALL, JEREMY, *The Media Are American.* New York: Columbia University Press, 1977.

UNESCO, "Film as a Universal Mass Medium," in Heinz-Dietrich Fischer and John C. Merrill, eds., *International and Intercultural Communication,* 2nd ed. New York: Hastings House, 1976.

Chapter 14
Advertising and Public Relations

Advertising is the all-important connection between the mass media and the world of commerce. Without advertising, neither the media nor the commercial establishment could survive in the form we know them today. By molding the behavior and attitudes of individuals, advertising also helps shape the character of American society itself. This enormous power is firmly in the hands of advertising's practitioners, working within government regulations and ethical standards that forbid outright fraud but not more subtle manipulation of the American psyche.

In 1954 the net profits of Revlon, Inc., a cosmetics company, stood at $1,297,826. In 1955 CBS introduced a new TV quiz program, "The $64,000 Question." Revlon sponsored the show, as well as its twin, "The $64,000 Challenge." Both programs were on the air until 1958, when evidence began emerging that the programs were rigged (see p. 146). During those four years, Revlon's net profits rose to $3,655,950 in 1955, $8,375,502 in 1956, and $9,688,307 in 1958. When a Senate committee asked Martin Revson, owner of Revlon, whether his phenomenal success was due to sponsoring the two

shows, he answered musingly: "It helped. It helped."[1]

In 1963 the Clark Oil and Refining Company spent its entire $1.6-million advertising budget on television. Until then, Clark had limped along with annual earnings of $1.5 million or so. The first year following the TV campaign, the company earned $2.1 million. It committed itself permanently to television—and in 1969 Clark Oil earned $13.0 million. Said one Clark executive: "That's really advertising power."[2]

ADVERTISING AND BUSINESS

American institutions—mostly profit-making institutions—spend more than $50 billion a year on advertising, about two-thirds of it in the mass media. This figure represents the raw cost of buying time or space in the media, plus the cost of comparable campaigns through billboards, direct mailings, etc. It does not include the salaries of many of the 400,000 Americans now employed in advertising, and it leaves out a lot of "incidental" expenses such as market research, commercial production, and the like. With these items included, the actual cost of advertising is closer to $70 billion a year—more than $300 for every man, woman, and child in the country.

What does the advertiser get in return? Increased sales, of course. The "success stories" of Revlon and Clark are two of thousands that could be told. Frederick R. Gamble, former president of the American Association of Advertising Agencies, put it this way:

> Advertising is the counterpart in distribution of the machine in production. By the use of machines, our production of goods and services has been multiplied. By the use of the mass media, advertising multiplies the selling effort. . . . Reaching many people rapidly at low cost, advertising speeds up sales, turns prospects into customers in large numbers and at high speed. Hence, in a mass-production and high-consumption economy, advertising has the greatest opportunity and the greatest responsibility for finding customers.[3]

The purpose of most advertising, then, is to induce the buyer to purchase something that the seller has to sell—a product, a service, a political candidate, or whatever. A successful ad is an ad that sells.

Advertising can boost sales in two ways: by winning a bigger share of the market, or by increasing the size of the market itself (perhaps creating the market to start with). The first technique may be called competitive advertising; it says "Buy our brand of aspirin instead of the brand you're using now." The second is noncompetitive advertising; it says simply "Buy more aspirin." Most ads are a combination. They urge the consumer to switch brands and to buy more.

Business competition is not limited to advertising, of course. A manufacturer or a store may compete by cutting its prices, improving its products, or offering superior service. It is not hard to find examples of ads that are essentially "informational"—telling the public about a genuine competitive edge.

But these tactics have limited value. Aspirin is aspirin. It is nearly impossible to make a better aspirin. And price-cutting may lose more in profits than it gains in sales; how many people would switch brands to save a nickel? Competitive ads for aspirin—and many other products—have no real differences to talk about. The competition is not in the products, but in the ads themselves. Meyer Weinberg describes the big-money television advertisers this way:

> Having eschewed competition by cutting prices, the Top Fifty instead go all out to attract the consumer's attention by amusement or entertainment. There is no other way of driving consumers to prefer one substantially identical item over another. Thus advertising agencies specialize in the manufacture of spurious individuality. . . .[4]

In the language of advertising, this is called "positioning." Each manufacturer picks which segment of the market it wants to aim at, then designs its ads to capture that segment, forfeiting the rest of the market to other manufacturers with nearly identical products but quite different advertising. One perfume thus becomes the choice of independent women who think they're "worth it"; another appeals to would-be vamps looking for more "allure"; a third is marketed with the happily married in mind. One beer aims at serious drinkers who are having more than one; another at busy working people when they've got the time; a third at hosts hoping to add a little class to their entertaining. Once a market position is established, changing it is difficult and expensive—but possible. The "Marlboro Man" was created in the 1960s because mostly women were smoking Marlboros.

So much for competitive advertising. If the only way an advertiser could earn a dollar was by wooing it from the competition, America's gross national product would be at a permanent standstill and advertising would be less important than it is. In addition to slicing up the existing market, advertisers work hard to expand it. An ad for Ford may help you decide to switch from General Motors, but it may also help you decide you need a new car after all. An ad for Pepsi may seduce you away from Coke, but it may also remind you that you're almost out of soft drinks. An ad for McDonald's may get you to go there instead of to Burger King, but it may also get you to go there instead of staying home. You deserve a break today.

One way to expand the market is to create new uses for old products. In thirty years of phenomenal market expansion, jeans have evolved from the work clothes of the lower classes (at $3 a pair) to the play clothes of the young (at $10 a pair) to the party clothes of the stylishly informal (at $30 a pair). As we shall see in a few pages, even a seemingly eternal product like the household detergent can find new uses—and the presoak is born.

Another way to expand the market is to create a new consumer need, and a product to satisfy it. Cigarettes, spray deodorants, power lawnmowers, and aluminum cans are all products we didn't know we wanted until advertisers told us we did. Whether such products genuinely improve the quality of our lives is an unanswerable question. Either way, advertising built a market for them, and thus earned a profit for their manufacturers.

The overarching goal of all advertising is to get the consumer to consume. In the words of economist John Kenneth Galbraith, "the individual serves the industrial system by consuming its products. On no other matter, religious, political, or moral, is he so elaborately and expensively instructed."[5] Communications researcher Dallas Smythe recalls an ad in the *New York Times* that filled an entire page with the message: "Buy Something." Smythe comments: "The popular culture's imperative—'Buy Something'—is the most important educational influence in North America today."[6] Erich Fromm sums it all up in a phrase. The typical American, he says, is no longer *Homo sapiens,* but *Homo consumens*—Man the consumer.[7]

The United States is the wealthiest nation in the world. It is also the most wealth-

BIG-MONEY ADVERTISERS

Listed below are the top ten advertisers in the U.S. as of 1979, together with the percentage of total sales each spent on advertising.[8] What do most of these companies have in common? They compete on the basis of advertising rather than genuine product differences, and they grow by creating consumer needs for the products they manufacture.

Company	Ad costs	% of sales
Procter & Gamble	$614,900,000	5.7
General Foods	393,000,000	6.5
Sears, Roebuck	379,313,000	2.1
General Motors	323,395,000	0.5
Philip Morris	291,201,000	3.5
Kmart	287,095,000	2.3
R. J. Reynolds	258,115,000	2.9
Warner-Lambert	220,242,000	6.8
AT&T	219,756,000	0.4
Ford	215,000,000	0.5

conscious, the most materialistic. Advertising deserves much of the credit and much of the blame.

ADVERTISING AND THE MEDIA

If big business as we know it couldn't exist without advertising, neither could the mass media. Newspapers, magazines, television, and radio compete for every advertising dollar. As of 1979, newspapers had 29 percent of the total. Television had 20 percent; magazines (and specialized business and farm papers) had 9 percent; and radio had 7 percent. The other 35 percent went to direct mail, billboards, and the like. This division of the spoils is not a constant. The development of radio ate significantly into the percentage shared by newspapers and magazines. The development of television did a lot of damage to radio and magazines.

But as long as advertising continues to grow, there is plenty of money to go around. In 1941, the total cost of all advertising was less than $2 billion. Today, that figure is over $50 billion. A minute of time on network radio may now cost up to $8,000. A full-page ad in a major newspaper may run as high as $10,000. A full page in a national magazine may sell for more than $70,000. And thirty seconds on network television may go for a phenomenal $140,000 or more. Advertisers willingly pay the going rates, and all four media are earning good money.

The influence of advertising over media content has already been discussed in considerable detail (see Chapter 5). Direct threats and outright bribes are not unknown, but they are far less common than tacit "mutual understandings." The mass media, after all, depend on advertisers for their profits. They don't have to be threatened or bribed to keep the advertisers happy. It comes naturally.

None of this is inevitable. Take British television, for example. There are two networks, one commercial and the other government-sponsored. On the noncommercial network, no ads are permitted. On the commercial network, advertisers have only one choice—which station to give the ad to. Station managers schedule the ads as they please, and no commercials are permitted in the middle of a program. Unable to choose their show (much less to produce it), British advertisers have next to no influence on British programming.

GERMANY'S SNEAK ADVERTISERS

Most European countries strictly regulate television advertising. West Germany, for example, has three TV stations, all operated by public broadcasting corporations. One permits no advertising at all, while the other two allow commercials only under rigid restrictions. On ZDF, for instance, ads are run together in blocks, totaling no more than 20 minutes a day; all commercials must appear before 8 P.M. on weekdays, and never on Sundays.

To beat these restrictions, advertisers try to sneak their messages onto the air. In a 1974 soccer game between Hamburg and Frankfurt, the players wore ads for Remington shavers and Campari aperitifs on their uniforms. The station outwitted the sneak advertisers by carefully avoiding close-up shots. But when companies started putting their ads on movable billboards in the soccer stadiums, towing them in mid-game to wherever the action was, German television was stymied. It had no choice but to cancel the broadcasts of a few weekend soccer games. "We are not trying to be purists about this," explained a TV official, "but we felt we had to put a stop to the excesses at least."[9]

The American mass media do not just adjust their content to meet the needs of individual advertisers. They also adjust their attitudes to promote the interests of the business community as a whole. In an essay entitled "Mass Communication, Popular Taste and Organized Social Action," sociologists Paul Lazarsfeld and Robert Merton put the case this way:

> Since the mass media are supported by great business concerns geared into the current social and economic system, the media contribute to the maintenance of that system. This contribution is not found merely in the effective advertisement of the sponsor's product. It arises, rather, from the typical presence in magazine stories, radio programs and newspaper columns of some element of confirmation, some element of approval of the present structure of society. . . .
>
> Since our commercially sponsored mass media promote a largely unthinking allegiance to our social structure, they cannot be relied upon to work for changes, even minor changes, in that structure. . . . Social objectives are consistently surrendered by the commercialized media when they clash with economic gains.[10]

The point here is not that reporters, or the staff of entertainment programs, or even publishers and station managers take orders from advertisers. As a rule they don't. As a rule they don't have to—and that is precisely the point.

The mass media in the United States are an industry. The main product of that industry is your attention, and the sole customer for that product is, of course, the advertising business. When necessary, most of the media are prepared to carry content that may offend a particular advertiser. Though the advertiser understandably sees this as treachery, the practice maintains the self-respect and public credibility of the media, and thus serves the long-term interests of advertising as well. Media definitions of what is newsworthy and what is entertaining insure that the problem doesn't come up more often than necessary.

The vast majority of media content provides a perfect vehicle for advertising, not because the media are struggling to make it so, but because it has always been so. The business community complains about news coverage of business skulduggery, but the concept of a fundamentally anti-business commercial television station or daily newspaper is almost a contradiction in terms. The mass media *are* businesses. The standards of journalism and the customs of entertainment have developed in that context, and are consistent with that reality.

ADVERTISING AND THE PUBLIC

Several effects of advertising on the American public are already implied in what we have said about the impact of advertising on business and the media. Advertising creates and maintains an economic system that offers us a rich and bewildering choice of nearly identical consumer goods. Each time we make that choice, we do so largely on the basis of the thousands of ads we have seen and heard. Our selection is inevitably influenced by which ads have been repeated most frequently; which products have been tied most successfully to our innermost needs for status, security, sexuality, and the like; which endorsements by actors or athletes we have found most convincing; and a variety of other factors that have nothing to do with the quality of the product. Our response to the irrationality of this system of influences is typically a world-weary cynicism that makes us distrust all efforts to alter our attitudes or actions—yet we continue to buy.

Those of us who can, in fact, continue to buy more, and more, and more; while those of us who can't, justifiably resent our exclusion from the world of consumership. For rich and poor alike, advertising inculcates a firm conviction that the quality of our lives depends on the things we buy. In the late

1970s, ironically, the energy crisis and wors-
ening economic conditions forced the mass
media to pay increasingly respectful attention to an alternative value system, one that
prizes conservation and thrift over consumption and waste. Even some ads urged Americans to make do with less. But most ads continued to urge us to buy more, perpetuating
a culture of consumption to which the media seem inextricably tied.

There is much to admire in all this. The
United States does have the highest material
standard of living in the world. Though our
big cars and uninsulated homes are often
mocked (and are slowly disappearing), our
level of consumption is the envy of the vast
majority of the world's people. The harshest
domestic critics of American materialism are
themselves well-off—and might well be reluctant to give up their stereo systems and tape
collections. It is doubtful that they would
have stereo systems and tape collections
without advertising.

Bear in mind that advertising not only
sells us products; it also sells us ideas and
images. Number 9 on the list of the nation's
top advertisers is the American Telephone
and Telegraph Company, which in 1979
spent $220 million on advertising. Some
AT&T ads urged people to rent AT&T
phones instead of buying them from other
manufacturers—genuinely competitive advertising. More of them aimed at increasing the
size of the market. The phenomenally suc-

cessful "reach out and touch someone" campaign, for example, was launched in 1979 to
promote long-distance calls by softening
their emergencies-only image in the minds of
infrequent users. The remaining AT&T ads
were institutional, designed to create a favorable public attitude toward the company, to
sell the idea that AT&T is a well-run, public-
spirited organization. AT&T's institutional
advertising is considered a legitimate business expense. Since the company is a regulated monopoly, regulatory agencies set the
phone rates high enough to cover the cost.
You pay to have the phone company tell you
how terrific it is.

Institutional advertising is not limited to
AT&T and other regulated monopolies.
Many large corporations devote a significant
part of their advertising budgets to institutional ads. A good public image pays off not
just in sales, but also in stock market prices
and in public support for the company when
it comes into conflict with other companies
or with the government. Some of the nation's
largest corporations deal in high-technology
products that are sold only to other corporations. Their product ads are in the trade
press, their institutional ads in the mass
media.

And when a company has been hit with
some unfavorable publicity, institutional advertising is almost essential to take the edge
off. In 1979, for example, an American Airlines DC-10 crashed at Chicago's O'Hare Air-

port. For a while all DC-10s were grounded for testing. When the ban was lifted, the McDonnell Douglas Corporation began its "cleared for takeoff" advertising campaign. Airline passengers don't buy airplanes, but airlines do, and they prefer not to buy planes that passengers are afraid to fly in. The campaign was therefore designed "to reassure people that the DC-10 comes from a company skilled in technology and in building an advanced product," explained John Bickers, director of advertising for McDonnell Douglas.[12]

One variety of institutional ad that grew enormously in the 1970s is advocacy advertising—ads that argue a particular point of view on issues of public policy. The oil industry led the way, spending tens of millions of dollars a year throughout the decade to recommend the easing of environmental restrictions, the defeat of the windfall profits

tax, federal subsidies for oil shale development, etc. Mobil set the pace with a chatty ad each week opposite the editorial page of the *New York Times* and in other prestige newspapers. Soon other embattled industries—nuclear power, chemicals, cigarettes, etc.—began increasing their budgets for advocacy advertising.

The distinction between product advertising and institutional advertising is by no means airtight. Many institutional ads help sell a company's products, and many product ads help build its image. Even more important, product advertising often has a substantial impact on our attitudes and values, not just toward the product or the company, but toward every aspect of American society. Consider a snowmobile advertisement, for example. The goal of the ad may be to sell us a particular brand of snowmobile, but in the process the ad also tells us that snowmo-

ACCESS FOR ADVOCACY ADS

As many of the nation's largest corporations geared up in the 1970s to push their policy views through advertising, they encountered a somewhat unexpected obstacle. The television networks didn't want the ads. Though most newspapers happily accept advocacy advertisements, the networks regularly reject them—at worst they could provoke a costly fairness doctrine dispute, at best they might disturb the placid selling environment of TV entertainment (see p. 234). With advertisers lining up for the available time, the networks can afford to be choosy—and they generally choose to do without controversial advertising.

Incensed at the network censorship, the Mobil Corporation pled its case in print ads, and won some grudging editorial support to boot. "I hate Mobil's message," wrote Marvin Kitman of *Newsday*. "But they certainly have the right to their say." "Can the television industry dish it out but not take it?" asked the *Philadelphia Inquirer* in an editorial.[13] But the networks stood firm, arguing that commercials were the wrong place to discuss complicated issues.

So Mobil's feisty Vice President Herb Schmertz tried a new tack. In early 1980, the company bought time on 50 individual TV stations for a six-part series called "Edward and Mrs. Simpson"—Mobil's own series with Mobil's own advocacy ads already inserted. A few stations followed network policy and turned down the series because of the ads, but Mobil quickly lined up replacements.[14] The series went on as planned, and the fairness doctrine complaints came in as expected. Most stations granted free reply time to environmental or consumer groups. The Friends of the Earth reply was an unusually aggressive ad that closed: "You can buy their gas, but don't buy their line."[15]

biling is a safe, satisfying, red-blooded American sport, just the thing for someone who loves nature and the outdoors. Even if we have no intention of buying a snowmobile, the ad leaves us with a better image of snowmobiling. And when conservationists propose new restrictions on snowmobiles in order to protect the wilderness they sometimes destroy, we are that much less likely to support the proposals.

Government regulatory agencies and industry self-regulation groups seldom concern themselves with the impact of truthful advertising on social values. Their chief interest is the possibility that the ads might be fraudulent or misleading (see pp. 377-81). But other groups are increasingly concerned about the noncommercial effects of advertising. Among the most irate—and with considerable justice—is the feminist movement.

American advertising has traditionally treated women as sex objects. This isn't an arbitrary insult, but simply a good sales technique. Advertisers know that overtly sexy women help sell products to men, who enjoy the association, and even to women, many of whom have been persuaded (largely by advertising itself) that it's a good thing to be a sex object. An air-travel slump in the early 1970s, for example, prompted National Airlines to run a series of ads featuring attractive stewardesses who urged the would-be passenger to "Fly me." Continental Airlines responded with its own equally attractive women, who promised that "We'll really move our tail for you." Feminist groups pushed for a boycott against both companies, and a TV producer in Los Angeles—one of the very few women in the business—called the ads a "ridiculous attempt to portray women flight attendants as sexy, fun-promising amateur call girls."[16]

When they are not sex objects, women portrayed in advertising are often drudges. Professor Caryl Rivers writes:

The housewives in TV commercials stalk dirt, dust and stale air. . . . The Lysol lady sticks her nose in the sink and sniffs. . . . The women in the Joy commercials get their dishes so clean guests can see their faces in them. . . . The message is clear. Failure to perform a menial personal service properly brings rejection and the withdrawal of love and approval. Success at her assigned task brings her both approval and sex. . . . I like to think I am immune. . . . But I still wish my floors were shinier.[17]

Although television advertising often seems to be an endless succession of sex objects and drudges, as of the mid-1970s only 32 percent of the performers in TV commercials were women, according to research by women in the Screen Actors Guild. Even more significant, the same study found that only 7 percent of the off-camera voices in TV commercials were women.[18] Off-camera voices, of course, are the authority figures who tell the viewer what to do.

The advertising industry is not single-handedly responsible for the sexism in American society. Advertising merely uses that sexism to sell products. The ads will change when the society changes. In fact, spurred by the growth in women's consciousness and the lobbying of the feminist movement, the ads are beginning to change. For years, *Redbook* magazine advertised itself as "The Magazine for Young Mamas." In 1974, it coined a new slogan: "The Magazine of the New Management." Describing its readers as "the millions of young women who are now emerging from homebody to somebody," one 1975 *Redbook* advertisement declared: "Married or not, working or not, women run their own lives. They're the New Management."[19]

In the last half of the 1970s, advertising discovered the working woman. American Express commercials started featuring women cardholders as well as men. United Airlines put women executives in its planes, Equitable Life urged them to buy insurance, and Dreyfus Liquid Assets asked them "Is your money working too?" In a more subtle but perhaps more important transformation, women with lives outside the home started turning up in ads for consumer products—whipping up a quick dinner after work or hosting their own business parties instead of their husbands'. Says Alan Rosenshine of the B.B.D.&O. ad agency: "Male approval used to be the buzz word in all advertising directed to women. Today, the tendency is to show how a product will help a woman who lives for herself, rather than a man."[20]

The shift is real, but advertising still has a long way to go. "I honestly don't think there's been much change," says Rena Bartos of the J. Walter Thompson agency. "The images have consistently been the same old clichés—the housewives and the glamour girls."[21] To be sure, a new stereotype has been added—the "modern woman" who does it all, marriage, children, and career, and still manages to look sexy. But the old stereotypes remain plentiful, and the new one may yet prove just as oppressive. From a woman curled up next to a man as he drives to a woman driving herself while gazing seductively at the camera is modest progress at best.

As the 1980s dawned, TV viewers were greeted with the sexiest ads yet, for designer jeans. The women in the ads were obviously sex objects—but so were the men in the ads. This too is progress of a sort.

Advertisers are as willing to be anti-sexist as they are to be sexist, as long as it won't cut down on sales. The only *goal* of product advertising is that we buy what they're selling. But the *effects* of product advertising go far beyond that. When advertisers ground their sales pitch in sexism, they reinforce the sexism in American culture. The same may be said for elitism, competitiveness, status-seeking, violence, sexual insecurity, and many other facets of our lives that advertisers prey on to make us buy. Consumption is not the only American value maintained by advertising.

Who pays for all this commercial and social indoctrination? You do. The cost of advertising is passed on to the consumer in the form of increased prices. A bar of soap that sells for 39¢ might cost only 34¢ if Procter & Gamble didn't spend $615 million a year on advertising. In the early 1960s, Harry Skornia computed the cost of television advertising alone for a typical middle-class family. The annual "tax" for free TV, he found, was $53.[22] A similar calculation today yields a much higher figure—more than $150 per family. Ads in radio, newspapers, and magazines, of course, increase the total still further.

You get something for your money. By increasing the demand for consumer goods, advertising makes possible the economies of mass production and mass distribution—economies that are in part passed on to the consumer. Most economists today agree that advertising earns back more than its cost—especially when you throw in the value of the media.

Economically, then, advertising is a pretty good deal. Which leaves only one question unanswered: What do you think of the kinds of media that advertising gives you, the kinds of products that it offers you, and the kinds of values that it inculcates in you?

ADVERTISING PROFESSIONALS

Advertising professionals face their greatest challenge when introducing a new kind of product, creating a need that does not already exist. Enzyme soaps are a typical case. Developed in the late 1960s, enzyme soaps do essentially the same job as standard detergents, perhaps a little more effectively. But without exception, the companies that manufacture enzyme cleaners also make detergents, and bleaches to boot. Their goal, of course, is to sell the new product while maintaining the sales records of the old ones. How, then, did the hypothetical Brand X Detergent Company introduce Enzyme X?

The company's first move was to hire a

When the movie *Casablanca* appeared in theaters it ran 102 minutes. When it was shown by a New York television station on a Sunday afternoon in 1980, it lasted 150 minutes. That's 48 minutes of commercials, promos, and station IDs—nearly a minute of "break" for every two minutes of movie.[23] Prime-time television runs at about a one-to-five ratio of commercials to program—less cluttered, but still very noticeable indeed.

Clutter turns out to be the public's greatest objection to advertising, especially on TV. But people are philosophical about it. While almost three-fourths of the public feels there are too many commercials on television, the same percentage says commercials are a "fair price" to pay for TV.[24]

The content of the ads triggers surprisingly little opposition. Not that people like them all. Everyone knows of certain advertisements that he or she actually enjoys, certain others that he or she finds incredibly annoying or offensive. Most ads we accept as tolerable background noise. We don't especially trust them. In one Louis Harris survey, 46 percent of the respondents said that all or most TV commercials were seriously misleading, with another 36 percent saying that some were seriously misleading. Newspaper and magazine ads fared a little better; 28 percent said that all or most were seriously misleading, 50 percent that some were.[25] Despite these high levels of distrust, there has been no groundswell of public demand to clean up advertising. Most Americans apparently accept ads they consider misleading as an inevitable byproduct of capitalism.

A clue to this toleration can be found in the fact that most Americans do not believe that they themselves are misled. Feminists worry about the effects of advertising on social values, parents worry about the effects of advertising on their children—but very few people worry about the effects of advertising on themselves. Advertising, we think, is something that influences *other* people.

We are wrong, of course. One typical study found that the average food shopper is willing to pay 18.4 percent more for a major advertised brand than for an unadvertised "house" brand.[26] The food may be the same, but unless the price is overwhelmingly different we feel more comfortable with a brand we've heard of. How have we heard of it? Through advertising.

New York advertising agency, one of the big ones geared for national campaigns. Brand X was a major account, so an agency vice president was assigned the job of account executive. Like most account executives, he was a white male with an M.B.A. from a prestigious university. He had been catapulted to the vice presidency at the age of 38 by several phenomenally successful campaigns. He was earning in excess of $50,000 a year, and was already planning to quit and start his own agency, perhaps with Brand X as his first big client.

The job of an account executive is to act as liaison between the client and the agency's creative people. In this case, the executive planned to make use of the following departments: research, copy, art, layout, production, and media. Selecting one or two people from each department, the account executive put together a planning group that would stay with the account from start to finish.

It was a psychologist from the research department who pointed out the obvious: "We cannot base our advertisements on the superiority of enzymes over detergents, because our client manufactures detergents as well. We must therefore urge the consumers to add the enzyme product to the detergent and bleach they already use, in order to obtain an even cleaner wash than before." Everyone agreed that this appeal was essentially irrational (what is "cleaner than clean"?), but everyone agreed that it could work. The research department verified that many women are emotionally attached to their old detergents and will not give them up—but will cheerfully dump an extra ingredient into their wash if convinced that it will give them the cleanest clothes on the block.

Convincing them was, of course, the job of the copy, art, and layout departments. The media department, meanwhile, tentatively decided to stress national women's magazines and daytime TV soap operas. Work began on four different magazine ads and three television commercials, each in 60-second, 40-second, 30-second, and 10-second versions. Since the agency's movie production facilities were already working to capacity, an independent filmmaker was called in to help.

Throughout this period, the account executive was in constant contact with the Brand X advertising department. He obtained their approval for each ad and each commercial. He also got their permission to test-market the product in a dozen communities, trying out various appeals to see how they worked.

According to the research department, these tests produced one unexpected result. Housewives, it seems, were not only willing to add Enzyme X to their wash; they were also willing to use it as a pre-soak before washing. New commercials were designed to stress this additional function.

Now the media department went into action. Using data from the Audit Bureau of Circulations, the media people began deciding which ads to place in which newspapers and magazines, when and how often. Their main criteria were total circulation and total cost—how many readers per dollar could they

reach in each publication. But it wasn't that simple. The "enzyme-buying public" was obviously easier to reach in some magazines than in others; even newspapers vary in the number of women readers they attract. Quality and minority-group magazines required different ads from the mass magazines. There were back covers to be considered, and special editions, and regional magazines, and dozens of other factors.

But choosing the print media was child's play compared with placing broadcast commercials. The main tool here was the ratings, prepared by the A. C. Nielsen Company and the American Research Bureau. Broadcasters live and die by the Nielsen and ARB rating reports, simply because advertisers swear by them. In this case, the main candidates for commercials were the daytime network soap operas. Each show was carefully examined in terms of its cost per thousand viewers, its credibility as an advertising vehicle, its popularity with the sorts of people who might buy enzymes, and so forth. Consideration was also given to the possibility of commissioning and sponsoring a special program, but this was rejected. In the end, spot commercials were placed in seven different network serials.

The media department had plenty of help deciding where to place its ads—from the space and time sales representatives in the advertising department of each newspaper, magazine, and broadcast station and network. In theory, this is a cut-and-dried process. The media have their ad rates; the client pays the full rate; the agency remits 85 percent of it and keeps the other 15 percent as its commission. In reality, there's a lot of room for wheeling and dealing—to get the client a lower price and the agency a higher commission.

Media commissions account for about three-quarters of the income of most advertising agencies. The other quarter comes from surveys, production, and similar "expenses," for which the client pays a premium. After covering its own expenses, the average ad agency has a net profit of only 4 percent of the gross. Madison Avenue is not a cheap address, and advertising executives are well paid.

How did the enzyme campaign work out? Like many advertising campaigns, it was a success. Housewives diligently began adding enzyme products to their wash, or using them as pre-soaks; the more dutiful housewives did both. Enzyme X became a big money-maker for the Brand X Detergent Company. After a year or two, the company (and nearly all its competitors) decided to add enzymes to its detergent as well. Properly advertised, this gimmick helped to boost detergent sales without damaging the sales of nondetergent enzymes. By 1971, the cooperative American housewife did her wash in the following manner: first an enzyme pre-soak, then an enzyme detergent supplemented with more of the pre-soak and with bleach. Her clothes were cleaner than cleaner than clean, her self-image was ever more closely tied to the washbasket, and detergent-caused eutrophication had become a serious water-pollution problem.

That is not the end of the story, of course. Americans spend $2.2 billion a year on detergents, and detergent manufacturers never stop battling to expand the market and increase their share of it.

The company to beat is Procter & Gamble —number one in the nation in overall advertising, in television advertising, and in detergent profits. P&G's Tide rules the roost with 23 percent of the market; P&G's Cheer is number two with 9 percent. (Yes, Procter & Gamble like many companies competes with itself, positioning each product to appeal to a somewhat different sort of detergent user.) Unilever, number 23 in overall advertising, holds the third and fourth slots in the detergent derby, with Wisk at 7 percent and All at 6 percent. Back with the also-rans is Colgate-Palmolive. Though a respectably spendthrift advertiser (number 37), Colgate can do no better than a sixth-place finish with Dynamo.[27]

But it's making a Fresh Start. Back in 1975, Colgate conducted 300 in-depth interviews to discover how homemakers felt about their detergents. The company concluded that there was a big untapped market for a stronger detergent in a smaller package. It set its research and development team to work, and the result was Fresh Start, a heavy-duty detergent so concentrated that it could be (and was) packed in a small plastic bottle.

Fresh Start's packaging and advertising went through extensive tests. Possible packages, for example, were test-marketed in the Assessor, a mock-up minisupermarket run by Management Decisions Systems of Weston, Mass. Possible ads went to Bakersfield, Calif., where a company called Adtel operates a cable television system, one of several that ad agencies use often to evaluate the effectiveness of commercials. Commercial A is shown to viewers on one side of town, while viewers on the other side see Commercial B—and the sales records of each side's supermarkets tell the story. By mid-1977, Colgate was ready to introduce Fresh Start in its first urban market, New Orleans. Testing continued as the company introduced the product area-by-area, spending $20 million a year on sampling and advertising. By 1980, when Fresh Start hit New York, New England, and Atlanta, it was averaging a healthy five percent of the market in the areas where it had been around for a while.

Three-quarters of Fresh Start's advertising budget goes for television, both daytime and prime-time. The six-month introductory phase uses two 60-second commercials, with actor Skip Holmeier explaining the new product. The second-phase commercials tout performance, and stress the Fresh Start slogan: "Best of powders. Best of liquids. In one."[28]

And what are Procter & Gamble and Unilever doing to counter the new competition? Watch a soap opera tomorrow and see for yourself.

The first advertising agencies were founded in the 1840s. By 1860 there were thirty of them. As intermediaries between the advertisers and the publications, they were in an ideal position to cheat both—inflating prices, demanding kickbacks, and so on.

These abuses didn't improve until 1869, when George P. Rowell began publishing the *American Newspaper Directory*, an accurate listing of newspaper circulations and ad rates. Also in 1869, the N. W. Ayer & Son agency was founded to buy space for advertisers on a straight commission basis. Thereafter, it was not so easy for ad agencies to manipulate publishers and advertisers.

But manipulating the public was something else. Many ads at the turn of the century—especially those for patent medicines—were grossly misleading, often outright falsehoods. The public put up with them for a few decades, then began to complain. Several of the more ethical agencies joined in the campaign against misleading advertising. The Better Business Bureau was founded in 1913, the Audit Bureau of Circulations in 1914. The Association of Advertising Clubs developed a model "truth in advertising" law. It was championed by the trade journal *Printers' Ink,* and was soon adopted by several states.

The federal government entered the scene in 1914, when the Federal Trade Commission Act empowered the FTC to regulate false advertising. But the Commission's responsibility was limited to ads that could be shown to constitute unfair competition—that is, false advertising that hurt the sales of more truthful competitors. The Wheeler-Lea Amendment of 1938 broadened the FTC's mandate to include all false advertising regardless of its effects on competition, especially in the food, drug, and cosmetics industries. Still, the Commission was required to prove that an ad was fraudulent before it could take action against the advertiser.

This emphasis on consumer fraud is still characteristic of the FTC—but the definition of "fraud" has broadened considerably. Acknowledging that advertisers know how to mislead without lying, the Commission now considers what an ad implies as well as what it says. Profile bread, for example, was advertised for years as a diet bread that contained "fewer calories per slice" than ordinary breads. It did, but only because the bread was sliced thinner. In the 1950s such an ad would have been judged acceptable; in the 1970s the FTC ruled that it was misleading.

In dealing with false and misleading advertising, the FTC has always been most effective against marginal operators whose ads are clearly fraudulent. It sucessfully challenges many such ads every year, and thus helps insure that advertising does not return to the "patent medicine" standards of the turn of the century. But until the 1970s, the Commission's record against mainstream advertisers was a good deal less impressive, leading many critics to claim that it was subservient to the industry it was supposed to regulate. Quite apart from any subservience, the FTC found it difficult to surmount the legal delaying tactics that major advertisers can so easily employ. It typically took years for the FTC to collect evidence against a particular advertisement and then push the case through the courts. By then the ad had long since been junked and a new one put in its place.

In the 1970s an increasingly aggressive FTC found new ways to cope with advertiser delay. To speed the process of gathering evidence, it began collecting data from advertisers on the facts behind ad claims on a routine, industry-by-industry basis, even before there was a complaint to investigate. To insure that advertisers wouldn't escape justice by changing their ads at the last minute, it began imposing "corrective advertising" as a penalty, requiring the new ads to admit that the earlier ones were indeed misleading. In 1975, Congress helped con-

377

solidate this progress by authorizing the FTC to set advertising standards for entire industries in advance.

The change was remarkable. The FTC had first questioned the advertising claims of Listerine mouthwash in 1941. But nothing serious was done about Listerine until 1975, when the Commission ruled that it was ineffective against colds, and ordered Warner-Lambert to spend $10 million on corrective ads or stop advertising the product altogether. The company appealed the decision, but the federal courts upheld the FTC's authority to order corrective advertising, and in 1978 the Commission's victory was complete when the Supreme Court declined to review the case.[29]

FTC regulation of false advertising is backed up by the self-regulatory apparatus of the advertising industry and the media. Within the ad industry, the key regulator is the National Advertising Division of the Council of Better Business Bureaus, which investigates consumer complaints and announces its findings. An advertiser who disagrees may appeal to a five-member panel of the National Advertising Review Board. The NAD and NARB have no formal power to impose penalties, but when they decide against an advertiser the offending ad is almost always withdrawn or changed.

Like the FTC, the NAD and NARB have extended their definitions to include misleading ads as well as outright frauds. They tend to concentrate mostly on small national advertisers, the sort you find on matchbook covers and the back pages of comics. In May of 1980, for example, the NAD dealt with 12 cases. Five advertisers substantiated their claims; the other seven agreed to cancel or change their ads. Among the seven were two ads offering "solid gold" that was less than 24-carat, and an ad for Sad Sack Books that was asked to drop the "only" from its "only $1.98" price.[30]

The mass media, meanwhile, have a virtually ironclad right to reject advertising; by using that right they can be by far the speed-iest "regulator" of dishonest ads. They do use it, but sparingly. Somewhere in the bowels of most newspapers, magazines, and broadcast stations is a person responsible for reviewing advertisements and deciding which ones to accept. For the most part, stations rely on the judgment of the networks, and networks, newspapers, and magazines rely on the standards published by the Better Business Bureau—that is, by the advertising industry itself. A lot of obviously misleading ads do get weeded out this way. When a network or a major newspaper rejects an ad, the advertiser almost always revises it—and the problem is solved long before a complaint could be processed by the NAD or the FTC. But less obviously misleading ads must usually wait for NAD or FTC action. Only after that action will the media apply the new precedent to other advertisers.

All in all, this is a pretty good system for controlling dishonest advertising—an aggressive but slow-moving Federal Trade Commission, a speedy but conservative media rejection process, and an advertising industry that is in the middle on both dimensions. The philosophy that underlies the system is still *caveat emptor* ("let the buyer beware"). We assume that sellers will exaggerate the good points and ignore the bad points of what they're selling, and we assume that buyers (except perhaps children) will know this and make allowances for a certain amount of advertising puffery. But we no longer assume that advertisers will lie or mislead their audience on the facts. They usually do not. And when they do, they are quite likely to be caught and stopped.

So much for false and misleading ads. Unfortunately, many ads that consumers consider false or misleading are actually neither. Instead, they are merely manipulative, designed to appeal to emotional needs and irrational desires. Consider the "claim" that a particular toothpaste will improve your sex life. In legal terms, this isn't a claim at all. The quality of someone's sex life is a subjective judgment, and the ability of a toothpaste to improve it has more to do with the customer's self-confidence than the customer's teeth. Yet the selling power of such an ad is enormous. It appeals to deep-seated sexual and social insecurities in its audience. Even those who do not believe the ad intellectually may be persuaded by their own emotional needs to give the product a try.

SUBLIMINAL SEDUCTION?

Nearly everyone agrees that advertising successfully manipulates its audience's emotions, insecurities, and needs. Two of the most common words in ads are "love" and "friend"—"you have a friend at Chase Manhattan" who doubtless drinks "Amaretto di Sarronno, the rare liqueur of love."[31] Sex adds to the selling power of advertisements for jeans, cars, lipsticks, cigarette lighters, and hundreds of other products. Snob appeal, mob appeal, and innumerable other nonrational appeals dominate much of consumer advertising.

Such messages may sometimes be subtle, but they are not subliminal. You can see what's going on if you look for it. In the 1950s, on the other hand, marketing researcher James Vicary came up with the novel idea of flashing the message "Hungry? Eat Popcorn!" between the frames of a film in a Fort Lee, N.J. theater.[32] This is genuinely subliminal advertising. The message goes by too fast for the conscious mind to catch it, though Vicary claimed the unconscious mind noticed and popcorn sales increased. Vance Packard exposed Vicary's experiment in his popular book *The Hidden Persuaders*, beginning a debate that continues intermittently to this day. The debate centers on two questions: Does subliminal advertising occur often? And does it really work?

The leading advocate of the "yes" position is Wilson Bryan Key, whose *Subliminal Seduction* in 1973 and *Media Sexploitation* in 1977 were paperback best-sellers. Both books are prolifically illustrated with blow-ups of magazine advertisements, with arrows pointing to shadowy images of sex and death. According to Key, the unconscious mind picks up these taboo images and is motivated by them to purchase the product. American culture, says Key, is "one enormous, magnificent, self-service subliminal massage parlor."[33]

Most scholars don't think so. Many of the images Key finds in magazine ads could be sheer accidents, just as clouds and inkblots form pictures for the receptive mind. Some of the images are undoubtedly really there, but even these might have been airbrushed in by a bored ad agency artist. If there is an organized conspiracy to push sales with subliminal messages, so far the evidence of that conspiracy is subliminal itself.

The evidence on the actual effects of subliminal messages is inconclusive, and surprisingly scanty. Several studies in the late 1950s concluded that there was no effect,[34] but two more recent studies found evidence that subliminal messages did work.[35]

Further research is needed to settle the point. And it's not just an academic point. Subliminal advertising hit television in the 1970s, with a toy commercial that flashed the subliminal message "Get it!" The Federal Communications Commission responded with a warning against broadcasting subliminal ads. But except for a few state laws, no government body currently regulates subliminal advertising in print or film. Or in department stores: a company called the Behavioral Engineering Center now markets a background music system for department stores that carries subliminal messages like "I am honest" and "I will not steal."[36] If the method works to prevent theft, it will presumably work to promote sales as well. Regulation will be badly needed—*if* the method works.

Who regulates this sort of advertising? Nobody. At the height of its powers in the late 1970s, the Federal Trade Commission tried to control the use of psychological manipulation in advertising aimed at children—for example, the suggestion that other children will like you better if you buy a particular toy. The rationale for this regulatory initiative was that children's immaturity made them unfairly vulnerable to emotional and psychological manipulation. Any psychologist will tell you that adults are also vulnerable. But the American legal system is firmly rooted in the notion that adults are rational. It is illegal for advertisers to mislead an adult's mind with false information. But it is perfectly legal to ignore the mind and speak directly to the audience's needs and emotions.

This is probably the way it should be. The specter of a government agency that outlawed certain messages as "too emotional" or "unfairly appealing to needs" would come close to destroying the First Amendment. The assumption that adults are rational may be naive, but it is a lot safer than the contrary assumption that adults are children, to be protected by their government from potentially inflammatory advertisements. Big Brother government, most observers agree, is a more serious threat than manipulative advertising.

Of course the ad industry and the media could regulate themselves in this area without any such threat. So far they show no signs of doing so. Their position on advertising's "hidden persuaders," in fact, is that they don't exist. Advertising executives insist that their job is merely to tell people about the goods and services they have for sale. Of course they present this information in the most effective possible light; that's only common sense. But there's nothing underhanded, they say, about using sex to sell shaving cream, or athletes to sell aspirin, or snob appeal to sell soap. The media agree.

The psychological impact of advertising thus goes unregulated. What about its sociological impact, its effects on American values and American culture? Who regulates an advertisement that is demonstrably harmful to its audience, even though it may not mislead their minds or manipulate their emotions?

The Federal Trade Commission has long had some limited power to stop dangerous-though-accurate advertisements. It kept a razor blade company from attaching free samples to the Sunday newspaper, for example, on the grounds that people can cut themselves even on an honest ad. In the late 1970s it began gingerly to expand this power. In one case, an FTC administrative judge objected to the milk industry's use of baseball star Vida Blue as an advertising spokesman. The ads were honest enough, and the judge certainly wasn't attacking athletic endorsements in general. His point was that many blacks have trouble digesting milk, a genetic trait that means they shouldn't drink much of it. A black superstar in a milk commercial might therefore have a harmful effect.

Then the Commission went too far. Under pressure from Action for Children's Television and other citizens groups (see p. 227), it had agreed to take a look at sweetened food commercials aimed at children. In 1978 it expanded the investigation to consider the advisability of banning all television advertising for young children. The broadcasting, soft drink, candy, toy, cereal, and sugar industries exploded. The result was an intensive anti-FTC lobbying campaign—and in 1980 Congress voted to restrict the powers of the Commission.[37] The children's advertising inquiry continued on a much more modest scale.

For the next few years, at least, the FTC is unlikely to expand its powers; it will be lucky to keep those it has. And at best, expanded government regulation of advertising is a two-edged sword. It is tempting to seek new laws that would put an immediate stop to all advertising abuses. Say we start with the negative stereotyping of women.

Then what's to prevent the government from passing other regulations that outlaw negative images of politicians, of corporate executives, of Ku Klux Klansmen? For good reason, the First Amendment forbids the government to tell the media what images they are allowed to present . . . of anybody.

As with psychological manipulation, a better solution is voluntary self-regulation by the media and the advertising industry. Traditionally, both groups have been uninterested in the social effects of the ads. Advertising professionals often tell the story of an ill-fated TV commercial for a toy sub-machine gun. The commercial featured a trigger-happy child standing on a hill and cheerfully mowing down hundreds of toy soldiers. When the National Association of Broadcasters refused to approve the ad, the agency assumed at first that it was cracking down on super-violent advertising. Not so. The NAB's objection was that young viewers might be misled into believing that the toy soldiers (and the hill?) came with the gun.

This is an old story, and today the NAB might be worried about the violence as well. Advertisers and the media are susceptible to public pressure. The NAB's Radio and Television Codes say so in black and white, obliging broadcasters to turn down an ad if they have "good reason to believe [it] would be objectionable to a substantial and responsible segment of the community."[38] Many newspapers and broadcast stations refuse ads for liquors, suppositories, X-rated movies, condoms, fortune-tellers, and controversial ideas of various sorts, all in order to avoid offending readers or viewers. Under pressure from minority groups, advertisers have eliminated nearly all the racial slurs in advertising, and the media have learned to reject the ones that slip through. Under pressure from feminist groups, advertisers and the media are beginning to clean up their act in that area as well.

In short, the best hope for dealing with advertising abuses other than fraud is a vocal public that insists that such abuses be dealt with. Today, government regulation and industry ethics both forbid misleading advertising. Regulation is ill-fit to cope with accurate advertising that is psychologically manipulative or socially harmful. Ethics can do the job—but first public pressure will be needed to force a change in the ethical standards of advertising.

To sell their products and services, institutions use paid advertising. But when they want to sell themselves, they turn mostly to public relations. Public relations may be defined as the planned effort to create and maintain a favorable climate of opinion through communications, especially through free publicity in the mass media. Although it became a "science" only in the twentieth century, public relations has been a practical art in the U.S. for more than 300 years. Much of what we know about our government, corporations, and other institutions we have learned from the nation's PR professionals.

PR AND THE MEDIA

In 1641, Harvard College sent three preachers to England on a "begging mission." At their request, a fund-raising brochure, _New England's First Fruits,_ was prepared by the elders of the Massachusetts Bay Colony—the first public-relations pamphlet written in the New World. Press releases, pseudo-events, and the rest of the PR arsenal followed soon after. Though the first professional public-relations firm wasn't founded until 1904, the techniques were already well-established before the American Revolution.

The difference between advertising and public relations is one of methods, not goals. Martin Mayer puts it this way:

Advertising, whatever its faults, is a relatively open business; its messages appear in paid space or on bought time, and everybody can recognize it as special pleading. Public relations works behind the scenes. . . . The advertising man must know how many people he can reach *with* the media, the public relations man must know how many people he can reach *within* the media.[39]

This is a valid distinction, but advertising and public relations are often so intertwined that it is hard to tell where one leaves off and the other begins. When political candidates, for instance, put themselves in the hands of the professionals (as most of them do now), they hire not only advertising specialists to write their commercials, but also public-relations specialists to write their speeches. The two kinds of specialists work together to build a consistent (if unreal) image of the candidate they work for. Corporate advocacy advertising (see p. 371) represents a similar collaboration between advertising and public-relations experts.

If anything, public relations is a broader field than advertising. Every politician employs a full-time press secretary even after the election, though there may be no further need for an ad agency. Government departments don't advertise much, but they collectively employ thousands of professional PR people. And every college and every corporation has its own "public-information office" or "public-relations department."

Whatever their title and whoever their employer, public-relations people have just one job: through communications, to build in various publics the sorts of attitudes their client wants those publics to have. The job may include a company newsletter for employees, a speaker service for civic groups, a lobbying effort for Congress, and a variety of other specialized approaches. Invariably, it also includes an effort to reach the general public through the mass media.

PR techniques for influencing the media run the gamut from handouts to junkets, from press conferences to bribes. The main techniques are discussed in detail in Chapter 6. That chapter was entitled "Source Control" to stress the fundamental purpose of public relations—PR is what sources do to control the content of the media.

How much control do they actually exercise? By way of example, consider a 1971 study of news coverage of environmental issues in the San Francisco Bay Area. David B. Sachsman asked reporters and editors from twenty-five Bay Area media where they got their information for the 474 local environmental news stories they carried over a twelve-day period. He received answers for 200 of the stories. The breakdown was as follows:

Rewritten press releases	46
Business Wire	3
News film from PR people	2
Telephone or personal contact with PR people	26
Press releases plus additional reporting	28
No public-relations influence	95

In other words, 51 of the 200 stories were based entirely on PR material; the "reporter" did no reporting at all. Another 54 stories came as the result of an initial PR push—a phone call, a personal visit, or a press release—followed by some additional work on the reporter's part. Only 95 stories, less than half, were initiated by the reporter without significant public-relations input.[40]

Sachsman also asked eleven specialized environmental reporters to keep track of what they did with every press release they received over an eight-week period. The reporters logged an impressive total of 1,347 environmental releases. They wrote news stories based on 192 of them, and saved an additional 268 releases for possible later use.[41]

It is clear from these figures that distributing an environmental press release by no means guarantees the desired news story. PR people must compete with each other and with other sources of news (such as the wire services) for the limited space and time available in the media. On the other hand, the figures also demonstrate that PR exercises a very substantial influence over environmental news coverage in the San Francisco Bay Area. Sachsman concludes:

> The easy way for a Bay Area medium to cover the environment is to rely on information supplied by public relations. . . . It is reasonable to estimate that about 40 percent of the environmental content of the Bay Area media comes from public relations practitioners, and that about 20 percent of the environmental content consists of rewritten press releases. When a newsman uses a press release to help him investigate a story, he should not be accused of abandoning his job to the public relations man, but when he simply rewrites a press release or uses a PR wire story or film . . . it is the PR man who is really covering the story.[42]

Many other studies of public-relations influence have reached similar conclusions. During a one-month period in 1973, for example, a group of Pentagon reporters produced 155 news stories. Of these, 47 were based primarily on the words of Pentagon information officers. And 42 more reported the statements of high-ranking Defense Department officials at events engineered by the Pentagon's public-information office, such as press conferences, arranged interviews, and congressional appearances.[43] Military public relations, in short, dominated well over half the Pentagon news stories published during this typical month.

A 1976 study of the press releases of state senatorial candidates found that the average release was used by only 8 percent of the weekly newspapers in the candidate's district—but 76 percent (over three-quarters) of the campaign coverage in the weeklies originated with the candidates' releases.[44] In one 1979 issue of the *Wall Street Journal*, as many as 45 percent of all the articles in the paper were based on press releases.[45]

Writing in 1962, Professor Scott M. Cutlip

estimated that 35 percent of the news in the average newspaper came from public-relations sources. He contended further that as the content of news became more complex, making it increasingly difficult for reporters to understand fully what they were writing about, the percentage would increase.[46] A fair estimate of how much of today's news is directly inspired by public relations would probably run between 40 and 50 percent.

Journalists are understandably ambivalent about this extensive PR influence. Most reporters are keenly aware of the fact that public-relations people have an axe to grind. They don't especially enjoy rewriting press releases day after day. They'd much rather investigate and write their own stories.

But a reporter's time and expertise are both extremely limited, and without public relations many stories would never get reported at all. The most efficient way to cover a minor event (such as a corporate promotion or a garden club meeting) is to publish the releases submitted by the participants. The most efficient way to cover a technical issue (such as an air-pollution ruling or the introduction of a new missile) is to publish the expert statements supplied by the agencies. The most efficient way to cover a public controversy (such as a zoning dispute or a close vote in Congress) is to publish the conflicting PR claims of both sides. Public-relations professionals report the routine stories for the media, and help them report the important ones. Few journalists relish their dependence on PR, but nearly all agree that there is simply no other way to get their business done on time.

PR AND THE PUBLIC

Since the media depend largely on public relations for news, the public inevitably does too. Of course reporters decide which press releases to publish, which PR people to talk with, which questions to ask, which answers to include, and which stories to investigate

ADVICE FROM THE PROS

The top PR professionals—the ones who handle presidential candidates and giant corporations—are far beyond routine lists of pointers. They concentrate on advanced problems like how to get around the equal time law or how to avoid an unflattering segment on "60 Minutes."

But beginners need manuals. In 1979, a handbook on "the art of press relations" was distributed to Democratic candidates for the New Jersey Assembly, offering nuggets like the following.

On exclusives: "Never play favorites with newsmen. If you begin a pattern of feeding one or two reporters the choice items, the others will rightfully downplay the routine stories you send them. Reporters who are regularly scooped look bad to their management, and few actions make them more resentful. That's not to say there isn't a place for exclusives in the campaign. Just make sure the exclusive placements are spread around so that everyone has his share."

On news conferences: "Find an easily accessible place for the conference. If it happens to be the campaign headquarters, make sure it is bustling and exudes the air of impending victory."

On photographs: "Never, never have a photograph taken of the candidate holding a cocktail. Even with rapidly increasing tolerance by the public of a candidate's weaknesses, it can hurt. The same goes for cigarettes. . . . Incidentally, even an innocent hug can be misunderstood, so be careful with the opposite sex, especially with a camera in the vicinity."[47]

Real beginners need even more basic advice than this. Many newspapers, especially suburban ones, rely heavily on amateur PR for their coverage of groups that aren't important or controversial enough to merit a reporter's attention. To help local organizations get their story into the paper, editors often run workshops on how to write and

more thoroughly and report more interpretively. Nonetheless, any point of view that does not have expert PR help faces an uphill battle for favorable coverage in the media. And any point of view that is blessed with a superlative PR apparatus has an almost unbeatable advantage.

It is customary to blame every example of biased news coverage on the news media themselves. We tend to say that this newspaper was biased against labor in that strike, that this broadcast station was biased in favor of that candidate in the election, etc. Sometimes the bias is just that, an intentional or unintentional distortion on the part of the media. But most of the bias in the news is not the bias of the reporter, but rather the bias of the sources who knew best how to meet the needs of the reporter. Imbalances in news coverage, in other words, usually result from imbalances in public-relations skill; the reporter is as much a victim as the rest of us.

Not that reporters should be let off the hook entirely. We have a right to insist that the media work especially hard to cover those viewpoints that are not represented by effective PR professionals, and that they struggle to lessen the influence of those viewpoints whose PR is especially expert. But all that takes time, and time is the media's scarcest commodity. As long as reporters continue to rely heavily on public relations, the groups that achieve the most favorable coverage will be the groups that employ the most effective PR people.

It is in this sense that public relations must be viewed as a potent social force, as a

submit press releases. Many also publish guidelines for publicity heads. The following is the "Guide for Publicity Chairmen" provided by the *Somerset Spectator,* a suburban New Jersey weekly.[48]

1. The deadline for all copy is Monday noon each week (except on holidays when an earlier deadline may be announced in the paper). We would appreciate your timing all publicity to appear in area newspapers on the same day.
2. Releases should be mailed to the *Spectator,* P. O. Box 336, Somerset, N.J. 08873, dropped in the mailbox in the downstairs lobby at 900 Hamilton Street or submitted at our office in Room 11 (second floor) on Mondays between the hours of 9 A.M. and 12 noon.
3. Releases should be typed, *double-spaced* (to permit editing between lines, if necessary) and should contain the name and telephone number of the person who can be contacted for additional information. Carbons are acceptable if they are truly legible.
4. We prefer that you take photographs of most club events. Polaroids are fine as long as they are clear and sharp. All photographs should be black and white. Be sure to include complete information for a caption on a separate sheet of paper attached to the back of the photograph with a piece of tape. If something special is coming up, please give us a few weeks notice and we will try to send a photographer.
5. Please check and double check the spelling of all names in your releases. Always include first names (not *Mr. Jones* or *Mrs. Smith*). We prefer that women, married or not, be referred to simply as Marilyn Jones.
6. News items that are submitted on time will automatically be included in "Week at a Glance" or you may submit items specifically for the weekly calendar. The deadline for each month's "Looking Ahead" is announced under the column on page 3 (around the middle of each month for the subsequent month).
7. Since our readers do not want to read the same news more than once, please submit only one release about a particular event unless you have new information. The date, however, can be announced in advance (see no. 6 above).
8. Let us know well in advance about any event or activity you think might make an interesting feature story.

mass medium in its own right. How much do you know about, say, the Bell Telephone system? And where did you learn what you know? You learned a little of it from personal experience and conversations with friends. You learned a great deal more from those charming and impressive AT&T ads. And you learned by far the most from the efforts of the Bell PR department. Those efforts range from the little "newsletter" that comes with your bill every month to upbeat newspaper articles about Bell's work in minority recruiting. They range from Bell-sponsored science films distributed free to primary schools to cute magazine fillers about the adventures of a long-distance operator. They range from widely publicized grants to educational TV stations to county-fair exhibits of telephone technology.

There is nothing dishonest about all this. Public-relations people seldom lie. They don't even have to distort the truth all that often. They simply distract the public's attention from disagreeable facts and concentrate its attention on agreeable ones—agreeable to the client, that is. Bell Telephone really does impressive things technologically; it is generous in its support of education; it doubtless has thousands of courteous, helpful operators who love people. But Bell Telephone is other things as well—things you seldom hear about unless an opponent of Bell starts generating its own PR.

The success of a PR campaign is measured in two ways. First, it must be covered by the media; the more news stories a campaign generates, the more successful it is. Second, it must contribute to a favorable climate of public opinion; if sales go up and friendly letters pour in, the campaign is truly successful. As a fairly typical success, consider the story of Lucky Breweries, a West Coast beer company. Lucky's PR expert, Bert Casey, calls it the story of the company's decision to "live and exploit its sense of corporate public responsibility."[49]

Lucky was one of the first companies to discover the public-relations potential of the nation's rising concern about the quality of the environment. In 1969, Casey began publicizing the company's efforts at environmental cleanup. The results were good, and by September, 1970, Lucky had developed a workable bottle-recycling program in Seattle. With Casey's help, the program received wide press coverage; sales started climbing, and Lucky immediately began recycling efforts in other areas. By mid-June, 1971, the company had redeemed more than ten million containers. As a result of its recycling program, Lucky sales were up as much as 20 percent in some areas, and the company had accumulated literally thousands of letters of congratulations in its files.

Casey's biggest coup was undoubtedly his glasphalt campaign. There is nothing fake about glasphalt. A mixture of asphalt and glass chips, it is a paving material with substantial promise. Though making glasphalt out of old bottles isn't nearly as good for the environment as refilling the bottles and using them again, it's a lot better than tossing them into the garbage.

On May 20, 1971, Lucky Breweries paved its first glasphalt parking lot. About forty journalists were there for the occasion. They watched the paving, attended a press conference, received a Lucky press kit, and left with the story Lucky wanted them to have. They were there, of course, because Casey got them there—by mailing 120 invitations to West Coast media and telephoning reminders to dozens of editors.

The story was a natural. It tied the growing public interest in recycling to the novel idea of paving a parking lot with broken glass. Lucky would have considered the campaign a success even if the story had been confined to those newspapers and broadcast stations that sent their own reporters. But Casey was after wider coverage than that. He hired the Business Wire (a public-relations wire service) to telegraph his press release to every subscriber. And as soon as the paving was over and the reporters were gone, the big push came. Casey explains:

> We selected two photos to be released in a saturation mailing. These were produced overnight, pasted to captions, stuffed along with the news release and mailed May 21 to 2,250 radio stations, television stations, daily newspapers and weekly newspapers in the west. Additionally, we released a 120-second television film clip to 35 western stations.[50]

The results were predictable. The glasphalt story moved on both the AP and the UPI wire. In the San Francisco area (where the event took place), the story appeared in all the metropolitan papers and most of the suburban dailies; it was on most of the area's TV stations and many of its larger radio stations. Overall, more than a hundred newspapers ran a glasphalt story, and twenty television stations used Casey's film clip.

The total cost of the glasphalt campaign was $4,000—a drop in the bucket in Lucky's 1971 PR budget of $150,000. Yet the campaign brought the company more favorable publicity than it could have purchased with $100,000 in advertising. On the strength of glasphalt and several similar successes, Casey soon went into business as Bert Casey & Company, an independent public-relations consulting firm with one major client, Lucky Breweries.

There is nothing unusual about Lucky Breweries and Bell Telephone. Every company, union, government, charity, and political movement uses the same techniques. Much of what we know about our world comes to us (free of charge) courtesy of the nation's more than 115,000 public-relations professionals.

Back in 1906, PR pioneer Ivy Lee sent the following "Declaration of Principles" to newspaper publishers:

> This is not a secret news bureau. All our work is done in the open. We aim to supply news. This is not an advertising agency; if you think any of our matter ought properly to go to your business office, do not use it. Our matter is accurate. Further details of any subject will be supplied promptly, and any editor will be assisted most cheerfully in verifying directly any statement of fact. . . . In brief, our plan is frankly and openly, on behalf of business concerns and public institutions, to supply to the press and public of the United States prompt and accurate information concerning subjects which it is of value and interest to the public to know about.[51]

This declaration is, in effect, a public-relations handout on behalf of public relations. It forms the basis for the Public Relations Code of the Public Relations Society of America.

Even taking Lee's declaration at face value, PR still raises serious problems. Consider Lee's claim that public relations is done in the open. This is true so far as reporters are concerned; they know a publicist when they see one. But so far as the audience is concerned, PR *is* secret. It does not carry the unspoken *caveat emptor* of paid advertising. Similarly, Lee's promise of accurate information is honored by most PR professionals—"never lie to the press" is a cardinal principle of public relations. But PR people do stretch the truth from time to time, and telling half the truth is an integral part of their business.

And unlike advertising, public relations is almost completely unregulated by the government. It doesn't even have a self-policing body like advertising's NAD and NARB. The only real "regulation" of PR comes from skeptical reporters and PR people for opposing interests. These may be enough when reporters are on their toes and opposing interests can afford effective PR peo-

ple of their own. But when the reporter is busy with "more important" stories and the other side is still struggling to learn the game, one PR professional can single-handedly control the news.

Among journalists, the slang word for a PR person is "flack." The derivation of this unflattering term is disputed, but most dictionaries trace it to World War II anti-aircraft fire—that incessant ack-ack-ack that befuddles the mind before destroying its victim. As you think about the effects of public relations on the public, consider the following aspects of flacking:

Junkets. In 1977, roughly 1,900 journalists were guests of the Taiwanese government for a week, funded by something called the Pacific Cultural Foundation. Some insisted on picking up their own tabs, but most accepted free airfare, free luxury rooms, and free gourmet meals for themselves and their spouses.[52] In February, 1978, Braniff International Airlines hosted more than 50 journalists on a pre-inaugural celebration of its newly approved Dallas-to-London flight. Braniff dubbed its 747 "Fat Albert" for the trip.[53] The payoff for junkets like these is publicity, presumably favorable publicity. Whether reporters should accept them is a hotly debated ethical issue (see pp. 95-96). But no one questions the ethics of offering them.

Borrowed credibility. In 1978, the White House began producing taped radio spots that sounded just like news reports, except that they were naturally favorable to President Carter. Some 600 radio stations were invited to call a toll-free number to record the spots for their own use. "We're leaving it up to the radio stations to identify the source of the tapes," explained Walt Wurfel, an aide to Presidential press secretary Jody Powell.[54] Stations that didn't bother to do so, of course, could pretend to have a White House reporter on staff, while the White House borrowed the credibility of journalism for its PR.

Stonewalling and Misdirection. PR people struggle mightily to avoid lying to the media, but when faced with a tough question it's acceptable to decline to answer, to say you'll have to check into it, or to answer the question you wish you'd been asked instead. In extremis, you can even bend the truth a bit. In 1980 when Jimmy Carter decided to go ahead with plans to rescue the hostages in Iran, White House spokesman Jody Powell decided that the best way to keep the plans secret was to supply the press with misleading information. Powell actually told reporters to look for possible military action in mid-May—many weeks later than the date already planned for the rescue attempt. When journalists questioned Powell's credibility following the failure of the mission, he said, "I gave responses to questions that I felt were necessary to protect our mission. . . . If I had it to do over again, I'd do it."[55]

Ballyhoo. In 1977, Paramount Pictures helped stage a three-inning baseball game in New York's Central Park between a team from its new movie *The Bad News Bears in Breaking Training* and a team of "orphan girls" from the Broadway musical *Annie.* This typical publicity stunt produced the normal ration of local coverage—but Paramount was after more. It videotaped the game and hired sportscaster Heywood Hale Broun to do the commentary. Out of the tape it made two TV news spots, and sent them to stations around the country. Fifteen stations ran the spots immediately, and Paramount estimated that a hundred stations would use them eventually. ABC's "A.M. America" inserted its own narration and gave the stunt nationwide play.[56]

Our purpose in telling these stories is not to suggest that public-relations people are unethical. The point, rather, is that few public-relations people would find anything unethical in these stories. It is up to journalists to cover Taiwan and Braniff without feeling indebted for a free trip, to identify the White House spots as coming from the White House, to dig elsewhere for clues to the rescue plans, and to give Paramount's baseball game only as much coverage as it deserves. That journalists sometimes fail to live up to these high standards, that the seamier tactics of public relations are so often successful, is merely the publicist's good fortune.

PR PROFESSIONALS

The 1960 Census listed 31,141 public-relations people. By 1970 the figure had more than doubled to 75,852. The Department of Labor estimated 115,000 PR people in 1976, and predicted a climb to at least 134,000 by 1985. Public relations, obviously, is a growth field.

The largest single employer of PR people is the federal government. The armed services lead the list with 1,340 public-information specialists. The Department of Health, Education and Welfare employed about a thousand PR professionals when it was a single agency; now that the Department of Education has splintered off, the combined total is probably higher. Even the unsung Department of Agriculture employs more than 750 public-relations personnel.[57]

The largest public-relations operations outside of government are Hill & Knowlton (with 672 employees and $22.5 million in billings in 1978) and Burson-Marstoller (with 670 employees and $22.1 million in billings in the same year).[58] Both are PR agencies with a wide range of corporate and institutional clients. Next come the PR departments of major corporations—General Motors with 180 PR people, AT&T with 130, etc.

But the typical PR person does not work for these giants. According to a survey conducted in 1976-77 by Scott M. Cutlip and Allen H. Center, roughly a third of the nation's PR people work for the thousand largest operations, while "the larger part of the remaining two-thirds is spread among thousands of departments and counseling firms having fewer than six employees."[59]

On the average, PR people are both better paid and better educated than newspaper journalists. They are also happier with their jobs.[60] The typical PR professional is between 30 and 50 years old, and earns between $20,000 and $35,000 a year. Years ago virtually every PR person was an ex-journalist—and plenty of reporters still make the mid-career shift into public relations. But most new PR employees today have never worked as reporters. Many college and university journalism departments, in fact, now send more students each year to PR jobs than to newspapers.

What do they do in these jobs? Many write press releases, stage pseudo-events, plan junkets, arrange interviews, and engage in various other efforts to influence the content of the mass media. But while this sort of general public relations is undoubtedly the most important aspect of PR from the nonprofessional's perspective, it probably doesn't employ the largest number of PR people. Consider the following activities well below the tip of the iceberg.

PR people write annual reports, quarterly reports, profits-and-earnings statements, and other information for stockholders and potential stockholders. They also disseminate this information to the specialized financial press, and directly to stock brokers, pension funds, and the rest of the investment community. And they plan the annual stockholders' meetings.

PR people staff the customer relations departments of manufacturing companies and retail stores. They're the ones who have to read your letters of complaint, and who eventually get around to answering them.

PR people write and edit the tens of thousands of employee newsletters produced in this country. They deal with the suggestion box at the factory, the bulletin board in the office, the company picnic and the company Little League team.

PR people plan and execute the slide shows that turn up at trade conventions, the filmstrips that are distributed free to school systems, the "shorts" that stretch out the program at some movie theaters, the videotapes that are used to train new employees and indoctrinate old ones, the photo displays that hang on the walls of public libraries, and dozens of other visual media of all sorts.

PR people coordinate the mountains of documentation that precede government approval to market a new drug, open a new airline route, or build a new factory. And if approval is hard to get, they turn up as lobbyists at the appropriate regulatory agency or legislative committee.

PR people send specialized press releases on products and services to the trade magazines that circulate to potential customers. They send the same information to potential customers themselves, in countless form letters and sales brochures.

PR people give speeches to the Elks Club and the Junior Chamber of Commerce. They produce the directions for assembling a bicycle and taking a medicine. They ghost-write the policy statements of top executives. They take school children on guided tours of company headquarters. They give corporate money to some charities and politely turn down others. Whatever needs doing to keep the organization looking good to all its various constituencies, PR people do it.

A lot of this may sound a bit dreary to you. Certainly there is plenty of routine work to be done in public relations, as in most occupations. But increasingly, PR is as much involved in making policy as in carrying it out.

Until the 1960s, public relations was essentially a fancy name for publicity. The goal of media PR, for example, was simply to get the employer's name into the papers in a favorable context, in the hope that this would somehow contribute to product recognition, good will, and ultimately sales and profits. Public relations began changing when business, government, and other institutions began encountering powerful adver-

CRISIS PR

A week after the nuclear accident at Three Mile Island, the Metropolitan Edison utility retained the nation's largest PR agency, Hill & Knowlton. There wasn't a lot the agency could do in the face of such monumental bad publicity, but it tried. "We advised them on what they might expect," explained senior vice-president Richard C. Hyde.

The advice would have helped more before the accident. Knowing that a crisis inevitably comes along from time to time, many corporations ship their top executives off for advance training in coping with an angry public. The trainers, of course, are the big PR agencies like Hill & Knowlton.

Burson-Marsteller, for example, operates "Crisisport," a hypothetical community where executives find themselves defending their companies before actors playing skeptical city council members, enraged environmentalists, or cynical TV interviewers.[61]

In a 1979 column, syndicated humorist Art Buchwald imagined what such training might be like. Buchwald's class is taught by Prof. Heinrich Applebaum of the Stonewall School of Business. The student, Bensinger, represents the Windfall Oil Company:

"Mr. Bensinger, the DOE says that you overcharged your customers by $1 billion. What do you say to that?"

Bensinger wet his lips. "It's a dirty, contemptible lie."

Applebaum broke in: "No, Bensinger, a company spokesman must keep his cool under media questioning. Your response should be, 'We don't wish to comment on the matter until we've read the charges.' " . . .

"Do you intend to return any of that money to your customers?"

Bensinger answered, "These are political charges made by a vindictive administration whose one aim is to get a large tax on all oil profits."

"Very good, Bensinger," said Applebaum. "How did you come up with that one?"

"I saw it on the Cronkite show last night." . . .

"Mr. Bensinger, the people think the oil companies are ripping them off. The report from the DOE seems to confirm this. How can you establish your credibility?"

"You've seen our TV commercials. It's up to the public to decide whether they want to believe Bob Hope or some flunky who works for the government."

"Bravo," said Applebaum. "I'm giving you a B—. I might have given you an A if you weren't perspiring so much. . . ."[62]

As usual, Buchwald's burlesque is close to the mark. At a genuine 1980 training session for utility executives, the Reddy Communications agency rehearsed its students in such techniques as restating hostile questions in neutral language, directing answers at the audience instead of the questioner (so a follow-up question is harder to get in), and using body language to project sincerity and concern.

saries. In the pressure-cooker environment of the 1970s, the views of various publics on a wide range of issues had a direct, visible impact on the fortunes of companies and agencies. It was no longer enough for PR people to publicize what the employer was doing; they were now expected to suggest what the employer *ought* to be doing in order to build and maintain public support. PR moved from tactics to strategy, and PR people started speaking up in top-level staff meetings.

"Fifteen or twenty years ago, you could be in this business with a mimeograph machine," explains Harold Burson, chairman of Burson-Marsteller. "There was no real thought of why you wanted the client's name in the paper or what it would accomplish other than recognition and goodwill. Now you want to communicate such-and-such to such-and-such audience so you will be able to do thus-and-so better."[63] *Business Week* summarized the trend in a special 1979 report entitled "The Corporate Image: PR to the Rescue." Top executives, the magazine said, "now recognize public relations as a tool for problem-solving as well as attention-getting."[64]

This is undoubtedly good news for PR people, who have often been stuck between a public that distrusted them and an employer that ignored them. Whether it is good news for the public remains to be seen. Perhaps increasingly powerful PR professionals will convince their employers to be more responsive to public views and needs. Or perhaps they will simply hone their manipulative skills and try to engineer public views and needs to accord with those of their employers.

Either way, public relations is here to stay. So is advertising. The mass media and the economic system depend on them both, and society as we know it could not exist without them. The power of advertising and PR—for good or for harm—is unquestionable. When you make a list of mass media and related institutions, do not forget to include them. And if your list is in order of influence on American civilization, do not forget to put them near the top.

Notes

1 Meyer Weinberg, *TV in America* (New York: Ballantine Books, 1962), pp. 46-47.

2 Lawrence B. Christopher, "Clark Oil Finds Out TV Really Works," *Broadcasting*, March 2, 1970, pp. 42-44.

3 Theodore Peterson, Jay W. Jensen, and William L. Rivers, *The Mass Media and Modern Society* (New York: Holt, Rinehart and Winston, 1965), p. 191.

4 Weinberg, *TV in America*, p. 194.

5 John Kenneth Galbraith, *The New Industrial State* (Boston: Houghton Mifflin, 1967), pp. 37-38, 201.

6 Dallas Smythe, "Five Myths of Consumership," *Nation*, January 20, 1969, p. 82.

7 Erich Fromm, *Escape from Freedom* (New York: Farrar & Rinehart, 1941).

8 *The World Almanac and Book of Facts 1981* (New York: Newspaper Enterprise Association, 1980), p. 415.

9 Craig R. Whitney, "Germans Upset about TV Commercials," *New York Times*, September 22, 1974, p. 20.

10 Bernard Rosenberg and David Manning White, eds., *Mass Culture: The Popular Arts in America* (New York: The Free Press, 1957), pp. 465-66.

11 "The Art of Selling," *Newsweek*, December 20, 1971, p. 85.

12 Edwin McDowell, "The Reselling of the DC-10," *New York Times*, July 22, 1979, pp. F1, F11.

13 Joel Swerdlow, "Mobil Fables—Volume II," *Washington Journalism Review*, June, 1980, p. 13.

14 Les Brown, "3 Stations Bar Mobil Series Over Ads," *New York Times*, January 24, 1980, p. C19. "Sponsorship and Censorship," *Time*, February 11, 1980, pp. 67, 69.

15 Swerdlow, "Mobil Fables," p. 13.

16 "Airlines' Sexy Ads May Cause 'Spontaneous Lack of Enthusiasm,'" *New Brunswick* (N.J.) *Home News*, June 30, 1974, p. A8 (Associated Press).

17 Caryl Rivers, "How To Be Spotless, Sexy, and Loved," *New York Times*, April 28, 1974, p. D15.

18 Philip H. Dougherty, "Female Role in TV Spots Studied," *New York Times*, November 14, 1974, p. 82.

19 Philip H. Dougherty, "Redbook's Approach to Women," *New York Times*, December 9, 1974, p. 60.

20 Barbara Lovenheim, "Admen Woo the Working Woman," *New York Times*, June 18, 1978, business section, pp. 1, 13.

21 Anne Quindlen, "Women in TV Ads: The Old Image Lingers," *New York Times*, May 16, 1978.

22 Harry J. Skornia, *Television and Society* (New York: McGraw-Hill, 1965), p. 96.

23 John Leonard, "Private Lives," *New York Times*, February 27, 1980.

24 George Comstock, "The Impact of Television on American Institutions," in Michael Emery and Ted Smythe, eds., *Readings in Mass Communication*, 4th ed. (Dubuque, Iowa: Wm. C. Brown, 1980), pp. 39-40.

25 Charlene Brown, Trevor R. Brown, and William L. Rivers, *The Media and the People* (New York: Holt, Rinehart & Winston, 1978), p. 406.

26 S. W. Dunn and A. M. Barban, *Advertising: Its Role in Modern Marketing*, 4th ed. (Hinsdale, Ill.: Dryden Press, 1978), pp. 75-76.

27 Philip H. Dougherty, "Fresh Start: Colgate's Best Effort," *New York Times*, June 9, 1980, p. D12.

28 *Ibid.*

29 "F.T.C. Upheld on Listerine's Ads as Supreme Court Bars a Review," *New York Times*, April 4, 1978.

30 Philip H. Dougherty, "Advertising," *New York Times*, June 16, 1980, p. D9.

31 Ralph Keyes, "Love Bug Bite Rise," *More*, February, 1977, p. 33.

32 "Secret Voices," *Time*, September 10, 1979, p. 71.

33 Wilson Bryan Key, *Subliminal Seduction* (New York: Signet, 1973), p. 11.

34 Allen D. Calvin, "Subliminal Perception: Some Negative Findings," *Journal of Applied Psychology*, 1959.

35 Joel Saegert, "Another Look at Subliminal Perception," *Journal of Advertising Research*, February, 1979. Lloyd H. Silverman, "Psychoanalytic Theory: The Reports of My Death Are Greatly Exaggerated," *American Psychologist*, September, 1976.

36 "Secret Voices," p. 71.

37 "Open Season on the FTC," *Time*, December 3, 1979, p. 84. Irwin B. Arieff, "Should the FTC Ban Children's Commercials?" *TV Guide*, April 21, 1979, pp. 8-14. A. O. Sulzberger Jr., "House, in Compromise, Votes to Restrain F.T.C.," *New York Times*, May 21, 1980, p. D10. A. O. Sulzberger Jr., "Will F.T.C. Battle Inhibit Regulation?" *New York Times*, May 22, 1980, pp. D1, D6.

38 Radio and Television Codes.

39 Peterson, Jensen, and Rivers, *Mass Media and Modern Society*, p. 191.

40 David B. Sachsman, *Public Relations Influence on Environmental Coverage* (Ph.D. dissertation, Stanford University, 1973), pp. 276-80.

41 *Ibid.*, pp. 50, 275.

42 *Ibid.*, pp. 278-79.

43 Brit Hume and Mark McIntyre, "Polishing Up the Brass," [*MORE*], May, 1973, p. 6.

44 Lynda Lee Kaid, "Newspaper Treatment of a Candidate's News Releases," *Journalism Quarterly*, Spring, 1976, pp. 135-137.

45 Joanne A. Ambrosio, "It's in the Journal. But This is Reporting?" *Columbia Journalism Review*, March/April, 1980, pp. 34-35.

46 Scott M. Cutlip, "Third of Newspapers' Content PR-Inspired," *Editor & Publisher*, May 26, 1962, p. 68.

47 James Manion, "Handbook Defines Press Rela-

tions," *New Brunswick* (N.J.) *Home News*, October 11, 1979, p. 46 (Associated Press).

48 "Guide for Publicity Chairmen," *Somerset* (N.J.) *Spectator*, December 30, 1971, p. 4.

49 Sachsman, *Public Relations Influence on Environmental Coverage*, pp. 256-59.

50 *Ibid.*

51 Sherman Morse, "An Awakening in Wall Street," *American Magazine*, September, 1906, p. 460.

52 "Taiwan Woos Press with 7-Day Junkets," *Editor & Publisher*, June 24, 1978, p. 22.

53 Dave McNeely, "Come Along on Fat Albert's Big Junket," *Quill*, April, 1978, p. 30.

54 Terence Smith, "Free Taped Radio Spots Will Be Provided By the White House to 600 U.S. Stations," *New York Times*, December 2, 1978, p. 12.

55 Steven R. Weisman, "How Jody Powell Misled Press on U.S. Aim in Iran," *New York Times*, May 2, 1980.

56 "Par Publicity Tests Video Feed; Stunt Baseball Proves Effective," *Variety*, August 3, 1977, p. 6.

57 Dom Bonafede, "Uncle Sam: The Flimflam Man?" *Washington Journalism Review*, April/May, 1978, pp. 70-71.

58 Elizabeth M. Fowler, "A Guide to Public Relations," *New York Times*, October 17, 1979.

59 Scott M. Cutlip and Allen H. Center, *Effective Public Relations*, 5th ed. (Englewood Cliffs, N.J.: Prentice-Hall, 1978), p. 21.

60 Oguz Nayman, Blaine K. McKee, and Dan L. Lattimore, "PR Personnel and Print Journalists: A Comparison of Professionalism," *Journalism Quarterly*, Autumn, 1977, pp. 492-497.

61 Stan Luxenberg, "Image Agencies Thrive on Crises," *New York Times*, July 29, 1979, p. F9.

62 Art Buchwald, "How to Be a Corporation Spokesman," November 20, 1979.

63 "The Corporate Image: PR to the Rescue," *Business Week*, January 22, 1979, p. 49.

64 *Ibid.*, p. 56.

Suggested Readings

ARLEN, MICHAEL J., *Thirty Seconds*. New York: Farrar, Straus & Giroux, 1980.

BARNOUW, ERIK, *The Sponsor*. New York: Oxford University Press, 1978.

BONAFEDE, DOM, "Uncle Sam: The Flimflam Man?" *Washington Journalism Review*, April/May, 1978.

"The Corporate Image: PR to the Rescue," *Business Week,* January 22, 1979.

CUTLIP, SCOTT M., and ALLEN H. CENTER, *Effective Public Relations,* 5th ed. Englewood Cliffs, N.J.: Prentice-Hall, 1978.

DELLA FEMINA, JERRY, *From Those Wonderful Folks Who Gave You Pearl Harbor.* New York: Pocket Books, 1970.

DUNN, S. W., and A. M. BARBAN, *Advertising: Its Role in Modern Marketing,* 4th ed. Hinsdale, Ill.: Dryden Press, 1978.

KEY, WILSON BRYAN, *Subliminal Seduction.* New York: Signet, 1973.

KLEPPNER, OTTO, *Advertising Procedure,* 7th ed. Englewood Cliffs, N.J.: Prentice-Hall, 1979.

McCLURE, DONOVAN, "The Woes of a Government PR Man," *Washington Monthly,* February, 1978.

NAYMAN, OGUZ, BLAINE K. McKEE, and DAN L. LATTIMORE, "PR Personnel and Print Journalists: A Comparison of Professionalism," *Journalism Quarterly,* Autumn, 1977.

OGILVY, DAVID, *Confessions of an Advertising Man.* New York: Ballantine, 1963.

PACKARD, VANCE, *The Hidden Persuaders.* New York: Pocket Books, 1957.

PATTON, PHIL, "Fowl Play: The Great Chicken War," *New York,* November 19, 1979.

RUBIN, DAVID M., "Anatomy of a Snow Job," *[MORE],* March, 1974.

SACHSMAN, DAVID B., "Public Relations Influence on Coverage of Environment in San Francisco Area," *Journalism Quarterly,* Spring, 1976.

TAN, ALEXIS S., "TV Beauty Ads and Role Expectations of Adolescent Female Viewers," *Journalism Quarterly,* Summer, 1979.

PART IV
COVERAGE

We come now to the last section of the book, "Coverage." In earlier sections we talked about the functions and effects of the media. We detailed their history. We traced the patterns of media control by various groups and individuals, from governments to publishers. We examined each medium in turn to see what made it unique. Now, finally, it is time to turn to content. In a sense, the first three-quarters of the book was intended to show why the media perform the way they do. This section is intended to evaluate the performance itself.

Nearly 400 pages ago, we listed four functions of the mass media—to serve the economic system, to inform, to entertain, and to influence. It should be obvious by now that the authors consider the second of these functions by far the most important. In the chapters that follow, therefore, we will be interested in only one question: How well do the mass media inform the public?

Before evaluating the quality of news coverage, it is essential to consider standards of evaluation. Nothing is good or bad in itself; it is good or bad with respect to some standard. The following are the most important of the many standards that have been proposed and used by the media and media critics.

1. Profitability. The American mass media are, for the most part, privately owned and privately financed. Unless they earn a profit, they will fail. And a newspaper or broadcast station in imminent danger of failure is unlikely to spend much money improving its news operation. A mass medium that earns a lot of money may still do a poor job of covering the news. But one that loses money almost always does a poor job.

2. Audience Satisfaction. Like profitability, audience satisfaction is a necessary but not a sufficient condition for media quality. If nobody reads a newspaper article it can accomplish nothing—but many articles are well read and still accomplish nothing.

3. Accuracy. An inaccurate news story is always, without exception, a poor news story. Most editors and reporters know this, and strive mightily to spell the names right, even if they do not fully understand what their sources are saying.

4. Objectivity. Nearly all responsible journalists aim at objectivity, and quite often they fail. Words have connotations as well as denotations; they imply more than they say. As long as reporters must work with words, complete objectivity is impossible. And even an "objective" reporter must decide whom to interview, what to ask, and which facts to include in the story. Fairness is a reasonable standard to ask of journalists. Literal objectivity is not.

5. Advocacy. Ideologically committed journalists often complain that where one side is right and the other is wrong, objectivity is a false god. Was objectivity a good thing in the 1950s, when it forced the media to be "fair" to the self-serving allegations of the leader of that decade's anti-communist witch hunt, Senator Joseph McCarthy? Journalists whose goal is advocacy, who wish to convince their readers of some point of view, have little use for objectivity.

6. Unusualness. Most editors urge their reporters to find stories that are distinctive, dramatic, or in some way unusual. If overused, this standard becomes more a definition of sensationalism than of news. If the media ignore what is typical and stress what is weird, they inevitably present us with a weird picture of the world. Nonetheless, "man bites dog" is still a bigger story than "dog bites man."

7. Relevance. Relevant news is important news. What kinds of stories are most relevant?—those that are local, timely, and directly useful to the audience. This standard, too, is sometimes overemphasized. The most local, timely, and useful stories around, after all, are the supermarket ads.

8. Completeness. The *New York Times* is the most complete newspaper in the country. But not for everything—it is weak in sports, photos, and editorial cartoons. And is the most complete medium always the best medium? A three-hour TV news show is

hardly three times as good as a one-hour show, especially if you're waiting for a particular story. When we demand completeness, what we are really asking for is a sample of the news that is adequately large and appropriately varied. We are talking about selection.

9. Independence. However a medium selects its news, its judgments should be its own, and should not be influenced by outside pressures. If a newspaper kills a story because a big advertiser insists on it, then it is a poor newspaper—not because it killed the story (maybe it didn't deserve to run), but because it deferred to the wishes of an advertiser. Independence is absolutely essential for good journalism.

10. Propriety. The mass media have an obligation to keep within the bounds of propriety and good taste. But what are those bounds? Some business executives think it's in poor taste to report declining sales figures. Some revolutionaries think it's in good taste to report do-it-yourself bomb-making techniques. Most editors disagree—on both counts.

11. Comprehensibility. As the world grows more complicated, it becomes less and less adequate for reporters to stick to the bare facts in their reporting. The facts of the energy crisis, the facts of inflation, the facts of racial unrest, are not the entire story of these events. Interpretation is essential to put the facts into a meaningful context, to make them comprehensible to the reader or viewer.

12. Uniqueness. Democracy is predicated on the assumption that all kinds of news and opinions are available to the public, competing in the free market of ideas. The trouble with this assumption is that most of the media today are not ideological competitors. They all say pretty much the same things, and that isn't healthy. We therefore propose the standard of uniqueness. Any mass medium that is significantly different from its competitors is in this sense "better" than one that is undifferentiated. New York City is better off with both the *Times* and the *Daily News* than it would be with two papers like the *Times*. Offbeat media should be cherished.

We have listed a dozen standards. We could list a hundred, but this isn't the place for it. The point to be stressed here is that judgments of quality are meaningless without explicit criteria. Go ahead and criticize the mass media; you're as qualified as anyone else. But first make sure you know what your standards are.

Chapter 15
Coverage of National Government

According to the libertarian theory of press-government relations, the media serve the public best when they act as aggressive watchdogs over government activities. But in practice this adversary relationship is very difficult to achieve and sustain. The government official most often subjected to an adversary press is undoubtedly the president of the United States. Yet news coverage of the president is at least as much a product of White House news management as of aggressive, independent reporting.

The heroic, hard-drinking "typical" journalist of movie fame had a lot of flaws. But in at least one way this stereotype captured an American ideal. The movie reporter's attitude toward government officials was always magnificently suspicious and uncompromising. Inevitably, our hero wound up the third reel with a crusading exposé on the abuse of public trust by a public official—and to hell with the repercussions.

This movie stereotype is solidly grounded in historical reality. "The United States had a press before it had a foreign policy," notes *New York Times* columnist James Reston. "The American press was telling the coun-

try and the world where to get off before there was a State Department. . . . In their more amiable moods, [early American journalists] no doubt conceded that the press should serve the country, but they insisted that the best way to serve it was to criticize its every act and thought, and something of this pugnacious spirit has persisted until now."[1]

THE ADVERSARY RELATIONSHIP

Critic and scholar William L. Rivers has a name for this attitude. He calls it "the adversary relationship," and he considers it the basis for all good coverage of government.[2] Every government official, Rivers explains, has a job to do—passing laws, running a federal agency, or whatever. Reporters also have a job to do—informing the public about everything that goes on, including what goes on within the government. Sometimes the reporter's job and the official's job coincide; they work together and everybody is happy. But sometimes their jobs come into conflict. Either the official wants to publish something that the reporter considers inaccurate or unnewsworthy, or the reporter wants to publish something that the official would prefer to keep secret. That's when the adversary relationship comes into play.

If the reporter goes along with the official's view on what should and should not be printed, then he or she is not a good reporter. A journalist who consistently complies with the wishes of government officials has abdicated the responsibility of the media to act as the public's watchdog. A good reporter, by definition, does not take official statements at face value, refuses to protect the image of office-holders, persists in asking embarrassing questions, and fights for the answers. A good reporter, in short, is an adversary.

The adversary relationship doesn't mean simply that reporters and government officials should get mad at each other occasionally. It means that they should both respect the inevitability—even the desirability—of conflict. Officials often have good reasons for hiding or distorting the truth, at least temporarily. Journalists have good reasons for seeking the truth and releasing it to the public. For the adversary relationship to function properly, each must accept as valid the goals of the other, and the conflict that results.

It is worth stressing that the adversary relationship is a peculiarly American notion of the proper attitude of the media vis-à-vis the government. Throughout most of the world and most of history, the job of the media has been to publish whatever the government wants published. A good reporter in seventeenth-century England or twentieth-century Russia is defined as a reporter who gets the official line right and repeats it effectively.

Only in libertarian societies are the mass media a sort of "fourth branch of government," assigned the task of checking up on the other three branches. And only in a democracy must a good reporter be a hard-headed, two-fisted uncompromising skeptic— the kind of person you might make a movie about.

Journalism professors have been talking about the concept of an adversary relationship for decades. Between 1969 and 1974, lots of other people started talking about it too—and not always with approval. A series of bloody battles between the Nixon administration and the media during this period led many observers to question the value of an adversary press. The media's longstanding dislike for Richard Nixon, they charged, was producing exaggerated and sensational coverage of the illegal burglary, wiretapping, and cover-up activities now known as Watergate. And Richard Nixon's longstanding dislike for the media, they added, was largely responsible for the very abuses that eventually led to the president's downfall.

For the first time in recent history, Americans had a president who announced to his subordinates that the press is the enemy, meant it, and acted upon it. And for the first time in recent history, it seemed that the press really was the enemy, successfully hounding the nation's chief executive out of office. If this is what the adversary relationship is all about, many Americans concluded, then it is the wrong model for press-government relations in the United States.

First Amendment expert Harry Kalven believes that the media should treat the government as an adversary, but that the government must not fight back by criticizing the media. "There is no way the government can operate in this area as a polite critic," he says, "and a less-than-polite critic is bound to produce a chilling effect upon those being criticized. . . . The Constitution really does intend to guarantee one-way tension, through a one-way adversary system."[3]

Despite Kalven's argument, it seems unrealistic to expect a president to welcome an adversary press. In any battle between president and press, the Constitution protects the press much more than the president. But when the media use that protection to attack the president, the president will inevitably fight back with secrecy, harassment, news management, and any other available weapon. Not every president will resort to illegal tactics, as Richard Nixon did. But the temptation will always be there. That, too, is part of the adversary relationship.

Another danger of the adversary relationship is the ever-present possibility that in a battle between the press and the government, the people may wind up on the government's side, and may strip the media of their cherished freedoms. Political scientist Ithiel de Sola Pool expresses this fear most cogently:

> No nation will indefinitely tolerate a freedom of the press that serves to divide the country and to open the floodgates of criticism against the freely chosen government that leads it. The notion among some newsmen that the press can be at one with the people in combat with the common enemy, the government, is a self-destructive delusion. More often in a democracy the government is the true expression of the nation's feelings. The press may be surprised at who is St. George and who is the dragon. . . . If the press is the government's enemy, it is the free press that will end up being destroyed.[4]

The events of the Nixon years provide some support for this analysis. Vice President Agnew's early attacks on the media, for example, struck a responsive chord in many Americans. As the Watergate revelations began to dominate the news, the issue of government credibility slowly replaced the issue of media credibility in the public consciousness. But a poll of California residents in May, 1974, found that 51 percent of them felt there had been too much Watergate coverage, while only 11 percent felt there had been too little. And 31 percent believed the coverage had been unfair and biased against the president.[5]

Even after Nixon resigned, some people viewed his demise as a media plot. "Congratulations," wrote one woman to the *New York Times*, "on the wonderful hatchet job you did on Richard Nixon! You staged a beautiful crucifixion all the way."[6]

But remember that it took two years of sustained coverage, an aroused Congress and public, an honest special prosecutor, an incredible collection of incriminating tapes, and a dozen participants-turned-witnesses to topple the only president ever to resign from that office. Though the Watergate experience does demonstrate the power of the media, it also demonstrates the almost inexhaustible news-management resources of the government. The wonder is not so much that Nixon was finally forced to resign; the wonder is that he almost got away with it.

The mass media's violent hostility to President Nixon during his final years did pose a danger, but it was not the danger that the media could destroy any president who came along. Rather, it was the danger that the media might adopt a Watergate standard of consistent opposition as their new definition of the adversary relationship between press and government. If that had happened, the public might well have turned on its media, and the government would certainly have done so.

But tempers on both sides cooled considerably during the Ford and Carter administrations. Not that either president enjoyed a placid press corps. Ford's "honeymoon" with the media ended after only a few weeks, when he pardoned his predecessor. Carter's lasted a bit longer, then he too was subjected to extensive press criticism—not just for his handling of policy matters, but also for his problems with budget director Bert Lance (charged with financial irregularities while a Georgia bank president), chief of staff Hamilton Jordan (accused of illegal drug use but never tried for lack of evidence), and brother Billy (forced to register as a lobbyist for the Libyan government). Ford and Carter both found the media less compliant than they'd have liked. But this is merely business as usual for press-president relations. In place of the implacable hatred of the late Nixon years, wariness and skepticism once again characterize the attitude of each adversary toward the other. And that, we think, is the way it should be.

Some observers disagree, fearing that the

adversary relationship still proceeds at too high a level of tension. James Reston, among others, has worried in print that "maybe criticism in this country is going too far, and that, in the process, we are harming the institutions we need the most." For good reasons, Reston acknowledges, the press is determined "to expose the weakness and corruption of government at all levels, but in the process tends to dramatize the worst in everything and everybody."[7]

Critic Tom Bethell takes the opposite stance. In an article entitled "The Myth of an Adversary Press," he argues that "media and government alternately dance together in close embrace and break apart to make confusing gestures of mutual defiance. Much of the time what we are witnessing is the equivalent of a marathon dance, in which media and government lean on each other because they need each other to survive and prosper."[8]

There is truth on both sides. The media *are* more comfortable tearing down than building up, especially when the object of their attention sits in the White House. But the president is not defenseless in this battle. He makes the news, after all, and reporters have little choice but to cover what he says and does. Out of the mix of iconoclasm and collaboration, ideally, comes an adversary relationship that neither goes too far nor falls too short.

BARRIERS TO ADVERSARITY

The problem of too much adversarity surfaced during the Nixon administration for the first time in generations. The more usual problem in news coverage of the government, even today, is too little adversarity. In the real world, as opposed to movies and theories, the adversary relationship has a tough time surviving. Many of the reasons for this will come up later in the chapter, but we will list some of the more important ones now.

1. Friendship. Most government reporters are specialists; they cover the Justice Department or City Hall or the Pentagon full-time. Specialization has many advantages, but one big disadvantage: Reporters are likely to become close personal friends of their news sources. "The more you go out to dinner," said Drew Pearson, "the more friends you make and the more you diminish the number of people you can write about without qualms of conscience or rebukes from your wife."[9] Friendly reporters seldom write embarrassing articles about their friends.

2. Sympathy. Closely related to friendship is the sympathy that often develops between reporters and their major sources. It is good to understand the official's point of view, but if the reporter understands it too well for too long, he or she may come to accept it. It is for this reason that most New York newspapers impose a mid-season shuffle on the reporters who cover the Yankees and the Mets. Such a shuffle would do wonders for Washington coverage.

3. Dependence. Government reporters depend on their sources for everything from front-page scoops to last-paragraph quotes. They are understandably reluctant to do anything to offend them. For years the Senate press corps overlooked the growing financial fortunes of Bobby Baker, a $19,000-a-year Senate employee. It was an outsider who got wind of the story, pursued it, and turned it into a national scandal. The Senate regulars viewed Baker as a vital source of information; they viewed the exposé as a nuisance.

4. Alliance. Many a reporter starts out covering a government agency and winds up working for it—unofficially. Washington is full of such part-time officials. They draft bills, guide press conferences, suggest handouts, and otherwise join in the process of governing. Their reporting, of course, suffers.

5. Complexity. There was a time when most reporters understood (or thought they understood) most news. No longer. Today a government reporter must deal with more than politics. Political writers must discuss the intricacies of inflation, the arms race, energy, pollution, and hundreds of similar topics. To make sense of these issues, they rely heavily on the help of government experts. It is hard to be aggressive and independent in covering a story you don't understand to start with.

6. Secrecy. Government secrecy has already been discussed in considerable detail (see Chapter 6). All we need say here is that a reporter who tries to dig for the truth is very likely to run into an endless series of classified documents and closemouthed sources.

7. Time. Adversary reporting takes time—time to pore over documents and gather statistics, time to find and interview sources who dispute the party line, time to figure out the story behind the story. The typical government reporter, covering breaking news under deadline pressure, barely has time enough to write up the news conferences and edit the press releases. That notebook full of investigative leads, saved for a slow news day, tends to get fuller and fuller.

8. News Management. A large fraction of the public-relations people in the country are employed by government. Their job (see Chapter 6 and Chapter 14) is to manage the news in the best interests of their employer. A PR staff is like a dam. The reporter who uses it as an information source saves a lot of time and effort. But it is the PR people who manage the flow of news; they can drown the reporter with facts or make the reporter die of thirst. And behind the dam, they may be hiding the dirtiest water of all.

These eight barriers to adversarity apply at all levels of government, from the White House to the statehouse to the precinct house. At the lower and less visible levels, they virtually rule out adversary reporting. A journalist who covers, say, the agriculture, labor, and commerce departments is under enormous pressure to get along with sources and get the routine news; there is little counter-pressure to go looking for dirt. A journalist who covers the president, on the other hand, feels both kinds of pressure.

The extraordinary visibility of the president thus gives the adversary relationship a fighting chance. But visibility is a double-edged sword—it also adds to presidential news management. Though presidents inevitably find their total lack of privacy a personal annoyance and a political hindrance, it is very valuable to them as well. To the extent that a president can influence what is written about him, he thereby influences public opinion. The president needs the press—and uses the press—to help him rally support for his programs, opposition for his enemies, and respect for his office. The history of president-press relations is the history of presidential efforts to control the press.

For the first eighty years of American history, presidents controlled the press by sponsoring their own newspapers. President John Adams offered the official Federalist party line in the *Gazette of the United States*. President Thomas Jefferson did the same for the Republicans in the *National Intelligencer*. Each administration supported its party papers with government advertising and joblot printing contracts. Opposition papers had to scrounge for private funds.

This state of affairs continued until 1860, when President-elect Lincoln refused to establish an official newspaper. Instead, he utilized the Government Printing Office, thus ending the use of printing contracts as hidden subsidies. Suddenly the president was on his own in his relations with reporters. During the Civil War, Henry Villard of the Associated Press became the first reporter assigned to cover the president full-time. A few years later, in the wake of Lincoln's assassination, Andrew Johnson became the first president to be formally interviewed by an independent, unaligned reporter.

After the Civil War, Congress grew in importance and the presidency declined. Press relations were casual. One reporter won a five-dollar bet by ringing up President Grover Cleveland on the new telephone to ask if there was any news. Cleveland reportedly answered the phone himself, and told the reporter he could safely go to bed.

In the 1880s, public interest in the president began to rise again. The stage was set for a president who could capitalize on that interest to wrest control of the government from Congress. That president was Theodore Roosevelt.

Roosevelt was the first president to realize that he could manipulate the media to mold the public. He set up permanent White House quarters for the press. He permitted several reporters to interview him every day while he was being shaved. He ordered his secretary, William Loeb Jr., to act as press liaison. He invented the tactic of releasing news on Sunday to take advantage of the wide-open Monday-morning front page. Comments Elmer E. Cornwell Jr.: "T.R. did not just provide bully entertainment for an enthralled public, but dramatized the potential of the office for affecting the course of public policy by means of a dynamic relationship with the electorate via the mass media."[10]

Roosevelt knew how to take the press off the scent of an embarrassing story. When T.R. backed a Panamanian revolution against Colombia in an effort to get the Canal Zone, the opposition press began to growl. So the president immediately ordered all military officers in Washington to get out and run in the park as part of a physical fitness program. The hilarious misadventures of pot-bellied generals and admirals kept the press corps busy for a week—by which time it had forgotten all about the Canal Zone.

Presidential press relations after Roosevelt are characterized by three tactics: the press conference, the press secretary, and direct use of the broadcast media.

THE PRESS CONFERENCE

The presidential press conference was invented by Woodrow Wilson as a way of giving every reporter a chance and still leaving time in the day for other matters. At first it worked out very well for everybody. Wilson's press conferences were scheduled twice a week and were open to all accredited reporters.

Franklin Roosevelt made great use of Wilson's invention, holding over 900 press conferences in his thirteen years in office. Unlike Wilson, F.D.R. refused to be quoted directly. But he was unfailingly frank and open with reporters, often devoting an entire conference to a single topic. At this point, the press conference was still a convenience for both the reporter and the president.

Then came Truman. Faced with an increasingly huge press corps, including more and more foreign journalists, Truman gradually abandoned Roosevelt's easygoing press conference style. He stopped trying to explain the thinking behind his decisions, stopped concentrating on a single topic in each conference, and stopped chatting informally with reporters before and after. Everything became much more formal. A reporter would rise, ask a question, and sit; the president would carefully recite his answer, then turn to the next reporter.

The crowning blow came in 1951, when Truman began taping his press conferences for release to radio. Forced to weigh every word for its possible effects, Truman made the conferences even less lively, less useful than before. He ignored the information needs of the press and public, and concentrated on making a good performance. The press conference was becoming a tool of news management.

Two new wrinkles were added in the

Eisenhower years. First, Ike began using the first few minutes of each half-hour conference to read a prepared statement, encouraging reporters to stress that statement in their articles. Second, Eisenhower had his press secretary, James Hagerty, arrange for friendly reporters to ask the questions the president wanted to answer. Both the prepared statement and the planted question have since become press conference staples.

The Kennedy administration was the first to permit live television broadcasts of press conferences, and this too has become standard procedure. Television has reduced the reporter to a participant in a stage show. It is not unusual to see newspaper journalists at press conferences not bothering to take notes; many readers will see the thing on TV anyhow, and a complete transcript will be available minutes after the end. It is also quite common for reporters to ask pointless questions (or sit next to someone who asks intelligent ones) simply in order to be seen on TV by their editors.

Press conferences today are scheduled at the president's pleasure, and are conducted according to the president's rules. The ingredients are now pretty well standardized: a big room, hundreds of reporters, dozens of cameras and microphones, a prepared statement, several planted questions with prepared answers, and perhaps four or five spontaneous questions with little discussion or follow-up. It's not surprising that Tom Wicker of the *New York Times* calls the press conference "more an instrument of presidential power than a useful tool of the press."[11]

Even so, presidents are not always anxious to hold one. The frequency of presidential press conferences hit its height at the beginning, with Wilson's twice-a-week schedule. Roosevelt averaged 83 conferences a year; Truman, 40; Eisenhower, 20; Kennedy, 21; Johnson, 25. Then came Richard Nixon, the most reclusive of all recent presidents. He averaged eight press conferences a year

until Watergate, then avoided the Washington press corps almost completely.

Ford and Carter both tried to revive the press conference as a useful way to communicate with press and public. Carter managed 51 conferences in his first 30 months in office, about tied with Eisenhower and Kennedy. But in July, 1979, he faced the first major PR crisis of his term, public dissatisfaction with his handling of inflation, recession, and energy. He retreated to Camp David to think, then emerged and announced that the Washington press corps was part of the problem. He was doing a good job, the president and his aides maintained, but somehow the media coverage wasn't reflecting the reality. In the next eight months—before he took to the stump to campaign for re-election—Carter held only five Washington press conferences.[12]

Instead, Carter adopted a Nixon innovation—local and regional press conferences to escape the "insular mentality" (i.e. critical approach) of the Washington press corps. He also arranged "town meetings" at which he answered questions from private citizens, with reporters limited to covering the proceedings. And he borrowed a time-tested technique that dates back at least to Franklin Roosevelt—private talks with reporters from the major media, under a ground rule that forbade them to reveal that the president was their source. All three tactics, Carter felt, served his needs better than the traditional Washington press conference.

Since the Johnson years press conferences had become rather chaotic affairs, with reporters fighting noisily for the chance to put their questions to the president. In the early months of his presidency, Ronald Reagan tried to solve the problem. In the interests of decorum, he said, reporters would raise their hands silently and wait to be called on.

Most political reporters feel that the presidential press conference has become largely an empty ritual, one that no longer helps the public get "the truth" from its president.

But most recent presidents have avoided the ritual, preferring other techniques that they could control even more thoroughly. And so the White House press corps winds up fighting—half-heartedly—for more press conferences.

THE PRESS SECRETARY

While President Wilson conducted his twice-weekly press conferences, Joseph P. Tumulty (Wilson's adviser) held daily briefings for reporters. From that time on, presidents came to rely more and more on their press secretaries.

So did reporters. From 1933 to 1945, President Roosevelt's press secretaries were never once quoted in the media. Truman's press secretaries were quoted only once. But James Hagerty, Eisenhower's press secretary, was named hundreds of times as a source of news about the president.[13] And the names of later press secretaries—Pierre Salinger, George Christian, Bill Moyers, Ron Ziegler, Ron Nessen, Jody Powell—were as well known to the public as those of the more prominent Senators and cabinet officials.

As the number of presidential press conferences has declined, the importance of the press secretary has soared. The average White House correspondent writes at least a story a day. Yet most reporters count themselves lucky if they actually get to talk to the president once a month. The bulk of the news about the president therefore comes, not from the president, but from his press secretary.

Press secretaries have a tricky job. They

WHY WOODWARD AND BERNSTEIN?

The two journalistic sleuths who did the most to unravel the mysteries of Watergate were Bob Woodward and Carl Bernstein, both young *Washington Post* reporters whose regular beats were not the White House or even the federal government. Woodward had done some investigative pieces on police corruption and unsanitary Washington restaurants; Bernstein had written on rock music and covered the local courts and city hall. For lack of anyone else, they were assigned to cover the odd break-in at the Democratic National Committee headquarters in the Watergate complex on Saturday, June 17, 1972.[15]

With very little help from the rest of the Washington press corps, and almost none at all from the White House press corps, the two reporters bit by bit established the relationship between the seven burglars and the Oval Office. Why did dozens of White House reporters ignore the biggest news story of the decade that was right under their noses? How did two neophyte journalists succeed where seasoned veterans failed? The answers explain much about the deficiencies of presidential news coverage.

First, White House correspondents are responsible for covering the endless flood of presidential news releases, statements, and speeches, leaving little time for investigation. President Nixon was typical in this regard. He generated roughly 500,000 words a year in his speeches, statements, messages to Congress, press conferences, and interviews. Nor was it unusual that in the seven weeks before the 1972 election, when Watergate was just beginning to heat up, Nixon made forty-one speeches; issued eighteen statements, eighteen proclamations, and twelve declarations; announced eight resignations and thirty-four appointments; and sent ten messages to Congress.[16] That didn't leave White House reporters much time for Watergate.

Second, the White House press corps feels duty-bound to travel with the president wherever he goes, killing substantial periods of time in airplanes and hotel lobbies. This is sometimes called the "assassination mentality"—no one wants to miss out on *that* story.

dare not antagonize the press corps or justify charges of a "credibility gap." So they try to be genuinely useful. They answer factual questions, help set up interviews with presidential assistants, and even use their influence to get important stories released on time. But their first allegiance is, of course, to the president.

The most talented press secretary of modern times was probably James Hagerty. One of his favorite tricks was to release good news from the White House, bad news from anyplace else. A State Department triumph, for example, would always be announced by the president himself; a State Department flop would be announced by the State Department.

Hagerty always held back a few middling stories—the appointment of a new ambassador, say—for the inevitable day when Eisenhower would take off on a golfing trip. Russell Baker explains the ploy:

> If editors demanded a presidential story a day, it follows that reporters will be found to satisfy them one way or another. On days when there is no news, they will poke around darkened rooms, look under the carpet, or start staring at the west wall and adding two and two in news stories. When that sort of thing happens, the White House is in trouble. Hagerty prevented this by seeing to it that there was rarely a newsless day. If there was no news, he made a little.[14]

There is nothing especially evil about these techniques. Most reporters understand

---

Third, the White House press corps is no exception to the rule that reporters eventually come to identify with their sources. Many White House journalists simply couldn't believe that a president would have anything to do with breaking and entering, wiretapping, or obstruction of justice. They were reluctant to face the emerging pattern in the miscellaneous pieces of Watergate information that slowly unfolded.

Fourth, White House reporters are accustomed to dealing with top-level sources. Woodward and Bernstein got most of their information from low-level officials far from the public eye—from secretaries and clerks, from anonymous bureaucrats, from Hugh Sloan, Jr., treasurer of the Committee to Re-Elect the President, etc. The White House press corps, meanwhile, tried to get answers from the big guns, such as Nixon aides H. R. Haldeman and John Ehrlichman. Even before Watergate, these people were pretty inaccessible; R. W. Apple, chief political writer of the New York Times, once spent the day calling seventeen White House officials, and was never called back by any of them.[17] After Watergate, Nixon's top aides were virtually invisible—and so White House reporters had nobody to ask.

Finally, many White House correspondents were afraid of the president's power to make their jobs impossible. When the Washington Post refused to let up on the Watergate story, its longtime society columnist was dropped from the press pool for three White House social events.[18] And several exclusive presidential "scoops" found their way to the Post's competitor, Garnett D. Horner of the Washington Star-News. Horner and his paper were not rocking the boat with Watergate stories.[19] Since they were not assigned to the White House on a daily basis, Woodward and Bernstein cared little about these reprisals. But for the White House press corps, the pressure to conform was strong.

Bill Moyers, presidential press secretary under Lyndon Johnson, sums up the situation this way: "The White House press corps is more stenographic than entrepreneurial in its approach to news gathering. Too many of them are sheep. Sheep with short attention spans. They move on to tomorrow's story without pausing to investigate today's."[20]

that a press secretary's job includes more than a little news management. Good press secretaries, like Hagerty, are able to maintain their reputation for integrity even when protecting their boss's interests.

But Richard Nixon's press secretary, Ron Ziegler, proved incapable of balancing his loyalties to the president against his obligations to the press. A former advertising executive with no prior news experience, Ziegler misled reporters for nearly two years on the involvement of the White House in Watergate. His deteriorating relationship with the media culminated on April 17, 1973, when events forced him to admit that everything he had said about Watergate (including his attacks on the reporters who covered it) was "inoperative." The word instantly became a part of the American vocabulary of satire.

Jimmy Carter's press secretary, Jody Powell, earned high marks from reporters. One of the president's most trusted advisers, Powell usually knew what Carter and the White House inner circle were thinking— and he was able to distinguish their thinking from his own. Though Powell took care not to mislead the media, there were exceptions. His reputation sagged a bit after the hostage rescue mission in Iran; while the White House was planning the mission, Powell had intentionally implied that it was some months off. But even though the mission proved a fiasco, most reporters sympathized with Powell's desire to avoid alerting the Iranian terrorists. Said John Osborne of the *New Republic:* "Only permanent adolescents, idiots and ignoramuses expect a press secretary—or any other governmental spokesman—to tell the whole truth and nothing but the truth all the time." Osborne, who covered presidents for nearly 50 years before his death in 1981, ranked Powell as perhaps the best press secretary with whom he had worked.[21]

Powell had 44 people working for him, about as many as in previous administrations. They were divided into five divisions— news and information; speechwriting; the president's news summaries; liaison with non-Washington media; and logistics for broadcasting.[22] But these 44 people were just the tip of the iceberg. About half of the 500-odd White House employees are engaged in some sort of public information work, including congressional liaison, intergovernmental affairs, correspondence, and relations with such special-interest groups as women, Hispanics, Jews, and labor.[23]

But it is the press secretary, not the staff, who directs the presidential news operation and sets its tone. Any lingering doubts about the importance of the secretary were set to rest in 1981, when an assassination attempt against President Reagan seriously wounded Reagan's press secretary, James Brady. In the hectic hours after the attempt, White House officials gave the media several conflicting and inaccurate stories, including at one point the misinformation that Brady himself was dead. Without Brady's access to the top, Deputy Press Secretary Larry Speakes was unable to sort truth from rumor for reporters.

During the Nixon years, relations between reporters and press secretary Ron Ziegler were often overtly hostile. Though they are much less so today, some members of the White House press corps still use the press secretary's daily briefings as opportunities to bait him into a shouting match. Columnist Meg Greenfield has called these "excesses . . . pretty awful to behold." But she also points out that testiness is not the essence of the adversary relationship, and that reporters and press secretaries must inevitably get along:

> The White House press, having missed some of the major stories of the decade that were taking place under its collective nose, is understandably more prosecutorial in tone these days. But sooner or later it will stop seeing "liars" and "cover-ups" everywhere. . . . The central problem, however, will remain: an institutionalized relationship between White House press and White House press spokesman that is based on mutual necessity, mutual dependence and mutual dissatisfaction.[24]

And it *is* mutual. Press secretaries distrust reporters with as much vehemence, and for as much reason, as reporters distrust press secretaries—yet neither can perform without the other's help. The ambivalence is clear in the following "open memo" to Jody Powell, written in early 1977 for *Newsweek* by President Ford's outgoing press secretary, Ron Nessen:

1. Don't make any jokes. White House reporters don't find much funny these days. So what is meant as a joke is treated as a serious statement.

2. Don't say anything you are not willing to see reduced to a six-word headline.

3. Don't play the "yes or no" game. You lose, no matter what you say. I was asked repeatedly for a "yes" or "no" to the question: "Will you rule out the possibility that the United States will ever use military force in the Middle East to preserve its oil supply?" If I answer an honest "no" the headline reads: "WHITE HOUSE HINTS MIDEAST INVASION." If I answer "yes" the headline reads: "FORD PROMISES HANDS OFF ARABS."

4. Watch out for the "dog did not bite man" story. Reporters get upset when the president does not live up to his press-created image.

5. Watch out for the "man did not bite dog" story. Reporters also get upset when the president does exactly what they expect him to do.

6. Don't do the unexpected. Reporters don't like surprises. Even if a decision has been under consideration by the president for weeks or months, it is reported as a "last-minute move" by correspondents who never heard of it before.

7. Don't try to find the "White House source" who is always telling reporters what's really going on. Sometimes it's nobody. Sometimes it's an assistant to an assistant who doesn't really know what's going on, but is ashamed to admit that to the reporter. And sometimes it's you.

8. Confess. Confess. If the press thinks you or the president made a mistake, you might as well agree and apologize, even if you don't think it was a mistake. The story will haunt you from the front page and the evening news until you make a public confession.

9. Don't screw up on a slow news day.

10. Don't criticize the press. It always has the last word.[25]

LIVE AND IN COLOR

Franklin Roosevelt was the first president to demand a chunk of broadcast time to speak directly to the public without a reporter in the middle. Roosevelt averaged only two or three radio "fireside chats" a year—yet their effect on public confidence and support was substantial.

By the Eisenhower years, television was available for the same purpose. Yet both Eisenhower and Kennedy used TV only for emergencies, such as the Cuban missile crisis of 1962. Presidents Johnson and Nixon adopted a different approach. Both resorted to television regularly to circumvent the questions and interpretations of the press corps. Nixon, for example, took to the air twenty-five times in his first twenty-two months in office. In January, 1970, he became the first president ever to deliver a routine veto message (an HEW appropriations bill) live and in color. In January, 1972, Nixon starred in four television specials—first an exclusive interview with Dan Rather on CBS, then a speech on troop withdrawals from Vietnam, then his State of the Union address, and finally a new peace proposal.

There are two dangers here. First, the president's opponents cannot so easily obtain free air time for rebuttal. Only after sharp controversy did the networks offer some time to critics of the war, and critics of the HEW veto were not able to talk back. Perhaps more important, people automatically tend to support the president in times of crisis—and a direct television address gives the impression of crisis. Public-opinion polls showed increased approval of President Nixon after every major TV speech before Watergate. Nixon tried the same direct appeal to the public after Watergate, with rather less success. Still, historian Clinton Rossiter is on solid ground in claiming that immeasurable power has flowed from Congress to the president because of the latter's ability to reach the people directly via television.[26]

If opponents have grounds for griping about presidential TV appearances, so do the media. When the president goes directly to the public, he runs the show. It is hard for a reporter to be an adversary when he or she isn't even there.

Broadcast news executives are increasingly sensitive to the charge that presidents use TV to manipulate public opinion. But they often feel they have no choice in the matter. In October, 1974, all three networks decided not to carry a speech by President Ford in Kansas City, on the topic of inflation. The president had addressed the nation (via TV) on economic matters some weeks earlier, and the networks doubted that the Kansas City address would add very much. Then the White House formally requested that they carry the speech live. So they did. The president of ABC News, William Sheehan, explained: "Historically, any time a president flat-out asks for air time, he'll get it. That's what the party out of power always complains about, but when the president wants to speak to the nation there's no way we can deny him the air."[27]

By the time Jimmy Carter took office, the networks were beginning to exercise more discretion. Carter spent his first presidential New Year's Eve as the guest of the Shah of Iran in Teheran; when he asked for a live network feed to wish the American people a happy new year, all three networks flatly refused.[28] In 1978, Carter scheduled a prime-time "fireside chat" on the pending Panama Canal treaty; ABC and NBC went along, but CBS delayed the broadcast until 11:30 that night, insisting that there was "no indication of special urgency or dramatic change in President Carter's position" on the treaty.[29] And when Carter held a press conference

just before the 1980 Illinois primary, it was ABC that refused to carry the conference live, fearing that the president might misuse his incumbency to influence the voting.

But in general Carter, too, got the air time he asked for. It's hard to say no to the president.

PRESIDENTIAL COVERAGE

The president of the United States receives more attention from more reporters than any other person in the world. More than thirty news organizations cover the president's activities on a daily basis, and hundreds more pop up regularly at the White House when something of special interest is brewing. Hordes of journalists hungry for a story surround the president and his family at every public appearance, from the ski slopes to the church pews. And when the president does not appear in public, these same reporters bombard his representatives with demands for news of his actions, policies, thoughts, feelings, and moods.

Thus, presidents may safely take the quantity of their news coverage for granted, and concentrate on its quality. For a president, of course, good news coverage is favorable news coverage. To make sure that that's what they get, presidents manage the news. Press conferences, press secretaries, and television appearances are among their tools for doing so.

Comments one correspondent: "The White House has absolute control. They draw up the agenda; they decide today is regulatory reform day. That's the day's news. If you're not interested, okay. There are scores of other papers. The reporters vent their frustrations on the press secretary, but that's not really aggressive journalism."[30]

This is true as far as it goes. The president—any president—can guarantee himself a steady flow of favorable news, which reporters must cover simply because it is what the president said or did today. What the president cannot do is to stop the parallel flow of unfavorable news. This second flow is not nearly as voluminous as the first, but it too is steady.

Even when White House reporters are too busy for real investigative reporting—which is most of the time—they are seldom too busy to ask an irreverent question at a briefing or press conference. Even when they are reluctant to offend high-level sources, they are seldom reluctant to listen to opposing sources, on the record or off. Even when they feel obliged to parrot the president's most self-serving statement as though it were golden words of wisdom, they seldom feel afraid to quote an opponent that the statement was self-serving. The president, in short, cannot control all the news from the White House—only most of it.

Since presidents would like to control it all, they typically go through three stages in their relations with the media. First is the period of alliance, the "honeymoon" during which reporters cooperate in publicizing the hopes and goals of the new administration. Second comes the period of competition. Reporters start covering leaks and criticisms as well as the official line; the White House retaliates by curtailing access to officials. This leads to the third stage, the period of detachment. The president meets with the Washington press corps only in rigidly controlled situations, preferring to plead his case to the non-Washington media or directly to the public.[31] President Reagan will doubtless go through these stages, as did Presidents Carter, Ford, Nixon, and Johnson before him.

In whatever time it can spare from presidential coverage, the Washington press corps must also report on Congress, the Supreme Court, and the federal executive agencies. All three tend to get lost in the shuffle. The less flamboyant members of Congress are ignored; Supreme Court coverage is plagued by a pointless quest for speed; the executive agencies are reported mainly by means of press releases. Adding more Washington reporters could go a long way toward solving these problems—but Washington already boasts more reporters than any other city in the world.

THE WASHINGTON PRESS CORPS

Washington, D.C. is the news capital of the world, a Mecca for every ambitious political journalist. At this moment, there are roughly 3,000 full-time reporters at work in Washington—the largest, most talented, and most experienced press corps anywhere.

It wasn't always that way. The first Washington correspondent reached the city in 1822. He was Nathaniel Carter of the *New York Statesman and Evening Advertiser,* and his job was to supply readers with "the latest intelligence of every description which can be obtained at the seat of government."[32] Carter was soon joined by others, but it wasn't until the Civil War that Washington became a really important source of news. By 1867 there were forty-nine correspondents listed in the Congressional Press Galleries.

As the government grew, so did the press corps. And so did the importance of news from Washington. Elmer E. Cornwell Jr. has analyzed six weeks worth of front pages from two newspapers (the *New York Times* and the *Providence Journal*) for every year from 1885 to 1957. Cornwell's sample for 1885 yielded 447 column inches of news about Congress and the president. By 1909 the figure had increased to 508 column inches. By 1925, it was up to 1,235. And in 1933, the height of the Depression, it reached an incredible 1,914 column inches.[33] Today's figure is probably somewhat lower—but not much. Three thousand reporters can cover a lot of news.

The size of the Washington press corps is a mixed blessing. Public officials couldn't grant personal interviews to 3,000 journalists even if they wanted to. Instead, they resort to mass press conferences—with batteries of microphones, shouted questions, and very little dialogue. In this impersonal, hurried environment, news management is much, much easier.

Even 3,000 reporters may not be enough. The vast majority of American newspapers and broadcast stations have no representative in Washington. Of course the three networks, the nation's top newspapers, and the major newsmagazines all employ substantial Washington staffs; the *New York Times* Washington bureau, for example, includes 75 journalists. The larger newspaper chains (Gannett, Copley, Hearst, Newhouse, Knight-Ridder, and the like) have long maintained a Washington window for their members, and in recent years broadcast chains have begun to do the same. But it's expensive. The Cox chain's Washington bureau—consisting of two TV reporters, a radio reporter, two cameramen, and a secretary—is budgeted at $300,000 a year.[34] Most non-chain stations and papers forgo the expense and depend on two sources for their news of the federal government: the Associated Press and United Press International.

With 80-odd reporters and editors each, the AP and UPI Washington bureaus do their best to staff every executive department, subcommittee hearing, and diplomatic reception. Not surprisingly, they fail—there is simply too much to cover. The major events of the day get reported well enough, but the minor ones are rewritten from press releases or ignored entirely. "When I went to Washington," recalls a former AP bureau chief, "I had seventeen men. When I left I had seventy-seven. And the whole time I was there, I was one man short."[35]

Besides covering the news for those media without their own Washington correspondents, the wire services also backstop the media that have their own reporters. A newspaper with one or two Washington staffers wants more for its investment than a duplication of the wires. In the mid-1970s, for example, Lee Catterall was a one-man Washington bureau for eleven Wyoming daily newspapers, including the *Cody Enterprise* and the *Jackson Hole News*. Catterall focused on the implications for Wyoming of federal legislation and court decisions, and kept abreast of the activities of the state's two senators and one representative. He paid particular attention to government decisions affecting oil shale, cattle ranching, and other special interests of Wyoming residents. He also provided his clients with a weekly column and a summary of the votes of the Wyoming delegation.[36] News of more general interest he naturally left to the wires.

Most of what's wrong with national government news could be cured with more reporters—more AP and UPI staffers to dig into the under-examined executive agencies, more bureaus from individual papers and stations to watchdog their congressional delegations. But Washington already has more reporters than any other city in the world, and the federal government already receives more coverage than any other news source in the world. Other beats also could use added personnel—local government, international affairs, minorities, business. Does Washington really deserve a higher media priority than it already gets?

What is the Washington press corps? It is scores of reporters hanging around the White House press room, and one visit a year to the Federal Maritime Administration. It is CBS at a news conference, UPI rewriting a handout, *Newsweek* looking for color, and the *Los Angeles Times* on the trail of an exposé. It is a newspaper stringer interviewing a hometown business executive who has been invited to testify before a congressional committee about the threat of cotton imports. It is an industrial lobbyist masquerading as a reporter for a trade magazine. It is a freelance photographer trying to sell a photo essay on the president's dog. It is a syndicated columnist telling the country what it ought to think about Pakistan. It is a Pakistani reporter telling the people back home what they ought to think about Washington. It is a documentary film crew recording the night-life at a fashionable party.

It is 3,000 journalists covering the news capital of the world—doing the best job they can, a better job than we have any right to expect, but still in many respects an inadequate job.

CONGRESS AND THE PRESS

The United States has only one president—but it has 535 members of Congress. This simple fact has several important implications. For one thing, it makes it extremely difficult for a senator or representative to manage the news as the president does. For another, it puts every member of Congress in competition with every other member of Congress for the limited amount of available publicity. And members of Congress *need* publicity. They need it to get re-elected in their districts; they need it to gain stature as possible candidates for higher office; they need it to bring their views to the attention of the president and the party leaders. The Capitol Hill reporter, unlike the White House correspondent, is operating in a buyer's market for news.

In 1963, only six senators employed full-time press secretaries; today all 100 have them. Many members of the House, where staffs are smaller, combine the job with something else—but everyone has a staffer handling press relations. The job is significantly different from that of the president's press secretary. Presidents assume they will be covered, and work to make the coverage favorable. Members of Congress struggle to get covered, period. Says reporter Al Hunt of the *Wall Street Journal:* "There are 535 publicity hounds on Capitol Hill. . . . The House *gets* less coverage, but their lust for headlines is just as great."[37]

To win the attention of the 300 or so reporters who cover Congress regularly, senators and representatives tailor their activi-ties to the journalists' preferences. James Reston comments:

The influence of reporters on the conduct of individual members of the House and Senate, particularly the House, is much greater than is generally realized. For example, if reporters tend to play up the spectacular charges or statements of extremists on Capitol Hill and to play down or ignore the careful, analytical speeches of the more moderate and responsible members—as, unfortunately, they do most of the time—this inevitably has its influence on many other members, particularly new members. . . . [T]he new Congressman often draws the obvious conclusion and begins spouting nonsense to attract attention.[38]

The days when reporters were unwelcome on Capitol Hill are long gone. The House of Representatives opened its doors to journalists in 1789; the Senate followed suit in 1795. There were occasional squabbles in the early 1800s, but by 1841 the right of reporters to roam freely through the Capitol was well established. Once admitted, the reporter is treated like visiting royalty. The press gallery hovers directly over the presiding officer's desk in both Houses, providing a box-seat view of the proceedings. Wire-service reporters have special muted telephones within the chambers themselves. Pages are available for journalists who wish to summon legislators from their seats for interviews or off-the-record consultations. And few members of Congress ignore such a summons.

Behind the press gallery, reporters have an extensive suite of rooms for work and relaxation, with staff assistants whose salaries are paid by the government. Every possible piece of equipment—from typewriters to reference books to swank leather couches—is provided for the convenience of the press. Symbolic of the easy access of reporters to congressional news is a sign over one of the elevators in the House wing of the Capitol. It reads: "Reserved for Members and the Press."[39]

Broadcasters are less free than the print

MAKING THE HEADLINES

The following are some of the tactics used by publicity-hungry members of Congress to woo the attention of reporters, as described by Joseph Nocera in the *Washington Monthly*.[40] It is interesting to compare Nocera's list with the advice of presidential press secretary Ron Nessen to his successor (see p. 407). Nessen is worried about avoiding bad press; Nocera's sources want to achieve almost any press at all.

1. Forget about standards.   Nebraska Senator Ed Zorinsky took the door off his Senate office to dramatize—in photos—his open-door policy.

2. Abuse the wires.   Local papers are more likely to run congressional press releases if they come from the wire services instead of direct from the mimeograph machine. The wires do a little rewriting, then move the releases locally or regionally, giving them a gloss of respectability.

3. Quote Shakespeare.   Be a little flakey. Pennsylvania Congressman Daniel Flood wore bow ties, told jokes, waxed his moustache. The media called him colorful, and gave him more coverage than workaholic colleagues.

4. Feud your way to the top.   Reporters like a good argument. Picking a fight with the president is best; if you write him a tough letter, make sure you send a copy to the media.

5. Go to the White House often.   There are always reporters at the White House. Massachusetts Congresswoman Margaret Heckler usually positioned herself on-camera behind the president for bill-signing ceremonies. Ohio Senator Howard ("Headline Howie") Metzenbaum left White House meetings early to get first crack at the waiting reporters.

6. Take up jogging. Get a big kitchen. Go to the scene of the crime.   Good coverage requires good photo and film opportunities, and providing them is the Congressmember's job. Pennsylvania Senator John Heinz criticized the Carter administration's bridge repair program speaking from a creaky Pennsylvania bridge, strategically located near the state's major media markets.

7. Be a leaker.   Reporters always think a story is better if it's leaked.

---

media in their coverage of Congress. Although both chambers permit TV cameras at many committee hearings (in fact, many committee hearings are designed for TV cameras), the Senate forbids TV coverage of floor debate. The House permitted it for the first time in March, 1979. In a 1980 poll of House members, more than half said they were pleased with the change. Many local stations air excerpts from the proceedings on the news, and members themselves use the system to monitor the course of debate from their offices. But 48 percent agreed that more amendments were being introduced from the floor as a result, and 10 percent admitted making more speeches to please the home-

town audience.[41] House Speaker Tip O'Neill called the system a "disaster" and urged its elimination.[42]

If members of Congress are so desperate for publicity, why are many of them skeptical about the televising of floor debate? Senators and representatives are accustomed to their clubbish privacy. Though they are tired of being ignored by the media, many are afraid that the public might disapprove of such congressional traditions as political compromise and reciprocal back-scratching. Though increased coverage would aid the national careers of the grandstanders in Congress, many fear it might damage the reelection chances of the more flexible deal-makers. Most members of Congress are reasonably pleased now with the *quality* of congressional news; it's only the quantity they want changed. They want more media attention, but not at the cost of more media (and public) criticism.

The content of important but non-controversial laws may tend to go under-reported— but so does the influence of lobbyists on congressional action. The press may overlook a member's noninflammatory policy initiative, but it also overlooks the member's hypocrisy in saying one thing to constituents while doing another when it comes time to vote. The grueling labor of drafting legislation may get less media play than the rituals of political posturing—but the quiet compromises, mutual favors, and constant logrolling get even less play than the labor.

When members of Congress want to say something to the people back home, they can use their free postal franking privilege to mail a "newsletter" to every constituent, or at least a press release to every newspaper. Or they can use the $500,000 congressional broadcast studios to prepare a tape for hometown radio and TV stations. When they want to reach a national audience, they can try introducing a controversial bill, or giving an inflammatory floor speech, or issuing a carefully timed comment on the actions of some more newsworthy personage. These techniques may not provide enough publicity to satisfy the ambitions of some Congressmen and Congresswomen, but at least it's all "good" publicity, controlled by the members themselves.

THE SUPREME COURT

When the Supreme Court has a batch of decisions to announce, the Court goes into session, some opinions are read aloud, and

---

CONGRESSIONAL COMMITTEES

Like the rest of the government, Congress uses two main styles of news management— publicity and secrecy. Congressional committees demonstrate both.

When a committee of Congress schedules a series of public hearings, the show is usually staged with the media in mind. In theory, congressional investigations are supposed to collect information for use in the legislative process. In practice, publicity is the main purpose of many investigations. The late Senator Joseph McCarthy built his reputation as a fearsome hunter of communists primarily through his activities as chairman of the Senate Permanent Investigating Subcommittee. A more recent example was the Senate Watergate hearings of 1973, chaired by Sam Ervin (D.-N.C.). Ostensibly set up to gather material that would help in the drafting of a campaign reform bill, the Watergate hearings revealed additional information, eroded public support for President Nixon, and thus paved the way for an impeachment vote in the House Judiciary Committee. It also made an instant folk hero of Senator Ervin.

The real work of Congress, meanwhile, is accomplished in the working sessions of congressional committees. This is where bills are written and political deals are consummated. More often than not, congressional conflicts are compromised and the final decisions are made in committee, long before the floor show begins. Traditionally, these committee sessions have been closed to the media. In 1973, however, the House voted 370-27 to open all committee meetings to the press, unless a committee votes to keep a particular meeting closed.[43] The Senate considered a similar change, but decided instead to stick with its current rule, which keeps committee meetings closed unless the committee votes to open them.[44]

printed copies of all the opinions are distributed to reporters. That's it until the next batch.

There are few news beats more clearly defined than this one. A single press officer is available, but is permitted to discuss only the Court in general, not specific decisions. Interviews with the Justices and their staffs are not often granted. Speculation on the backstage negotiations that produce a majority opinion is frowned upon, and generally avoided by reporters. *The Brethren,* a 1979 bestseller on the Court, caused a stir precisely because that sort of gossipy, anecdotal coverage of the Supreme Court is so rare. By contrast, comparable books on Congress, the presidency, and the federal executive agencies are published frequently.

Supreme Court reporters write their stories from court-supplied background materials, briefs, and the printed opinions. To help them prepare, the Association of American Law Schools, the American Law Institute, and the American Bar Association jointly produce a legal analysis of each case pending before the Court. That's it—no irreverent interviews, no jazzy pseudo-events, no dramatic confrontations. This is such a difficult assignment that no more than 35 or 40 journalists appear regularly enough to rate term passes. The vast majority of the print and broadcast media rely exclusively on the wire services for their Supreme Court news.

The hallmark of wire-service reporting is speed. On decision days, AP has three reporters assigned to the Court. One sits in the courtroom, collects the written opinions, and shoots them via pneumatic tube to the press room below. The other two have the job of wading through thousands of words of legal jargon. They must identify the case, determine the decision, pinpoint the majority and minority opinions, select the quotes, and fill in the background—all in a matter of minutes. As always, AP tries frantically to beat UPI with the first bulletin. If a dissenting opinion gets muddled in the process, that's only to be expected.

There are some kinds of news for which speed is a sensible goal—but it is doubtful that the Supreme Court is one of them. Most cases are pending for years before the Court reaches a decision; one would think the public could wait a few minutes more to find out what the decision was. It takes a trained lawyer hours of careful checking to figure out the significance of a judicial opinion. Wire-service reporters do the job in minutes.

Not surprisingly, they often make mistakes. In 1962, AP reported that the Supreme Court had ruled that "a state or city may not interfere in any fashion with peaceful racial integration demonstrations in public places of business." This was simply wrong. The Court had actually decided that any city that officially supported segregation could not prosecute Negroes for seeking service in privately owned stores. The decision applied only to those areas where segregation was official policy.[45] Such errors and misinterpretations are quite frequent.

Former AP manager Wes Gallagher once proposed that the Supreme Court lock its doors on decision day—with the press corps inside. Half an hour or so later, the doors would be opened, and everyone would be released at the same time. So far the Court has refused to go along. The wire services would like to be forced to spend some time studying the decisions. But neither is willing to do so voluntarily, and let the other get the story on the teletype first.

What do the media do with Supreme Court stories? The broadcast media do very little with them—a complex legal issue without pictures is tough for television to handle. The networks typically pick one decision out of each batch to summarize in 30 seconds or so, while local broadcasters ignore the Court altogether unless a case originated locally.

Newspaper coverage is more variable. One study examined coverage of all 145 Court decisions in the 1974 term. The *New York Times,* with its own full-time Court reporter, mentioned 112 of the 145 decisions; it offered readers at least the essentials on 63 of them, and printed detailed accounts of 32. The

Detroit News was more typical. It mentioned only 44 of the 145 decisions, providing detail on 12. Only six of the *Detroit News* stories were staff-written; the rest came from the wires. "The quantity and quality of coverage of a given decision were highly associated," the study's author concluded. "The 'average' decision was either covered by no article or by articles of such short length that on its face the quality of coverage was poor. Only 'major' decisions were covered by articles of sufficient length to bring quality of coverage into question."[46]

THE EXECUTIVE AGENCIES

More than 90 percent of the federal bureaucracy in Washington is made up of the personnel of executive agencies—from the State Department and the Defense Department all the way down to the Food and Drug Administration and the Civil Aeronautics Board. The job of these agencies is to put into operation the policies dictated by the president and Congress.

An overwhelming amount of news is generated each day by the executive agencies. Reporting that news aggressively and independently would be a hard job for the entire Washington press corps. And the entire Washington press corps isn't available. Except for the Pentagon and the State Department, agency assignments are the least glamorous of all. The media count on the wire services for just about all their agency news. And the wire services count on a handful of overworked reporters.

In staffing terms alone, the press is beaten before it begins. A UPI reporter, say, assigned to cover the Departments of Labor, Commerce, and Agriculture, may get as many as forty handouts a day from the three departments. There is barely enough time to rewrite a quarter of the releases—if no time is wasted on additional research. Every telephone call to get more information on one story means ignoring another story entirely.

A really careful look at one story means forgetting the whole rest of the day's events.

A second impediment to investigative coverage is the attitude of most civil servants toward the press. While Congress and the president seek out publicity, most agency employees wouldn't mind if they never saw their names in print. They are polite and friendly with reporters, but suspicious and closemouthed. In 1970, consumer affairs writer Trudy Lieberman of the *Detroit Free Press* asked the Agriculture Department for the names of those manufacturers whose hot dogs exceeded the government limit of 30 percent fat. It took many weeks (and the combined efforts of Nixon aide Herb Klein, the American Society of Newspaper Editors, the Freedom of Information Center, and a formal appeal) to pry the list loose.[47]

Occasionally disgruntled civil servants will tell reporters (often anonymously) about some agency action of which they disapprove. And even more occasionally a stubborn journalist will dig to the bottom of an agency story. But only the most important executive departments receive investigative coverage more than once or twice a year. The typical executive agency seldom gets even routine coverage.

Consider the Nuclear Regulatory Commission, comfortably ensconced in suburban Bethesda, Maryland, a forbidding half-hour trip from downtown Washington. Despite the raging debate over nuclear power, very few reporters found time to cover the NRC before the 1979 Three Mile Island accident made it front-page news. There were important NRC stories there for the looking, such as poor supervision of reactor operator training, safety requirements that were willingly bent on utility request, total lack of planning for a major accident, and pro-nuclear bias among the staff. All these and more came out in the months immediately after Three Mile Island. Then the NRC returned to the shadows, probably not to emerge again until the next nuclear accident.

According to one researcher, 22 percent of all news coming out of Washington can be traced to handouts from the executive agencies.[48] That still leaves hundreds of handouts that are never made into news stories at all. As for investigative reporting, journalists covering the agencies simply haven't got the time.

CONVENTIONS OF GOVERNMENT REPORTING

When a news source agrees to talk to a reporter, it is the source, not the reporter, who decides the rules of the game. And in official Washington, the rules are often aimed at protecting the source. Hence the government tradition of interviews that are not entirely on the record. Top Washington officials, including the president and his cabinet, use such interviews to float "trial balloons" that they can later deny if it becomes convenient to do so. Lower-level officials, such as the bureaucrats in the executive agencies, use such interviews to "leak" information that might cost them their jobs if published with their names attached.

Over the years, a number of interview conventions have developed in Washington to cover these sorts of situations. Reporters who want to keep their sources must obey the conventions. In a 1972 survey, the Associated Press Managing Editors listed seven of them, as follows.[49]

On the record. This is the most open (and still the most common) of the categories. The reporter may quote the source verbatim and by name, with no restrictions.

Check quotes. As the label implies, this convention still permits reporters to quote their source by name, but they must check their quotations with the interviewee before publishing them. Such a restriction is typically imposed by sources of technical information, but it is available to anyone who distrusts the reporter's memory or wants a second chance to withdraw or modify earlier statements.

Not for direct quotation. Interviews in this category may be attributed to their source, but must be paraphrased instead of quoted. Before television, many presidents held "not for direct quotation" press conferences; if their statements backfired they could always claim that wasn't quite what they meant. Lesser officials still resort to this convention for the same reason.

Not for attribution. This convention permits the reporter to quote the source directly, but not by name. Instead, the remarks must be attributed to "a reliable official," or "a State Department representative," or "persons close to the president," or whatever. The "not for attribution" interview is an ideal way to launch a trial balloon or a leak (see p. 153). Those in the know can usually figure out who was talking, but the general public can't, and the source can always claim it must have been somebody else. So can the reporter; the "not for attribution" convention enables journalists to hide behind blind quotes (see p. 199).

Background. The typical background interview is a combination of "not for direct quotation" and "not for attribution." The reporter must paraphrase what was said, and attribute it to "a Pentagon official" or whatever. This leaves the source free to insist that the reporter misunderstood, or that it must have been someone else talking, or both.

Deep background. Journalists reporting on a "deep backgrounder" may not quote the source; they can't even imply that there is a source. They must use the information essentially on their own authority. This convention provides the greatest safety for low-level government employees who want to attack a decision without losing their jobs, and for high-level ones who want to test public reaction to an undeclared policy.

Off the record. This is the convention of greatest secrecy. Reporters at "off the record" briefings may not publish what they hear, even anonymously. Officials use this device to keep journalists up to date on developing stories. They also use it to plug leaks. One reporter emerged from an exclusive interview with President Theodore Roosevelt and told his colleagues: "I've just seen the President. He told me everything I knew already, and all that I was preparing to write—but he pledged me to secrecy on every fact I had, and now I can't write the blooming story."[50]

These interview ground rules aren't confined to Washington; they have been widely copied by local and state governments as well, and even by nongovernment sources. But the precise meaning of each convention varies from city to city, from year to year, and from official to official. Many reporters and sources use the word "background" loosely to cover everything from "not for attribution" to "deep background." A reporter who isn't sure what the ground rules are for a particular interview simply has to ask in advance—or assume that everything is on the record and risk a battle if the source was assuming something quite different.

The value of the interview conventions is obvious. They offer the conscientious government official a middle ground between complete openness and complete secrecy. It is fair to say that many important stories would never reach the public at all if it were not for these conventions.

Their danger is just as obvious. Alfred Friendly, former managing editor of the *Washington Post,* points out that backgrounders are useful "when a person of considerable importance or delicate position is discussing a matter in circumstances in which his name cannot be used for reasons of public policy or personal vulnerability." Fair enough. But Friendly adds that backgrounders are also used "by persons who want to sink a knife or do a job without risking their own position or facing the consequences to themselves."[51]

BACKGROUND BY KISSINGER

One of the things for which Secretary of State Henry Kissinger was justly famous—at least among the media—was his fondness for backgrounders. The lengths to which the press went to protect his identity (not very successfully) were comic in their intricacy. This attribution, for example, appeared in a *New York Times* story of December 15, 1974: "A high American official who often briefs reporters on major foreign-policy issues said, aboard the President's plane during the flight here. . . ."[52]

Kissinger was also at the center of the most serious backgrounding controversy to date. In late 1971, he briefed the reporters chosen to travel with him (known as the "pool") on the conflict between India and Pakistan over Bangladesh. He said that if the Soviet Union did not restrain the Indians, "the entire United States–Soviet relationship might well be re-examined" and "a new look might have to be taken at the President's summitry plans." These were strong words, and Kissinger made it clear they were not to be used with his name.

A *Washington Post* reporter who was not part of the pool, and therefore not directly pledged to adhere to the interview agreement, published the statements and attributed them to Kissinger. The *Post* might well have questioned the propriety of the top U.S. foreign-policy official challenging the Russians on a not-for-attribution basis. But the White House was furious at the *Post* for its breach of journalistic etiquette.[53]

So were the other reporters. Shortly thereafter, in an obvious rebuke to the *Post,* the White House Correspondents Association called on all its members to respect the rules of anonymous briefings.[54]

James Reston of the *New York Times* offers a similarly qualified defense:

It leaves room for honest dissenters. It is the refuge of conscience. It can be used for good or evil: to disclose the murders of My Lai, the secret bombings of Cambodia, the cover-up of Watergate. Or it can be used to disrupt elections, to vilify and destroy the political opposition. It is a powerful, ambitious, and sometimes dangerous instrument. . . . When Washington and Paris get into an awkward argument over policy and consultation, Secretary of State Kissinger can either call a press conference and denounce the French, or both sides can "inspire" articles that make their points clear, and still leave room for maneuver.[55]

Whatever their misgivings, reporters usually honor the interview conventions meticulously. If they did not, they would have a great deal less political news to report.

Like so much in this chapter, the interview conventions demonstrate a high level of cooperation between government officials and the reporters who cover them. Such cooperation is essential if the media are to do their jobs properly. But conflict—an adversary relationship—is equally essential. The trick is to find the balance.

Throughout most of the world, the mass media are considered essentially a tool of the government. The United States is nearly unique in the role it assigns to the media: not only to tell the public what government officials are saying, but also to tell the public what government officials are doing—even if the officials would rather the public didn't know. The media in America are expected to inform the people so that the people can select and instruct the officials.

Perhaps this is too much to expect. Limited by news management, friendship with sources, understaffing, and other factors, the media find it hard enough to do an adequate job of routine reporting. Independent and aggressive journalism often seems out of the question. The American media do investi-

gate their government more thoroughly than the media of any other country in the world. But too frequently, even in the U.S., the public's watchdog winds up thumping its tail to the government's music.

———————

The most important political role of the mass media, at least in theory, is to provide the information on which public opinion is based. But through news of polls, the media also report— and misreport—public opinion itself. And when it comes time for the public to act out its opinions in an election, the media pay more attention to political maneuvers and preference trends than to the issues on which informed votes are presumed to rest. Americans can often learn more about the policy stances of the candidates from campaign advertising than from campaign news.

PUBLIC OPINION

In a televised news conference on December 2, 1974, President Gerald Ford stated that he did not favor a stiff new tax on gasoline as a way of reducing American consumption of imported oil from the Middle East. The president justified his position by noting that more than 80 percent of the American people, according to a recent public-opinion poll, opposed such a tax. It would be unwise, said Ford, to flout the wishes of so large a majority.

This sort of deference to "the will of the people" is not a uniquely American phenomenon. As leader of the Second Empire of France, Napoleon III commissioned weekly public-opinion reports from agents all over the country. In 1866 he was thinking about intervening on the side of Austria in the Austro-Prussian war. But his sources told him that most French citizens wanted peace, so Napoleon decided to stay out of the conflict. Four years later, having disposed of

Austria, Prussia went to war against France, leading to the defeat of Napoleon III and the downfall of the Second Empire.[56]

Despite such overseas precedents, the American government undoubtedly pays more attention to public opinion than any other government in the world. It always has. Back in 1837, European visitor Harriet Martinu wrote that "the worship of Opinion is, at this day, the established religion of the United States."[57] Many visitors since have made the same observation.

What is public opinion? Political scientist V. O. Key, Jr. offers this definition: "Public opinion may simply be taken to mean opinion held by private persons which governments find it prudent to heed. Governments may be impelled toward action or inaction by such opinion; in other instances they may ignore it, perhaps at their peril; they may attempt to alter it; or they may divert or pacify it."[58] Note that Key doesn't claim that governments always obey public opinion, only that they always "heed" it. After threatening rationing and a variety of even less palatable policies, President Ford eventually did propose a new excise tax on gasoline. By that time he had engineered enough public support for the move to make it politically acceptable.

American politicians almost invariably justify their actions on the basis of public opinion. They may do their best first to manipulate the public so that it supports their views. But when politicians cannot change the public's opinion, they generally change their own, or at least keep very quiet about it. It is extremely rare for an American political figure to declare: "Most people disagree, but *I* believe thus-and-such!"

Of course public opinion doesn't always mean everybody's opinion. On any given issue, some people are more interested and more powerful than others. Inevitably, their opinion counts more. Lester Markel commented that "public opinion in a democracy is a collective viewpoint powerful enough, if the power is exerted, to influence public policy. It may be the viewpoint of a majority of the people, or, in the absence of an effective majority, the viewpoint of an effective minority."[59] The government officials responsible for American policy toward imported textiles, for example, are no doubt very responsive to public opinion on the issue—which turns out to be the opinion of textile manufacturers, textile wholesalers, textile retailers, and textile unions.

Although the "public opinion" of interested minorities dominates many government decisions, it is important not to underestimate the power—at least the potential power—of majority opinion. Especially in this post-Watergate era of suspicion, no government official wants to be accused of subservience to special interests. When mass public opinion is successfully mobilized on behalf of one side of an issue, it stands a very good chance indeed of defeating entrenched powers on the other side. The problem, of course, is that it is very difficult to mobilize mass public opinion. Most of us care very little about most issues. And most of us know very little about most issues, except what the entrenched powers have told us through their public-relations efforts.

Two other factors add significantly to the importance of mass public opinion in the United States. The first is public-opinion polling, a relatively new science (and media fad) that gives government officials more information than they ever had before about what the rest of us are thinking. The second is voting, an opportunity for every adult American, interested and uninterested, informed and uninformed, to take a stand on the public issues of the moment. Since the rest of this chapter is devoted to mass-media coverage of polls and elections, and since polls and elections contribute enormously to the importance of mass public opinion, it is appropriate to start with this question: What do we know about mass public opinion in the United States?

First of all, we know that it is often egregiously uninformed. In 1965, 73 percent of a national sample failed a CBS News test on current events, judged according to tenth-grade standards. A month after the presidential nominating conventions of 1968, 28 percent of the public could not name the Democratic nominee for vice president, Edmund Muskie, and 33 percent couldn't name his Republican counterpart, Spiro Agnew.[60] In 1970, a California Congressman easily won re-election to his tenth consecutive term; a poll taken just before the election revealed that after eighteen years fewer than half the voters knew his name. A 1973 survey showed that only 39 percent of Americans could name both U.S. Senators from their home state, and only 46 percent could name their Representative. Even more startling, only 62 percent knew that Congress was composed of two chambers, the Senate and the House of Representatives.[61]

Psychologists tell us that public opinion, especially when it's strong, is often based on emotion rather than facts. Moreover, people's opinions are very hard to change. We tend to interpret new realities in terms of old values without re-examining the values—and whatever doesn't fit we simply forget. Walter Lippmann argued that most people consistently make decisions based on their comfortable stereotypes of the world, not on the world itself. Lippmann didn't blame the public for these flaws in public opinion, but he did worry about their implications:

> The environment with which our public opinions deal is refracted in many ways, by censorship and privacy at the source, by physical and social barriers at the other end, by scanty attention, by the poverty of language, by distraction, by unconscious constellations of feeling, by wear and tear, violence, monotony. These limitations upon our access to that environment combine with the obscurity and complexity of the facts themselves to thwart clearness and justice of perception, to substitute misleading fictions for workable ideas, and to deprive us of adequate checks upon those who consciously strive to mislead.[62]

Public opinion has a myriad of sources. We learn our opinions from our parents and early childhood experiences, from primary schooling and religious training, from friends and college courses, from traveling and other influences. The mass media play a particularly vital role. It is through the media that Americans acquire the current information they need to test old opinions and form new ones. If the American public is uninterested in many important issues, and uninformed on those issues, psychology cannot take all the blame. Some of it belongs to the media, whose difficult job it is to interest and inform us.

POLLS AND THE MEDIA

Several decades ago, President Woodrow Wilson voiced the following heartfelt complaint about his job: "I do not know what the people are thinking about; I have the most imperfect means of finding out, yet I must act as if I knew. I'm not put here to do what I please."[63] If Wilson were president today, he would be an avid reader of public-opinion polls.

Most of us alternately deplore and applaud the reliance of government officials on poll results. When the results differ from our own opinions, we complain that our officials ought to think for themselves more, or at least listen to the people (like us) who really understand the issue. When the results support our views, we congratulate the officials for finally acknowledging the will of the public.

However we feel about it, the fact is that government officials are greatly influenced by public-opinion polls. And here is a more disquieting fact: The public is greatly influenced by public-opinion polls. People like to be in the majority when they can; on issues where they have no firm opinion of their own, they are quite willing to adopt the viewpoint of their neighbors. How poll results are reported in the media is therefore an issue of some importance.

The biggest controversy over polls used to concern the size and representativeness of the sample. Many people still doubt that a survey of just a few thousand citizens can accurately reflect the opinions of millions of others who have never even met a pollster. This was a genuine problem in the 1920s and 1930s, the early years of polling. Today, pollsters know how to select a large enough random sample to serve as a cross-section of Americans. Particularly with the various "weighting" techniques now used to insure that minority groups are properly represented, sampling just isn't a big problem any more.

The choice of questions is. In fact, it's three problems. First, most poll questions are too simple. They typically state a very complicated issue in oversimplified terms, then insist on a one-dimensional yes-or-no answer— no essays allowed. Second, many poll questions are biased. During the Vietnam war, for example, it made a big difference whether you asked people if they supported "unilateral troop withdrawal" (sounds bad) or if they thought "the U.S. should make the first move toward peace" (sounds good). By how they phrase their questions, pollsters can carelessly or intentionally predetermine the answers. Third, some poll questions are so poorly phrased that *any* answer is meaningless. Take this question from a 1973 Gallup Poll: "Do you think President Nixon should be impeached and compelled to leave the Presidency, or not?" It is possible to answer either half of this question yes, and the other half no—except that Gallup won't let you. Such a question may actually mislead people into thinking that impeachment (indictment in the House of Representatives) is the same as removal of the president (conviction in the Senate or resignation).

To help readers and viewers cope with such dilemmas, the American Association for Public Opinion Research offers its code of disclosure standards. The code requires pollsters to identify the sponsoring group, give the exact wording of the question, describe the nature and size of the sample, discuss how far off the results might be (the sampling error), state the date of the polling interviews, etc.[64] But of course not all media present this information with every poll. When it is presented, it may not be read. And how many readers would understand its implications for the credibility of the poll?

Perhaps the most serious defect of polls is that they assume everybody has an opinion in the first place. Most people have never thought about, say, whether food processing companies are responsible for the high price of groceries—but there's nothing to keep a pollster from asking them anyhow. "In effect," says one critic, "the pollster is asking people what their opinion would be if they had one. Then he takes this 'information' to the food processors or the farmers (or both) as a demonstration of powerful popular forces that can affect their planning."[65] Because of this defect, argues political observer Henry Fairlie, poll results are "necessarily an exaggeration of the strength of popular conviction on any issue."[66]

There is something terribly circular about all this. A politician pondering a policy choice commissions a poll to find out "what the people think." The people don't think much of anything on the topic, but they graciously answer the pollster's questions anyhow. In due time the politician announces the new policy, citing the poll data as evidence of its wisdom, and the media duly publish the story. We read in the paper that thus-and-such will happen because we (the people) want it that way. And if we don't much care one way or the other, we may obediently conclude that we do want it that way. The public tells the pollster, who tells the politician, who tells the press, which tells the public—with no need for a real decision at any stage in the cycle.

Polling has become so important to the political process that Jimmy Carter's pollster, Patrick Caddell, was literally the only non-Georgian in Carter's inner circle, with frequent access to the president. And polling has become just as important to the media. Louis Harris polls for ABC, Daniel Yankelovich for *Time;* The Associated Press and NBC run a joint poll, as do CBS and the *New York Times;* George Gallup—a founder of the modern polling industry—has a syndicated newspaper column. The media used to be skeptical about publishing politicians' polls. Now that they are paying for their own, the skepticism is forgotten and the results automatically get big play.

Election time is when the polls are most prominent, and a candidate is likely to attribute all sorts of gains and losses to their influence. Trailing far behind in the polls, it is said, can hurt fund-raising; running far ahead can make the staff lethargic and overconfident; closing fast near election day can produce a bandwagon effect and a final victory spurt; leading substantially near election day can induce supporters to stay home and not vote at all. Much of this post-election assessment of the effects of the polls is little more than a reading of tea leaves. We really don't know what the effects are.

But certainly there are effects, sometimes visible and far-reaching ones. In 1972, going into the New Hampshire primary, the polls showed Edmund Muskie with a wide lead for the Democratic presidential nomination. He won the primary, but not by as much as the polls had predicted. Political reporters then interpreted the outcome as a Muskie setback, and asked the senator why he had not done as well as the polls had said. Muskie was understandably peeved.[67] When he failed to live up to the polls in succeeding primaries as well, reporters made that failure the main theme of their coverage. Clearly, reporters were viewing the polls as the most important fact of Muskie's campaign. When the polls turned out to be wrong, the candidate, not the pollsters, suffered.

Notice that what we are examining here is not just the effects of the polls, but the effects of media attention to the polls. An unreported poll may guide—or misguide— the politician who commissions it, but it can-

not affect the public opinion it purports to measure. A reported poll can and does affect public opinion—especially when reporters interpret the results as evidence of strength or weakness, momentum or decline.

Once again the process is circular. When John Anderson was considering running for president in 1980 as an independent, reporters looked at poll results showing substantial disenchantment with Carter and Reagan, and wrote endless columns suggesting he just might pull it off. The media enthusiasm helped Anderson attract endorsements, contributions, campaign workers— which the media reported, which helped attract more. Anderson moved up in the polls; he had momentum. The media reported that, too, which gave him more momentum.

But as election day approached, Anderson began slipping in the polls. People learned that he was slipping from the media, of course. Potential supporters decided that he couldn't win after all. This led to a further decline in his poll numbers, which led to news stories about the decline, which led to more decline and then more news stories, until election day put an end to the cycle. Anderson rose, in large part, because the media told us he was rising, and he fell because the media told us he was falling. Rise and fall alike were largely products of the media's insatiable appetite for polls.

PICKING THE CANDIDATES

Long before a political campaign begins, the media are busy picking the candidates, acting as a combination "handicapper" and "scout." Some politicians are ignored or rejected. Others are identified for the public as political "comers."

Political satirist Russell Baker calls the media "The Great Mentioner." It was The Great Mentioner that first suggested George Romney as an ideal Republican presidential candidate for 1968. And it was The Great Mentioner that ruled Romney out of the race after he claimed he had been "brain-washed" by the U.S. military in Vietnam. Similarly, the presidential aspirations of Senator Edward Kennedy have risen and fallen twice as The Great Mentioner gave or withheld approval.

Why do the media play such a crucial role in the selection and winnowing of political candidates? We have already discussed one major reason—the polls. Throughout the now-continuous campaign process, polls provide the essential news pegs for media discussions of which candidates may survive and which are bound to get weeded out early.[68]

Even more importantly, the media have gained influence because of the collapse of the party system in American politics. Throughout most of American history, would-be politicians needed the approval of the party regulars to run for office; only then, with the party behind them, did they compete for the votes of ordinary citizens. But now, says Anthony Lewis of the New York Times, "we are in the age of atomized politics, without structure, without process except what the press supplies—accidentally and inadequately."[69] When the parties were strong, a candidate's first priority was to build alliances with other politicians and coalitions with organized interest groups. But a candidate who "has his modern priorities straight," comments political scientist James David Barber, "is first and foremost a seeker after favorable notice from the journalists who can make or break his progress."[70]

When Jimmy Carter was still a relatively unknown dark horse candidate for the 1976 Democratic presidential nomination, he won 29 percent of the delegates in January's Iowa party caucuses. This unexpectedly good showing led Roger Mudd, then of CBS, to declare Carter the winner and to place his candidacy at the head of the pack. What boosted Carter several giant steps toward the presidency was not 29 percent of Iowa's convention delegates, but the fact that Mudd and others saw these delegates as evidence that Carter was ahead in the race. Surprisingly, Mudd leveled with his viewers:

It's not exactly the precise figures that will be important, it's whether or not the media and the politicians agree that this man won and this man lost. . . . Does Carter have to win by ten or must he win by only one to be a front-runner? During the night, it will be the collective wisdom, or misjudgment, of the media and the politicians that's going to determine who actually comes off well out here.[71]

The early caucuses and state primaries, in short, have become like the polls. The handful of delegates each candidate wins at these events turns out to be almost a trivial consideration. Their main impact is the chance they give the media to talk about which candidates are pulling ahead and which are falling by the wayside—information that is carefully attended to by the citizens who will vote in the next round of caucuses and primaries. Political bosses used to pick the candidates. Now they watch, while the media tell the public which candidates it will pick.

COVERING THE CAMPAIGN

The mass media are not the most important influence on voting decision. Family background, economic status, geographical location, and other demographic factors are far better predictors of an individual's vote than what he or she reads in the papers or sees on TV. But most elections are decided by a small "swing vote" which is able to overcome demographics and change its mind during the campaign. And swing voters are greatly influenced by the media.

Even the average voter may be significantly affected by media content. A 1969 study found that 70 percent of American adults make regular use of television for information on candidates and campaigns; 50 percent use newspapers and 25 percent turn to

TV AT THE CONVENTIONS

When parties controlled the political system, the presidential nominating conventions were events of enormous importance, and the media naturally covered them thoroughly. There were complaints even then that the parties manipulated the media to advance their own interests, and that coverage focused on the self-serving show and missed the back-room deals. But no one doubted that the conventions deserved the media's undivided attention. They were where the presidential candidates were selected.

But now the presidential candidates are selected in state primaries, and the conventions merely rubber-stamp the choice. In 1980, for example, everyone knew that Ronald Reagan would be the Republicans' nominee in Detroit, and Jimmy Carter the Democratic choice in New York. Yet the media sent 15,000 people to Detroit to cover the work of 1,993 Republican delegates; 11,500 media representatives went to New York to cover 3,381 Democratic delegates.[72] The three television networks alone spent $60 million on the conventions.[73] CBS, for example, took 700 people to Detroit, with 14 cameras, five minicam units, four mobile units, five control rooms, 204 TV monitors and 750 telephones.[74]

Why so much investment for so little news? "What audiences get, or what they ought to get, is a civics lesson," says NBC anchor John Chancellor. "The conventions give us time . . . to raise and discuss the most important issues of the day."[75] Maybe so, but there are other reasons. Live convention coverage is one of the few substantial blocks of time the news divisions have won from the entertainment divisions, and they are loath to give it up. Future ratings may be involved, since network newscasters believe the audience they attract at convention time tends to stick with them for the news over the next four years. And prestige is certainly involved. "How would it have been perceived," asked ABC executive producer Jeff Gralnik, "if ABC had said, journalistically, this convention is worth 45 minutes each night and the rest of it is going to be Mork, Mindy, Laverne and Shirley?"[76]

Overcoverage of the convention can have serious side effects, as floor reporters scramble for every scrap of news. This happened in Detroit concerning Reagan's last-minute bid to woo Gerald Ford onto the ticket as vice presidential nominee. The scramble started when Walter Cronkite was interviewing Ford on CBS. The ex-president did not close the door to a vice presidential offer, but indicated that certain conditions would have to be met. While Ford and Reagan representatives discussed the possibility, network newspeople interviewed everyone they could find to see if the bargain had been consummated. At one point Michigan Governor William G. Milliken told Bob Schieffer of CBS that "the reports I'm getting from the networks and radio are that the deal hasn't been done."[77] Sources were feeding TV rumors back to TV as confirmation.

As long as each network knows instantly what the others have reported, and victories are measured in seconds, it will be hard to break this cycle of rumors. The networks defend themselves by pointing out that they only report what their sources tell them. What they don't say is that in print journalism there is time to evaluate what sources have said, to compare stories and sort out truth from rumor. In live television there is no time, and the viewer must do the sorting.

magazines.[78] An earlier study, completed in 1960, revealed that four-fifths of all Americans learned more about national election campaigns from newspapers and television than from interpersonal conversation.[79] It is still quite likely that most Americans are more influenced by their friends than by the media when it comes to political opinions and attitudes (see pp. 4-5), but political information appears to come largely from the media.

Traditionally, the media have been as unfair in election coverage as they thought they could get away with. In 1952, for example, several researchers found that newspapers that supported Eisenhower on their editorial page tended to give him more and better coverage on their news pages as well. Papers that supported Stevenson were equally biased in favor of their candidate. Since there were many more Republican than Democratic papers, this raised a serious ethical problem.

The problem is much less serious today. Guido H. Stempel III studied campaign coverage in fifteen metropolitan dailies for 1960 and 1964, and found that both parties were given roughly equal news space.[80] The same was true in 1968; even third-party candidate George Wallace was treated fairly.[81] And a content analysis of 1972 campaign coverage in the three networks, the *Philadelphia Inquirer,* the *Philadelphia Evening Bulletin,* and the *New York Times* showed the same even-handed pattern. In fact, the three newspapers gave more space to the candidate they didn't endorse than to the one they did.[82] Obviously, professional news judgment was determining coverage, not the prerogatives of ownership.

The same pattern continued throughout the 1970s, including the 1980 campaign. With only occasional exceptions, the media proved themselves admirably even-handed in their coverage of political candidates, regardless of editorial endorsements. Even in local campaigns, where news bias has traditionally been heaviest, the trend of the 1970s was to bend over backwards to be fair. A 1978 study of eleven mayoral elections in various Texas cities, for example, found that newspapers gave *more* space overall to the candidates they opposed editorially than to the ones they endorsed.[83] Bias is no longer a serious problem in campaign coverage.

There is one huge exception to this statement: the media are unalterably biased against "minor" candidates. The unspoken assumption of virtually all political journalists is that candidates deserve coverage only to the extent that they are likely to be elected. The reasoning is circular, of course—candidates who the media judge cannot win receive scanty media attention, which in turn guarantees that they cannot win, which justifies the scanty attention.

We have already discussed this dynamic as it bore on the 1980 chances of John Anderson. Among the primary candidates of 1980 who received short shrift in the media because they couldn't win were Edmund G. Brown, Howard Baker, Robert Dole, and Philip Crane.[84] And after the primaries, presidential candidates of the "minor parties" were similarly ignored—Barry Commoner of the Citizens Party, Ed Clark of the Libertarian Party, and a host of others.

It is easy to sympathize with the media position on minor candidates—why squander valuable news time and space on a candidate who can never win? But it is also easy to understand the anger of candidates who have been treated so cavalierly. Their positions on the issues may well merit public attention, regardless of their electoral chances. Are reporters covering an election or a horse race?

The answer is that they are covering a horse race. Coverage of the major candidates, too, avoids evaluating their competence, their integrity, their consistency on the issues, or even their positions on the issues. Instead, it focuses on the techniques of the campaign—who is winning, who is losing, and what they are doing that is causing them to win or lose. It focuses, in short, on the horse race.

A study of CBS coverage of the 1980 pri-maries, for example, found that 54 percent of the content was devoted to who's winning and who's losing, versus only 17 percent to the substantive issues. This proportion was about the same as in the 1972 and 1976 cam-paigns, a consistent three-to-one ratio of horse race to issues.[85] Another 1980 study of the *New York Times, Washington Post* and *Chicago Tribune* found ratios ranging from five-to-one to two-to-one, all in favor of the horse race. To be sure, the newspapers also ran many solid stories about the issues, but "the reader had to wade through reams of column inches" to find them. Overall, the researchers concluded, the three papers showed "an uncontrollable addiction to fore-casting results" and "a subjugation of stories about issues by stories about pithy speeches, tactics, style, and above all else, who was ahead."[86]

The same problems that limit the effective-ness of the White House press corps in its coverage of the president also constrain the reporters who handle presidential campaigns. Obliged to cover the candidate minute by minute, reporters see thousands of trees and miss the forest. They hear the same speeches over and over again, ask the same questions, read the same polls, see the same babies kissed. Halfway through the campaign they are so exhausted that it's all they can do to file a story of any sort. But their employers are paying a small fortune so they can parade around the country in the wake of the candi-date, so they must file every day, even if nothing important has happened. For the most part they file on the horse race.

In 1972 one reporter, Hunter Thompson of *Rolling Stone* magazine, earned a national reputation with his free-wheeling stories on the meaning and direction of the campaign.

TV ON THE CAMPAIGN TRAIL

Political campaigns are won and lost on television. During Ronald Reagan's 1980 presi-dential race, for example, 22 out of 51 press seats on the candidate's plane were re-served for the three networks. Press secretary Lyn Nofziger sometimes gave the networks releases and transcripts that he withheld from the other reporters. "The most effective thing we can do is put [Reagan] on television whenever we can," Nofziger explained. "Each of the three networks has tremendously bigger circulation than any individual newspaper or magazine."[87]

Television is just as important on the local and state levels. Two Washington lawyers studied TV coverage of races in Massachusetts, Tennessee, and Indiana and came up with the following recommendations on how to handle the medium:

1. Make sure the camera crew can shoot the story and get back to the studio in time for the late afternoon news.
2. Provide some sort of visual angle.
3. Divide the electoral district up into media markets and visit each one on a regular basis.
4. If an event isn't going to be covered, cover it yourself by providing footage to the stations.
5. Don't do anything until the cameras arrive.
6. Keep statements short and simple. In this way you can control the 30 to 60 seconds the reporter will select to use in the newscast.
7. If a reporter asks a tough question, make your answer so long and confusing that it cannot be put on the air.
8. Don't overestimate the ability of local TV newspeople. Most of them won't catch your mistakes.[88]

Readers appreciated Thompson's behind-the-scenes interpretations, and reporters envied his journalistic freedom. Thompson's tendency to mix fact, opinion, and imagination without telling the reader which is which represents a potentially dangerous style of political journalism. But at least he tried to explain where the campaign was going, and why. Most election reporting merely tells us that the campaign is still going.

Ironically enough, one main reason for this stress on the horse race is the new-found objectivity of political coverage. "It is easier to avoid being called biased," write Charles Self and Jim Stovall of the University of Alabama, "if one avoids what is said and concentrates instead on the *fact that something was said,* the circumstances under which it was said and the possible reasons the candidate might have had for saying it—in other words, to concentrate on the techniques of the campaign."[89] The tendency is exacerbated by the fact that political reporters, not issue specialists, handle most of the coverage. Comments the *New Republic:* "For many political reporters, issues are merely the playing field on which the game of politics is performed."[90]

In the absence of serious attention to issues, reporters become obsessed with trivia. The possible "blunders" of candidates seem especially newsworthy—Gerald Ford's debate misstatement in 1976 that Poland was not under Soviet domination; Jimmy Carter's admission to *Playboy,* also in 1976, that he had lust in his heart; Ronald Reagan's ethnic joke on the campaign plane in 1980. Each of these incidents occupied the press corps for days.

Once again a vicious cycle is at work. The media overcover such campaign blunders not because reporters consider them important, but because reporters think voters will consider them important. They are overcovered because they may affect the horse race. But if they do in fact affect the race—a question no one can answer—they do so only because the media thought they might and therefore

focused on them. By avoiding the issues, in other words, the media encourage voters to base their decisions on other grounds, which then justifies the media's tendency to avoid the issues.

It is almost as if the newspaper reader and the television viewer were not voters at all, but rather disinterested observers of the political process. The media offer us an incredibly detailed blow-by-blow account of the campaign. They keep us right up to the minute on who's winning and how. But they tell us almost nothing about who ought to win, about how the world might change if one candidate won instead of the other. As amateur political scientists, we can learn a lot from the media. As voters, we seldom learn enough.

POLITICAL ADVERTISING

For many people the main source of "news" about political candidates is not the news at all. It is political advertising, especially television advertising. One study of TV viewers, for example, found no relationship between what they learned about the candidates and how much network news they watched—but those who saw a large number of political ads learned more than those who saw fewer ads.[91]

This use of broadcasting is a fairly recent phenomenon. Presidential candidates spent only $6.1 million on TV and radio time in 1952, but by 1972 the figure had climbed to $59.6 million. Federal limits on campaign funding forced the figure down by 1980, but no serious political candidate today fails to allocate a sizeable percentage of the campaign budget—usually the largest single chunk—to political advertising.

The typical political ad is a 30-second or one-minute TV spot inserted between two popular entertainment programs. It is designed and produced by a professional advertising agency. Candidates retain a veto power, but they don't use it very often if they want to win. After all, in the business of packaging and marketing products the ad agencies are pros. The candidates are merely the products, and act accordingly. They do what they're told.

A classic case of political advertising was the 1966 re-election bid of New York Governor (later Vice President) Nelson Rockefeller. The incumbent, Rockefeller was extremely unpopular with the electorate, and early polls indicated that literally any Democrat could defeat him. Frank D. O'Connor was picked for the job.

Rocky won the election (by 400,000 votes) on the strength of a massive media campaign. He spent well over $2 million on television ads alone. On WNBC in New York City, Rockefeller ran 208 commercials at a cost of $237,000; O'Connor bought 23 ads on this station, spending only $41,000. It was that way throughout the state. In the rural city of Watertown, the Rockefeller campaign spent $3,067 on 99 TV spots; O'Connor spent $1,307 on a mere 18 spots.

Jack Tinker & Partners (of Alka-Seltzer fame) designed the commercials. Rockefeller's face and voice were seldom used. A typical early ad featured a talking fish in an underwater news interview. The reporter asks the fish about the governor's Pure Waters Program. The fish says that things are still pretty smelly, but thanks to Rocky they're getting better. "I would say, uh, next to a fish. . . . I'd say he's the best gov. . . ."

Later the campaign took a nasty turn. One script read: "Frank O'Connor, the man who led the fight against the New York State Thruway, is running for governor. Get in your car. Drive down to the polls, and vote." Actually, O'Connor had fought for a free thruway against Rockefeller's plan for a tollroad. But the O'Connor campaign lacked the money to clear up the record.[92]

Campaigns such as the Rockefeller-O'Connor race raise two important questions. First, what does it mean for democracy when only the wealthiest candidates (or those who can raise the cash from supporters) are able to mount an effective, "modern" campaign?

And second, what does it mean for democracy when political candidates are sold to the public like Alka-Seltzer?

Of course there is another side to the argument. Political advertising does give the candidates a chance to address the public directly on the issues. This circumvents both the failure of many citizens to pay attention to political news and the tendency of the media to stress the horse race instead of the issues. Better 30 slick seconds on Candidate X's opinions about inflation than no information at all. In addition, it is said with some justice that television advertising permits an unknown candidate to reach the public and thus defeat a well-established incumbent. Since the news invariably focuses on known candidates, advertising becomes a much-needed vehicle for unknowns to *become* known.

The designers of political ads rely heavily on the polls, of course, but they rely just as heavily on experience, intuition, and luck. Many schools of thought on what works and what doesn't flourish simultaneously, waxing or waning temporarily with the success or failure of a particular campaign. In the wake of Watergate, political ad campaigns have tended to shy away from "dirty tricks," focusing more on the candidate's personal integrity, record of performance, and stand (oversimplified, of course) on the issues. But many ads still lack substantive content. In 1980, consultant Robert Goodman sold Wyoming Senator Malcolm Wallop by putting him on a horse in front of 75 other horsemen, backed by stirring western music and the slogan "Ride with us, Wyoming." And Goodman strapped a cameraman to a tree for three hours to photograph a sunset behind an 11,000-foot ridge in New Mexico to help sell Senator Peter V. Domenici.[93]

Presidential campaign ads in 1980 lacked the razzle-dazzle of some earlier campaigns, perhaps because political reporters now monitor the ads carefully for news of campaign strategy. Carter's ads alternately tried to frighten voters about Ronald Reagan and to wrap Carter in the mantle of the presidency (with lots of shots of the president at work). Reagan's ads attacked the Carter record, demanded fiscal responsibility and military strength, and stressed the candidate's experience as governor of California. The most controversial presidential ad of 1980 came from minor-party candidate Barry Commoner, who used a taboo eight-letter word (seldom before heard on television) to describe his view of the Carter and Reagan campaigns.

Controversial or not, slick or strident or straightforward, one prediction is a sure bet. Political advertising will continue to play an important role in American election campaigns.

ELECTION NIGHT

The broadcast media devote an incredible amount of money and time to election-night coverage. The networks let out all the stops, hiring every computer programmer and news analyst in sight. Local broadcasters do the same thing on a smaller scale. No expense is spared to make sure that viewers are told who won and who lost at the earliest possible second. A great deal of network prestige rides on the question of which one makes the important predictions first.

This election-night performance certainly provides the most accurate, detailed, up-to-the-minute information about election results that any viewer could possibly demand. In fact, the criticism has centered on the notion that it might be *too* up-to-the-minute. Relying on computers, sophisticated sampling techniques, and exit polling of voters, NBC in 1980 was able to predict Ronald Reagan's victory by 8:15 p.m. eastern time, long before the polls were due to close in the west. Nobody knows how many western voters decided to stay home as a result, and nobody knows how their staying home affected close local races. But NBC's achievement revived suggestions that the U.S. copy a Canadian law forbidding broadcasters to announce any results until the polls are closed everywhere.

CAMPAIGNING IN BRITAIN

Despite the shared political heritage of Britain and the United States, politicking in Britain is vastly different from the American experience. The 1974 British elections provide a case in point.

As soon as Parliament was dissolved and an election called, all broadcast political advertising immediately ceased, as required by British law. Instead, the two major parties, Labour and Conservative, were given five free TV appearances each, while the minority Liberal Party got three. That was it—no extra time may be purchasd during a campaign.

Extra time wasn't really needed, since the British media devoted extraordinary attention to the campaign. Both the BBC and the Independent Broadcasting Authority allocated all their public-affairs time to the election. For three days Radio London offered four minutes of free time to each of 300 parliamentary candidates.

The three prospective prime ministers—Harold Wilson, Edward Heath, and Jeremy Thorpe—held daily press conferences at their London headquarters. This effectively limited campaigning to day trips throughout Britain. Thus reporters (and candidates) did not have to undergo the wearying experience of months on the road, American style.

The whole campaign, from the dissolution of Parliament to election day, took three weeks. The average parliamentary candidate was permitted to spend only $4,000—and most spent less. The entire cost for all 1,800 candidates, including Wilson, Heath, and Thorpe, was a mere $5.5 million.[94]

Daniel Henninger of the *Wall Street Journal* comments:

What we were really watching election night was three enormously wealthy networks whose news divisions had made large investments in computer technology, on-camera talent and a vast web of precinct pollsters for the primary purpose of being able to say that a particular network was first, by minutes, in projecting the outcome of a campaign whose results would within minutes be common knowledge. On its own terms this may be no small achievement, but on its own terms it isn't much to begin with. Perhaps it's time the networks started listening to people within their organizations who have some fresh ideas about the business.[95]

Of the thousands upon thousands of news stories about national government, the best-covered story of them all may well be election night. This in itself tells us something important about the mass media. They are at their best with the concrete details of a dramatic competition, where they can impartially record the battle and impartially announce the winner. No story involves less news management than the results of an election. No story is less influenced by friendships with news sources. No story makes so few demands for independence, integrity, and the adversary relationship. That is why the media do such a good job with election results.

Notes

[1] Laura Longley Babb, ed., *Of the Press, By the Press, For the Press (And Others, Too)* (New York: Dell, 1974), p. 117.

[2] William L. Rivers, *The Adversaries* (Boston: Beacon Press, 1970).

[3] Harry S. Ashmore, *Fear in the Air. Broadcasting and the First Amendment: The Anatomy of a Constitutional Crisis* (New York: W. W. Norton, 1973), p. 59.

[4] William L. Rivers and Michael Nyhan, eds., *Aspen Notebook on Government and the Media* (New York: Praeger, 1973), p. 16.

[5] "California Poll," *Time,* June 17, 1974, p. 42.

[6] Edith Baumann, letter to the editor, *New York Times,* August 13, 1974, p. 34.

[7] James Reston, "The Age of Destruction," *New York Times,* December 7, 1979, p. A31.

[8] Tom Bethell, "The Myth of an Adversary Press," *Harper's,* January, 1977, p. 33.

[9] Leo C. Rosten, *The Washington Correspondents* (New York: Harcourt, Brace and Company, 1937), p. 249.

[10] Elmer E. Cornwell Jr., *Presidential Leadership of Public Opinion* (Bloomington, Ind.: Indiana University Press, 1965), p. 14.

[11] James E. Pollard, "The Kennedy Administration and the Press," *Journalism Quarterly,* Winter, 1964, p. 14.

[12] Terence Smith, "On Carter and the Washington Press Corps," *New York Times,* August 2, 1979, p. A14.

[13] Cornwell, *Presidential Leadership,* p. 220.

[14] William L. Rivers, *The Opinionmakers* (Boston: Beacon Press, 1965), p. 144.

[15] Carl Bernstein and Bob Woodward, *All the President's Men* (New York: Simon and Schuster, 1974).

[16] "Mum's the Word at White House These Days," *Miami Herald,* January 14, 1973, p. 5K.

[17] Charles Peters, "Why the White House Press Didn't Get the Watergate Story," *Washington Monthly,* July/August, 1973, p. 14.

[18] "White House Disputes a Report of Washington Post 'Exclusion,'" *New York Times,* December 19, 1972, p. 30.

[19] "Horner's Corner," *Newsweek,* December 25, 1972, pp. 51-52.

[20] Peters, "Why the White House Press," p. 8.

[21] John Osborne, "The White House Watch—In Jody's Shop (II)," *New Republic,* March 25, 1978, p. 10.

[22] John Osborne, "The White House Watch—In Jody's Shop (I)," *New Republic,* March 18, 1978, p. 18.

[23] Dom Bonafede, "The President's Publicity Machine," *Washington Journalism Review,* May, 1980, p. 44.

[24] Meg Greenfield, "Shotgun Marriage," *Newsweek,* July 21, 1975, p. 72.

[25] Ron Nessen, "Poor Jody Powell," *Newsweek,* January 31, 1977, p. 9.

[26] Clinton Rossiter, *The American Presidency* (New York: Harcourt Brace Jovanovich, 1956), p. 114.

[27] "TV Networks, in a Shift, Air Ford at His Request," *New York Times,* October 16, 1974, p. 20.

28 Charles Mohr, "TV Rings Out a Carter Show," *New York Times,* December 10, 1977.

29 Les Brown, "Timing of Carter Speech on TV Questioned," *New York Times,* February 2, 1978, p. C16.

30 Bonafede, "The President's Publicity Machine," p. 49.

31 Michael Grossman and Martha Kumar, "Why Relations Between the Press and the President Will Get Worse If Carter Is Reelected and Better If Reagan (or Anyone Else) Is Elected," *Washington Journalism Review,* May, 1980, pp. 51-56.

32 Douglass Cater, *The Fourth Branch of Government* (New York: Vintage Books, 1959), p. 78.

33 Elmer E. Cornwell Jr., "Presidential News: The Expanding Public Image," *Journalism Quarterly,* Summer, 1959, p. 278.

34 Edmund B. Lambeth, "A Cooperative Approach to Research and Media Criticism: A Case Study of Washington's Special TV Correspondents," paper presented to the Association for Education in Journalism, Boston, Mass., 1980, pp. 5, 8.

35 Rivers, *The Opinionmakers,* pp. 22-23.

36 "Lee Catterall—Wyoming's 1-Man Washington Bureau," *Editor & Publisher,* December 15, 1973, pp. 35-36.

37 Susan H. Miller, "The Collaborators: Congress and the Press," unpublished manuscript, p. 16.

38 James Reston, *The Artillery of the Press* (New York: Harper Colophon Books, 1966), p. 73.

39 George Barnes Galloway, *The Legislative Process in Congress* (New York: Crowell, 1953), p. 222.

40 Joseph Nocera, "How to Make the Front Page," *Washington Monthly,* October, 1978, pp. 12-23.

41 "The House Likes its TV System," *Broadcasting,* March 31, 1980, p. 78.

42 "O'Neill Rates Television in US House 'a Disaster,'" *Boston Globe,* August 4, 1979, p. 9.

43 "House Restricts Secret Meetings of Its Own Panels," *New York Times,* March 8, 1973, p. 1.

44 "Senate, 47 to 38, Retains a Limit on Open Hearings," *New York Times,* March 7, 1973, p. 1.

45 Wallace Carroll, "Essence, Not Angle," *Columbia Journalism Review,* Summer, 1965, p. 5.

46 David Ericson, "Newspaper Coverage of the Supreme Court: A Case Study," *Journalism Quarterly,* Autumn, 1977, pp. 605-607.

47 *Archibald Newsletter,* Freedom of Information Center, Columbia, Mo., no. 5, August, 1970, pp. 2-3.

48 Edward M. Glick, "Press-Government Relationships," *Journalism Quarterly,* Spring, 1966, pp. 53-54.

49 Courtney Sheldon, "A Vote of No Confidence for Background Briefings," *APME News,* June, 1972, p. 3.

50 "Politicians and the Press," p. 72.

51 Alfred Friendly, "Attribution of News," *Nieman Reports,* July, 1958, p. 12.

52 "U.S. and France: Two Views on Oil," *New York Times,* December 15, 1974, p. 3.

53 Tom Wicker, "Background Blues," *New York Times,* December 16, 1971, p. 35.

54 "White House Newsmen's Group Affirms 'Backgrounder' Rules," *New York Times,* January 4, 1972, p. 28.

55 James Reston, "In Defense of Leaks," *New York Times,* June 21, 1974, p. 37.

56 Paul F. Lazarsfeld, "Public Opinion and the Classical Tradition," in Charles S. Steinberg, ed., *Mass Media and Communication* (New York: Hastings House, 1966), pp. 79-93.

57 Seymour Martin Lipset, *The First New Nation* (Garden City, N.Y.: Anchor Books, 1967), p. 123.

58 Lester Markel, *What You Don't Know Can Hurt You* (New York: Quadrangle, 1972), pp. 8-9.

59 *Ibid.,* p. 9.

60 *Ibid.,* p. 31.

61 "39% of Americans in Poll Named Their 2 Senators," *New York Times,* December 3, 1973, p. 34.

62 Walter Lippmann, *Public Opinion* (New York: Free Press Paperbacks, 1965), pp. 48-49.

63 Markel, *What You Don't Know Can Hurt You,* p. 19.

64 *Ibid.,* p. 17.

65 Stephen Chapman, "The Public Opinion Hustle," *New Republic,* November 25, 1978, p. 15.

66 Henry Fairlie, "Galluping Toward Dead Center," *New Republic,* April 8, 1978, p. 19.

67 Timothy Crouse, *The Boys on the Bus* (New York: Random House, 1972), pp. 45-46.

68 Irving Crespi, "The Case of Presidential Popularity," in Albert H. Cantril, ed., *Polling on the Issues* (Washington, D.C.: Seven Locks Press, 1980), p. 29.

69 Anthony Lewis, Second Annual Chet Huntley Memorial Address, New York University, New York, N.Y., November 13, 1980, p. 17.

70 *Ibid.,* pp. 8-9.

71 Paul H. Weaver, "Captives of Melodrama," *New York Times Magazine,* August 29, 1976, p. 6.

72 Bernard Weinraub, "Party Delegates Outnumbered by News Media's Delegates," *New York Times,* August 12, 1980, p. B14.

73 *Ibid.* Steven Rattner, "Extent of News Coverage

Questioned at Convention," *New York Times,* July 17, 1980, p. B8.

74 Tony Schwartz, "Networks Are Running Hard for the Viewer's Acclamation," *New York Times,* July 14, 1980, p. A11.

75 *Ibid.*

76 Rattner, "Extent of News Coverage Questioned at Convention," p. B8.

77 Daniel Henninger, "The Night the TV News Dam Broke," *Wall Street Journal,* July 18, 1980, p. 12.

78 Serena Wade and Wilbur Schramm, "The Mass Media as Sources of Public Affairs, Science and Health Knowledge," *Public Opinion Quarterly,* Summer, 1969, p. 198.

79 Dan Nimmo, *The Political Persuaders* (Englewood Cliffs, N.J.: Prentice-Hall, 1970), p. 113.

80 Guido H. Stempel III, "The Prestige Press in Two Presidential Elections," *Journalism Quarterly,* Winter, 1965, p. 21.

81 Guido H. Stempel III, "The Prestige Press Meets the Third Party Challenge," *Journalism Quarterly,* Winter, 1969, p. 701.

82 Robert G. Meadow, "Cross Media Comparison of Coverage of the 1972 Presidential Campaign," *Journalism Quarterly,* Autumn, 1973, pp. 482-88.

83 J. Sean McCleneghan, "Effects of Endorsements on News Space in Texas Papers," *Journalism Quarterly,* Winter, 1978, pp. 792-93.

84 Douglas Lowenstein, "Covering the Primaries," *Washington Journalism Review,* September, 1980, pp. 38-42.

85 "Study Finds TV Devotes More Time to 'Horse Race' Than to Campaign Issues," *Broadcasting,* July 7, 1980, p. 47.

86 Lowenstein, "Covering the Primaries," pp. 38-42.

87 Howell Raines, "Reporter's Notebook: Ghost in Reagan Camp," *New York Times,* October 5, 1980, p. 11.

88 Rick Neustadt and Richard Paisner, "How to Run on TV," *New York Times Magazine,* December 15, 1974, pp. 20, 72-74.

89 Charles Self and Jim Stovall, "Mass Media and Consensus Politics," paper presented to the Association for Education in Journalism, Boston, Mass., 1980, p. 7.

90 "The Permanent Campaign," *New Republic,* May 19, 1979, p. 6.

91 Thomas E. Patterson and Robert D. McClure, *The Unseeing Eye: The Myth of Television Power in National Elections* (New York: G.P. Putnam's Sons, 1976), *passim.*

92 James M. Perry, *The New Politics* (New York: Clarkson N. Potter, 1968), pp. 107-37.

93 Bernard Weinraub, "Bush Gets Lessons in Performing on TV," *New York Times,* January 13, 1980, p. 23.

94 Penn Kimball, "British Elections: The Old Boys on the Bus," *Columbia Journalism Review,* May/June, 1974, pp. 28-32. "Campaigning in Britain Requires Less Time and Money Than in U.S.," *New York Times,* February 18, 1974, p. 3.

95 Daniel Henninger, "Can Television Find a Better Way to Cover Our Elections?" *Wall Street Journal,* November 7, 1980, p. 27.

Suggested Readings

BAGDIKIAN, BEN H., "Congress and the Media: Partners in Propaganda," *Columbia Journalism Review,* January/February, 1974.

BARBER, JAMES DAVID, *Race For The Presidency: The Media and the Nominating Process.* Englewood Cliffs, N.J.: Prentice-Hall, 1978.

BERNSTEIN, CARL, and BOB WOODWARD, *All The President's Men.* New York: Simon & Schuster, 1974.

BETHELL, TOM, "The Myth Of An Adversary Press," *Harper's,* January, 1977.

BONAFEDE, DOM, "The President's Publicity Machine . . . The Press," *Washington Journalism Review,* May, 1980.

CATER, DOUGLASS, *The Fourth Branch of Government.* New York: Vintage Books, 1959.

CROUSE, TIMOTHY, *The Boys on the Bus.* New York: Random House, 1972.

ERICSON, DAVID, "Newspaper Coverage of the Supreme Court: A Case Study," *Journalism Quarterly,* Autumn, 1977.

HEISE, JUERGEN ARTHUR, *Minimum Disclosure: How The Pentagon Manipulates the News.* New York: Norton, 1979.

HESS, STEPHEN, *The Washington Reporters.* Washington, D.C.: The Brookings Institution, 1981.

KOTZ, NICK, et al., "Horsefeathers: The Media, the Campaign and the Economic Crisis," *Columbia Journalism Review,* July/August, 1980.

LOVELL, RON, "Keepers of the Flame," *The Quill,* February, 1981.

MARBUT, F. B., *News from the Capital: The Story of Washington Reporting.* Carbondale and Edwardsville, Ill.: Southern Illinois University Press, 1971.

McGINNISS, JOE, *The Selling of the President 1968*. New York: Trident Press, 1969.

NOCERA, JOSEPH, "How to Make the Front Page," *The Washington Monthly*, October, 1978.

PETERS, CHARLES, "Why the White House Press Didn't Get the Watergate Story," *The Washington Monthly*, July/August, 1973.

RIVERS, WILLIAM L., *The Adversaries*. Boston: Beacon Press, 1970.

SIGAL, LEON V., *The Organization and Politics of Newsmaking*. Lexington, Mass.: D. C. Heath, 1973.

THOMPSON, HUNTER S., *Fear and Loathing: On the Campaign Trail '72*. New York: Popular Library, 1973.

WEAVER, PAUL H., "Captives of Melodrama," *The New York Times Magazine*, August 29, 1976.

Chapter 16
Coverage of Local News

Most journalists do not cover national government. Instead, they cover mayors and school boards, burglaries and bond issues—the local hard news stories that fill America's newspapers and local newscasts. Journalistic neophytes cut their teeth on suburban zoning board hearings, while seasoned veterans patrol city hall. Our local mass media may owe their popularity to comics, service features, and syndicated columns, but their responsibility—the essential job only they can do—is covering local hard news. When this news is provided by local officials, they cover it well enough. But when officials keep mum, coverage of local issues is often scanty.

The news from Teheran, Paris, Washington, and even the state capital reaches its audience courtesy of the wire services, the broadcast networks, the newsmagazines, and a small number of truly national newspapers. This non-local news often seems to dominate our media, but it does not dominate the work of journalism. A mere handful of reporters can adequately cover, say, a Supreme Court decision on school busing—but it takes hundreds of reporters to cover the way school boards around the country implement the decision. Only local media can cover local news, and covering local news is the job that preoccupies the vast majority of reporters and editors.

To the average American, furthermore, busing problems at the local schools are far more important than a Supreme Court decision on busing. A proposed toxic wastes dump across town is far more important than new toxics regulations at the Environmental Protection Agency. The threatened closing of the nearest hospital is far more important than the national crisis in health care delivery. Nothing can replace these local hard news stories.

This said, we will paradoxically begin our discussion of local coverage with crime—the most thoroughly covered of all local news beats, and the only local story that is actually *over*-reported. Yet the defects of crime coverage mirror the more serious defects of other areas of local coverage—the emphasis on events instead of issues, the reliance on official sources, and the scarcity of investigative and interpretive reporting.

America has always been profoundly interested in violence and lawlessness—a holdover, perhaps, from its revolutionary and frontier beginnings. Nowhere is this preoccupation more clearly reflected than in the content of the nation's local mass media. The average newspaper or broadcast station may or may not cover a new city ordinance or a school bond issue. But a bank robbery, a kidnaping, or a rape/murder is sure to get extensive play.

It has always been that way. The first specialized reporter in American journalism, hired in 1833, covered the police beat. The most typical article in the Yellow Press at the turn of the century was the crime story, with headlines like "Death Rides the Blast," "Love and Cold Poison," "Screaming for Mercy," and "Baptized in Blood." The tabloid papers of the 1920s followed the same tradition. They are still at it today. So are many standard-sized newspapers, though their headlines may be smaller and less enticing. Even the *New York Times* cannot resist a juicy murder now and then.

The worst offenders today are local television newscasts, many of which lead with violent crime stories almost every night. Inflation and unemployment may be up, the arms race may be spiraling, the city may be teetering on the edge of bankruptcy, but the solemn-voiced promo still intones "bizarre ice-pick murder on the north side . . . news at eleven." And sure enough, if you are seduced into watching, you are rewarded with an almost mythic tale of good versus evil: the gritty street scene, the flashing lights and screaming sirens, the stolid cop discoursing on perpetrators and alleged victims, the distraught relative howling about injustice, the bemused bystander recounting how scary it was, perhaps even a quick shot of the body or the accused in handcuffs. Inflation, unemployment, the arms race, and municipal bankruptcy will be squeezed in after the first set of commercials.

Obviously, editors believe crime news sells newspapers and news programs. They are probably right. A series of .44 caliber murders terrorized New Yorkers in 1976 and 1977. On the day "Son of Sam" was finally captured, the *New York Post* sold 391,000 extra copies, and the *Daily News* sold 350,000 more than usual.[1] No school bond issue ever accomplished that.

But why is the media audience so preoccupied with violent crime in the first place? The easy answer is that Americans are bored and crave excitement. There is probably some truth to this charge, but social scientists have repeatedly found that the public's interest in crime is grounded less in excitement than in fear. Crime in the streets is a genuine and serious problem in American cities and suburbs. And the fear of crime is stark, widespread, and very, very real.

The mass media did not create the fear of crime. But by catering to that fear, they perpetuate, exaggerate, and distort it. The prototypic black, teenaged mugger of middle-class white women is not a figment of the media's imagination, but he is a great deal less common than the media imply. Most crimes committed by blacks are committed against blacks, and many violent crimes take place between people who know each other. Yet the media underplay crimes against blacks and crimes arising from family quarrels, and grossly overplay street crimes against the white middle class. They thus increase the fear that justifies the coverage that increases the fear—and so the cycle continues, apparently forever.

Apart from the public's insatiable interest, there is another reason for lavishing time and space on crime news: It is ridiculously easy to cover. A reporter sits at a desk in the police station, listens to the police radio, and chats with various friends on the force. Every once in a while the reporter telephones the smaller police stations in the area, and asks the desk sergeant to check the blotter. Just before deadline, the reporter calls the newsroom and dictates any grue-

THE ETHICS OF CRIME NEWS

Crime news raises a number of specialized ethical issues that reporters and editors must attempt to solve. Four of the thorniest problems are the names of juvenile offenders, the race of suspects, the names of witnesses and victims, and the pressure to ignore some crime news altogether.

Juveniles. Some editors argue that young people are more likely to "go straight" if they are not publicly identified as criminals. They therefore withhold the names of juvenile offenders. Other editors believe that readers have a right to know the names of criminals in their midst, and that the embarrassment of publicity may actually aid in their redemption. Government officials also disagree on this point. In some states all juvenile records are confidential. Other states leave it up to the editor, and still others let the judge decide in each individual case.

Race. Until the 1960s, it was customary for the media to include the race of minority suspects in crime stories. Today this practice is frowned upon, sometimes on the grounds that race is irrelevant, and sometimes on the grounds that its relevance, though genuine, is subject to misinterpretation by a fearful white middle class. In 1970 the *San Francisco Examiner* editorialized:

> Crimes are committed by individuals, not races. Race is not an inherent factor in criminal tendencies. This is basically why we adopted several years ago the practice of omitting race from crime stories unless race has pertinence.
> If a crime is racial in nature we say so and identify the principals by race. If a criminal is at large and the printing of his race will aid in catching him, we print it.[2]

Of course most newspapers still give the names and addresses of suspects, making a tentative racial identification possible if the reader wants to work at it. And fearful white readers can and possibly do assume that most unidentified criminals are black. It might do more good for the media to publicize the fact that crimes against whites are usually committed by whites.

Names. The mass media seldom publish the names of rape victims, but aside from that the media are diverse and inconsistent in their policies on using the names of victims and witnesses. The *St. Louis Post-Dispatch* is one of the few newspapers in the country with formal guidelines in this area. Unless the victim asks to be identified, the paper omits the name in all cases where publicity might embarrass or degrade the victim, such as sex crimes. Burglary victims, however, are always identified by name and block number. Except in major cases, witnesses aren't identified at all.[3] Other media have decided these questions differently, and most simply haven't decided them.

Blackouts. The pressure to withhold crime news comes from many different sources, and with many different justifications—spectacular crimes spawn a raft of imitators; criminals thrive on the notoriety given their handiwork; too much crime news creates a mood of fear and a bad image of the community. The media are sometimes persuaded by these arguments, sometimes not. In 1974, the *Daily Freeman-Journal* in Webster City, Iowa, revealed that it had joined with radio station KQWC in a three-month moratorium on local news stories about vandalism. Despite the blackout, the paper reported, vandalism had increased. It concluded: "An uninformed public often harbors a false sense of self-security. The outcome of the past three months is proof of that."[4]

some facts to a rewrite specialist, who puts them into paragraphs. Photographers are dispatched to the more photogenic crime scenes—the same ones that TV crews turn up at.

This technique for handling crime news results in several abuses. Since the reporter works hand in glove with the police, crime stories almost invariably favor the official point of view. On a minor story, the reporter is unlikely to meet the accused at all; the suspect's protestations of innocence or charges of police brutality therefore go unreported. Moreover, a journalist whose research is confined to the police blotter will never learn much about the underlying causes of crime, or even the motives for a particular crime. Many criminal acts today are a reflection of social unrest, of racial discrimination or political repression, of poverty, joblessness, and systematic exclusion from "the good life." Such factors are far too seldom adequately covered by the media.

The blood-and-guts approach to crime news and the dependence on police sources also result in far greater coverage of arrests than of trials. News of an arrest is both absorbing and easy to get. News of a trial requires a lot more work on the reporter's part, and is interesting to the audience only if the case is especially important or especially juicy. And when a suspect is acquitted or charges are dropped, that's hardly news at all.

While many media continue to rely on the police blotter for crime news, others are beginning to cover more important aspects of crime. Some papers and stations have explained how people can protect themselves against burglaries, muggings, and rapes. Some have discussed the growth of neighborhood crime-prevention groups. Some have examined crimes against the poor in inner-city ghettos and high-rise low-income developments. Some have looked seriously at white-collar crime. Some have even analyzed the sociology of crime, the relationship between criminal violence and intolerable social conditions.

Not all crime news, in other words, is a waste of time and space. When crime reporter Don Bolles of the *Arizona Republic* was murdered by underworld figures, a consortium of reporters from around the country organized into Investigative Reporters and Editors. The group's 23-part series on organized crime in Arizona, published in 1977, focused largely on underworld ties to corporate and political leaders. It was clearly a valuable undertaking, as was the *Republic*'s 16-page special section on the same subject a year later.[5]

But as currently reported, most crime news *is* a waste of time and space. It may even be harmful. As early as 1801, observers were already protesting the excesses of media sensationalism:

> Some of the shocking articles in the paper raise simple, very simple wonder; some terror; and some horror and disgust. . . . Do they not shock tender minds and addle shallow brains? They make a thousand old maids and ten thousand booby boys afraid to go to bed alone.[6]

Crimes like the .44 caliber killings in New York must be covered, but the public is not well served by headlines like the *New York Post*'s "NO ONE IS SAFE FROM THE SON OF SAM!" And sensationalism aside, most crime stories are not particularly valuable to the society as a whole. Unexplained and uninterpreted, a mugging or a robbery just isn't as important as a school bond issue.

THE SYSTEM OF JUSTICE

In contrast to their incessant attention to crime itself, the daily media have little to say about the American system of justice. Each criminal act is treated as an isolated event that begins at the moment of violence and ends at the moment of arrest. How society deals with the criminal is a matter of little interest to the mass media.

Consider the police department. Though most crime news is obtained from police sources, the police department itself is seldom adequately covered. Are police officers poorly trained? Are they underpaid and overworked? How many are on the take, and why? How many despise poor people, or black people, or all people not in uniform, and how does this affect their treatment of suspects and witnesses? What are the policies and practices of your local police department concerning the harassment of suspected criminals, the use of guns and violence, the reporting of corrupt officers, etc.? How much stress is put by the police on white-collar crime and organized crime, as opposed to pornography, marijuana, and similar offenses? Why do so many noncriminals hate the police? With occasional exceptions—the *Philadelphia Inquirer* and the *Miami Herald,* for example, have published award-winning series on the problems of their police departments—the media rarely raise these sorts of questions.

Why? For one thing, the complexities of police-community relations are a lot less enticing to most readers and viewers than the details of a spicy crime. And covering these sorts of issues requires aggressive investigative reporting, which takes a lot more time and skill than copying the police blotter. Perhaps most important, police reporters understand, admire, and depend on their police sources. They are not generally enthusiastic about the idea of provoking a scandal. Significantly, the 1977 *Philadelphia Inquirer* series on police brutality that won a Pulitzer Prize was not the work of police reporters at all; Jonathan Neumann and William K. Marimow, who normally covered the courts, spent four months on the investigation. For the most part it takes a renegade cop, an independent commission, or the accidental shooting of a bystander to force the media to examine the police as an institution.

When the police are finished with a crime, the courts are ready to begin. We have already noted that court reporting is a lot less extensive than police reporting, because trial news takes more work to cover and is less interesting to the audience. And that's routine

court reporting, the sort that merely reconstructs the crime itself in the words of witnesses and attorneys. Investigative court reporting is rarer still. One 1978 study found 193 reporter-written court stories in 428 issues of various newspapers—a little under one story every other issue. All but 14 of the articles were spot news coverage of specific trials; 13 were features and one was an editorial. Not a single investigative article on the court system turned up in the sample.[7]

In recent years the media have slowly come to grips with the conflict between complete reporting of crime news and the defendant's right to a fair trial (see pp. 191-94). Despite many setbacks and exceptions, reporters today are more careful than they used to be about trying not to prejudice their audience against a suspect or defendant. Perhaps as a result of this caution, the once common practice of journalistic detective work is now a rarity. It does happen—in 1978 an Arkansas newspaper editor proved that a local resident could not have been in Texas on the date a crime was committed in Houston, thus freeing the suspect.[8] But today it is the unusual newspaper or station that digs up its own witnesses and evidence to challenge (or support) the prosecution's interpretation of a crime.

When the courts are honest and capable, this new journalistic restraint protects the innocent. When the courts are corrupt or incompetent, it protects the judicial system instead. The media audience, unfortunately, is unlikely to find out which is the case, because reporting of the courts as an institution is almost nonexistent. How much do judges differ in the sentences they mete out for the same offense? Which judges are senile, or arbitrary, or consistently overruled on appeal? How long does the average defendant languish in jail before trial, and what staffing needs are responsible for the delay? How adequate are the prosecutors and public defenders, the parole officers and other agents of the judicial system? How are juries chosen, and what sorts of people wind up on them? Why are so many cases settled by an agreement to plead guilty to a lesser charge? And when was the last time you read a news story on these topics in the paper, or saw one on television?

For an example of what court reporting can be like, consider the career of Selwyn Raab, one of the best court reporters in the United States.

In 1964, the New York City police accused George Whitmore, Jr. of attempting to rape Elba Borrero, a practical nurse. The police announced that under questioning the young Brooklyn black had confessed to three murders as well—but Whitmore said the confessions had been beaten out of him. Raab's investigation proved that on the day of two of the murders, Whitmore had been 150 miles from the scene. Eventually a drug addict confessed to the two murders. Whitmore's trial on the third murder charge ended in a hung jury, but he was convicted of assaulting Borrero.

On the Borrero case, Raab found a secret FBI lab report that disproved the prosecution's claim that the button Borrero had torn from her assailant had come from Whitmore's coat. Raab kept digging. Finally, in 1972, he helped locate Borrero's sister-in-law, who said that Borrero had first identified her attacker from a police mug shot—at a time when no mug shots of Whitmore existed. Faced with this new evidence, the Brooklyn prosecutor asked that the conviction be set aside, and in 1973 Whitmore was released.[9]

After helping to clear Whitmore, Raab moved from WNET, New York's public TV station, to the *New York Times,* where he offered *Times* readers unusual in-depth examinations of the courts as an institution. In 1975, for example, he reported that eight out of ten New York City homicide cases were settled by plea-bargaining, and that most defendants who agreed to plead guilty to a lesser charge were released on probation or given short sentences. An amateur sociologist as well as a detective, Raab is a model of what court reporting can be but seldom is.

The final step in the criminal justice system is the prison. Traditionally, prisons have received no news coverage at all—in part because authorities limit reporters' access to prisons (see pp. 195-97) but mostly because our society's obsessive interest in criminals fades to nothing the moment they are jailed. The 1971 Attica prison revolt served notice on the media that prison conditions are important, and triggered some reporters to take a look at conditions in their own local prisons. A rash of investigative stories followed, some of them written from the inside by reporters posing as prisoners or guards. Then the furor died down. Today, once again, most of the media wait for a local prison uprising before they get around to investigating prison problems.

The typical big-city paper, after all, has several police reporters to cover current crimes, perhaps one court reporter to rehash old crimes, and no prison reporter to find out what happened to the criminals.

Crime news is unique among local news beats in the sheer quantity of its coverage. In many cities the police department gets more newspaper space and broadcast time than the mayor's office, and in all cities it gets more space and time than the other municipal departments. But in the *character* of its coverage, crime news is absolutely typical. Spot news dominates, most of it obtained from official sources, the easy way. Interpretive reporting of underlying issues and investigative reporting of official conduct are rare. The media, in other words, cover individual crimes, not the social problem of crime or the system of criminal justice.

In all fairness, reporters are perfectly willing to cover crime as an issue and criminal justice as an institution if sources manage to turn these topics into spot news. A municipal task force report on the causes of crime or a political battle over the leniency of judges isn't as "good" a story as an ice-pick murder, but it's a good enough story, and even television will give it 40 seconds or so. The problem is that the real issues of crime become hard news only once in a while, while individual crimes are hard news every day. Official sources could remedy this imbalance by addressing the real issues in their statements and actions. When they do, reporters cover the real issues. But usually they do not—and usually no reporter is available to do the tough investigative and interpretive work necessary to cover the real issues without such a hard news peg. And so crime coverage deteriorates into coverage of crimes.

CITY HALL

News of municipal government is somewhat less extensive than crime news, but still reasonably plentiful because it, too, is easy to cover.

Metropolitan government reporters do not have to go looking for stories. Elected officials want as much coverage as they can get,

so they hold regular news conferences, participate in endless pseudo-events, and issue a steady stream of press releases. Attending the conferences and pseudo-events and rewriting the releases occupy the bulk of the typical local government reporter's time, guaranteeing a constant supply of news.

The newspaper is the workhorse of local government coverage. Most big-city papers employ several full-time city hall reporters, including at least one who camps out in the mayor's office and another who hounds the city council. Typically these specialists occupy their own office (the "press room") at city hall itself, from which they can conveniently cover the nitty-gritty of local government and local politics.

The broadcast media cannot match the

STATE GOVERNMENT COVERAGE

Everyone agrees that media coverage of state government is generally poor, and everyone agrees why: no one wants to pay for good coverage. As John Burns put it in his book *The Sometime Governments*, "The media generally do not value state government news very highly. Such news usually ranks a poor third behind national and local news."[11] Editors send their best political reporters to Washington or to city hall. They sometimes staff the statehouse with cynical old-timers who couldn't make it and inexperienced youngsters who have yet to try.

And not too many of those. In the mid-1970s, for example, the *New York Times* had 33 journalists in Washington—but only four in Albany. The entire Albany press corps (not counting the local media) was made up of fewer than 40 reporters, representing 23 different news organizations. They covered the governor, the state legislature, and a multi-billion-dollar bureaucracy of state agencies. The typical statehouse reporter in Albany filed an average of four to five stories a day, generally checking in about ten in the morning and often working until midnight.[12] (That sort of overtime is essential just to stay on top of the routine news—and besides, what else is there for a reporter to do in Albany?) Said one *New York Times* staffer: "Our Albany bureau is a vale of tears to pass through en route to someplace else."[13]

The typical statehouse reporter works for a large daily newspaper or a wire service, often alone and sometimes part-time. Broadcast stations and smaller papers may cover major state government stories directly, but they usually rely on the wires for day-to-day coverage. Not surprisingly, statehouse reporting is dominated by spot news stories on important developments, with little time to spare for in-depth or investigative reporting.

The understaffed statehouse bureaus are often up against state PR offices that are fully stocked with skilled publicists. In New Jersey, for example, the governor's chief press officer oversees some 40 PR specialists who staff the various executive agencies of

papers for routine coverage. Few stations have a large enough staff to keep a crew at city hall. Instead, they show up—cameras, microphones, and all—for prearranged events that guarantee usable tape or film. Since the prearranged events are frequent, radio and television wind up with a substantial quantity of local government news. A 1976 content analysis of local TV newscasts in Pennsylvania, for example, found that the typical half-hour early evening news program devoted 9.6 minutes to local and state government.[10] In total words that's undoubtedly less than the average newspaper; 9.6 minutes of talking would fit on half a newspaper front page with space to spare. But after subtracting for commercials, sports, and weather, 9.6 minutes of local and state government news comes out to more than half the news in the newscast.

On the whole, then, critics of local government coverage can't really complain about quantity—at least so far as big-city government is concerned. Suburban government, unfortunately, is a different story. The typical suburban area is a hodgepodge of small cities, townships, villages, and whatnot, each with its own government. Superimposed on this system are networks of county governments, water and sewerage districts, school boards, and regional authorities of various sorts. A suburban daily newspaper may thus include as many as 60 separate governmental units in its circulation area, each of considerable importance to a small group of readers and no importance to the rest.

state government; their 1979 budget totalled $610,000.[14] Legislative leaders employ additional PR people of their own, of course. Given the media's skimpy investment in state government coverage, that's news management overkill.

State government reporters are not only outgunned by their sources; they're also very tempted to begin thinking like their sources. Most state capitals are small towns, physically and emotionally. Officials and reporters work together and play together; they eat at the same restaurants, drink at the same bars, and live in the same hotels. The following admission from an Oregon reporter is probably typical of the views of most statehouse journalists:

> I wouldn't report it if a member were drunk all session . . . so long as he was doing a good job for the state. I wouldn't report it, I mean, unless . . . somebody else would, so it would become general knowledge anyway. Or if I knew a legislator was getting his liquor from the dog-race lobbyists, I wouldn't write that up. . . . I'd have to tell all the good about him—all the good things he's done—if I told the bad.[15]

Yet state government officials are not especially pleased with statehouse coverage. According to a Rutgers University seminar of leading state legislators, statehouse reporters tend to focus too much on superficial political ploys, on the obviously "big" stories, and on the antics of publicity-minded celebrities within the government.[16] Similarly, members of the Pennsylvania General Assembly told one survey that the press "over-publicizes controversial issues" in the legislature, while "ignoring routine legislative business."[17]

The criticism is undoubtedly accurate, but so is the answer any statehouse reporter would give: If you were trying to cover the whole state government single-handedly, and then fighting to get your copy into the paper, you'd focus on big stories and controversial characters too. State officials should count themselves lucky that statehouse reporters lack the time (and in some cases the inclination) for investigative digging.

Faced with this intrinsically impossible situation, suburban newspapers do the best they can. They tell their government reporters to hit the high spots, so the reporters wind up driving from town to town and meeting to meeting, trying to figure out what is going on. Less crucial meetings merit only a part-time stringer (a high school civics teacher, perhaps), who phones in with a nuts-and-bolts summary of the new town ordinance or the village budget dispute. Or if nonprofessional reporting scares the suburban editor, the paper prints a press release from the municipal clerk, or nothing at all.

Nothing at all is precisely what television has to say about suburban government. A big-city TV (or radio) station may reach literally hundreds of suburban municipalities; short of a major or photogenic crisis, it ignores them all. Suburban radio stations have fewer communities to cover, but far fewer reporters to cover them. The typical suburban station employs only one or two journalists; it offers five-minute news summaries culled from the wire services and the front page of the nearest daily. Only the biggest local stories merit on-the-spot reporting.

Next to the big cities, in fact, the most extensive local government coverage is found in small, isolated communities with their own weekly newspapers. A small-town weekly may find nothing critical to say about the mayor—ever—but at least it covers the mayor. By contrast, the mayor of a suburban village served only by a nearby daily paper may go weeks without seeing a reporter at all.

Back in the big cities, meanwhile, government coverage is fairly extensive. But just as crime news comes almost exclusively from police sources, city hall news comes from the releases and news conferences of city officials. This leads to several important distortions in local government coverage.

First, the news inevitably focuses on the highest-ranking elected officials, usually the mayor and the city council. These are the people who actively court media attention, the ones who arrange the news conferences and issue the news releases. Lesser elected officials tend to get lost in the shuffle—their news conferences are sparsely attended, their releases cut to a paragraph or two.

Appointed officials, the professional civil servants who run the city day-by-day, are often ignored altogether. The bureaucrats who manage the budget and the bus system, the sewers and the schools, the housing projects and the hospitals, do not normally seek publicity. The rising cost and falling quality of these city services add up to a well-known indictment, summarized as "urban decay." Obviously, the officials who run the services should be under constant media scrutiny. But in practice they go about their business with little fear of public accountability. Unless there's a scandal or a visible crisis, or an appointed official actively pursues publicity (usually in preparation for running for elective office), the media concentrate on elected officials and leave the bureaucrats alone.

A second distortion results largely from the first. Elected officials are politicians first and foremost. Since elected officials dominate government coverage, the coverage winds up dominated by politics.

The distinction between government and politics is hard for Americans to grasp, so accustomed are we to government officials who are primarily politicians. To be sure, the two are closely tied, and *should* be closely tied: politics is how we keep our government accountable. But there is still an important distinction. Whether the welfare system, say, is efficiently run, whether its clients receive enough support to live decent lives, whether its bureaucrats tolerate too much cheating— these are not just issues of electoral politics, but also crucial issues of the quality of government. But since these issues are most frequently raised by elected officials or candidates for elective office, we come to think of them as exclusively matters of political rhetoric. And so do reporters—who cover them that way.

Coverage of government, in short, often deteriorates into coverage of politics, because the sources are politicians and what they say and do is interpreted by the media as political statements and political acts.

And when the government does something that is hard to interpret in political terms— a zoning board decision, for example—the media tend to downplay the story. If they cover it at all, the resulting article is often unbearably dull. Stuart A. Dunham of the *Camden* (N.J.) *Courier-Post* has described such coverage as "a vast gray monotony, lit only occasionally by a spark of interest." The straight news of city hall, according to Dunham, is invariably written "in the terms of procedure and in the language of city ordinances."[18] Readers naturally shy away from such articles, and editors respond by emphasizing politics and de-emphasizing government all the more.

Probably the most significant distortion in local government coverage is the emphasis on events instead of issues. Just as crime news focuses on individual crimes instead of the criminal justice system, so too government news concentrates on individual ordinances and political battles instead of the system of government and the issues it faces.

Consider, for example, a 1972 study of community development issues (land use, housing, transportation, etc.) in newspaper stories. Three papers were analyzed—the *Christian Science Monitor* (a national newspaper), the *Kansas City Times* (a metropolitan newspaper), and the *Manhattan* (Kansas) *Mercury* (a small-town newspaper). Overall, for every thousand column-inches of space, the *Monitor* ran 34 inches on community development versus 27 inches on sports; the *Times* carried 10 inches on development and 53 inches on sports; and the *Mercury* included 8 inches on development and 100 inches on sports. Clearly sports seemed more newsworthy than community development, especially to the local papers.

The study went on to subdivide the community development coverage into articles focusing on programs and articles focusing on problems. Over two-thirds of the content

focused on programs.[19] When a government official announces a new bus route or housing project, in other words, newspapers cover the announcement—but only occasionally do they go beyond the announcement to explore community development issues.

LOCAL ISSUES

In 1980, northern New Jersey suffered a drought. For months, as the reservoirs gradually dried up, a variety of local governments waited, and watched, and hoped. They didn't hide the drought (how do you hide a drought?), but they didn't try to make news about it either, so the media ignored it. Finally the governor declared a state of emergency and instituted mandatory rationing. Then the media "discovered" the crisis, with news accounts and feature stories galore.

In their coverage of local issues, in short, the media are strictly reactive, waiting for the government to do something or say something. For the audience, the result is a roller-coaster ride of crises that come without warning and disappear without explanation. But before blaming the media for this unfortunate state of affairs, ask yourself whether you would read a detailed feature on reservoir levels, long-term weather predictions, antiquated pipelines, interlocking water companies, standby planning, and the other ingredients of water shortage . . . before the shortage. Editors figure you wouldn't. So they wait for the crisis and the hard news peg.

Although all local issues are vulnerable to this pattern of reactive and crisis-oriented coverage, some suffer more than others. The best-covered issues are those that have a specialized reporter assigned to them and that directly and visibly affect the daily lives of many readers and viewers—education, for example. The worst-covered, like the welfare system, lack a specialized reporter and directly affect only a minority of the audience.

Let's look briefly at a sample of local issues and see how they fare.

1. Education. In the 1940s and early 1950s, school boards and educational issues rarely made headlines. Only 10 out of 52 major metropolitan newspapers employed an education specialist in 1945. And in the early 1950s, education news filled only 1.4 percent of the average paper, and was read by only 16.6 percent of the readers. Then came *Brown v. Board of Education,* the Supreme Court decision that outlawed school segregation. The responses of local school boards became front-page news, and by 1966 49 of the 52 major metro dailies had an education specialist.[20]

Of all local issues, education has the best shot at adequate coverage. Not only is the local paper likely to have a specialized education beat, but the topic also looms large in the lives of many readers, especially the parents of school-age children. And there are even elected government officials—the school board—whose public statements and meetings provide continual news pegs for education stories.

Yet even education coverage tends to be reactive. A controversy over busing or a violent incident in the high school gets big play—even on television—as does the threat of a teacher strike, a battle over sex education, or the closing of a neighborhood school. But the key issues of educational policy (as opposed to school management) are matters like class size, "basics" versus "frills," student work load, and individualized instruction. The media rarely report these issues from the local angle; even radical shifts in school policy may go unreported. Similarly, the economics of education receive little attention until a budget crisis forces a cutback in services or a tax hike. And the success or failure of the schools (How much are the children actually learning? How do they feel about their schooling? Why?) is seldom examined until it becomes a political issue in a school board election.

Training is part of the problem. Few local education reporters feel confident of their ability to explore the technicalities of declining SAT scores or curriculum reform. But they would try, and learn on the job, if they thought that was what the beat was all about.

They don't. The job is defined, first and foremost, as covering the hot public controversies like busing, school violence, and sex education. Between controversies, TV has nothing, and newspapers keep busy with routine articles on routine school board meetings—decisions to purchase new uniforms for the cheerleaders and the like. If the education specialist has time left over, he or she fills it with cute features—Mrs. Smith's class on their trip to the planetarium—complete with three-column photographs. In the competition for the reporter's time and the paper's space, educational issues lose.

2. Health Care. A survey conducted in 1958 revealed the startling fact that 37 percent of newspaper readers read all the medical news they could find in the paper, and 42 percent wanted more. These numbers were far higher than the comparable figures for crime, national politics, and other "popular" topics.[21] Obviously, there was a ready market for news about medicine and health.

To meet this market, most big-city newspapers employ a science and medicine reporter, who usually devotes more than half of his or her time to medical news. And medical reporting matured substantially in the 1970s, moving steadily from the gee-whiz enthusiasm of the past to a more skeptical approach (see box on p. 445).

Unfortunately, health-care reporting has made a lot less progress than medical reporting. How well-staffed is the emergency room of your local hospital? Did the hospital really need that expensive CAT scanner it bought last year? Has the nearest medical school changed its curriculum to respond to new approaches? What are conditions like at local old-age homes and mental health facili-

In 1980, eight science and medical journalists gathered in San Francisco to discuss the future of their craft. An end to innocence was the recurring theme of the discussion, summarized by Cristine Russell of the *Washington Star* when she commented: "I'll bet no one at this table has used the word 'breakthrough' in the last five years."[22] No one wanted to bet.

When Dr. Christiaan Barnard of Cape Town became the first surgeon to perform a successful heart transplant in the late 1960s, the mass media turned him into an instant celebrity. The medical and legal complications of the story were almost ignored; so was the fact that twenty surgical teams around the world were ready to perform the same operation; so was the question of whether such heroic surgery was a better use of health-care money than, say, screening ghetto children for lead poisoning. *Time* put Dr. Barnard on its cover, CBS brought him to America to appear on "Face the Nation," and NBC was dismayed to learn that he would not allow it to film his next operation.[23] Medical reporting in the 1960s was show biz, and "breakthroughs" were nearly weekly events.

Skepticism hit science and medical reporting in the 1970s. No longer was a promising piece of basic cancer research likely to be overblown into tomorrow's cure, embarrassing the researcher and outraging the medical establishment. Medical journalists learned to wait until the research was published in a refereed journal or discussed at a major conference, and they learned to ask expert sources for a cautious evaluation of the new work's real potential. By the end of the 1970s, in fact, the opposite complaint was beginning to be heard—that non-establishment medical research is unfairly underplayed.

But the media do cover maverick medicine—the battles over laetrile and vitamin C therapies, for example. By covering such matters as controversies rather than ignoring them as frauds or ballyhooing them as breakthroughs, reporters annoy both sides in the contest, but serve the public well. Even the political dimension of medical science—the fact that there *is* a medical establishment that controls the flow of research money according to its own biases and commitments—is beginning to get some media play.

ties? How does the local medical ethics committee deal with patient complaints? What are local physicians and hospitals doing to hold down the price of health care? While the medicine reporter looks into the pros and cons of laetrile, these local health-care issues are likely to go unreported—until a hospital strike, a big malpractice suit, or some other newsworthy event forces the media to react.

And local health threats often receive even less media attention than local health care. Most local media in the textile states of North and South Carolina paid scanty attention to brown lung disease among textile workers until the national media picked up the story in 1977. Then the locals followed suit. Commented Chip Hughes, an organizer for the Carolina Brown Lung Association: "The really fantastic thing was how the national television and press legitimized the story for local papers in the Carolinas."[24]

3. Housing and Land Use. Most newspapers have a daily real estate page or a weekly real estate section, rich with advertisements for new housing developments and condominiums. News stories are needed to separate the ads—a perfect chance to cover housing and land-use issues in the community.

Newspapers and broadcast stations are, of course, businesses, avidly seeking to make a profit. This goal can easily conflict with hard-hitting coverage of local government and local problems—especially when the topic is urban growth.

The economic future of a news medium is intertwined with the future of the community it serves. As population increases, newspaper circulation and broadcast ratings go up. As more business and industry is attracted to the area, advertising goes up. Thus a medium's self-interest generally dictates that it adopt a civic-booster "chamber of commerce" attitude and promote the growth of the community.

In the 1960s, San Jose, California, grew from a sleepy orchard town to a major metropolitan area. The two San Jose newspapers—the *Mercury* and the *News,* both owned by the Ridder chain—profited enormously from this boom. The papers became so committed to the "growth for growth's sake" philosophy that they provided consistently biased coverage of such topics as airport expansion and mass-transit construction. If you knew whether a particular policy would make San Jose grow bigger or not, you could reliably guess whether the *Mercury* and *News* were promoting it or ignoring it.

The activities of the papers' executives and editors provide some indication of their commitment to economic expansion:

- A yearly "Progress Issue" was used by the city government to recruit new industry to the San Jose area.
- The business manager of the papers was a member of the Greater San Jose Chamber of Commerce, working with representatives of such corporations as the Pacific Gas and Electric Company, Bank of America, and General Electric.
- The real estate editor was a member of the Greeters Committee of the San Jose Real Estate Board.
- The business and financial editor was an honorary member of the Board of Realty.
- The city hall reporter became an administrative assistant to the growth-oriented mayor.
- The papers' general manager was airport development chairman for the Chamber of Commerce, and a member of numerous special committees devoted to making San Jose grow.

Reporters at the two papers quickly became aware of the extracurricular interests of their editors and executives. Self-censorship took over, and stories dealing with zoning, planning, environmental deterioration, and the like often took on a pro-growth slant. Only occasionally was top-down censorship required.[25]

In the mid-1970s, the papers' policy toward growth began to change. A new publisher, Anthony Ridder, questioned the "growth at any price" philosophy, freeing reporters to cover the alternatives. When the Ridder chain merged with Knight in 1977, the papers became champions of "managed growth," and began investigating the business relationships between some land developers and public officials. In 1978 San Jose's chief government planner, Gary Schoennauer, was moved to comment: "When the Knight organization came in, it had a tremendous impact; the editorial policies were like night and day."[26]

Most papers pass up the chance, filling the section instead with model-home plans and the press releases of local developers. "Our real estate section is 99 percent puff," admitted the city editor of a suburban California newspaper. "It is a developer-oriented section. Most of its stories come from our classified ad department."[27]

In all fairness, the media took housing and land-use issues much more seriously in the 1970s than they did in the 1960s. Many papers and stations ran thoughtful analyses on the impacts of urban renewal, the problems of public housing, the environmental effects of development, the economics of the housing industry, and the like. The middle class had fled the cities in the 1950s and 1960s without much media attention; when the middle class started returning in the 1970s (a phenomenon called "gentrification"), city papers tried to tell the story. Suburban papers, meanwhile, focused on mortgage scarcity and the dwindling minority of readers who could afford to buy a new home.

But for the most part these stories came in infrequent spurts—a single series or documentary on a currently hot issue, then months of silence until the next major controversy. Only a few local media followed the lead of papers like the *Danbury* (Connecticut) *News-Times,* which regularly frees reporters to provide in-depth coverage of growth and land development.[28] For most editors, civic boosterism is still the name of the game in day-to-day coverage. New housing starts are automatically cause for rejoicing. Local zoning boards (if they are covered at all) get routine stories on the inside pages, heavy with legalese and written by the greenest reporter on the staff. And the real estate pages, which could provide real continuity in coverage of housing and land use, keep publishing pap instead.

4. Poverty and Welfare. America's more than 24 million poor people are concentrated in urban and rural areas. America's middle class lives mostly in the suburbs.

Most middle-class people, therefore, have little first-hand experience with poverty. What they know about the poor they know from the mass media.

Until the 1960s, the media ignored the poor. Then came President Lyndon Johnson's "war on poverty," huge increases in crime and violent unrest among the poor, and equally huge increases in the size and scope of the welfare system. All three were mostly urban phenomena. Frightened and resentful, the middle class wanted to know what was going on. And so the media began to cover urban poverty, while continuing to pay little attention to the rural poor.

All too often, however, the media's approach to the urban poor played to—and increased—the fear and resentment of the middle class. Stories about pimps and drug pushers and ghetto gangs have been more common than stories about poor people struggling to escape poverty. Stories about welfare cheats and the inefficiency and waste of the welfare system have been more common than stories about welfare payments that fall steadily further behind inflation and welfare regulations that demean the clients they are designed to help. Middle-class audiences have been allowed, even encouraged, to see poverty as uniquely a problem of urban minorities, and as the fault of the poor.

All this has to do with explaining poverty to the middle class—a crucial job that the media fail to do adequately. But the media also fail to serve the poor. When was the last time you saw a story about how to apply for food stamps, or about the procedure for filing grievances against the welfare department, or about the waiting lists for subsidized housing? These, too, are aspects of the story of poverty.

We have looked briefly at four local issues—education, health care, housing and land use, and poverty and welfare. This is by no means the full range of important local issues. We will discuss some of the other major ones (environment, energy, consumer affairs) in Chapter 19 on "Coverage of Specialized News."

For almost any issue you pick, the pattern is the same. Local newspapers and local broadcasting do a fairly creditable job of covering the hot public controversies, the political footballs of the community. And the papers, at least, report the bare-bones facts of government action even when no controversy is brewing. But despite a few happy exceptions, such as transportation, background coverage of the underlying issues is scanty at best, biased or nonexistent at worst. In short, the media tell us a great deal about what politicians are saying and doing about local issues, but relatively little about the issues themselves.

As we have said before, this imbalance results inevitably from journalism's dedication to hard news. To tell us more about the issues themselves, reporters would have to become amateur sociologists. This is a tall order, but an important one.

LOCAL ADVERSARITY

Though local reporters are reluctant to play sociologist, to dig beneath the public controversies to the underlying issues, they are at least willing to cover the controversies. Sometimes they even trigger the controversies, by adopting an adversary stance toward the government officials who provide the bulk of local news.

It wasn't always that way. Until the 1970s, in fact, the "adversary relationship" concept (see pp. 397-400) made far more sense to most national government reporters than to their colleagues at city hall. In 1961, for example, Robert Judd investigated the attitudes of West Coast reporters toward local government officials. The reporters, he found, were content to act as "passive gatekeepers" between the officials and their editors. They emphatically denied the existence—or desirability—of any sort of adversary relationship.[29] No doubt the officials agreed.

Similarly, a 1968 study of 88 Minnesota

newspapers revealed the startling fact that most editors saw themselves as promoters of civic virtue. Few thought they ought to serve as "watchdogs" over local government, and only two discussed the regular reporting of local controversy. Most wanted to advance the fortunes of their communities.[30]

Civic boosterism was the name of the game. In 1968, *McCall's* magazine ran an article on the quality of American drinking water. The article named 102 cities whose water supplies were rated as only "provisionally approved" by the U.S. Public Health Service. For newspapers in those cities, it was a big story. Eighty percent of the papers covered it, and half of them ran two or more articles on the subject.

But how did they cover it? Only one paper in five approached the Public Health Service for comment. Only one in five discussed the matter with local water-pollution experts. And a grand total of two reporters got in touch with the *McCall's* author for clarification.

Four-fifths of the papers built their articles around the reactions of local waterworks officials—the sources least likely to admit a problem. The *Topeka* (Kansas) *Daily Capital* was typical of this approach. It left unchallenged this statement from the local superintendent of utilities: "For this guy to pick on our water supply, I am inclined to think he doesn't know what is going on. . . . I just can't see how some guy can come out and say something like this. This is the same water I drink, that I give my wife and kids—even my dog." The vast majority of the papers responded to the *McCall's* article as an insult to their cities. They set out to discredit the article, not to examine the issue.[31]

The mid-1970s saw a decline in civic boosterism and a rise in local investigative reporting. It is hard to know what caused the change. Some attribute it to the mounting economic, social, and environmental problems of the cities and suburbs, which the media could no longer ignore. Others credit the precedent of Watergate, which led some editors to set up their own local investigative teams and which inspired many young reporters to look to the *Washington Post*'s Woodward and Bernstein as role models.

Whatever the causes, the results were quickly visible. In 1974, for example, a team of *Philadelphia Inquirer* reporters, Donald L. Barlett and James B. Steele, published a series of articles exposing serious inequities in Philadelphia's criminal court system. The series relied heavily on an innovative computer analysis of each judge's sentencing record, combined with more traditional journalistic legwork. It led to the eventual defeat of Philadelphia's district attorney.[32]

Chicago Today, an afternoon tabloid that folded in 1974, published two searing exposés before it died. The first led to the indictment and conviction of former Governor Otto Kerner, on charges that he had bought stock in an Illinois race track at bargain prices and sold it at a huge profit, in return for giving the track the racing dates it wanted. The second revealed that Chicago Mayor Richard Daley had ordered the city to award valuable insurance contracts to a firm that employed his son.[33]

Deciding to pursue corruption at a more everyday level, an investigative team from the *Chicago Sun-Times* created a bar called The Mirage in 1977 (see p. 90). For many months the team recorded kickback demands from a variety of municipal agencies, then published the results in a blockbuster 1978 series.[34]

Local broadcasters also turned toward investigative reporting in the 1970s. WLPG-TV in Miami filmed a political fixer meeting secretly with city officials. KOMO-TV in Seattle revealed the detrimental effects of the Alaska oil pipeline on Puget Sound. WCVB-TV in Boston forced the removal of a Bicentennial Commission director for lack of progress and planning. WLS-TV in Chicago successfully exposed scandalous conditions in local nursing homes.[35]

Weekly newspapers provided some of the most daring coverage of local government. One such paper was the *Mountain Eagle,* published in the Whitesburg, Kentucky area by Tom Gish. Gish has taken on the school board, the coal companies, the electric power utilities, and the state, county, and local police—often all at once. In retaliation, his printing plant was burned to the ground by an arsonist in August of 1974. Gish continued to print out of his home, changing the paper's motto from "The Mountain Eagle: It Screams" to "The Mountain Eagle: It Still Screams."[36] As of mid-1980, at least, it still did.

Don't make too much of this new enthusiasm for local investigative reporting—at least not yet. Even in the mid-1970s, Tom Gish was an exception. He was "balanced" by dozens of reporters who still skimmed the surface of municipal news, reporting only what local officials want reported and not too much of that, and by dozens of publishers who still worshipped at the shrine of my-city-right-or-wrong, refusing to spend the money that investigative reporting requires. And by 1980 some critics were already speculating that the wave had crested, that local coverage was retreating to its former stance of civic boosterism. The reporters who begin their careers in the next few years will determine whether the exposés of the 1970s were the start of a trend or a temporary fad.

At best, investigative exposés raise issues that officials would prefer to leave submerged. The real question about local coverage in the 1980s is how reporters will deal with the issues once they have surfaced. The pattern of the past is clear—heavy coverage of hot controversies, moderate coverage of political rhetoric, routine coverage of government action, and practically no coverage of underlying issues. Will reporters in the 1980s improve on that record?

Notes

[1] Carey Winfrey, " 'Son of Sam' Case Poses Thorny Issues for Press," *New York Times,* August 22, 1977, p. 38.

[2] *San Francisco Examiner,* January 11, 1970, p. B2.

[3] Gerald B. Healy, "St. Louis P-D to Leave Out Some

Crime News Details," *Editor & Publisher,* February 8, 1975, p. 17.

4 "So Much for Conventional Wisdom," *New York Times,* March 3, 1974, p. 13.

5 Grace Lichtenstein, "Arizona Paper Does Not Publish First Articles Prompted by Slaying of Its Reporter," *New York Times,* March 15, 1977, p. 12. "Arizona Hoods Exposed by Republic," *Editor & Publisher,* July 8, 1978, p. 35.

6 John Lofton, "Trial by Fury—A Projection of the Public Mood," unpublished draft, p. 5.

7 Robert Drechsel, Kermit Netteburg, and Bisi Aborisade, "Community Size and Newspaper Reporting of Local Courts," *Journalism Quarterly,* Spring, 1980, pp. 71-78.

8 John Wallworth, "Arkansas Editor's Probe Frees Imprisoned Man," *Editor & Publisher,* August 5, 1978, p. 9.

9 "Uncaped Crusader," *Newsweek,* April 23, 1973, p. 48.

10 William C. Adams, "Local Public Affairs Content of TV News," *Journalism Quarterly,* Winter, 1978, pp. 690-95.

11 Ralph Whitehead, Jr. and Howard M. Ziff, "Statehouse Coverage: Lobbyists Outlast Journalists," *Columbia Journalism Review,* January/February, 1974, p. 11.

12 Thomas Collins, "For the Press, a Lonely Outpost," *Newsday,* March 6, 1974, pp. 5A, 15A.

13 Whitehead and Ziff, "Statehouse Coverage," pp. 11-12.

14 Patrick Breslin, "Press Reps Answer All Questions," *New Brunswick* (N.J.) *Home News,* August 30, 1979 (AP).

15 John F. Valleau, "Oregon Legislative Reporting: The Newsmen and their Methods," *Journalism Quarterly,* Spring, 1952, p. 167.

16 Tom Littlewood, "The Trials of Statehouse Journalism," *Saturday Review,* December 10, 1966, p. 82.

17 "Press Coverage Criticized by Pa. Lawmakers," *Editor & Publisher,* February 9, 1980, p. 32.

18 Stuart A. Dunham, "Local News Coverage: A Vast, Gray, Dull Monotony," *ASNE Bulletin,* May, 1966, p. 3.

19 Sandra Williams Ernst, "Baseball or Brickbats: A Content Analysis of Community Development," *Journalism Quarterly,* Spring, 1972, pp. 86-90.

20 C. T. Duncan, "The 'Education Beat' on 52 Major Newspapers," *Journalism Quarterly,* Summer, 1966, pp. 336-38. Charles E. Swanson, "What They Read in 130 Daily Newspapers," *Journalism Quarterly,* Fall, 1955, p. 417.

21 Chilton R. Bush, ed., *News Research for Better Newspapers* (New York: American Newspaper Publishers Association Foundation, 1967), II, pp. 37-38.

22 "Science, Technology, and the Press: Must the 'Age of Innocence' End?" *Technology Review,* March/April, 1980, p. 52.

23 Hillier Krieghbaum, "Dr. Barnard as a Human Pseudo-Event," *Columbia Journalism Review,* Summer, 1968, pp. 24-25.

24 Bob Hall, "The Brown-Lung Controversy," *Columbia Journalism Review,* March/April, 1978, pp. 27-28.

25 David W. Jones, "The Press and the Growth Establishment," in David M. Rubin and David P. Sachs, eds., *Mass Media and the Environment* (New York: Praeger Special Studies, 1973), pp. 191-247.

26 Robert Lindsey, "San Jose Moves to Manage Its Growth," *New York Times,* December 30, 1978, p. 7.

27 David B. Sachsman, *Public Relations Influence on Environmental Coverage,* unpublished Ph.D. dissertation, Stanford University, 1973, pp. 187-88.

28 John S. Rosenberg, "Land-Use Coverage: A Connecticut Sampler," *Columbia Journalism Review,* May/June, 1978, pp. 39-40.

29 Robert P. Judd, "The Newspaper Reporter in a Suburban City," *Journalism Quarterly,* Winter, 1961, pp. 40-42.

30 Clarice N. Olien, George A. Donohue, and Phillip J. Tichenor, "The Community Editor's Power and the Reporting of Conflict," *Journalism Quarterly,* Summer, 1968, p. 250.

31 David M. Rubin and Stephen Landers, "National Exposure and Local Cover-Up: A Case Study," *Columbia Journalism Review,* Summer, 1969, pp. 17-22.

32 "The Inquirer's Inquirers," *Newsweek,* December 30, 1974, p. 55.

33 Gary Cummings, "The Last 'Front Page,'" *Columbia Journalism Review,* November/December, 1974, pp. 46-47.

34 "Sun-Times Runs Chicago Bar to Detail Corruption," *Editor & Publisher,* January 14, 1978, p. 12.

35 "TV and the Local Watergates," *Variety,* May 23, 1973, p. 42.

36 "An Eagle That Just Won't Stop Screaming," *New York Times,* August 25, 1974, p. 47.

Suggested Readings

ADAMS, WILLIAM C., "Local Public Affairs Content of TV News," *Journalism Quarterly,* Winter, 1978.

ATWOOD, L. ERWIN, ARDYTH B. SOHN, and HAROLD SOHN, "Daily Newspaper Contributions to Community Discussion," *Journalism Quarterly,* Autumn, 1978.

DRECHSEL, ROBERT, KERMIT NETTEBURG, and BISI ABORISADE, "Community Size and Newspaper Reporting of Local Courts," *Journalism Quarterly*, Spring, 1980.

EISENDRATH, CHARLES R., "Back to the People with the Mom-and-Pop Press," *Columbia Journalism Review*, November/December, 1979.

EMERY, MICHAEL, and SUZANNE STEINER EMERY, "Reporting Proposition 13: Business as Usual," *Columbia Journalism Review*, November/December, 1978.

GALLOWAY, PAUL, "The Mirage," *The Quill*, February, 1978.

HALL, BOB, "The Brown-Lung Controversy," *Columbia Journalism Review*, March/April, 1978.

MENCHER, MELVIN, "The Arizona Project: An Appraisal," *Columbia Journalism Review*, November/December, 1977.

MORGAN, DAVID, *The Capitol Press Corps: Newsmen and the Governing of New York State.* Westport, Conn.: Greenwood Press, 1978.

ROSENBERG, JOHN S., "Land-Use Coverage: A Connecticut Sampler," *Columbia Journalism Review*, May/June, 1978.

RUBIN, DAVID M., and STEPHEN LANDERS, "National Exposure and Local Cover-Up: A Case Study," *Columbia Journalism Review*, Summer, 1969.

SACHSMAN, DAVID B., "Mass Media and the Urban Environment," *Mass Comm Review*, July, 1974.

SHAW, EUGENE F., and DANIEL RIFFE, "Newspaper Reading in Two Towns," *Journalism Quarterly*, Autumn, 1979.

WHITEHEAD, RALPH JR., and HOWARD M. ZIFF, "Statehouse Coverage: Lobbyists Outlast Journalists," *Columbia Journalism Review*, January/February, 1974.

Chapter 17
Coverage
of International Affairs
and National Security

For the most part, the American mass media are profoundly uninterested in international affairs. Foreign news is thoroughly covered only when it is sensational or directly affects this country. Political terrorism and war meet both criteria; though their coverage reflects consistent biases, at least they are covered. The remaining international news in our media is actually news of our own government—of national security issues and the U.S. intelligence apparatus. On these critical topics the media have progressed from censorship and cooperation to a more adversary stance that exposes many secrets of U.S. foreign policy.

When Egyptian President Anwar Sadat made his historic visit to Jerusalem in 1977, more than 1500 journalists from around the world converged on Israel. The largest contingent of visiting reporters was American—580 "special correspondents" for a week.[1] Similarly, the mass suicide in Guyana attracted scores of American reporters. So did the hostage crisis in Iran. And when a Pope dies, Rome fills with American journalists.

These are exceptions. Also exceptions are the *New York Times,* which gives nearly 20 percent of its news hole to international affairs, and the *Christian Science Monitor,* which devotes about 30 percent of its space to foreign news. For the average daily newspaper on an average day, the figure is less than 10 percent. Local broadcasters ignore international news altogether, leaving such coverage to the networks. And the typical network evening newscast between 1970 and 1975 contained only five international items, including the war in Vietnam.[2]

For the occasional international event of compelling interest, in other words, the American media pull out all the stops. But usually they give short shrift to the rest of the world.

INTERNATIONAL NEWS

When editors compare notes on audience response, they often disagree on which kinds of news are the most popular—sports, politics, "human interest," or what. But they agree on at least one point. Readers and viewers, they feel certain, care very little about foreign news.

As evidence of audience apathy, editors

may point to many studies dating back to the 1950s. A typical one found that the average adult reads only 12 column inches of foreign news a day, spending roughly 140 seconds doing so. When the readers were asked if they'd like to see more international news in their papers, only eight percent answered yes. Fourteen percent had no opinion and 78 percent said definitely not.[3] As recently as 1979, a survey of newspaper readers yielded strong criticism of editors for being too preoccupied with international news at the expense of local coverage.[4]

Studies occasionally produce different results. A 1978 Louis Harris survey, for example, found that 41 percent of those interviewed expressed deep interest in news of world affairs; journalists had predicted that five percent would say they were deeply interested.[5] The view that Americans don't like international news is thus open to debate. What is not debatable is that most editors are convinced that Americans don't like international news, and therefore cut their foreign coverage to the bone.

Besides their belief in public indifference, editors have another good reason for downplaying foreign news: It is difficult and expensive to cover. A good foreign correspondent needs special training in the culture, politics, and language of the country (or more likely the countries) he or she is to cover. But journalists with such training command higher salaries—not to mention the added costs of food, lodging, and "hardship pay" for an American forced to live and work overseas. To make matters worse, the host country may impose severe restrictions on where the reporter may travel and whom the reporter may interview. Stories may be censored to the point of uselessness; the reporter may even be kicked out of the country entirely. It seems a lot of trouble to go to for an article that few will read anyhow.

War zones aside, there are only about 500 full-time American journalists abroad. The wire services have the largest foreign staffs, and supply the vast majority of the interna-

tional news in the American media. Only a half-dozen newspapers have more than one or two reporters overseas. So do the three television networks and a handful of magazines. The typical local newspaper or broadcast station, of course, has no foreign staff at all.

On the whole, American foreign correspondents are topnotch reporters, skilled and experienced in their trade. The swashbuckling loner of movie fame has pretty much disappeared. Leo Bogart notes that the modern overseas reporter "works as part of a bureau team, and . . . is rooted to his station by long residence, an established family life, and a comfortable income."[6]

Nevertheless, 500 reporters spread over an entire world make a thin network. True, they are aided by hundreds of part-timers, freelancers, and foreign nationals working as stringers. But on the other hand, they are heavily concentrated in Western Europe, and spend most of their time reporting the same stories. England, France, and Germany are reasonably well covered. Not so Ecuador, Finland, and Ghana.

Nearly all the foreign news that reaches the American public falls into one of three categories. In order of importance, these are: the political, the sensational, and the colorful.

Political news is the most common largely because it is the easiest to gather. Government officials are happy to explain their viewpoint, and to supplement the explanation with handouts and other documents (many of them already translated into English). Local newspaper reports, which often reflect official government thinking, are another important source. The opposition stance, of course, is harder to find and more dangerous to report. Many reporters are content to make do without it.

Sensational news is popular with reporters because it is popular with readers. "For the A wire," writes a former AP bureau chief in Colombia, "I file earthquakes, student riots, general strikes, assassination attempts, and plane crashes. These I send 'urgent' if a rea-

CHAUVINISM

Four-fifths of all U.S. foreign correspondents, according to one study, believe their reports should not be influenced by American foreign policy.[7] This is an admirable stance —but also a somewhat naive one. Reporters are people, and so they inevitably carry a built-in nationalistic bias. So do editors and publishers—and for that matter so do readers. The bias is expressed in the kinds of countries reporters get assigned to, in the kinds of stories they choose to write, and in the kinds of information they include in the stories. There is no more reason to trust an American journalist writing about Cuba than a Cuban journalist writing about America.

In a classic study of the *New York Times,* Walter Lippmann and Charles Merz documented this bias with respect to the Russian Revolution. Most Americans, and hence most American reporters, wanted Bolshevism to fail. Between 1917 and 1919, therefore, the *Times* reported no less than ninety-one times that the new Soviet government was about to fall. The authors termed this "a case of seeing not what was, but what men wished to see."[8] The Lippmann-Merz conclusion is as valid today as it was in 1919.

British journalist Alexander Cockburn argues that Americans overseas must write so as "to confirm existing prejudice, rather than contradict it." His advice to aspiring foreign correspondents on "How To Earn Your Trench Coat" is cynical, stressing the use of clichés:

> The proper adjectival adornment for leaders is a vast and complex subject. If he is one of our dictators then use words like *dynamic, strong man, able.* He *laughs* a great deal, is always *on the move, in a hurry.* He *brushes impatiently aside* questions about franchise and civil liberties: "my people are not yet ready for these amenities you in the West feel free to enjoy. . . ." If, on the other hand, he is one of *their* dictators, then use words like *unstable, brooding, erratic, bloodthirsty, indolent.* He seldom ventures out of his palace unless under *heavy guard.* He is *rumored to be ailing.* Oddly enough he is often *charismatic.* At the moment it is particularly dangerous to use any adjectives about Arab leaders. Stick to general concepts in this case, like *converted to Western ways* or *deeply religious.*[9]

Even if reporters were able to shed their free-world bias, few editors or readers in the U.S. would appreciate the change. A reporter who learned "to float free and almost denationalize himself," writes Christopher Rand, "would be rushed home to be reindoctrinated."[10]

The chauvinism of American reporters may be inevitable, but it does distort the international knowledge of American readers and viewers. It also enrages editors, audiences, and government officials in other nations, especially in third world countries whose media rely largely on American wire services for worldwide coverage. In the late 1970s, third world critics moved beyond criticism to political action (see pp. 256-57). If AP and UPI respond to the pressure by becoming more sensitive and less chauvinistic in their coverage of the third world, the change will benefit American audiences as well.

But it will be a difficult change to accomplish. Third world media are also chauvinistic. A truly international perspective on international news—if it could be achieved—might wind up pleasing no one.

sonable number of people have been killed. For the regional and secondary news wires I include items about coffee, oil—Texas is most interested—and banditry."[11]

Colorful news is prized for its human-interest value, though it may give little insight into the people it describes. Typical topics include Japanese geishas and African safaris. Often these items have a strong American angle: "Hamburgers Big Hit in Paris" or "Bolivians Find New Uses for Saran Wrap."

Often, of course, the categories are combined. When President Nixon visited China in 1972, the story was obviously political. But the media—especially the networks—had made big plans for covering the visit, and there wasn't enough political hard news to fill the allotted time and space. Nor could reporters find anything sensational to cover. So they resorted to colorful travelogs, generally trivial anecdotes, and often flimsy attempts at interpretation. "One after another," commented *Newsweek*'s Joseph Morgenstern, "the networks' brightest news stars popped up with hundred-year-old egg on their faces."[12]

COVERING TERRORISM

Terrorism is perhaps the prototypical international news story. It is at once political, sensational, and—in a macabre sort of way—colorful; it genuinely affects American interests and is consumingly interesting to the American public. Not surprisingly, acts of terrorism receive blanket coverage in the American media.

Whether it is good coverage is more debatable. Often the media overplay terrorist acts, providing the exposure many terrorists seek and thus encouraging terrorism itself. And sometimes they underplay the issues that motivate terrorist activities, stressing the "terror" and ignoring the "ism." Besides cheating the audience of a proper understanding of world events, this too may en-

courage terrorism, by forcing terrorists to ever more extreme actions to compel media attention to their grievances, goals, and ideologies.

Terrorism is not a new phenomenon. Acts of terrorism are recorded in the Bible and throughout the history of civilization. Nor is American history free from terrorism—witness the Ku Klux Klan. Yet the media were unprepared for the modern-day terrorists who captured headlines in the 1970s. Early in 1974, American intelligence experts noted that 432 major acts of international political terrorism had occurred in the previous six years, including 235 bombings, 94 hijackings, and 57 kidnappings.[13] Terrorism continued to climb throughout the rest of the decade, not just in places like Belfast and Jerusalem, but in New York and Washington as well. One group of experts counted 6,294 acts of terrorism between 1970 and 1979, and a CIA study found that 587 people were killed by terrorist attacks in 1979 alone.[14]

News coverage of international terrorism typically depends on the politics of the terrorists and the politics of the country whose media are doing the coverage. In countries where the viewpoint of the terrorists is unpopular, political bombings and kidnappings are treated as shocking and spectacular crimes, period. In countries where the ideology of the terrorists is more acceptable, the same events are treated as regrettably extreme ways of making a political statement.

Consider, for example, news coverage of the Palestinian guerrilla movement. Terrorism has played an important role in Palestinian strategy for decades. But in 1970, fearful that they were being frozen out of Arab decision-making, activists in the Palestinian movement stepped up their terrorist activities and aimed at worldwide publicity. They hijacked planes in Europe, killed Israeli Olympic athletes in Munich, staged spectacular massacres inside Israel, and in a variety of other violent ways demonstrated their dedication to the Palestinian cause. As a result, Europe, the third world, and above all the Arab nations began to take the Palestinians seriously. Reporters begged the guerrilla leaders for interviews, hailed them as Arab independence fighters, and reported their grievances in detail.

In 1974, largely because of this publicity, Yasir Arafat of the Palestine Liberation Organization was invited to address the United Nations General Assembly. One Palestinian offered this comment on the success of the terrorist strategy: "We had been forgotten by the world, and we vowed never to be forgotten again. I believe we have kept that vow."[15]

Most American newspapers and broadcast stations did not join in the worldwide enthusiasm for the PLO. Coverage of Palestinian terrorism in the U.S. press was shocked and disapproving; it oversimplified the politics of the Middle East and tended to treat the bombings, hijackings, and massacres simply as crimes. But in 1973, the tone of U.S. coverage began to change. Interviews with terrorist leaders and analyses of their ideology became more common. A list of the twenty-five most intriguing people of 1974, published in *People* magazine, included Yasir Arafat—but no mention of PLO terrorism.[16]

The reasons for the change were the 1973 Middle East war, the oil crisis, and the rapprochement between the United States and the Arab world that these events precipitated. As some Americans began taking the Arab nations and the Palestinian political viewpoint more seriously, a crime story became a political story.

By way of contrast, the American mass media covered terrorism in Northern Ireland as a political story from the very beginning. The struggle was viewed not just as a succession of bombings and shootings, but as a genuine civil war, and so the positions of both Catholics and Protestants were carefully examined. Before 1973, in other words, the American press generally treated Arab guerrillas as criminals and Irish guerrillas

as revolutionaries. After 1973, it generally treated them both as revolutionaries.

What about American revolutionary terrorists? Small groups of militant American radicals used bombs as a political weapon beginning in the late 1960s. Between 1969 and January of 1975, the Weather Underground claimed responsibility for twenty bombings, including explosions at the Capitol (1971), the Pentagon (1972), and the State Department (1975). The underground press treated the terrorists as a legitimate revolutionary movement. Adopting the "orthodox" approach to domestic terrorism, the Establishment press did not.

Soon after the State Department bombing in 1975, the *New York Times* published an eloquent editorial on terrorism here and abroad. Its title embodies its theme: "The Violence Plague."

> Like a dread plague in medieval times that moved relentlessly and invisibly from one walled town to another and that walls were powerless to keep out, terrorist violence breaks out today in one great city after another and sophisticated security systems are powerless to prevent it. Within days a bomb goes off in the State Department in Washington, there is a murderous explosion at Fraunces Tavern in New York, planes are shot up and hostages seized in an airport in Paris. No city—Stockholm or Rome, Birmingham or Buenos Aires—is immune, and in the least favored, such as Belfast, violence has become endemic. . . .
>
> The political senselessness and moral nihilism of these terrorist acts may be clues to their essential nature. The fanatics are rebels against —not only a particular grievance or injustice— but against the modern world itself.[17]

This sort of editorial must be immensely frustrating to terrorists who view themselves as serious political revolutionaries, not senseless nihilists. It is immensely comforting, on the other hand, to government officials, who prefer to depict their violent enemies as lunatics. The very word "terrorist" has come to connote senseless violence; those whose violence makes sense to the media become "guerrillas" or even (if they oppose communist governments) "freedom fighters." Guerrillas have grievances, goals, and ideologies. Terrorists just kill people.

Some terrorists, of course, *are* lunatics who just kill people. Authorities are right in their claim that massive media attention to terrorism encourages a chain reaction of still more terrorism. Like any spectacular crime, a bombing, kidnapping, or hijacking can spawn a flurry of imitators, often motivated by nothing more than a twisted need for notoriety. In 1974, as the House Judiciary Committee debated presidential impeachment charges before millions of television viewers, a bomb threat came into the Capitol switchboard. While the hearing room was cleared and searched, the networks reported the threat to their viewers. In the next several days, according to then FBI Director Clarence Kelley, there were seven telephoned bomb threats against the committee, "all apparently generated by the instant, nationwide exposure given the initial threat."[18] Perhaps the first threat was genuinely political, but what about the other seven?

In 1977, CBS became the first major news organization to issue specific guidelines for coverage of terrorism. CBS News President Richard Salant announced that "except in the most compelling circumstances . . . there should be no live coverage of the terrorist-kidnapper, since we may fall into the trap of providing an unedited platform for him." CBS reporters were also advised to check with authorities before making direct contact with terrorists, and to seek official guidance in order to avoid reporting anything that might exacerbate the situation. The guidelines were widely applauded by broadcasters and government officials.[19]

But guidelines or no guidelines, terrorism continues to be a big story for the media, too alluring to resist. In late 1979, NBC made a deal with the Iranians holding 53 American hostages in Teheran. In return for an interview with one of the hostages, the network agreed to air a statement from their captors. ABC News President Roone Arledge called the NBC decision "a setback for those of us trying to operate responsibly in a sensitive terrain."[20]

Responsibility in news coverage of terrorism turns out to be very difficult to define. It is easy to criticize the media for sensation-mongering, for overplaying terrorist acts and thus encouraging more terrorist acts. But when terrorism really is political, the media owe it to their audience to report the story fully, including the ideology behind it. Was NBC right or wrong, then, when it allowed itself to be used by Iranian terrorists as a pulpit for their preachings?

One thing is certain. The American media can do a far better job than they now do of covering nonviolent political dissidence around the world. Background stories on ideological battles in other countries would inform the American audience without encouraging terrorism. Such stories would even eliminate one motive for terrorism, the sense that only violence can catch the media's attention. To achieve this goal, of course, American journalists—and American audiences—will have to develop a taste for international news without the spice of violence.

Terrorism aside, much of the international news in the American media is about Americans—issues of American national security, American military actions, and American intelligence-gathering. We turn now to these topics.

NATIONAL SECURITY

For more than a year, James Reston of the *New York Times* knew that the United States was flying high-altitude spy planes (U-2s) over the Soviet Union. His paper did not report the fact. Then, in 1960, a U-2 was shot down and its pilot captured. President Eisenhower denied everything. The *Times,* which knew the denials were lies, printed them without comment. Only after the president finally admitted the truth did the *Times* finally publish the truth.

Reston defended this judgment in 1966. He agreed that it was contrary to the traditional journalistic ethic, but he added: "In this time of half-war and half-peace that old principle of publish-and-be-damned, while very romantic, bold and hairy, can often damage the national interest."[21]

No doubt there are times when American military adventures should not be reported by the mass media. Equally clearly, there are times when it is vitally important that those adventures be reported. The problem is telling one from the other.

Consider two other instances when the *Times* neglected to report what it knew—the Bay of Pigs invasion of 1961 and the Cuban missile crisis of 1962.

Tad Szulc's article on the planned invasion was already dummied into the front page of the *Times,* under a four-column headline. But managing editor Turner Catledge and publisher Orvil Dreyfoos had grave reservations. They feared that the story might give Castro the warning he needed to repel the invasion, thus endangering the lives of the CIA-supported invaders and damaging the national security of the United States. After much heated debate, the article was toned down. References to the CIA and to the "imminence" of the invasion were dropped, and the whole thing was run under a single-column headline. There were no immediate repercussions.

When the invasion took place, it was a total failure, a serious blow to U.S. prestige. A month later President Kennedy confided to Catledge: "If you had printed more about the operation you would have saved us from a colossal mistake."

The Cuban missile crisis was another kettle of fish. The *Times* Washington bureau knew that there were Russian missiles inside Cuba, and that Kennedy was planning to do something about them. The president telephoned Dreyfoos and asked him to hold off on the story. Dreyfoos agreed. The result was a spectacularly successful blockade, a triumph for American diplomacy (which badly needed a triumph). Kennedy generously gave the *Times* part of the credit for that success.[22]

The Cuban crises of 1961 and 1962 illustrate two important points. First, it is extremely difficult for the media to know when they should kill a story for reasons of national security. Kennedy felt that the *Times* made a bad mistake in 1961, but showed extraordinary wisdom in 1962—by doing precisely the same thing. Second, when faced with this sort of dilemma, the media have typically killed the story. With the benefit of hindsight, we can find hundreds of articles that should have been published and weren't. But there are very few cases of published articles that did serious damage to national security.

American journalists have traditionally drawn a hard-and-fast line between wartime and peacetime. When the nation is at war, censorship has been accepted without argument. But in time of peace, reporters have viewed the public's right to know as the paramount consideration in deciding what to publish. An informed public, after all, is a cornerstone of democracy. How then can the truth be detrimental to the national interest?

This once-unquestioned distinction is now permanently muddled. Modern warfare is no longer a matter of clear-cut enemies and established battlefronts. The next formal, declared war the United States fights will probably be the world's last. The conflict in Southeast Asia was a war. The ongoing struggle against the "communist menace" is a war. The battle between Israel and its neighbors in the Middle East is a war. The stockpiling of missiles and atomic bombs is a war. In these terms, the United States has been constantly at war since the 1940s, and will remain at war for the foreseeable future. Does this mean that wartime standards of self-censorship should go forever unopposed?

In 1961, Douglass Cater listed four kinds

of stories that should not be reported (even in "peacetime") because of national security:

1. Advance disclosures of the U.S. government's position on issues to be negotiated at the international conference table.

2. Leaks on security matters which include the built-in bias of those who did the leaking.

3. Technical data of little interest to the ordinary reader but of immense value to the "enemy."

4. The clandestine operations of our government, both diplomatic and military.[23]

By and large, the American media abided by these standards until the end of the 1960s. As we shall see later, the fact that they did so contributed significantly to the increasing American involvement in Vietnam.

GOVERNMENT CENSORSHIP

Throughout most of American history, the media seldom faced for themselves the key question of news versus national security—to publish or not to publish. Instead, they allowed the government to make that decision, and to enforce it through censorship.

The history of wartime censorship is as old as the history of war itself. In this country it starts with the Revolution. Loyalist newspapers were persecuted throughout the war, and many were forced to stop publishing altogether. Patriot papers fared just as badly in Tory-held territory.

Soon after the Revolution, troops under the command of Major General Arthur St. Clair were attacked by Indians. A congressional committee convened to study the disaster, and asked President Washington to furnish the relevant documents. Washington replied that the executive branch of government had a right to withhold any information that might injure the public if disclosed. Although Washington did hand over the records, the principle soon took root. Very early in American history, then, the right of the government to withhold information for rea-

sons of national security was asserted. And the difficulty of distinguishing between wartime and peacetime was demonstrated.

Coverage of the War of 1812 was casual, and based mostly on official reports. Censorship was thus unnecessary. Much the same thing was true during the Mexican-American War. News reports were colorful and heavily pro-American, and by the time they were published—often weeks later—they posed little threat to military security. The government felt no need to interfere. But the Civil War was a different story. It was the most heavily and most speedily reported war up to that point in American history, and by far the most divisive.

In July of 1861, the Union Army issued an order forbidding telegraph companies to send reports on military affairs. The goal of this measure was to restrict the communications of spies and to prevent the Confederacy from learning about troop movements and the like through Northern newspapers. For several months the ban was extended to nonmilitary reporting as well, but Congress objected and the earlier rule was reinstated. Even this was a serious infringement on freedom of the press, but the Supreme Court was in no mood to defend the First Amendment at the expense of the war effort.

In order to transmit news by telegraph, reporters were required to submit their stories for government censorship. In theory only information of military value to the enemy was to be excised, but many field commanders used their censorship powers to eliminate unfavorable publicity as well. Reporters who wrote glowingly about their favorite generals were free to work without restriction. Those who were more critical of military tactics found themselves out in the cold; a few were actually accused of treason.

Critical newspapers were similarly harassed. The federal government temporarily shut down the *New York World,* the *Journal of Commerce,* and the *Chicago Times* for publishing stories deemed detrimental to the war effort. Confederate soldiers dealt even more harshly with the *North Carolina Standard* and other "union-screamers." None of these papers supported the enemy, but any criticism seems perilously close to treason in time of war.

The Spanish-American War was so short and so successful that censorship never got off the ground. Strangely enough, there was need for it. The Yellow Press gleefully printed any news it could find, including news of troop movements and strategy planning. Commented *The Journalist:* "We gave the Spaniards no use for spies, for our yellow journals became themselves the spies of Spain."[24] Sensationalism was at its height; William Randolph Hearst sailed his own yacht to war, and actually captured a few hapless Spanish sailors off the coast of Cuba. High jinks and hoaxes inevitably impeded the war effort, but the confident U.S. military voiced no serious objections. For the press, at least, it was a fun war.

World War I was not fun. Censorship and news management were merciless. Reporters had to be accredited by the Allied forces, and needed special permission to move from one location to another. Every dispatch from the front was ruthlessly censored in the interests of troop morale and domestic enthusiasm, as well as national security.

Back home, meanwhile, the government's Committee on Public Information was organized under George Creel. During the course of the war, the CPI set up standards of voluntary press censorship and issued more than 6,000 press releases, many heavily larded with patriotic propaganda. The press observed the voluntary codes, and many American newspapers printed all 6,000 of Creel's releases.

Just to make sure, the government nationalized the infant radio industry, calling a halt to all wireless experimentation. It also passed the Espionage Act, the Trading-with-the-Enemy Act, and the Sedition Act, all of which limited the kinds of news and opinions the mass media were permitted to publish. The Sedition Act was by far the most expansive of the three. It prohibited "any disloyal, profane, scurrilous, or abusive language about the form of government of the United States, or the Constitution, military or naval forces, flag, or the uniform of the army or navy of the United States." More than seventy-five socialist and German-language publications were prosecuted or threatened under these acts.

But World War I was "the war to end all wars," and very few reporters or editors objected to government censorship. Raymond S. Tompkins comments:

> The censorship irked them and they hated it at first, but gradually they grew used to it and wrote what they could, working up all the "human interest stuff" available and learning quickly that the censors loved it and almost invariably passed it—provided it said nothing about the drinking, stealing and rugged *amours* of the *soldat Américain.* . . . Dragooned into thinking about and observing the war in terms of what would get printed [the correspondent] went on exuding larger and larger gobs of slush, to the continual delight of the appreciative censor, the supreme satisfaction of his managing editor and the glory of the paper that had sent him.[25]

In World War II, voluntary self-censorship was instituted once again. The government issued codes urging the media to censor their reports of shipping, planes, troops, fortifications, armaments, war production, and even the weather. The program was largely successful. No American paper reported the German submarine blockade of 1942. Radar and the atomic bomb were both developed in absolute secrecy, though there were reporters and editors in the know.

The CPI was revived in the form of the Office of War Information, and once again patriotic press releases filled the media. The same agency examined all communications entering or leaving the United States, and deleted whatever it thought was detrimental to the national interest. In one case this included the word "God-damned" in an Ernie Pyle dispatch. Like its predecessors, World War II had its share of unreported stories.

The Espionage Act was still in force. Though it was used sparingly, America's few pro-Nazi media were soon suppressed.

The Korean conflict was America's first full-fledged undeclared foreign war, and the first generally unpopular war in the twentieth century. The government censors soon became less concerned with national security than with troop morale and military prestige. In 1950, AP's Tom Lambert and UP's Peter Kalischer were forced to return to Tokyo for "reorientation." And the Eighth Army announced that "criticism of Command decisions or of the conduct of Allied soldiers on the battlefield will not be tolerated."[26]

The censorship grew worse after General MacArthur's drive into North Korea brought the Chinese Communists into the war. In the face of intense criticism, MacArthur authorized censorship of all dispatches that might injure military morale or embarrass the U.S. government. Only after President Truman removed MacArthur from command was some measure of freedom of the press restored.

Throughout this entire period, from the start of the Revolution to the end of the Korean War, the American media were basically passive in their response to government censorship. Of course there were occasional newspapers that opposed a particular war, and therefore opposed the censorship that accompanied it. And there were frequent skirmishes to keep military censorship from expanding beyond national security to cover the self-interest of battlefield commanders. But on two fundamental points the media and the government agreed: News damaging to the war effort should not be published, and the government should be the one to decide which news is damaging to the war effort.

This happy consensus began its slow collapse during the cold war of the 1950s. It was an undeclared, civilian war of threats and diplomacy, and the traditions of wartime censorship were neither obviously applicable nor obviously irrelevant. The media, by and large, were still willing to adhere to government definitions of national security, but the government was no longer willing to trust the media that far. Military precedents were too shaky, issues were too complex, events

---

RADIO IN EUROPE

World War II was radio's finest hour. The entire country thrilled and chilled as Edward R. Murrow and his colleagues reported, live, the air blitz over London, the invasion of France, and other critical events that changed the face of Europe:

This is Edward Murrow speaking from Vienna. It's now nearly 2:30 in the morning and Herr Hitler has not yet arrived. No one seems to know just when he will get here, but most people expect him sometime after ten o'clock tomorrow morning. . . .

Young storm troopers are riding about the streets, riding about in trucks and vehicles of all sorts, singing and tossing oranges out to the crowd. Nearly every principal building has its armed guard, including the one from which I am speaking. . . . There's a certain air of expectancy about the city, everyone waiting and wondering where and at what time Herr Hitler will arrive.[27]

Murrow was seldom censored by the government. He seldom needed to be. He was a superb reporter and an independent one; after the war he would do more than any other journalist to end the demagogic career of Senator Joseph McCarthy. But like most reporters (and most Americans), he supported the war and did what he could to help.

were too fast-moving, and the stakes—the ever-present possibility of nuclear holocaust—were too high.

And so, with increasing frequency, the government resorted to lying. At the time of the Cuban missile crisis, Assistant Secretary of Defense Arthur Sylvester, a former reporter himself, explicitly defended this tactic: "It's inherent in government's right, if necessary, to lie to save itself when it's going up into a nuclear war. That seems to me basic—basic."[28]

That right was also assumed by the American government when faced with something less than the threat of nuclear disaster.[29] Politically sophisticated Americans came to expect lies and half-lies from the Departments of Defense and State. So did the media—but they published them nonetheless.

Then came Vietnam.

VIETNAM AND THE MEDIA

The story of the U.S. commitment in Southeast Asia begins in the 1950s. By 1961, it was already American policy to camouflage the shortcomings of the Diem regime in South Vietnam. As one U.S. "adviser" put it: "Bad news hurts morale."[30]

He didn't say *whose* morale—and it's a pertinent question, since at that point U.S. officials claimed there were no Americans fighting in Vietnam. When an American aircraft carrier was observed in action on the Saigon River, a U.S. information officer merely said, "I don't see any aircraft carrier."[31] In 1962, the State Department sent a secret cable to Saigon:

CORRESPONDENTS SHOULD NOT BE TAKEN ON MISSIONS WHOSE NATURE IS SUCH THAT UNDESIRABLE DISPATCHES WOULD BE HIGHLY PROBABLE. . . . WE RECOGNIZE IT NATURAL THAT AMERICAN NEWSMEN WILL CONCENTRATE ON ACTIVITIES OF AMERICANS. IT IS NOT—REPEAT

NOT—IN OUR INTEREST, HOWEVER, TO HAVE STORIES INDICATING THAT AMERICANS ARE LEADING AND DIRECTING COMBAT MISSIONS AGAINST VIET CONG.[32]

As the war intensified throughout 1963, this policy could not hold up. A band of young correspondents (Neil Sheehan of UPI, Malcolm Browne of AP, David Halberstam of the *New York Times,* Charles Mohr of *Time*) reported again and again that Americans were indeed fighting in Vietnam—and losing.

Such articles were not popular back home. President Kennedy suggested that the *Times* replace Halberstam. Mme. Ngo Dinh Nhu, in the midst of a good-will tour of the U.S., commented that the reporter "should be barbecued and I would be glad to supply the fluid and the match."[33] The *Times* resisted both proposals, and Halberstam remained in Vietnam. Charles Mohr was not so fortunate. *Time* freely altered the sense of his dispatches, and eventually published a special article charging the Saigon press corps with "helping to compound the very confusion that it should be untangling for its readers at home."[34] Mohr immediately quit his job in protest, and later moved to the *Times* himself.

Halberstam and Mohr were part of a small minority. Most of the reporters in Southeast Asia acted more as mail carriers than as journalists. They faithfully delivered to their readers the messages of U.S. diplomatic and military sources. Many depended heavily on the daily government briefings and propaganda sessions—the famous "Five O'Clock Follies." Some never got out into the field at all.

Dependence on official sources was, in fact, the great sin of the media throughout the mid-1960s. Consider the following statements from Defense Secretary Robert McNamara:

1962: "There is no plan for introducing combat forces into South Vietnam."

1963: "We have every reason to believe that [United States military] plans will be successful in 1964."

1964: "Reliance on military pressure upon the North would not be a proper response."

1965: "We have stopped losing the war."

1967: "Substantial progress has been achieved on virtually all fronts—political, economic, and military."[35]

Some of these statements were errors in judgment. Some were probably outright lies. In either case, the vast majority of reporters in Vietnam knew better—but very few of them saw fit to set the record straight.

In November of 1967, the government undertook a supreme effort to reassure the American people about Vietnam. Ambassador Ellsworth Bunker and General William Westmoreland were put on public display. Westmoreland described the situation as "very, very encouraging"; Bunker spoke of "steady progress" and declared that two-thirds of South Vietnam was now under control. A scant two months later came the Tet offensive against the South.

The Tet offensive was not a North Vietnamese military victory. In fact, as journalist Peter Braestrup pointed out nearly 10 years later in his book *Big Story,* it was actually a military setback for Hanoi. But to American reporters who had accepted (and covered) Westmoreland's and Bunker's assurances that such an invasion could not happen, the Tet offensive looked like proof of two crucial points—that the U.S. was not winning the war, and that the U.S. was lying about it.[36] Though the government's "credibility gap" had opened long before, it was only after Tet that the gap was mentioned frequently in the press. Ironically, then, a North Vietnamese setback fueled American media skepticism. From 1968 on, coverage of the war in Southeast Asia grew more and more aggressive, independent, and critical.

To read the American press before Tet, U.S. forces in Vietnam had no deserters, no racial conflict, no drug problem, and no

crimes or atrocities. It is a comment on the Saigon press corps that even after Tet, when many "unreportable" stories were beginning to receive coverage, the news of the My Lai massacre first broke as a result of the independent efforts of Seymour Hersh, then a freelance writer working out of Washington.

Vietnam was an undeclared war, and so outright censorship played only a minor role. The underground press was free even to support North Vietnam without federal prosecution. Individual correspondents were free to write what they pleased. To be sure, uncritical reporters had an easier time hitching rides to the front, and found their sources more cooperative when they got there. Harassment of the most bitter war critics was common. But on the whole, the government had little use for censorship in Vietnam. It lied instead. It lied to the reporters, and it lied to the public.

And when (as frequently happened) the lies of the authorities were contradicted by events in the field, an embargo was placed on all reporting of those events. The most flagrant embargo came during the invasion of Laos in 1971. For six days, the media were forbidden to report any events taking place on the Laos-Vietnam border. Afterward, the Associated Press wrote:

> The U.S. Command in South Vietnam has placed an embargo on certain news from the northern part of the country. Embargoes are nothing new in Vietnam, but available information indicates the one imposed last week is the strictest yet seen. . . .
>
> In this case, officials informed newsmen of the embargo but prohibited them from mentioning it and did not brief them until later—thus, in effect, placing an embargo on the embargo. . . .[37]

The embargo quite clearly had nothing to do with national security. Its goal was to forestall public protest against widening the war. But the Nixon administration claimed that national security was at stake, and with-

TELEVISION IN VIETNAM

Vietnam was television's war—the first time in history parents watched their sons suffer and die on the six o'clock news. Not that there was much suffering and dying to be seen. In the interests of decency and propriety, the networks managed to present a uniquely antiseptic picture of modern warfare. We saw flag-draped coffins loaded onto helicopters with all due pomp and ceremony—not headless G.I.s in plastic bags. Yet despite the trivialization of violence (and the inevitable oversimplification of issues), television did bring the war home.

Before the Tet offensive, broadcasting (like the rest of the media) docilely accepted the official version of events in Vietnam. On many occasions filmclips that seemed to contradict that version were simply dropped from the nightly news. And documentaries were uniformly patriotic, with perhaps a three-minute interview with Senator Fulbright to acknowledge the existence of "responsible dissent."

All that changed after Tet. The following excerpt from the CBS Evening News of June 27, 1970, is in many ways typical of Vietnam broadcast reporting in the early 1970s. The Cambodian invasion has just ended, a party is underway, and Morely Safer is interviewing a young American soldier on his way out:

> Safer: What was the morale like in the field among the men?
>
> Soldier: It was pretty bad. These clothes, I've had these clothes on for about 40 days now. We can't get clothes. We can't—mail is slow, it's pretty bad. There were a lot of people killed, and a lot of people were sad. Why this [party] at the end, you know? We're supposed to forget about it, something like that.
>
> Safer: A lot of men smoking marijuana. Was that common in your outfit?
>
> Soldier: Pretty common, I'd say. Just about everybody I know smokes marijuana in my outfit. There is nothing else to do.
>
> Safer: But the beer flows on and the band plays on and the girls are sympathetic and cheerful in that sweet, hometown way. . . . This attempt by the Army to put a nice neat World War II finish to the war in Cambodia makes for very good, very appealing propaganda pictures, but as one tanker asked me as we arrived here back at Katum, who's paying for all those ghosts we left behind? Morely Safer, CBS News, at Katum on the Cambodian border.[38]

If you opposed the war and distrusted the government, this was interpretive reporting at its finest. But even those who supported the war and the government—and deplored Safer's coverage—were forced to admit that at long last television had begun to speak its mind.

---

out exception the media went along with the embargo. Though opposed to the war, they were unwilling to second-guess the president on a question of national security. Bay of Pigs all over again.

Later in 1971, a former Defense Department consultant delivered to the *New York Times* a top-secret government report on

U.S. Vietnam policy-making in the 1950s and 1960s. The report documented the war's "credibility gap" in fantastic detail, revealing many discrepancies between official policies and official statements. Despite its top-secret status, the *Times* decided to publish the report. A temporary injunction forbidding publication was fought before the

Supreme Court, which granted the *Times* the right to publish (see pp. 159-60).

The significance of the Pentagon Papers (as the report came to be called) is twofold. On the one hand, the incident represents an unsuccessful government attempt at precensorship of the press—a hallmark of authoritarian control. Perhaps more important, it represents a decision by the nation's foremost newspaper to reveal the wartime secrets of the government. The *Times* determined to its own satisfaction that the Pentagon Papers contained little or nothing damaging to American national security. Although the Pentagon hotly disputed this conclusion, the *Times* stood firm on its opinion and published the report. The lesson of Bay of Pigs was beginning to take hold.

In January, 1973, after months of private negotiations, an "Agreement on Ending the War and Restoring Peace in Vietnam" was signed in Paris. The Paris accords did not bring peace to Southeast Asia. The wars in Vietnam and Cambodia continued, and the United States continued to supply military aid. But as American soldiers came home, American interest in the war as a war waned. Vietnam became a political story.

By the time the Paris accords were signed, public support for past Vietnam policies was almost nonexistent, and public debate over current Vietnam policies was widespread. Opponents of the war within the government could now be counted on for nearly daily revelations, and the media were free to report these revelations without concern for national security. In July, 1973, for example, the Senate Armed Services Committee began an investigation of charges that the U.S. had secretly begun its bombing raids into Cambodia in 1969, when that country was still officially neutral. The media joined Congress in pressuring the Defense Department to reveal the truth—that some 3,500 secret bombing raids had occurred during the fourteen-month period before the United States sent combat troops into Cambodia.

Similarly, in 1975, news coverage of the collapse of the Thieu regime and the evacuation of the last Americans from South Vietnam was characterized by a nearly total disregard for traditional considerations of national security and national self-image. Apparently convinced that there was no legitimate American national interest left in Southeast Asia, the media reported what they saw with total candor, and what they were told with considerable skepticism.

THE INTELLIGENCE APPARATUS

The Central Intelligence Agency was founded after World War II to improve the quality and quantity of information available on the plans of foreign governments. It is the organization that sent U-2 spy planes over the Soviet Union and helped plan the Bay of Pigs invasion of Cuba. For many years it was considered "untouchable" by most American reporters. Throughout the 1950s and 1960s, the media generally accepted the government position that almost any news story about CIA activities would endanger the national security of the United States.

Journalistic skepticism about the CIA grew enormously during the Vietnam conflict, as reporters discovered bits and pieces of various CIA exploits in Southeast Asia. But the story remained untouchable until Watergate. When it was learned that several Watergate burglars had worked for the CIA in the past, and when further investigation raised the possibility that even more direct links existed between Watergate and the CIA, American journalists finally began questioning what really went on behind the closed doors of the secret spy agency.

In September, 1973, a successful coup toppled the government of Marxist President Salvador Allende of Chile. The Nixon administration insisted that the U.S. had played no role in the coup. But in April, 1974, CIA Director William E. Colby told a top-secret

ISRAEL CONTROLS WAR NEWS

Over the long history of Arab-Israeli conflict, most foreign correspondents came to consider Israel a more reliable information source than the Arab countries. But during the first few days of the October, 1973 war, when Israel appeared to be losing, Israeli information was anything but reliable. While the Arabs provided a "barrage of information," Israeli handouts were bland and often false. Israeli leaders, for example, told the Israeli television audience that all but three Egyptian bridges over the Suez Canal had been destroyed—but when viewers turned to the Arab TV channels, they *saw* more than three bridges left standing. Not until the fourth night of the war, as the tide began to turn, did Israel begin to tell the truth.[39]

On the fifth day, Israeli reporters were allowed to go to the front lines, where they joined tank charges on the Golan Heights, missile-boat missions in Egyptian waters, and the Israeli crossing to the west bank of the Suez. When Arab TV stations celebrated the large number of captured Israeli soldiers, Israeli television countered with battle footage —plus hours and hours of extra entertainment programming. Foreign journalists—some 800 of them from more than thirty nations—were permitted to visit the Golan, where Israel had already broken the Syrian offensive, but they were not allowed near the action on the Sinai front. Unable to observe for themselves what was really happening, American journalists had no choice but to report the sharply conflicting information provided by Arab and Israeli government sources.[40]

Both Israel and Egypt practiced strict news censorship throughout the war. Israeli censors, for example, would not permit stories that Defense Minister Moshe Dayan was extremely worried during the early fighting; Egyptian censors refused to allow stories that the Egyptian Third Army had been "encircled."[41] On the whole, Israeli information was most misleading in the early days of the war, when the Arabs were making significant gains. Later, when Israel went on the offensive, Arab information proved undependable. When a country—any country—is at war and losing, accurate information, freedom from censorship, and the free movement of journalists may be too much to expect.

---

congressional hearing that the administration had authorized the CIA to spend more than $8 million between 1970 and 1973 for covert activities designed to bring down the Allende government (including financial support for the Chilean opposition press). The story was leaked to the *New York Times,* and in September, 1974, the *Times* published it.[42] Ten years earlier the *Times* almost certainly would have sat on the story. But by 1974 the media were deciding for themselves what should and should not be run in the interests of national security—and they were in no mood to protect the CIA.

The *Times* article was written by Seymour Hersh, the investigative reporter who had broken the My Lai massacre story, then moved to the *Times* and provided it with a number of Watergate exclusives. Now Hersh was on the CIA's trail. In December, 1974, he reported that the CIA had conducted "a massive, illegal domestic intelligence operation during the Nixon administration against the antiwar movement and other dissident groups in the United States."[43] President Ford appointed a commission to look into the agency's activities, and CIA Director Colby released a statement admitting a wide range of domestic efforts against dissenting and antiwar groups.

In 1975 the *Washington Star* reported that CIA Director Colby had just briefed President Ford on the extent of the agency's past involvement in plans to assassinate foreign leaders.[44] The role of the CIA in political assassinations had been an untouchable story throughout the 1960s. Now even this most sensitive information was coming out.

Another taboo was broken in 1976, when several journalists revealed that they had worked for the CIA while employed as reporters. In previous decades this had been viewed as acceptable behavior for a reporter. Now it seemed so reprehensible in retrospect that the media set about house-cleaning in public (see p. 97). In 1977, Carl Bernstein reported in *Rolling Stone* magazine that some 400 American journalists had worked secretly with the CIA over the preceding 25 years. Three months later, the *New York Times* ran a three-part series on the agency's involvement with the news media. Responding to the pressure, the CIA announced that it would no longer pay American reporters except in unusual circumstances. Voluntary cooperation, the agency said, was still acceptable.[45] But it was no longer acceptable to most journalists—a telling shift in attitude that demonstrated the low esteem in which the nation's media now held the nation's intelligence apparatus.

In early 1977, President Jimmy Carter learned that the *Washington Post* was planning an article revealing that the CIA had paid millions of dollars to Jordan's King Hussein over the previous 20 years. Carter asked *Post* executive editor Ben Bradlee and reporter Bob Woodward to come to the White House, where he pointed out the damaging impact such a revelation might have. He did not explicitly ask them to kill the story, but he did make his preference clear—and he asked for 24 hours' notice if they decided to run the story anyhow. The next day, the *Post* gave the new president his notice.[46] The media usually go easy on a president in his first few months in office—but there was to be no "honeymoon" on intelligence issues.

When journalism professors asked their

THE EXCEPTION THAT PROVES THE RULE

The media still keep the government's secrets on occasion. By early 1975, for example, the *Los Angeles Times* had discovered that the CIA had contracted with Howard Hughes to raise a sunken Soviet submarine in the Pacific. The attempt had been only partly successful, and most of the sub was still under water. Afraid that the *New York Times* had the story and would publish it, the Los Angeles paper did run an article in early February, but reported that the sub had been recovered in the North Atlantic instead of the Pacific. When the CIA asked the paper to kill the story, it was moved from the front page to the inside.[47]

No less than 11 American news organizations were putting together more extensive sub stories in February and March, but the CIA was able to convince them to delay publication until the salvage operation was either completed or dropped. On March 18, Jack Anderson finally decided to break the story. He did so only after determining that the Soviet government already knew, and that what was involved was "not national security but international etiquette."[48] But for many weeks, most of the nation's prestige news organizations had willingly cooperated with the CIA to button up the Soviet sub story.

students whether there was any information the media should withhold on national security grounds, a common response in the 1970s was "not much—except how to build the Bomb." But in 1979 the *Progressive* magazine decided that even the Bomb wasn't off limits. The Justice Department initially won a temporary restraining order preventing the *Progressive* from publishing Howard Morland's "The H-Bomb Secret: How We Got It, Why We're Telling It," then dropped the suit when a Wisconsin newspaper published some of the same information in a letter to the editor (see p. 180).

The case split the journalistic community. While many editors supported the *Progressive*'s right to publish on First Amendment grounds, others sided with the restraining order in the interests of national security. Even among those who reluctantly endorsed the *Progressive*'s right to publish, few said their own publications would have run such an article.[49] The exposés of ex-CIA agent Philip Agee, revealing the names of other agents around the world, also troubled many journalists. "His writings have made intelligence much more hazardous," said the *New York Times* in a 1980 editorial.[50]

As the United States entered the 1980s, in short, there were still a few government secrets that most reporters were inclined to honor for the sake of national security—but only a few.

For the most part, the media today reserve for themselves the right to decide what to publish and what not to publish in the interests of national security. After two centuries of letting the government make that decision for them, the media are understandably unsure about what standards to use when making it themselves. But the important point is that they *are* making it themselves. The days when government officials could safely take reporters into their confidence, secure in the knowledge that the media would honor their secrets, are over. The media must now fight for what they

know, and must then decide what—if anything—to hold back.

Notes

1 Allen Alter, "580 U.S. News People Cover Sadat's Visit," *Editor & Publisher,* November 26, 1977, p. 9.

2 George Gerbner and George Marvanyi, "The Many Worlds of the World's Press," *Journal of Communication,* Winter, 1977, pp. 54-57. "Study Shows U.S. Media Distort Foreign News," *Editor & Publisher,* May 3, 1980, p. 17.

3 Bernard C. Cohen, "The Press, The Public and Foreign Policy," in Bernard Berelson and Morris Janowitz, eds., *Reader in Public Opinion and Communication,* 2nd ed. (New York: The Free Press, 1966), pp. 134-35, 142.

4 "Ties That Bind Readers to Papers," *Editor & Publisher,* July 21, 1979, p. 16.

5 Louis Harris, "Press Underplays News, Overdoes Sports: Readers," *Editor & Publisher,* January 21, 1978, p. 33.

6 Leo Bogart, "The Overseas Newsman: A 1967 Profile Study," *Journalism Quarterly,* Summer, 1968, p. 305.

7 Frederick T. C. Yu and John Luter, "The Foreign Correspondent and His Work," *Columbia Journalism Review,* Spring, 1964, pp. 5-12.

8 Walter Lippmann and Charles Merz, "A Test of the News," *New Republic,* August 4, 1920, pp. 1-42.

9 Alexander Cockburn, "How To Earn Your Trench Coat," *More,* May, 1974, pp. 24-25.

10 James R. Whelan, "The Agencies and the Issues," *Nieman Reports,* December, 1967, pp. 8-9.

11 Peter Barnes, "The Wire Services in Latin America," *Nieman Reports,* March, 1964, p. 5.

12 "TV: An Eyeful of China, a Thimbleful of Insight," *Newsweek,* March 6, 1972, p. 27.

13 "The 'Morality' of Terrorism," *Newsweek,* February 25, 1974, p. 21.

14 Blanche Cordelia Alston, "Scholars Foresee New Age of International Terrorism," *New York Times,* December 13, 1979. Drew Middleton, "1979 Terrorist Toll Put at a Record 587," *New York Times,* May 11, 1980, p. 14.

15 "The 'Morality' of Terrorism," p. 22.

16 Sol Stern, "Has the Press Abandoned Israel?" *More,* February, 1975, pp. 7-8.

17 "The Violence Plague," *New York Times,* Feb. 2, 1975, p. E14.

18 Clarence Kelley, "Television Is Armed and Dangerous," *TV Guide,* March 8, 1975, p. 6.

19 "CBS Sets Guidelines for Terrorist Stories," *New Brunswick* (N.J.) *Home News,* April 22, 1977, p. 3 (Washington Post/Los Angeles Times News Service). "Survey Shows Approval of Terrorism Guidelines," *Editor & Publisher,* November 26, 1977, p. 23.

20 "NBC News Interviews Marine Hostage," *Editor & Publisher,* December 15, 1979, p. 41.

21 James Reston, *The Artillery of the Press* (New York: Harper Colophon Books, 1966), pp. 20-21.

22 William McGaffin and Erwin Knoll, *Anything But the Truth* (New York: G. P. Putnam's Sons, 1968), pp. 205-209.

23 Douglass Cater, "News and the Nation's Security," *Montana Journalism Review,* 1961, pp. 2-3.

24 Frank Luther Mott, *American Journalism,* 3rd ed. (New York: Macmillan, 1962), p. 536.

25 Joseph J. Mathews, *Reporting the Wars* (Minneapolis: University of Minnesota Press, 1957), pp. 157-58.

26 Mott, *American Journalism,* p. 853.

27 Erik Barnouw, *The Golden Web* (New York: Oxford University Press, 1968), pp. 77-78.

28 David Wise, *The Politics of Lying* (New York: Vintage Books, 1973), p. 56.

29 Martin Goodman, "Numbers Game," *Columbia Journalism Review,* Summer, 1965, pp. 16-18.

30 Stanley Karnow, "The Newsmen's War in Vietnam," *Nieman Reports,* December, 1963, p. 4.

31 *Ibid.,* p. 6.

32 McGaffin and Knoll, *Anything But the Truth,* p. 79.

33 Gay Talese, *The Kingdom and the Power* (New York: World, 1969), pp. 466-67.

34 Karnow, "The Newsmen's War in Vietnam," p. 3.

35 Bruce Ladd, *Crisis in Credibility* (New York: New American Library, 1969), pp. 167-68.

36 Noam Chomsky, "10 Years After Tet: The Big Story That Got Away," *More,* June, 1978, p. 16.

37 Associated Press, February 5, 1971.

38 Marvin Barrett, ed., *Survey of Broadcast Journalism 1969-1970* (New York: Grosset & Dunlap, 1970), pp. 145-46.

39 Philip Gillon, "Israeli TV Comes of Age," *Hadassah Magazine,* February, 1974, p. 26.

40 *Ibid.,* pp. 26-27. Terence Smith, "Israel's Curbs on Press Impair Her Credibility in Current War," *New York Times,* October 17, 1973, p. C15.

41 Richard M. Smith, "Censorship in the Middle East," *Columbia Journalism Review,* January/February, 1974, pp. 44-46.

42 Seymour M. Hersh, "C.I.A. Chief Tells House of $8-Million Campaign Against Allende in '70-73," *New York Times,* September 8, 1974, pp. 1, 26.

43 Seymour M. Hersh, "Huge C.I.A. Operation Reported in U.S. Against Antiwar Forces, Other Dissidents in Nixon Years," *New York Times,* December 22, 1974, p. 1.

44 "Colby Oral Fill-In to Ford on Assassination Reported," *New York Times,* March 5, 1975, p. 1.

45 Robert U. Brown, "Pressure on CIA," *Editor & Publisher,* January 22, 1977, p. 56. "Journalists Linked to CIA," *New Brunswick* (N.J.) *Home News,* September 12, 1977, p. 3 (AP). "CIA Issues New Rules for Dealing with Press," *Editor & Publisher,* December 17, 1977, p. 9. "Report Tells How CIA Used the News Media," *Editor & Publisher,* December 31, 1977, p. 9. Deirdre Carmody, "C.I.A. Head Defends Approving Use of Journalists," *New York Times,* April 11, 1980.

46 "Carter Discouraged an Article on Hussein," *New York Times,* February 26, 1977, pp. 1, 45 (AP).

47 James Phelan, "An Easy Burglary Led to the Disclosure of Hughes-C.I.A. Plan to Salvage Soviet Sub," *New York Times,* March 27, 1975, p. 18. "Salvaging the Sub Story," *Newsweek,* March 31, 1975, p. 66.

48 "Anderson Says Soviet Knew Submarine Story," *New York Times,* March 26, 1975, p. 13. Phelan, "An Easy Burglary," p. 18.

49 "Bad Cases Make Bad Law," *Editor & Publisher,* March 17, 1979, p. 6.

50 "Trial by Agee," *New York Times,* January 7, 1980, p. A18.

Suggested Readings

ARLEN, MICHAEL J., *Living-Room War.* New York: Viking Press, 1969.

BAGDIKIAN, BEN H., "A Most Insidious Case," *The Quill,* June, 1979.

BELL, J. BOYER, "Terrorist Scripts and Live-Action Spectaculars," *Columbia Journalism Review,* May/June, 1978.

BRAESTRUP, PETER, *Big Story: How the American Press and Television Reported and Interpreted the Crisis of Tet 1968 in Vietnam and Washington.* Boulder, Colo.: Westview Press, 1977.

CHOMSKY, NOAM, "10 Years After Tet: The Big Story That Got Away," [*MORE*], June, 1978.

DIAMOND, EDWIN, and PAULA CASSIDY, "Arabs vs. Israelis: Has Television Taken Sides?" *TV Guide*, January 6, 1979.

EMERY, EDWIN, "The Press in the Vietnam Quagmire," *Journalism Quarterly*, Winter, 1971.

ERLANGER, STEVEN, "Vietnam Now," *Columbia Journalism Review*, July/August, 1978.

FRIEDMAN, ROBERT, "The Reporter Who Came In From the Cold," [*MORE*], March, 1977.

GERBNER, GEORGE, and GEORGE MARVANYI, "The Many Worlds of the World's Press," *Journal of Communication*, Winter, 1977.

HARRIS, JOHN D., *War Reporter*. New York: Manor Books, 1979.

HOWE, RUSSELL WARREN, "Asset Unwitting: Covering the World for the CIA," [*MORE*], May, 1978.

KNIGHTLEY, PHILLIP, *The First Casualty*. New York: Harcourt Brace Jovanovich, 1975.

MARCHETTI, VICTOR L., and JOHN D. MARKS, "Uncovering the CIA," [*MORE*], April, 1974.

MORRIS, ROGER, "Reporting for Duty: The Pentagon and the Press," *Columbia Journalism Review*, July/August, 1980.

THE NEW YORK TIMES, *The Pentagon Papers*. New York: Bantam Books, 1971.

RESTON, JAMES, *The Artillery of the Press*. New York: Harper Colophon Books, 1966.

SCHORR, DANIEL, *Clearing the Air*. New York: Berkeley Medallion Books, 1977.

TUNSTALL, JEREMY, *The Media are American*. New York: Columbia University Press, 1977.

UNGAR, SANFORD J., "The Forgotten Case of Sam Jaffe," *Columbia Journalism Review*, November/December, 1976.

"Vietnam: What Lessons?" *Columbia Journalism Review*, Winter, 1970-1971.

WISE, DAVID, *The Politics of Lying*. New York: Vintage Books, 1973.

As long as there has been an America, there have been racial, ethnic, economic, and sexual groups that the American mass media ignored or mistreated. Chief among these today are blacks. In recent years the media have improved greatly in their coverage of blacks, women, and other oppressed groups, but they still have a long way to go. Public indifference to the plight of these groups is both reflected in and exacerbated by media performance.

In July of 1967, in the middle of a long, hot summer of ghetto riots, President Lyndon B. Johnson appointed the National Advisory Commission on Civil Disorders. Headed by Governor Otto Kerner of Illinois, the commission was charged with the task of determining why blacks were rioting in the streets. Its final report placed a good deal of the blame on the mass media:

> The media report and write from the standpoint of a white man's world. The ills of the ghetto, the difficulties of life there, the Negro's burning sense of grievance, are seldom conveyed. Slights and indignities are part of the Negro's daily life, and many of them come from what he now calls "the white press"—a press that repeatedly, if unconsciously, reflects the biases, the paternalism, the indifference of white America.[1]

The Kerner Commission argued forcefully that the media alternately ignored and abused the black community. White readers were not forced to come to grips with the problems of the ghetto and their own bigotry. Blacks were afforded little opportunity to make known their grievances and lifestyles. Two separate and unequal societies were thus perpetuated, with little communication between them. Unable to make themselves heard in any other way, blacks took to the streets. Uninformed about the realities of ghetto life, whites were surprised. And so were the media, which should have known better.

Considerable progress has been made since the Kerner Commission's searing indictment of the media. But when a Miami ghetto exploded into violence in the summer of 1980, media inadequacies once again came in for part of the blame (along with police misconduct, rampant unemployment, and other inequities the media expose only occasionally). More progress, obviously, is needed.

MINORITY MEDIA

Minority groups have always been discriminated against in this country—by American society in general and by the American mass media in particular. Denied access to the majority media, and in many cases unable to understand the language of the majority media, ethnic minorities have traditionally organized their own. Though they could not speak to the WASPs, they could at least speak to each other.

The first foreign-language newspaper in America, the *Philadelphia Zeitung,* was founded in 1732. By 1914, the height of American immigration, there were more than 1,300 foreign-language publications in the country. The German press led the list, followed by the French, Italian, Japanese, Polish, Yiddish, and Scandinavian. War, depression, and assimilation soon took their toll. In 1979, according to *Editor & Publisher,* there were only 215 regularly published foreign-language newspapers in the United States.

The foreign-language media exist for the unassimilated, for ghetto groups that are still not a part of mainstream America. Today, this means primarily the Spanish-speaking— the Puerto Ricans and Cubans in the East, the Mexican-Americans in the West. *El Diario-La Prensa,* for example, is a Spanish-language tabloid daily in New York City, with the biggest circulation of any foreign-language publication in the country.

How is *El Diario* different from other New York City newspapers? One analysis found the following:

> *El Diario* showed 50% Latin orientation on its front page, 46% on its "important" news pages, 78% in its inside news space, and 75% of its sports space. In addition, *El Diario,* on

occasion, added a Latin slant to its coverage of essentially nonethnic news items. . . .

What this means quite simply is that the Puerto Rican butcher, baker and taxi driver in New York City is reading, more often than not, different news than that read by his *New York Daily News*-reading counterpart. He, a member of the minority, is not reading much of the news read by the majority of New York City newspaper readers.[2]

Miami, like New York, supports a thriving Spanish-language media system, including a daily newspaper (*Diario Las Americas*), five radio stations, and two television stations. It is also a center for Spanish-language magazine publishing, including several magazines published simultaneously in Latin America.

And in more than 40 cities from Miami to New York to Los Angeles, Spanish-speaking TV viewers can now watch Latin soap operas, Latin entertainers, and Latin news anchored in Mexico City. The Spanish International Network, three-quarters owned by a Mexican television company, reaches more than two million American homes daily, offering satellite transmissions of Latin American and European broadcasts.[3]

Black Americans speak English. Unlike many Mexican-Americans, Puerto Ricans, and Cubans, they can read the white media. But they have traditionally found so little there of relevance to their lives that they have supported a second, independent system of black media as well.

The first Negro newspaper in America was *Freedom's Journal,* founded in New York in 1827. More than twenty others, mostly devoted to the slavery issue, were established before the Civil War, including Frederick Douglass' *North Star.* Untypical but indicative was the case of one Willie A. Hodges, who in 1847 sought to have his opinions published in the *New York Sun.* He was told that if he wanted to see his ideas in print he would have to print them himself. So he did, in a newspaper he called the *Ram's Horn.*[4]

From 1850 to 1980, nearly 3,000 Negro publications were founded in the United States. Most were short-lived, but some survived for generations, exercising a tremendous influence on the development of the black community. Among the most successful were the *Chicago Defender* (1905), the *New York Amsterdam News* (1909), the *Pittsburgh Courier* (1910), and the *Norfolk Journal and Guide* (1911). Like most black papers, these four emerged from the inner-city ghetto. But they were really national newspapers, available at ghetto newsstands across the country.

In 1945, the *Pittsburgh Courier* boasted a circulation of 250,000. The *Chicago Defender* (202,000) and the *Baltimore Afro-American* (137,000) were close behind. Whites and blacks alike considered the editors of these papers to be the leaders of the Negro community. Presidents Roosevelt and Truman read the papers almost as faithfully as the typical ghetto black. Gunnar Myrdal could justly comment in his book, *An American Dilemma,* that "the Negro press . . . is rightly characterized as the greatest single power in the Negro race."[5]

Today, there are about 200 black-owned newspapers in the U.S., roughly the same as in 1945. But the *Courier's* circulation has dropped to around 16,000, and the *Afro-American* has suffered a similar readership decline. The *Defender,* which turned daily in the 1950s, now has a circulation of 21,000. Only two other black newspapers are dailies, the *Atlanta Daily World* and the *New York Challenge.* Presidents no longer pay much attention to these newspapers, nor does the black American look to them for leadership.

What happened? Rising costs and increased competition from black-oriented radio stations were part of the problem. But the Negro press lost most of its clout in the turbulent sixties, when it failed to keep pace with the black revolution. Notice the apologetic tone of these 1970 quotations from black publishers. John Murphy of the *Afro-*

American: "Newspapers are small businesses and publishers are businessmen. Surely you'd have to describe black publishers as conservatives, I suppose. In earlier years, black newspapers were spearheads of protest. Today we're much more informational." And C. B. Powell of the *Amsterdam News:* "You've got to realize that we don't see our role as leaders. We are not out to revolutionize. When the *Amsterdam News* sees issues that are too revolutionary, we speak out against them."[6]

Most black newspapers have changed very little since the 1950s. They still feature crime and sensationalism on page one, black sports and black society on the inside pages. Meanwhile, the movement around them was changing constantly—from civil rights and freedom someday to Black Power and Freedom Now!

Carl Morris, former general manager of the *New Pittsburgh Courier,* summarized the situation in a 1978 article in the *Pittsburgh Post-Gazette.* "Black publishers today are no longer crusaders," he wrote, "but ultra-conservative news chroniclers and penurious businessmen living with a glorious past but facing an uncertain future. Circulation and advertising revenues are tumbling as the mainly family-owned enterprises, rife with nepotism, scramble to find a way out of their problem." Morris's own move from the black *Courier* to a general assignment spot on the establishment *Post-Gazette* was not untypical. "The black press may well become a victim of integration," he noted, "because white media are providing jobs for black journalists in increasing numbers."[7]

Fed up with the traditional black press, many urban blacks looked for alternatives in the late 1960s and early 1970s. During that period the militant *Muhammad Speaks* claimed a circulation of more than 400,000. Together with the *Black Panther* and a number of local anti-establishment papers, it was seen as standing in the forefront of the revolution. Today the teachings of the Nation of Islam have become more moderate,

THE PHOENIX RISES

The first American Indian newspaper, the *Cherokee Phoenix,* was founded in 1828, published in both Cherokee and English by Elias Boudinot. The Cherokee nation was then in Georgia, but white Georgians wanted the Indians out. The Cherokees split into factions over the emigration issue, with Boudinot supporting the proposed move west. In 1832, Boudinot was forced out of the editorship by the tribal chief. In 1838, Georgia troops attacked the Cherokees, driving the nation onto the Trail of Tears. The presses of the *Cherokee Phoenix* were dismantled and buried. A year later in Oklahoma, Boudinot was murdered by political opponents within his own tribe.[8]

The Oklahoma Territory was to become a center for the Indian press. The *Cherokee Advocate* was launched in the 1840s, and other tribal newspapers developed as their nations evolved written alphabets. The first Indian editors' association was founded in the 1870s, and by the turn of the century more than a hundred newspapers had played a role in Indian life from Florida to Alaska.[9]

Today dozens of weekly newspapers—including the *Cherokee Advocate*—serve the Native American community. Indians now control six radio stations, one of which, KMDX-FM in Parker, Arizona, is commercial; Indian programming is carried by another 48 radio stations and a score of TV stations. There are even several Indian news services. Almost all the Native American media are now in English, although a number of publications run tribal language columns.

and so has the newspaper, renamed the *Bilalian News.* Its circulation is now down to about 150,000—still number one among black newspapers. The other circulation leaders are traditional papers. Four black newspaper chains boast combined circulations over 100,000, and 16 other chains and papers have circulations over 50,000. Despite their economic troubles and their lack of influence, traditional black newspapers may yet survive the 1980s.

While the national circulations of traditional black newspapers have all but disappeared, national black magazines have found a secure niche. John H. Johnson founded *Ebony,* a black picture magazine similar to *Life,* in 1945. *Ebony* now has a 1,270,000 monthly circulation, and the Johnson empire has grown to include *Jet* (700,000) and *Black World* (100,000).

In the mid-1960s, most black magazines were as conservative as the traditional black newspapers. Since then, many have changed their content in order to retain their standing in the black community. Still, they tend to shy away from hard political news and commentary, leaning instead toward the cultural "Black is Beautiful" side of social change. For example *Essence,* a women's magazine with the slogan "subscribe to blackness," specializes in fiction, fashion, and beauty. Its columns show an awareness and acceptance of black militancy, but they do not generally report or promote it.

Advertising is the lifeblood of the American media, and the black press is no exception. For many decades the vast majority of the ads in the black media were for specialized black-oriented products. But by the 1970s, many mainstream companies had discovered the purchasing power of black Americans. In 1972, *Ebony, Jet, Essence, Tuesday,* and *Black Enterprise* (then the five biggest black magazines) boasted a combined circulation of more than five million, and a total of 166 pages of advertising per issue.[10]

Black radio is clearly the most successful medium today in speaking to the black community. With some exceptions, however, that medium does not speak *for* the black community. As many as 800 commercial radio stations in the country program "the soul sound," but no more than a hundred of them are black-owned. Even that figure represents progress; the number of black-owned stations more than doubled from 1965 to 1975, and then tripled from 1975 to 1980. In the typical black-oriented radio station of the 1960s, only the disc jockeys and the janitors were black. Though employment opportunities have improved in recent years, there are still comparatively few black managers with real decision-making power.

There is reason for hope. The National Black Network and the Sheridan Broadcasting Network, both owned and operated by blacks, now offer hourly news feeds to black-oriented radio stations around the country. And today there are three VHF television stations under black control, where a decade ago there were none.

The real tragedy of the minority media is that they need to exist at all—that the mainstream media have been unable or unwilling to meet the needs of minorities. Almost as tragic is the fact that so many minority media have failed to serve their own communi-ties. The minority media speak to the people, but few speak for them.

COVERING THE REVOLUTION

The history of white coverage of blacks prior to 1954 is brief and undistinguished. From time to time a movie or radio drama would feature a black character (almost always stereotyped as a bumbling, laughable menial). And newspapers and magazines carried their share of hard news about black criminals and features about black athletes. For the most part that was it for the Negro.

Then, in 1954, the Supreme Court announced its school desegregation decision and the modern civil rights movement was born. As far as the white media were concerned, it was a virgin birth—the movement came out of nowhere, with no hint of long-standing grievances. Arthur B. Bertelson of the *St. Louis Post-Dispatch* described the rude awakening:

> At first, we self-consciously proffered tidbits with a heavy coating of soothing syrup. We dredged up sticky little features about those few Negroes who had made it. . . . In our

---

MOTOWN

The rise of Motown is the black media success story of the 1960s and 1970s. Berry Gordy, Jr. founded the Detroit-based record company with an $800 loan. He went on to discover Diana Ross and the Supremes, Martha and the Vandellas, and Stevie Wonder; and with them he created a distinct sound: "Motown." In 1973, Motown Industries had sales of more than $46 million. In 1974 *Black Enterprise* named Motown as the biggest black-owned and black-managed business in the U.S.

Motown Records is still the heart of the company, but three other divisions now earn additional profits. Jobete Music publishes music. Multi-Media manages entertainers. And Motown Productions puts together television specials and feature films, including *Lady Sings the Blues,* which won five Academy Award nominations and grossed over $10 million.[11]

At the end of the decade Motown still led the *Black Enterprise* list with annual sales of $58 million. Number two, by the way, was the Johnson Publishing Company (*Ebony, Jet, Black World*), with sales of more than $55 million.[12]

news columns, God forgive us, we quoted those "leaders" who counseled the Negro community to be patient, that we were all good fellows, that all would be well before they knew it.

When it became obvious that [the civil rights movement] wasn't going to assimilate this kind of pap, some of us began to try a little harder and discovered that what was required was a steady diet of raw—and, more often than not, unpalatable—truth.[13]

The "truth" as served up by the nation's newspapers and TV stations told of blacks valiantly struggling for their freedom from Southern oppressors. Reporters on the so-called "seg beat" were sent south for months at a time. They were horrified by what they saw, and their sense of outrage permeated their stories.

After a burst of gunfire stitched holes in a University of Mississippi doorsill, *Newsweek* reporter Karl Fleming turned to a companion and said, "You know, if I were Meredith, I wouldn't go to school with these bastards."[14] Millions of *Newsweek* readers experienced the same revulsion. So did anyone who watched television or read a newspaper.

From *Brown v. Board of Education* in 1954 to the Watts riot of 1965, the civil rights movement was centered in the South. The Northern media (which means the national media) did a commendable job of covering that movement. It was an easy story to cover—the heroes and villains clearly identified, the whole mess conveniently far away. Throughout the decade, those very same media managed to ignore completely the festering sores of their own local ghettos. Civil rights reporters invaded Mississippi and Alabama by the hundreds, but only an occasional crime writer bothered to visit Harlem, Watts, or Hough.

The Southern media didn't have it so easy. The violence was in their own back yard; the challenge was to their own way of life. On the whole, they acquitted themselves well. Ted Poston, later a reporter for the *New York Post,* wrote:

There have always been, and there still are, some fine and courageous Southern papers. As a native Kentuckian, I was reared from my earliest days on the *Louisville Courier-Journal.* As a college student, Pullman porter, and dining-car waiter, I received a valuable adjunct to my education through the *Nashville Tennessean,* the *Atlanta Constitution,* the *St. Louis Post-Dispatch,* and other pillars of liberal journalism in the South.[15]

Ralph E. McGill of the *Constitution* and Harry E. Ashmore of the *Little Rock* (Ark.) *Gazette* both won Pulitzer Prizes for their coverage of Southern racial unrest.

After the Watts riot of 1965, the focus of the story moved north. And the media discovered all over again that black people were big news. Newspapers and broadcast stations moved mountains in a frantic effort to cover the tragic succession of riots, demonstrations, and confrontations that characterized the last half of the 1960s.

COVERING A RIOT

It was Sunday, July 23, 1967. The *Detroit Free Press* had only a skeleton staff in the office when reports of looting and arson in the black section of town began filtering in. Police reporter Red Griffith told the newsroom the demonstrations had begun with a police raid the night before. Griffith also reported that the violence was spreading rapidly—despite police claims that it was under control. One *Free Press* reporter had already been struck by a bottle and sent to the hospital.

The deadline for Monday morning's first edition was fast approaching. Tom De Lisle, the youngest reporter on the staff, was toying with the lead for his rundown on the worst damage areas. "Can I call it a riot?" he asked assistant city editor Wayne King. Determined not to contribute to the trouble, King said no. Shortly afterward, Michigan Governor George Romney called out the national guard, making the riot condition official. Even so, the word "riot" appeared only three times on the front page of Monday morning's paper.[16]

This was only the first of thousands of journalistic decisions that faced the *Free Press* during the next four days of uncontrolled violence. The paper acquitted itself well, and its coverage of Detroit's unrest was later hailed as a model for American journalism.

"The truth, the whole truth, and nothing but the truth" isn't a bad motto for the mass media—but it is a very difficult motto to live up to in covering a riot. Nine times out of ten, the media get their first word of a civil disturbance from one of two sources: the police radio or the wire services. Both are more concerned with speed than with accuracy. And both are notoriously unreliable in a crisis, mixing fact and rumor in about equal proportion.

In Tampa, Florida, for example, a deputy sheriff died in the early stages of a disturbance. AP and UPI immediately bulletined the news that he had been killed by rioters. Half an hour later reporters discovered that the man had suffered a heart attack.[17] In 1969, the Third World Liberation Front organized a student strike on the Berkeley campus of the University of California. Mike Culbert, editor of the *Berkeley Gazette*, noted that "the wire services didn't know what was going on. The early leads in the first days of the strike were atrocious. At one point AP was taking down my *speculation* on what was happening and moving it as the early lead."[18]

Not that newspapers and broadcast stations have a much better record on riot rumors. During the Watts riot of 1965, radio station KTLA sent a reporter aloft in a helicopter. In the space of a few hours he told his audience that the Shrine Auditorium was on fire, that communists were directing the uprising, and that the Minute Men were about to invade the ghetto. All were unsubstantiated rumors, and all turned out to be false. The reporter hedged his statements with phrases like "police believe" and "it is thought that"—but few listeners noticed the qualifiers.[19]

As the media grew more experienced with civil disruption, they became more cautious about publishing unproved rumors. Some editors and broadcasters went even further.

LEARNING TO USE THE MEDIA

The plight of the American Indian was dramatized in 1972 by a week-long takeover of the Bureau of Indian Affairs in Washington. Although the publicity was generally unfavorable, there was plenty of it—the grievances of Native Americans received little coverage, but at least the public became aware of the fact that there were grievances. Coverage of the seventy-one-day armed occupation of Wounded Knee, South Dakota, was even more extensive. Again the news was generally less than favorable, concentrating on violent incidents instead of fundamental issues. But it was clear that American Indians were not happy with their lot, and at least a few people started asking why.[20]

The 1975 occupation of a deserted Roman Catholic novitiate in Wisconsin demonstrated that militant Indians had learned still more about using the media. The armed Menominee Indians staged their takeover shortly after the New Year began, thus taking advantage of the slow holiday news period. The month-long occupation was much less violent than Wounded Knee. It ended in an agreement to deed the novitiate to the Menominee Nation, and produced a good deal of favorable publicity for the Native American cause.

They began withholding the established facts of explosive incidents, in the hope that those incidents would not escalate into full-fledged riots.

These news blackouts may or may not have prevented a few disturbances. Certainly the cost was high (see p. 93). People who could have avoided the scene of an incident if informed blundered into it instead. Word-of-mouth rumors were often less accurate and more inflammatory than the media reports would have been. And the public—black and white—was denied information it needed to understand the seriousness of racial unrest. After a few years most editors abandoned their blackout policies and resolved to cover the whole truth.

"The whole truth" about a riot includes a lot more than what happened and how much damage was done. In particular, it includes the "background" of the riot. Why did a group of people suddenly explode? What were their grievances, and how legitimate were they? What could the community have done to attack the underlying issues and prevent the outburst? What can the community do now to keep the same thing from happening again?

Ideally, of course, these questions should be discussed by the media long before any riot. Every civil disturbance is proof that some problem has gone unattended, and usually this means the media have failed to expose the problem for the community to see. The riot itself is a desperate form of communication. When people are able to air their grievances effectively in a peaceful manner, they do not riot.

Once the riot begins, it is up to the media to make up for lost time and begin reporting the issues. It shouldn't take a riot to make editors aware of this responsibility, but sometimes it does. The very least we can expect is decent coverage of the underlying issues during and after the explosion.

Quite often we don't even get that. The reporters and editors who work for the establishment media are predominantly white

and middle-class. Their principal audience is also white and middle-class. And so coverage of the riots of the 1960s reflected white middle-class fear of blacks and black rage. Stories about ghetto riots, the Black Panthers, and similar topics stressed the impending destruction of (white middle-class) civilization at the hands of angry blacks. This was not just a racial matter. Antiwar demonstrators and young radicals also seemed to threaten the fabric of American society. The media's way of coping with that threat was to concentrate on violent acts, rather than the issues behind the violence.

Much the same pattern was repeated in the 1970s. In the early years of the decade, reporters covered the culmination of the antiwar movement, the Attica prison uprising, the Native American occupation of Wounded Knee, and dozens of similar incidents. The media were also confronted with political terrorism—bombings and airplane hijackings, the Weather Underground and the Symbionese Liberation Army. Seeing their society threatened, many reporters downplayed the issues and stressed the violence.

The problem is partly a matter of sources. In the middle of a full-scale riot, it is hard enough for a reporter to figure out who speaks for the police. And the reporter *knows* the police, has worked closely with them for years, and has built up a relationship of mutual trust and cooperation. By contrast, the reporter is likely to have no sources at all (let alone cooperative ones) among the rioters—the blacks, students, radicals, or whatever. So the reporter relies heavily on police sources, and the story turns out like a play-by-play account of a ball game: all action and no motivation.

And no inaction either. The media, like the police, are interested primarily in what's happening. They don't much care why, and they don't much care how limited the action is. A single incident of violence in a long, peaceful demonstration is fated to be the only incident that makes the evening news.

"By focusing on a handful of violent activists," admitted Frank Stanton, then of CBS, "we may give the impression that that's the way it is all over. This is the danger in all kinds of demonstrations. Our tendency is to try to go where the action is."[21]

In nearly every demonstration and civil disturbance, the media rely on official sources for most of their information. They stress action and violence, and downplay the underlying issues. Writing in the late 1960s, Nathan Blumberg used the adjective "orthodox" to describe this tendency. "Perhaps it is too much to expect," he concluded, "that a press with an undeniable stake in the economic and political system would report fairly on those who are fundamentally dissatisfied with the status quo."[22]

Racial confrontations, in short, have not always received fair and ample treatment in the media. Local activist leaders have sometimes been ignored by local papers and stations. Peaceful demonstrations have been dismissed in a few sentences or made to look violent. Police sources have been taken at their word even when directly contradicted by minority witnesses. And events of tremendous significance have been underplayed or misplayed. In 1968, three black students were shot and killed by police in Orangeburg, South Carolina. The national media barely mentioned the incident. Two years later, when four white students were killed at Kent State University, the story filled front pages for days.

Nevertheless, media coverage of the facts of minority unrest has been magnificent in comparison with coverage of the grievances that underlie that unrest. As the Kerner Commission report stressed again and again: "The Commission's major concern with the news media is not in riot reporting as such, but in the failure to report adequately on race relations and ghetto problems."[23] More than a decade later, after the 1980 Miami riots, Joseph Boyce, *Time*'s Atlanta bureau chief and himself a black, repeated the point. "Blacks are like artifacts in a room seldom used," he said. "They are dusted off periodically for a look, especially after a riot, then replaced in the cabinet. The doors close again until the next time."[24]

COVERING MINORITY LIFE

There are three criticisms frequently voiced about media coverage (and noncoverage) of black people. First, the media have failed to make clear to white people the problems, frustrations, and tensions of the ghetto. Second, the media have exhibited bias or racism in their approach to black news. And third, the media have ignored the everyday life of the black person, the "good news" that comes out of black America.

We have said enough already about the first criticism. As a rule, the media are much better at covering a crisis after it arrives than they are at seeing it on the way. The 1980 racial crisis in Miami was a reminder of the 1960s. As long as the black community kept its suffering and anger to itself, the media were content to leave well enough alone. Only after the inevitable explosion did they suddenly wake to the issue of race. And even then, they concentrated on the explosion itself, devoting far less time and space to the underlying grievances.

The charge of racism is a hard one to document. In 1968, black militants in Oakland, California, organized a boycott of a white-owned ghetto shopping center. In response, the *Oakland Tribune* printed a cartoon of a gloved hand pointing a pistol at the reader. "What would *you* do in a case like this?" asked the caption. "Think it over carefully because soon you may have to decide whether you want to run a business with a gun to your head or close up shop." Two black reporters resigned in protest, charging *Tribune* publisher William Knowland with racism.[25] At best, the cartoon seems a rather extreme response to the time-honored pressure tactic of a boycott.

Oakland, by the way, was fast becoming a

There are more than 24 million poor people in the United States. Over 16 million of the poor are white, and almost half of the poor whites live in rural areas. Fewer than 5 million poor blacks live in central cities. Anyone who finds these facts surprising has been cheated by the mass media.

When the media imply, as they often do, that poverty is uniquely a problem of urban blacks, they make themselves vulnerable to two serious charges—the charge of racism from the black community, and the charge of indifference from the poor nonblack community.

Why do the media ignore the needs and interests of poor people? The simple, economic answer is that poor people have very little to offer the media in return. Poor people spend more time watching television than the general population, but they buy less—and so TV ads and programs are aimed at the middle class. For the same financial reason, newspapers and magazines try to attract middle-class readers and avoid poor ones. It is true that poor people read fewer newspapers and magazines than the general public, but the difference isn't huge; 75 percent of all low-income families subscribe to a newspaper.[26] Yet there have been many more news stories published about welfare cheats and vandalism in public housing than about how to apply for welfare or housing assistance.

black-majority city, as white middle-class residents fled to the suburbs. The *Tribune* changed ownership in the 1970s, improved its coverage of minorities, and eventually hired a black editor. But many other newspapers responded to the white middle-class exodus by expanding suburban coverage and cutting down on inner-city reporting. The strategy makes sense economically; advertisers are more interested in the wealthy suburbs. But from the viewpoint of the ghetto resident, it smacks of racism.

In 1980 and 1981, a large number of black children and teenagers in Atlanta were murdered. Once the media picked up the story they covered it sympathetically, even spectacularly, including the fears of the black community. No rumor, no charge went unreported. Comedian Dick Gregory earned front-page space with a wholly unsubstantiated allegation that Atlanta's Center for Disease Control might have abducted the youths for medical experiments. But the media had been slow to see a big story in the Atlanta murders, slower, some claimed, than they would have been if the victims had been white.

The third criticism is in many ways the most important. It is almost a prerequisite for white acceptance of blacks that the everyday reality of black living, the good and the bad, be made clear to white people. It is also essential to black self-acceptance (and black pride) that this everyday reality be portrayed by the media. As the Kerner Commission put it: "It would be a contribution of inestimable importance to race relations in the United States simply to treat ordinary news about Negroes as news of other groups is now treated."[27] The Commission went on to specify the need for black content in newspapers, magazines, movies, radio, television, and advertising.

The print media have made the least progress of all. Even today, newspapers seldom carry much in the way of black club news, black society, black engagements and marriages, even black obituaries. And when a black civic group plans a dance, say, or opens a youth club, it is extremely unlikely to get much publicity from the white press.

Reporter Bill Sloat, who left the *Fort Myers* (Florida) *News-Press* in 1978, had this to say about coverage of the neighboring black community of Dunbar: "The only time Dunbar ever got covered was the murders out there. Nobody was interested in going out to look at the zoning violations for example. They [the *News-Press*] never treated it as a community." Shortly after Sloat left the paper a new managing editor turned the *News-Press* around, beginning with a 33-article series on the local black community.[28]

Despite real improvement throughout the 1970s, newspapers kept making tell-tale slips. In one newspaper article about Detroit's churches, for example, all the ministers interviewed were white—though half of Detroit's churches are black. And a chart in the *Los Angeles Times* on the impact of Proposition 13 on taxpayers included only those earning over $15,000 a year—leaving out all low-income readers and many minority readers.[29] When they focus on poor people or black people, most media today make a good-faith effort to "say the right things." But too often still the media simply forget to look for news—especially good news—among poor people and black people.

Film and broadcasting have a somewhat better record. From *Gone With the Wind* to *Guess Who's Coming to Dinner* was a big step for the movies, and from *Shaft* to *Sounder* and *Lady Sings the Blues* was an even bigger one (see pp. 353-54). The same change was reflected on television—from black menial to black super-hero to black human being. In 1970, actor Bill Cosby, formerly of "I Spy" (a super-hero show), inaugurated his own comedy series, in which he played an average schmo who just happened to be black. By 1970, also, blacks had begun appearing as journalists in TV news shows, and as consumers in TV commercials. These were major achievements for television.

The early 1970s saw further progress, notably series programs such as "Sanford and Son," "Good Times," and "The Jeffersons." Though some critics complained the shows were stereotyped, they dealt regularly, if superficially, with real economic and social problems, and they all featured characters who were proud to be black. Enormously popular with black audiences, they earned good ratings from white audiences as well. As of 1980, "The Jeffersons" was still going strong, "Sanford" was back on NBC in a slightly revised format, and "Good Times" could still be seen in reruns.

In 1977, ABC broadcast "Roots," a 12-hour dramatization of Alex Haley's best-seller on the struggles and triumphs of one black family. During the eight-night period, 130 million Americans stayed tuned to ABC, and an unprecedented 85 percent of the TV audience watched at least one episode of the mini-series. The program dominated conversations, talk shows, classrooms, and sermons for weeks. "It was a remarkable phenomenon," said Eugene Bohi of WGHP-TV in High Point, N.C. "Over and over we kept hearing people remark that the enthusiasm for 'Roots' proved how far we've come in black-white acceptance."[30]

"Roots" may not have been great theater, but it was as good as American television gets. Its portrayal of the black experience was sensitive, gripping, and uplifting. While a study by the U.S. Commission on Civil Rights reported in the late 1970s that blacks continued to be seen on TV in a "disproportionately high number of immature, demeaning and comical roles," "Roots" was spawning other serious dramatizations of black American life—among them "Roots: The Next Generations" and "Backstairs at the White House."[31]

Change was coming, but it would not be without setbacks. Comparatively few whites watched "King," a six-hour made-for-TV movie about Martin Luther King Jr.[32] And "Freedom Road," which starred Muhammad

Ali as a former slave who becomes a U.S. Senator and then fights the Ku Klux Klan, was not shown by the NBC affiliate in Boston for fear that the film might heighten that city's racial tension.[33]

Ironically, TV news improved rather less than TV entertainment in the 1970s. Black newscasters became common, but black news remained scarce except in times of crisis. And black-oriented public-affairs programs were still few and far between. Admirable though it is, "Roots" is no substitute for news and documentary coverage of minority issues.

There are 7.1 million Mexican-Americans in the United States; the more than two million who live in California comprise that state's largest ethnic minority. There have been Chicano entertainers and movie stars—Delores Del Rio and Ramon Novarro, Anthony Quinn and Ricardo Montalban, Trini Lopez and Vikki Carr. But for the most part,

the media image of Mexican-Americans has been less than positive. Said TV critic Dwight Newton: "On movie screens, and later television screens, they were pictured as loiterers, loafers, cowhands, revolutionaries, assassins, bad guys."[34] And in the news, of course, they were ignored.

Little wonder, then, that the Chicano organization Nosotros (founded by Montalban) objected strenuously to the corn chip advertising campaign featuring the "Frito Bandito." Most stations self-righteously resisted the pressure, but a few agreed to eliminate the ads, and eventually the advertiser abandoned the character.

After the Los Angeles disruptions of 1970 and 1971, Chicanos began to get some serious attention in the news media. In 1978, for example, the *Arizona Daily Star* ran a 28-page special section on "Tucson's Barrios: A View from Inside." But the coverage accorded Spanish-speaking people has not al-

A LITTLE HELP FROM THE LAW

A minority organization that believes a local broadcast station has failed to serve the needs of minorities can ask the FCC to take away the station's license. Since the landmark WLBT-TV case in the mid-1960s (see pp. 229-30), well over a hundred minority groups have done precisely that. In a number of cases they actually succeeded in getting the FCC to act. In 1975, for example, the Commission refused to renew the Alabama state government's educational TV licenses, because the state-run stations had too few black employees and too little black-oriented programming.[35] And in 1979 the WLBT license was finally awarded to a black-majority coalition.

But more frequently what the minority groups have won is a deal (see p. 230). In response to license-challenge threats from local citizen groups, all but six of Atlanta's 28 radio and TV stations agreed to employ more blacks. WNBC and WABC in New York promised to provide regularly scheduled black-oriented programming. McGraw-Hill pledged to hire more Mexican-Americans at the four television stations it was planning to buy, and to run more Mexican-American programming on the stations. When faced with the possibility of a reasonable challenge from an organized minority, most broadcasters would rather make concessions than fight for the license.

In 1978 the FCC adopted two policies designed to promote minority ownership of broadcast stations. It offered special tax relief to owners who sell their stations to minorities, and permitted broadcasters in danger of losing their licenses to sell to minority purchasers at a "distressed price."[36] When the policies were adopted there were about 70 stations in minority hands. By 1980 the total was around 100 and growing steadily.

ways been sympathetic. Articles on Mexican immigrants in the 1970s sometimes carried racist headlines like "State Threatened by Alien Horde" (*Los Angeles Herald-Examiner*).[37] The sudden influx of Cuban refugees in 1980 yielded a similar mix of thoughtful coverage and unconscious racism. And between crises, the most usual coverage was still no coverage at all.

On network television, meanwhile, programs featuring Spanish-heritage characters tended toward light entertainment like "Chico and the Man" and "Fantasy Island"—a modest improvement over nothing at all. No Hispanic "Roots" has so far emerged.

Just as confrontations forced the media to pay more attention to blacks and Chicanos, the same pattern began to affect the media's treatment of Native Americans in the 1970s. According to movies and television, nineteenth-century Indians were savage warriors, and twentieth-century Indians were incompetent drunks. White story-tellers rewrote American history to make Indians the villains, then hired white actors to play the parts. Only after Native American groups began taking over buildings and towns did the media begin taking Indians seriously. In the 1970s there were a few thoughtful films about Indian history and Indian reality, occasionally with Indian actors in the major roles. As for news, the demonstrations and confrontations were fully covered, of course. They were the first news about Indians that most white Americans had ever seen. But by the end of the decade, Indians once again appeared to be out of sight and out of mind, and if the black experience is any guide it will take continued prodding to remind the media that Native Americans exist.

Whatever minority group you examine, the pattern seems the same. American entertainment uses minority groups for comic relief, while American news ignores them. Only when frustration explodes into violence do the media wake up. Then they cover the violence in news, tone down the stereotypes in entertainment, and go back to sleep if they

can. It takes constant pressure to keep the media focused on the grievances and lifestyles of American minorities.

WOMEN AND THE MEDIA

Since the nineteenth century, there have been specialized mass media in this country that catered to the women's market. Special magazines, special sections of newspapers, and special daytime TV shows are designed to capture the attention of women—but until the 1970s these media were rarely designed to serve the needs of women.

Women's magazines, for example, have traditionally pictured their audience as fashion-conscious ladies, compulsive housewives, or devoted mothers. These were essentially the only roles for women the magazines were willing to discuss. But with the success of *Ms.* in the early 1970s, more traditional women's magazines began to change. *Cosmopolitan* ran articles like "How To Make a Man's Pay," in addition to its usual fare such as "The Poor Girl's Guide to America's Rich Young Men" and "Women, Men and Kinky Sex."[38] And *Redbook,* which used to call itself "The Magazine for Young Mamas," adopted a new slogan, "The Magazine of the New Management." The changes were less than many feminists wanted, but at least most women's magazines have stopped putting down women who are employed outside the home.

These changes reflected not only a growth in consciousness, but also a recognition that working women are an important market. By the end of the 1970s, three-fifths of all women between the ages of 18 and 64 were employed. Even many working women, of course, want to read about beauty, fashion, and homemaking. In fact, six of the ten top-circulation magazines are traditional women's periodicals: *Better Homes & Gardens, Family Circle, Woman's Day, McCall's, Ladies' Home Journal,* and *Good Housekeeping.* But today most of these traditional "big slicks" carry articles on finance and abortion as well, and their beauty and fashion lay-outs are often designed with working women in mind. Even the steadfastly home-oriented *Good Housekeeping* has responded in its own way—"not by giving articles related to working women," explains editor John Mack Carter, "but articles on how to manage the home with more limited time."[39] And as the 1970s ended, new magazines like *Working Woman* and *Self* were created to fill the gulf between *Good Housekeeping* and *Ms*. Some of them are sure to survive the eighties.

The women's section of the typical news-paper has also changed. It used to contain no news at all—only recipes, fashions, beauty and homemaking tips, wedding and engage-ment announcements, society features and advice columns. These are still the staples of the section, even though most papers have now changed its name to something like "Family Life" or "Life Styles." But progress has been made. Women's sections today run frequent profiles on local women who have thought, said, or done interesting things. This was an important first step, publicly ac-knowledging that women *do* think, say, and do interesting things. The next step, which many papers have begun to take, is running serious features on such topics as day care, abortion, divorce, and sex discrimination. And when the editors of women's sections begin taking responsibility for hard news stories on these topics, the women's pages will have achieved an important break-through.

Daytime television soap operas are still full of traditionally stereotyped women, but they're increasingly full of professional women and serious issues as well. Free-lance writer Beth R. Gutcheon reports:

SEX AND LANGUAGE

A society's language reflects its values and its history. The language of American society is sexist.

In the late 1960s, feminist groups began an all-out assault on sexist language in the media. At first, the campaign had only modest success. Many editors who willingly acknowledged that sex discrimination was an important social issue balked at changing "Miss" and "Mrs." to "Ms.," or substituting "Congressperson" for "Congressman," or cluttering their sentences with phrases like "he or she" and "his or her." They insisted that the media should follow conventional language usage, not try to change or create it. They stood firm for conciseness and against awkwardness. In response, feminists argued that taking the sexism out of language was not just a symbolic achievement, but also a way of raising people's consciousness about the sexism in American society.

In 1974, the McGraw-Hill Book Company came up with a suitable compromise. In sixteen pages of "Guidelines for Equal Treatment of the Sexes in McGraw-Hill Book Company Publications," the publisher suggested changes like the following:

Instead of	Use
the fair sex, the weaker sex	women
lady lawyer, lady doctor	lawyer, doctor
authoress, poetess, usherette	author, poet, usher
libber	feminist, liberationist
mankind, manmade, manpower	human beings, manufactured, workers
the best man for the job	the best person for the job
businessman, salesman, mailman, camera-man, fireman	business executive, sales representative, mail carrier, camera operator, fire fighter

There are more women doctors, lawyers, writers, judges, nurses, District Attorneys and corporate executives on daytime television than were ever dreamed of on prime time. . . . There is also more consistent, serious effort to deal sensitively with the red-hot issues of the day, from abortion to homosexuality, than is ever seen on prime time, except in occasional documentaries.[40]

Women's magazines, women's newspaper sections, and daytime television are not all that they should be—but in their treatment of women they are miles ahead of the rest of the media.

Film, for example, is dominated by a male perspective (see pp. 354-56). Even the list of movie super-stars, which was evenly divided between men and women in the

1930s, today includes mostly men. Molly Haskell summed up the change in the title of her 1974 book, *From Reverence to Rape: The Treatment of Women in the Movies*.[41] For the most part, she noted, "the great women's roles of the decade are whores, quasi-whores, jilted mistresses, emotional cripples, drunks, daffy ingenues, Lolitas, kooks, sex-starved spinsters, psychotics, ice-bergs, zombies. . . ."[42] That relatively few women are employed as movie producers, directors, and writers has clearly contributed to the stereotyping of female film characters. Though the late 1970s saw a marked improvement with films like *The Turning Point* and *Julia*, only time will tell if serious women's movies catch on.

Prime-time television, meanwhile, manages to take at least one step backward for

| the average American drinks his coffee black | most Americans drink their coffee black, the average American drinks coffee black |
| chairman | chair, head, coordinator |

Essentially, the McGraw-Hill guidelines attempt to keep assumptions about sex out of the language. They don't insist on obtrusively anti-sexist writing, but they do insist on getting rid of obtrusively sexist writing. Thus it is probably acceptable to refer to "Congressman Bob Jones" because we know Jones is a man. But "write your Congressman" should become "write Congress," or "write your Senator and Representative." In McGraw-Hill's view, it is almost always possible to avoid sexism without resorting to awkward phrases like "write your Congressperson."

The guidelines also urge authors to put an end to sexual stereotyping. Books designed for children, for example, should show married women who work outside the home as well as those who don't. Both men and women should be depicted as cooking, cleaning, fixing things, washing the car, etc. Both sexes should be portrayed as sometimes independent, courageous, and decisive; sometimes aggressive and insensitive; sometimes thoughtful, loving, and intuitive; sometimes fearful and illogical.[43]

The 1977 publication of a new *Associated Press Stylebook* marked the beginning of the end of sexist language in American journalism. According to the bible of newspaper copy editing, "fire fighter" and "letter carrier" are now the preferred terms, and "Ms." is an acceptable alternate. "Women should receive the same treatment as men in all areas of coverage," the stylebook dictates. "Physical descriptions, sexist references, demeaning stereotypes and condescending phrases should not be used." Subliminal male chauvinism did not disappear overnight. For example, female politicians are still referred to by first name—Jane (Byrne), Bella (Abzug), Bess (Myerson)—much more frequently than their male counterparts. But sexist usage is no longer considered conventional or even correct. Nonsexist language is the accepted style of the 1980s.

every two steps forward. The proportion of females in leading roles was higher in 1980 than in the 1960s, but men still outnumbered women three to one.[44] And starring women were often seen in "jiggly" shows like "Charlie's Angels" and "Three's Company." There are more working women on prime time today than in the 1960s, but occupations are still stereotyped, and most female roles continue to center on romance, marriage, and family.

In all fairness, the 1970s were the decade of Mary Tyler Moore, who stood her ground as a professional woman; of "Family" and "The Waltons," which dealt seriously with marriage and family; of episodes on "All In the Family" and "Maude" that tackled issues like breast cancer and abortion. But the 1970s were also the decade when the zany antics of housewife (later secretary) "Lucy" were replaced by the zany antics of bottle-cappers "Laverne and Shirley," and when the character played by Suzanne Somers in "Three's Company" reached a combination of sexiness and imbecility seldom before seen on television. Prime-time TV changes season by season, so it is at least possible that women's roles will improve. But according to one television writer, what the networks really want is women who are "good looking, well-endowed and running toward the camera."[45]

The treatment of women in advertising did improve substantially in the 1970s (see pp. 372-73). Or at least it changed, as advertisers discovered the working woman and featured her prominently in ads for credit cards, airlines, insurance companies, and the like. She even found her way into commercials for consumer products, whipping up dinner after a hard day on the job. Advertising thus created a new stereotype—the "modern woman" who does it all and still manages to look sexy —while downplaying, but certainly not eliminating, the less complicated stereotypes of the past.

The image of women in media entertainment and advertising is a critically important topic, because it will undoubtedly be reflected in society's attitudes toward women ten and twenty years from now. Equally important, and even more important in the short term, is news coverage of issues of special relevance to women. And the media's track record in this area is weak.

When the National Organization for Women challenged the license of WABC-TV in 1972, it stated that the New York station's "Eyewitness News" did not even report the passage of the Equal Rights Amendment by Congress.[46] Most activists in the feminist movement can recall similar lapses on the part of local stations and papers.

In the early 1970s, hard news coverage was still almost entirely controlled by men, both in broadcasting and in newspapers. Female reporters and editors handled mostly feature stories. When the feminist movement began making waves, the men of the media turned the story over to the women on the feature desk, where it received the inevitable "soft" coverage. The front page—and hard news in general—remained a male preserve.

The media establishment's response to the women's movement was thus quite different from its response to the black movement. Both were ignored until they began confronting society. But black confrontation earned instant coverage, while black lifestyles continued to be neglected. Women's confrontation, by contrast, was ignored or at best converted by the media into a matter of lifestyles, relegated to the features in the women's section.

Women's issues invaded hard news only after women broke into hard news reporting in substantial numbers. The change was most visible on television, but it was just as important in the print media. By the end of the 1970s, editors no longer expected female reporters to limit women's issues to feature treatment. The increased presence of women in all areas of the newsroom—even sports—gradually raised the consciousness of many male editors and reporters as well. Although women's issues, like minority issues, are still underreported, they are no longer trivialized or handled flippantly. Although men still control most newsrooms, the number and influence of female hard-news editors is growing. In the 1980s, issues like sex discrimination, abortion, and child care may finally be recognized as serious concerns for all readers and viewers.

EMPLOYMENT

One of the most obvious signs of racism in the media—and one of the most important reasons that racism has survived so long—has been the ludicrously small number of minority reporters. The 1968 Kerner Commission report hit this point hard:

> The journalistic profession has been shockingly backward in seeking out, hiring, training, and promoting Negroes. Fewer than 5 percent of the people employed by the news business in editorial jobs in the United States today are Negroes. Fewer than 1 percent of editors and supervisors are Negroes, and most of them work for Negro-owned organizations. . . . News organizations must employ enough Negroes in positions of significant responsibility to establish an effective link to Negro actions and ideas and to meet legitimate employment expectations.[47]

Spurred on by the commission, the mass media began searching frantically for minority reporters. Not surprisingly, they found few blacks or Hispanics with both the interest and the training; no one had ever bothered to encourage the former or provide the latter. At a California Newspaper Publishers Association convention in the early 1970s, one talented black college junior was extended half a dozen firm job offers, while his white counterparts were informed that money was tight and jobs were scarce. The black student was forced to turn down all his offers; he had already accepted one from a Northern California television station.

This frenzy of recruiting activity raised several questions. First, was it legitimate or was it tokenism? There was reason to suspect the latter. For one thing, the very media that scurried to hire a black or two were reluctant to support large-scale journalism training programs for minorities. And they hesitated to place their minority employees in policy-making positions.

Consider the following incident from the late 1960s. Ben Gilbert, then city editor of the *Washington Post,* received a telephone call from a *New York Times* executive. How many blacks had the *Post* hired, he wanted to know, and where did it find so many? Gilbert told him that the *Post* had twelve, and then asked how many blacks the *Times* employed. "Three," came the response, "but we won't lower our standards."[48]

Tokenism or not, minority employment in the media improved significantly in the early 1970s. According to one study, an astounding 72 percent of all new employees hired by commercial television stations between 1971 and 1974 were members of minority groups. That's an impressive figure, but consider it in the context of two other figures. Roughly 20 percent of America's TV stations had yet to hire their first minority person. And in 1974 minorities still constituted only 9 percent of commercial television's managerial, professional, technical, and sales personnel—a big improvement over 1971's 6 percent, but well below the proportion of minorities in the big cities where many stations are based.[49]

The second half of the 1970s saw continued improvement. Pressured by the FCC, broadcasters hired minority managers, professionals, and technicians in larger numbers than ever before. When the U.S. Commission on Civil Rights investigated 40 television stations in 1977, it found that all 40 had met the FCC's standards for black males in the higher job classifications, and 32 of them had satisfied the guidelines for black females.[50]

Progress in the newspaper industry has been slower, but real. In 1968, just after the Kerner Commission report was released, a study of metropolitan dailies found that only 2.6 percent of the reporters, editors, and photographers were black. Ten years later when the study was repeated, blacks accounted for 5.7 percent of newsroom personnel. The *Washington Post* now had 35 minority journalists; the *New York Times,* 40.[51]

The news isn't all good. Two-thirds of the nation's daily newspapers still had not hired a single minority news professional as of 1978. And they could no longer excuse themselves on the grounds that qualified candidates were not available. The number of minority journalism and broadcasting students has increased substantially since the 1960s, and the pool of eager beginners and experienced veterans gets larger every year.[52]

Media employment of women also improved in the 1970s. In 1971, 22 percent of the employees of commercial television stations were women, but only 6 percent of the stations' managers, professionals, technicians, and salespeople were women. Over the next three years, women comprised 58 percent of all newly hired employees. This raised the proportion of women in the higher job classifications to 11 percent in 1974.[53]

Broadcasting made further progress in the late seventies, most of it on-camera. Between 1974 and 1977, the number of women reporting for the three TV networks nearly doubled to 25. And in 1977, 90 percent of the TV stations in one survey said they employed women as newscasters, and more than half said they had women producers as well. (For radio the figures were 72 percent with women newscasters and one-third with women producers.) The most visible change came in the high-pay, high-prestige news anchor jobs on local television. Anchorwomen were few and far between in the early 1970s. By 1978, 77 anchorwomen were employed in the 75 largest TV markets; by 1980, 156 women held anchor positions in the top 90 markets.[54]

Newspapers have hired women for years, but mostly as secretaries and women's page writers. This, too, changed in the 1970s. By 1975 there were already more than 20,000 female journalists working for American newspapers.[55] And by 1977, one-third of all newspaper employees were women. Newspaper management proved a tougher nut for women to crack (except for the weeklies, one-third of which are now edited by women), but by 1980 10 percent of the women working for daily newspapers were in editorial or managerial slots.[56]

No matter which of the mass media you look at, the pattern is pretty much the same. Women and minorities are moving into entry-level professional positions in increasing numbers. In time, if the pressure keeps up, their representation in the media will begin to approach their representation in the audience. But they are moving into managerial positions much more slowly—leaving policy-making, at least for now, mostly in the hands of white males.

The media deserve a lot of credit for their efforts to make up for past employment inequities, but it is important to remember that these efforts came only in the face of pressure—pressure from government agencies and commissions, pressure from citizen groups, and pressure from minority and women's caucuses within the media. By the mid-1970s, many publishers and broadcasters seemed genuinely committed to affirmative action. But it still *takes* affirmative action; equal employment of women and minorities does not come automatically.

In 1974, William Ewald of Pocket Books boasted of the paperback industry's progress in the employment of women. "It's where the action is," he said, "and a lot of young bright women have gone into it because there's a lot of room to swing around in. It's not calcified the way some of the hardcover business is." True enough, but the analysis of Bantam Books Senior Editor Nancy Hardin strikes deep: "It's nice that those women are there, and it's nice that attention is being paid to them, but it would be nicer still if it were just taken for granted that exceptional women had exceptional jobs."[57]

Discrimination in employment is usually

considered an issue of social justice. Women and minorities have a legal and moral right to their fair share of jobs in the media. But employment in the media is not only a matter of justice; it is also a matter of coverage. The way the media treat minorities and women in entertainment, advertising, and news is inevitably a product of the sorts of people who work for the media. Black screenwriters, Mexican-American advertising executives, and female reporters are a good deal less likely than their nonminority male counterparts to continue the sorts of coverage problems we have been discussing in this chapter.

What then should minority and female reporters be doing once they're hired? When the *Washington Post* hired its first black reporter in 1952, it was careful to assign him only nonracial stories, where his presence and copy would stir up no controversy. But during the riots of the late 1960s, many newspapers found that their white reporters were ineffective in the ghetto. When these papers got around to hiring their first black, they naturally assigned him or her to the "civil rights" beat.

Many minority reporters today devote a significant percentage of their time to minority news. Some are glad to do so, but others object to this form of segregation. The conflict is summed up by Chris Campbell, a former AP and UPI reporter who now works as a television associate producer: "Editors always tend to stick minorities with covering minorities, and you feel insulted and limited by that. But when you try to move out, that means you don't know who is going to cover minorities, and sometimes that coverage is worse than having no coverage at all. So you want to move and you don't want to move."[58]

For female reporters the question is especially puzzling. The media traditionally assigned women to "women's stories"—soft features on food, fashion, and the like. Professional progress for a woman reporter usually meant moving from the women's section to the front page, where she could cover the same stories as everyone else. But now that newspapers and broadcast stations are offering hard news coverage of the issues that underlie the feminist movement, should female reporters hold onto that specialty? Or should they avoid it?

Ideally, of course, minorities and women ought to be covering all kinds of stories, both those that do and those that do not concern race and sex. But ours is not an ideal world. Perhaps the biggest contribution minority and female journalists can make today is to help their papers and stations do what they should have been doing long ago—covering minorities and women completely, fairly, and sensitively.

"What we now seek," says editor Robert Maynard of the *Oakland Tribune,* himself a black, "is portrayal of our communities as places inhabited by real people, not pathological fragments. We are not asking to be romanticized. Where there is disease, report disease; crime, report crime. But where there is health, report health; creativity, report creativity."[59] This is a just demand, long overdue for both minorities and women. It will require good faith and hard work from reporters of all races and both sexes to achieve.

Notes

1 *Report of the National Advisory Commission on Civil Disorders* (Kerner Commission) (New York: Bantam Books, 1968), p. 366.

2 David Sachsman, "Two New York Newspapers," unpublished paper, Stanford University, 1968, p. 11.

3 "Special TV Networks for Special Audiences," *New York Times,* April 8, 1980.

4 Jack Lyle, ed., *The Black American and the Press* (Los Angeles: Ward Ritchie Press, 1968), p. 3.

5 L. F. Palmer, Jr., "The Black Press in Transition," *Columbia Journalism Review,* Spring, 1970, p. 31.

6 *Ibid.,* pp. 33-34.

7 Dennis Schatzman, "The Black Press and Its Role in Modern Society," *Editor & Publisher,* April 21, 1979, p. 16.

8 "Media Milestone: Indian Journalists Mark 150th

Year of Publishing," *Red Current,* Spring, 1978, pp. 1, 9. Richard La Course, *"Cherokee Phoenix:* First Newspaper Born on Eve of Infamous 'Trail of Tears,' " *Red Current,* Spring, 1978, p. 3.

9 "Media Milestone: Indian Journalists Mark 150th Year," p. 1.

10 "Black Market," *Newsweek,* July 17, 1972, p. 71.

11 Robert A. Wright, "The Dominant Color Is Green," *New York Times,* July 7, 1974, p. F3.

12 "A Billion-Dollar Baby," *Black Enterprise,* June, 1979, p. 145.

13 Arthur B. Bertelson, "Keeper of a Monster," in Paul L. Fisher and Ralph L. Lowenstein, eds., *Race and the News Media* (New York: Anti-Defamation League of B'nai B'rith, 1967), pp. 61-62.

14 Ray Jenkins, "Open Season in Alabama," *Nieman Reports,* March, 1965, p. 8.

15 Ted Poston, "The American Negro and Newspaper Myths," in Fisher and Lowenstein, *Race and the News Media,* p. 64.

16 *Reporting the Detroit Riot* (New York: American Newspaper Publishers Association, 1968), pp. 3-4.

17 *Report of the National Advisory Commission on Civil Disorders,* p. 373.

18 William L. Rivers and David M. Rubin, *A Region's Press: Anatomy of Newspapers in the San Francisco Bay Area* (Berkeley, Calif.: Institute of Governmental Studies, University of California at Berkeley, 1971), p. 125.

19 William L. Rivers, "Jim Crow Journalism," *Seminar,* March, 1968, p. 16.

20 "Indians Feel They May Be on the Verge of Some Major Gains," *New Brunswick* (N.J.) *Home News,* January 22, 1975, p. 16 (Washington Post—Los Angeles Times Service).

21 Letter from CBS President Frank Stanton to Pennsylvania Senator Hugh Scott, August 9, 1967, p. 3.

22 Nathan B. Blumberg, "A Study of the Orthodox Press: The Reporting of Dissent," *Montana Journalism Review,* 1968, pp. 7-9.

23 *Report of the National Advisory Commission on Civil Disorders,* p. 382.

24 " 'I Feel So Helpless, So Hopeless,' " *Time,* June 16, 1980, p. 23.

25 "Is Oakland There?" *Newsweek,* May 18, 1970, p. 100.

26 Bradley Greenberg and Brenda Dervin, "Mass Communication Among the Urban Poor," *Public Opinion Quarterly,* Summer, 1970, pp. 224-35.

27 *Report of the National Advisory Commission on Civil Disorders,* p. 385.

28 "Deep South Daily Admits It Ignored Racial Affairs," *Editor & Publisher,* April 7, 1979, p. 15.

29 "Initiative and Interest: Keys to Desegregation," *Editor & Publisher,* March 10, 1979, p. 15. Félix Gutiérrez and Clint C. Wilson II, "The Demographic Dilemma," *Columbia Journalism Review,* January/February, 1979, p. 54.

30 Roscoe C. Brown Jr., "Let's Uproot TV's Image of Blacks," *New York Times,* February 18, 1979, p. D35. Les Brown, " 'Roots' Success in South Held a Sign of Change," *New York Times,* February 10, 1977, p. 18.

31 Brown, "Let's Uproot TV's Image of Blacks," p. D35.

32 John J. O'Connor, "Was 'King' Too Much for the Audience?" *New York Times,* February 26, 1978.

33 Aljean Harmetz, " 'Freedom Road'—The Long Haul to TV," *New York Times,* October 28, 1979, sec. 2, pp. 1, 23.

34 Dwight Newton, "A Minority Seldom Seen," *San Francisco Sunday Examiner and Chronicle,* February 14, 1971, p. B4.

35 Alabama Educational TV Denied License Renewal," *New York Times,* January 9, 1975, p. 71.

36 Ernest Holsendolph, "F.C.C. Acts on Minority Broadcasting," *New York Times,* May 18, 1978.

37 "Comment," *Columbia Journalism Review,* November/December, 1978, p. 22. Félix Gutiérrez, "Latinos and the Media," in Michael Emery and Ted C. Smythe, *Readings in Mass Communication,* 4th ed. (Dubuque, Iowa: Wm. C. Brown, 1980), p. 364.

38 Stephanie Harrington, "Ms. Versus Cosmo: Two Faces of the Same Eve," *New York Times Magazine,* August 11, 1974, p. 11.

39 "Survey Spots Changes in Women's Media Use," *Editor & Publisher,* January 19, 1980, p. 23. N. R. Kleinfield, "What Do Women Want? They Want Lots to Read!" *New York Times,* January 20, 1980.

40 Beth R. Gutcheon, "Look for Cop-Outs on Prime Time, Not on 'Soaps,' " *New York Times,* December 16, 1973, p. D21.

41 Molly Haskell, *From Reverence to Rape: The Treatment of Women in the Movies* (New York: Holt, Rinehart and Winston, 1974).

42 Anatole Broyard, "From Star to Satellite," *New York Times,* March 5, 1974, p. 31.

43 "Guidelines for Equal Treatment of the Sexes in McGraw-Hill Book Company Publications," New York, 1974 (pamphlet). " 'Man!' Memo From a Publisher," *New York Times Magazine,* October 20, 1974, pp. 38, 104-108.

44 "How Many of These 16,888 TV Characters Are Women?" *Pennsylvania Gazette,* February, 1980, p. 17.

45 U.S. Commission on Civil Rights, *Window Dressing on the Set: An Update* (Washington, D.C.: U.S.

Government Printing Office, January, 1979), pp. 5-22, 60-61.

46 George Gent, "Women's Group Challenges WABC-TV's Renewal," *New York Times*, May 2, 1972, p. 87.

47 *Report of the National Advisory Commission on Civil Disorders*, pp. 384-85.

48 Jules Witcover, "Washington's White Press Corps," *Columbia Journalism Review*, Winter, 1969-1970, p. 44.

49 Les Brown, "Women and Minority Groups Increase Again in TV, Study Shows," *New York Times*, December 2, 1974, p. 66. Ralph M. Jennings and David A. Tillyer, *Television Station Employment Practices: The Status of Minorities and Women* (New York: Office of Communications, United Church of Christ, 1973).

50 *Window Dressing on the Set: An Update*, pp. 33-39.

51 Edward J. Trayes, "Black Journalists on U.S. Metropolitan Daily Newspapers: A Follow-Up Study," *Journalism Quarterly*, Winter, 1979, pp. 711-14.

52 Nick Kotz, "The Minority Struggle for a Place in the Newsroom," *Columbia Journalism Review*, March/April, 1979, pp. 23-31.

53 Brown, "Women and Minority Groups Increase Again," p. 66.

54 Barbara Murray Eddings, "Women in Broadcasting (U.S.): De Jure, De Facto," in Helen Baehr, ed., *Women's Studies International Quarterly Special Issue on Women and Media* (New York: Pergamon Press, 1980), p. 1. "Prime Time for TV Newswomen," *Time*, March 21, 1977, pp. 85-86.

55 Robert U. Brown, "New Job Vistas for Women," *Editor & Publisher*, February 1, 1975, p. 32.

56 Barbara Reed, "Sexism in the Media World," in Emery and Smythe, *Readings in Mass Communication*, 4th ed., pp. 352-53.

57 Eric Pace, "In the Paperback Field, It's Getting to Be a Women's World," *New York Times*, February 12, 1974, p. 28.

58 Kotz, "The Minority Struggle for a Place in the Newsroom," p. 28.

59 *Ibid.*, p. 28.

Suggested Readings

Baehr, Helen, ed., *Women's Studies International Quarterly Special Issue on Women and Media*. New York: Pergamon Press, 1980.

Bogle, Donald, *Toms, Coons, Mullatoes, Mammies, and Bucks: An Interpretive History of Blacks in American Films*. New York: Viking Press, 1973.

Brown, Cynthia, "Strong-Arming the Hispanic Press," *Columbia Journalism Review*, July/August, 1980.

Ferretti, Fred, "The White Captivity of Black Radio," *Columbia Journalism Review*, Summer, 1970.

Greenberg, Bradley, and Brenda Dervin, "Mass Communication Among the Urban Poor," *Public Opinion Quarterly*, Summer, 1970.

Gutiérrez, Félix, and Clint C. Wilson II, "The Demographic Dilemma," *Columbia Journalism Review*, January/February, 1979.

Haskell, Molly, *From Reverence to Rape: The Treatment of Women in the Movies*. New York: Holt, Rinehart & Winston, 1974.

Hur, Kenneth K., and John P. Robinson, "The Social Impact of 'Roots,'" *Journalism Quarterly*, Spring, 1978.

Jeffres, Leo W., and K. Kyoon Hur, "The Forgotten Media Consumer—The American Ethnic," *Journalism Quarterly*, Spring, 1980.

Kotz, Nick, "The Minority Struggle for a Place in the Newsroom," *Columbia Journalism Review*, March/April, 1979.

"'Man!' Memo From a Publisher," *New York Times Magazine*, October 20, 1974.

Palmer, L. F. Jr., "The Black Press in Transition," *Columbia Journalism Review*, Spring, 1970.

Reed, Barbara, "Sexism in the Media World," in Michael Emery and Ted C. Smythe, eds., *Readings in Mass Communication*, 4th ed. Dubuque, Iowa: Wm. C. Brown, 1980.

Report of the National Advisory Commission on Civil Disorders (Kerner Commission). New York: Bantam Books, 1968.

Schatzman, Dennis, "The Black Press and Its Role in Modern Society," *Editor & Publisher*, April 21, 1979.

Smith, Robert E., "They Still Write It White," *Columbia Journalism Review*, Spring, 1969.

Strainchamps, Ethel, ed., *Rooms With No View: A Woman's Guide to the Man's World of the Media*. New York: Harper & Row, 1974.

Tan, Alexis S., "Evaluation of Newspapers and Television by Blacks and Mexican-Americans," *Journalism Quarterly*, Winter, 1978.

TRAYES, EDWARD J., "Black Journalists on U.S. Metropolitan Daily Newspapers: A Follow-Up Study," *Journalism Quarterly,* Winter, 1979.

TUCHMAN, GAYE, ARLENE K. DANIELS, and JAMES BENÉT, *Hearth and Home: Images of Women in the Mass Media.* New York: Oxford University Press, 1978.

U.S. Commission on Civil Rights, *Window Dressing on the Set: An Update.* Washington, D.C.: Government Printing Office, 1979.

WITCOVER, JULES, "Washington's White Press Corps," *Columbia Journalism Review,* Winter, 1969-1970.

Chapter 19
Coverage of Specialized News

The typical American is only indirectly involved with traditional news topics like government and international affairs. We are far more involved with our economic prospects and our recreational activities. Though the American media have always devoted some attention to such topics as business and lifestyles, that attention has grown substantially in recent years. Some of the resulting content is fluff; much is service features; and some is genuine news.

For many decades American newspaper journalism maintained a clear distinction between the Sunday paper and the daily paper. Sunday newspapers contained as many as a dozen sections, filled with timeless features on everything from boating to stamp collecting. Daily newspapers concentrated on hard news. Of course the daily paper had some special sections too. But the daily sports section stressed sports news rather than features, and the daily business section was little more than a page or two of stock quotations. Only the daily women's section was identical to its Sunday counterpart.

The 1970s virtually eliminated the distinc-

tion. By early in the decade, many newspapers were experimenting with feature supplements on gardening, the arts, food, travel, homemaking, fashion, and entertainment—all on days other than Sunday. The supplements were popular with readers and advertisers alike. Within a few years they had become regular sections of many daily papers, filling as much as half the available space in some of them. Hard news reporters tended to resent the gaudy feature sections, pointing with pride to holdouts like the *New York Times* that refused to cater so obviously to the "Me Generation."

In 1976 the *Times* took the plunge, and the distinction between Sunday feature writing and daily newspaper writing disappeared. The daily *Times* is now a four-section newspaper. The first section carries national and international news; the second section is the "Metropolitan Report." The fourth section is "Business Day," reflecting vastly expanded attention to economic trends and corporate behavior. The third section, the timeless feature section, changes daily. On Monday it's "Sports Monday"; Tuesday brings "Science Times"; Wednesday's "The Living Section" emphasizes cooking; Thursday's "The

Home" specializes in decorating; on Friday comes "Weekend," devoted to entertainment.

It is easy to see these new sections as many old-line journalists see them: the flourishing of fluff, the triumph of the Me Generation over hard news. To be sure, much of their content is pure entertainment. But service features are *not* pure entertainment. Though not exactly news in the traditional sense (it could run as well next week as this week), an article on how to insulate your attic is genuinely useful to the audience—arguably more useful than an article on the latest pronouncements of the Secretary of State.

Furthermore, a special section devoted to a topic encourages increased media attention to that topic. Only some of the extra coverage is given over to entertainment and service pieces. The rest of it goes to serious background features, investigative reporting, and even hard news. The media, in short, are not only paying more attention to business, lifestyles, sports, and the like. They are also paying more *serious* attention to these topics. The change has toppled the dominance of political news, and thus understandably upset political reporters. But whether it is a change for the better or for the worse depends on how this specialized coverage matures in the coming years. A whole section of advertiser-supplied recipes is a step down from an occasional page of them. But a serious food section—with shopping tips, nutritional information, and the latest on chemical additives in addition to recipes—is a step up. Most specialized sections are still deciding which way to go.

BUSINESS

The April, 1980, issue of the *Washington Journalism Review* carried a full-page ad from Coors, the Colorado brewing company. "We used to say no comment," the ad reads. "Now we're asking for your questions." Admitting that Coors "must talk to the media"

to survive, the ad provides two toll-free numbers for journalists to call and promises that officials will talk "openly and frankly."[1]

After 107 years in business, why did Coors suddenly change its "no comment" policy? The company was responding to a significant change in its environment: a huge increase in media attention to business. In 1970, "no comment" usually meant no story; in 1980 it meant a story that lacked the Coors point of view. Spurred on by persistent inflation and recession, by energy shortages and volatile interest rates, by unemployment and corporate bankruptcies, American editors decided in the late 1970s that business was big news. No longer would it be sufficient to cover the business community with stock tables, investment advice, and corporate press releases. The news media were coming to agree with Ralph Nader's dictum: "If the 1950s focused on the role of labor in America and the 1970s on government, then the 1980s should scrutinize the role and reach of big business in America."[2]

Improvement has come first in the big-city newspapers, newsmagazines, and broadcast networks. The daily business section of the *New York Times* has a staff of 70. The *Chicago Tribune,* which publishes a special business section on Wednesdays, grew from eight business reporters and editors in 1977 to 26 of them in 1980.[3] In 1980 alone, the *Los Angeles Times,* the *Boston Globe,* and the *Washington Post* all added business sections, with comparable increases in staffing.[4] *Forbes,* a leading business magazine, grew from 2,600 pages a year to 4,500 pages between 1975 and 1979, while *Time* more than doubled its coverage of business and economics to an average of five to seven pages per issue.[5] And all three broadcast networks hired business correspondents; in 1971 NBC was the only network with a business specialist.

Hobart Rowan, economics columnist for the *Washington Post,* describes the change:

The quality and quantity of business/economics reporting has made vast strides in the past 20 to 25 years, and especially in the last few. There was a time when the business editor of the typical American daily was one step up or down in the pecking order from the church editor—and in some places, maybe was the same person. If he had a function, it was to be responsive to local business interests who also were the main advertisers. He often operated alone, with no support from management, no background and no prospect of personal advancement—unless he got the hell out of the job as fast as he could.

Today, things are different, especially on big-city papers. More and more, managers and editors understand the pervasive importance of economic developments, and the close connection between what goes on in the economy and political/social trends. There is freedom from the influence of the advertising dollar. In some places, the financial desk is actually the fastest growth area of the newspaper. There is more analysis and commentary.[6]

The new attention to business is not all serious journalism. The *Chicago Tribune*'s "Midweek Business Report," for example, includes lots of features on executive recreation, health, clothing, and entertainment, becoming largely a lifestyle section for the gray flannel set.[7] But on the whole, increased coverage of business has meant more serious coverage of business. Even political reporters are not complaining.

Business executives, on the other hand, are complaining. Many see an anti-business bias in the media, a tendency to depict corporations (especially big ones) as greedy and irresponsible, and "profit" as a dirty word. It isn't hard to find examples of anti-business stories, such as an NBC series on improprieties in the oil industry that the National News Council called "biased and at times deceitful."[8] But it isn't hard, either, to find examples of media deference to business. When Mobil Oil produced a TV report on "Energy at the Crossroads," putting oil industry activities in the best possible light, 62 stations aired the propaganda as news, re-

vealing Mobil's role only in a credit line at the end.[9]

Overall, the evidence supports neither the charge of anti-business bias nor the accusation of pro-business subservience. A University of Minnesota study, for example, found that business stories in Minneapolis and St. Paul newspapers were neutral 56 percent of the time, pro-business 25 percent of the time, and anti-business only 19 percent of the time. A similar study of business coverage in Raleigh, North Carolina found 54 percent neutral stories, 20 percent favorable, and 26 percent unfavorable.[10]

Such a study in the 1950s or 1960s would probably have shown a substantial pro-business tilt, not so much because the media were ideologically pro-business but because business coverage was scanty and underbudgeted, relying mostly on press releases from the business community. Reporters still get much of their business news directly from business—quarterly earnings statements, announcements of personnel changes, features on new products and new policies. But much of this news today is intrinsically negative—plant closings, product recalls, reduced earnings. Regulatory agencies and citizen pressure groups are available to reporters as sources of non-business perspectives on business. And reporters increasingly have both the time and the inclination to seek out these non-business perspectives.

So business news is becoming more hard-nosed, more objective, more news-oriented. To corporate executives who rose to power in an era of verbatim press releases, advertiser pressure, boozy junkets, and cheerleading business reporters, this looks like an anti-business bias.

For many smaller newspapers and local broadcast stations, in fact, business coverage is still business as usual. A 1979 survey of 186 daily newspapers revealed both the improvement and the need for more improvement. On the one hand, more than two-thirds of the papers said they devoted more space to business news in 1979 than in 1974, and more than a third had added part-time staff during this period. On the other hand, 71 percent of the papers said they still did not employ a single full-time business/financial reporter.[11]

Such papers fill the bulk of their business sections with stock tables and syndicated investment advice, plus wire stories on national and regional business trends. This material is inexpensive, easy, and guaranteed not to offend an advertiser. Serious reporting on local business developments, on the other hand, is expensive, difficult, and potentially controversial. You can't do too much of it without a full-time reporter.

Chris Welles, a financial journalist who runs a fellowship program in business writing at Columbia University, puts the progress in perspective: "In lesser papers there has been very little change at all. Economic news among the middle level papers, with few exceptions like the *Louisville Courier-*

STOCKS AND STRIKES

The staple of the newspaper business section has long been the stock market listings. Though other kinds of business news are improving at many papers, investment information remains the core of the section. There are many reasons for this emphasis—the mercantile origins of the newspaper industry, the investment interests of most publishers, the inexpensiveness of stock market news services. The biggest reason is probably that investors are dedicated readers; many buy their afternoon papers solely to check the stock market.

Investors are also dedicated viewers. Perhaps the best broadcast coverage of business has come in "Wall Street Week," a half-hour program hosted by Louis Rukeyser and carried by 250 public television stations. Its audience of ten million viewers makes it the most popular regularly scheduled show on public TV.[12]

There are more than twice as many labor union members as stockholders in the United States, but they are apparently less interested in their unions than stockholders are in their stocks. While business news has flourished, labor news has fallen on hard times. In 1951, *Editor & Publisher Yearbook* listed 154 newspaper labor reporters. In 1980, according to AFL-CIO public relations director Albert J. Zack, there were only 25 full-time labor reporters at American newspapers.[13]

Labor news concentrates on strikes. This is particularly true in broadcasting, which cannot resist the visual appeal of a picket line. But it is true even in newspapers, as former Secretary of Labor W. Willard Wirtz complained back in 1967: "A strike is invariably the subject of extended coverage, with pictures, and usually with accompanying editorials. The peaceful signing of a new collective bargaining agreement, even in a major industry, is at best a one-day story, usually on an inside page."[14] Zack singles out three publications for solid labor coverage that goes beyond strike reporting—the *Washington Post,* the *Wall Street Journal,* and *Business Week.*

More broadly, union leaders are angry that the media devote more attention to executives and the interests of the affluent than to workers and the interests of the working class. Everything from network entertainment to service features seems to suggest that the U.S. population is composed mostly of white-collar professionals. The *Chicago Tribune* used to be one of the few newspapers in the country to focus on working-class issues, with a twice-weekly column entitled "Blue Collar View." The column was dropped in 1979.[15]

Journal or the great investigative work being done by the *Philadelphia Inquirer,* is as desolate as ever; it's a wasteland. There is an assumption among them that economics is boring and dull, which it ain't. Or that it can get the editor and publisher in trouble with their friends."[16]

ENVIRONMENT/CONSUMERS/ENERGY

In June of 1969, ABC commentator Edward P. Morgan addressed a journalism conference at Stanford University. "In the 1950s," he mused, "reporters covered the cold war in depth, but they missed completely the civil rights movement and the racial crisis of the 1960s. What crisis of the 1970s, I wonder, are the mass media failing to report now?" Morgan then answered his own question: environmental deterioration.

He could as well have said consumer problems or the energy crisis. All three issues—and they are interconnected, of course—caught the media unprepared when they emerged in the 1970s.

There are several reasons for this failure.

1. Until the 1970s, there were few national or local groups devoted to these issues and powerful enough to fight for coverage.

2. The short-run economic interests of the media favored inattention; advertisers don't like stories on industrial pollution or shoddy products.

3. The story was virtually invisible. Consumer complaints were individual events; the environment deteriorated and energy problems worsened slowly, imperceptibly. Only when the various crises had emerged full-blown did government agencies and others start acting, providing the news pegs that justified media attention.

4. Reporters had no background in the issues. Without specialized training in a dozen fields at once, they were at the mercy of their sources. And the sources, as often as not, provided conflicting facts and theories that reporters had enough trouble comprehending, let alone explaining to the public.

Given these barriers to effective coverage, the media did a good job of gearing up in the 1970s to cover the environment, consumers, and energy. But by 1980, some experts were complaining that the media were already gearing down again. Francis Pollock, former editor of *Media & Consumer* magazine, estimates that there are only 200 full-time consumer reporters in the U.S. today, down from 500 at the peak in 1974.[17] The number of environmental reporters has suffered a similar decline. Energy reporting has taken up some of the slack, but even in the energy area coverage is remarkably trendy. Reporters pay careful attention to nuclear power for a few months after an accident, careful attention to fossil fuels for a few months after a gas shortage. Then coverage declines until the next crisis.

The question is whether environmental, consumer, and energy news will become institutionalized in the 1980s. There is some reason to hope that they will—not like business with a special section of their own, and perhaps not even with specialized reporters of their own, but as a consistent emphasis in nearly all reporting.

They are, after all, intrinsically interdisciplinary fields. The proposed construction of a nuclear power plant, for example, is obviously an energy story. But it is also a consumer story (how will the plant affect electric rates?) and an environmental story (how will it affect air and water quality?) And it's a business story (what impact on the utility?), a labor story (how many jobs?), and a science story (how safe is the plant? how will it work?). And of course it's a major political story as well, involving literally dozens of government agencies, advocacy groups, and legal proceedings. It is hard to find an environmental, consumer, or energy story that does not belong, like nuclear power, to half a dozen news beats at once.

The economics of journalism make it un-

SCIENCE IS SEXY

Like business and financial journalism, reporting on science and technology is a growth area. At the end of the 1970s, a number of newspapers added special science sections, and hired science reporters to staff them. Half a dozen new science magazines hit the market, with publishers ranging from *Penthouse* to Time, Inc. to the American Association for the Advancement of Science. CBS inaugurated a new science program called "Universe," while public television supplemented its highly successful "Nova" with a children's science show, "3-2-1 Contact," and a new adult mini-series hosted by Carl Sagan, "Cosmos."

In a 1971 newspaper readership study, science did not place among the top 17 categories in reader interest. But when the study was repeated in 1977, science ranked eleventh, and the related topics of energy, health, and environment ranked first, third, and sixth respectively. Even nutrition proved more popular than sports (or politics) in the readers' rankings of which topics deserved the most newspaper space.[18]

This increased interest in science is all the more impressive because it comes at a time when science journalism is no longer dominated by the gee-whiz enthusiasm of the 1950s and 1960s. Says science writer David Perlman of the *San Francisco Chronicle*, "I think our experiences have lowered our thresholds of suspicion, increased our skepticism, and taught us that the great hopes, new cures, and technological fixes on the horizon haven't proved so foolproof."[19] Science writers today are thoroughly enmeshed in environmental, consumer, and energy reporting, not to mention the economics of research and the politics of health care. And the audience is more enthusiastic than ever about science news.

---

likely that teams of specialized reporters will cover such stories. The next best alternative is a single reporter with a broad perspective, willing to look at all the implications of the power plant. Viewed in this light, the decreased number of consumer and environmental specialists may not reflect a decline in media attention to these topics, but rather an increase in the sophistication with which the media cover them. Environmental considerations turn up in the middle of a story in the business section, written by a business reporter. Hard-nosed consumer journalism finds its way into the lifestyle section, written by a lifestyle reporter. This may be the direction of the 1980s.

Not all predictions are so rosy, of course. Press critic Ben Bagdikian believes that coverage of such topics as pollution and hazards in the workplace inevitably declines as economic conditions worsen; protecting the en-

vironment and the consumer comes to be seen as a luxury the economic system can no longer afford.[20] Glenda Daniels, a Chicago-based environmental columnist, says the media are beginning to cover the environment the way they cover Latin American politics: "If there's a revolution, we throw a lot of people in for a short time, and then nothing."[21] Certainly this tendency to overstress dramatic confrontations and hot breaking stories must be overcome if the media are to mature in their coverage of environmental, consumer, and energy news.

So must the tendency to settle for cheap shots. Robert B. Reich, director of the Office of Policy Planning of the Federal Trade Commission, complains that consumer reporters too seldom tackle the difficult structural problems that confront consumers. Instead, he says, they "tend to go after the marginal operators, the home siding salesmen, the mail order firms and the usual sort of sleazy operations."[22]

Toby J. McIntosh, a reporter for the Bureau of National Affairs, was a judge in the 1979 National Press Club competition for consumer reporting. McIntosh said he found plenty of educational pieces on how to be a good consumer (don't shop when you're hungry; beware of chain letters), and plenty of Action Line columns dealing with specific (and usually minor) consumer complaints. But he found far too little of two other kinds of consumer reporting—comparison shopping to assess the relative merits of different health spas, auto repair shops, or whatever; and investigative pieces on significant consumer hazards.[23] The most consistent source of these latter sorts of consumer reporting continues to be the Consumers Union, which publishes *Consumer Reports* magazine, syndicates a radio program to 60 stations across the country, and provides a three-times-a-week consumer column to 300 newspapers.[24]

Yet serious, investigative coverage of environment, energy, and consumer problems is still alive, even flourishing at some papers and stations. Among the submissions to the National Press Club competition were stories on radiation, dental care, inflation, veterans' disability treatment, art fraud, arson, and generic drugs.[25] The *Niagara Falls* (N.Y.) *Gazette* helped break the Love Canal story about toxic wastes buried by the Hooker Chemical Company. The *Philadelphia Inquirer* won a Pulitzer Prize for its massive coverage of the accident at the Three Mile Island nuclear power plant. The *Charlotte* (N.C.) *Observer* published a courageous series on byssinosis, a cotton dust disease that threatens the lungs of mill workers in the area. The *Louisville Courier-Journal* investigated toxic waste facilities in Kentucky and Indiana, with reporters posing as truckers to find out which dumps would accept wastes in violation of government regulations.[26]

Environmental, consumer, and energy problems will not go away in the 1980s. They will continue to surface in the news, not always as stories in their own right but often as crucial aspects of business, science, lifestyle, and political stories. Will the media continue to improve in their coverage of these issues, despite the diminished cadre of specialized reporters and the lack of a special section for their work? Or will the environment, consumers, and energy get lost in the cracks between more traditional journalistic specialties?

LIFESTYLES

Business and financial journalism is a traditional news topic that won expanded, serious media attention in the 1970s. Environmental, consumer, and energy journalism are untraditional news topics that flourished briefly in the 1970s, and are now poised on the brink of either decline or institutionalization as parts of other news beats. Lifestyles journalism also expanded in the 1970s, but unlike the other areas we have discussed so far, it expanded chiefly through service features, not news. When political reporters complain about the unbridled growth of specialized coverage, they are not objecting to stories on business, environment, consumers, or energy. They are objecting to stories on home decorating, fashion, entertainment, and travel—to the growth of lifestyles journalism.

To traditional journalists, service features are "mere" entertainment. It is enough, they argue, that television, film, recordings, and radio are entertainment media, that entertainment is what sells most magazines and many books. News should be different, pure, unsullied by the effort to amuse.

Of course news has never been quite that pure. The whimsical features of the Penny Press in the 1830s attracted readers with the promise of entertainment. So did the scandal, gossip, sex, and pseudo-science of the great circulation war between Pulitzer's *World* and Hearst's *Journal* in the 1890s. The *World* was the first newspaper to feature a cartoon comic, "The Yellow Kid of Hogan's

Alley." During the circulation war both newspapers carried "Yellow Kid" cartoons, bequeathing the name "yellow journalism" to all such efforts to win readers through gimcrackery and sensationalism. Cartoon strips remain among the most widely read items in American newspapers.

But until the 1970s, print journalists thought they had entertainment under control. A page of comics was okay, an occasional crime splurge on the front page was okay, even the no-news women's section was okay. The rest of the daily paper, including the sports section, was news. Only on Sundays, when nothing happened anyway, did entertainment and service dominate the newspaper.

But in the 1970s, entertainment and service came to dominate many newspapers all week long. The change was heralded by the success of the city magazines. These began their lives as restaurant, theater, and television guides, like *Cue* (now part of *New York*) and *Chicago Guide* (now *Chicago*). *New York* added classy graphics, political gossip, "New Journalism," and service features for the affluent (shopping guides to vintage wines, divorce lawyers, private schools, European vacations). The result was a model for the chic lifestyles journalism that became the hallmark of the 1970s. Today there are roughly a hundred city and regional magazines helping upper-income readers spend their money. Most are extremely attractive to advertisers. J. Stanley Heuisler, publisher of *Baltimore Magazine,* explains why: "As ad agency people become increasingly selective in their strategy, city magazines become increasingly economical—if they're looking for the household earning $25,000 a year or more."[27]

The same logic persuaded newspaper publishers to expand their attention to lifestyles journalism. Readers, especially younger and more affluent readers, wanted a newspaper that was attentive to their personal needs, crammed with advice on what to buy and where to play. And advertisers wanted a newspaper that appealed to those sorts of readers, and that encouraged them to buy and play more.

The newspaper prototype for all this was, of course, the women's section. To a greater extent than many men realize, women have long had their own separate media. Women's magazines are among the top sellers in the country—*Better Homes & Gardens, Family Circle, Woman's Day, McCall's, Ladies' Home Journal, Good Housekeeping,* etc. From ten in the morning to four in the afternoon, television is aimed predominantly at women. And in newspapers there is the women's section.

The content of the section changed very little from the 1880s to the early 1970s. The most common topics according to one 1969 survey were club news, food preparation, homemaking, recipes, beauty tips, weddings and engagements, fashion, society, and decorating.[28] In addition, many editors put their etiquette and advice columns (always the most popular columns in the paper) in the women's section. And if the paper could afford to use color anywhere, this was the place —food and fashion in full color.

Everything practical, all the service features, all the information readers could actually use in daily living was isolated in the women's section. Men were presumed to be interested only in news of the "real world" of city councils and wars and football games.

The segregation began ending when editors realized that male readers too were interested in service features. So they broadened the scope of the section, adding entertainment, celebrity gossip, travel, home repairs, even science and health. The change to a coeducational lifestyles section was often accompanied by a change in name, from "Women" to something like "Style" or "Family Life." By 1980, the staff of the *Los Angeles Times* included specialists in art, architecture and design, auto, classical music, drama, human behavior, jazz, literature, medicine, media, popular music, religion, science, and television, all in addition to the traditional women's topics.

The popularity of this expanded section led to the next step, the creation of more specialized weekly lifestyles sections. The *St. Louis Post-Dispatch,* for example, added a "Dollar/Sense" consumer magazine supplement on Tuesdays, traditionally lowest in weekday circulation. Thanks to the new section, Tuesday circulation rose to the second highest of the week, topped only by the Wednesday edition, which features the food pages.[29]

Newspapers of all sizes have found that specialized lifestyles sections attract both readers and advertisers. When the *Paragould* (Ark.) *Daily Press* proposed a special section on gardening, so many advertisers wanted in that the paper had to add more pages.

"When I broke into the newspaper business in Kansas," commented editor and publisher Fred Wulfekuhler, "we had an unwritten law. We did no special sections. Today we've gone just the opposite. We are special section crazy."[30]

The proliferation of lifestyles sections raises three issues worth pondering. The first we have already mentioned—traditional journalists deplore the growing ascendancy of service features over hard news. This is a battle that is already settled, at least for now. The traditional journalists lost. Future definitions of news will have to include service features.

The second issue is still in doubt: Who will be served by all those service features? The media's traditional answer—and still for the most part their current answer—is advertisers and high-income readers. Back in

---

CELEBRITY GOSSIP

Service features are more than just entertainment; though they are not news, they are useful. This cannot be said for celebrity gossip, which also found new respectability in the media of the 1970s.

Gossip has traditionally been considered the soft underbelly of American journalism. It was confined to tabloid columnists, movie magazines, and publications like the *National Enquirer,* which rose to a weekly circulation of five million in 1980 on the strength of outrageous headlines like "Pushing 40 and Shunned by Hollywood: Raquel Welch Weds Out of Desperation."[31]

But in the 1970s, gossip went legit. To compete with the *Washington Star's* successful "Ear" column, the *Washington Post* added tantalizing tidbits on the private lives of public figures to the name-dropping and gushy fashion reports in its society coverage. Time, Inc. came out in 1974 with *People;* by the end of the decade it was ranked among the top ten U.S. magazines in total revenues, proving that celebrity gossip could be packaged to attract high-income readers and name-brand advertisers.[32]

Small wonder that ABC picked celebrity gossip Rona Barrett to help "Good Morning America" fight the ratings battle against NBC's solidly entrenched "Today" show. At the start it was a classic showdown: entertainment-oriented "Good Morning America" versus news-style "Today." But when ABC started picking up ratings points, "Today" moved to a less newsy format. And when "Good Morning America" actually pulled ahead in the ratings, NBC hired away Rona Barrett. The ultimate winner of the morning network battle was entertainment over news—by a knockout.

1964, a critic of the women's sections noted their subservience to advertisers with only mild objections:

> So far as food is concerned, most of the "coverage" consists of recipes. In some instances, the recipes are tied in with the foods being advertised in that day's paper. This is done particularly on Thursdays, when food advertising is heavy before the traditional shopping day, Friday. This is fine, but it isn't enough.[33]

Today it isn't fine, though it still happens on occasion. In 1973, the Newspaper Food Editors and Writers Association was founded, aimed at lessening commercial pressures. In 1975, the Association adopted a code of ethics.[34] Nowadays big-city food editors steer clear of advertisers, while their small-city colleagues remain vulnerable. Some food editors today even write about the nutritional harm of snack foods or the health risks of additives. But food coverage is still predomi-

nantly recipes, and food advertisers are still happy.

Travel writing has changed even less. The following 1970 critique of the *New York Times* travel section would apply nearly as well today:

> A *Times* travel article on Haiti spoke of "an optimistic spirit" among the Haitian people, who "give the impression that even though they lack the material abundance of some parts of the world, they share the pride that comes with independence." Not only is this description directly contradicted by articles on Haiti in the *Times'* regular news columns, but the travel story also fails to point out that dollars spent by visitors to Haiti go into the pocket of [now deceased] dictator François Duvalier, who desperately needs hard currency to prop up his repressive regime.[35]

Perhaps you feel a travel story has no business talking about dictators and repressive

COVERING ENTERTAINMENT

Like most lifestyles journalism, entertainment coverage is a mixture of service items and light features, with very, very little serious reporting. This is true of most entertainment magazines. It is true of television interview programs, on which entertainers are by far the most frequent guests. And it is true of the newspaper entertainment section.

Virtually every major newspaper has such a section, averaging several pages a day and as many as a dozen pages on Fridays and Sundays. At least half of its content is strictly service—radio and TV logs, movie listings, nightclub directories, and such. This material is of real value to readers. It is also of real value to the entertainment industry, which shows its appreciation by advertising generously. Interspersed among the ads and the logs are PR releases touting the virtues of this or that extravaganza and human-interest features on the lives and views of successful entertainers. The entertainment editor seasons this cheerful blend with a dollop of celebrity gossip.

The saving grace of entertainment coverage is the reviews. Most movie reviewers, for example, are fiercely independent. Some would rather pan than praise a picture (it's more fun, especially on television), and few are affected by Hollywood hoopla or the endless flow of free tickets. Movie theater owners are advertisers, but their complaints about unfavorable reviews usually prove fruitless. Newspaper reviews of television programs are similarly independent, and generally negative. Except for amateur theater, which is sacrosanct in most communities, entertainment reviewers are generally free to dip their pens in poison—a nice contrast to the unfailing enthusiasm of the rest of entertainment coverage.

regimes anyhow. But it could at least talk about poor accommodations, overcrowded airplanes, rude customs officials, or the fact that some idyllic vacation isle has just been destroyed by a hurricane. You won't often find these stories, either, in the travel section of your local paper. Nor will you find them on radio or television, or in specialized magazines like *Holiday* and *Travel News*.

It hardly needs to be added that part of the service feature's deference to advertisers is its stress on the interests of upper-income readers—the sorts of readers advertisers want to reach. When the food section talks about how to apply for food stamps and the travel section deals with local parks accessible by bus, the service feature will have achieved a quantum leap in maturity.

The third issue raised by lifestyles sections is the fate of lifestyles *news*—hard news on topics ranging from crisis centers for battered wives to the Equal Rights Amendment, from the regulation of deceptive advertising to the recall of dangerous products. Before the 1970s such stories were relatively scarce. They normally wound up buried in the back of the regular news section (because they weren't about a traditional news topic) or treated as a feature in the women's section (because that wasn't the place for hard news). The growth of consumerism, environmentalism, and feminism in the 1970s made hard news about lifestyles far more common. But the media still haven't figured out how to handle this journalistic hybrid. The various lifestyles sections continue to be built around light backgrounders and service features, not serious reporting about lifestyles. Look for this to change in the 1980s, as lifestyles reporters insist on covering their beats with solid journalism as well as reader service.

SPORTS

Spectator sports are probably America's foremost recreational activity. And since most spectators can't get to the game in person, they rely instead on the mass media.

Every sporting event of any significance at all is carried live on radio or television. The networks bid in the millions of dollars for the right to broadcast the most important games. Given this strong economic interest in the continued popularity of big-money sports, it should come as no surprise that TV sports announcers and commentators have more in common with promoters than with journalists: the game is always exciting and the players are always in top form.

The exception to the rule is ABC's Howard Cosell, always ready to jump in with scandals, rumors, and informed critiques of the players and teams. A 1978 poll found that Cosell was the most popular network sports announcer—and the most unpopular.[36] ABC is obviously happy to have one controversial sportscaster . . . but only one. Cosell is the pinch of spice in an otherwise bland stew, not the forerunner of a new trend.

Many television sportscasters, by the way, are paid by the team, not by the station—a sure sign that sports announcing is not journalism.

But sports journalism does exist. It fills up to one-quarter of many broadcast news programs, at least half a dozen pages in most daily newspapers, and a host of specialized magazines led by *Sports Illustrated*. With all that time and space, we have a right to expect sports news as detailed and comprehensive as news of the government. In a sense, that's what we get. Certainly every game, every injury, and every trade receives wide attention in the media. But until the 1970s it was one-sided attention. Sports journalists were no more likely than sports announcers to tell the fans that an athlete was traded because he couldn't get along with his teammates, or that a coach was being investigated for drugging his team, or even that a game was poorly played and deadly dull. Like the lifestyles sections, sports news was uniformly positive and enthusiastic—and it didn't even include service features.

In the 1970s it became harder and harder for sportswriters to maintain this happy optimism. Player strikes, recruiting scandals,

Religion gets a lot less news coverage than sports in the American media, but the quality of the coverage is remarkably similar: often celebratory, rarely critical. Just as most sportswriters are fans, most religion writers are deeply sympathetic to organized religion. They tend to view themselves as lone bastions of idealism in a cynical age and a cynical occupation, and they are understandably reluctant to use what little space they get to write critically about religious organizations. And so the weekly religion page is usually a schedule of upcoming services, a smattering of local church news, and a guest column by a clergyman.

Even secular reporters turn reverent on those rare occasions when they write about religion. In 1979 when the Pope reached Chicago, the *Chicago Sun-Times* headlined its story: "A City Nestles in the Hands of a Gentle Pilgrim."[37] Imagine a similar headline about the visit of a political leader.

But religion coverage, too, is changing. It began changing in the 1970s, when religion writers found themselves writing about a wide range of cults that seemed to merit more alarm than reverence. More traditional groups remained inviolable, however. The left-leaning political activities of some national religious organizations, for example, were seldom mentioned. But by the end of the decade, the growing connections between religion and politics were too important to ignore.

A major contributor to the change, ironically, was religious broadcasting. Ever since the earliest days of radio, many stations have carried Sunday morning services. Some religious groups operated their own stations, and a few preachers developed syndicated programs. But until the 1960s, about half of the airtime used for religious programming was donated by the stations, mostly to mainstream religious groups. Today, by contrast, more than 90 percent of religious broadcasting time is *sold*—and evangelists are the buyers.[38]

Members of the Evangelical-Fundamentalist-Pentecostal wing of Protestantism now own roughly 1,400 radio stations and 35 television stations in the U.S. Religious networks use satellites to send their programs to stations and cable systems nationwide. And religious programmers spend about $600 million a year to buy time on commercial stations. In all, religious programs attract an estimated 14 million TV viewers and more than 100 million radio listeners each week. Not all the programs are preaching. Two of the most successful TV offerings, Pat Robertson's "700 Club" and Jim Bakker's "PTL Club," are Johnny Carson-style talk shows. And Rex Humbard's hour uses a variety show format.[39]

This "Electronic Church" solicits audience donations, often very successfully; some broadcast evangelists take in tens of millions of dollars a year. In addition to financing the programs themselves, the money supports other activities, such as missionary work abroad.

Some evangelists have used their TV fame, off the air, to promote and raise money for conservative political causes in the U.S. This is no different in principle from the liberal political activities of many churches in the 1960s and 1970s; Martin Luther King was a political preacher too. But it is significantly larger in scale, and in the 1980 presidential campaign it became a political issue in its own right—an issue that the media were forced to cover.

financial problems, and courtroom battles absolutely demanded objective coverage. Many sportswriters resented this necessity, and reverted as quickly as possible to covering the games they loved.

Sportswriters are, first and foremost, fans. As Leonard Shecter put it: "The man who covers a baseball team year after year spends a good deal more time with the management of the ball club than with his own editors; indeed, with his own wife. He becomes, if he is interested enough in his job to want to keep it, more involved with the fortunes of the team than that of his newspaper."[40]

There is nothing so terrible about this as long as it is confined to the amateur level. Who can quarrel with a local paper that refers to the town's star Little Leaguer as a pint-sized Ted Williams, and makes excuses for the 0-23 record of the high school basketball team? But professional athletics—and much of college athletics—is big business. Working to fill a 60,000-seat stadium is not the same thing as helping to support the Little League. On that level the fans have a right to know why seat prices were raised, or why the coach kept the star halfback on the bench. And nonfans have a right to know about illegal recruiting, drug misuse, and the like. Slowly, reluctantly, sportswriters are beginning to meet these information needs, to cover sports as journalists rather than as promoters and fans.

We have dealt with a number of kinds of specialized news in this chapter—business, labor, environment, consumers, energy, science, lifestyles, entertainment, sports, religion. They are not all the same, but they all share two important characteristics. First, they have more to do with the daily lives of the media audience than many more traditional news categories. And second, because they are *not* traditional news categories, they have tended to be covered less objectively and less aggressively than politics or government.

The first characteristic justifies the increased media attention these topics started receiving in the 1970s. But the second characteristic requires further improvement. No newspaper needs to apologize for giving space to a stamp-and-coin column. But even the stamp-and-coin columnist has an obligation to be honest, aggressive, accurate, and independent. Most specialized news sections are only beginning to live up to that obligation.

Notes

1 *Washington Journalism Review,* April, 1980, p. 45.

2 Randall Poe, "Masters of the Advertorial," *Across The Board* (The Conference Board Magazine), September, 1980, p. 15.

3 Dom Bonafede, "The Bull Market in Business/Economics Reporting," *Washington Journalism Review,* July/August, 1980, p. 25.

4 Deirdre Carmody, "More Newspapers Are Starting Special Sections for Business News," *New York Times,* April 19, 1980, p. 25.

5 Bonafede, "The Bull Market in Business/Economics Reporting," pp. 24, 26.

6 "Reporters on Economics," *Washington Journalism Review,* July/August, 1980, p. 28.

7 "New Business," *Columbia Journalism Review,* July/August, 1978, p. 6.

8 A. Kent MacDougall, "TV Business Coverage Is Struggle Against Superficiality," *Los Angeles Times,* February 5, 1980.

9 A. Kent MacDougall, "Advocacy: Business Increasingly Uses (in Both Senses) Media to Push Views," *Los Angeles Times,* November 16, 1980.

10 A. Kent MacDougall, "Flaws in Press Coverage Plus Business Sensitivity Stir Bitter Debate," *Los Angeles Times,* February 3, 1980.

11 Ernest C. Hynds, "Business Coverage Is Getting Better," *Journalism Quarterly,* Summer, 1980, pp. 297-304, 368.

12 Steven Rattner, "Making Wall Street A Television Hit," *New York Times,* July 20, 1980, sec. 3, pp. 1, 16.

13 Newsletter of the National Center for Business and Economic Communication, American University, Washington, D.C., April 1, 1980, p. 4.

14 Sam Zagoria, "Equal Breaks for Labor News," *Columbia Journalism Review,* Fall, 1967, p. 44.

15 A. Kent MacDougall, "Labor Is Also Unhappy About Media Coverage," *Los Angeles Times,* February 4, 1980.

16 Bonafede, "The Bull Market in Business/Economics Reporting," p. 27.

17 MacDougall, "Flaws in Press Coverage Plus Business Sensitivity Stir Bitter Debate."

18 Clyde Z. Nunn, "Readership and Coverage of Science and Technology in Newspapers," *Journalism Quarterly*, Spring, 1979, pp. 28-29.

19 "Science, Technology and the Press: Must the 'Age of Innocence' End?" *Technology Review*, March/April, 1980, p. 52.

20 Willard Sterne Randall, "Cancer Country: Where Newspapers Fear to Tread," *Columbia Journalism Review*, September/October, 1979, p. 70.

21 *Ibid.*

22 Toby J. McIntosh, "Chronic Insignificance," *Quill*, September, 1980, p. 19.

23 *Ibid.*, pp. 18-19.

24 Denis M. Hurley, "Beyond Nader: Consumer Reporting Is Maturing," *Quill*, September, 1980, pp. 18-19.

25 McIntosh, "Chronic Insignificance," p. 18.

26 A. Kent MacDougall, "Reporting Environmental Hazards, Job Dangers Poses Risk for Media," *Los Angeles Times*, November 23, 1980.

27 Alan D. Fletcher, "City Magazines Find a Niche in the Media Marketplace," *Journalism Quarterly*, Winter, 1977, pp. 740-42.

28 Chilton R. Bush, ed., *News Research for Better Newspapers* (New York: American Newspaper Publishers Association Foundation, 1969), IV, pp. 28-29.

29 Hugh Morton, "Special Section Craze Sweeping the Country," *Editor & Publisher*, March 29, 1980, p. 31.

30 *Ibid.*

31 Aljean Harmetz, "Hollywood Stars Are Fighting Back Against Enquirer," *New York Times*, November 12, 1980, pp. C1, C20-21.

32 Robert Friedman, " 'Life,' 'Look,' and the Pursuit of the Perfect Picture Layout," *New York*, September 25, 1978, p. 91.

33 Sister M. Seraphim, "The Women's Section," *Nieman Reports*, March, 1964, p. 13.

34 Philly Murtha, "New Breed of Food Editors Rally for News, not Commercialism," *Editor & Publisher*, October 12, 1974, pp. 17, 20, 22. Carla Marie Rupp, "Food Editors Urged to Give Advertisers a 'Fair Shake,' " *Editor & Publisher*, March 1, 1975, pp. 10, 28. "Majority of Food Editors Endorse New Ethics Code," *Editor & Publisher*, March 8, 1975, p. 19.

35 Stanford N. Sesser, "The Fantasy World of Travel Sections," *Columbia Journalism Review*, Spring, 1970, p. 46.

36 Neil Amdur, "TV Sports Still Walks a Delicate Tightrope," *New York Times*, January 7, 1979, p. 35.

37 Gary Wills, "The Greatest Story Ever Told," *Columbia Journalism Review*, January/February, 1980, p. 25.

38 Tala Skari, "The New Revival in Radio," *Washington Journalism Review*, October, 1980, pp. 29-31.

39 "Stars of the Cathode Church," *Time*, February 4, 1980, pp. 64-65.

40 Leonard Shecter, *The Jocks* (New York: Paperback Library, 1969), p. 23.

Suggested Readings

ADONI, HANNA, and AKIBA A. COHEN, "Television Economic News and the Social Construction of Economic Reality," *Journal of Communication*, Autumn, 1978.

BANKS, LOUIS, "Taking on the Hostile Media," *Harvard Business Review*, March-April, 1978.

BONAFEDE, DOM, "The Bull Market in Business/Economics Reporting," *Washington Journalism Review*, July/August, 1980.

BORDEWICH, FERGUS M., "Supermarketing the Newspaper," *Columbia Journalism Review*, September/October, 1977.

DIAMOND, EDWIN, "The Dark Side of Moonshot Coverage," *Columbia Journalism Review*, Fall, 1969.

HURLEY, DENIS M., "Beyond Nader. Consumer Reporting Is Maturing," *The Quill*, September, 1980.

HYNDS, ERNEST, "Business Coverage Is Getting Better," *Journalism Quarterly*, Summer, 1980.

MacDOUGALL, A. KENT, "Flaws in Press Coverage Plus Business Sensitivity Stir Bitter Debate," *The Los Angeles Times*, February 3, 1980, p. 1.

MERRITT, SHARYNE, and HARRIET GROSS, "Women's Page/Lifestyle Editors: Does Sex Make a Difference?" *Journalism Quarterly*, Fall, 1978.

NUNN, CLYDE Z., "Readership and Coverage of Science and Technology in Newspapers," *Journalism Quarterly*, Spring, 1979.

POE, RANDALL, "The Writing of Sports," *Esquire*, October, 1974.

———, "Masters of the Advertorial," *The Conference Board Magazine*, September, 1980.

POLLOCK, FRANCIS, "Towards Protecting Consumers," *Columbia Journalism Review*, March/April, 1974.

Report Of The Public's Right to Information

Task Force, Staff Report to The President's Commission on the Accident at Three Mile Island. Washington, D.C.: Government Printing Office (#052-003-00734-7), October, 1979.

SCHOENFELD, A. CLAY, "Newspersons and the Environment Today," *Journalism Quarterly,* Autumn, 1980.

"Science: News, Controversy, Drama," *Journal of Communication,* Spring, 1981.

"Science, Technology and the Press: Must the 'Age of Innocence' End?" *Technology Review,* March/April, 1980.

SERAPHIM, SISTER M., "The Women's Section," *Nieman Reports,* March, 1964.

SESSER, STANFORD N., "The Fantasy World of Travel Sections," *Columbia Journalism Review,* Spring, 1970.

SIMONS, HOWARD, and JOSEPH A. CALIFANO, JR., *The Media and Business.* New York: Vintage Paperback, 1979.

SKARI, TALA, "The New Revival in Radio," *Washington Journalism Review,* October, 1980.

STOUT, ROBERT JOE, "Sportswriters: The New Breed," *The Quill,* November, 1980.

WILLS, GARY, "The Greatest Story Ever Told," *Columbia Journalism Review,* January/February, 1980.

Epilogue

For the most part, this book has been highly critical of the American mass media—for two reasons. First, the media deserve and need criticism. Second, it is vitally important that future journalists (and future community leaders in all occupations) be aware of what is wrong with the media and how they must change to better serve the public.

But it is equally important to preserve a sense of perspective. With all their flaws, the American media are among the most independent and the most responsible media in the world. The best of modern American journalism is unsurpassed anywhere else in history or in the world today. The rest of modern American journalism must be helped to live up to those high standards.

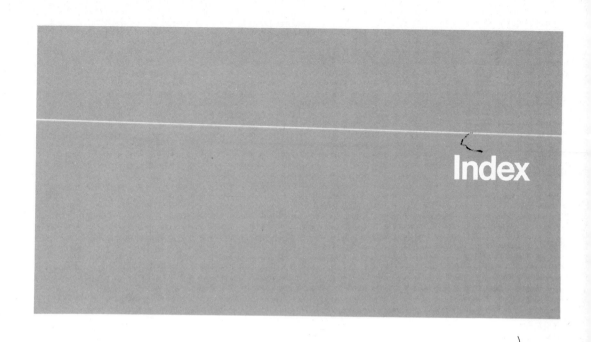

Index

ABC. *See* American Broadcasting
  Company
ABC News, 408
"ABC News Nightline," 330
Academy Awards, 301
Acceptance, latitude of, 19
Access: getting, 233–35; right of,
  231–33
Access, 226
*Access to the Press—A New First
  Amendment Right,* 231
Accountability, media, 221–25
Accuracy in Media, 208, 227
Ackerman, Martin, 282
Action for Children's Television
  (ACT), 225, 226, 380
Action on Smoking and Health,
  (ASH), 228
Adams, John, 401
Adams, Samuel, 37–38
Addison, Joseph, 32
Administrative Procedures, Act,
  161
Adversary relationship, 397–402,
  448–49
Advertisement: advertiser control
  of, 139–42; consumer access to,
  226
Advertiser control, 136–47;
  broadcasting, 145–47; company
  and product image, 139–42;
  controversy, avoiding, 142–44;
  patterns of, 138–42; power
  over content of media, 138;
  product and nonadvertising
  content, 138–39; threats, bribes,

and understandings, 144–45
Advertiser(s): big-money, 367;
  sneak, German, 368
Advertising, 9, 12, 189–90, 365–
  81; account executive, 374; advocacy, 208, 371; black, 319–20;
  boycotts, 143; and business,
  365–68; children's TV, 226;
  consumer cost of, 373; controversial, 234; coverage of, 448–
  49; election night, 429–30;
  ethics and regulation, 377–81;
  fairness doctrine, 229; false,
  377; ideological, 190; ideology
  vs. business, 137–38; institutional, 371; and media, 368–69;
  media department, 375; newspaper origins of, 41; plugs, 140;
  policing, 82; political, 427–29;
  price for, 145; product, 371;
  professionals, 373–76; protest,
  234; psychologist, 374; and
  public, 369–73; radio, 58; regulation, 189–90; research department, 375; revenue, 137;
  scatter plan system, 146; subliminal, 379; subservice of
  news, 140; TV, 226; and women,
  372–73
Advertising Age, 224
Advertising agencies. *See* specific
  agency
Advocacy advertising, 208, 371
Agence France-Presse, 247
Agenda-setting, 20–21
Agnew, Spiro, 113, 420

Agostino, Don, 317
Agriculture, Department of, 388,
  415
Airplane, 352, 356
Akis, 289
Alaska Public Interest Research
  Group, 226
Ali, Muhammad, 303, 481–82
Alice's Restaurant, 348
Alien, 351
Alka-Seltzer, 428
Allen, Robert S., 65
Allen, Woody, 347
Allende, Salvatore, 465
"All in the Family," 303, 313, 486
"All Things Considered," 337
Alphabet, first, 30
Alternative Media Center, 228
Altman, Robert, 349, 350
"Amazing Howard Hughes, The,"
  339
Ambrosio, Joanne A., 152
American Airlines, 370
American Association for the Ad-
  vancement of Science, 498
American Association for Public
  Opinion Research, 421
American Association of Adver-
  tising Agencies, 138, 366
American Bar Association, 192,
  414
American Broadcasting Company
  (ABC), 65, 69, 141, 147, 173,
  178, 179, 220, 234, 235, 303, 309,
  312, 314, 316, 321, 326, 330, 336,
  338, 352, 408, 422, 424, 457, 481,